www.wadsworth.com

wadsworth.com is the World Wide Web site for
Wadsworth and is your direct source to dozens of
online resources.

At *wadsworth.com* you can find out about
supplements, demonstration software, and
student resources. You can also send email to many of
our authors and preview new publications and exciting
new technologies.

wadsworth.com
Changing the way the world learns®

From the Wadsworth Series in Broadcasting

Albarran, Alan B., *Management of Electronic Media,* 2nd Ed.

Alten, Stanley R., *Audio in Media,* 6th Ed.

Armer, Alan A., *Writing the Screenplay,* 2nd Ed.

Craft, John, Frederic Leigh, and Donald Godfrey, *Electronic Media*

Eastman, Susan Tyler, and Douglas A. Ferguson, *Broadcast/Cable/Web Programming: Strategies and Practices,* 6th Ed.

Gross, Lynne S., and Larry W. Ward, *Electronic Moviemaking,* 4th Ed.

Hausman, Carl, Philip Benoit, and Lewis B. O'Donnell, *Modern Radio Production,* 5th Ed.

Hausman, Carl, Lewis B. O'Donnell, and Philip Benoit, *Announcing: Broadcast Communicating Today,* 4th Ed.

Hilliard, Robert L., *Writing for Television, Radio, and New Media,* 7th Ed.

Hilmes, Michele, *Connections: A Broadcast History Reader*

Hilmes, Michele, *Only Connect: A Cultural History of Broadcasting in the United States*

Mamer, Bruce, *Film Production Technique: Creating the Accomplished Image,* 3rd Ed.

Meeske, Milan D., *Copywriting for the Electronic Media: A Practical Guide,* 4th Ed.

Stephens, Mitchell, *Broadcast News,* 3rd Ed.

Stephens, Mitchell, *A History of News,* 2nd Ed.

Viera, Dave, *Lighting for Film and Electronic Cinematography*

Zettl, Herbert, *Sight Sound Motion,* 3rd Ed.

Zettl, Herbert, *Television Production Handbook,* 8th Ed.

Zettl, Herbert, *Television Production Workbook,* 8th Ed.

Zettl, Herbert, *Video Basics,* 3rd Ed.

Zettl, Herbert, *Video Basics Workbook,* 3rd Ed.

Zettl, Herbert, *Zettl's VideoLab 2.1*

Connections

A Broadcast History Reader

MICHELE HILMES
University of Wisconsin–Madison

THOMSON

WADSWORTH

Australia • Canada • Mexico • Singapore • Spain
United Kingdom • United States

THOMSON

™

WADSWORTH

Publisher: *Holly J. Allen*
Assistant Editor: *Nicole George*
Editorial Assistant: *Amber Fawson*
Technology Project Manager: *Jeanette Wiseman*
Marketing Manager: *Kimberly Russell*
Marketing Assistant: *Neena Chandra*
Advertising Project Manager: *Shemika Britt*
Project Manager, Editorial Production: *Karen Haga*

Print/Media Buyer: *Karen Hunt*
Permissions Editor: *Bob Kauser*
Production Service and Compositor: *Shepherd, Inc.*
Copy Editor: *Patterson Lamb*
Cover Designer: *Jennifer Dunn*
Cover Image: *©Corbis*
Text and Cover Printer: *Webcom Ltd.*

Printed in Canada
1 2 3 4 5 6 7 06 05 04 03 02

For more information about our products,
contact us at:
Thomson Learning Academic Resource Center
1-800-423-0563

For permission to use material from this text,
contact us by:
Phone: 1-800-730-2214 **Fax:** 1-800-730-2215
Web: http://www.thomsonrights.com

Library of Congress Control Number: 2002111516

Student Edition with InfoTrac College Edition:
ISBN 0-534-55217-X
Student Edition without InfoTrac College Edition:
ISBN 0-534-55218-8

Wadsworth/Thomson Learning
10 Davis Drive
Belmont, CA 94002-3098
USA

Asia
Thomson Learning
5 Shenton Way #01-01
UIC Building
Singapore 068808

Australia
Nelson Thomson Learning
102 Dodds Street
South Melbourne, Victoria 3205
Australia

Canada
Nelson Thomson Learning
1120 Birchmount Road
Toronto, Ontario M1K 5G4
Canada

Europe/Middle East/Africa
Thomson Learning
High Holborn House
50/51 Bedford Row
London WC1R 4LR
United Kingdom

Latin America
Thomson Learning
Seneca, 53
Colonia Polanco
11560 Mexico D.F.
Mexico

Spain
Paraninfo Thomson Learning
Calle/Magallanes, 25
28015 Madrid, Spain

Contents

Preface

onnections is an attempt to bring together some of the best work that has been published over the last 15 years in the field of U.S. broadcasting history. It is meant to be used in a course covering cultural issues in broadcast history and can be a companion to my text, *Only Connect: A Cultural History of Broadcasting,* but it is also designed to stand alone as a survey of broadcasting history research. In the process of researching and writing over the last three years, I began to get a sense of what scholars in the field of media study regarded as the most seminal works in the historical field, in terms of both influence on their own research and usefulness in the classroom. Other articles, though perhaps less known, help to fill in knowledge in particularly essential areas. Certainly many of the scholars represented here have had a large influence over my own work, and I am grateful to them for having published their writings in the first place, as well as for giving me permission to reprint their articles in this book. I am also grateful to the reviewers who gave me feedback on their use of the readings in their own classrooms.

The book is intended as an overview of the development of American broadcasting, from its earliest radio days to the present moment of global outreach and transnational influence. The articles are arranged chronologically, in terms of their subject matter, in four parts: Fundamental Concepts and Radio Days, covering the early period of radio broadcasting; Transition to Television, dealing with television's stylistic, social, and industrial development out of radio; The Classic Network System, tracing the shift to the three-network era of the 1960s through the early 1980s; and The Multichannel Universe, dealing with the more recent period of technological innovation, diversity, and cultural negotiation. Many articles, however, exceed these rather arbitrary time categories, as they look backward to an earlier period of establishment and social context, or forward to future developments.

Part I of *Connections* begins with Brian Winston's seminal article "How Are Media Born?" This popular article examines the impact of theoretical approaches to media history on our thinking about technology, communication, and cultural consequences. It encourages readers to think about the processes and practices of history writing and reading as they embark on a study of broadcasting's role in the twentieth century. Its clarity and excellent use of examples make it a most accessible discussion of media theory for scholars and undergraduates alike. Mark Goodman and Mark Gring next contribute an excellent analysis of the Progressive movement roots in "The Radio Act of 1927," helping to round out the social and political context within which broadcasting developed. Robert McChesney's article "Crusade against Mammon," centering on Father Harney of WLWL, fills in some detail on the regulatory battles of the early 1930s and makes the complex contentious issues of the reform movement clear in the way that only a close case study can. Eileen Meehan's "Why We Don't Count" combines an in-depth historical overview of the development of broadcast ratings systems with an incisive critique of the methodical exclusions and cultural consequences such an invisible and under-studied aspect of the media business brings.

Part II begins with Kristine Brunovska Karnick's analysis of early network news. In "NBC and the Innovation of Television News, 1945–1953," she argues that film-based news-gathering techniques had to be coordinated with radio's styles and practices in order for "the network news" to emerge as a form in its own right on NBC in the early 1950s. George Lipsitz takes the discussion toward fictional programs in "The Meaning of Memory," his examination of working-class and ethnic situation comedies on network TV, including such shows as *Mama, The Goldbergs, Amos 'n' Andy, The Honeymooners, Hey Jeannie, Life with Luigi,* and *The Life of Riley.* Placing the predominance of such shows in the early network period within their industrial and social context, Lipsitz argues that the invocation of a vanishing past negotiated not only economic but ideological and cultural tensions in 1950s American life. Mary Beth Haralovich's groundbreaking and much-reprinted article "Sitcoms and Suburbs" extends this deeply contextual approach to the construction of the 1950s homemaker. National social and political priorities, marketing research, and television's developing economic framework created representations of American families and the women at their center that continue to resonate today.

Part III looks at key events within the period of Big Three network dominance. Lynn Spigel analyzes a key program genre of the high-network period, the fantastic family sitcom, in "From Domestic Space to Outer Space," linking such programs as *I Dream of Jeannie, My Favorite Martian, Lost in Space,* and *Bewitched* to the American space race and the middle-class suburban lifestyle.

Chester Pach, Jr.'s revealing discussion of television network coverage of the Vietnam War, "And That's the Way It Was," explores the dark side of television's representational universe, as the first "living room war" entered American homes and placed television at the center of national political life. Gary Edgerton's detailed history of the made-for-TV movie and the miniseries, "High Concept, Small Screen," examines the origins of one of network television's most creative innovations and its considerable social impact. And in "Feeding Off the Past," Phil Williams traces the rise of the rerun, or syndicated program, within the changing network system as networks and producers began to compete in an expanding television marketplace.

Part IV enters the more recent period of technological innovation and shifting industry relationships as well as social struggle over television representation. Patricia Aufderheide's "Cable Television and the Public Interest" brings forward the type of political debate that often surrounds the introduction of new technologies. She argues that cable's potential for developing a community-based public sphere has been undercut by commercial economics and pro-industry legislation in a pattern that will repeat itself with later technologies. Herman Gray criticizes the limited universe of commercial network television in "Recodings: Possibilities and Limitations in Commercial Television Representations of African-American Culture." Examining the innovative program *Frank's Place* and its struggles to find its own place on the network TV schedule, Gray demonstrates the pressures that restrict and contain discussion of race in mainstream media, even as cable television promised to provide alternatives—and often broke that promise. Willard Rowland, Jr., reviews the history of U.S. broadcasting regulation in terms of its ongoing tension between industry and public interest, in "U.S. Broadcasting and the Public Interest in the Multichannel Era." By placing the Telecommunications Act of 1996 within this critical framework he reveals contemporary legislation not as a break with the past but as an entirely consistent continuity. In a related vein, Ron Becker examines the breakthrough of gay representations on television in "Prime-Time Television in the Gay '90s," linking it to marketing strategies in the deregulated post-network era.

The final two articles extend attention to American television in a global setting. William Boddy's "U.S. Television Abroad: Market Power and National Introspection" looks at both U.S. media expansion and national efforts at resistance and recuperation of national cultural identity, particularly in Europe. Michael Curtin looks toward Asia for his examination of U.S. cultural influence on mediated forms originating elsewhere, and particularly at their contradictory social messages. In "Feminine Desire in the Age of Satellite Television" he suggests that female audiences and artists, in particular, may be able to use the expanded universe of feminine representation drawn from global imagery in culturally specific and socially liberating ways.

Taken together, these essays represent the significant change that media study has undergone in the last decades of the twentieth century, continuing into the twenty-first. They offer insightful critical analysis of media practices, social contexts, and texts in a theoretical framework that integrates economics, industry structures, regulations and policies, social pressures and negotiations, cultural forms, and audience constructions to come to a better understanding of key media decisions, characteristics and events. Though not all of them are written from a cultural studies framework, they carry out the project of cultural studies as it examines the uses of power in cultural production and the inclusions and exclusions, the emphases and absences, that it engenders. They open up the discussion of radio and television and their related technologies to a form of discussion and debate that exceeds the boundaries of media debunking that has so often passed for informed criticism throughout U.S. history. Radio and television, now expanding globally to include all manner of electronic communication, have formed the central nervous system of modern national life. Limited effects models and simple denunciations of television's power over our lives cannot sufficiently address the complex web of relationships and cultural hierarchies that have produced and circulated meanings about and in our lives over the last century. These key essays prove how much more complicated the issues are and give us better ideas about how to comprehend this vital aspect of our mediated experience. They make connections that help us to think through the past into the present, and to imagine the future.

ACKNOWLEDGMENTS

My very sincere thanks go to the scholars who have allowed me to reprint their articles in this volume. I hope this republication will bring renewed attention to their excellent work. Thanks also to Norma Coates, now at the University of Wisconsin–Whitewater, for her assistance in writing the introductions to each article. Thanks to my editor at Wadsworth, Holly Allen, for seeing this project through. And I would like to extend special thanks for the invaluable suggestions of this book's reviewers, who did so much to help shape it:

Steven Classen, California State University–Los Angeles

Sylvia Hope Daniels, Columbia College, Chicago

Christina S. Drale, Southwest Missouri State University

Katherine Giuffre, Colorado College

Geoffrey Hammill, Eastern Michigan University

Susan Murray, New York University

Thomas Rosteck, University of Arkansas–Fayetteville

Contributors

Pat Aufderheide is professor and director of the Center for Social Media at American University in Washington, D.C. She is the author of, among others, a collection of critical essays on media and society, *The Daily Planet* (Minnesota, 1999) and of *Communications Policy and the Public Interest* (Guilford, 1995).

Ron Becker is a Ph.D. candidate in the Department of Communication Arts' Media and Cultural Studies Program at the University of Wisconsin-Madison. His dissertation examines the industrial and social contexts surrounding the rise of gay material on prime-time network television in the 1990s.

William Boddy is a professor in the Department of Communication Studies at Baruch College and in the Certificate Program in Film Studies of the Graduate Center, both of the City University of New York. He is the author of *Fifties Television: The Industry and Its Critics* (University of Illinois Press, 1990) and of *New Media and Popular Imagination* (Oxford University Press, forthcoming).

Michael Curtin is professor of Communication Arts at the University of Wisconsin-Madison. His books include *Redeeming the Wasteland: Television Documentary and Cold War Politics* (Rutgers, 1995), *Making and Selling Culture* (co-editor, Wesleyan, 1996), and *The Revolution Wasn't Televised: Sixties Television and Social Conflict* (co-editor, Routledge, 1997). He is writing a book about the globalization of Chinese film and television and, with Paul McDonald, co-editing a book series for the British Film Institute called *International Screen Industries.*

Gary Edgerton is professor and chair of the Communication and Theatre Arts Department at Old Dominion University. He is the co-editor of the *Journal of Popular Film and Television,* and has published five books and more than fifty essays on a wide assortment of film, television, and culture topics in a variety of books and scholarly journals. His latest volume, *Ken Burns's America* (Palgrave for St. Martin's Press) received Honorable Mention (Second Place) in the 2001 John G. Cawelti National Book Award of the American Culture Association for Outstanding Scholarly Inquiry into American Cultural Studies.

Mark Goodman is an associate professor in the Communication Department at Mississippi State University. He received his Ph.D. in Communication from the University of Missouri in 1993. Most of his research is in media law history and media effects.

Herman Gray is the author of *Watching Race.* Gray teaches courses in cultural politics and media at the University of Californai at Santa Cruz where he is a professor of sociology. He is completing a book on black cultural politcs at the end of the 20th century.

Mark A. Gring received his Ph.D. from The Ohio State University and is an assistant professor at Texas Tech University in the Department of Communication Studies. His research interests focus on the study of rhetoric and its implications for epistemology, religion, and sociopolitical change.

Mary Beth Haralovich is associate professor of media arts at the University of Arizona in Tucson. In television, she has published studies of the popular appeal of *Magnum P.I.* and the geo-politics of civil rights in *I Spy.* In film, she is the author of articles on film advertising and the proletarian women's film of the 1930s. She is co-editor of *Television, History, and American Culture: Feminist Critical Essays* (Duke, 1999) and a founder of the International Conference on Television, Video, New Media, and Feminisim: Console-ing Passions. She is working on a history of local film advertising in the 1930s.

Kristine Brunovska Karnick is an associate professor in the Department of Communication Studies and Adjunct Associate Professor in the Departments of English and of New Media at Indiana University-Purdue University at Indianapolis. She is co-editor (with Henry Jenkins) of *Classical Hollywood Comedy* (Routledge, 1994) and is completing an anthology *Life of the Party: Female Comedians in Hollywood* for New York University Press. Her work on media history has appeared most recently in *Continuum: Journal of Media and Cultural Studies.*

George Lipsitz is professor of ethnic studies at the University of California San Diego where he directs the Thurgood Marshall Institute. His books include *American Studies in a Moment of Danger, The Possessive Investment in Whiteness, Time Passages, Dangerous Crossroads,* and *A Rainbow at Midnight.*

Robert W. McChesney is research professor of communication at the University of Illinois at Urbana-Champaign. He is the author of nine books and over 125 book chapters and journal articles. His work has been translated into twelve languages. McChesney hosts a weekly radio program, Media Matters, on WILL-AM radio, and is the co-editor of *Monthly Review,* the independent socialist magazine founded by Paul Sweezy and Leo Huberman in 1949.

Eileen R. Meehan is an associate professor of media arts at the University of Arizona. Her research examines the political economy of culture. She co-edited *Sex and Money: Feminism and Political Economy in the Media* with Ellen Riordan, and *Dazzled by Disney? The Global Disney Audiences Project* with Janet Wasko and Mark Phillips.

Chester J. Pach, Jr. is the author of *Arming the Free World: The Origins of United States Military Assistance Program, 1945–1950* and *The Presidency of Dwight D. Eisenhower,* rev. ed. He is completing a book titled, *The First Television War: TV News, the White House, and Vietnam.* He has written several articles about television coverage of Vietnam and international affairs including, most recently, "Television," in the *Encyclopedia of American Foreign Policy,* 2nd ed.

Willard D. ("Wick") Rowland, Jr. is president and general manager of Colorado Public Television, KBDI-TV/12 in Denver, Colorado. He also is professor and the former dean of the School of Journalism and Mass Communication at the University of Colorado. His teaching and research focus on media history and policy, the TV violence debates, public broadcasting, and the history of communication studies.

Lynn Spigel is professor at the School of Cinema-Television, University of Southern California. She is author of *Make Room for TV* and *Welcome to the Dreamhouse.*

Phil Williams was, at the time of writing this article, a master's degree candidate studying twentieth century popular culture in the American Studies program at Purdue University.

Brian Winston is director of the School of Communication and Creative Industries at the University of Westminster. He is the author of numerous works on media, including *Lies, Damn Lies, and Documentaries; Media, Technology and Society;* and *Misunderstanding Media.*

PART I

❖

Fundamental Concepts
and Radio Days

1

How Are Media Born?

BRIAN WINSTON

The history of broadcasting is tightly tied to the history of technological innovation—from the invention of the earliest wireless telegraphy using Morse code, running through a series of refinements of transmission and reception technology, up to the advent of television and beyond. Historian Brian Winston makes the point that often this history of *technological* development becomes so prominent that it obscures, rather than reveals, the more complex history of broadcasting as a medium of culture and communication. He calls this kind of history *technological determinism,* after a term coined by social theorist Raymond Williams, and demonstrates how such technology-based accounts are themselves shaped by powerful, distorting assumptions about the ways that technological change occurs and what effects it has, even though they *seem* neutral and objective.

Using examples taken from various histories, he demonstrates the shortcomings of the *technological determinist* approach, and argues for a more complex, socially and politically nuanced *cultural determinist* view of history. His concept of the "suppression of radical potential" that so often plays a part in the development of a new medium is particularly useful for students of media history, as it helps to account for what *doesn't* happen, or what intriguing yet threatening possibilities get sidelined and repressed as media innovations occur.

This article originally appeared in *Questioning the Media* (2nd ed) edited by John Downing and Annabelle Sreberny-Mohammadi (Sage, 1990). Reprinted by permission of Sage Publications, Inc.

This chapter addresses two related questions: (a) How does technological change occur in mass communication? (b) What effect, if any, does the technology have on the content, the output, of mass communication? These questions are related in that they both deal with the historical relationship of technology to communication processes.

The first question is clearly historical. There are various accounts available to explain the nature of these changes. In some, technological developments are isolated: The technology is the dominant, *determining* factor in the process. I will be calling such accounts of change *technological determinist*. Other accounts place a greater emphasis on socioeconomic factors. In these accounts, technology is but one of many forces, influenced by and influencing social, economic, and cultural developments. I will be calling accounts of this sort *cultural determinist*.

The second question, about the effect of technology on communication, can also be thought of as historical. The only way a judgment can be made as to the effect of a technology on the content of communications is by comparing the content before and after the technology is introduced. Thus the second question, which seems to address only the issue of effects, is also really addressing the issue of change and, in so doing, is historical.

These two questions are linked in another way. Technological determinist accounts of media history tend to stress the role of media technology in governing the content of communication. Conversely, cultural determinist accounts tend to deny technology this determining role. So the answer to the first question above is likely to condition the answer given to the second.

This chapter presents four successive accounts of the genesis of communications technology. It is not, clearly, a full-blown history of media technology, although you may well find some new information on the subject. It is designed to encourage you to think more carefully about that history, to learn how to evaluate the problems in historical explanations and not just accept them because a scholar has published them.

TECHNOLOGICAL DETERMINIST ACCOUNT A

Technological determinism, wrote Raymond Williams (1974),

> is an immensely powerful and now largely orthodox view of the nature of social change. New technologies are discovered by an essentially internal process of research and development, which then sets the conditions of social change and progress. Progress, in particular, is the history of these inventions which "created the modern world." The effect of the technologies, whether direct or indirect, foreseen or unforeseen, are as it were the rest of history. (p. 13)

In its simplest form, this dominant theory explains the "essentially internal process of research and development" as nothing more than the biographies of the scientists and technologists involved, arranged chronologically. This account sees the development and impact of technology as "the progress of great men" (women and people of non-White cultures tend not to figure).

Here, presented as a case study, is a short history of the cinema written as "the progress of great men," based on a classic history of film (Ramsaye, 1926).

Case 1: Cinematic Projection

One essential element of the cinema is the idea of projection. The line that leads to projection begins with Della Porta, an Italian, who put a lens on the front of the earliest camera—a simple box. An image was produced on a glass screen set in the back wall of the box. Della Porta made this device in 1555. Next, Athanasius Kircher, a German, produced a magic lantern that projected an image onto a screen (1649).

Peter Roget, an Englishman, theorized in 1824 that the retina of the eye retains an image for a fraction of a second after the image is removed or changed. This "persistence of vision" can be used to fool the eye into believing a succession of separate and slightly different images to be actually one moving image. Toys to exploit "persistence of vision" by animating drawings were then "invented" by men like Paris (English, 1824), Plateau (Belgian, early 1830s), and von Stampfer (German, 1832). In 1852, von Uchatius, another German, put an animated strip of drawing (done on glass) into a magic lantern and projected the resulting moving image onto a screen. A substitute for glass now had to be found. The line leading to this part of the cinematographic apparatus goes back to early experiments with substances that change their color, essentially by darkening, in response to light. More research, like that of Wedgewood (English, 1802), led to the first photograms—images made by laying objects, such as leaves, directly onto materials, like paper or leather, treated with light-sensitive substances. But these images were not "fixed" and would disappear into black if further exposed to the light.

Scientists undertook the discovery of a chemical that would halt the darkening process. In 1837 a Frenchman, Nicephore Niepce, found a way of doing this and, with his partner Daguerre, produced a type of photograph known as the daguerreotype. Meanwhile, an Englishman, Fox-Talbot, invented a photographic process that produced first a negative, made of chemically treated paper oiled to transparency, and then a positive copy.

This, the essence of modern photography, was then refined. A wood pulp extract called cellulose was used instead of paper. Celluloid film finally allowed George Eastman to "invent," in 1888, a camera that anybody could use.

Back to the cinema. It was Edison who took photography and melded it with the development in animated drawing and magic lanterns to produce the kinetoscope in 1892. There were British, French, and other claimants for the honor of "inventing" the first motion picture device. Two Frenchmen, the Lumiere brothers, gave the first public cinema (their term) show, using a projector to throw a moving image onto a screen, before an audience, arranged as in a live theater, in 1895.

So was the cinema invented.

There are numerous problems with this account. In its eagerness to create "great men," the story becomes highly selective. For instance, Roget's explanation of why we see apparent motion, "persistence of vision," is not really physiologically accurate (Nichols & Liderman, cited in DeLauretis & Heath, 1980, pp. 97ff.), but even very recent histories still begin with Roget and his idea (see, e.g., Beaver, 1983; Mast, 1981).

Real contributions are seen as coming solely from the genius of a single figure, when, in fact, they are the product of collective inventiveness. For instance, it took more than 30 years to go from the development of celluloid, which was originally produced during the U.S. Civil War as a dressing for wounds, to the Kodak. The full story of those years reveals a number of innovations and dead ends. It involves many, many more people than just George Eastman, who successfully marketed a technology to which a lot of hands had contributed.

Edison's role in this process needs to be revised. Edison at Menlo Park was running one of the earliest modern industrial laboratories and pursuing a range of experiments, including investigations into the moving image. His method was to delegate much of the work to his assistants. In the case of the cinema, the work was actually done by a man named Dickson (Hendricks, 1961). Edison knew this full well, but that never prevented him from accepting credit for the "invention" of the kinetoscope.

The poverty, or "thinness," of great-man histories is not based simply on the desire to create heroes. Another crucial factor is the implicit insistence on the primacy of the West. For instance, the camera does not begin with Della Porta but with Arab astronomers at least 300 years earlier. There is even a reference to projected images in China in 121 B.C. It has been suggested that the first magic lantern lecture in Europe was given by a Jesuit who had learned the technique while a missionary in China, and that Kircher had nothing to do with it (Temple, 1986, p. 86). Even without this, it is possible that the camera was in existence in Italy over a century before Della Porta (Winston, 1987, p. 199).

You might also have wondered why, in this account, such emphasis has been placed on nationality. In part, it has to do with national pride. But establishing who did something first has more to it than that. Modern patent rights depend on registering an invention first, and that implies financial advantages.

The failure of the great-man style of technological determinism cannot be corrected simply by writing more comprehensive histories. This sort of history really cannot answer the question of *how* technological change occurs; instead, it simply tells us *when*. The only explanation offered as to *how* is that great men, out of their genius, think of them.

TECHNOLOGICAL DETERMINIST ACCOUNT B

There is a more sophisticated version of the technological determinist approach that we need to explore in order to see if these "how/why" questions can be better answered. Here, the changes listed in Case 1 would be treated as a sequence of developments causally related to each other. The "inventors" would be left out, or their parts downplayed. Such a history of the cinema would view its technological development as the inevitable result of scientific progress, part of the never-ending advancement of human knowledge in Western culture. Such an account would suggest that the independent existence of the camera, the lantern, and the lens had to combine to produce the magic lantern. In turn, this development inevitably melded with the development of photography to create cinematography.

The arrival of sound in film provides us with a case study in this more sophisticated mode. This account is based on Ong (1982).

Case 2: Sound in Film

Sound recording developed using wax cylinders, discs, and wire before the turn of the twentieth century at the same time as the cinema itself was being perfected. However, these were mechanical recording devices without amplification that would not, therefore, work well in a theatrical environment.

Electronic devices that enabled sound to be amplified evolved out of experiments on the nature of electricity itself, then at the cutting edge of physics. By 1906, a number of independent researchers had produced a tube rather like the electric light bulb then being generally manufactured, but this specialized version could reproduce and amplify electrical signals.

The application of this technology to silent cinema was interrupted by World War I, but experiments continued using various systems. Running film projectors synchronously with phonographs was one. Another, more complicated, converted sound waves, via a microphone linked to a light bulb, into light waves to which the film could be exposed.

The technology was therefore awaiting its moment. That came in 1926, when the industry finally realized that the public would accept sound. Earlier attempts had failed because the technology was not quite developed and because there was inertia about changing over from the commercially successful method of having live music at each screening.

The introduction of sound also made easier the introduction of faster (i.e., more light-sensitive) film stocks. The very bright arc lights used in the silent studios used to hiss. This was acceptable in silent shooting but bothersome if sound was being recorded. Incandescent lights were then introduced because they made no noise, but they were also less powerful, so the industry needed faster stocks. More sensitive film had been available but unused since before World War I.

This new stock was black-and-white but panchromatic—equally sensitive to all colors, unlike the slower orthochromatic stock it replaced. "Ortho" was blind to red, which it therefore photographed as black. The introduction of panchromatic film affected makeup, costume, and set design. It also helped, therefore, to put in place production procedures that would facilitate the next major technical advance—color.

Such an account presents a seamless sequence of technical events, each automatically triggering its successor. Each can be delayed by external factors, such as World War I and industrial inertia. But in the end the technology triumphs.

Yet important clues as to *how* technical change occurs can be gained by thinking of *why* a change occurs at a particular time. This is a more complicated issue than it might seem to be at first sight. Changes do not occur simply when the materials and the scientific knowledge necessary for an advance are at hand. The history of the cinema is a good illustration of this.

The great-man account in Case 1 revealed that there was nothing to prevent Kircher from doing, two centuries earlier, what Ustachius did. Kircher could draw and he had glass. And he had just "invented," or borrowed from the Chinese, the lantern that Ustachius was to use.

Such questions can be extended. Why did Della Porta not place a light where he had put his ground-glass screen? Had he done so, he could have created the magic lantern a century before Kircher. And why did the Arab astronomers not pursue these developments centuries before that? Or the Chinese even earlier?

The great-man style of technological determinism cannot help us to answer such questions. It is equally clear that the sophisticated technological determinism of Case 2 is no better. We do not know from Case 2 why early films did not have sound, since sound-recording techniques and motion picture devices developed simultaneously (Hendricks, 1961, p. 111). And we are no nearer to understanding why the Arabs failed to exploit the camera, why Kircher did not invent the camera, and so on.

A better way we can begin to answer these questions is, however, hinted at in Case 2. There we started to hear about forces other than the technological, such as World War I and attitudes in the film industry. In a technological determinist account these are treated as incidentals, but cultural determinists will take these external factors as significant.

CULTURAL DETERMINIST ACCOUNT A

To take a cultural determinist view, it becomes necessary to examine the social context of the technology. This implies an examination of the circumstances into which the technology is introduced and diffused through society. In turn, then, a cultural determinist would need to look at the circumstances preceding the development of a technology. Note that the word *development* is preferred to the word *invention* because invention implies a single moment—but these single moments always obscure long-term developments involving many hands. Thus the cultural determinist will at least be an economic historian.

Let us take an economic history type of account of the introduction of sound in film and see how it compares with the technological determinist account offered in Case 2. Here, in Case 3, the key player becomes a corporation (Warner Brothers), but this key player is not a corporate great man. Rather, the struggle to introduce sound is located within corporate competition (Allen & Gomery, 1985, pp. 105ff.).

Case 3: The Economics of Sound in Film

In the mid-1920s Warner Brothers was a small studio. It obtained from a New York bank, Goldman Sachs, a line of credit to expand its operations and used this money primarily to acquire movie theaters. Warner's biggest rivals were vertically integrated in this way; that is, studios owned chains of theaters and thus had ready markets for their products. Studios that did not own theaters were at a considerable disadvantage in marketing their films.

Warner's also used the money to buy into the new radio industry by acquiring a radio station. This was done because radio was increasingly being used to promote movies. By this acquisition the company gained familiarity with sound-recording techniques.

It was this changing capital infrastructure in the movie industry that constituted the enabling ground for the introduction of sound. Warner, smaller than the five major Hollywood studios, decided after much internal debate to gamble that sound in its newly acquired theaters would give it an edge. The introduction of sound was thus an attempt to improve market share. Acquisition of a chain of theaters alone was not enough to do this; the chain had to attract audiences by offering something different.

It was the potential disruption to their profitable silent film business, reinforced by their experience of failed experiments with sound dating back to the period before 1914, that "caused" Warner's rivals, the Big Five, not to exploit sound. The technology was available, but the commercial desire and need were not.

Warner successfully demonstrated that sound could be popular with audiences by making a series of variety shorts. Fox, another company struggling to catch up with the Big Five, then demonstrated that sound news films could also be popular.

As a result of this challenge, the Big Five agreed to introduce sound film using a common system. The technology they agreed upon, sound on film, was the most complex and expensive, but, because the Big Five had agreed upon it, it was well placed to become the industry standard. It was thus also designed to prevent Fox and Warner, who were using slightly different versions, from continuing to make gains. Warner and Fox fell into line.

The Big Five sound system is the one in use up to the present day.

There are a number of differences between the accounts in Case 3 and Case 2. In Case 3 the development of sound film critically depends on the period before its introduction. In Case 2 this period is seen as a lull, a pause before the inevitable triumph of the technology. In Case 3 it becomes instead a period of struggle of the sort that determines not only the pace at which the technology is introduced, but also its form. It is a struggle waged first within Warner, then between Warner and its rivals, to maximize profits and to have a particular technical solution dominate.

The explanation given in Case 3 is not a substitute for the information in Case 2. It is not that we are writing economic history instead of technological history. Rather, we are attempting to combine the "thinness" of the account in Case 2 by trying to write a "thicker" history, one that describes both. Economic historians, in effect, would add a mass of new information about Warner as a business.

However, economics is a crucial element, but not the end of the matter. Case 3 assumes that the main engines of technical change are the corporation and the market, and that the corporation's motivation will always be to increase the "bottom line." There are two problems with this. One is that technical innovation has not always depended upon the existence of corporations seeking profits. Case 3 is good at explaining sound, but it still does not help us understand why the Arabs, Della Porta, Kircher, and the others did not create the cinema.

Second, much innovation is designed to protect corporations and preserve existing markets, rather than to produce new goods and services for profit. Bell Laboratories is a good case in point. Often considered the most effective industrial innovator in history, Bell Labs was actually established to protect AT&T, the telephone monopoly, from new technologies, specifically radio. By 1878 Bell himself had built a good telephone receiver, but his transmitter was terrible. Edison, by contrast, had patented a superior transmitter, but his receiver was not as effective as Bell's. In this patent standoff, Bell and his business partners hired Emile Berliner to get the infant phone company out of trouble. Berliner, who later built the first device for playing records (the phonograph), did just this. In six weeks' time, he produced a good transmitter without infringing on Edison's patents. Thereafter this pattern of threat averted by patentable innovation was repeated often until, in the radio era, AT&T's research programs were finally organized into Bell Labs.

The result of Bell's research program is that every telecommunications innovation has relied to some extent on Bell patents. This includes radio, television, sound film, fax systems, and space communications. No innovation has occurred in the telecommunications field without Bell both agreeing to it and profiting from it. The expenditures lavished on Bell Labs were not therefore simply to maximize profit. They were designed to suppress the disruptive—to Bell—possibilities of innovation.

Thus we need to go beyond the economic historian's version of cultural determinism to something "thicker" still. Central to my argument is that *all* technological communication innovation can be thought of as a series of events taking place in the realm of technology, but influenced by and reacting to events taking place (a) in the realm of pure science and (b) in society in general. This model has to be rendered even more complex, because society also influences science, which in turn influences the technology. However, for present purposes I will include society's influences on science as part of science itself.

CULTURAL DETERMINIST ACCOUNT B

Let us take another case—television—to illustrate this "thicker" cultural determinism.

Case 4: Television

As industrial capitalism, from the end of the eighteenth century onward, began to stimulate scientists' inquiries into more practical and profitable applications, so substances were discovered that responded to light in various ways. The basic chemistry of photography emerged, as Case 1 showed, because it was known that some substances darken when exposed to light. Here we will be concerned with the fact that a group of substances alter their resistance to electric current according to the amount of light that falls on them.

Selenium was noted as such a substance by 1839, but no theoretical understanding of why this occurs was offered and no immediate applications suggested themselves for about 40 years. Then it became possible to theorize a device that would translate an optical image (light waves) into a variable electric current, using selenium as a sensor. This idea was prompted by parallel developments that used the variable resistance of carbon to electricity to construct a device that translated sound waves into a variable electric current—a telephone.

The problem for "seeing by telephone," as it was called, was that it had no practical application except perhaps as a facsimile device. But facsimile devices, which allowed for images to be sent by telegraph, were already in existence and worked better, because with the selenium versions there was no apparent way of creating a hard copy. Nevertheless, a device for turning images into an electrical wave analogue using a selenium sensor was patented in Berlin in 1884. Use of the word *television* as a description of this process dates from 1903.

Various researchers all over the world realized that television could transmit moving pictures. But what use would that be? The live theater had been industrialized in the nineteenth century by the creation of theatrical circuits that brought entertainment to the masses. Film had partially mechanized theater and would eventually largely substitute for it. There was no social need for television at that time.

Nor did any researcher think money could be made by delivering entertainment to the home. The masses, given the long hours they worked and the poor pay they received, had not yet the means to use it. The consumerist economy was still around the corner.

Thus by the turn of this century television existed as a technical possibility. It was grounded in scientific research but seemingly had no practical application. By 1908 the actual electronic system used to produce TV images had been outlined. The first image was transmitted in 1911 to a cathode ray tube in St. Petersburg, now Leningrad. Major firms were interested, because the technology could potentially be used as an alternative to radio and film, and because of its possible threat to established facsimile systems. Research programs were set up, but they were underfunded. Nevertheless, by 1923 an RCA team, led by Vladimir Zworykin, patented the basic TV camera tube of today.

Further development during the 1920s and 1930s was confused because the major radio industry players were not interested and because other solutions than a purely electronic TV system were also under consideration. These mechanical/electronic systems, which dated back to the 1884 patent, were being explored by a group of researchers largely outside the radio industry.

The confusion persisted because the capital necessary to diffuse TV was then being applied to the movies—by now the talkies—and to radio. The very same firms were interested in all three areas, and judged that TV would be a threat to current business but had interesting future possibilities. Nevertheless, in both Britain and Nazi Germany public television, using a fully electronic system, began in 1936. In Germany it was seen only rarely for theatrical purposes, for the regime continued to focus more on radio, film, and the press to get across its propaganda. In Britain the economic difficulties of the Depression decade prevented its widespread use.

A major factor in the delay in the United States was that RCA so controlled the patents that the Federal Communications Commission was worried about the survival of the other firms that could make TV equipment. It therefore stood in the path of RCA's development of TV from 1936 to 1941. The FCC was trying to prevent the AT&T telephone monopoly from being reproduced by RCA in this area. By 1941 the necessary agreements had been struck, but U.S. entry into the war that year halted further development.

At the end of the war the situation was quite different. The radio industry was looking for a new technology to exploit, having saturated the market with radio sets. In general, the war had greatly expanded the electronic manufacturing capacity of the country, and if that capacity were not to be lost, the public would have to begin to "need" a range of domestic electrical appliances that it had lived without previously. Further, the opportunities for advertising these and other products via TV seemed wide open. The Depression decade seemed to have fixed in policymakers' minds that if consumer demand was flat, no economic growth was possible; and after the many sacrifices of the war, a return to Depression would have been political dynamite.

However, it was not an overnight process. The FCC again suppressed the free development of TV by limiting the number of stations that could be built, even instituting a "freeze" on new construction from 1948 to 1952. There were technical reasons for doing this, including the decision as to which color system was to be used, the power and location of TV masts, and the question of VHF and UHF wavebands. But the reasons were not simply technical.

It is often suggested that TV destroyed Hollywood. The great studios are a thing of the past. But where does most TV production still take place? Hollywood. The FCC freeze also allowed Hollywood to maintain its position as supplier to the new TV industry, for it was during that period that the terms of this trade were worked out.

Case 4 attempts to meld all of the elements used in the other cases—the individual contribution, the triggering effects of increasing knowledge in science, and the application of other technologies, economic forces, political considerations, social policy, and general cultural factors. These various elements can be thought of as relating in the following way.

Imagine the realm of science as a line going from the past to the future:

past _____ future

science

Now imagine a parallel line, which we will call "technology":

technology

past   future

science

These two lines are connected in the mind of the technologist, the person who has an idea for an application:

technology

past   future

science

The idea is triggered by the understanding of science but is expressed "in the metal" as a technological device. History shows the technologist is likely to build a whole series of devices, some slightly, some radically, different from each other. The device we commonly call the "invention" does not differ from the others because it works and they do not. Often the "preinventions" work just as well. What makes the difference is that a point is reached where one of these contrivances is seen to have a real use. After that recognition of the *application* the device is considered an "invention"; before, as a "prototype." I will call the emergence of an application *supervening social necessity.*

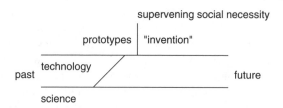

supervening social necessity

prototypes | "invention"

technology

past   future

science

Supervening social necessities are the accelerators pushing the development of media and other technology.

In Case 4 the supervening social necessities that influenced the development of television include the rise of the home market, the dominance of the nuclear family, and the political and economic need to maintain full employment after World War II. Because of these, the device finally moved out of the limbo of being an experiment to being a widely diffused consumer product.

Supervening social necessities are at the interface between society and technology. They can exist because of the needs of corporations, as when Kodak introduced Super 8 film because ordinary 8mm film had saturated the market. Or they can become a force because of another technology. Railroad development required instant signaling systems, and so enabled the telegraph to develop. Or, as in Case 4, there can be general social forces that act as supervening social necessities. Telephones emerged in the late 1870s because the modern corporation was emerging and with it the modern office. Not only telephones but elevators, typewriters, and adding machines were all "invented" during this period, although the first typewriter was patented 150 years earlier, the adding machine dated back some 250 years, and the modern hydraulic elevator had been available for over 20 years.

But if there are accelerators, there are also brakes. These work to slow the disruptive impact of new technology. I describe the operation of these brakes as the *"law" of the suppression of radical potential,* using "law" in its standard social science sense to denote a regular and powerful general tendency.

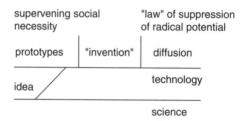

The brakes in Case 4, which caused television to be nearly a century in development, show its radical potential being suppressed, and are thus an instance of this "law." The brakes ensure that a technology's introduction does not disrupt the social or corporate status quo. Thus in the case of TV, the existence of facsimile systems, the rise of radio, the dominance of RCA, and the need not to destroy the film industry all acted to suppress the speed at which the new medium was introduced, to minimize disruption. The result is that all the main film and radio interests of the 1930s are still in business today, and television can be found in practically every house in the nation, sometimes in almost every room.

This concept of supervening social necessities and a "law" of the suppression of radical potential represents one way in which a cultural determinist would seek to understand the nature of change in media technology. I would argue it to be a more effective, more *powerful* way of explaining these matters than any that the technological determinists can produce.

For instance, we can now, using this model, answer our questions about the Arabs and the Chinese. The Arab astronomers who pioneered the camera did so for astronomical reasons, which were their supervening social necessity. Furthermore, their Islamic faith by then forbade the making of realistic images of living beings, so that culturally they would have been prohibited from exploring the camera's image-making potential. That was how the "law" of the suppression of radical potential operated on their research agenda. The Chinese produced these technologies in the context of an imperial system that used them as marks of distinction for the court. The culture made the technologies elite and limited and therefore suppressed their further development. It is these sorts of factors, not scientific knowledge or technological know-how, that condition technological developments.

EFFECTS OF TECHNOLOGY
ON COMMUNICATION CONTENT

We can now begin to address our second question. All communication modes except face-to-face speech depend on technology. Mass communication requires technologies of a sophisticated kind. The question is whether any such technologies determine what gets communicated.

Answers come in weaker and stronger forms. The weakest form is also the easiest to agree with, namely, that it is obvious that not all technologies can do the same thing. A typewriter cannot convey the same information as a photo. But can we go further?

In his article on cultural imperialism, Mohammadi (1995) reviews a well-known study by Daniel Lerner (1958) that argued, based upon research in the Near East, that when modern media were suddenly injected into a traditional village environment in the Third World, they had the effect of expanding many villagers' horizons and expectations quite dramatically. This is a stronger version of the claim that media technology determines the communication that takes place. Mohammadi notes the highly questionable assumptions also carried with this theory, but we might agree that the theory's basic assertion is plausible, even if we might want to rein it in with further "buts" and "if sos." Similarly, Sreberny-Mohammadi's argument about forms of media (1990) is an intermediate version of the argument that media technologies must be incorporated into the analysis of media effects. So far there may be room for dispute on individual points, but not on the basic position.

However, the stronger versions are quite frequently to be met with in the generalized pronouncements about media influence in the world today that commentators and editorial writers reproduce from time to time. The most renowned exponent of the strong position was Canadian media theorist Marshall McLuhan, who—even though I am now about to attack his arguments—has the distinction of having first encouraged the general public to think seriously about the impact of media technology on society. He was one of a group of Canadian historians, anthropologists, and literary critics who developed a body of ideas that suggested that in communications, technology was the determining influence. His most frequently quoted aphorism is that "the *medium* is the message" (McLuhan, 1964, chap. 1). He meant by this that media content (the explicit message) explains far less about communication than the communicative impact of the technical medium as such, viewed in terms of its effects on whole societies and cultures over centuries of their development. Actual media output therefore was of comparatively little interest to McLuhan. Here is how he describes the impact of printing press technology:

Socially, the typographic extension of man brought in nationalism, industrialism, mass markets, and universal literacy and education. For print presented an image of repeatable precision that inspired totally new forms of extending social energies. . . . The same spirit of private enterprise that emboldened authors and artists to cultivate self-expression led other men to create giant corporations, both military and commercial. (p. 157)

The key words here are that "print *presented an image* of repeatable precision that *inspired*." It is a claim not merely that the printing press determined the content of books or pamphlets, but that leading aspects of our communicative culture (literacy, education, self-expression by authors and artists), our institutions (industrialism, giant corporations, mass markets), and our political self-understanding (nationalism) were summoned into being by this media technology. It goes beyond a technical explanation of how media technology developed to provide a media-technological explanation of modern society.

But McLuhan's approach, although grounded in his reading of history, is difficult to sustain on the basis of the historical evidence. All the effects of the printing press he outlines took centuries to manifest themselves. Nationalism, in its modern form, dates from after the American and French revolutions. How then can a device introduced nearly 300 years earlier have "caused" nationalism? Similarly, universal literacy and the rise of great corporations date from the second half of the nineteenth century, some 400 years after the printing press had been introduced into the West.

McLuhan's technological determinism depends upon a very loose idea of historical causality. "Perhaps the most significant of the gifts of typography to man is that of detachment and non–involvement," he asserts (p. 157). This assertion is built upon his prior claim that the printing press gave birth to the individual author and artist. But his position is untenable. In what sense are modern people more communicatively uninvolved and detached than they were in the past, specifically the medieval European past? Certainly our sensitivity to human cruelty toward other people and animals is vastly increased, although we can be just as brutal, and now on an industrial scale, as our ancestors. How could it be shown that before print there were no authors, artists, or ordinary people who thought of themselves as individuals in the way we think of ourselves today?

Furthermore, McLuhan's basic mode of reasoning may have important ideological effects. If technology is an external force, like nature, it cannot easily be subjected to social control. It implies we are helpless in the face of such a force, rather than that we can adapt and use technology for our own freely determined purposes.

One last example: For the technological determinist, the fact that color film does not easily photograph Black skin tones is the result of the technical properties of the dyes used in those films. The cultural determinist will want to explore this matter a little more thoroughly. I would begin with the fact that color film was largely created by White scientists to photograph White skin tones. These products do not simply reproduce nature. Each color film stock the chemists designed contained a different solution to the basic problem of representing—or, better, re-presenting—natural colors. Each produces a slightly but noticeably different result.

In doing the creative work involved, the chemists are forced to make choices as to which colors their film will respond to best. For reasons grounded in the fundamental physiology of color perception within the human eye, any one set of choices will result in a film that cannot represent Black skin tones as well as it represents White. Color film stocks in general tend to give Black people a greenish hue. Indeed, the research literature on the development of such stocks reveals that the chemists were primarily interested in getting so-called White (i.e., Caucasian) skin tones as acceptable as possible. They simply did not concern themselves with how Black people would be photographed (Winston, 1985, pp. 195ff.). In this way we see once again that it is the social context, not the technology, that determines the content of communication forms.

CONCLUSIONS

At the outset, we noted that the answers given to the question as to how media technologies develop will in turn condition the answers given to the parallel question of what impact technology has on the content of communication. The technological determinist, who wants to see the technology as all-powerful, operating as though in a historical vacuum, will tend to see the influence of media technology on content as overwhelming. The cultural determinist, who wants to place the technology firmly in its social context, will also want to see that context as the primary factor determining both media technology and media content.

Technological determinism tends to present us as being comparatively impotent, as malleable consumers, unthinking and unprotesting, in the face of media technology power. The cultural determinist view, by contrast, is empowering. By drawing attention to the ways in which society constantly conditions technological developments, this view gives us the power to evaluate media technologies and to understand that we are not in the grip of forces totally beyond our control.

These implications also show us why theories in general are important. Theories can help or hinder us in coming to an understanding of the world. Without that understanding we cannot act. Thus theory is critical to action.

WORKS CITED

Allen, R. and Gomery, D. (1985). *Film History: Theory and Practice*. New York: Knopf.

Beaver, F. (1983). *A History of the Motion Picture*. New York: McGraw-Hill.

De Lauretis, T. and Heath, S. (Eds.). (1980). *The Cinematic Apparatus*. New York: St. Martin's.

Hendricks, G. (1961). *The Edison Motion Picture Myth*. Berkeley: University of California Press.

Lerner, D. (1958). *The Passing of Traditional Society*. New York: Free Press.

Mast, G. (1981). *A Short History of the Movies* (3rd ed.). New York: Bobbs-Merrill.

McLuhan, M. (1964). *Understanding Media*. London: Methuen.

Mohammadi, Ali. (1995). "Cultural Imperialism and Cultural Identity." In J. Downing, A. Mohammadi, and A. Sreberny-Mohammadi, eds., *Questioning the Media: A Critical Introduction.* Thousand Oaks, Calif.: Sage.

Ong, W. (1982). *Orality and Literacy.* New York: Methuen.

Ramsaye, T. (1926). *A Million and One Nights.* New York: Simon & Schuster.

Sreberny-Mohammadi, Annabelle. (1990). "Forms of Media as Ways of Knowing." In J. Downing, A. Mohammadi, and A. Sreberny-Mohammadi, eds., *Questioning the Media: A Critical Introduction.* Thousand Oaks, CA: Sage.

Temple, R. (1986). *The Genius of China.* New York: Simon & Schuster.

Williams (1975). *Television: Technology and Cultural Form.* New York: Schocken Books.

Winston, B. (1987). "A Mirror for Brunelleschi." *Daedelus,* 116(3). 18–36.

QUESTIONS FOR DISCUSSION

1. How do some popular accounts of broadcasting history, such as Ken Burns's PBS documentary *Empire of the Air,* employ a "technological determinist" narrative strategy? What gets left out? What gets overemphasized, according to Winston's critique?

2. Trace the process the author describes with the Internet (or VCRs, or MP3, or DVDs). Has the "suppression of radical potential" stage occurred yet?

3. Many times, "suppression" is justified through invocation of cultural "hot buttons" like race, sex, or a threat to the nation (e.g., jazz and radio, communism and TV, pornography and cable television). What "hot buttons" are currently being pushed to raise fears about the Internet or other new technological/cultural forms?

 INFOTRAC® COLLEGE EDITION

Search InfoTrac College Edition for articles on "new media and technology." Also, search under the author's name for reviews of his book on this topic.

2

The Radio Act of 1927
Progressive Ideology, Epistemology, and Praxis

MARK GOODMAN
MARK GRING

This article brings out—along the lines prescribed by Winston in the previous piece—some of the complex swirl of political and social ideas around one of broadcasting's landmark moments: passage of the Radio Act of 1927. It makes the important connection between a series of decisions usually regarded as driven by technology (chiefly the technological *scarcity* of the radio spectrum) and a dominant framework of social thought, Progressivism, that played a vital role in shaping broadcasting's structure and functions. The authors demonstrate that the cultural concerns of the Progressives, intent on maintaining the existing social order by carefully controlling who might be allowed to speak on the air, determined how radio's technology was understood and how its immense power was restricted to the hands of a few: the suppression of radio's radical potential.

Particularly interesting is Goodman and Gring's analysis of how the new radio law conflicted with our First Amendment freedom of speech protections, and how Progressives redefined this freedom into a more passive "freedom to listen" concept. Goodman and Gring's discussion of *praxis,* the "working out of the law," shows how the ideology of an elite group worked to bring radio under tighter social and governmental control than any other medium in history, despite First

This article originally appeared in *Rhetoric and Public Affairs* 3, no. 3 (2000): 397–418. Published by Michigan University Press. Used by permission.

Amendment freedoms. Under the standard of "public interest, convenience, and necessity" the rights of the public were reduced to the right to receive radio programs, while "only those voices fitting into the framework of the dominant ideology, as defined by the Progressives, were granted easy access to the media." They point to Progressivism's continuing impact on media policy today.

The Radio Act of 1927, the cornerstone of broadcasting regulation in the United States, reflects the Progressive ideology of its writers. This article explains the limited rights Progressives assigned to broadcasters when guaranteeing them "freedom of speech."

The Progressive movement, and the propaganda analysis that grew out of it, remains among our most worthy traditions of scholarship and one from which there remains much to be learned.[1]

The Radio Act of 1927 is one of the most influential pieces of legislation in U.S. history. This bill was the first law that regulated radio broadcasting as a mass medium; therefore, the Radio Act became the legal foundation for the development of the broadcasting industry. Further, the Radio Act was incorporated almost word for word into the Communications Act of 1934, extending the reach of the law into television and telephone. The Telecommunications Act of 1996, despite adding sections dealing with newer forms of telecommunications, was a series of amendments to that 1934 law. When the 1996 Act was graphed onto the language of the old, the new law incorporated many past assumptions. In effect, The Radio Act of 1927 remains the legislative cornerstone governing broadcasting in the United States today.

Our goal in this paper is to understand the Progressive mindset which influenced the way Congress wrote the Radio Act. Our approach casts a rhetorical light on this law to illuminate the ideological influences on the people who created the cause and effect relationships. Yet, we do not seek to perform a traditional rhetorical criticism on the text, because we do not believe that the words or structure of the law (the codification of the ideas) provide much new insight unless the ideological framework of Congress in 1927 is understood. Ideological analyses such as this one lend themselves to cultural studies approaches, but our scope is more limited. Our historical, rhetorical, cultural approach pries open this law in search of its Progressivist assumptions.

In light of the current communication revolution and the continued influence of the Radio Act on current regulation, a reconsideration of the epistemological and ontological assumptions within the Radio Act of 1927 is in order, particularly since this act redefined "free speech" along ideological lines. We argue that a prima facie definition of free speech inadequately explains the intent of Congress in 1927. Instead, a Progressive sense of the meaning of free speech in 1927 needs to be understood, to clarify the Radio Act. By understanding the "subtle, ambiguous, nuanced, retrospective, and/or suggestive" use of power,[2] we can go beyond the words of the law or the law makers to uncover a more comprehensive intent inherent in the law.

We contend that the interaction among epistemology, power, and praxis expresses the cultural understanding of what Progressives meant in 1927 by the concept of "free speech." Congress in 1927 never intended for radio to become an unregulated part of the marketplace of ideas. In an unregulated marketplace, all voices would be heard and through unimpeded discussion and debate the truth would be discovered. We argue that what Congress had in mind for the radio industry was a system free of direct government interference, but predicated on continual governmental surveillance. Congress intended radio to be the voice for the dominant values in American culture as those values were understood by the Progressives and by much of middle-class America.

In some ways, the tasks we have set for ourselves are hopelessly complex. To "prove" our contention that Congress sought to use radio to present the dominant values of the middle class would require us to do the following: (1) prove what values the middle class held (as if cultural solidarity existed); and (2) prove that all members of Congress who voted or debated radio legislation knew what these values were, agreed with them, and wrote specific provisions to achieve those ideological ends. Even thousands of interviews, all of which included a "smoking gun" statement that supported our thesis, would not prove our contentions. Instead, we make a circumstantial case that supports our contention, not necessarily proving we are "right," but rather that our contentions are worthy of consideration because they do shed additional light on the Radio Act of 1927.

Specifically, we will present the following arguments:

1. The principal players in writing the legislation—Representative Wallace White, Senator Clarence Dill, and Secretary of Commerce Herbert Hoover—were either Progressives or influenced by Progressive ideology, as were the two strongest congressional opponents, Representative Edwin Davis and Senator Key Pittman.

2. The language of the act had its precedents in Progressive legislation, particularly the legal cornerstone of "public interest, convenience, and necessity."

3. Parts of the congressional debate dealing with free speech issues for broadcasters expressed Progressive concepts of epistemology and ideology. The language of the act put into praxis Progressive concepts of epistemology and ideology; as a result, the solutions contained within the Radio Act to resolve points of contention likewise reflect Progressive concepts of epistemology and ideology.

4. Members of the public interested in radio legislation accepted a Progressive concept of regulation based on a "public interest" standard.

5. A Progressive concept of free speech coincided with contemporary rulings of the U.S. Supreme Court, which sought to define free speech rights.

Once we have presented our evidence on these five points, we believe we will have made a prima facie case that *radio was intended to be the voice for the dominant values in American culture as those values were understood by the Progressives and by many middle-class Americans.* Therefore, it is reasonable to conclude that Congress never intended for radio broadcasting to be an unfettered marketplace of ideas.

THE PROGRESSIVES

Progressivism is a controversial term in American history because it describes a wide range of people who frequently disagreed with each other.[3] On one extreme of the movement were Midwestern and Southern farmers (the old populists). On the other were the immigrants who came to the United States by the millions after 1880 to work in the factories and live in the urban slums of America. A third social and economic force were the "captains of capitalism," pushing America into the 20th century through technology and industrialism. Progressivism began as a grassroots reform movement in the 1800s, alternatively identified with the aspirations of farmers, immigrants, and industrialists but also members of the middle class threatened by the corruption and immorality of changing social systems.

The Progressive members of the middle class sought to define their place in this new order. Oscar Handlin describes them as holding the traditional Protestant values of the agrarian populists; yet, they staked their economic future on the business values of the wealthy industrialists by going to work for and investing in their operations. As the middle class joined the factory force and business classes as managers, they were brought into contact with an immigrant labor force frequently composed of Jews and Catholics from eastern Europe.[4] These non-Protestants held on to their ethnic identities, creating inner-city neighborhoods where, from the perspective of the middle class, crime, poverty, and sin flourished.

In the competition for control of this social order, Robert H. Wiebe argues, the middle class led the way in a shift from rural, agricultural, small town thinking to urban, industrial, big-government solutions. Middle-class Progressives placed power and authority in government bureaucracy, which was to manage the new order by limiting the power of corporations in the business marketplace. Only government could conceivably protect what Progressives perceived to be the public welfare, which was permitting individuals to manage their own affairs by freeing them from the abuses of monopolies.[5] That individualism, to David Danbom, was a product of the Victorian age in which the Progressives had grown up and of the Victorian faith in individualism. Explains Danbom, "The individual . . . was the shaper of his own destiny. His economic success was dependent upon his own efforts, as was his social position."[6] Yet, as David N. Rabban notes, Progressives found that too much individualism and too much freedom threatened social harmony:

> More broadly, the shared Progressive commitment to social harmony implied limitations on free speech. Many Progressives appreciated free speech and even dissent as qualities that contributed to, and should be nurtured by, a Progressive democratic society. But they saw no value in, and occasionally expressed hostility toward, dissent that was not directed at positive social reconstruction.[7]

By the 1920s, conflicts between "urban life and rural sentiments" made the creation of a broad-based Progressive coalition impossible.[8] Some senators remained Progressive activists, such as Robert La Follette of Wisconsin, who ran a credible third-party candidacy in 1924. La Follette and Senators George Norris, William Borah, Hiram Johnson, Burton Wheeler, and Fiorello La Guardia earned the nickname "Sons of the Wild Jackass"[9] for their insurgent, Progressive positions.

These senators, however, did not reflect the totality of Progressivism in the 1920s. The movement had changed after World War I. John Chamberlain says Progressivism "ceased to be critical; it contented itself with following the drift of events" and then satisfied itself by "calling the drift decision."[10] Richard Hofstadter contends that World War I led to the "liquidation of the Progressive spirit," allowing the dark side of the movement to flourish in the 1920s.[11] Progressives were no longer the reformers they had been in the early part of the century; however, in many ways they were more powerful. After 50 years of public debate, the Progressive ideal of societal control through federal power was accepted—and still is. McCraw calls "the bureaucratization of American life" one of the continuing legacies of the Progressives.[12] In relationship to the Radio Act of 1927, what is crucial is that congressmen, regardless of party, accepted a Progressive way of thinking about the role and mechanisms of government.[13]

THE PRAXIS OF IDEOLOGY

Progressivism was one of the competing/emerging ideologies within the hegemony of the 1920s. Antonio Gramsci defines hegemony as the societal interplay of groups which compete for dominance.[14] His emphasis is on the progression of the development of those who are in power and those who are on the fringes of power. This perspective recognizes a dominant group whose ideas maintain the dominant position within the social system while acknowledging the existence of competing ideologies (some of which are "coming into power" while others are "waning in power").

Raymond Williams, building on Gramsci, claims that hegemony "is a concept which at once includes and goes beyond the terms 'culture' and 'ideology.'"[15] One way in which hegemony goes beyond "culture" and "ideology" is in its recognition of process. There is no assumption of a culture or an ideology as static because "hegemony is always a process."[16] As a process, hegemony does not just passively exist as a form of dominance. It has continually to be renewed, recreated, defended, and modified. It is also continually resisted, limited, altered, and challenged by pressures not at all its own. We have then to add to the concept of hegemony the concepts of counter-hegemony and alternative hegemony which are real and persistent elements of practice.[17] The absence of a singular, dominant hegemony does not mean that there is not a "dominant hegemony"; it only means that an hegemonic dominance is "never either total or exclusive."[18]

Just as Progressivism was one of several competing political movements within its social milieu, so, too, were there competing positions under the rubric "Progressivism." Despite these competing perspectives, commonality existed among Progressives. They argued for societal regulation exerted by the combined forces of the federal government, "experts" from the area, and business. By the 1920s, these regulatory agencies were accepted. Fights over the nature of the regulation and the radio commission nearly wrecked the chances for legislation in 1926, but both houses of Congress, the listening public, and the industry accepted the concept of regulation through commission. Only a handful of amateur radio operators protested.

Through governmental regulation, Progressives had found ways to bring those outside the morality of Progressive ideology under surveillance, even silencing some voices. The U.S. Supreme Court found convictions under the Espionage Act of 1917 constitutional during World War I, even though the justices recognized that the state was silencing voices of protest. Later the Supreme Court extended to the states the authority to silence other radicals.

The forces of silence and surveillance were unified when the Progressives codified their assumptions into the Radio Act of 1927. Our concern is with this legal codification of the Progressive ideology as praxis. This is the actual proposal of law, not just the words used to justify why the law is needed, but the actual working out of the law. It is in the "working out of the law" with which we are intrigued, because here we find the "performance of ideology." Within any ideology there must be the carrying out of one's ideas, the attempt to implement one's epistemological and power assumptions upon the rest of the sociopolitical system. As Nikolaus Lobkowicz, Jacques Ellul, Kenneth Minogue, and Clodovis Boff argue, it is within the praxis, the sociopolitical implementation of the ideas, that one becomes ideological and where the actual *doing* begins to inform the philosophical assumptions.[19]

We contend that the Radio Act's "public interest, convenience, and necessity" standard and the creation of the Federal Radio Commission performed ideological functions for the Progressives. Broadcasters and the listening public were told in 1927 that the Radio Act guaranteed "free speech."[20] Everyone could listen to radio programming as they chose and no government agency would create programming. Monopolies would be prevented from controlling the airwaves. Radio seemed to benefit everyone, but in reality only those voices fitting into the framework of the dominant ideology, as defined by the Progressives, were granted easy access to the media. Our critical analysis of the discourse which brought about the Radio Act of 1927 reveals the ideological assumptions of the Progressives, who were the primary promoters of this and the dominant force behind the ensuing Federal Radio Commission (FRC).

THE PRINCIPAL PLAYERS

The four principal players in writing the Radio Act of 1927 reflected the diversity among those falling under the rubric of Progressive. Clarence Dill had aligned himself with the insurgents in the Senate.[21] Herbert Hoover, an engineer by training and profession, believed in the power of disinterested experts to work for and achieve the public good.[22] During the 1920s, Hoover used his position as Secretary of Commerce to nurture the growth of radio. President Coolidge[23] and Congressman Wallace White both opposed the creation of another regulatory commision.[24] However, both listened to the concerns of the "captains" of the radio industry and were anxious for some kind of government regulation.

Dill had been a Progressive before World War I, serving one term in the House of Representatives before losing his seat because he voted against the declaration of war against Germany. Washington voters sent him to the Senate in 1922 on the promise he would join the farm bloc directed by Senator George Norris of Nebraska.

Dill's first radio bill generally copied White's bill introduced in the House. White's 1926 bill, and Dill's Senate version, derive from other bills introduced that date back to 1922. William Borah, however, introduced competing legislation, labeled an "anti-administration bill" by the *New York Times,* because Borah wanted a new radio commission to assume the authority being exercised by Hoover. Dill reintroduced his bill with the Borah provisions. This was the bill passed by the Senate in the spring of 1926.

Hoover opposed Dill's commission because he considered control of radio important to the functioning of the federal government. In naming individuals to the radio conferences of 1922–1925, Hoover always asked representatives from several governmental agencies to attend. H. C. Smither, chief coordinator of the Interdepartment Radio Advisory, wrote in a 1925 memo to Hoover that radio policy directly affected the following government agencies and cabinet offices: State Department, Treasury, War, Department of Justice, Post Office, Navy Department, Interior, Department of Agriculture, Bureau of Standards, Department of Labor, ICC, Shipping Board, "dissemination of information by the federal government and potential for national defense."[25] While the interest of the listening public may have focused on entertainment, to Hoover, the federal government needed radio to be effective, and that would require direct government control over some aspects of broadcasting. Hoover sought to explain this concept to the participants of the third radio conference: "Through these policies we have established, the Government, and therefore the people, have to-day the control of the channels through the ether just as we have control of our channels of navigation; but outside this fundamental reservation radio activities are largely free."[26] Now Dill and the insurgent Progressives in the Senate sought to remove the administration of radio from the executive branch and place it under five commissioners who were answerable to no one. Hoover needed to prevent that from happening.

Another factor to consider in understanding the battle over the commission was Hoover's role in the development of radio. While he was secretary of commerce, radio had boomed. His careful, bipartisan approach to regulation had helped radio grow and evolve. His radio conferences had paved the way for meaningful regulation. If elected president in 1928, Hoover could continue to nurture radio, guiding it with the moral hand so necessary for it to become an instrument of public good. C. M. Jansky argues that Hoover predicated his concept of free speech and public service upon the existence of the moral hand. If radio served the public interest, then programming would not have to be regulated.[27] Hoover explained this point at the Third Radio Conference: "We will maintain them [radio activities] free—free of monopoly, free in program, and free in speech—but we must also maintain them free of malice and unwholesomeness."[28] This is Hoover the Progressive and the engineer speaking. His biographer Joan Hoff Wilson describes Hoover as a "Progressive engineer."[29] Richard Hofstadter calls Hoover a self-described "independent Progressive" who identified with "efficiency, enterprise, opportunity, individualism, substantial laissez-faire, personal success, and material welfare."[30]

As a Progressive, Hoover believed that engineers should not just be designers, but should seek to maximize opportunities and efficiency for the cooperative good. In 1926, radio was literally and figuratively an engineering project. Its structure needed to be built; its utility needed to be maximized for the greatest good, which would be serving the needs of the listeners. Hoover raised this issue often. One example was in November 1925: "The ether is a public medium, and its use must be for the public benefit. The use of a radio channel is justified only if there is public benefit." Those listeners needed government to protect them from the immoral, the indecent, the lies, and the propaganda that unscrupulous people could broadcast. If radio regulation was in the hands of the secretary of commerce, then Hoover, the engineer, could continue to build radio and ensure that it was quality product for the public. Under an independent commission such responsibility would rest with individuals who would not have Hoover's background and training, or perhaps even the right moral fiber. Hoover would solve this problem in 1927 by sending commissioners' names to Coolidge. In his *Memoirs,* Hoover describes his choices: "They were all men of technical and legal experience in the art, and none of them were politicians."[31]

If Hoover believed so much depended on the proper administration of radio, then why did he agree to a compromise with Senator Dill in January 1927? A consideration to Hoover could have been the one-year expiration placed on the Federal Radio Commission (FRC). Within a year, Hoover planned to be president-elect. When the FRC expired, he would be in a position to influence what would replace it. Meanwhile, the main task of the FRC was to assign broadcasting licenses, a task Hoover planned all along to give to his administrative commission, since he did not believe that one person should make those decisions.[32] Nor should the intense lobbying from the radio industry for almost any regulation be forgotten. In a few months, the RCA/GE chief executive officer Owen Young, his protégé, David Sarnoff, and others would create the National Broadcasting Corporation, the first major permanent radio network and a project worth millions. Chaos threatened that economic future in ways that a commission did not and radio chaos had only increase since a state court decision *(United States v. Zenith)* had undercut Hoover's authority.[33] A decision by acting Attorney General William J. Donovan stated that the court's decision limited Hoover's power to assigning licenses, that he had no authority to assign wavelengths, hours of operation, or put limits on power.[34] If Hoover accepted Dill's compromise, a mechanism existed to restore order to the airwaves, please the radio corporations, let the commission accomplish a task he wanted the commission to do, and position himself to guide radio's future. He could outsmart the Progressive senators in the end.

Hoover's influence extended beyond that of commerce secretary. White and Coolidge relied heavily on Hoover's radio expertise. Coolidge looked to Hoover to develop radio policy. Although Coolidge would speak out often on radio legislation, on at least one occasion Hoover wrote Coolidge's speech.[35] White also looked to Hoover.[36] White had conferred with Hoover on radio legislation as early as 1921.[37] During the 1926 debate over the Radio Act, Hoover marked up a copy of the Senate bill[38] and a copy of the legislation labeled "Confidential Conference Draft."[39] It requires little stretch to presume Hoover shared with White his comments in the margins of the draft.

While Congressman E. L. Davis and Senator Key Pittman presented the populist side of Progressivism, White and Hoover preferred to work with the captains of the radio industry. During the Radio Act debate, RCA kept its views known to both Hoover and White. The Radio Corporation of America had been founded in 1919 when General Electric, Westinghouse, American Telephone and Telegraph, and United Fruit took over the assets of American Marconi. Each corporation took shares in RCA and divided the marketing of products.[40] The president of RCA was J. G. Harbord, who corresponded with both Hoover and White on radio legislation.[41] In addition, David Sarnoff, the rising star at RCA, met with White to discuss radio legislation.[42] Publicly, AT&T, General Electric, and the National Association of Broadcaster stated their support for the White bill.[43]

From these interconnections, meetings, and correspondences, a conclusion can be drawn that the White bill not only reflected the congressman's thinking, but also the influence of RCA and Hoover, with the agreement of President Coolidge.

Even though passage of the Radio Act would pit the insurgent Republicans like Dill against the populists like Key and Davis and against the Coolidge administration, the key point is that Hoover, Coolidge, the senators, and White agreed on what federal regulation could achieve and sought similar goals for radio; the disagreement was over what mechanism of government to use to achieve those goals. The arguments among the principal players were between different shades of Progressive thought.

THE NEED FOR LEGISLATION

By 1927, the technology and growth of radio had outpaced existing congressional regulation, written in 1912 when radio meant ship-to-shore communication. Radio was loosely regulated through its growth years in the 1920s. By mailing a postcard to Secretary of Commerce Herbert Hoover, anyone with a radio transmitter—ranging from college students experimenting in science classes, to amateur inventors who ordered kits, to newspaper-operated stations— could broadcast on the frequency chosen by Hoover. The airwaves by 1927 were an open forum for anyone with the expertise and equipment[44] to reach an audience with 25 million potential listeners.[45]

Radio's open forum, however, became unmanageable in 1926 after an Attorney General's decision said the Radio Act of 1912 did not give the secretary of commerce authority to assign specific wave lengths.[46] By 1926, radio in the United States included 15,111 amateur stations, 1,902 ship stations, 553 land stations for maritime use, and 536 broadcasting stations.[47] Geographical separation and power restrictions would make it possible to place six stations per broadcasting channel for a total of 534 stations. In addition, 425 more licensing applications were under consideration by the department of commerce, which had no legal authority to reject any request for a license. White warned his colleagues in 1926 that radio stations were jamming the airwaves, causing interference between stations in many locations. In the words of the *New York Times,* the radio signal almost anywhere on the dial sounded like "the whistle of the peanut stand."[48] Radio had become what Erik Barnouw calls "A Tower of Babel."[49] The "babel" threatened the emerging economics of radio. The undisciplined and unregulated voice of the public interfered with corporate goals of delivering programming and advertising on a dependable schedule to a mass audience.

Congress faced many difficulties in trying to write legislation. No precedent existed for managing broadcasting except the powerless Radio Act of 1912. No one knew in 1926 where the technology was going nor what radio would be like even the next year, so Congress was trying to write law to cover potentialities. Senator Key Pittman of Nevada expressed his frustration to the Senate chair:

> I do not think, sir, that in the 14 years I have been here there has ever been a question before the Senate that in the very nature of the thing Senators can know so little about as this subject.[50]

Nor was the public much better informed, Pittman noted, even though he received telegrams daily urging passage.

> I am receiving many telegrams from my State urging me to vote for this conference report, and informing me that things will go to pieces, that there will be a terrible situation in this country that cannot be coped with unless this report is adopted. Those telegrams come from people, most of whom, I know, know nothing on earth about this bill.[51]

Offering to bring order out of this chaos were White and Dill. These two congressional radio experts led the year-long fight in 1926 to pass legislation to regulate radio, leading to the Radio Act, signed by Calvin Coolidge in February 1927.

THE HISTORICAL ARGUMENT

Other historians have considered congressional intent in the Radio Act and evaluated Progressive influences, most notably Louise Benjamin and Donald Godfrey. Benjamin's dissertation on free speech in the Radio Act considered the issues of censorship, creation of a regulatory agency, monopoly, and the right of broadcasters to use the medium. In trying to resolve who should be allowed to broadcast, Benjamin argues, Congress placed itself into a larger social debate. A free speech debate existed within American society over those who "saw 'abuses' of free speech as intolerable and those who wished to use speech to further social and economic goals."[52] As Benjamin would later argue, these conflicts were resolved by Secretary of Commerce Herbert Hoover and the radio industry during the 1920s radio conferences conducted by Hoover prior to passage of the Radio

Act. The end result of these agreements was "to transform the industry from amateur communication to nationwide broadcasting," which met the economic needs of the major radio corporations.[53]

Godfrey spent some time in his dissertation looking at Progressive influence on the Radio Act. He makes particular note of the Progressive roots of Senator Dill and his identification with Progressive Senators James Watson, William Borah, Robert La Follette, Hiram Johnson, and Burton Wheeler. According to Godfrey, one of the areas of Progressive influence was in the selection of the language "public interest, convenience, and necessity." These words were a way of balancing industrial control of radio against the potential for government censorship. To Godfrey, "The founders of the legislation sought to provide a degree of regulation that would preserve industrial freedom and the public interest."[54] Another way that Progressive senators specifically shaped the Radio Act was in the creation of the Federal Radio Commission, contends Godfrey in a later article.[55] Influenced by Borah and Watson, Dill rewrote his first draft of the 1926 Senate version of the bill to create the FRC. Borah and Watson objected to putting radio control into the hands of the secretary of commerce, for fear that person would use radio for political purposes. Kerry Irish notes that these Progressive senators were not happy with the final version of the Radio Act. George Norris, for example, wanted governmental control of radio. Despite getting the FRC and the public interest standard, Irish claims that Dill, Norris, Borah and others would not have called the Radio Act a Progressive victory, because White and Coolidge refused to permit government ownership.[56] To an extent, Irish is correct. Coolidge told Hoover to turn to the "successful elements of the industry" for advice.[57] White discussed regulation with representatives from the National Association of Broadcasters, RCA, and even David Sarnoff.[58] In the final analysis, however, whether Borah and other Progressive senators were happy, the fact remains that the Radio Act includes many provisions, particularly the creation of an independent commission and the public interest standard, borrowed from the Progressive model of federal regulation.

White and Dill agreed that the public interest standard was the heart of the Radio Act.[59] The FRC, armed with the "hidden teeth" of the public interest standard, had all the authority it needed to create the machinery for censorship.[60] Public interest provided a criterion for the commission to determine who was fit to broadcast, notes C. B. Rose, but without creating specific guidelines. Without guidelines to follow, the commission could favor large "capital interests."[61] Ultimately, the public interest standard represented "prior restraint" of broadcasters, argues Fred H. Cate, and, therefore, "The First Amendment is nowhere to be found" in the Radio Act of 1927.[62]

However, Progressives would not have seen themselves as violators of free speech. Rabban notes that free speech carried with it moral obligations that were to keep free speech checked. For Goodman these unspoken moral obligations are as much a part of understanding the free speech issues of the Radio Act as are the free speech statements in the language of the law.[63] The congressional goal in the Radio Act was not government censorship, but many in Congress feared the power of radio, Goodman argues. If the FRC licensed the right kind of people with the right moral values, then Congress would have nothing to fear.

THE FREE SPEECH DEBATE

Before radio legislation could be passed, competing Progressive factions debated who would control radio. Senator Pittman and Representative E. L. Davis of Tennessee represented the voice of the common man of rural America. Pittman and Davis believed that RCA was conspiring to turn radio into a monopoly. The monopoly would not only be worth millions, but to Pittman and Davis, RCA would use the voice of radio to gain great political power and to shape though in America.

RCA was not the first corporation to be targeted by Progressives. Monopolies had long been a principal target of rural Progressives, dating back to their populist roots. This eventually led to the Sherman Antitrust Act of 1890, which sought to prevent the destruction of "free capitalism and restraint of trade."[64]

Dill and White were spokesmen for those who believed progress and technology needed to move forward and that regulation would prevent the evils predicted by Davis and Pittman. White considered the public interest standard to be one of the seven key elements in the law to prevent monopolies.[65]

Free speech under the First Amendment had traditionally meant that everyone had the right to express opinion, creating an uninhibited marketplace of ideas. However, the limited number of radio channels made the old definition obsolete from the viewpoint of Congress. Noting that free speech needed to be "inviolate," White argued that a new concept of free speech was required.

> We [Radio Conference of 1924] have reached the definite conclusion that the right of all of our people to enjoy this means of communication can be preserved only by the repudiation of the idea underlying the 1912 law that anyone who will may transmit and *by the assertion in its stead of the doctrine that the right of the public to service is superior to the right of any individual to use the ether* [emphasis added.][66]

In effect, White was creating a right to listen and equating it with freedom of speech. Such an equation would work, Dill argued,[67] because of the "public interest, convenience, or necessity" standard written into the act.[68]

Proper use of the radio was a second free speech issue debated. The power of the FRC would become the instrument for ensuring that radio was not used for improper speech. Specifically, the Radio Act banned "obscene, indecent, or profane language."[69] In addition, those who would use radio for radical change also could be silenced, White and Dill told their colleagues.

Attempts were made in writing the bill to guarantee that only the "right" kind of material was communicated to the audience. Senator Hiram Bingham of Connecticut thought the commerce department should handle the technical aspects of radio while the Post Office could handle "improper" communication of thought, since it already had expertise.[70] Senator Coleman L. Blease of South Carolina was willing to create the FRC as long as he knew what the politics and religion of the commissioners were. Blease wanted to know if someone could go on the air and say "he came from a monkey."[71] Blease's amendment to prohibit all radio discussion of evolution failed.

At one point during congressional debate, Senator Earle B. Mayfield of Texas wanted to know what was going to keep "bolshevism or communism" off the air.[72] Dill believed that radicals could be excluded from the airwaves since the law[73] only discussed air time for legally qualified candidates.[74] Congressional intent was to give voice to the political parties supported by the middle class while the candidates of immigrants, many of whom supported unions or radical political change, would have limited access to the airwaves.

As praxis in the Radio Act, regulated free speech meant that the only discussions to be heard over the radio would be those consistent with the ideology of the Progressives. In this way, the Progressive agenda could be presented to the public. Unions, socialists, communists, evolutionists, improper thinkers, non-Christians, and immigrants, could be marginalized by keeping these ideas off radio, outside of "public interest, convenience, and necessity." Progressives silenced opposition during World War I with the Espionage Act, and the Supreme Court extended the law during the 1920s through its rulings to control the voice of radicals. Within such an historical and ideological context, the Radio Act of 1927 becomes a performance of Progressive ideology.

The Radio Act put the mechanism in place for control of the airwaves through surveillance and silence. The FRC would review all station logs and programming to determine if each broadcaster was acting in the "public interest, convenience, and necessity." That determination would be based on the assumptions that listeners did not have a right to speak, only a right to hear. Through regulatory agencies, Rabban explains, controls on individualism could be instituted that "would permit a benevolent government to participate actively in creating a society in which all citizens have the resources to exercise effective freedom and to develop their individual capacities for the common good."[75]

The "benevolent" efforts of White and Dill had been successful. They had given both the public and the corporations essentially what they wanted, but the real control of radio would be in the hands of the Progressives' representative: the FRC. The people would be guaranteed access to radio programs that would be entertaining, but they were effectively denied access to the airwaves. Radio station owners had lost the right to speak for themselves, but in return they could use the electromagnetic spectrum to make money through advertising. For Progressives such as Dill, White, and Hoover, technology and progress could go forward, controlled by the moralistic hand of the middle class and the power of "public interest, convenience, and necessity."

PUBLIC INTEREST, CONVENIENCE, AND NECESSITY

Dill claims the language "public interest, convenience, and necessity" was a late addition to the Radio Act, that the term resulted from his meetings with White to write the final version of the bill.[76] Yet, the concept of radio operating in the public interest dates back at least to the first radio conference of 1922 when

Hoover, in his opening comments, stated that radio should be presenting information of the "public interest." In 1925, he described "the ether" as "a public medium, and its use must be for public benefit."[77]

Dill acknowledged that the public interest concept was not original but was borrowed from the Interstate Commerce Commission (ICC).[78] White, in a letter, credited parts of the Radio Act to the ICC.[79] Dill served on the Senate's ICC committee while White served on the House committee overseeing railroad regulation. Since Hoover was secretary of commerce, he worked extensively with the ICC and railroad regulation. All three were familiar with the traditions of regulation under a public interest standard before writing the Radio Act.

All three also shared a presumption that a public interest standard conferred on the government the right to limit who spoke. Dill went so far as to admit that the public interest standard created a "twilight zone" between serving the public interest and permitting the federal government the right to censor radio, although he did not believe that public interest, convenience, and necessity gave the government the right to control programming.[80] Rather, the goal of public interest was to "empower the Commission to limit the amount of advertising, prohibit programs that it decided were harmful to the public as a whole, and to refuse to renew licenses of those who disregarded its rulings."[81] To Dill, such use of the language by the FRC did not violate the First Amendment because it protected the listeners. White told the House that the free speech provisions of the Radio Act of 1912 had to be repudiated to be replaced by "the right of the public to service."[82] White also did not believe that protecting the public interest was censorship but that it was "about as far as we can go in permanent legislation" to regulate broadcasters.[83]

Like White and Dill, Hoover did not try to explain apparent free speech restrictions created by implementing a public interest standard. Hoover described the state of radio before the 1927 act as "a policy of absolute freedom and untrammeled operation, a field open to all who wished to broadcast for whatever purpose desired." However, the only way to end radio chaos was "to keep the best stations." Freedom of speech had two parties, Hoover explained, the speaker and the listener. "Certainly in radio I believe in freedom for the listener," Hoover told the 1924 radio conference. "The greatest public interest must be the deciding factor."[84]

Willard D. Rowland's essay on the public interest standard of broadcasting further explains the perspectives of Hoover, White, and Dill. Rowland points out that a public interest standard dated back nearly a century by 1927. State regulatory agencies had been created early in the 1800s to regulate railroads, and many of these agencies used a public interest standard. The U.S. Supreme Court upheld the standard in 1837.[85] "Convenience and necessity" became associated with the public interest as a provision for the granting of licenses to railroads and utilities, Rowland explains. The federal government adopted a public interest standard for the first time in the Interstate Commerce Act of 1887. Congress also relied on public interest in creating the Federal Reserve Board in 1912 and the Federal Trade Commission in 1927. As Rowland explains, "Having become an integral part of the state regulatory philosophy and having been sustained in the courts, the public interest standard readily migrated into the new federal policy."[86]

Rowland disagrees with those historians who have labeled public interest as a vague standard. "In fact, however, it turns out that the public interest standard was neither vague nor undetermined in meaning or practice when introduced into broadcasting legislation," writes Rowland. Its long use as regulatory language provided the writers of the Radio Act a "well-rehearsed doctrine," which was widely understood as the authority for a regulatory agency. Regulators liked the way the standard finessed the balance between the interests of the public in protection and the need for corporate profits. On the surface, public interest language placed regulators on the side of the public. In practice, regulators protected the profits of corporations, since the public interest would not be served if those who served the public failed to survive. This regulatory approach created a need for commission experts to meet regularly with corporate leaders to discuss their needs.

The finesse worked well in creating support for the Radio Act. Dill had his commission which would serve the public interest by protecting the public from an RCA monopoly. Meanwhile, Hoover and White conferred with Sarnoff and other radio industry leaders to discuss their needs. The Radio Act protected profits, which in the long run served the public's demand for entertainment. The public interest standard of the Radio Act symbolizes the Progressive experience, writes Rowland, because it accomplishes the "social and legal compromises" of Progressive "reform and the appeal to public service and welfare."[87]

THE PUBLIC PERSPECTIVE

Despite the limitations placed on free speech by the Radio Act, most of the listening public and those in radio accepted the Progressive concept of free speech. A typical example of Progressive thinking was J. H. Morecraft, who wrote a regular column, "The March of Radio," in the industry magazine *Radio Broadcast*. "We need to protect freedom of speech," Morecraft argued, "but our rights cannot interfere with the rights of others."[88] Congestion on the airwaves was a bigger problem than free speech concerns, Morecraft held. "At this writing, we fear more no legislation at all, than the harmful effects of any particular bill or method of control."[89] Radio offered an easy solution to any legislative limitations on the speaking public. "If you have something to say," he told his readers, "go to an existing broadcaster and buy time."[90] Later, Morecraft wrote: "Freedom of the air does not require that everyone who wishes to impress himself on the radio audience need have his private microphone to do so."[91] He reiterated the point in a later column: "Radio waves cannot be freely used by everyone," Morecraft wrote. "Unlimited use will lead to its destruction."[92]

Many others concerned with radio also believed that radio could not be an unfettered marketplace of ideas. As *The Literary Digest* stated in 1924, "[T]he power of one man through a broadcasting station must be curbed if that man persists in affronting the sensibilities of a large or a small part of the population." While censorship was not appealing, the article continued, radio should not appeal to "vulgarities" or morbid affairs. Therefore, broadcasters should be businessmen of the highest class so that radio would remain "clean and fit for the common consumption."[93] When the wrong people were allowed to broadcast, then the listening public suffered, *The Literary Digest* noted in another article. "Propagandists, religious zealots, and unprincipled persons" are using radio to "grind their own axes."[94] Once the Radio Act passed, *The Literary Digest* called upon the new radio commission to assign licenses only to the "high type" that would operate the station for public service by providing "well-rounded" programming.[95]

FREE SPEECH: THE U.S. SUPREME COURT CONCEPT

A congressional concept of limited free speech was consistent with several contemporary U.S. Supreme Court rulings, including opinions written by Justices Oliver Wendell Holmes and Louis Brandeis, two Progressives on the Court. Beginning in 1919, the U.S. Supreme Court upheld the constitutionality of the Espionage Act as a tool to quiet discontent against the U.S. effort in World War I, first in *Schenck v. United States* and later in *Frohwerk v. United States* and *Debs v. United States*. Eventually, the Supreme Court extended limitations on free speech beyond the context of World War I to include radicalism and anarchy *(Gitlow v. New York; Whitney v. California)*.

Rabban argues that the Espionage Act under which Frohwerk, Schenck, and Debs were convicted held similar ideological assumptions as those we ascribe to the Radio Act. Rabban based his conclusions on a review of the writings of John Dewey, Herbert Croly, and Roscoe Pound, three Progressive intellectuals. Rabban notes that Progressives found that too much individualism and too much freedom threatened social harmony.

> More broadly, the shared Progressive commitment to social harmony implied limitations on free speech. Many Progressives appreciated free speech and even dissent as qualities that contributed to, and should be nurtured by, a Progressive democratic society. But they saw no value in, and occasionally expressed hostility toward, dissent that was not directed at positive social reconstruction.[96]

In light of the writings of Progressive leaders, Supreme Court decisions, and the actions of the federal government during the Red Scare, the concept of free speech as understood in 1927 did not include a marketplace of robust debate and extremist views. Free speech was protected for those who used it responsibly, in ways consistent with the dominant ideology. Therefore, a discussion of radical political change would not only seem to violate the Radio Act's standard of "public interest, convenience, and necessity," but could also be illegal.

CONCLUSIONS

We have laid out our circumstantial case. The three people most responsible for writing the Radio Act of 1927 approached radio regulation from a Progressive perspective. White and Hoover sought to balance the profit needs of the radio industry against the entertainment requirements of the public. They relied on the Progressive concept of public interest, convenience, and necessity to achieve and maintain that balance. Dill, the third major player, took a more insurgent approach, forcing Hoover and White to accept the Federal Radio Commission, which Dill hoped would protect the public interest from the monopolist designs of RCA, while encouraging the development of the art of radio. Despite the firm opposition of Hoover and White to Dill's FRC, they both also wanted a commission to play a role in radio regulation. More fundamentally, the difference was over *which branch of the federal government* should provide surveillance over the radio voices, not *if* there should be surveillance. None of the three designers of the law envisioned a free and uninhibited marketplace of ideas over the airwaves. They did not consider surveillance as being a restriction on free speech. Nor did they object to the silencing of radical or immoral voices.

From a Progressive perspective, free speech meant the freedom to behave in a responsible manner. This was the argument made by the U.S. Supreme Court in several contemporary decisions. Further, it was a definition of free speech accepted by the listening public as represented by magazine and newspaper writers of the time. Progressive epistemological and ideological assumptions were put into praxis through public interest, convenience, and necessity and the creation of the FRC. The radio industry accepted limitations because it was given a free hand in developing networks and making radio a profitable industry driven by advertising sales. The public was satisfied as long as it could listen nightly to its favorite programs without the "whistles of the peanut stand" created by station interference.

Since the Radio Act of 1927 remains the cornerstone of broadcasting regulation in America, a fair presumption is that some of the Progressive ideological and epistemological assumptions continue to influence regulation today. The challenge remains for scholars to review the Telecommunications Act of 1996, the U.S. Supreme Court decision in *ACLU v. Reno*, as well as other recent regulatory decisions to discover how Progressivism continues to influence broadcasting today.

NOTES

1. James Carey, "Communications and the Progressives," in *Critical Perspectives on Media and Society*, ed. Robert K. Avery and David Eason (New York: Guilford Press, 1991), 28–48.

2. Ronald F. Wendt, "Answers to the Gaze: A Genealogical Poaching of Resistances," *Quarterly Journal of Speech* 82 (1996): 251–73.

3. Many historians make note of the conflicts within Progressivism, including Arthur Link and Richard McCormick, Robert Wiebe, Richard Hofstadter, Robert Murray, Joan Hoff Wilson, LeRoy Ashby, Kenneth MacKay.

4. Oscar Handlin in the foreword of David P. Thelen, *Robert La Follette and the Insurgent Spirit* (Boston: Little, Brown and Co., 1976), v.

5. Robert H. Wiebe, *The Search for Order 1877–1920* (New York: Hill and Wang, 1967), 297.

6. David B. Danbom, *The World of Hope: Progressives and the Struggle for an Ethical Public Life* (Philadelphia: Temple University Press, 1987), 5–6.

7. David N. Rabban, "Free Speech in Progressive Social Thought," *Texas Law Review* 74 (1996): 955.

8. LeRoy Ashby, *The Spearless Leader: Senator Borah and the Progressive Movement in the 1920s* (Urbana: University of Illinois Press, 1972), 8.

9. Ray Tucker and Frederick R. Barkley, *Sons of the Wild Jackass* (Seattle: University of Washington Press, 1932).

10. John Chamberlain, *The Rise, Life and Decay of the Progressive Mind in America,* 2nd ed. (New York: John Day Co., 1933), 305.

11. Richard Hofstadter, *The Age of Reform: From Bryan to F.D.R.* (New York: Knopf, 1955), 273.

12. Thomas K. McCraw, "The Progressive Legacy," in *The Progressive Era,* ed. Lewis L. Gould (Syracuse, N.Y.: Syracuse University Press, 1974), 182.

13. Key Pittman, for example, was always identified as a party line Democrat, but in 1925 and 1926 he pushed for passage of a Progressive-like piece of governmental regulation, the Long and Short Haul amendment to the Interstate Commerce Act with the help of Progressive leader William Borah. Betty Glad, *Key Pittman: The Tragedy of a Senate Insider* (New York: Columbia University Press, 1986), 139.

14. Antonio Gramsci, *Selections from the Prison Notebooks,* ed. and trans. by Quintin Hoare and Geoffrey Nowell Smith (New York: International Publishers, 1971).

15. Raymond Williams, *Marxism and Literature* (New York: Oxford University Press, 1985), 108.

16. Williams, 112.

17. Williams, 112–113.

18. Williams, 113.

19. Nikolaus Lobkowicz, *Theory and Practice: History of a Concept from Aristotle to Marx* (Notre Dame, Ind.: University of Notre Dame Press, 1967). Jacques Ellul, *Jesus and Marx: From Gospel to Ideology* (Grand Rapids, Mich.: Eerdman Publishing, 1988). Kenneth Minogue, *Alien Powers: The Pure Theory of Ideology* (London: Weidenfeld and Nicholson Ltd., 1985). Clodovis Boff, *Theology and Praxis: Epistemological Foundations* (Maryknoll, New York: Orbis Books, 1987).

20. Radio Act of 1927, Sec. 29. *Congressional Record,* 1927, 1173.

21. Clarence Dill, *Where the Water Falls* (Spokane: C. W. Hill, 1970), 74.

22. Joan Hoff Wilson, *Herbert Hoover: Forgotten Progressive* (Boston: Little, Brown and Co., 1975), 31.

23. "Coolidge Opposes More Commissions," *The New York Times,* April 28, 1926, 24.

24. "Hoover Backs Radio Bill," *The New York Times,* January 7, 1926, 41.

25. H. C. Smither, Chief Coordinator, Interdepartment Radio Advisory Committee to Herbert Hoover, Secretary of Commerce. May 20, 1925. Box 501: Radio—Interdepartmental Problems, 1923–27. Herbert Hoover Papers; Herbert Hoover Library, West Branch, Iowa (hereafter HHL).

26. "Recommendations for Regulation of Radio, Adopted by the Third National Radio Conference, October 6–10, 1924," p. 2. Box 496: Radio—Conferences; Folder: Radio—Conferences, National—third (Oct. 6, 1924), Herbert Hoover Papers, HHL.

27. C. M. Jansky. "The Contribution of Herbert Hoover to Broadcasting," *Journal of Broadcasting* 1 (1957): 241–49.

28. Hoover, Third Radio Conference, 2, Herbert Hoover Papers, HHL.

29. Wilson, 31.

30. Hofstadter, 286.

31. Herbert Hoover, *The Memoirs of Herbert Hoover: The Cabinet and the Presidency 1920–1933,* vol. 2 (New York: Macmillan, 1952), 144.

32. Hoover, *Memoirs,* 145.

33. *United States v. Zenith,* No. 14257, District Court of the U.S., Northern District of Illinois, Eastern Division. Box 502: Radio—Zenith Radio Corporation 1925. Hoover Papers, HHL.

34. Decision by William J. Donovan, Acting Attorney General, July 9, 1926. Box 501: Radio—Legislation, 1926, Herbert Hoover Papers, HHL.

35. See Box 478: President Coolidge 1926, August–November. Herbert Hoover Papers; HHL. On Nov. 20, 1926, Hoover sent a draft of a speech on radio legislation to Coolidge. Coolidge delivered that speech in December 1926 without modification.

36. Hoover and White apparently met socially, since the Hoover files include a handwritten note inviting Mr. and Mrs. Hoover to the Whites' home. Box 501: Radio—Legislation, 1926; Folder—Radio: Federal Radio Commission Legislation, 1925–1928 & Undated. Herbert Hoover Papers; HHL.

37. To Herbert Hoover from Wallace White, April 12, 1921. Box 283: House of Representatives—White, Wallace H., 1921–28 and undated. Herbert Hoover Papers; HHL.

38. S. 4156, May 3, 1926. Box 501: Radio—Interdepartmental Problems, 1923–27; Herbert Hoover Papers; HHL.

39. Confidential Draft, Radio Act. Box 501: Radio—Interdepartmental Problems, 1923–27; Herbert Hoover Papers; HHL.

40. Erik Barnouw, *Tower of Babel: A History of Broadcasting in the United States,* vol. 1 (New York: Oxford University Press, 1966), 59.

41. Harbord letters to White and Hoover. J. G. Harbord to Herbert Hoover, April 4, 1923. Box 496: Radio—Conferences, National—second (March 20–24, 1923). Herbert Hoover Papers, HHL. J. G. Harbord to Wallace White, July 26, 1926. Box 651: Folder—Radio, Miscellaneous #2. Wallace H. White Collection, Library of Congress.

42. From William Brown to Wallace White, October 26, 1926. Box 54: Folder—Radio, Miscellaneous #2. Wallace H. White Collection, Library of Congress, Washington, D.C.

43. "Bill Provides for Control of Radio Motion Pictures," *The New York Times,* January 17, 1926, 41.

44. An indication of this are the following numbers reported in *New York Times,* February 25, 1927. In 1927, there were 733 public entertainment stations and 18,119 amateur radio sending stations.

45. Dill, "A Traffic Cop for the Air," *The American Review of Reviews,* February 1927, 183.

46. Herbert Hoover, perhaps to force Congress to pass legislation, asked for an opinion ending his authority to regulate radio after the Zenith court decision undermined his authority. See C. C. Dill, "Hope to Stretch Ether Channels," *New York Times,* September 12, 1926; sec. R, 2.

47. *Congressional Record,* 1927, 5478.

48. "Expect New Radio Law to Be Shaped This Month," *New York Times,* November 7, 1926, sec. XX, 18.

49. Barnouw's title for Volume One of his history of broadcasting.

50. *Congressional Record,* 1927, 3027. Another indicator of the complexity of the issues is that Clarence Dill and Wallace White were ultimately assigned the task of writing the final version of the Radio Act because no others in Congress understood the issues. See *New York Times,* December 17, 1926, 44. Dill referred to himself as a "one-eyed man among the blind." See Dill, *Water Falls,*114.

51. *Congressional Record,* 1927, 3570.

52. Louise Benjamin, "Radio Regulation in the 1920s: Free Speech Issues in the Development of Radio and the Radio Act of 1927" (Ph.D. diss., University of Iowa, 1985), 116–117.

53. Louise Benjamin, "Working It Out Together: Radio Policy from Hoover to the Radio Act of 1927," *Journal of Broadcasting & Electronic Media* 42 (1998): 233.

54. Donald G. Godfrey, "A Rhetorical Analysis of the Congressional Debates on Broadcast Regulation in the United States, 1927" (Ph.D. diss., University of Washington, 1975), 33.

55. Donald G. Godfrey, "Senator Dill and the 1927 Radio Act," *Journal of Broadcasting* 23 (1979): 477–89.

56. Kerry Irish, "Clarence Dill: The Life of a Western Politician" (Ph.D. diss., University of Washington, 1994), 168.

57. Barnouw, 178.

58. Wallace H. White to L. S. Baker, managing director, National Association of Broadcasters, December 2, 1927, Box 50: Folder—Radio, Miscellaneous, Wallace H. White Collection, Library of Congress.

Wallace H. White to William Brown, vice president and general attorney, RCA, November 24, 1926, Box 51: Folder—Radio, Miscellaneous, Wallace H. White Collection, Library of Congress.

Wallace H. White to H. G. Harbord, president, RCA, September 22, 1926, Box 5: Folder—Radio, Miscellaneous, Wallace H. White Collection, Library of Congress.

Wallace H. White to Paul B. Klugh, ex-chairman, National Association of Broadcasters, September 2, 1926, Box 651: Folder—Radio, Miscellaneous #2, Wallace H. White Collection, Library of Congress.

Telegram from William Brown to Wallace White, arranging meeting with "SARNOFF," October 26, 1926, Box 651: Folder—Radio, Miscellaneous #2, Wallace H. White Collection, Library of Congress.

59. Frederick W. Ford, "The Meaning of Public Interest, Convenience, or Necessity," *Journal of Broadcasting* 5 (1961): 207.

60. Francis Chase, Jr., *Sound and Fury: An Informal History of Broadcasting* (New York: Harper, 1942), 233.

61. C. B. Rose, Jr., *National Policy for Radio Broadcasting: 1940* (reprint, New York: Arno Press, 1971), 6.

62. Fred H. Cate, "A Law Antecedent and Paramount," *Federal Communication Law Journal* 47 (1994): 207.

63. Mark Goodman, "The Radio Act of 1927 as a Product of Progressivism," *Mass Media Monographs* 2 (1999): 1.

64. John Braeman, "The Square Deal in Action: A Case Study in the Growth of the 'National Police Power,' " in *Change and Continuity in Twentieth-Century America,* ed. John Braeman, Robert H. Bremner, and David Brody (Columbus: Ohio State University Press, 1964, 41).

65. Wallace H. White, "Monopoly," undated handwritten notes. Box 64: Folder—Federal Control or Radio, undated. Wallace H. White Collection, Library of Congress.

66. *Congressional Record,* 1926, 5479.

67. *Congressional Record,* 1927, 4111.

68. Barnouw, 305–306.

69. *Congressional Record,* 1927, 1173.

70. *Congressional Record,* 1926, 12357.

71. *Congressional Record,* 1926, 12615.

72. *Congressional Record,* 1926, 12502.

73. *Congressional Record,* 1927, 1170.

74. *Congressional Record,* 1926, 12502.

75. David M. Rabban, "Free Speech in Progressive Social Thought," *Texas Law Review* 74 (1996): 967.

76. Dill, *Radio Law: Practice and Procedure* (Washington, D.C.: National Law Book Co., 1938), 110.

77. Hoover, *Memoirs,* vol. 2, 140, 144.

78. Dill, *Water Falls,* 109.

79. Wallace H. White to W. C. Alley, managing editor, Radio Retailing (October 25, 1926), Box 51: File—Radio, Miscellaneous. Wallace H. White Collection, Library of Congress.

80. Dill, *Radio Law,* 85, 92.

81. Dill, *Water Falls,* 110.

82. Wallace H. White, "Radio Communications," House of Representatives (March 12, 1926). Box 67: Folder—Speeches, Articles, Remarks. Wallace H. White Collection, Library of Congress.

83. Wallace H. White to Willis Kingsley Wing, editor, *Radio Broadcast* (December 28, 1926). Box 50: File—Radio, Miscellaneous. Wallace H. White Collection, Library of Congress.

84. Hoover, *Memoirs,* 6–8.

85. William D. Rowland, Jr. "The Meaning of 'The Public Interest' in Communications Policy, Part I: Its Origins in State and Federal Regulation," *Communication Law & Policy* 2 (1997): 318.

86. Rowland, 323.

87. Rowland, 324.

88. J. H. Morecraft, "March of Radio," *Radio Broadcast,* July 1926, 118.

89. Morecraft, "The March of Radio," *Radio Broadcast,* August 1926, 296.

90. Morecraft, "The March of Radio," *Radio Broadcast,* May 1926, 24.

91. Morecraft, "March of Radio," *Radio Broadcast,* April 1926, 555.

92. Morecraft, "March of Radio," *Radio Broadcast,* October 1926, 475.

93. "Radio Censorship," *The Literary Digest,* October 4, 1924, 28.

94. "The Fight for 'Freedom of the Air,'" *The Literary Digest,* March 22, 1924, 9.

95. "To Kill Off Broadcasting 'Pirates.'" May 7, 1927, *The Literary Digest,* 13–14.

96. Rabban, 955.

QUESTIONS FOR DISCUSSION

1. How does considering the ways in which free speech protection has been (or has not been) applied to other media help us to understand the Progressive influence on radio? For example, how was the press influenced by Progressive values? How did movies fare under Progressive beliefs?

2. Does understanding radio regulation as an expression of Progressive ideology help to explain why legislators favored big business over amateurs, or why jazz became such a hot topic in a way that affected early radio rules? How?

3. Relate Winston's article to this one by thinking of the Progressive influence of key legislators as part of the suppression of radio's radical potential. What "radical potential" was suppressed? How might radio have been differently structured if this had not happened?

 INFOTRAC COLLEGE EDITION

Search InfoTrac College Edition under the keyword "Progressivism" for more perspectives on this important cultural and political influence. Also search for "radio regulation" under subject headings.

3

Crusade against Mammon

Father Harney, WLWL, and the Debate over Radio in the 1930s

ROBERT W. MCCHESNEY

The story of Father Harney of the Paulist Fathers and his fight to keep a renegade radio voice on the air is related in detail by Robert W. McChesney. Here we can see a countervailing force to the Progressive ideology traced in the preceding essay, in the form of American pluralistic populism. Though the populist tradition is not an organized movement like Progressivism, it is a powerful strain in American social thought that brings together a host of varied and often conflicting agents and agendas—religious, political, cultural, critical, and economic—with only their resistance to centralized social power uniting them. However, populist dissenters from the status quo should not be understood as endorsers of unqualified broadcasting freedom; most educational and religious groups would have been happy with strict government controls—as long as those controls gave *them* power and kept their rivals in place.

Father Harney's and other educational broadcasters' support for the Wagner-Hatfield amendment to the Communications Act of 1934, though defeated, set forth a model for protection of nonprofit broadcasting that would be influential in later years. McChesney calls our attention to the suppressed side of U.S. broadcasting history: its critics, reformers, renegades, and rebels who never

Reprinted from *Journalism History* 14 (Winter 1987): 118–30. Reprinted by permission.

acceded to the commercial network system that would soon rule the day. The story of WLWL also showcases some of the underlying fissures in the broadcast reform movement: religious broadcasters' troubled relationship with the separation of church and state; the regulatory distinction between general public service and propaganda stations set forth by the Federal Radio Commission (FRC), and the elite Progressive vision of public service broadcasting versus a more pluralistic, varied, and uncontrolled model that might have allowed voices like Father Harney's, among others, to take to the air.

On May 15, 1934, the U.S. Senate defeated the Wagner-Hatfield amendment on a vote of 42–43. The amendment would have required the newly created Federal Communications Commission (FCC) to void all radio licenses within 90 days, for there to be a complete reallocation of the airwaves, and for the FCC to allocate a minimum of 25 percent of the channels to non-profit and educational broadcasters. This was the most serious challenge ever to the private, oligopolistic and commercially subsidized nature of American broadcasting; it was opposed with extraordinary vigor by the commercial broadcasting industry. Later the same day the Senate passed the Communications Act of 1934 by a voice vote. This is still the guiding statute regarding broadcast regulation, and no challenge to the status quo along the lines of the Wagner-Hatfield amendment has arisen since that spring day in 1934.

By all accounts, the person most responsible for getting the Wagner-Hatfield amendment to the floor of the Senate and, indeed, to near passage was the Very Reverend John B. Harney, the superior general of the Missionary Society of St. Paul the Apostle. The amendment was first introduced by Harney and initially referred to as the "Harney amendment." Harney was commonly referred to as Father Harney and this New York-based order of 93 priests was commonly called the Paulist Fathers. The Paulist Fathers had established the first Catholic radio station in the United States, WLWL, in New York City in 1925. Within two years WLWL was struggling to survive amidst efforts to seize its valuable frequency by commercial broadcasting companies. In these struggles WLWL found little support from the Federal Radio Commission (FRC), which had been established by the Radio Act of 1927 to bring order to the airwaves. It was these bitter experiences that led Father Harney to the forefront of the battle to reform radio in 1934.

This article briefly narrates the saga of WLWL and, more important, discusses the impact Father Harney and WLWL had upon the debate over radio policy in 1934 and, specifically, the Wagner-Hatfield amendment. First, the article reviews the establishment of WLWL and its financial problems and run-ins with commercial broadcasters and the FRC in the late 1920s and early 1930s. Second, it discusses Harney's 1934 activities to gain passage of the Wagner-Hatfield amendment. Third, it concludes with some cursory and rather broad observations about the significance of this episode and the reform movement it represented for American broadcasting history. The author argues that the WLWL experience can assist in a fundamental reconstruction of American broadcasting history as well as providing insight for a modern generation of media scholars, critics and activists.

WLWL: 1924–33

On December 16, 1924, the Paulist General Council approved plans for the Paulist Fathers to establish a radio station.[1] The plans for the station received support and encouragement from Patrick Cardinal Hayes, the archbishop of New York, as well as other church authorities.[2] During 1924 and 1925 the Paulists raised nearly $100,000 in private donations to get the station off the ground. Western Electric built the station, which was established in Paulist rectory in Manhattan, for a cost of $65,000.[3]

The Paulist order, which was established in the 19th Century as a distinctly American order dedicated to teaching and democracy, had extremely high hopes for the station as a vehicle for its works.[4] The Paulists cited their goal with the station as the presentation of "talks on religious, social and literary subjects and discussions of interest of the present day."[5] While Sundays would feature Paulist services and sermons by "distinguished preachers," the balance of the programming was meant to be accessible to people of all faiths as well as to non-church people. In particular, the Paulists identified their audience as being of the working class.[6]

In July 1925 the Department of Commerce, at that time responsible for the licensing of radio stations, granted the Paulist Fathers a Class B commercial license to operate on the 1040 frequency with 5,000 watts power and unlimited time.[7] WLWL formally began broadcasting on September 24, 1925; at the time it was among the 25 most powerful stations in the nation.[8] However, in just over one year, in October 1926, the Department of Commerce licensed the Starlight Amusement Park of the Bronx to broadcast over the 1040 frequency being used by WLWL. WLWL was outraged; Father Harney commented that this

> act of the Department of Commerce was an overt, deliberate and outrageous discrimination against a high-grade non-commercial radio station with an unrivalled program of cultural entertainment and of instractive talks on religious, ethical, educational, economic and social questions, in favor of a mere dispenser of jazz and cheap amusement.[9]

The Department of Commerce, however, claimed it was powerless to discriminate against any group that sought a broadcast license. This was during the infamous "breakdown of the law" period that developed in late 1926 after an Appeals Court ruled the Department of Commerce's selective licensing of broadcasting stations was unconstitutional.[10] In this context WLWL sought out a new frequency, 780, where it would have no-nearby rival and could enjoy unlimited time. The Department of Commerce approved WLWL's move to the 780 frequency on October 13, 1926.[11]

In February 1927 Congress passed the Radio Act of 1927, which had been rushed through to no small extent to address the breakdown in regulation created by the Appeals Court decision. Some 200 new broadcasters had entered the fray with the elimination of selective licensing in the last few months of 1926. Broadcasters were using any frequency they desired and a general chaos had ensued. The Radio Act of 1927 created the FRC to bring order to the airwaves by allocating licenses among the plethora of contending broadcasters. The only criteria the legislation provided the FRC to use in determining which stations were to receive licenses was that it was to show preference for stations that best served the "public interest, convenience, or necessity." With so many stations the FRC would eventually opt for having two stations sharing the same frequency; it would then determine how the air time would be allocated between the two broadcasters using the "public interest" criteria. There was no indication of what Congress meant by this phrase. All that was certain was that its inclusion was necessary to render the law constitutional.[12]

The first step taken by the FRC in February 1927 was to request that every station designate the bare minimum of hours they needed. Complying faithfully, WLWL declared a minimum of 21 hours per week, including the evening hours Sunday through Friday, as absolutely necessary. In June 1927 the FRC shifted WLWL to 1020, which the Paulists regarded as undesirable due to its proximity to other New York area broadcasters. They protested and within a few days the FRC reassigned WLWL to the 810 frequency, which it would have to share with commercial station WMCA. Initially, the two stations split the time evenly but, at the request of FRC member Henry A. Bellows, WLWL agreed to temporarily grant WMCA a larger share of the hours to protect its commercial programming. However, in December 1927 the FRC sent WLWL a telegram notifying it that the station's hours had been reduced to two hours per day with WMCA receiving the balance of the air time.[13]

At this point the Paulist Fathers, who had been optimistic about their relationship with the new regulatory agency entered into battle with the FRC regarding their frequency and the allocation of air hours. This battle lasted until the FRC was abolished and replaced by the FCC in 1934. When WMCA was granted the lion's share of the hours, it was operating at only 500 watts power and had decidedly inferior equipment; in fact it had been negotiating with the Paulists to obtain the use of WLWL's markedly superior transmitter. Father Harney characterized the FRC's favoritism toward WMCA as

> a serious, injurious, and deadly discrimination against a non-profit making station of high character and of indubitable cultural and educational value, in favor of one which unquestionably was not broadcasting for the "public interest, convenience, or necessity," but for the fattening of its shareholders' pocketbooks.

Harney noted that by 1934, "thanks to the manifold favors of the Radio Commission," WMCA had an estimated market value of four million dollars while WLWL "might net five thousand dollars" for the sale of its transmission and studio equipment.[14]

In the autumn of 1928 the FRC instituted General Order No. 40, which was a comprehensive reallocation of wavelengths. WLWL was assigned to the 1100 frequency, which it was to share with another 5,000-watt station, WPG, a municipally owned station based in Atlantic City. WPG soon was owned and operated by the Columbia Broadcasting System (CBS). The FRC assigned WLWL 15½ hours of air time per week while WPG was assigned 110 hours.

For the following five years, WLWL constantly and unsuccessfully tried to persuade the FRC to expand its hours on the 1100 frequency.[15]

Although the Paulists were prone to regarding the motives of the FRC in sinister and diabolical terms, the rationale for favoring for-profit, commercial broadcasters was spelled out succinctly in the FRC's *Third Annual Report* in 1929. The FRC argued that in the allocation of licenses it would favor "general public service" broadcasters over those inclined toward promoting their own "private or selfish interests." Advertising was not characterized by the FRC as a private or selfish use of the airwaves since it "furnishes the economic support for the service and thus makes it possible." General public service stations were those that attempted to serve the "entire listening public within the service area of a station." These preferred stations were expected to provide "a well-rounded program" of entertainment as well as cultural and educational programming. The FRC was not interested in stating what, precisely, constituted "well-rounded" programming; rather, that would be left to broadcasters scurrying to meet the desires of listeners in the competitive marketplace.[16]

Stations that earned the FRC's disfavor, in contrast to the "general public service" stations, were termed "propaganda" stations by the commission. The FRC emphasized that the term was not meant derogatorily but was intended to stress that these broadcasters were more interested in spreading their particular viewpoints or interest than in reaching the broadest possible audience with whatever programming was most attractive. They observed: "There is no room in the broadcast band for every school of thought, religious, political, social, and economic, each to have its separate broadcasting station, its mouthpiece in the ether."[17]

Consequently, since every group could not have its own "mouthpiece," then, according to the FRC, *no* such group should be entitled to have the privilege of a broadcast license. If a group's message was desired by the public, the reasoning went, the listeners would make this known through the marketplace and "general public service" broadcasters would provide this type of material as part of their "well-rounded" programming. The FRC deemed the programming offered by WLWL as being carried "to a considerable extent" by the commercial broadcasters in the New York area.[18]

In short, the FRC position was a clear endorsement of the private, commercial development of the airwaves. The only non-profit stations not living on borrowed time were those few with ample finding or extensive commercial support.[19] Harney rejected the idea that a for-profit commercial station automatically served the "public interest" while a non-profit station like WLWL, no matter how well-intentioned, was some sort of "special interest" of which the public needed to be wary. He argued that WLWL

> is not a special interest, unless you want to say that those who are working for public welfare are pursuing special interests and that the gentlemen who are working for their own pockets are not. Why not the other way about, with all due respect to Judge Sykes [chairman of the FRC] and others, why not say that those who are working for their own pocketbooks are the gentlemen who are working for special interests?[20]

Harney became superior general of the Paulist order in 1929 at the age of 54. He would hold the position until 1940. He was also designated director-general of WLWL in 1929 in the hope of giving the station more lobbying effectiveness in Washington, but he enjoyed little success in his arguments before the FRC. By the early 1930s the Paulist Fathers began to solicit public support for their case. In September 1931, for example, WLWL appealed over the air for letters of support for the station that could be given to the FRC to provide evidence of listener support. As a WLWL representative commented:

> Our principal object in requesting these letters is to strengthen our plea that the Paulist Fathers' station should have more advantageous hours on the air. At present we must broadcast when most of our New York area listeners are on their way home from work.[21]

The plea generated 25,000 letters within one week. In addition, the auxiliary bishop of the Archdiocese of New York, with the approval of Cardinal Hayes, sent a letter to the pastor of each of the Archdiocese's 452 churches asking them to request that parishioners write letters of support for WLWL.[22] But these and other campaigns of public support failed to move the FRC.[23] Harney did begin to attract attention in Washington, however. In June 1933 a White House aide began to consult with the secretary of the FRC regarding WLWL.[24] While nothing came of this, it provides some indication of WLWL's ability to publicize its case.

WLWL also had to look increasingly for financial assistance to keep the station afloat. In 1927 the Paulists built a $38,000 transmitting facility in New Jersey, which the FRC mandated if WLWL wished to maintain 5,000 watts power.[25] This construction placed the station in debt from which it never emerged. The annual expenses of WLWL ran close to $75,000 in the late 1920s and, after budget cutbacks of close to $17,000 in 1930, ran at $40,000–$50,000 in the ensuing years.[26] After 1927, WLWL received annual loans and grants from the Paulist Fathers and Catholic groups including the Catholic Missionary Union, the Central Verein, the Holy Name Society, the Catholic Daughters of America and the Knights of Columbus.[27]

WLWL attempted to sell commercial advertising with little success; at most these efforts generated some $3,000 per year.[28] The Paulist Fathers also had a plea for support read at masses at their church in Manhattan.[29] Commercial interests were eager to "assist" WLWL with its financial problems with offers to purchase their broadcast license and facilities. In 1930, CBS offered to purchase WLWL outright. In 1931, Hearst radio interests offered the Paulists $500,000 for WLWL due to its "excellent frequency." In each case the Paulists refused.[30]

EMERGENCE OF OPPOSITION
TO THE STATUS QUO

The financial problems experienced by WLWL in its dealings with commercial interests and in its hearings before the FRC were similar to those experienced by numerous other non-profit broadcasters. In 1927, for example, there had been

95 broadcasting stations affiliated with educational institutions as well as another 115 managed by religious and non-profit organizations.[31] Some scholars have termed the educational broadcasters as the true "pioneers" of broadcasting.[32] By the beginning of 1934, however, the number of non-profit broadcasters overall was down to 65. At the same time, the two major networks, CBS and the National Broadcasting Company (NBC), moved from virtual non-existence in 1927 to enormous prosperity by 1934. Philip Rosen has described this period as one of "prosperous, almost triumphant expansion" for the commercial broadcasting industry.[33]

These displaced and struggling educational broadcasters felt they were left "unprotected" by the FRC as their frequencies were "attacked constantly by commercial broadcasters."[34] In 1930 nine prominent national educational groups formed the National Committee on Education by Radio (NCER) to defend the rights of educational broadcasters. NCER was formed, among other things, to explicitly press Congress for a law that would require that 15 percent of the airwaves be set aside for educational broadcasters. Legislation to this effect was introduced by Senator Simeon Fess of Ohio in 1931 and 1932, but it never left committee. By 1933 NCER had given up hope of having any specific legislation passed by Congress due to the strength of the radio lobby and the opposition of Senator C. C. Dill, Democrat from Washington and chairman of the critical Senate Interstate Commerce Committee, which handled all radio legislation.[35] Rather, NCER began to push for a bill that would establish a non-partisan panel to evaluate American broadcasting and suggest substantive reforms. Such a study had been conducted in Canada in the early 1930s and had come out decisively against the commercial use of radio. NCER believed that any independent study could *only* recommend a radical move away from the private, commercial status quo.[36]

NCER generated a critique of the commercial status quo that was quite similar to that of Father Harney and WLWL. Both derided what they regarded as the cheap commercialism and debased character of the network programming and both argued that it was absurd to turn over a vital public resource to private interests for private gain. Nevertheless, the two sides never worked together; by 1934 NCER had given up its lobbying efforts in Congress and prior to that year WLWL had been consumed in its own dealings with the FRC. At the same time, several other displaced broadcasters, intellectuals and civic groups such as the American Civil Liberties Union were waging their own independent battles against the status quo. These groups were ineffectual and, like NCER, were largely observers to the 1934 deliberations in Congress regarding radio.[37] Standing opposite this divided opposition were the two networks and the National Association of Broadcasters (NAB)—a trade association of commercial broadcasters generally recognized as one of the most powerful lobbying groups in Washington.[38]

The only opposition to the status quo that the Paulists ever worked with during this period were certain elements of organized labor. In the mid-1920s, the Chicago Federation of Labor had established WCFL to be the "voice of labor" and to fight the "appropriation of the lanes of the air for the propaganda of Big Biz for deadening the minds of the masses."[39] WCFL experienced the same sorts of problems with commercial interests and the FRC as did WLWL and other non-profit broadcasters. WCFL and its general manager, Edward Nockels, led the fight for radio reform in Congress in 1930 and 1931 but abandoned these efforts when NBC and the FRC agreed to give WCFL increased power and air time.[40] In 1932, WLWL and representatives of the American Federation of Labor (AFL) sought permission for the AFL to establish a labor station on WLWL's share of the 1100 frequency if WLWL would be switched to full-time on 810. The FRC rejected the request.[41]

FATHER HARNEY AND
BROADCAST REFORM

The FRC had always been a temporary body; each year it had to be renewed by Congress or its duties would be returned to the Department of Commerce. By 1933 there was considerable pressure for the establishment of a permanent body to regulate not only broadcasting but the entire range of communications industries. The commercial broadcasters, in particular, were eager to establish a permanent basis for government regulation of broadcasting. The FRC had, in effect, served its function; the airwaves had been cleared for profitable development and now the dislocation of 1928–31 had given way to a far more stable environment.[42]

In 1933 President Roosevelt appointed an interdepartmental committee under Secretary of Commerce Daniel C. Roper to study the issue of how best to regulate communications and to suggest permanent legislation. The group essentially recommended the maintenance of the status quo with all regulatory bodies merged into a new super-agency.[43] But the Roper Committee neglected to consider broadcasting in its deliberations and President Roosevelt even authorized a separate study of broadcasting to generate radio legislation. He quickly withdrew those plans on the advice of Senator Dill and Representative Rayburn; to do so would have meant postponing any possibility of getting legislation passed by the end of the current session. The broadcasting industry made its displeasure with the proposed study known as well, particularly when it became clear that "anti-broadcasting groups" like NCER intended to use the proposed study as an opportunity to present their case.[44]

The legislation was prepared by Senator Dill and Representative Rayburn in consultation with White House staff members in February 1934. Dill and Rayburn were the chairmen of the relevant Congressional committees and each prepared slightly different bills. As far as radio was concerned, however, both bills almost totally re-enacted the provisions of the Radio Act of 1927. President Roosevelet issued a formal statement to Congress in late February announcing his support for the legislation and urging its passage. To assuage those in Congress concerned that the bill was being rushed through without any careful consideration, Roosevelt argued that the proposed communications commission "should, in addition, be given full power to investigate and study the business of existing companies and make recommendations to the Congress for additional legislation at the next session."[45] Senator Dill was more blunt: "If we leave out the controversial matters the bill can be passed at this session."[46]

The commercial broadcasters were enthusiastic about the proposed legislation; their goal was simply the establishment of the Radio Act of 1927 on a permanent basis and under a different name. Furthermore, they were in complete favor of having Congress ignore the issue of broadcast reform; they felt far more comfortable letting a regulatory agency handle these matters.[47] They were on extremely solid footing with both Senator Dill and Representative Rayburn. Indeed, Henry Bellows, who after leaving the FRC had become a CBS executive and the chief lobbyist for the NAB, pronounced at the NAB national convention in September 1934 that "the entire broadcasting industry is deeply indebted" to both of them.[48] Furthermore, President Roosevelt showed no inclination to antagonize the commercial broadcasters by engaging in any reform effort.[49] In short, especially in view of the lack of organized opposition, the commercial broadcasters were in the proverbial catbird seat.

It was in this context that Father Harney entered the picture. In February 1934 the FRC denied another request by WLWL to share equally the hours on the 1100 frequency with WPG. WLWL then began to air programming sharply critical of commercial radio. One address argued that radio was

> begotten of a spawning and not too choosey commercialism. And in this devotion to commercialism radio has fallen from its high estate, and has become in large measure the competitor of the comic strip and the cheap vaudeville theater.

The talk outlined the sharp decrease in the number of non-profit stations since the mid 1920s and concluded on this note:

> But, in the name of the worthy things for which our national ideals and aspirations stand, in the name of the new born realizations, that charity and justice and kindliness and a deep pervading sense of right and wrong must assume a necessary and powerful place in the everyday affairs of our land, may we not believe that those instruments which are given in sworn purpose to such a cause shall not be wiped out in a tide of sordid commercialism, but shall be given the opportunity of continuing on a new and greater scale, the work which they have gathered to their hearts.[50]

A copy of this speech was published and circulated by the Paulists in Washington.

Father Harney went on the air in March and argued that the FRC "discriminated not only against our station, but against other educational agencies in the allotment of broadcasting facilities."[51] He proposed what would become known as the Wagner-Hatfield amendment, the gist of which was presented at the outset of this article. Nonetheless, it is difficult to ascertain precisely how deep Harney's commitment was to this new-found interest in radio reform. In early April WLWL announced that it was planning to apply before the FRC to be shifted to the frequency of 810 and be given six continuous hours on a daily basis in the late afternoon and evening.[52] To accomplish this move, WLWL would have to contend with Minneapolis CBS outlet WCCO, which had no desire to sacrifice such lucrative hours to WLWL. To some extent, Harney's sudden interest in radio reform may have been a last-gasp effort to frighten CBS and the FRC and force them accede to WLWL's demands, rather than being a tremendous commitment to the welfare of all non-profit broadcasters.

The Senate Interstate Commerce Committee hearings on S. 2910, as the Dill legislation was numbered, took place in March 1934. Nineteen witnesses testified over the course of five days; the vast majority of them were either corporate executives, representatives of industry groups or government officials. Only five of the witnesses discussed broadcasting: two government officials, Henry Bellows and David Sarnoff, the president of the Radio Corporation of America (RCA), representing the broadcasting industry, and Father Harney. Bellows and Sarnoff were satisfied with the legislation and expressed particular delight that the new regulatory agency, and not Congress, would take up any thorny reform questions.[53]

Harney submitted his amendment to the committee on March 15. The amendment specifically called for the new regulatory commission, after 90 days, to allocate 25 percent of the channels to non-profit broadcasters. Harney estimated that non-profit broadcasting accounted for only 2½ percent of the air time by 1934. He argued that this measure was necessary to

forestall the possibility of a monopolistic control of radio communications facilities, and to secure permanently for responsible religious, educational, cultural, social service, and other human welfare agencies of a non-profit-making type such an assignment of radio facilities as is in keeping with their high character and unselfish aims; such also as will give them all a chance to be decently self-supporting and free from overlordship of the mere commercialists whose dominant purpose is to accumulate wealth even at the cost of human decay.[54]

Harney was specifically challenged by committee members on two points. First, Senator James Couzens of Michigan asked him to explain how these non-profit broadcasters would support themselves and be viable economic entitles. Harney argued that the non-profit broadcasters would have to be permitted to sell advertising. He commented:

These licensees should have the right to sell some of their time so as to obtain enough to live on; not to make a profit, but enough to support themselves, so they will not be dependent on charity all the while and will not have to be beggars.[55]

Harney emphasized that his amendment would not permit the non-profit broadcasters to sell their licenses for a profit. Nonetheless, this point—that non-profit broadcasters would be able to sell advertising—proved a major stumbling block for the legislation when it reached the Senate floor as the Wagner-Hatfield amendment. Indeed, this had been one of the reasons that NCER had lost its enthusiasm for the fixed percentage concept in the early 1930s: It adamantly opposed the sale of time by non-profit broadcasters on principle and believed that any sensible solution would necessitate that the funding issue be resolved directly.[56]

Senator Dill then stepped in and tried to impress upon Harney his idea of having the to-be-created communications commission study his fixed percentage proposal and then report back to Congress with its recommendations the following year. Harney dismissed this, outlined what he regarded as the FRC's dismal record on behalf of non-profit broadcasters and emphasized that it was Congress' duty, not that of the regulatory agency, to determine fundamental broadcast policy. He then asked in return:

May I ask if this information from publication is correct, that when the Radio Act of 1927 was drawn up and the Federal Radio Commission was created, the original draft contained a clause requesting—rather ordering—the giving of preference to educational stations? And that one of the Senators said, "Oh, that is not at all necessary, because we can trust the Radio Commission to conserve the interests of those educational and other similar agencies."

Senator White acknowledged that while something along those lines had been considered in an earlier draft, it proved too "controversial" and had to be removed.[57] In fact, educational broadcasters were led to believe in 1927 that the wording "public interest, convenience, or necessity" was meant to be interrupted by the FRC to favor educational broadcasters.[58]

The Interstate Commerce Committee rejected Harney's amendment in private deliberations a few weeks later. Only two senators voted on its behalf: Democrat Robert Wagner of New York and Republican Henry Hatfield of West Virginia. Nevertheless, perhaps sensing impending problems on the Senate floor where Harney was in the process of drawing considerable support, Dill had the Committee insert a passage that specifically instructed the new commission to study Harney's "fixed percentage" proposal and then report back to Congress in early 1935 with its recommendations. This would become Section 307(c) of the Communications Act of 1934. Dill reported the new bill, now numbered S. 3285, to the Senate on April 19 and called it a "good bill."[59]

LOBBYING EFFORTS IN SPRING 1934

Father Harney and the Paulist Fathers were undaunted by this defeat. Indeed, in late March they launched an extensive campaign to gain public support for the "Harney amendment." The Paulists actively sought support, particularly from Catholic groups, for the legislation. By the end of April the Senate had received over 60,000 signatures on petitions supporting the amendment in addition to thousands of letters and telegrams.[60] One petition was titled "Save Catholic Radio." Another concluded:

Our children listen to the radio and if there were some restrictions on some of the junk commercialized over the various stations, we would have a better country to live in. We think it is about time we Catholics of America get some representation and protection from our government.[61]

Most of the petitions, however, were formal representations of the "Harney amendment" and were signed by chapters of such groups as the Knights of Columbus, the Ancient Order of Hibernians, the Catholic Ladies' Relief Society and the National Council of Catholic Women. One speaker informed the Catholic Daughters of America that WLWL was "being crowded off the air" and that the fight for "good clean radio programs" was a "serious part of the program of Catholic action."[62] In addition, both the White House and the Federal Radio Commission received thousands of petitions, letters and telegrams supporting the proposed legislation.[63]

In April the Paulists also published a pamphlet by Father Harney titled "Education and Religion vs. Commercial Radio." In addition to recounting the saga of WLWL and Harney's critique to the FRC, the pamphlet provided a polemic against the network-dominated, commercially subsidized status quo for the free speech requirements of a democratic society. To Harney the status quo inexorably precluded opinion and programming that challenged the prerogatives of big business; the only solution was to preserve air channels for non-profit use.[64] Some 20,000 copies of the pamphlet were published and mailed to Catholic parishes across the nation.[65]

Harney met with several Catholic members of Congress in early April to press his argument. He also met with New York senators Robert Wagner and Royal Copeland, who had received a considerable portion of the petitions. His eloquence carried the day. Representative Rudd introduced the "Harney amendment" to the House in early April and attributed it directly to Father Harney.[66] On April 27 senators Wagner and Henry Hatfield of West Virginia introduced a slightly revised version of the same amendment to the Senate and their names replaced Harney's as the sponsor.[67] By the end of April the momentum had seemingly shifted to the side of the reformers; *Variety* observed that the sentiment on Capitol Hill was that the Wagner-Hatfield amendment stood "better that a 50-50 chance of being adopted."[68] The NAB newsletter to commercial broadcasters noted that the amendment "brings to a head a campaign against the present broadcasting set-up which has been smoldering in Congress for several years.[69]

Harney found two allies for his campaign to reform American radio. Michael Flynn of the AFL and Edward Nockels of WCFL, who was the AFL's official representative on radio matters, actively lobbied on behalf of the Wagner-Hatfield amendment. Nockels even helped Harney draft the final version and he wrote all the member unions of the AFL urging them to actively support this bill that would "destroy the monopoly and dictatorship of the air" by the "two chains on the air." While Nockels would inform Congress that organized labor was "solidly behind" the Wagner-Hatfield amendment, he would confess in a meeting of the Chicago Federation of Labor that "It is often very discouraging and disappointing to find how little response we get from our affiliated organizations when we call upon them for cooperation."[70]

The second ally for Father Harney was found, in all places, on the FRC. James Hanley, President Roosevelt's first appointment to the body in 1933, was a reform-minded Democrat who became WLWL's sole supporter in its effort to win full-time on the air in hearings before the FRC. On April 14, 1934, Hanley issued a statement to mark his first anniversary on the FRC that was critical of commercial broadcasting and called for setting "aside a liberal number of channels for the exclusive use of education and educational institutions." Hanley's statement was immediately repudiated by high administration officials and the balance of the FRC.[71] Harney became a "frequent visitor" to Hanley's office, according to *Broadcasting* magazine, which characterized Hanley as a "staunch supporter" of the amendment.[72]

The radio lobby attacked the Wagner-Hatfield amendment between April 27 and May 15 as if, as Henry Bellows later put it, its passage "obviously would have destroyed the whole structure of broadcasting in America."[73] Philip Loucks of the

NAB characterized matters as "a fight between life and death."[74] Telegrams were sent to all broadcasters informing them that, if passed, the Wagner-Hatfield amendment "would cancel your license in 90 days." Broadcasters were given no other information about the legislation and they were urged to contact their representatives in Congress.[75] *Variety* noted that the NAB was "in panic checking off names of Senators and trying to pull wires and get votes."[76] The chairman of the FRC even advised members of Congress to oppose the legislation.[77]

The campaign was quite effective; on May 12 the NAB noted that "the Wagner-Hatfield amendment vote, if its proponents permit it to come to a vote, will be overwhelmingly against its adoption." Similarly, the NAB noted that the Dill Communications bill faced certain passage.[78] NBC's vice-president in charge of legislative matters, Frank Russell, reported to headquarters that he "had taken every opportunity to work against" the Wagner-Hatfield amendment. By May 5, he was confident that the legislation did not have "the slightest chance of enactment into law."[79]

CBS also became actively involved in the fight. At the end of April, Ivy Lee, representing CBS, approached the attorney for WLWL and indicated that CBS was willing to grant WLWL more air time opposite WPG on the 1100 frequency—as much as five hours per day.[80] Harney and his advisors interpreted the move to mean that the networks were "scared" and that it would be wise "to let them worry somewhat longer." A few days later, Harney advised his attorney to inform CBS that WLWL rejected the offer and found it "seriously unsatisfactory." He suggested that he would, however, be open to further negotiations on the matter.[81]

Nevertheless, on May 2 Harney discovered on a trip to Washington that a rumor had surfaced that WLWL had accepted the preposition made by CBS. He was told by Senator Wagner that a government official had told him to take no further steps on the Wagner-Hatfield amendment "in view of the fact that the difficulties between Columbia Broadcasting System and WLWL were at the point of settlement." While Harney corrected Wagner on the true state of affairs and told him to push on with the bill, it is difficult to gauge how much damage this did the reform effort. In any case, CBS did not attempt to resume negotiations with WLWL.[82]

In the second week of May the House Interstate and Foreign Commerce Committee began hearings on the Rayburn communications bill. Henry Bellows appeared May 8 on behalf of the NAB and argued vociferously against the inclusion of something like the Watner-Hatfield amendment in the House communications bill. Bellows refused to accept Harney's argument chastising the status quo as being inimical to free speech:

> The National Association of Broadcasters is as jealously determined to safeguard the right of free speech by radio as the newspapers are to safeguard their rights in the same field . . . there is no such thing as radio "censorship." Freedom of speech can be maintained in radio only by insisting that every station shall serve every listener within its normal range, whether Democrat or Republican, conservative or radical, rich or poor, Catholic or Jew, city dweller or farmer. It can most quickly be destroyed by assigning facilities to a favored few groups which seek to appeal to a special and limited audience.[83]

Father Harney appeared before the committee the following day. His frustration with the success of the radio lobby in turning the tide against the amendment was apparent.

> Now, of course there will be much opposition and there is much opposition to this amendment. Yet, I would say this, not one man has dared to come out and find fault with or condemn what I will call the heart of the amendment, namely that one fourth of the radio broadcasting facilities shall be reserved for human welfare agencies. No man has done it. No man dares to do it. One would make himself a laughing stock of the American public, which has its heart set upon education, if one would dare to get up and say that education should not have any opportunity to make use of the radio; should be debarred from that exceedingly powerful means of reaching, instructing, elevating, and improving the minds and morals of men.

In particular, Harney was upset with the NAB's claim that the American public was opposed to the amendment, when indeed the only publicity attending to the amendment was that generated by the Paulist Fathers.

> The National Association of Broadcasters has absolutely no warrant for declaring it speaks in the name of millions of radio listeners, whereas millions of listeners have written and expressed their wishes to Congress in favor of this amendment. They have not dared to do it. However brazen they may be, they will never dare to do it now or later because they know full well that if millions of listeners were acquainted with the provisions of this amendment and with the facts that have called for its presentation, the majority of their listeners, as all real thinking American people will do, would say that the amendment is fair and just and ought to be law.[84]

Harney also dismissed the notion that the new communications commission could be trusted to undertake a fair study of the Wagner-Hatfield provisions as called for by Section 307(c) of the Senate bill. He referred to the disappointing experiences that non-profit broadcasters had faced with the FRC:

> It was once thought that the Federal Radio Commission could be trusted to make due provision for these human welfare agencies, but the Radio Commission's own acts prove that no such trust can be placed in its hands. If Congress wants to protect the radio future of human welfare agencies it must lay down an emphatic law to that effect and give clear, definite mandates which the Commission will have to carry out.[85]

The eventual House bill did not include a fixed percentage amendment or even something along the lines of the Senate bill's Section 307(c).

At this point, it was abundantly clear to the radio lobby that they could do as they pleased with the legislation. Some, like NBC President Merlin Aylesworth, wished to have the legislation withdrawn for fear that "too many victories go wrong on a vote." Russell argued, on the other hand, that it would be a "danger" if the proponents of the amendment were able to return the legislation to committee to mount another campaign in the next session of Congress. Indeed,

Russell convinced Aylesworth of the soundness of his argument and his approach carried the day. As he informed Aylesworth on May 11, "some of our friends in the Senate have indicated they will force a vote in order to dispose of this matter for all time."[86]

THE WAGNER-HATFIELD AMENDMENT

The Senate took up consideration of S. 3285 and the Wagner-Hatfield amendment on May 15. Senator Dill, as Bellows later commented, "splendidly assumed" the floor leadership against the amendment.[87] After Senator Wagner offered his amendment and briefly argued on its behalf, Dill interjected that the amendment was flawed because it permitted what he termed "so-called" non-profit broadcasters to sell advertising time to support themselves. Thus, he observed,

> It is proposed by this amendment to grant 25 percent of the radio facilities to those who call themselves educational, religious, nonprofit stations, but who in reality are planning to enter the commercial field and sell a tremendous amount of their time for commercial purposes.

Senator Couzens responded to the spirit of this argument by noting that the amendment did not make any specific programming requirements of the non-profit stations. Thus, "After having once gotten a license under the provisions of the amendment, the whole time allotted to the station can be used for commercial purposes."[88]

After senators Wagner and Copeland challenged the significance of this argument, Dill proceeded to another line of attack. He called attention to a recent conference conducted by NCER in which the group did not discuss, consider or act upon the Wagner-Hatfield amendment. Rather, the NCER conference called for the President to appoint an independent committee to conduct a sweeping study of American broadcasting and generate a plan for its radical reconstruction.[89] Senator Dill pointed out that "they do not recommend the adoption of this amendment. They recommend, rather, a study." Dill then provided his own interpretation of why NCER was "not ready to recommend that 25 percent of the facilities be set aside for educational and religious institutions":

> Let me call to the attention of the Senator why what they [NCER] say is so. It costs a tremendous amount of money to build large radio stations. The religious and educational and cultural organizations do not have the money necessary, and they are trying to work out some system whereby existing stations may be used, probably in addition to the 63 stations which are already in operation, of an educational and non-profit nature, and still not be burdened with the great expense of building stations.[90]

Senator Dill had blatantly misconstrued the position of NCER, which had always seen cooperation between educators and commercial broadcasters as unworkable, into opponents of the Wagner-Hatfield amendment and proponents, if not of the status quo, then at least of Section 307(c). Senator Hatfield then took the floor and, in the process of a lengthy speech on behalf of the amendment, cited articles published by NCER to clarify their position. It is unclear what effect this had.[91]

At this point Dill began to make a series of observations regarding the amendment. He pressed for letting the new commission make its own study of the matter as called for in Section 307(c) of his bill. He also emphasized his commitment to educational and non-profit broadcasting. He concluded by delving into some of the conceivable administrative problems involved with the amendment. In the following exchange with Senator Logan he stressed the problem of allocating the 25 percent to the various non-profit broadcasters:

> **Dill:** "If we should provide that 25 percent of time shall be allocated to non-profit organizations, someone would have to determine—Congress or somebody else—how much of that 25 percent should go to education, how much of it to religion, and how much of it to agriculture, how much of it to labor, how much of it to fraternal organizations, and so forth. When we enter this field we must determine how much to give to the Catholics probably and how much to give to the Protestants and how much to the Jews."
>
> **Logan:** "And to the Hindus."
>
> **Dill:** "Yes; and probably the infidels would want some time."
>
> **Logan:** "Yes; there is a national association of atheists. The perhaps would want some time."[92]

The Wagner-Hatfield amendment was defeated shortly thereafter on a vote of 42-23. Without any additional debate, S. 3285 was passed on a voice vote and without a roll call later that day. Philip Rosen has argued that Dill's inclusion of Section 307(c) probably stemmed the tide of sentiment in the amendment's behalf. He also noted that the White House played a critical behind-the-scenes role in defeating the Wagner-Hatfield amendment: "Quick action from the Roosevelt administration overwhelmed its opposition."[93] Certainly Dill was a key factor himself; he was generally acknowledged as the Congress' foremost authority on radio. His call for Section 307(c) probably influenced enough wavering votes. In addition, Dill raised a number of legitimate questions regarding the suitability of the Wagner-Hatfield amendment. Nonetheless, despite his claims to the contrary, one cannot find many instances of his attempting to resolve the plight of non-profit broadcasting in any constructive manner. Indeed his conduct lends itself far more to an interpretation that he was attempting to squash the Wagner-Hatfield amendment by any means at his disposal.

The House debate over the Rayburn bill was anti-climatic in comparison to the Senate debate over the Wagner-Hatfield amendment. The reform forces were much weaker in the House and were unable to get the amendment either attached to the bill or brought to the floor. Representative Rayburn managed to restrict debate to two hours and on June 2 the bill passed on a voice vote.[94] The bill then went to conference to iron out several differences between the bills.

When the conference committee completed its work Senator Dill informed Henry Bellows over the telephone: "We have been very generous to you fellows." Bellows would later comment: "When we read it, we saw that every major point we had asked for was there."[95]

On June 18 President Roosevelt signed the Communications Act of 1934 into law. Within two weeks be appointed the seven members of the new Federal Communications Commission; both the chairman and vice-chairman were holdovers from the FRC, Hanley, the "radical" on the FRC, was not among those appointed to the new FCC.[96] At its first meeting on July 11, the FCC voted to "retain the status quo insofar as broadcasting regulation is concerned" and to move "cautiously" toward any reform.[97] The commercial broadcasters were delighted; the era of legitimately challenging the private, commercial basis of American broadcasting had passed.[98]

Ironically, the Paulist Fathers and Father Harney revealed no interest in the FCC hearings mandated by Section 307(c) of the Communications Act of 1934. These hearings were to determine the desirability of allocating 25 percent of the wave lengths to non-profit broadcasters and were scheduled to begin on October 1. Most reformers were dubious about how fair any hearing before the FCC could possibly be. In September, two of the three FCC commissioners who were on the "broadcast division" that would conduct these hearings informed the NAB convention that they were opposed to any alteration of the status quo.[99] Indeed, Father Harney only testified before the hearings in an unscheduled appearance on October 8. He requested an appearance only to refute a vitriolic anti-Catholic and anti-Harney diatribe made by a representative of the Jehovah's Witnesses on October 4. He spoke briefly and provided no additional testimony at the hearings.[100]

In January 1935, to the surprise of no one and certainly not the Paulist Fathers, the FCC recommended against the fixed percentage concept to Congress. It suggested, instead, that commercial broadcasters and educators learn to cooperate using the existing system and announced that it would call a conference to get the sides working together.[101] NCER attended the first of these meetings, in May 1935, and formally proposed the establishment of a government network. The idea went nowhere as it became increasingly clear that there was little hope for reform. In January 1936 NCER reorganized and announced that it would accept the status quo and attempt to work in cooperation with the commercial broadcasters and the FCC.[102] By this time most of the other reform groups had collapsed as well or had come to accept the status quo as irreversible.

WLWL did not entirely dispense with its efforts at reform, but now they had a clearly opportunistic cast; their purpose was quite explicitly to force CBS and the FCC to accommodate the Paulist Fathers with a clear-channel station and unlimited time. Thus, on January 15, 1935, WLWL formally applied to the FCC for the 810 frequency. This "junior reallocation" would have forced several stations to move as well and was opposed by all of them. For the next two years WLWL attempted fruitlessly to gain full-time status on the air, all the while struggling to stay afloat financially. Finally, the Paulists elected to sell WLWL to Arde Bulova, the watch manufacturer, for $275,000 when, as an internal Paulist memo stated, "all plans to make it self-supporting had failed."[103] On March 4, 1937, the FCC approved the sale of WLWL to Bulova and the Paulists went off the air. A White House memo at the time noted that with the Paulists' departure from broadcasting, much of the incentive for reform of radio on Capitol Hill would vanish: "Anyone familiar with radio and Congress knows that 90 percent of the adverse talk of radio on Capitol Hill has been caused by the Paulist Fathers."[104]

CONCLUDING OBSERVATIONS

The primary purpose of this article has been to shed light on a critical period in the history of American broadcasting: the passage of the Communications Act of 1934 and the movement to gain passage of the Wagner-Hatfield amendment. As such, the sagas of Father Harney, the Paulist Fathers and station WLWL have been highlighted. Beyond this aim, however, this article has argued for a basic re-construction of American broadcasting history in three ways.

First, the experience of WLWL was by no means isolated. Scores of non-profit and educational broadcasters started with high ideals and lofty ambitions in an era when few forecast that within a decade American broadcasting would be irretrievably cast as an oligopolistic and commercially subsidized system. Almost all of these broadcasters, arguably the "true pioneers" of the medium, faced a se-ries of economic crises and conflicts with the FRC and commercial broadcasters that made it virtually impossible for them to succeed. This non-profit experience could almost be termed the hidden history of American broadcasting.[105]

Second, this experience implies that the development of the American sys-tem of network-dominated and commercially subsidized broadcasting was every bit as much the product of conflict as it was of consensus. Furthermore, there was never a coherent study and debate over how best to structure broadcasting as transpired, for example, in Canada. Rather, the dominant system emerged for the most part as the result of the actions of small self-serving elites acting in a sea of public ignorance. Indeed, the basic effort of Harney and the other reformers was simply to put the issue of broadcast policy before the American people. At this task they were largely unsuccessful as the dominant interests were able to keep radio policy *out* of the public spotlight.

Finally, many of the concerns of Father Harney and the other reformers re-garding the limitations of an oligopolistic and commercially subsidized media sys-tem for a democratic society have been raised again over the past generation by a new wave of media scholars and activists. These contemporary media critics need to realize that they are not reinventing the proverbial wheel, nor are they necessar-ily relying upon "foreign" ideologies to criticize "American" institutions. As the experience of Father Harney and the other reformers of the early 1930s reveals, radical criticism of the status quo can be derived from long-standing American democratic traditions and values. This tradition of dissent and criticism has been ignored or trivialized, by and large, to the extent that the self-serving rhetoric of the commercial broadcasters has been taken at face value.

NOTES

1. James McVann, *The Paulists, 1958–1970* (New York: Society of St. Paul the Apostle, 1983), p. 875.

2. C. Joseph Pusateri, *Enterprise in Radio* (Washington, D.C.: University Press of America, 1980), p. 187.

3. McVann, *Paulists,* p. 876; Pusateri, *Enterprise,* p. 167.

4. For discussions of the theological and intellectual origins of the Paulist order see John Farina, *An American Experience of God* (New York: Paulist Press, 1981); John Farina, *Hecker Studies* (New York: Paulist Press, 1983).

5. Pusateri, *Enterprise,* p. 167.

6. *In the Matter of Section 307(c) of the Federal Communications Act of 1934; Brief on behalf of Radio Station WLWL. Submitted by the Very Rev. John B. Harney, C.S.P.* (Washington, D.C.: Federal Communications Commission, 1934), p. 27. (Hereafter *Harney Brief.*)

7. *Ibid.,* p. 25.

8. McVann, *Paulists,* p. 877.

9. *Harney Brief,* p. 25.

10. This was the famous Zenith decision of 1926. For a discussion of this case and its significance see Marvin R. Bensman, "The Zenith-WJAZ Case and the Chaos of 1926–27," *Journal of Broadcasting* 14 (Fall 1970): 423–40. For a discussion of the "breakdown of the law" period see "Pending Litigation Marks Beginning of Radio Jurisprudence," *American Bar Association Journal* 15 (March 1929): 173–78.

11. *Harney Brief,* p. 25.

12. This point is developed in Louis G. Caldwell, "The Standard of Public Interest, Convenience or Necessity as Used in the Radio Act of 1927," *Air Law Review* 1 (July 1930): 295–330.

13. *Harney Brief,* p. 26.

14. *Ibid.*

15. *Ibid.*

16. *Third Annual Report of the Federal Radio Commission to the Congress of the United States* (Washington, D.C.: United States Government Printing Office, 929), 32. [HEREAFTER, *FRC 3rd Report*]

17. *Ibid,* p. 34.

18. Cited in Pusateri, *Enterprise,* p. 168.

19. An example is WWL. In New Orleans, which was a Jesuit station that would eventually affiliate with CBS. See Pusateri, *Enterprise.*

20. *Hearings Before the Committee on Interstate and Foreign Commence House of Representatives 73rd Congress 2nd Session on H.R. 8301, 1934* (Washington, D.C.: United States Printing Office, 1934), p. 161. [HEREAFTER *House Hearings 1934*]

21. "25,000 Praise WLWL, Asking for More Time," *New York Times,* September 29, 1931, p. 23.

22. "Catholic Aid Asked for Station WLWL," *New York Times,* September 28, 1931, p. 26.

23. "WLWL Asks More Time," *New York Times,* November 5, 1931, p. 30; "Protest WLWL Decision," *New York Times,* June 14, 1932, p. 2.

24. H. M. McIntyre to Herbert Pettey, June 1, 1933, Franklin Delano Roosevelt Papers, Franklin D. Roosevelt Presidential Library, Hyde Park, New York, OF 136, Box 1, 1933. [HEREAFTER Roosevelt Mss]

25. McVann, *Paulists,* p. 882.

26. *House Hearings 1934,* p. 160; McVann, *Paulists,* p. 891.

27. McVann, *Paulists,* p. 890.

28. *House Hearings 1934,* p. 166.

29. "Paulists Seek Radio Aid," *New York Times,* November 11, 1929, p. 32.

30. "Hearst Negotiating to Acquire WLWL," *Broadcasting,* November 15, 1931, p. 16.

31. *Digest of Hearings, Federal Communications Commission Broadcast Division, under Sec. 307(c) of "The Communications Act of 1934" October 1–20, November 7–12, 1934* (Washington, D.C.: Federal Communications Commission, 1935), pp. 180–249.

32. See Werner J. Severin, "Commercial vs. Non-Commercial Radio During Broadcasting's Early Years," *Journal of Broadcasting* 22 (Fall 1978): 491–504.

33. Philip T. Rosen, *The Modern Stentors; Radio Broadcasters and the Federal Government 1920–1934* (Westport, Conn.: Greenwood Press, 1980), p. 12.

34. Armstrong Perry, "The College Station and the Federal Radio Commission," in *Education on the Air: Second Yearbook of the Institute for Education by Radio,* Josephine H. McLatchy, ed. (Columbia: Ohio States University, 1931), pp. 16–17.

35. Roger Baldwin to Tracy Tyler, October 24, 1933; Tracy Tyler to Roger Baldwin, October 26, 1933, American Civil Liberties Union Manuscripts. Princeton University Library, Princeton, New Jersey, 1933, Volume 599. [HEREAFTER ACLU Mss]

36. NCER's activities are discussed at considerable length in Robert W. McChesney, "Enemy of the Status Quo: The National Committee on Education by Radio and the Debate over the Control and Structure of American Broadcasting in the Early 1930s," paper presented to History Division, Association for Education in Journalism and Mass Communication, 1967 Annual Convention, San Antonio, Texas.

37. The activities of the ACLU's Radio Committee are discussed in Robert W. McChesney, "Constant Retreat: The American Civil Liberties Union and the Debate Over the Meaning of Free Speech for Radio Broadcasting in the 1930s," In *Free Speech Yearbook, Volume* 26, Stephen A. Smithy, ed. (Speech Communication Association, 1988).

38. Eddie Dowling, the adviser to President Roosevelt who was in charge of his relations with broadcasters during the 1932 presidential campaign, observed: "Radio is credited with one of the strongest of the swarming lobbies in Washington—one with substance behind it. Members of Congress are dominated by tactics which are constantly under the direction of private interests." From Eddie Dowling, "Radio Needs A Revolution." *Forum* 91 (February 1934): 69.

39. "Keeping Public Opinion for Big Biz," *Federation News,* May 30, 1931, p. 4.; See also Nathan Godfried, "The Origins of Labor Radio: WCFL, the 'Voice of Labor', 1925–1928," *Historical Journal of Film, Radio and Television* 7 (1987): 143–59.

40. "Labor Wins Victory in Long Air Fight," *Federation News,* June 4, 1932, p. 6.

41. "Labor Group Asks New York Station," *Broadcasting,* September 1, 1932, p. 10; "Labor Asks Right to Radio Outlet," *Federation News,* August 27, 1932, p. 8.

42. This point is developed in Rosen, *Stentors,* pp. 173–74.

43. *Study of Communications By an Interdepartmental Committee, Letter from the President of the United States to the Chairman of the Committee on Interstate Commerce Transmitting a Memorandum from the Secretary of Commerce Relative to a Study of Communications by an Interdepartmental Committee* (Washington, D.C.: United States Government Printing Office, 1934).

44. Roper to Roosevelt, January 25, 1934, Roosevelt Mss, OF 3, X Refs 1934; "Broadcasting Survey Postponed," *NAB Reports,* February 24, 1934, p. 309.; Sol Talshoff, "Roosevelt Demands Communications Bill," *Broadcasting,* February 15, 1934, p. 6.

45. "Asks Body to Rule Wires and Radio," *New York Times,* February 27, 1934, p. 1.

46. 'Roosevelt Approves Communications Board to Rule Radio, Telephone, Telegraph, Cable,' *New York Times,* February 10, 1934, p. 12.

47. See testimony of Henry Bellows and David Sarnoff in *Hearings before the Committee on Interstate Commerce United States Senate 73rd Session on S. 2910 1934* (Washington, D.C.: United States Government Printing Office, 1934), pp. 53–54, 106. [HEREAFTER *Senate Hearings 1934*]

48. Henry A. Bellows, "Report of Legislative Committee," *NAB Reports,* November 15, 1934, p. 618.

49. This point will become clear later in the text. For a more thorough discussion of Roosevelt see Robert W. McChesney, "President Franklin D. Roosevelt and the Communications Act of 1934," paper presented to 1987 West Coast Journalism Historians Conference, Berkeley, CA. A revised version will be published in *American Journalism.*

50. Address by Rev. Doctor Joseph A. Daly, February 11, 1934, *WLWL Press Release.* Roosevelt Mss, OF 138, Box 1, 1934.

51. Pusateri, *Enterprise,* p. 168.

52. "WLWL Seeks New Law," *New York Times,* April 11, 1934, p. 15.

53. *Senate Hearings 1934,* March 13, 1934, p. 106.

54. *Ibid.,* March 15, 1934, p. 185.

55. *Ibid.,* p. 186.

56. "Boring From Within," *Education By Radio,* August 18, 1932, p. 92.

57. *Senate Hearings 1934,* March 15, 1934, p. 186.

58. Perry, *Education on the Air 1931,* p. 33; see also Joy Elmer Morgan. "The National Committee on Education by Radio," in *Education on the Air 1931,* p. 24.

59. "Wire-Radio Bill Up to President," *New York Times,* April 14, 1934, p. 7.

60. McVann, *Paulists,* p. 896.

61. United States Senate Interstate Commerce Committee Papers. National Archives, Washington, D.C., Sen 73A-J28, tray 155. [HEREAFTER *ICC Mss*]

62. "Plea for Radio Station," *New York Times,* March 26, 1934, p. 26.

63. Federal Communications Commission Papers, National Archives, Suitland, MD., National Archives Record Group 173, Box 38, File 15-3a. [HEREAFTER FCC Mss]

64. John B. Harney, *Education and Religion vs. Commercial Radio* (New York: Paulist Fathers, 1934).

65. "WLWL Seeks New Law," *New York Times,* April 11, 1934, p. 15.

66. *Congressional Record,* April 19, 1934, p. 6898.

67. *Congressional Record,* April 27, 1934, p. 7509.

68. "Air Enemies Units Forces," *Variety,* May 6, 1934, pp. 37, 45.

69. "Wagner Amendment Up Next Week," *NAB Reports,* May 5, 1934, p. 375.

70. "Labor Aids Bill for Free Radio," *Federation News,* April 7, 1934, p. 6; "Labor Toils for Radio Freedom," *Federation News,* May 26, 1934, pp. 1, 3.

71. "Hanley Criticism of Broadcasting Setup Denied by Administration Colleagues," *Broadcasting,* May 1, 1934, p. 22.

72. Sol Talshoff, "Powerful Lobby Threatens Radio Structure," *Broadcasting,* May 15, 1934, pp. 5, 6.

73. *Bellows,* "Report," *NAB Reports,* November 15, 1934, p. 618.

74. *Broadcasting,* May 15, 1934, pp. 5, 6.

75. *House Hearings 1934,* pp. 116, 345.

76. *Variety,* May 8, 1934, p. 45.

77. Maloney to Sykes, April 25, 1934; Sykes to Maloney, April 28, 1934, FCC Mss, NARG 173, Legislation, Acts-Radio, FCC General Correspondence, Box 38.

78. "Senate to Pass Dill Bill," *NAB Reports,* May 12, 1934, p. 387.

79. Russell to Patterson, May 5, 1934, National Broadcasting Company Papers, Wisconsin Historical Society, Madison, Box 90, Folder 53. [HEREAFTER NBC Mss]

80. McVann, *Paulists,* p. 897.

81. Harney to Harry, May 2, 1934; Harney to MacDonald, May 3, 1934, Society of St. Paul the Apostle Manuscripts, Catholic University, Washington, D.C., WLWL file. [HEREAFTER Paulist Mss]

82. Harney to Gillepsie, May 3, 1934; Gillepsie to Harney, May 17th, 1934, Paulist Mss.

83. *House Hearings 1934,* May 9, 1934, p. 162.

84. *Ibid.*

85. *Ibid.*

86. Russell to Aylesworth, May 11, 1934; Aylesworth to Russell, May 15, 1934, NBC Mss, Box 90, Folder 53.

87. Bellows, "Report," *NAB Reports,* p. 617.

88. *Congressional Record,* May 15, 1934, p. 8830.

89. The proceedings of the NCER conference were published in June, 1934: *Radio as a Cultural Agency in a Democracy,* Tracy F. Tyler, ed. (Washington, D.C.: The National Committee on Education by Radio, 1934).

90. *Congressional Record,* May 15, 1934, p. 8831.

91. *Ibid.,* pp. 8832–33.

92. *Ibid.,* p. 8843.

93. Rosen, *Stentors,* p. 179.

94. *Congressional Record,* June 2, 1934, pp. 10315–23.

95. Bellows, "Report," *NAB Reports,* November 15, 1934, p. 618.

96. Sol Taishoff, "Fate of FCC Measure Hangs in Balance," *Broadcasting,* June 1, 1934, p. 6.

97. Sol Taishoff, "Radio Status Quo as FCC Convenes," *Broadcasting,* July 15, 1934, p. 7.

98. An editorial in *Broadcasting* noted: "Any fears harbored by those in broadcasting that an immediate upheaval of radio might result from the creation of the new FCC are dispelled with the organization of that agency into divisions. The Broadcasting Division . . . is a conservative group. It can be expected to carry on the basic policies of the old Radio Commission, for, indeed, two of its members were on the former agency." (August 1, 1934, p. 22.)

99. "Government Interference Fear Groundless, Say Commissioners," *Broadcasting,* October 1, 1934, p. 18.

100. *Official Report of the Proceedings before the Federal Communications Commission,* Smith & Hulse, Official Reporters (Washington, D.C.: n.p., 1934), pp. 580–85.

101. "Federal Communications Commission Reports to Congress," *Education by Radio,* January 31, 1935, p. 5.

102. "New Program for NCER," *Education by Radio,* January–February 1936, p. 1.

103. Joseph Malloy, "History of the Negotiations Leading to Sale of WLWL" Paulist Mss. WLWL file.

104. Confidential Memo Re: George Henry Payne, April 29, 1937, Roosevelt Mss. OF 2001.

105. For a comprehensive review of educational broadcasters see S. E. Frost, *Education's Own Stations* (Chicago: University of Chicago Press, 1937).

QUESTIONS FOR DISCUSSION

1. Why was the declared intention of WLWL to sell some time for commercial advertising so contentious? Are "public service" and "commercial" broadcasting necessarily contradictory? Why did the FRC, and also many in the reform movement, reinforce this distinction?

2. Relate the ideas of Winston and Goodman and Gring to this debate. How did Progressive beliefs enter into the distinction made above? What radical potential was being suppressed in the case of WLWL?

3. Would assignment of a broadcasting license to a religious organization have violated the separation of church and state? What if another religious group applied and did not receive a license? How has this issue been resolved in today's broadcasting universe?

 INFOTRAC COLLEGE EDITION

Search InfoTrac College Edition for more articles by Robert W. McChesney. Also, search under "religious broadcasters" for an update on the issue today.

4

Why We Don't Count
The Commodity Audience

EILEEN R. MEEHAN

Commercial broadcasters in the United States like to promote the notion that they slavishly serve the interests of the American public when it comes to programming: "We give the public what they want." But Eileen Meehan's article reminds us that there is an important middleman in this process. The ratings system, supported by its corporate sponsors, is not a transparent device for magically and objectively measuring exactly what the public wants but instead a complicated, self-interested, deeply biased and flawed mechanism that has been developed over the years to serve its clients' interests, not the public's.

Meehan traces the history of the various ratings systems for both radio and television, showing us how ratings produce a "commodity audience" that is sold to advertisers. She shows us the "hidden economics" of both ratings process and technology, demonstrating the ways that ratings providers put advertisers' and broadcasters' agendas first—and why we don't count.

From *Logics of Television: Essays on Cultural Criticism*, edited by Patricia Mellencamp
(Indiana University Press, 1990). Reprinted by permission of Indiana University Press.

US intellectuals have little influence in shaping popular taste or in designing the cultural commodities that are mass-distributed to the US public. This is not simply a reflection of the esteem accorded to our intellectual minority by the general populace. Nor is it simply a reflection of differences in training, temperament, and taste that separate the professional intellectual from the average television viewer. Of the 86.3 million households owning television sets,[1] one can safely assume that only a narrow slice of those households shelter our intellectual minority, with a still narrower slice sheltering scholars of cinematic or televisual texts. Perhaps, as Dr. Frank Stanton of CBS argued,[2] our tiny numbers mitigate against a role for us in a democratic mass medium such as television. But where other nations have sought to ensure minority participation in mass media by creating structural openings in their media systems,[3] the commercial nature of the US system leaves few, if any, structural openings for minorities—intellectual or otherwise. In the US, then, intellectuals have no formal role in the multimillion-dollar industry that produces and distributes television to masses and intellectuals alike. In our television industry, intellectuals simply don't count.

But if we don't, who does? According to national networks, national advertisers, and national ratings firms, the answer is democratic in the extreme: the people count.[4] The preferences of millions of viewers, as scientifically measured in the ratings, determine what gets on and what stays on. Perhaps we may not like *Alf, Murder, She Wrote,* or *Wheel of Fortune,* but millions of people do, as demonstrated by the ratings. With raters measuring the people's choices in programming and programmers selecting shows that conform to these demonstrated preferences, then surely television reflects the public's taste.

All this rests on the claim that ratings are research—a claim that has been cultivated by raters in their promotional materials, in the trade press, before congressional committees, and in the mass circulation press.[5] If that claim is accurate, then the ratings firm's scientific sample is representative of television viewers. If that claim is accurate, then television programming reflects the forced choice behaviors of the mass of television viewers. That would mean that most people's preferences would count in the television industry, even if any particular individual was not in the sample. In short, we would all count, although only our forced choice behaviors would matter.

Most critics of television ratings and television taste have accepted the basic claim that ratings are research. Hence, their work has focused on the manipulation of network schedules to skew ratings, whether because of greed[6] or the desire to "prove" that a certain genre or particular show is not popular.[7] Others, equally accepting of the objectivity of ratings, have focused on the use of ratings to measure the naturally occurring viewership in order to package that viewership for sale to advertisers as the commodity audience.[8] But to accept the claim of scientificity without scrutinizing the historical development of ratings and the economic conditions that constrain ratings production is naive.

The purpose of this essay is to dissolve that naiveté. By examining the historical development of the market for ratings, I will demonstrate how ratings become fully commoditized through producers' manipulation of continuities and discontinuities in corporate demand for estimates of the commodity audience. I will show

how economic self-interest restricts and reformulates measurement techniques, transforming these techniques from scientific measures into business practices, into corporate tactics in the struggle for market control, profitability, and low production costs. From this perspective, ratings do not count the viewers, but only the commodity audience which is saleable to national advertisers and networks. In fact, within the closed market where raters sell their commodities—the ratings— to national advertisers and networks, only the commodity audience counts. In this way, both intellectuals and masses have been defined out of this market and out of the audience. Neither intellectuals nor masses count.

Let me anticipate some objections: we all know that television is the massest of mass media. Millions of people watch television for eight to sixteen hours a day; programs are constructed to play to the lowest common denominator in taste and understanding. We all know that in millions of homes—maybe even our own—the set is not watched but remains on as constant soundtrack and moving wallpaper. We know all this as professional intellectuals, and we know it as everyday folks.

We know it, but does it make a difference? Do these behaviors, does this knowledge count? Consider another bit of common knowledge: television shows live and die by the numbers—that is, the ratings currently produced by the A. C. Nielsen Company and sold to national networks and national advertisers. These numbers are used by the networks to cancel shows, rearrange schedules, commission new shows, and set prices for advertising slots. The same ratings are used by advertisers to buy commercial time and target subgroups of consumers. The result is a cultural system run by magic numbers, numbers that shape content, creation, and availability. The question then becomes: Who counts in the ratings?

To answer that question, we need to develop a historical and analytic perspective on the macroeconomic structure of US commercial broadcasting. Constraints of space, however, preclude a full account, which would require a detailed examination of the internal struggles and national security connections of the Radio-Telephone Patent Pool, an essentially illegal cartel that dominated and defined US telecommunications from World War I into the 1930s.[9] Instead, I will look briefly at the Pool's radio operations directly after the Armistice. I will examine AT&T's innovation of "toll" broadcasting and the creation of corporate demand for audience measurements and program ratings in the late 1920s and early 1930s. I will analyze the structure of that demand and show how the measurement methods were selected by raters to both serve continuities in demand and manipulate discontinuities in demand.[10] I do this to demonstrate the artificial nature, the manufacturedness of the market for ratings, of the ratings themselves, and of the rating's object—the commodity audience. Finally, I will offer a brief observation on the people meter controversy.

The point of all this is to uncover the underlying macroeconomic structure that has set and continues to set the limits, parameters, and operating rules of national broadcasting as show *business*. In this corporate "game," players come and go. The balance of power between players shifts. But the basic structure of the game remains, and the longevity or success of any particular corporate player depends on its ability to adapt to and creatively manipulate the underlying structure.

TELEPHONY VS. RADIO: TAKING THE TOLL

So let me begin by noting that the Patent Poolers had divided the world into two territories: wired telephony controlled by AT&T and wireless or radio telephony controlled by General Electric (GE) and Westinghouse.[11] To manufacture equipment, AT&T had its wholly owned subsidiary, Western Electric; to distribute and sell radio equipment, GE and Westinghouse used RCA (co-owned by AT&T, GE, and Westinghouse). All three principals had research units, and all three dabbled in the experimental application of wireless telephony which we now call radio.[12]

Throughout World War I, the three had manufactured equipment for radio telephony for the armed forces, but the Armistice in 1918 meant a dramatic decrease in the military's demand for radio equipment. This left AT&T, GE, and Westinghouse geared up to produce radio equipment at levels that far exceeded civilian demand. At this time, radio was primarily a hobby that attracted college students, engineers, and tinkerers of all ages who built their own sets in order to communicate with other "ham" operators. GE and Westinghouse funneled their components through RCA into the home market where they competed with independent inventors but not with AT&T, since AT&T had agreed not to produce or sell radio sets in this market, just as its two partners had agreed to stay out of telephone manufacture. In 1922, GE and Westinghouse began selling fully assembled radios in the hope of expanding their equipment sales from do-it-yourselfers to the general consumers who lacked the ham's mechanical skills.

However, consumers had little incentive to buy radio sets in order to eavesdrop on conversations between hams or hear occasional experimental transmissions.[13] To persuade people to buy sets, manufacturers and retailers realized that they needed to provide something to hear on a regularly scheduled basis. Programs, then, were used to promote the sale of radio sets. Thus, radio broadcasting earned no direct revenues for itself; instead, it was an advertising devise that earned indirect revenues by boosting set sales. The strategy was successful; sales rose from 100,000 sets in 1922 to 500,000 in 1923, and shot to 1.5 million only a year later.[14] Clearly, programming sold sets.

AT&T enjoyed none of the revenues from set sales. Despite this, the company remained active in broadcasting research and pioneered the use of long-distance telephone lines to link its station in New York (WEAF) to other AT&T stations. AT&T proposed to form a great chain of stations across the country that would serve as common carriers bringing to listeners the messages of any person or company that would pay the necessary "toll" for transmission. Rather than provide programs itself, AT&T would network the programs of any sponsor wishing to advertise its wares to a national listening audience. This proposal was the foundation of commercial broadcasting. It also signaled the start of a serious crisis for the cartel as AT&T sought to change the basic definitions upon which GE, Westinghouse, and AT&T had divided radio from telephony. AT&T essentially argued that toll broadcasting made radio a form of telephony and hence part of AT&T's territory.

The story of that crisis rivals the best spy fiction for intrigue, complexity, and drama. Unfortunately, that means I cannot delve into its web of detail;[15] suffice it to say that the outcome was a reaffirmation of the split between telephony and radio. AT&T would continue to monopolize telephony, but added to its activities the exclusive right to interconnect broadcast networks. GE and Westinghouse retained their hold on radio, especially in manufacturing. RCA secured a more independent role, taking over AT&T's network and coordinating those stations with GE's and Westinghouse's through RCA's new subsidiary, the National Broadcasting Company (NBC). The resulting NBC-Red and NBC-Blue networks would earn income by selling time to national manufacturers. These advertisers would produce programs to persuade consumers to buy their products, programs which listeners would receive free of charge.

This reorganization of the radio business was so promising that other networks were started on national and regional bases, with CBS emerging as NBC's strongest rival.[16] By 1927, then, through the struggles of private corporate interests, the basic structure of both radio and television broadcasting had largely emerged: three national networks, advertisers as the basic source of revenues, access to audiences as the basic commodity sold by networks. But if AT&T had solved the problem of direct revenue, the company had created a new problem by doing so—namely, how to figure out the cost of that access.

INFORMATION, PLEASE

The cost of such access hinged on advertisers' demand for listeners. However, because advertisers were being asked to pay per listener, not any listener would do. Clearly, the listeners worth paying for were those most likely to buy the product—in short, potential consumers. Since advertisers also bore the costs of programming, the number of potential consumers listening would have to be sufficiently large for advertisers to shoulder the combined costs of programming and access.

Advertisers, then, needed information about the radio audience in order to select a time slot that would reach their targeted subgroup, to assess the performance of their shows, and to evaluate the costs charged by networks for the time slot and its audience. Similarly, broadcasters needed information about the size and the value of the audience in order to both set and justify prices. Advertisers and broadcasters both needed information on the size and demographics of radio's audience in order to establish radio's ability to produce the right audience—an audience of consumers rather than of listeners.

This posed a problem: how to measure radio's productivity, that is, its ability to produce the invisible "commodity audience." The obvious solution was for CBS and NBC to measure their own productivity, reporting the aggregate numbers of listening consumers and describing the demographics of these consumers. The networks did this through their research departments which consistently found that radio drew vast audiences of eager consumers.[17] Such reports were used to justify the rates that networks charged advertisers.

For advertisers, however, these reports were simply promotional material. How could advertisers trust such glowing numbers when those numbers served the networks' economic self-interest? Since prices were tied to reaching the right audience in the right numbers, higher estimates of that audience's size meant higher prices. Although advertisers wanted fairly accurate demographics describing targeted listeners, their economic interests lay in methods of measurement that focused on the commodity audience yet underestimated the size of that audience, and thereby kept network prices down. This bifurcation of demand has persisted to the present. Advertisers and networks share an interest in ratings that measure audience *quality;* but their interests conflict over the accuracy of ratings that measure audience *quantity.*

In the face of the networks' self-reports, advertisers decided to do their own measuring. By 1928, the Association of National Advertisers (ANA) hired Archibald Crossley to devise a means to measure radio listening.[18] One year later, the ANA accepted Crossley's findings and officially institutionalized his suggestions in a new organizations, the Cooperative Analysis of Broadcasting (CAB), which began operation in 1930. The CAB was directly under the control of the ANA, its members, and representatives of their advertising agencies. Using Crossley's method, CAB produced radio ratings that were circulated only to advertisers. Although the numbers usually leaked out to the networks and the trade press, CBS and NBC were barred by the ANA from buying the numbers and from using them in price negotiations or for self-promotion.

But if the circulation of CAB ratings was a problem for the networks, so too were the ratings themselves. Crossley's method favored the advertisers but offered no trade-offs to the networks. Let me briefly consider Crossley's methods and the socio-cultural setting in which he used them.

First, we need to remember that by 1929 radios had become a mass medium; more than 50% of the nation's homes were equipped with a radio, and sets were located in many public places (diners, bars, soup kitchens, etc.).[19] In all, 13 million sets had been sold, and sales had remained strong even during the recession of 1924 and 1927 when other commodities had suffered sales decreases. Radio was well on its way to universality by 1929.

In contrast, telephony remained a rather somber medium. Still connected in the public mind with business and middle-class status, residential telephone subscription had nevertheless climbed to 41% of the nation's households.[20] While having a radio was taken for granted, having a telephone listing was still a mark of prestige. The acceptance of radio outstripped that of telephony so that radio homes were not necessarily also telephone homes. However, having a radio *and* a telephone was a mark of membership in the thoroughly modern, consumer-oriented middle class. Those were the homes that Crossley's methods targeted—not radio homes *per se,* but telephone homes with radios, the homes of the new consumer consciousness.

Crossley did this by using a telephone survey.[21] He randomly selected residential listings from directories and then called these households to inquire about their radio listening. Specifically, the interview followed a two-prong pattern: first, ask if anyone listened to the radio yesterday; then, ask for the titles of the shows and the names of the sponsors. Since many programs were only fifteen minutes long, Crossley was asking people to perform an incredible feat of memory. But it was not memory alone that served to bias Crossley's ratings in the advertisers' favor; social mores also skewed his results.

Crossley was dealing with a state of society whose code of conduct emphasized politeness, indirection, and avoidance of conflict in interpersonal relations.[22] When confronted by unpleasant situations, one tried to extract oneself gracefully, often by the use of polite lies. If one did not wish to speak with a particular telephone caller, one might be "indisposed" or "unable to come to the telephone" or forever "in a meeting." Often criticized as hypocritical, these conventions had important implications for Crossley's measurements. Should householders find onerous the task of detailing twenty-four hours' worth of listening for a perfect stranger on the telephone, they could politely escape the situation by suddenly remembering that they hadn't listened yesterday, that they had confused yesterday with the day before. Crossley could not tell real nonlistening from police claims of nonlistening. Thus, reluctant respondents could systematically deflate the size of this middle-class audience. Indeed, ratings produced by these methods "found" that radio audiences were rather small.

Given Crossley's reliance on telephone households, his reports were systematically limited to those consumers that advertisers wanted. Given the interaction of socio-cultural codes and the difficulty of the task, his methodology deflated the number of listeners. In this way, Crossley and CAB produced ratings limited to the type of audience that advertisers wanted and delivered a quantity of audience that suited advertisers' interest in depressing network prices. No wonder the networks were quick to support an alternative, independent ratings service.

HOOPLA AND HOOPERATINGS

As early as 1930, C. E. Hooper contemplated a challenge to CAB.[23] The problem was to craft a measurement method that would rebalance the interests of both advertisers and networks in a way that would make the new ratings more attractive than CAB's numbers. Hooper's solution was based on changing economic conditions and on the bifurcation of demand. Where networks and advertisers shared an interest in better measures of the middle-class consumer at a time of downward socio-economic mobility, Hooper offered a sampling method that would further constrict the definition of the commodity audience. Where networks' interests conflicted with advertisers' interests over the accuracy of estimates of audience quantity, Hooper offered networks an interview that increased the number of listeners. To balance this, advertisers were offered a higher quality of listener at a lower price. Since Hooper sold his ratings to all comers—advertisers, agencies, networks, and local stations—he could decrease the cost for any single unit of information by spreading the production costs over more ratings consumers. (This is, of course, a central tenet of mass production.) Hooper gambled that advertisers would accept higher estimates of audience size (and thus higher network prices) if the sample was more carefully constricted to potential consumers and if unit costs were low. Essentially, Hooper promised both higher quality and larger quantity in ratings production, but a lower prices.

He achieved these manufacturing goals by selecting a particular form of measurement. Like CAB, Hooper used telephone listings to restrict his sample to the middle class. With the Great Depression in full swing, residential telephone subscription had fallen 10% in only three years (1929–1931).[24] But Hooper further restricted that sample by using only urban directories. The big cities, although seriously hurt by the Great Depression, remained centers of consumption, especially when compared with small towns or rural areas.[25] The concentration of people in cities meant that the cities housed more potential consumers, more members of the middle class with sufficient disposable income who were willing and able to purchase name-brand goods. From an economic perspective, ratings that measured the preferences of the urban middle class were more cost-efficient than ratings that measured the entire middle class. Consumers in New York City, Chicago, and San Francisco were a more valuable audience than consumers in Bangor, Sheuyville, or Rio Osso. In this way, Hooper further restricted who counted, but did so in a manner consonant with advertisers' preferences.

Hooper also redesigned the interview.[26] Rather than ask people to recall yesterday's listening, he first inquired whether the radio was on when the telephone rang. If so, the respondent was asked to identify the program and sponsor. Respondents were also asked for simple demographic information about themselves and anybody else who might be listening with them. Finally, they were asked if they had been listening fifteen minutes earlier; if so, the same information was solicited for that program. These changes had an immediate effect on the results that Hooper gathered: suddenly people were listening to radio in droves. Clearly, this played into the networks' interests.

From 1932 to 1936, Hooper struggled to oust CAB from its monopoly over ratings. On the scientific front, he conducted a series of proprietorial studies to demonstrate the superiority of his interview, christened the "telephone coincidental," over Crossley's "recall interview." This culminated in Chappell and Hooper's *Radio Audience Measurement*[27] in 1942, the definitive attack on the recall interview, published long after that method had fallen from advertisers' favor. The book, however, does provide a systematic account of Hooper's criticisms.

Hooper argued that the CAB's method was flawed by its reliance on the human memory. In contrast, his coincidental method was cast as directly tapping the listening behaviors of respondents. To illustrate this, Hooper contrasted his ratings with CAB's, arguing that differences in ratings reflected the weaknesses of CAB's methodology. He claimed that the ability to remember a program varied with the age of the program, its previous status in the ratings, and the status of its network. Hooper reported that CAB's methods favored older shows on NBC that had long placed in CAB's top ten. People simply remembered them better having been exposed to more information about them and thus reported them as the shows heard the previous day. But memory was even more slippery than that; Hooper also found that people could not reliably recall when they were home. However, by substituting memory for direct report of behavior, he promised a scientific breakthrough to advertisers and networks alike.

The ANA responded to this challenge by reorganizing the CAB and changing its interview to more closely resemble Hooper's coincidental. This *de facto* admission of methodological inferiority may have improved its measurement of the commodity audience, but it did little to stem the tide of Hooper's criticism or his in-house studies.

On the promotional front, the self-effacing image dictated for the CAB by ANA was easily overwhelmed by the outgoing Mr. Hooper. Known as both "Mr. Ratings" and "Hoop" in the trades and the popular press, Hooper challenged CAB's ratings secrecy by holding weekly press conferences in which he would unveil the ratings winners. "Hoop" was often featured in the gossip columns, particularly in Walter Winchell's column after Winchell dubbed Hooper's product the "Hooperatings." While he constructed his public persona as the approachable, affable, and honest fellow in the ratings business, Hooper used these public occasions to assert the objectivity and scientificity of his product. Hooper established himself as a "show biz personality," but always as a personality whose work was in scientific audience measurement.

Overall, his blend of showmanship and scientificity complemented his careful balance of advertiser and network interests. And after four years of two raters producing different ratings for the same shows, public confidence in ratings generally may have been shaken. Certainly the business of buying and selling audiences had suffered from the wealth of contradictory ratings. Hooper's stance as the objective scientist provided a rationale for dumping CAB: it was not that ratings *per se* were faulty, only the particular methods used by the partisan CAB. By 1936, Hooper emerged as an objective third party, able to mediate between advertisers and networks through the scientific production of ratings. By 1936, then, Hooper effectively monopolized ratings production for national, networked radio. Hooperatings were *the* determination of sponsors' programming decisions and *the* basis for network prices. This monopoly remained firmly entrenched until 1942.

THE HIDDEN ECONOMICS OF RATINGS

With Hooper's success, the macroeconomic structure of the market for ratings is set into place. First, there is a bifurcation of demand. Demand for ratings is unified in that advertisers and networks want measures only of potential consumers; this means that the audience to be measured is only a subgroup of the listening public. However, demand for ratings is disunified by the connections between price and size of the saleable audience; a big audience means a higher price. Thus, if ratings underestimate the size of the commodity audience, they work in the advertisers' economic interest; if ratings overestimate the size of the commodity audience, they work in the networks' economic interest. This discontinuity in demand opens up the possibility of independence for a ratings producer. And that possibility is strengthened by the fact that advertisers and networks need only *one* set of numbers as the basis for their transactions.

This crucial second element in the macroeconomic structure is made clear by the CAB-Hooper rivalry. Different methods will produce different ratings for the same program, partly as an artifact of the methods themselves. For Hooper, the selection of a particular method was a decision guiding both ratings production and the marketing of Hooper's particular brand of ratings. The selection of a method both positions a company in the ratings market *and* differentiates that company's number from those of its rival. Because ratings serve as the basis on which audiences are bought by advertisers and sold by networks in routinized transactions, having multiple, contradictory ratings for any single time slot complicates and disrupts the routine business of buying and selling the commodity audience. Only a single set of official numbers is required. This predisposes networks and advertisers to accept a monopoly in ratings production. If a ratings firm can take advantage of this predisposition and of bifurcation in demand in a way that satisfies continuities while balancing discontinuities in demand, that firm may gain control of national ratings production.

Such control also depends on the ability to discredit the methodology of any prior monopolist. Crucial to such an attempt is the selection and redesign of measurement methods to emphasize those groups of consumers that are targeted by advertisers. This brings up the worrisome problem that ratings may, in some sense, be tautological—that the design of the sample and measurements may determine the results. It should be clear from the analysis that the selection of the sampling method sets the definition for the commodity audience, which excludes some of the listening public in deference to continuities in demand. It should also be clear that methods can favor some networks over others, thus making the state of network rivalry another factor that must be weighed by ratings firms. However, for a ratings firm to remain independent and thereby retain its control over its own pricing policies, production costs, and profits, it must be able to sell its product to all comers interested in the commodity audience regardless of whether these purchasers are rivals in advertising, manufacturing, or broadcasting. Bitter rivals read the same reports, and for the ratings firm to succeed, such rivals must be willing to subscribe to those reports for years. This provides an economic reason for relative honesty in ratings within the limits set by economic considerations. The ratings may fairly be said to reflect the forced choice behavior of the commodity audience within limitations set by continuities in demand, market conditions, production costs, and changing conditions in the general economy.

The effect of this tripartite structure is important, but usually hidden behind a wall of clichés. We are constantly told by the networks, advertisers, and ratings monopolist that free programming is a reflection of what we want, that scientific measurements determine how people "vote" on content, that programming is just a mirror of public taste. If you don't like what's on, that means you're out of step with the people. While this may insult the populists among us, it is somewhat flattering for intellectuals to be out of step with those who find their cultural satisfaction in returns of *Gilligan's Island* or repeats of *Entertainment Tonight*. However, whether insulting or flattering, the effect of such claims is to brand as elitist those who would change the programming policies of national, networked television and to trivialize serious criticism of televisual programming by making it a function of membership in the intellectual elite.

By analyzing the macroeconomic structures beneath the programming, it becomes obvious that the clichés have no basis in economic reality. Ratings are tools designed by firms to achieve economic success—control over ratings production. Forms of measurement are selected on the basis of economic goals, not according to the rules of social science. Not everybody is wanted by advertisers, so a ratings firm must try to exclude those persons who are not in demand. Programs, then, reflect the forced choices of the commodity audience when its constituents select between networked offerings. The differences between the commodity audience and the public viewership, between manufacturing the commodity audience through ratings and measuring the public taste through social research, cannot be overemphasized.

I have concentrated on the emergence of the market for ratings and the commodity audience. For most analysis of the televisual text, if the names Crossley and Hooper ring a bell, the chimes are very faint indeed. Yet Crossley and Hooper, in conjunction with the national advertisers and national networks in the 1920s and 1930s, effectively defined the market structure for the production of two commodities still crucial to broadcasting and cable—commodity ratings and the commodity audience.

THE TRANSITION TO TELEVISION
AND METERS

Into this preexisting market structure came the best-known of the ratings firms, the A. C. Nielsen Company (ACN), which entered the market in 1942 and achieved its monopoly position in 1950. It is important to note that ACN did not invent the market for ratings. The company spent six years developing its measurement techniques and promotional strategy[28] in order to challenge Hooper's monopoly of that preexisting market. Like any firm entering a new market, ACN crafted its production techniques in terms of existing demand structures, established products, and current rivalries.

Three examples are particularly noteworthy in suggesting the care that ACN took in constructing its measurement practices as business strategies. Like Hooper, ACN promoted its method as the latest breakthrough in the scientific measurement of audiences and produced numerous in-house studies to show the superiority of the meter over any other method, including the telephone coincidental. But by grounding its ratings in a metered sample, ACN enjoyed a promotional advantage over Hooper in the technology-minded postwar era. ACN's Audimeters were promoted as impartial machines recording the facts about viewers, facts that viewers might be embarrassed to reveal to interviewers. The meters thus produced numbers untainted by human interaction. Furthermore, meters, unlike interviews, could be protected by patents and patent litigation. Thus, ACN could draw on the legal intricacies of the patent system and infringement litigation to forestall the entry of other firms into metered ratings production.[29] This gave ACN a new defense against rival ratings firms.

But ACN's strategies were also mindful of rivalries between clients, both within and across its client industries. For example, the metered sample went beyond the cities, where Hooper still found NBC preferred over CBS, to include the small towns and rural areas of the US, where CBS outdrew NBC. But where the particular sample might favor CBS, ACN's meters generally favored networks by treating tuning as if it were listening, thereby skewing audience estimates overall in the networks' favor. Finally, the metered sample offered advertisers a minute-by-minute account of audience tuning over a twenty-four-hour period. This capability would become more important to advertisers as they moved out of sponsorship and into spot advertising on television.

Importantly, ACN did not achieve industry dominance until after the networks took effective control over their schedules and after the nation entered the post-World War II economic boom. With economic imperialism abroad and real economic growth at home—plus the employment and inflationary effect of the limited war economies generated by various "police actions"—mass consumption in the US entered an expansionist phase. As more categories of people became bona fide consumers, advertisers sought media with greater coverage of the general population than ever before. The postwar boom shifted housing patterns so that more of these consumers became suburbanites, thus shifting advertisers' focus away from marketing strategies that emphasized urban living to those of suburban domesticity. Placing television at the center of the family room, the networks (NBC, CBS, and ABC rising out of NBC's divested second network) cast television in the role of the massest mass medium. With many advertisers reluctant to finance the expense of televising their radio shows but eager to advertise on television,[30] the networks took control over their schedules. Replacing sponsorship with the practice of selling sixty-second spots to advertisers, they manipulated their program schedules according to "flow," and created programs designed to appeal to the lowest common denominator.[31] With millions more people promoted to consumer status and suburban living and with network control over scheduling, ACN's particular methods of measurement suited the shifting relations between advertisers and broadcasters.

The upshot was simple and of great significance for television programming. In 1950, ACN achieved monopoly status when its two years of rivalry with Hooper culminated in its buying his national ratings operation and securing a promise from him that his company would never again produce national ratings for television or radio. With Hooper pushed out of national production, ACN's fixed sample of 1,200 designated households became *the* audience. And that sample was based on radio homes—not television households—some of which had participated in ACN's field tests as far back as 1938.[32] The company simply waited for its radio sample to buy television sets and then metered the televisions. This pool of radio households formed the backbone of the ACN sample until the mid-1960s. With investigations by the House Special Subcommittee on Investigations, Federal Trade Commission, and Federal Communications Commission plus pressures from advertisers and networks (especially ABC and NBC) for an updated sample, ACN announced plans for raising its quality controls on ratings production generally and for updating its sample specifically to reflect changes in housing patterns since the end of World War II.[33] ACN promised to begin turning over sample households and to turn over the entire sample by 1970, replacing the old radio homes with households that would be younger and more urban. The effect on programming was dramatic: ex-vaudevillians and radio stars who had moved from network radio to network television were replaced by a flood of youthful protagonists dealing with modern problems in urban settings—resulting in television's "Year of Relevance."[34] However, despite such turnover and regardless of increases from 1,200 to 1,700 households over the years, the definition of the commodity audience has remained synonymous with the people in the ACN metered sample. Only their forced choice preferences count.[35]

THE NEW SELECTIVITY: PEOPLE METERS

A downshift in economic conditions, changing relations between networks and advertisers vis-à-vis cable and satellite superstations, and emerging rivalry in ratings production, however, have had significant effects on the industrial definition of the commodity audience. The confluence of these forces has produced a redefinition that uses cable subscription as a barrier to inclusion much as CAB and Hooper once used telephone subscription, thereby narrowing the definition of the commodity audience and introducing a new selectivity into the ACN ratings operation. To see how this affects us and the definition of who counts, I will briefly review the current state of affairs.

With the advent of cable and superstations, the number of effective television networks has more than tripled for the 35,444,000 households subscribing to cable television.[36] The households paying for this expansion of channel choice constitute roughly 41% of the total 86.3 million television homes. Access to cable subscriptions, however, is neither randomly nor universally available to every television household. In some municipalities, city government and potential cable operators have disagreed on terms, typically leaving an area unwired as long as a franchise is not granted. In other areas, cable operators have bypassed opportunities when the potential for profit seemed surpassed by the high costs of capitalization involved in wiring a small town or rural area. While this has created a space in the cable industry for small companies similar to the "mom and pop" operations of 1950s CATV, the industry remains dominated by large companies that have secured franchises across the nation (called multiple system operators or MSOs in the trade press). Control over the cable industry has been concentrated in the hands of these MSOs, most of which are themselves divisions of even larger media conglomerates.[37] Thus, cable is generally available where cable operations are deemed profitable by MSOs and their parent corporations. And profitability is determined by the relations between cost of capitalization, density of potential subscribers within the population, and the changing balance between the ability of local government of require services and federal commitments to deregulation.

When MSOs do make cable available to a community, only about 50% of the households usually subscribe to the service. Cable subscribers, then, are households with sufficient discretionary income and sufficient interest in television programming that they pay for access to expanded television service. This separates them from ordinary viewers and marks them as active consumers. With 41% acceptance nationally, this pool of cable subscribers is now sufficiently large enough to merit special attention from advertisers. Yet the pool is also somewhat selective since subscribers must live within economically attractive areas and must pay monthly fees for service. Presumably, after subscribing to cable service, these households will organize a significant slice of their leisure around watching television. In this way, cable subscribers have come to be regarded by advertisers as an increasingly, desirable part of the viewership.

But where advertisers have come to regard cable with interest, networks have not. With 40–50% acceptance, cable has attracted serious interest from advertisers and seems poised to expand the oligopoly that networks have long enjoyed in the distribution by expanding the number of available channels. Previously, advertisers had little interest in paying for ratings that included cable channels. Network demand for ratings did not include measures of rival cable channels, particularly during the period when regulation forbade network participation in cable. When neither advertisers nor networks wanted the numbers on cable, there was little in the marketplace to encourage ACN to measure cable viewers.

However, which cable's subscription rate reaching acceptable levels, advertisers' interest expanded to include cable consumers. Also, the proliferation of cable channels created a new clientele for ratings, ranging from the superstations (WTBS, WGN, WOR, KTVU) to satellite-distributed channels (ESPN, CBN, FNN, MTV, etc.), some of which were wholly or partially owned by the networks (CBS Cable Arts, A&E). Eventually, ACN was persuaded by Turner Broadcasting System's willingness to pay for extra measures to begin reporting cable as part of television's commodity audience. Thus began the official decline in network audiences.

We are now beginning to see the cumulative effect of these shifting relations between networks, broadcasters, cablecasters, and advertisers. At a time when classes are polarizing into yuppies and yuffies, when the middle class is increasingly pushed into the underclass, when wealth increasingly flows into the hands of the sparsely populated ruling class, cable subscription in the late 1980s provides the sort of barrier that telephone subscription provided in the late 1920s and early 1930s. Cable subscription can be used as a guarantee of consumer status; hence, cabled households are more in demand by advertisers even as cable channels seek to purchase more cable ratings.

With these pressures on ACN, compounded by the entrance of aggressive new competitors (AGB and Percy) pushing people meters, ACN has turned to a metering technology that deflates the numbers in a sample that emphasizes consumers, i.e., to people meters in a sample emphasizing cable. Here the task discourages long-term viewers from recording their viewing, as people are expected to press a button every fifteen minutes to record their presence, without any

Skinnerian reinforcement. Further, ACN has adjusted its sample to the new balance in the marketplace by emphasizing cable households in the installation of its new people-metered sample.

The networks have fought this redefinition of the commodity audience and gained some concessions for the short run.[38] At this point, ABC agreed to pay ACN $500,000 to gain various considerations, including the right for its ratings to be based on households reporting useable data and not on the number of households with people meters or designated for the people meter sample. ACN has agreed to make the same service available to NBC and CBS. However, AGB's recent withdrawal from the US ratings market will probably weaken the networks' bargaining position.

The current trend suggests that ACN's people meters will in the long run eschew broadcast households to embrace cable households as the commodity audience. Network programming practices will thus necessarily shift as the networks and the satellite-distributed channels begin competing for the newly redefined commodity audience. This should produce another programming shift, à la the Year of Relevance, but whether that shift will mean an increase in the number of forced choices or a greater diversity in the content of those forced choices remains to be seen.[39] However, the driving force behind such a change will again be essentially economic, not cultural.

WHO COUNTS

The implications of this analysis are startling. Unless you have a meter, you don't count. Unless you live in a cable area and subscribe, you have almost no opportunity to count. In market terms, then, the Great American Public—washed or not, intellectual or mass, textual analyst or couch potato—is irrelevant. All that counts are the meters. The decision to install the meters is a function of demand in the closed market for ratings. There, advertisers, networks, and now cable channels buy ratings from a ratings firm whose success rests on the ability to serve continuities in demand, to manipulate discontinuities through measurement practices, and to design measurement practiced as strategies for market control. This means that ratings and the commodity audience are themselves manufactured in the strictest sense of the word. And it is only the manufactured commodity audience, measured by commodity ratings, that counts.

In social scientific terms, the metered group is not a scientific sample of the viewing public since it is not randomly selected from and not representative of that public. Hence, the forced choice behavior of the metered group cannot be generalized to the viewing public. Nor can the choices of that metered group be taken as representative of public taste. In short, the massest of mass media, television, is programmed for a narrow slice of the total viewership—for the commodity audience.

Thus it is macroeconomic structure—not taste, not training, not temperament—that determines who counts in television.

NOTES

1. United States Bureau of the Census, *Statistical Abstract of the United States* (Washington: GPO, 1978), p. 534.

2. Frank Stanton, "Parallel Paths," in *Culture for the Millions?* ed. Norman Jacobs (1959; Boston: Beacon, 1964), p. 90.

3. For examples, see Anthony Smith's discussion of Dutch broadcasting in *The Shadow in the Cave: The Broadcaster, His Audience, and the State* (Urbana: University of Illinois Press, 1973), pp. 264–78; Gertrude J. Robinson, *Tito's Maverick Media* (Urbana: University of Illinois Press, 1977); and Armand Mattelart and Seth Siegelaub, *Communication Liberation, Socialism,* vol. 2 of *Liberation and Class Struggle* (New York: International General, 1983).

4. Perhaps the strongest articulation of this view is by Arthur C. Nielsen, Jr., *If Not the People . . . Who?,* an address to the Oklahoma City Advertising Club, June 20, 1966. See also Stanton, "Parallel Paths." For a slightly cynical presentation of the same argument, see Paul Klein, "The Men Who Run TV Aren't That Stupid—They Know Us Better Than You Think," *New York Magazine* 25 Jan. 1971:20.

5. Cf. A. C. Nielsen Company, *Everything you've always wanted to know about TV ratings (but were maybe too skeptical to ask)* (Northbrook, Ill.: A. C. Nielsen Company, 1985); Arbitron, *Understanding and Using Radio Audience Estimates: Inside the Arbitron Television Report* (New York: Arbitron, 1985); testimony given by representatives from A. C. Nielsen Company, C. E. Hooper Company, Arbitron, Sindlinger & Co., Trendex, Plus, and Bideodex first to the US Congress, Senate, Committee on Interstate and Foreign Commerce, *Televisión Inquiry, Part 7: The Television Ratings Services,* 85th Congress, 2nd session, June 1958 (Washington: GPO, 1959), and later to the US Congress, House, Committee on Interstate and Foreign Commerce, *Broadcast Ratings,* Hearings before the Special Subcommittee on Investigations, 88th Congress, 1st and 2nd session, 1963–1964 (Washington: GPO, 1964 and 1965). See also US Congress, House, Committee on Interstate and Foreign Commerce, *Evaluation of Statistical Methods Used in Obtaining Broadcast Ratings,* House Report 193, 87th Congress, 1st session, 1961 (Washington: GPO, 1961), generally known as the Madow Report.

6. Erik Barnouw, *The Sponsor: Notes on a Modern Potentate* (Oxford: Oxford University Press, 1978); Harry J. Skornia, *Television and Society: An Inquest and Agenda for Improvement* (New York: McGraw-Hill, 1965), p. 120.

7. Erik Barnouw, *Tube of Plenty: The Evolution of Television* (Oxford: Oxford University Press, 1975), p. 160 on dramatic anthologies; Barnouw, *The Sponsor,* pp. 101–109 on the episodic series; Laurence Bergreen, *Look Now, Pay Later: The Rise of Network Broadcasting* (Garden City: Doubleday, 1980), p. 173 on anthologies and *Omnibus;* and Danae Clark, "The State vs. Asner in the Killing of Lou Grant." *Journal of Communication Inquiry* 11.2 (Summer 1987):87.

8. Dallas Smythe, "Communications: Blindspot of Western Marxism," *Canadian Journal of Political and Social Theory* 1(1977):1; Graham Murdock, "Blindspots about Western Marxism: A Reply to Dallas Smythe," *Canadian Journal of Political and Social Theory* 2(1978):109; Bill Livant, "The Audience Commodity: On the 'Blindspot' Debate," *Canadian Journal of Political and Social Theory* 3(1978):91.

9. The definitive account remains that of N. R. Danielian, *AT&T: The Story of Industrial Conquest* (New York: Vanguard, 1939).

10. Demand is often defined in one of three different ways: as the desire, willingness, and ability of a buyer to purchase a particular good (cf. Douglas Greenwald and Associates, *McGraw Hill Dictionary of Modern Economics* [New York: McGraw Hill, 3rd edition, 1983], p. 126); as the quantity of a good or service that a buyer or group of buyers desire at the prevailing price (David W. Pearce, *The MIT Dictionary of Modern Economics* [Cambridge: MIT Press, 1986], p. 100); or as the amount of a commodity or service that will be bought at a certain price (Alan Gilpin, *Dictionary of Economic Terms* [London: Butterworths, 3rd edition, 1973], p. 49). None of these dictionary definitions capture the sense of the term that emerges

from Adam Smith, *The Wealth of Nations,* ed. Edwin Cannan (London: Methuen, 1961), where Smith clearly sees demand, supply, and market transactions as human processes—that is, as negotiated, argumentative, conspiratorial, and fractious (see vol. 1, pp. 144 and 278; vol. 2, p. 284). Recapturing Smith's notion of demand, then, allows one to thoroughly examine the demand for ratings, discovering in it a complex and sometimes contradictory expression of vested interests that both conflict and coincide. For ratings, this is particularly important since ratings form the basis for a second transaction between the buyers of ratings, national advertisers, and networks, in which the price demanded by networks rests squarely on the ratings. To capture some of the complexity in demand for ratings, I have selected the phrase "continuity in demand" to indicate those parts of demand where the interests of national advertisers and national networks coincide. By extension, to indicate where their interests diverge, I use the term "discontinuity in demand." This seems consonant with Smith, but it also draws on the spirit, if not the phrasing, of Paul A. Baran and Paul M. Sweezy, *Monopoly Capital: An Essay on the American Economic and Social Order* (1966; New York: Monthly Review Press, 1968), pp. 79–217; John Eaton, *Political Economy* (New York: International Publishers, 1979, new revised edition), p. 29; Karl Marx, *A Contribution to the Critique of Political Economy,* ed. Maurice Dobb (New York: International Publishers, 1981), pp. 27–53 and 188–99, originally published in German in 1859; Karl Marx, *Capital,* vol. 3 *The Process of Capitalist Production as a Whole,* ed. Frederick Engels (New York: International Publishers, 1967), pp. 171–98, originally published in 1894; and Howard J. Sherman, *Elementary Aggregate Economics* (New York: Appleton, 1966), pp. 28–63.

11. The Patent Pool was originally composed of American Marconi, AT&T, its wholly owned subsidiary Western Electric, GE, Westinghouse, and United Fruit. American Marconi was forced to sell out to its fellow poolers when the Navy Department refused to return American Marconi's ship-to-shore stations after the Armistice on grounds of national security. United Fruit restricted its operations and its radio applications to its plantations in Central America. In the United States, the division of industrial territories was reflected in corporate policies on equipment: while AT&T offered its equipment for rental only, GE and Westinghouse sold both transceivers and receiving sets outright. Besides Danielian's *AT&T,* this account is drawn from the following texts: William Banning, *Commercial Broadcasting Pioneer: The WEAF Experiment* (Cambridge: Harvard University Press, 1946); Erik Barnouw, *A Tower in Babel: A History of Broadcasting in the United States to 1933* (Oxford: Oxford University Press, 1966); George Blake, *The History of Radio Telegraphy and Telephony* (1928; London: Arno, 1974); John Hammond, *Men and Volts: The Story of General Electric* (Philadelphia: Lippincott, 1941); Hiram L. Jome, *Economics of the Radio Industry* (Chicago: Shaw, 1925); W. Rupert Maclaurin, *Invention and Innovation in the Radio Industry* (New York: Macmillan, 1949); Paul Schubert, *The Electric Word: The Rise of Radio* (New York: Macmillan, 1928). The aggregate analysis, however, is entirely my own.

12. For an insider's account of AT&T's radio operations, see Banning.

13. Early broadcasts were generally organized around materials that were freely available (Barnouw, *Tube of Plenty,* pp. 27–31). Pioneering broadcaster Frank Conrad, a Westinghouse employee, became well known for his "evening phonograph concerts" (ibid., p. 21), which occasionally included recitations by his sons. One Conrad concert was reported as a news story in an advertisement by the Joseph Horne Department Store for a $10 radio. Similar phonograph concerts were offered by electrical engineer Fred Christian in Hollywood, contractor Fred M. Laxton in Charlotte, North Carolina, and others. Some pioneers, such as Professor Earle M. Terry of Madison, Wisconsin, and William E. Scripps, publisher of the *Detroit News,* reported weather, news, and sports events as well as playing phonographs. Occasionally, public speakers visited these pioneers or were visited by them, resulting in transmissions of church services, sermons, uplifting talks, and political oratory.

14. United States Bureau of the Census, *The Statistical History of the United States from Colonial Times to the Present* (New York: Basic, 1976), p. 796.

15. See Danielian, *AT&T,* or an excellent account of the negotiations given by Dane Yorke, "The Radio Octopus," *American Mercury* 23(1931):385.

16. See Bergreen, *Look Now,* p. 50.

17. Some of CBS's internal studies on radio audiences included *Does Radio Sell Goods?* (1931), *Has Radio Sold Goods in 1932?* (1932), *Ears and Incomes* (1934), and *Listeners at Half Cost* (n.d.). NBC's offerings included *Little Books on Broadcasting,* series 1–12 and A–F (1927–1931), *Straight across the Board* (1932), *Improving the Smiles of a Nation: The Ipana Story* (1928), and *A New Measurement of the Size, Location, and Occupations of NBC Radio Audiences, Supplemented by Dealers' Opinions of Radio Advertising* (n.d.).

18. The discussion of Crossley and the CAB is drawn from Archibald Crossley, *Watch Your Selling Dollar* (New York: B. C. Forbes, 1930); reports from Cooperative Analysis of Broadcasting: *The Invisible Audience: First Four Month Comprehensive Report* (New York: CAB, 1930); *Station Area Studies* (New York: CAB, 1933); *Ten Years of Network Program Analysis* (New York: CAB, 1939); Mark James Banks, "A History of Broadcast Audience Research in the United States, 1920–1980, with an Emphasis on the Rating Services," diss., University of Tennessee, Knoxville, 1981; A. B. Blankenship, *Professional Telephone Surveys* (New York: McGraw, 1977); Donald Lee Hurwitz, "Broadcast Ratings: The Rise and Development of Commercial Audience Research and Measurement in American Broadcasting," diss., University of Illinois, Urbana, 1983; Eileen Rose Meehan, "Neither Heroes nor Villains: Towards a Political Economy of the Ratings Industry," diss., University of Illinois, Urbana, 1983; and numerous articles in the serial trade publications *Variety, Broadcasting,* and *Advertising and Selling* for the years 1929–1930.

19. United States Bureau of Census, *Statistical History,* p. 796, and Frederick Lewis Allen, *Only Yesterday: An Informal History of the 1920s* (1931; New York: Harper, 1964), p. 137.

20. United States Bureau of the Census, *Statistical History,* pp. 783, 784.

21. See Crossley, etc., cited above.

22. Allen, p. 73; Boorstein, *The Americans: The Democratic Experience* (New York: Vintage, 1974), p. 525.

23. The discussion of Hooper and CEH is drawn from Matthew N. Chapell and C. E. Hooper, *Radio Audience Measurement* (New York: Stephen Daye, 1944); *Hooperatings Hi-lites* (CEH's newsletter); CEH's testimony to the Senate Committee and House Subcommittee investigating ratings; Banks, *History of Broadcast Audience Research;* Hurwitz, *Broadcast "Ratings";* Meehan, "Neither Heroes nor Villains"; numerous articles in the serial trade publications *Variety, Broadcasting,* and *Advertising and Selling* for the years 1930–1946; and "Behind the Ratings System, Part V: Hooper Riding the Big Radio Room," *Sponsor* 18 Oct. 1945:42.

24. United States Bureau of the Census, *Statistical History,* pp. 783, 784.

25. See Boorstein, *The Americans,* p. 89; Malcolm P. McNair, "Trends in Large-Scale Retailing," *Harvard Business Review* 10 (1931):6; and Irwin M. Heine, "The Influence of Geographic Factors in the Development of the Mail Order Business," *American Marketing Journal* 3 (Apr. 1936):127–30.

26. See *Hooperatings Hi-lites;* Chapell and Hooper, *Radio Audience;* CEH's testimony before the Senate and House; and the Madow Report for details of the methodology.

27. Chapell and Hooper, *Radio Audience;* for an analysis and concise summary of their case, see Blankenship, pp. 11–14.

28. The discussion of Nielsen and ACN is drawn from A. C. Nielsen, Sr.'s, published writings: *Advances in Scientific Marketing Research* (Chicago: ACN, 1944), *New Facts about Radio Research* (Chicago: ACN, 1946), *A Researcher Replies* (Northbrook, Ill.: ACN, 1963), and *Greater Prosperity through Market Research: The First Forty Years of the A. C. Nielsen Company* (Northbrook, Ill.: ACN, 1963), originally given as an address to the Newcomen Society, Chicago, Apr. 30, 1964; testimony by ACN representatives before the House and Senate; the Madow Report; Banks, *History of Broadcast Audience Research;* Hurwitz, *Broadcast "Ratings";* Meehan, "Neither Heroes nor Villains"; numerous articles in the serial trade publications *Variety, Broadcasting,* and *Advertising and Selling* from Jan. 1930–Aug. 1988.

29. See particularly testimony of Albert Sindlinger to the House Subcommittee and memoranda introduced into the record by Subcommittee counsel in the questioning of ACN's representatives, pp. 1592, 1596, 1587–603.

30. See Barnouw, *Tube,* pp. 190–95 on NBC's innovation of selling spots, and *Sponsor,* pp. 45–48 on the early move to network control; see Bergreen, *Look Now,* pp. 159–240 on network schedules.

31. See Klein, "The Men Who Run TV," p. 20, and Bergreen, p. 208; for an analysis of the cultural meaning of "flow," see Raymond Williams, *Television: Technology and Cultural Form* (1974; New York: Schocken, 1975).

32. See the questioning of ACN representatives by House Subcommittee 954–1618.

33. See ACN testimony, pp. 954–1019, House Subcommittee, pp. 1068–1618.

34. Barnouw, *Tube of Plenty,* p. 430; Morris Gelman, "A New Search of Relevance Next Season," *Variety* 17 Nov. 1969:52, 56; George Swisshehn, "CBS Inking of 3 New (Old) Stars Seen as Tipoff That Rube Image May Be Shucked in Next 2 Years," *Variety* 1 Oct. 1969:35.

35. The term "forced choice preferences" is widely used in research in psychology and marketing. It describes a situation in which respondents are required to select a single option (or good) from a limited numbers of options (or goods). The resulting selection is a choice, taken as reflecting a preference, but it is not a truly free choice since the range of possibilities is determined by the experimenter's interests. Skornia, *Television and Society,* p. 120, and Klein, "The Men Who Run TV," p. 20, extend the notion of "forced choice preference" to television viewing in the discussion of ratings and programming (120). The viewer picks one program from the roster that the networks have selected to offer. Instead of reflecting the desires and tastes of viewers, such forced choice selections are taken to reflect the least offensive program (Klein's LOP principle) or the program that resonates with the lowest common denominator of social experience. Most critical researchers would add to this an analysis of how the networks' economic agenda in selecting programming then feeds back to shape personal and cultural preferences in programming. For examples of such analysis see Philip Elliott, *The Making of a Television Series: A Case Study in the Sociology of Culture* (London: Constable, 1972, and Beverly Hills: Sage, 1979), or Herbert Schiller, *The Mind Managers* (Boston: Beacon, 1973), pp. 8–31 and 79–103.

36. United States Bureau of the Census, *Statistical Abstract,* p. 714.

37. The issues of corporate control, technologies of distribution, and diversity of programming/information have been taken up by critical researchers in a number of forums. For an analysis suggesting that economic concentration and new technologies will lead to more highly targeted and fractionalized commodity audiences, see Oscar H. Gandy, Jr., *Beyond Agenda Setting: Information Subsidies and Public Policy* (Norwood, N.J.: Ablex, 1980). For an analysis suggesting that the outcome will be a redesign of television as "more of the same" programming delivered to slightly fewer viewers, see Eileen R. Meehan, "Technical Capability vs. Corporate Imperatives: Toward a Political Economy of Cable Television and Information Diversity," in *The Political Economy of Information,* ed. Vincent Mosco and Janet Wasko (Madison: University of Wisconsin Press, 1988), and "Towards a Third Vision of the Information Society," *Media, Culture, and Society* 6 (1984):257.

38. At this point, directly prior to the 1988 fall season, ACN continues to install people meters with a projected sample of 4,000. The networks have received guarantees that houses will be turned over every two years rather than the three-to-five-year period originally envisioned by ACN, and that more households with children will be included in the people meter sample. ABC will receive rebates if the number of households in tabulation does not reflect the national population in terms of county size, men 18–49, women 18–49, and children 2–11. It is noteworthy that AGB has ceased operations in the US, claiming insufficient support from the networks, as the trade press indicates that the networks' ability to secure concessions from ACN rested on the threat of supporting AGB. For the trade discussions of the networks' attempts to

secure concessions from ACN over the people meter sample, see Morrie Gelman, "Gloom Looms for TV Webs As Woes Grow," *Variety* 8 July 1987:55, 71; Morrie Gelman, "NBC First Up at Bat with Peoplemeter: No Other Choice Available Now," *Variety* 29 July 1987:95, 118; Tom Bierbaum, "CBS" Poltrack Sez Meter Cooperation Key for Success," *Variety* 12 Aug. 1987:56, 84; Elizabeth Jensen, "Guarantees Yield Nielsen ABC-TV Pact—Will Have to Pony Up Extra $500,000," *Variety* 23 Sept. 1987:123, 154.

39. Compare Gandy and Meehan on programming. The possibility that cable channels will be programmed according to formats brings up serious issues of diversity and choice. The main question is clear: Will such formatting result in narrowcasting to consumers who fall in highly specified demographic groups, or will it result in slightly different content distributed to slightly fewer people? Where Gandy argues for the former, noting the ideological significance of such narrowcasting, Meehan suggests that media conglomeration, MSO control of cable systems, advertiser demand for generalized consumers, and the costs of narrowcasting militate against that practice. Perhaps some illumination on this question might be shed by the case of radio formats.

QUESTIONS FOR DISCUSSION

1. What social groups are most likely to be left out in television ratings' definition of the "commodity audience?" Is this exclusion reflected in programming?

2. What other means might be used to gauge the public's interests and wants in broadcasting programming if the ratings system is skewed toward economic interests?

3. Recent years have seen a dramatic decline in the network audience and a rise in cable audiences. How might this be at least partly a response to measurement methods?

4. What aspects of the modern ratings system does Meehan leave out of this article? (hint: what about local TV and radio?)

 INFOTRAC COLLEGE EDITION

Search InfoTrac College Edition for more articles on the ratings system; check under both "Nielsen ratings" and "Arbitron."

PART II

Transition to Television

5

NBC and the Innovation of Television News, 1945–1953

KRISTINE BRUNOVSKA KARNICK

Kristine Brunovska Karnick's article takes a form we know well—network television's nightly newscast—and deconstructs it by showing its historical roots. Behind the taken-for-granted combination of news anchors, live reporters on location, slick graphics, and video footage, interspersed with commercials, lies a history of uncertainty, experimentation, and awkward errors that show us how news *might* have been. Using NBC for her case study, Karnick shows how radio's commentators became TV's news personalities; how early television's blurred lines between content and advertising influenced news coverage; how filmed newsreels played a central role before videotape, yet posed problems for this "live" medium; and how networks began to expand coverage worldwide. She also explains the importance of internetwork rivalry, particularly between NBC and CBS, in TV news development, and how important, in return, network news coverage became in the competition for affiliates in the 1950s.

This article originally appeared in *Journalism History* 15 (Spring 1988): 26–34. Reprinted by permission.

As network executives debated the possibilities of television news in the early 1940s, questions and problems that had been absent from the radio news business quickly arose. One area of concern and debate was how to gather news for the new medium. How much of the news, planners asked, should resemble the action of newsreels and how much of it should present news for which no filmed material existed? Furthermore, if the news presented filmed material, would that material be gathered by the network or bought from existing newsreel companies? These concerns led directly to questions of format for television news. Would television news resemble radio, newsreels, newspapers, magazines, a combination of these, or none of them? Finally, networks needed to establish a clear policy for news presentation. How much would be "soft news" for which film was available, and how much would be "hard news," given the likelihood that it would be much more difficult to obtain film for "hard news" stories?

During the 1940s and early 1950s, television news developed in several different directions while producers and network executives looked for a structure that would prove suitable for the new medium. This early period was characterized by a complex set of accidents, experiments and necessities, as well as conscious choice about the direction in which television news should be headed. And current-day television news is the unmistakable legacy of this formative period.

The development of television news is often seen as a series of deliberate and conscious steps leading to the present. Influential books on the structure of today's news by such authors as Herbert Gans and Edward Epstein focus on its coherence as a unified set of economic and political imperatives that achieve the stable balance evident in today's news broadcasts.[1] But what is needed, in addition to such analyses of current-day network news practices, is an analysis of their formation. The formats of network news today are historically determined, and owe a great deal to the flexibility and experimentation of its first decade. This article attempts to add a historical perspective to the analysis of television network news by examining the National Broadcasting Company, the television network that, more than any other, innovated television news in the period of its infancy.

The most important period in the early development of NBC Television News is the period between 1945, the year in which NBC formed an organization for its news film, and 1953, when the network's attentions began turning from the expansion of its news operations to possible ways of cutting back on costs without giving up its dominance of television news to the Columbia Broadcasting Service's rapidly expanding news division. The innovation that NBC undertook during this period led to major problems in the mid-1950s. Since NBC was the first network to establish an organization for news-gathering, it experienced a good number of accidents and failed experiments. When CBS established its news film organization in the early 1950s, it was able to benefit from the lessons NBC had learned, while avoiding many of its mistakes.

Discussions of early television news too often begin and end with the contributions of Edward R. Murrow. NBC, however, was struggling to establish a quality television news network while CBS was still obtaining its news film from Telenews, and while Murrow was still presenting the news on radio. By examining the ways in which NBC personnel attempted to deal with questions of format, presentation policy and news-gathering, it is possible to better understand the rationale for the characteristics of television news today.

THE SEARCH FOR A FORMAT

NBC experimented with several different formats for the presentation of television news. One approach had its roots in the broadcasting of news on radio, and another was rooted in the theatrical newsreel. In this early period, programmers experimented with both of these formats, as well as with combinations taken from newspaper and magazine formats.

NBC began presenting regularly scheduled television news broadcasts on an experimental basis in 1940, with the introduction of "The Esso Television Reporter." The program was presented through a cooperative arrangement between NBC and Standard Oil, and offered still pictures that illustrated the words of the announcer as he spoke. Printed titles appeared between news items, accompanied by appropriate organ music.[2]

During World War II the Federal Communications Commission halted all such network experimentation. However, after the war, NBC embarked upon a course toward establishing a quality television news division. In May 1945, NBC set up an organization for the production of news film. The first program to emerge from this organization premiered on August 5, 1945, as the weekly "NBC Tele-Newsreel." During this early period of its newsreel development, NBC was forced to rely on material obtained from theatrical newsreel companies. The network's hope, however, was to become a self-sustaining news film producing entity, without having to rely on newsreels from these companies.[3]

While trying to build up its newsreel capabilities, NBC also experimented with television news formats other than the newsreel. "NBC Newsroom" premiered in January 1948, and was heavily influenced by NBC's radio network. The program, which featured three radio newsmen reading the news, was broadcast from the NBC radio newsroom. It was supposed to reflect the action taking place there in much the same way as televised news updates now are presented.[4]

However, even NBC admitted that the newsroom itself was very dull-looking and not what the public thought a newsroom should look like. NBC executive Anne Bachner wrote, "It just looks like an ordinary office which frankly is just what it is."[5] The program had an additional problem: If an important story was breaking during the television broadcast, the show would lose its commentators, who would leave to broadcast the news on NBC's much larger radio network.[6]

Criticisms of this format soon emerged. Paul White, a KFWB-AM-TV news executive, wrote in *Broadcasting*, "Let's face it—watching a man read the news or recite the news isn't much of a plus to understanding that news."[7]

Since NBC was attempting to establish its own newsreel organization at this time, the network's goals in this respect soon came into direct conflict with those of theatrical newsreel organizations. By the beginning of 1947, newsreel companies were setting up separate organizations to service television broadcasters with newsreel film, and therefore did not want competition from the networks. The major problem from the newsreel companies' perspective was the fact that their twice-weekly theatrical newsreels would face a dwindling market if the same information were carried daily on television.[8]

The newsreel companies' push into television news hit NBC News particularly hard in 1947, when sponsor R. J. Reynolds combined with 20th-Century Fox to produce a 10-minute daily newsreel on NBC titled "Camel Newsreel Theater." NBC had wanted to produce such a program itself, but did not yet have the capabilities to do so. NBC did not have long to wait; "Camel Newsreel Theater" aired for only one year. The sponsor complained of low ratings and technical inadequacies. NBC contributed to the problem by leaving the schedule empty before the telecasts, so that viewers watching their television sets before the program—which aired at 7:45 P.M. in the East—would be watching one of the other stations.[9]

Once this problem was recognized by the sponsor, NBC began scheduling programs earlier in the evening, and ratings increased markedly. However, R.J. Reynolds' advertising agency, the William Esty Company, also expressed dissatisfaction with the visual quality of Fox's program, for which Reynolds was paying $10,000 per week.[10] The filmed newsreels were much more sensitive to shadings of grey than were television receivers. As a result, newsreels with a variety of very light and very dark areas showed badly.[11]

When the NBC Television News Department heard of R.J. Reynolds' dissatisfaction with Fox, it immediately began pushing the sale of its own news program, developed by NBC and utilizing NBC film. This resulted in Reynolds cancelling its contract with Fox in favor of NBC's improved substitute, "Camel News Caravan."[12]

"Camel News Caravan" was scheduled to premier February 16, 1949. A press release announcing the program proclaimed:

> The complete news-gathering facilities of our network with more than 200 persons will be made available to this new television news show. We will be on the spot with our mobile units, cameras, and reporters whenever possible, to maintain the network's high standards of complete and accurate reporting.[13]

The "Camel News Caravan" acquired the services of radio commentator John Cameron Swayze, whom NBC already had under contract. When the program premiered, it was picked up by only 16 stations, primarily on the East Coast.[14] However, within eight months new stations were added, and by May of 1951 the program was being carried by 40 stations.[15]

Regardless of the tremendous growth of the network during this time, difficulties between NBC and Esty continued in much the same fashion as they had between Esty and Fox. NBC was extremely happy with the program. However, the Esty agency still complained of poor production quality and poor program content. In one letter to NBC, Kendall Foster, Esty vice president in charge of television, charged that "Camel News Caravan" was being used as a "training ground for technicians including lighting, camera, and boom men."[16] He also stated that some of the more experienced personnel in the studio referred to the program as "Siberia, where all new slaves are sent for indoctrination."[17] This did indeed appear to be the case, as technical personnel were rarely scheduled to work on the show two days in a row.[18]

"Camel News Caravan's" ratings indicated that the public liked the program. Reviews in the press, however, were not very favorable. Although initial reviews were positive,[19] critics such as Jack Gould of *Variety* and John Crosby of the *New York Herald Tribune* soon began to attack the show's emphasis on the pictorial, its heavy use of features, and its tendency to present "only the cream of the top news."[20] "Caravan" producer Frank McCall reacted to that charge by stating, "the basic tool of television news is film. We need more, and more, and more film coverage if NBC is to continue to be the outstanding television news network."[21] Another criticism, related to the first, was that NBC's news programs reflected the interests of their sponsors and were shaped by their concerns.[22]

NBC maintained that its goal was "to program news first, and *then* work to sell it."[23] The network's relationships with its various sponsors, however, only exacerbated this situation and lent evidence to its critics. NBC's contract with R.J. Reynolds, for example, stipulated that "Camel News Caravan" could be the only news program aired from 6:00 P.M. to 11:00 P.M. This was particularly frustrating during the Korean War, when, for a time, special bulletins could not be inserted in the nighttime schedule.[24]

"The Esso Television Reporter," "NBC Tele-Newsreel," "NBC Newsroom" and "Camel News Caravan" all were attempts at finding a suitable format for the presentation of news on television. When "Camel News Caravan" premiered in 1949, it was able to incorporate elements from each of these earlier efforts. Like "NBC Newsroom," it featured a visual reading of the news. However, it also relied heavily on newsreel footage, and usually emphasized the news for which there was such footage. With the introduction of "Camel News Caravan," NBC seemed to have found the ideal format for the presentation of news.

THE EXPANSION OF NEWS GATHERING

The format for the presentation of the news on the air was not the only area in which NBC experimented, or about which network executives disagreed. Conflicts existed over the direction in which the News and Public Affairs Division at NBC was moving. In terms of production, television news began its life as a stepchild of radio. More importantly, however, radio established television's access to news-gathering sources. Camera correspondents, commonly know as stringers, often were borrowed from radio, and early television reporting often was done by radio reporters. However, television also learned and incorporated elements from theatrical newsreels. When asked in 1950 what then-current practices newsmen found to be the best for television news presentation, they listed the following, in order of popularity: (1) remote on-the-spot coverage; (2) newsreel film; (3) still pictures; (4) headline shows (video: headline; audio: announcer); (5) TV newspapers (video: page; audio: music or announcer).[25]

The top three choices indicate a clear preference for the pictorial. They also represent the most expensive forms of news presentation.[26] NBC prided itself in these early years on the amount of newsreel footage it was able to shoot, and also on the high percentage of newsfilm that it showed on the air the same day it was shot.[27] However, since filmed material had to be either flown or mailed to the network, this goal was difficult to achieve.

By establishing newsfilm production in the late 1940s, NBC created a great financial burden for itself. It relied heavily on the financial assistance of its radio network, and also on the willingness of sponsors to foot the bill for this expansion.[28] In explaining the economic situation of the networks through the 1940s, WHAS-TV News Director Richard Oberlin, writing in *Broadcasting,* observed:

> There was so much money floating around in the early days of television and advertisers were so eager to buy time, any old time and any old program at all, that it must have been difficult to think in terms of profit and of balancing the budget.[29]

This situation, however, did not last for very long. In noting a shift in industry practice, Oberlin further observed:

> There seemed to be no limit to the money rolling in. If you needed a new camera, you bought it. If you needed another man, you hired him. If you wanted a new car, you ordered it. Eventually the day of reckoning had to come. It is [in 1953] with us now.[30]

In the case of NBC Television News, the great expansion that was undertaken was accomplished through the profits earned by NBC's radio news programs and "Camel News Caravan." In 1951, for example, these two sources alone supplied NBC with a profit of well over $200,000.[31]

The expansion that the network undertook during this time took many different forms. During the late 1940s and early-1950s, NBC Television News established seven main bureaus in New York, Chicago, Washington, Cleveland, Los Angeles, Dallas and San Francisco. It also recruited staff and stringers in 24 cities outside the United States.[32] To supplement this within the country, the network drew up exchange agreements with affiliate stations, and occasionally with independent stations, for news film. In the late 1940s, the NBC Television News Department hired an additional 24 photographers and editors to supplement its existing staff. For newsreel coverage alone, by mid-February of 1949 NBC had a crew of 56 with 38 cameras, 18 mobile units, and 16 reporters and correspondents.[33]

Even more impressive were NBC's efforts at establishing exclusive exchange agreements with newsreel companies in other countries. It worked out deals with such overseas entities as the British Broadcasting Corporation, Pathe, Radio Diffusione Italiano (RAI), and even the Soviet government. One thing which these agreements all had in common was that the newsreel material provided to NBC by these various entities would be provided to NBC exclusively.[34]

These deals were not immediately profitable to NBC. This is most clearly illustrated by the network's agreement with the Italian newsreel company, RAI, in which RAI paid NBC $.10 per foot for film, while NBC paid $1.00 per foot for RAI's film. However, NBC's interests here resided in more than just day-to-day acquisition and sale of newsreel film. By striking such deals, NBC gained an advantage over the other networks and newsreel companies, for it prohibited them from receiving the product of the overseas companies. NBC struck these deals in the late 1940s and early 1950s in order to gain an early advantage over the other networks before they could form newsreel organizations.[35]

In terms of newsreel production, then, NBC held a distinct advantage over its competitors. The results of this can be found in the fact that until 1952 Telenews tried, repeatedly, to convince NBC to abandon its own news film operations and utilize Telenews' newsreel service (as CBS was doing). In 1953, however, Telenews reversed its course and made an elaborate proposal to NBC, requesting the network produce film for it.[36]

Thus NBC's stress on improving the quality of its newsreel operations was meant as a financial investment in its future. However, while profit considerations appeared to be a prime mover for the direction in which NBC's Television News Department headed, its viewers appear to have benefited from the arrangement. NBC's focus, for example, on strengthening agreements with overseas film companies held advantages for NBC's viewers, who were able for the first time to see news developments brought by these overseas organizations.

Another area in which NBC's early Television News Department excelled was in the use of camera correspondents or stringers. While NBC Television's stringers were initially borrowed from its Radio News Division, the Television News Department soon began cultivating and establishing stringers of its own. By 1952, NBC had recruited stringers in 36 countries, including areas as familiar as Germany and as remote as Malaya and Indo-China.[37]

Although these sources were supplying NBC with a great deal of filmed coverage by the early 1950s, the network was not satisfied with the degree of coverage it obtained. This is evident in the observation by Frank McCall, director of television news and special events, that "we need more, and more, and more film coverage."[38] However, increases in filmed coverage necessarily entailed higher costs. Therefore, NBC began to seek out additional avenues of distribution. This led to its formation of its own newsreel syndication service, Daily News Syndication (DNS), in 1951. In introducing the service to a potential customer, McCall wrote:

> As you may have heard, NBC's Television News and Special Events is offering for the first time in television news history a completely scored daily news service. . . . All you have to do is put the reel in the projector and roll it.[39]

The service sounded promising, both to NBC and to independent and affiliate stations. Stations could benefit from the fact that the reel eliminated rehearsal and production problems at individual stations. NBC could benefit because, since the film had already been shot and NBC already owned it, DNS provided considerably more markets for the film than had previously existed. However, less than two months after beginning the service, NBC began receiving complaints from individual stations regarding the quality of the newsreel and soon more stations were cancelling the service than were picking it up. Even though DNS cost stations far less than similar services provided by Telenews or United Press, by April 1953 only 13 stations were carrying DNS.[40]

Individual stations expressed concern that they were often sent previously broadcast material and that shipments, which were sent through the mail, often arrived one or two days behind schedule. Stations also complained that they were not receiving enough footage to make up a five-minute newsreel, and that there was a lack of diversity and volume in story material when compared to wire service newsreels.[41] One customer, in cancelling the service, noted, "The NBC Daily and the NBC Weekly are the very poorest news shows on film released to date."[42]

Even though NBC continued to look upon DNS as a side operation, it was losing a considerable amount of money. In March 1953, for example, DNS income from the 13 participating stations was $8,000, while expenses reached $12,000.[43] By the end of the year, NBC executive Davidson Taylor had come to the realization that "if we went out of news film syndication it would save the network about $90,000 a year at the present rate of gain."[44] However, NBC continued to provide the service. Its head of public affairs film, Gene Juster, argued:

> If we discontinue the DNS, we are abandoning a field in which we pioneered—allowing CBS and others a free ride on our experience and ground work. This would make it extremely difficult for us to reenter the field even when [video] tape is a reality.[45]

Yet continuing the service proved to be a risky gamble for the network. Until this time, NBC Television News' importance within the hierarchy was evident in the emphasis that NBC placed on the development of a quality news-gathering organization.[46] The years 1952 and 1953, however, held many changes for the NBC Television News Department. The financial picture was altered due to the failure of DNS. It was further complicated when NBC Television's most profitable news show, "Camel News Caravan," began running into financial difficulties.[47] Suddenly, the television network had to find a way of consolidating costs and minimizing expenses.

THE END OF EXPANSION

Until the early 1950s, NBC had held a unique position among network news departments: It was the only network that maintained a complete news film service. CBS established its own news film service and library only in 1953. Until that time it received its newsreel material exclusively from Telenews.[48] However, NBC had not let its initial success limit the quality and scope of its television news operations. Instead, it approached the situation from the perspective that, in the words of network executive Joseph Heffernan, "so far, our competitors have been sitting around sucking their thumbs. Right now we are way ahead and the problem is to get even further ahead."[49]

However, these emerging financial difficulties caused NBC executives to reevaluate the situation. While the first years of "Camel News Caravan" had been successful ones, both for NBC and R. J. Reynolds, spiralling production costs began to take their toll on the Television News Department by 1952. The "Caravan's" primary problem was a sharp increase in production costs, which had more than doubled in three years. Although its ratings remained strong and net sales increased steadily, net profits declined due to these costs. This led sponsor R. J. Reynolds to cut back on costs, and in 1953 it slashed "Caravan's" total budget by $300,000. Such financial considerations led NBC executives to reconsider the amount of money they were investing in the News Department. In 1953, the enormous expansion that NBC News had undergone during the previous decade came to a quick halt.[50]

There was talk of consolidation between NBC's radio and television departments. This consolidation was not meant to aid in the expansion of the Television News Department, but rather to stifle its growth. Frank McCall confirmed the gravity of the consolidation in a letter to News and Special Affairs Director William McAndrew; "Originally the 'Camel News Caravan' had considerable [sic] more personnel than has [sic] been employed in the last year."[51] Talk of consolidation focused on the savings which could result if the radio and television news staffs were combined. Savings amounting to over $200,000 were estimated if writers, editors, clerical personnel, announcers, administrative personnel and supervisory personnel were common to television and radio news.[52]

Further cutbacks were made through the establishment of a Central News Desk, which centralized film procurement.[53] From here on every order for film to be shot by one of NBC's cameramen had to be cleared with New York's television news editor in charge of the Central News Desk.[54] The function of this office was to eliminate virtually all speculative shooting by staffers or stringers. Stories were to be covered only when a specific user was in mind. This system did indeed save the network money; what was lost in the shift, however, was the spontaneity in the work of the stringers. Stringers necessarily became more cautious, and would more often than not choose not to go out of their way to cover a story if the outcome was not certain to be newsworthy.[55]

Still additional economies instituted during this time of consolidation included the move from 35mm to 16mm film for all stories; cuts in overtime; reduction of length of leader; dropping cameramen, writers, and editors; and restricting cameramen to the arbitrary maximum of 200 feet of film for all routine stories.[56]

Such restrictions brought NBC Television News closer to the structure of television news today. Rather than concentrating on obtaining news material from as many varied sources as possible, the network's Television News Department began to concentrate much more heavily on pre-planned events. News department personnel, for example, requested that a permanent camera unit be set up at the White House and Congress, and in a letter to Washington correspondent Frank Russell, Public Affairs Director Davidson Taylor explored ways of increasing the visibility of television at House press conferences. For example, he requested that the President's weekly press conference be instead called a *news* conference and television and radio be permitted to be present.[57] He also explored the possibility of scheduling a weekly presidential press conference at a time convenient to the network.[58]

Whereas Herbert Gans, in his analysis of network news, states that 71 percent of today's network news stories focus on known figures ("knowns"), the most important of these being incumbent presidents,[59] this is not a new occurrence; the economic and perhaps even social rationale for this development can be traced back to the early 1950s and the economics of a constricting marketplace. The need to be able to predict where news was going to take place drove network news departments to focus on planned events such as press conferences, and it also compelled these news departments to concentrate on people who could be counted on to "make" news. "Knowns" such as the President provided the networks with such assurances.

By early 1953, economic conditions had reached a crisis point, and NBC considered abandoning its news film operation altogether. The network investigated the question of "whether Telenews could do our news film job for us better or for less money than we are now doing it."[60] The answer appeared to be, no. Davidson Taylor, in examining the situation, stated:

> The NBC news film organization is, in my opinion, the finest news film concern in the United States, and probably in the world. This view is shared by the AP. It would be a shame to destroy it and to abandon the field to our present competitors (Telenews and 20th Century Fox-UP) as well as our coming competitor, CBS.[61]

By May 1953, ideas that NBC had developed entered a period of diffusion, as CBS, NBC's most serious competition, began to adopt the practices that NBC had developed. At the same time that NBC entered a severe slump, CBS emerged with its own newsfilm organization.[62] As Gene Juster had predicted, CBS was able to build on the experience and background that NBC had furnished.

CBS established a National Assignment Desk, which was strikingly similar to NBC's Central News Desk. CBS began to compete with NBC in other areas as well. Within a month after establishing its newsfilm operation, and with fresh capital, CBS began luring affiliates away from NBC by undercutting NBC's prices and offering more control over acceptance of network programming.[63] In May 1953, *Broadcasting* reported that WTAR-AM-FM-TV in Norfolk, Virginia, "broke off a 19-year association with NBC by signing with CBS."[64] Several other stations followed WTAR's lead before NBC Chairman David Sarnoff was able to put a halt to the exodus.[65]

In 1954, CBS's news ratings for the first time surpassed those of NBC. Soon, time sales for CBS surpassed those of NBC as well. For the first two months of 1954, the total time sales for CBS Television were $20,678,810 while NBC's were $19,620,246.[66]

NBC executives soon began rethinking long-term plans for television news. This resulted in another transformation of NBC Television News in September 1953.[67] Under the new arrangement, the Television News Department became part of the much larger Public Affairs Organization. The organization was divided into four branches under the leadership of Public Affairs Director Davidson Taylor. The four branches would be Sports, Today, News and Special Affairs, and the newly created Television Documentaries.[68]

By the end of 1953, the News and Special Affairs Division had become a section within the larger Public Affairs Organization, a self-contained, highly structured organization. This structure was the result of a great deal of experimentation, especially in the earliest days of NBC Television News. In addition, economic imperatives and even mistakes played a crucial role in the development of the structure of the News and Special Affairs Division in 1954. The network's insistence on maintaining the unprofitable DNS service, for example, contributed to R. J. Reynolds' decision to cut back on its budget for "Camel News Caravan."

Finally, NBC's innovative role in television network newsfilm operations necessarily entailed a great many risks, and probably many more risks than advantages. While NBC was recovering from the losses it had incurred because of its experimentation, CBS was able to move in with fresh capital and, having learned from NBC's mistakes, benefit from the situation that NBC had created.

The network rivalry arising at this time came to replace the expansion of the previous decade. NBC, for the next several years, adopted a more moderate and mundane course for its news department. The emphasis now rested on trying to stay just ahead of the competition. In 1951, the network's goals had been expressed in its stated desire to obtain the greatest amount of newsreel coverage from as many different and varied sources as possible. Now its primary focus was the relative position of CBS, and to a much smaller extent, the American Broadcasting Company.[69] The network considered, for example, luring Edward R. Murrow away from CBS. Davidson Taylor expressed his opposition to this idea:

> The get-a-Murrow idea is not a valid one. We can't get him. If we could, I wouldn't want him. He has a Messianic streak, and I distrust Messiahs, even though he is a godfather of my daughter. Let's forget forever this get-a-Murrow thing.[70]

It took NBC until 1957 to get its own "Murrow," and to turn around the failing News and Special Affairs Division. During this time NBC again attempted to innovate in order to increase this sales. In 1953, for example, NBC Chairman Sarnoff exhibited videotape, and promised that it would be widely used within a few years.[71] Through the Radio Corporation of America, NBC also concentrated on the development of a compatible color system.[72]

Most critical analyses of television news during these years, however, focused on the presentation of news on the air, rather than on the gathering of news or on new developments in television technology.[73] This concern with news presentation over news gathering is exemplified by the following quote from *Variety:* "NBC"s shortcomings in its news-public affairs division. . . . [are due primarily to] its continued lack of a standout personality with the stature of an Ed Murrow or an Eric Severaid."[74]

In discussing a promotional plan for the "News Caravan," NBC's Kenneth Bilby argued:

> It is unlikely that *any* amount of promotion will appreciably affect that audience of a show which is now in its eighth year and which has exposure five times weekly—*unless* there are radical changes in the format and the talent on the show.[75]

In 1956 NBC began to make those changes. Late that year it hired Chet Huntley and David Brinkley, who soon became TV news' "first superstars"[76] when they replaced John Cameron Swayze on the evening news. By the end of 1956 NBC was beginning to rebound in the ratings. And while it had trailed CBS in gross time sales since 1953, the trend began to reverse by early 1957, when, for example, it found reliable and consistent sponsorship for the "Huntley-Brinkley Report."[77]

The NBC Television News of the 1940s and early 1950s was, in many ways, responsible for the form and structure of the news today. The emphasis, for example, on pictorial coverage of Washington politicians walking in and out of doorways, ostensibly going to or from conferences, stems from initial criticisms that the network encountered about its lack of up-to-date pictorial coverage of events. Similarly, the focus on disasters and tragedies for which there is news film, to the exclusion of similar occurrences not captured on film, also stems from these concerns.

Finally, today's emphasis on the charismatic news anchor can be traced to the problems NBC faced in the early 1950s. While it concentrated on expanding its newsgathering capabilities, critical discussions about television news often focused on personalities such as CBS's Murrow and Edwards, NBC's Swayze and Huntley-Brinkley, and ABC's John Daly. By the end of 1956, NBC began to respond to this emphasis on personalities. It cut back on its newsgathering organization and focused much more energy on developing its on-camera personnel.

Throughout the late 1940s and early 1950s, NBC developed procedures, structures and operational methods that were picked up and exploited by other networks in the diffusion process. By the mid-1950s the structures of television news organizations had entered a period of stability, and the practices that the other networks eventually adopted were based, to a large extent, on the ideas, experiments, mistakes and accidents that NBC had encountered during the previous decade.

NOTES

1. See for example Herbert Guns, *Deciding What's News: A Study of CBS Evening News, NBC Nightly News, Newsweek, and Time* (New York: Pantheon Books, 1979), and Edward J. Epstein, *News from Nowhere: Television and the News* (New York: Random House, 1974).

2. "Television Notes," *Broadcasting,* March 15, 1940, p. 69.

3. Interdepartmental Memorandum from John Williams, April 15, 1944, box 104, file 30, National Broadcasting Company Collection, State Historical Society of Wisconsin, Madison,

Wisconsin (Hereafter, "NBC"); "NBC's Hurry Up Job." *Variety*, May 29, 1946. p. 35; NBC Press Release, 1947, box 285, file 12, NBC; Edward J. Forrest, "A Historical and Interpretive Analysis of the Origins of Network News and Camel News Caravan" (Master's thesis, University of Wisconsin 1975), pp. 20–39.

4. Doan [sic], "NBC Television Newsroom," *Variety*, review, February 4, 1946, p. 28, Interdepartmental Memorandum from Anne Bachner, February 20, 1948, box 300, file 55, NBC; Interdepartmental Memorandum from N. Jordan, May 18, 1948, box 300, file 55, NBC.

5. Interdepartmental Memorandum from Anne Bachner, 20 May 1948, box 300, file 55, NBC.

6. Ibid.

7. Paul While, "Spot News is Better on Radio" *Broadcasting*, February 9, 1953, p. 35.

8. Bob Stahl, "Newsreels Seek Video Sales," *Variety*, March 12, 1947, p. 43.

9. Interdepartmental Memorandum from Harry Floyd, June 2, 1948, box 404, file 5, NBC; Program Schedule for the week of June 7, 1948, box 404, file 5, NBC; Interdepartmental Memorandum from Adolph Schneider, October 31, 1949, box 214, file 40, NBC.

10. Interdepartmental Memorandum from W. F. Brooks, May 28, 1951, box 130, file 21, NBC.

11. Ibid.

12. NBC Press Release, February 13, 1948, box 404, file 4, NBC; NBC Press Release, January 31, 1949, box 404, file 4, NBC; Letter from Robert Reld to William Brooks, October 25, 1948, box 284, file 19, NBC; Letter from Joseph McCall and William Brooks to Mr. Folsom, May 28, 1951, box 130, file 21, NBC.

13. NBC Press Release, January 31, 1949, box 404, file 4, NBC.

14. Interdepartmental Memorandum from Harry T. Floyd, June 14, 1949, box 310, file 50, NBC.

15. "Stations Carrying *Camel News Caravan*," May 3, 1951, box 310, file 50, NBC.

16. Letter from Kendall Foster, May 3, 1951, box 130, file 21, NBC.

17. Ibid.

18. "Directors Schedule," January 1, 1950, box 310, file 9, NBC.

19. "Camel News Caravan," *Variety*, review, February 23, 1948, pp.28.

20. John Crosby, "Radio in Review," *New York Herald Tribune*, February 22, 1949, pp. 17.

21. Interdepartmental Memorandum from Francis McCall, June 7, 1951, box 278, file 15, NBC.

22. Jack Gould, "Reporting the News," *Variety*, April 17, 1949, Section 2, p. 1; Letter from Kendall Foster to Frank McCall, May 3, 1951, box 130, file 21, NBC; Letter from Frank McCall to William McAndrew, April 30, 1952, box 311, file 20, NBC.

23. Interdepartmental Memorandum from William McAndrew, March 28, 1952, box 278, file 45, NBC.

24. Letter from Barney Weinberg to Dr. Thomas Coffin, December 3, 1950, box 190, file 11, NBC.

25. H. E. Heath, "News by Television: A Review of Practices and Possibilities," *Journalism Quarterly* 27 (Fall 1959): 409–417.

26. Ibid.

27. Interdepartmental Memorandum from Clarence Thoman, January 2, 1951, box 310, file 50, NBC; NBC Press Release, May 8, 1953, box 200, file 1, NBC.

28. Interdepartmental Memorandum from William Brooks, March 31, 1952, box 130, file 22, NBC; Richard Oberlin, "Television News Can Pay Off," *Broadcasting/Telecasting*, June 29, 1953, pp. 94–98.

29. Richard Oberlin, "Television News Can Pay Off," pp. 94–98.

30. Ibid., p. 94.

31. Letter from Kendall Foster to Davidson Taylor, June 6, 1952, box 278, file 45, NBC.

32. E. J. Forrest, "A Historical and Interpretive Analysis," p. 83.

33. Ibid.

34. "Tele News Best Score Sure to Rise Due to New NBC-Soviet Film Deal," *Variety,* March 26, 1947, pp. 33; Letter from Jack Begon to Dr. V. Sabel, October 20, 1952, box 314, file 18, NBC; Letter from Jack Begon to Len Allen, October 26, 1952, box 314, file 18, NBC; Letter from Romney Wheeler to Davidson Taylor, September 22, 1953, box 278, file 59, NBC; Letter from Romney Wheeler to William McAndrew, November 16, 1953, box 278, file 59, NBC.

35. Ibid.

36. Interdepartmental Memorandum from Davidson Taylor, September 1, 1953, box 278, file 18, NBC.

37. Interdepartmental Memorandum from Joe Mayers, April 29, 1952, box 314, file 6, NBC; Bruce Robertson, "Covering the World in TV News Film," *Broadcasting,* September 14, 1953, pp. 109–110; "Film Sources," undated, box 314, file 18, NBC; Forrest, pp. 83–88.

38. Letter from Francis McCall to Eloise Smith Hanna, WRC-TV, October 18, 1951, box 310, file 60, NBC; Interdepartmental Memorandum from Gene Juster, April 20, 1953, box 279, file 34, NBC.

39. Ibid.

40. Letter from Francis McCall to Eloise Smith Hanna, October 18, 1951, box 310, file 60, NBC.

41. Interdepartmental Memorandum from Gene Juster, April 20, 1953, box 279, file 34, NBC.

42. Interdepartmental Memorandum from Jack Cron, March 20, 1953, box 279, file 7, NBC.

43. Letter from Bernard Berth of WLW Cincinnati to Len Warager, May 26, 1953, box 297, file 7, NBC.

44. Interdepartmental Memorandum from Gene Juster, April 20, 1953, box 279, file 34, NBC.

45. Interdepartmental Memorandum from Davidson Taylor, September 1, 1953, box 278, file 18, NBC.

46. Interdepartmental Memorandum from Gene Juster, 20 April 1953, box 279, file 34, NBC.

47. Confidential Memorandum from Davidson Taylor, April 29, 1952, box 130, file 22, NBC; Letter from Joseph Heffernan to Gen. David Sarnoff, September 2, 1953, box 394, file 4, NBC; "Weekly Cost Structure—1954," box 394, file 4, NBC; Interdepartmental Memorandum from Robert McFadyen, September 20, 1955, box 137, file 37, NBC.

48. In early 1948, NBC had announced that it was expanding his video coverage by making radio reporters available to television. "The News by Television," *Newsweek,* February 2, 1946, 51; "NBC's Radio, TV Setups Dovetailed as Net Heaves All-Out Pitch for Video," *Variety,* April 28, 1948, p. 30. This integration, coming at a time when there were less than 14,000 television sets in the country, pointed up NBC's all-out emphasis on television.

49. Interdepartmental Memorandum from J. V. Heffernan, September 2, 1953, box 394, file 4, NBC.

50. Letter from Davidson Taylor to Frank White, August 4, 1952, box 278, file 15, NBC; Interdepartmental Memorandum from Len Allen, September 3, 1952, box 314, file 18, NBC; Interdepartmental Memorandum from Fred Wile, October 23, 1952, box 278, file 15, NBC; Letter from Francis McCall to William McAndrew, November 6, 1952, box 311, file 32, NBC; "Financial Review of News Film," September 1, 1953, box 279, file 18, NBC; Interdepartmental Memorandum from Leonard Hole, September 10, 1954, box 279, file 81, NBC.

51. Interdepartmental Memorandum from Davidson Taylor, July 20, 1951, box 310, file 78, NBC.

52. Letter from Francis McCall to William McAndrew, November 6, 1952, box 311, file 32, NBC.

53. Confidential Memorandum from Davidson Taylor, April 29, 1952, box 130, file 22, NBC.

54. Ibid.

55. Confidential Memorandum from Davidson Taylor, April 29, 1952, box 130, file 22, NBC; "Report of Investigation of Stringer Coverage," October 21, 1952, box 278, file 6, NBC; Forrest, p. 89.

56. E. J. Forrest, "A Historical and Interpretive Analysis," p. 89.

57. Letter from Davidson Taylor to Frank Russell, November 19, 1952, box 278, file 15, NBC.

58. Ibid.

59. Herbert Gans, *Deciding What's News,* pp. 11–17.

60. Letter from Davidson Taylor to Frank White, April 30, 1953, box 279, file 34, NBC.

61. Ibid.

62. CBS established its newsfilm department as a separate unit to supply networks' news departments with daily coverage of world events. See "CBS-TV Newsfilm Begins Operation," *Broadcasting,* May 18, 1953, p. 9.

63. "NBC Unrest Is Mounting; WTAR Changes to CBS," *Broadcasting/Telecasting,* May 25, 1953, pp. 27–29; "Radio Rehabilitation Is Sarnoff's Pledge," *Broadcasting/Telecasting,* September 21, 1953, pp. 29–31.

64. "NBC Unrest Is Mounting," pp. 27–29.

65. Ibid; "Radio Rehabilitation Is Sarnoff's Pledge, pp. 29–31.

66. "Radio, TV Networks' Combined Gross Exceeds $35 Million for February," *Broadcasting,* April 5, 1954, p. 33.

67. The biggest alteration in NBC's setup was the complete separation of the radio and television activities. This was aimed primarily at the reorganization of the radio network. Whereas network buying was quickly becoming the dominant form of television advertising, network sales in radio were declining quickly while local sales increased. See "Corporations: Big Push by RCA," *Newsweek,* September 7, 1953, pp. 63–64; "52 Radio Time Sales Reach $464 Million," *Broadcasting,* January 26, 1953, p. 27; "Timebuying in TV during '52 Reached $288.8 Million," *Broadcasting,* March 16, 1953, p. 27.

68. Public Affairs Organizational Chart, June 23, 1952, box 291, file 17, NBC.

69. Interdepartmental Memorandum from Len Allen, March 9, 1953, box 279, file 17, NBC; Letter from Romney Wheeler to William McAndrew, September 22, 1953, box 279, file 9, NBC; Interdepartmental Memorandum from William McAndrew, November 10, 1953, box 279, file 19, NBC; Interdepartmental Memorandum from Len Allen, October 26, 1954, box 280, file 1, NBC.

70. Interdepartment Memorandum from Davidson Taylor, July 28, 1954, box 123, file 39, NBC.

71. "NBC Unrest Is Mounting: WTAR Changes to CBS," *Broadcasting/Telecasting* May 25, 1953, pp. 27–28; "Corporations: Big Push by RCA," *Newsweek,* September 5, 1953, pp. 63–64.

72. Ibid.

73. See, for example, William Pfaff, "News on the Networks," *The Commonweal,* April 9, 1954, pp. 11–14.

74. "See Viewers Fed Up on Dull Feed," *Variety,* November 21, 1956, pp. 21, 34.

75. Letter from Kenneth Bilby to Davidson Taylor, January 3, 1956, box 174, file 25, NBC.

76. Barbara Matusow, *The Evening Stars: The Molding of the Network News Anchor* (Boston: Houghton Mifflin, 1963), p. 70.

77. "Radio, TV Networks' Combined Gross Exceeds $35 Million for February," *Broadcasting/Telecasting,* April 5, 1954, pp. 33.

QUESTIONS FOR DISCUSSION

1. By focusing on the early, unformed stage of television news coverage this article helps us re-think the relationships between TV news and "foreign" (but always present) elements like commercials, sponsors, and competing industries. How might "news" have developed differently? What elements of these factors remain, though obscured by later developments (such as spot advertising, the ethos of "objectivity," and network control)?

2. What form does conflict between commercial and public service principles take in today's news coverage?

3. How did network competition shape the development of TV news? How does comparison between networks and cable work similarly today? Did CNN go through a similar period of struggle and experimentation?

 INFOTRAC COLLEGE EDITION

Search InfoTrac College Edition for more information on the development of news. Try keywords such as "news and objectivity" and "news and competition."

6

The Meaning
of Memory
Family, Class, and Ethnicity
in Early Network
Television Programs

GEORGE LIPSITZ

In this influential and far-reaching study of early network television programs, George Lipsitz situates television's family sitcoms, in particular, at the juncture of complex social and cultural forces. He analyzes the presence of a "subgenre" of comedies focusing on ethnic, working-class families during television's first decade, a subgenre that had virtually disappeared by the late 1950s.

Lipsitz shows that such programs as *I Remember Mama, The Goldbergs, Amos 'n Andy, Life with Luigi,* and *The Honeymooners* hearkened back to a nostalgic vision of an earlier America, evoking traditional values and ways of life and then, crucially, linking them to the new era of middle-class consumption. This helped to smooth the transition to the assimilated, suburban consumer lifestyle embraced by so many Americans after the war, by legitimizing and "making comfortable" their new, affluent desires and expectations. It also downplayed and "silenced" other aspects of ethnic working-class life, such as labor struggles, racial and ethnic prejudice, Cold War political repression, and the continued economic plight of many excluded from the consumerist dream. These early sitcoms worked to obscure the economic and political underpinnings of the

Originally published in *Cultural Anthropology* 1 (November 1986): 355–87. Reproduced by permission of the American Anthropological Association. Not for sale or further reproduction.

middle-class suburban lifestyle by tying it to the traditional lifestyles of the past, by "putting the borrowed moral capital of the past at the service of the values of the present." Yet they also opened up the possibilities for a critique of postwar U.S. culture by reminding viewers of ethnic, familial, and class connections that the consumerist lifestyle wished to erase.

Almost every Friday night between 1949 and 1956, millions of Americans watched Rosemary Rice turn the pages of an old photograph album. With music from Edvard Grieg's "Holberg Suite" playing in the background, and with pictures of turn-of-the-century San Francisco displayed on the album pages, Rice assumed the identity of her television character, Katrin Hansen, on the CBS network program *Mama*. She told the audience about her memories of her girlhood, her family's house on Steiner Street, and her experiences there with her big brother Nels, her little sister Dagmar, her Papa, and her Mama—"most of all," she said, "when I remember that San Francisco of so long ago, I remember Mama" (Meehan and Ropes 1954).

Katrin Hansen's memories of her Norwegian immigrant working-class family had powerful appeal for viewers in the early years of commercial network broadcasting. *Mama* established itself as one of CBS' most popular programs during its first season on the air, and it retained high ratings for the duration of its prime time run (Mitz 1983:458). The show's popularity coincided with that of other situation comedies based on ethnic working-class family life—*The Goldbergs,* depicting the experiences of Jews in the Bronx; *Amos 'n Andy,* blacks in Harlem; *The Honeymooners* and *Hey Jeannie,* Irish working-class families in Brooklyn; *Life with Luigi,* Italian immigrants in Chicago; and *Life of Riley,* working-class migrants to Los Angeles during and after World War II.[1]

The presence of this subgenre of ethnic, working-class situation comedies on television network schedules seems to run contrary to the commercial and artistic properties of the medium. Television delivers audiences to advertisers by glorifying consumption, not only during commercial breaks but in the programs themselves (Barnouw 1979). The relative economic deprivation of ethnic working-class households would seem to provide an inappropriate setting for the display and promotion of commodities as desired by the networks and their commercial sponsors. Furthermore, the mass audience required to repay the expense of network programming encourages the depiction of a homogenized mass society, not the particularities and peculiarities of working-class communities. As an artistic medium, television's capacity for simultaneity conveys a sense of living in an infinitely renewable present—a quality inimical to the sense of history permeating shows about working-class life. Yet whether set in the distant past like *Mama,* or located in the contemporaneous present, the subgenre of ethnic working-class situation comedies in early network television evoked concrete historical associations and memories in their audiences (Boorstin 1973:392–397).

Table 1

Program	Ethnicity	Occupations	Location	Dwelling
Mama	Norwegian	Carpenter	San Francisco	house
The Goldbergs	Jewish	Tailor/Small Business	Bronx/Long Island	apartment/house
Amos 'n Andy	Black	Cab Driver/Hustler	Harlem	apartment
The Honeymooners	Irish	Bus Driver/Sewer Worker	Brooklyn	apartment
Life with Luigi	Italian	Shopkeeper	Chicago	apartment
Life of Riley	Irish	Machinist	Los Angeles	duplex/cottage
Hey Jeannie	Scottish/Irish	Cab Driver	Brooklyn	apartment

Anomalous to the commercial and artistic properties of television, these programs also ran counter to the dominant social trends in the era in which they were made. They presented ethnic families in working-class urban neighborhoods at the precise historical moment when a rising standard of living, urban renewal, and suburbanization contributed to declines in ethic and class identity.[2] They showed working-class families struggling for material satisfaction and advancement under conditions far removed from the *embourgeoisement* of the working class celebrated in popular literature about the postwar era. They displayed value conflicts about family identity, consumer spending, ethnicity, class, and gender roles that would appear to be disruptive and dysfunctional within a communications medium primarily devoted to stimulating commodity purchases (see Table 1).

The dissonance between ethnic working-class situation comedies and their artistic, commercial, and historical surroundings might be explained by the persistence of artistic clichés and the conservatism of the entertainment business. Though four of these seven television programs previously existed as radio serials, radio popularity did not guarantee adaptation to television: many successful radio series never made that transition, and television networks actually made more profit from productions specially created for the new medium (Allen 1985:126, 164; de Cordova 1985). Even when radio programs did become television shows, they underwent significant changes in plot and premise. Television versions of urban ethnic working-class situation comedies placed more emphasis on nuclear families and less on extended kinship relations and ethnicity than did their radio predecessors.[3] Those changes reflect more than the differences between television and radio as media: they illuminate as well significant transformations in U.S. society during the 1950s, and they underscore the important role played by television in explaining and legitimizing those transitions to a mass audience.

More than their shared history in radio or their reliance on common theatrical traditions from vaudeville and ethnic theater unites the subgenre of urban ethnic working-class situation comedies. Through indirect but powerful demonstration, all of these shows arbitrated complex tensions caused by economic and social change in postwar America. They evoked the experiences of the past to lend legitimacy to the dominant ideology of the present. In the process they served important social and cultural functions, not just in returning profits to investors or attracting audiences for advertisers, but most significantly as a means of ideological legitimation for a fundamental revolution in economic, social, and cultural life.

THE MEANING OF MEMORY

In the midst of extraordinary social change, television became the most important discursive medium in American culture. As such, it was charged with special responsibilities for making new economic and social relations credible and legitimate to audiences haunted by ghosts from the past. Urban ethnic working-class situation comedies provided one means of addressing the anxieties and contradictions emanating from the clash between the consumer present of the 1950s and collective social memory about the 1930s and 1940s.

The consumer consciousness emerging from economic and social change in postwar America conflicted with the lessons of historical experience for many middle- and working-class American families. The Great Depression of the 1930s had not only damaged the economy, it also undercut the political and cultural legitimacy of American capitalism. Herbert Hoover had been a national hero in the 1920s, with his credo of "rugged individualism" forming the basis for a widely shared cultural ideal. But the depression discredited Hoover's philosophy and made him a symbol of yesterday's blasted hopes to millions of Americans. In the 1930s, cultural ideals based on mutuality and collectivity eclipsed the previous decade's "rugged individualism" and helped propel massive union organizing drives, anti-eviction movements, and general strikes. President Roosevelt's New Deal attempted to harness and co-opt that grass roots mass activity in an attempt to restore social order and recapture credibility and legitimacy for the capitalist system (Romasco 1965). The social welfare legislation of the "Second New Deal" in 1935 went far beyond any measures previously favored by Roosevelt and most of his advisors, but radical action proved necessary for the Administration to contain the upsurge of activism that characterized the decade. Even in the private sector, industrial corporations made more concessions to workers than naked power realities necessitated because they feared the political consequences of mass disillusionment with the system (Berger 1982).

World War II ended the depression and brought prosperity, but it did so on a basis even more collective than the New Deal of the 1930s. Government intervention in the wartime economy reached unprecedented levels, bringing material reward and shared purpose to a generation raised on the deprivation and sacrifice of the depression. In the postwar years, the largest and most disruptive strike wave in American history won major improvements in the standard of living for the average worker, both through wage increases and through government commitments to insure full employment, decent housing, and expanded educational opportunities. Grass roots militancy and working-class direct action wrested concessions from a reluctant government and business elite—mostly because the public at large viewed workers' demands as more legitimate than the desires of capital (Lipsitz 1981).

Yet the collective nature of working-class mass activity in the postwar era posed severe problems for capital. In sympathy strikes and secondary boycotts, workers placed the interests of their class ahead of their own individual material aspirations. Strikes over safety and job control far outnumbered wage strikes, revealing aspirations to control the process of production that conflicted with capitalist labor-management relations. Mass demonstrations demanding government employment and housing programs indicated a collective political response to problems previously adjudicated on a personal level. Radical challenges to the authority of capital (like the 1946 United Auto Workers' strike demand that wage increases come out of corporate profits rather than from price hikes passed on to consumers), demonstrated a social responsibility and a commitment toward redistributing wealth, rare in the history of American labor (Lipsitz 1981:47–50).

Capital attempted to regain the initiative in the postwar years by making qualified concessions to working-class pressures for redistribution of wealth and power. Rather than paying wage increases out of corporate profits, business leaders instead worked to expand the economy through increases in government spending, foreign trade, and consumer debt. Such expansion could meet the demands of workers and consumers without undermining capital's dominant role in the economy. On the presumption that "a rising tide lifts all boats," business leaders sought to connect working-class aspirations for a better life to policies that insured a commensurate rise in corporate profits, thereby leaving the distribution of wealth unaffected. Federal defense spending, highway construction programs, and home loan policies expanded the economy at home in a manner conducive to the interests of capital, while the Truman Doctrine and Marshall Plan provided models for enhanced access to foreign markets and raw materials for American corporations. The Taft-Hartley Act of 1947 banned the class-conscious collective activities most threatening to capital (mass strikes, sympathy strikes, secondary boycotts); the leaders of labor, government, and business accepted as necessity the practice of paying wage hikes for organized workers out of the pockets of consumers and unorganized workers, in the form of higher prices (Lipsitz 1981).

Commercial network television played an important role in this emerging economy, functioning as a significant object of consumer purchases as well as an important marketing medium. Sales of sets jumped from three million during the entire decade of the 1940s to over five million *a year* during the 1950s (*TV Facts* 1980:141). But television's most important economic function came from its role as an instrument of legitimation for transformations in values initiated by the new economic imperatives of postwar America. For Americans to accept the new world of 1950s' consumerism, they had to make a break with the past. The depression years had helped generate fears about installment buying and excessive materialism, while the new Deal and wartime mobilization had provoked suspicions about individual acquisitiveness and upward mobility. Depression era and wartime scarcities of consumer goods had led workers to internalize discipline and frugality while nurturing networks of mutual support through family, ethnic, and class associations. Government policies after the war encouraged an atomized acquisitive consumerism at odds with the lessons of the past. At the same time, federal home loan policies stimulated migrations to the suburbs from traditional, urban ethnic working-class neighborhoods. The entry of television into the American home disrupted previous patterns of family life and encouraged fragmentation of the family into separate segments of the consumer market.[4] The priority of consumerism in the economy at large and on television may have seemed organic and unplanned, but conscious policy decisions by officials from both private and public sectors shaped the contours of the consumer economy and television's role within it.

COMMERCIAL TELEVISION
AND ECONOMIC CHANGE

Government policies during and after World War II shaped the basic contours of home television as an advertising medium. Government-sponsored research and development during the war perfected the technology of home television while federal tax policies solidified its economic base. The government allowed corporations to deduct the cost of advertising from their taxable incomes during the war, despite the fact that rationing and defense production left business with few products to market. Consequently, manufacturers kept the names of their products before the public while lowering their tax obligations on high wartime profits. Their advertising expenditures supplied radio networks and advertising agencies with the capital reserves and business infrastructure that enabled them to dominate the television industry in the postwar era. After the war, federal antitrust action against the motion picture studios broke up the "network" system in movies, while the FCC sanctioned the network system in television. In addition, FCC decisions to allocate stations on the narrow VHF band, to grant the networks ownership and operation rights over stations in prime markets, and to place a freeze on the licensing of new stations during the important years between 1948 and 1952 all combined to guarantee that advertising-oriented programming based on the model of radio would triumph over theater TV, educational TV, or any other form (Boddy 1985; Allen 1983). Government decisions, not market forces, established the dominance of commercial television, but these decisions reflected a view of the American economy and its needs which had become so well accepted at the top levels of business and government that it had virtually become the official state economic policy.

Fearing both renewed depression and awakened militancy among workers, influential corporate and business leaders considered increases in consumer spending—increases of 30% to 50%—to be necessary to perpetuate prosperity in the postwar era (Lipsitz 1981:46, 120–121). Defense spending for the Cold War and Korean Conflict had complemented an aggressive trade policy to improve the state of the economy, but it appeared that the key to an expanding economy rested in increased consumer spending fueled by an expansion of credit (Moore and Klein 1967; Jezer 1982). Here too, government policies led the way, especially with regard to stimulating credit purchases of homes and automobiles. During World War II, the marginal tax rate for most wage earners jumped from 4% to 25%, making the home ownership deduction more desirable. Federal housing loan policies favored construction of new single family detached suburban housing over renovation or construction of central city multifamily units. Debt-encumbered home ownership in accord with these policies stimulated construction of 30 million new housing units in just twenty years, bringing the percentage of home-owning Americans from below 40% in 1940 to more than 60% by 1960. Mortgage policies encouraging long term debt and low down payments freed capital for other consumer purchases, while government highway building policies undermined mass transit systems and contributed to increased demand for automobiles (Hartman 1982:165–168). Partly as a result of these policies, consumer spending on private cars averaged $7.5 billion per year in the 1930s and 1940s, but grew to $22 billion per year in 1950 and almost $30 billion by 1955 (Mollenkopf 1983:111).

For the first time in U.S. history, middle-class and working-class families could routinely expect to own homes or buy new cars every few years. Between 1946 and 1965 residential mortgage debt rose three times as fast as the gross national product and disposable income. Mortgage debt accounted for just under 18% of disposable income in 1946, but it grew to almost 55% by 1965 (Stone 1983:122). In order to insure eventual payment of current debts, the economy had to generate tremendous expansion and growth, further stimulating the need to increase consumer spending. Manufacturers had to find new ways of motivating consumers to buy ever increasing amounts of commodities, and television provided an important means of accomplishing that end.

Television advertised individual products, but it also provided a relentless flow of information and persuasion that placed acts of consumption at the core of everyday life. The physical fragmentation of suburban growth and declines in motion picture attendance created an audience more likely to stay at home and receive entertainment there than ever before. But television also provided a locus redefining American ethnic, class, and family identities into consumer identities. In order to accomplish this task effectively, television programs had to address some of the psychic, moral, and political obstacles to consumption among the public at large.

The television and advertising industries knew that they had to overcome these obstacles. Marketing expert and motivational specialist Ernest Dichter stated that "one of the basic problems of this prosperity is to give people that sanction and justification to enjoy it and to demonstrate that the hedonistic approach to life is a moral one, not an immoral one" (Jezer 1982:127). Dichter went on to note the many barriers that inhibited consumer acceptance of unrestrained hedonism, and he called on advertisers "to train the average citizen to accept growth of his country and its economy as *his* growth rather than as a strange and frightening event" (Dichter 1960:210). One method of encouraging that acceptance, according to Dichter, consisted of identifying new products and styles of consumption with traditional, historically sanctioned practices and behavior. He noted that such an approach held particular relevance in addressing consumers who had only recently acquired the means to spend freely and who might harbor a lingering conservatism based on their previous experiences (Dichter 1960:209).

Insecurities and anxieties among consumers compelled network television to address the complex legacies of the 1930s and 1940s in order to promote consumption in the 1950s. In the middle of its appeals to change the world in the present through purchase of the appropriate commodities, commercial network television in its early years also presented programs rooted in the historical experiences and aspirations of diverse working-class traditions. From the evocations of the depression era that permeated the world of *The Honeymooners,* to the recycled minstrel show stereotypes of *Amos 'n Andy,* from the textured layers of immigrant experience underpinning the drama and charm of *The Goldbergs* and *Mama,* to the reenactment of immigration in contemporaneous circumstances in *Life of Riley, Life with Luigi,* and *Hey Jeannie,* the medium of the infinitely renewable present turned to past traditions and practices in order to explain and legitimate fundamentally new social relations in the present.

FAMILY FORMATION AND THE ECONOMY—THE TELEVISION VIEW

Advertisers incorporated their messages into urban ethnic working-class comedies through indirect and direct means. Tensions developed in the programs often found indirect resolution in commercials. Thus Jeannie MacClennan's search for an American sweetheart in one episode of *Hey Jeannie* set up commercials proclaiming the abilities of Drene shampoo to keep one prepared to accept last minute dates and of Crest toothpaste to produce an attractive smile (*Hey Jeannie:* "The Rock and Roll Kid"). Conversations about shopping for new furniture in an episode of *The Goldbergs* directed viewers' attention to furnishings in the Goldberg home provided for the show by Macy's department store in exchange for a commercial acknowledgment (*The Goldbergs:* "The In-laws").

But the content of the shows themselves offered even more direct emphasis on consumer spending. In one episode of *The Goldbergs,* Molly expresses disapproval of her future daughter-in-law's plan to buy a washing machine on the installment plan. "I know Papa and me never bought anything unless we had the money to pay for it," she intones with logic familiar to a generation with memories of the Great Depression. Her son, Sammy, confronts this "deviance" by saying, "Listen, Ma, almost everybody in this country lives above their means—and everybody enjoys it." Doubtful at first, Molly eventually learns from her children and announces her conversion to the legitimacy of installment buying by proposing that the family buy two cars so as to "live above our means—the American way" (*The Goldbergs:* "The In-laws"). In a subsequent episode, Molly's daughter, Rosalie, assumes the role of ideological tutor to her mother. When planning a move out of their Bronx apartment to a new house in the suburbs, Molly ruminates about where to place her furniture in the new home. "You don't mean we're going to take all this junk with us into a brand new house?" asks an exasperated Rosalie. With traditionalist sentiment Molly answers, "Junk? My furniture's junk? My furniture that I lived with and loved for twenty years is junk?"

But in the end she accepts Rosalie's argument—even selling off all her old furniture to help meet the down payment on the new house, and deciding to buy new furniture on the installment plan (*The Goldbergs:* "Moving Day").

Chester A. Riley confronts similar choices about family and commodities in *The Life of Riley.* His wife complains that he only takes her out to the neighborhood bowling alley and restaurant, not to "interesting places." Riley searches for ways to impress her and discovers from a friend that a waiter at the fancy Club Morambo will let them eat first and pay later, at a dollar a week plus ten percent interest. "Ain't that dishonest?" asks Riley. "No, it's usury," his friend replies. Riley does not borrow the money, but he impresses his wife anyway by taking the family out to dinner on the proceeds of a prize that he received for being the one-thousandth customer in a local flower shop. Though we eventually learn that Peg Riley only wanted attention, not an expensive meal, the happy ending of the episode hinges totally on Riley's prestige, restored when he demonstrates his ability to provide a luxury outing for the family (*Life of Riley:* R228).

The same episode of *The Life of Riley* reveals another consumerist element common to this subgenre. When Riley protests that he lacks the money needed to fulfill Peg's desires, she answers that he would have plenty if he didn't spend so much on "needless gadgets." His shortage of cash becomes a personal failing caused by incompetent behavior as a consumer. Nowhere do we hear about the size of his paycheck, relations between his union and his employer, or, for that matter, the relationship between the value of his labor and the wages paid to him by the Stevenson Aircraft Company. Like Uncle David in *The Goldbergs*—who buys a statue of Hamlet shaking hands with Shakespeare and an elk's tooth with the Gettysburg address carved on it—Riley's comic character stems in part from a flaw which in theory could be attributed to the entire consumer economy: a preoccupation with "needless gadgets." By contrast, Peg Riley's desire for an evening out is portrayed as reasonable and modest—as reparation due her for the inevitable tedium of housework. The solution to her unhappiness, of course, comes from an evening out rather than from a change in her own work circumstances. Even within the home, television elevates consumption over production; production is assumed to be a constant—only consumption can be varied. But more than enjoyment is at stake: unless Riley can provide her with the desired night on the town, he will fail in his obligations as a husband (*Life of Riley:* R228; *The Goldbergs:* "Bad Companions").

A similar theme provides the crisis in an episode of *Mama.* Dagmar, the youngest child, "innocently" expresses envy of a friend whose father received a promotion and consequently put up new wallpaper in his house. "Why doesn't Papa get promoted?" Dagmar chirps, "Everyone else does." When Mama explains that a carpenter makes less money than other fathers, Dagmar asks if it wouldn't be smarter for Papa to work in a bank. Overhearing this dialogue, Papa decides to accept his boss' offer to promote him to foreman, even though he knows it will ruin his friendships with the other workers. The logic of the episode instructs us that fathers will lose their standing if they disappoint their families' desires for new commodities (*Mama:* "Mama and the Carpenter"). Shows exploring tensions between family obligations and commodity purchases routinely assert that money cannot *buy* love, but they seem less clear about whether one can trade material wealth for affection. Even the usually self-absorbed Kingfish on *Amos 'n Andy* gives in to his nephew Stanley's wish for "a birthday party with lots of expensive presents," while Jeannie MacClennan's search for romance suffers a setback when a prospective suitor sees her shabby apartment with its antiquated furniture (*Amos 'n Andy:* "Andy the Godfather"; *Hey Jeannie:* "The Rock and Roll Kid"). On *The Goldbergs,* a young woman is forbidden to marry the man she loves because, her mother says, "I didn't raise my daughter to be a butcher's wife" (*The Goldbergs:* "Die Fledermaus"); and Alice Kramden in *The Honeymooners* can always gain the upper hand in arguments with her husband by pointing to his inadequacies as a provider. In each of these programs, consumer choices close the ruptures in personal relations, enabling the episode to reach narrative and ideological closure.

One episode of *Mama* typifies the confusion between consumer purchases and family happiness pervading urban ethnic working-class situation comedies in early network television. "Mama's Birthday," broadcast in 1954, delineated the tensions between family loyalty and consumer desire endemic to modern capitalist society. The show begins with Mama teaching Katrin to make Norwegian potato balls, the kind she used long ago to "catch" Papa. Unimpressed by this accomplishment, Katrin changes the subject and asks Mama what she wants for her upcoming birthday. In an answer that locates Mama within the gender roles of the 1950s she replies, "Well, I think a fine new job for your Papa. You and Dagmar to marry nice young men and have a lot of wonderful children—just like I have. And Nels, well, Nels to become president of the United States" (Meehan and Ropes 1954). In one sentence Mama has summed up the dominant culture's version of legitimate female expectations: success at work for her husband, marriage and childrearing for her daughters, the presidency for her son—and nothing for herself.

But we learn that Mama does have some needs, although we do not hear it from her lips. Her sister, Jenny, asks Mama to attend a fashion show, but Mama cannot leave the house because she has to cook a roast for a guest whom Papa has invited to dinner. Jenny comments that Mama never seems to get out of the kitchen, adding that "it's a disgrace when a woman can't call her soul her own," and "it's a shame that a married woman can't have some time to herself." The complaint is a valid one, and we can imagine how it might have resonated for women in the 1950s. The increased availability of household appliances and the use of synthetic fibers and commercially processed food should have decreased the amount of time women spent in housework, but surveys showed that homemakers spent the same number of hours per week (51 to 56) doing housework as they had done in the 1920s. Advertising and marketing strategies undermined the potential of technological changes by upgrading standards of cleanliness in the home and expanding desires for more varied wardrobes and menus for the average family (Hartmann 1982: 168). In that context, Aunt Jenny would have been justified in launching into a tirade about the division of labor within the Hansen household or about the possibilities for cooperative housework, but network television specializes in a less social and more commodified dialogue about problems like housework: Aunt Jenny suggests that her sister's family buy her a "fireless cooker"—a cast iron stove—for her birthday. "They're wonderful," she tells them in language borrowed from the rhetoric of advertising. "You just put your dinner inside them, close 'em up, and go where you please. When you come back your dinner is all cooked" (Meehan and Ropes 1954). Papa protests that Mama likes to cook on her woodburning stove, but Jenny dismisses that objection with an insinuation about his motive, when she replies, "Well, I suppose it *would* cost a little more than you could afford, Hansen" (Meehan and Ropes 1954).

By identifying a commodity as the solution to Mama's problem, Aunt Jenny unites the inner voice of Mama with the outer voice of the sponsors of television programs. Mama's utility as an icon of maternal selflessness would be compromised if she asked for the stove herself, but Aunt Jenny's role in suggesting the gift removes that taint of selfishness while adding the authority of an outside expert. Aunt Jenny's suggestion of hypocrisy in Papa's reluctance to buy the stove encourages the audience to resent him for not making enough money and even to see his poverty as a form of selfishness—denying his wife the comforts due her. In reality, we know that Aunt Jenny's advice probably contains the usual distortions of advertising claims, that even if the fireless cooker enabled Mama to go where she pleased while dinner cooked, it would bring with it different kinds of tasks and escalating demands. But in the fantasy world of television, such considerations do not intervene. Prodded by their aunt, the Hansen children go shopping and purchase the fireless cooker from a storekeeper who calls the product "the new Emancipation Proclamation—setting housewives free from their old kitchen range" (Meehan and Ropes 1954). Our exposure to advertising hyperbole should not lead us to miss the analogy here: housework is compared to slavery, and the commercial product takes on the aura of Abraham Lincoln. The shopkeeper's appeal convinces the children to pool their resources and buy the stove for Mama. But we soon learn that Papa plans to make a fireless cooker for Mama with his tools. When Mama discovers Papa's intentions she persuades the children to buy her another gift. Even Papa admits that his stove will not be as efficient as the one made in a factory, but Mama nobly affirms that she will like his better because he made it himself. The children use their money to buy dishes for Mama, and Katrin remembers the episode as Mama's happiest birthday ever (Meehan and Ropes 1954).

The stated resolution of "Mama's Birthday" favors traditional values. Mama prefers to protect Papa's feelings rather than having a better stove, and the product built by a family member has more value than one sold as a commodity. Yet the entire development of the plot leads in the opposite direction. The "fireless cooker" is the star of the episode, setting in motion all the other characters, and it has unquestioned value even in the face of Jenny's meddlesome brashness, Papa's insensitivity, and Mama's old-fashioned ideals. Buying a product is unchallenged as the true means of changing the unpleasant realities or low status of women's work in the home.

This resolution of the conflict between consumer desires and family roles reflected television's social role as mediator between the family and the economy. Surveys of set ownership showed no pronounced stratification by class, but a clear correlation between family size and television purchases: households with three to five people were most likely to own television sets, while those with only one person were least likely to own them. (Swanson and Jones 1951). The television industry recognized and promoted its privileged place within families in advertisements like the one in the *New York Times* in 1950 that proclaimed, "Youngsters today need television for their morale as much as they need fresh air and sunshine for their health" (Wolfenstein 1951). Like previous communications media, television sets occupied honored places in family living rooms, and helped structure family time; unlike other previous communications media, they displayed available commodities in a way that transformed all their entertainment into a glorified shopping catalogue.

Publicity about television programs stressed the interconnections between family and economy as well. Viewers took the portrayals of motherhood on these shows so seriously that when Peggy Wood of *Mama* appeared on the *Garry Moore Show* and asked for questions from the audience, women asked for advice about raising their families, as if she were actually Mama, rather than an actress playing that role (*TV Guide* 1954:11). The *Ladies Home Journal* printed an article containing "Mama's Recipes," featuring photographs of Peggy Wood, while Gertrude Berg wrote an article as Molly Goldberg for *TV Guide* that contained her recipes for borscht and blintzes. "Your meal should suit the mood of your husband," Berg explained. "If he's nervous give him a heavy meal. If he's happy a salad will do" (*Ladies Home Journal* 1956:130–131; *TV Guide* 1953A:7). Actors on the shows also ignored the contradictions between their on-stage and off-stage roles. Actress Marjorie Reynolds told *TV Guide* that she enjoyed playing Mrs. Chester A. Riley, because "I've done just about everything in films from westerns to no-voice musicals, and now with the Riley show, I'm back in the kitchen. Where every wife belongs" (*TV Guide* 1953B:17).

The focus on the family in early network television situation comedies involved a special emphasis on mothers. Images of long-suffering but loving mothers pervaded these programs and publicity about them. Ostensibly representations of "tradition," these images actually spoke to a radical rupture with the past: the establishment of the isolated nuclear family of the 1950s with its attendant changes in family gender roles. The wartime economic mobilization that ended the depression stimulated an extraordinary period of family formation that was in sharp contrast to the experience of preceding decades. Americans married more frequently, formed families at a younger age, and had more children in the 1940s than they had in the 1920s and 1930s (Hartmann 1982:164–165). The combination of permissive recommendations for childrearing and social changes attendant to increases in consumer spending isolated mothers as never before. Work previously shared with extended kinship and neighbor networks now had to be done by machines, at home in isolation. Childrearing took up more time and responsibility, but inflation and expanded consumer desires encouraged women to work outside the home for pay. When the conflicting demands of permissivism created guilt and feelings of inadequacy, outside authorities—from child psychologists to television programs—stood ready to provide "therapeutic" images of desired maternal behavior.

While placing special burdens on women, changes in family identity in the postwar era transformed the roles of all family members. As psychoanalyst Joel Kovel demonstrates, the decomposition of extended kinship networks made the nuclear family the center of the personal world, "a location of desire and intimacy not previously conceptualized" (Kovel 1978:13–14). Kovel argues that participation in civil society can keep individuals from sliding back into total narcissism, but that separation of family from society in modern capitalism blocks access to the public realm. The family becomes the locus of all social demands, lauded all the more in theory as its traditional social function disappears in practice. The family appears to be private and voluntary, yet its isolation from neighborhood and class networks leave it subject to extraordinary regulation and manipulation by outside authorities like psychologists and advertisers. The family appears to be the repository of mutuality and affection, but commodity society has truncated its traditional functions into the egoism of possession. The family appears to maintain the privileges and authority of patriarchy, but "like a house nibbled by termites," the outwardly strong appearance of patriarchy masks a collapsing infrastructure no longer capable of wielding authority in an increasingly administered and institutionalized society. According to Kovel, the demise of the traditional family creates a need for authority that becomes filled by the "administrative mode"—the structure of domination that offers commodities as the key to solving personal problems (Kovel 1978:13–14). Sociologist Nancy Chodorow draws a similar formulation in her observation that "the decline of the oedipal father creates an orientation to external authority and behavioral obedience" (Chodorow 1978:189). Chodorow also points out that the idealization of masculinity inherent in the "distant father" role in the nuclear family gives ideological priority to men, while channeling rebellion and resentment against the power wielded by the accessible and proximate mother. Kovel and Chodorow both stress that these patterns are neither natural nor inevitable: they emerge in concrete social circumstances where the nuclear family serves as the main base of support for consumer society (Chodorow 1978:181; Kovel 1978:19).

Commercial network television emerged as the primary discursive medium in American society at the precise historical moment that the isolated nuclear family and its concerns eclipsed previous ethnic, class, and political forces as the crucible of personal identity. Television programs both reflected and shaped that translation, defining the good life in family-centric, asocial, and commodity-oriented ways. As Todd Gitlin argues, "What is hegemonic in consumer capitalist ideology is precisely the notion that happiness, or liberty, or equality, or fraternity can be affirmed through existing private commodity forms, under the benign protective eye of the national security state" (Newcomb 1978). Yet the denigration of public issues and the resulting overemphasis on the home contained contradictions of their own. If the harmonious and mutually supportive family of the past granted moral legitimacy to the consumer dilemmas of urban, ethnic working-class families, the tensions of the modern nuclear household revealed the emerging nuclear family to be a contested terrain of competing needs and desires.

Table 2

Program	Star's Gender	Children	Father or Male Lead	Mother or Female Lead	Extended Family
Mama	Female	Three	Distant but warm	Competent	Relatives/ neighbors
The Goldbergs	Female	Two	Distant but warm	Competent	Relatives/ neighbors
Amos 'n Andy	Male	None	Irresponsible	Hostile	Lodge brothers/ in-laws
The Honeymooners	Male	None	Irresponsible	Hostile	Neighbors
Life with Luigi	Male	None	Irresponsible	Warm	Neighbors
Life of Riley	Male	Two	Incompetent	Warm	Neighbors
Hey Jeannie	Female	None	Irresponsible	Competent	Neighbors/ boarder

The structural tensions basic to the "father absent-mother present" gender roles of the nuclear family identified by Chodorow pervaded television portrayals of urban ethnic working-class life in the 1950s. Peg Riley, Alice Kramden, and Sapphire Stevens heroically endure their husbands' failures to deliver on promises of wealth and upward mobility, and they earn the sympathy of the audience by compensating for the incompetent social performance of their spouses. Yet their nagging insistence on practical reason also marks them as "shrews," out to undercut male authority. Male insensitivity to female needs forms the focal point of humor and sardonic commentary—as in the episode of *The Life of Riley* where Riley can't understand Peg's complaints about staying home all the time. "I can't figure her out," he tells his son. "She's got a home to clean, meals to cook, dishes to wash, you two kids to look after, floors to scrub—what more does she want?" (*Life of Riley:* R228). Few shows displayed hostility between husbands and wives as openly as *The Honeymooners.* (Even the title functioned as bitter irony.) When Alice employs sarcasm in response to Ralph's "get rich quick" schemes and his neglect of her needs, Ralph invariably clenches his fist and says, "one of these days, Alice, one of these days, pow! right in the kisser!" Coupled with his threats to send her "to the moon," the intimation of wife-beating remains a recurring "comic" premise in the show. Jackie Gleason told one interviewer that he thought many husbands felt the way Ralph did about their wives. And an article in *TV Guide* quoted an unnamed "famous" psychiatrist who contended that the program's popularity rested on male perceptions that women had too much power, and on female perceptions that male immaturity demonstrated the superiority of women (*TV Guide* 1955:14). *The Honeymooners* might end with a humbled Ralph Kramden telling Alice, "Baby, you're the greatest," but the show clearly "worked" because tensions between men and women spoke to the experiences and fears of the audience (see Table 2).

Structural tensions within families, women betrayed by irresponsible and incompetent husbands, and men chafing under the domination of their wives:

hardly an ideal portrait of family life. These depictions reflected the fissures in a fundamentally new form of family, a form which increasingly dominated the world of television viewers. One might expect commercial television programs to ignore the problems of the nuclear family, but the industry's imperial ambition— the desire to have all households watching at all times—encouraged exploitation of the real problems confronting viewers. Censorship ruled out treatment of many subjects, but family tensions offered legitimate and fertile ground for television programs. Individuals cut off from previous forms of self-definition and assaulted by media images encouraging narcissistic anxieties had insatiable needs to survey the terrain of family problems, to seek relief from current tensions and assurance of the legitimacy of current social relations. In order to create subjects receptive to the appeals of advertisers and to achieve ideological and narrative closure for their own stories, the creators of television programs had to touch on real issues, albeit in truncated and idealized form. While they unfailingly offered only individual and codified solutions to those problems, the mere act of exposing the contradictions of the nuclear family created the structural potential for oppositional readings. Representation of generational and gender tensions undercut the legitimating authority of the televised traditional working-class family by demonstrating the chasm between memories of yesterday and the realities of today. If the programs remained true to the past, they lost their relevance to current tensions. Yet when they successfully addressed contemporary problems, they forfeited the legitimacy offered by the past and made it easier for their viewers to escape the pull of parochialism and paternal authority embedded in the traditional family form. This clash between the legitimizing promise of urban ethnic working-class shows and their propensity for exposing the shortcomings of both past and present social relations went beyond their treatment of family issues and extended as well to matters of work, class, and ethnicity.

WORK, CLASS, AND ETHNICITY

In addition to consumer issues, the changing nature of working-class identity also influenced the collective memory of viewers of ethnic urban working-class situation comedies in the 1950s. The decade of the 1940s not only witnessed an unprecedented transformation in the nature of the American family, but it also saw an extraordinary social upheaval among workers, which labor historian Stanley Aronowitz has characterized as "incipient class formation" (Aronowitz 1983). War mobilization reindustrialized the sagging U.S. economy, but also reconstituted the working class. Migrations to defense production centers and breakthroughs by women and blacks in securing industrial employment changed the composition of the work force. Traditional parochial loyalties waned as mass production and full employment created new work groups on the shop floor and new working-class communities outside the factory gates. Mass strikes and demonstrations united workers from diverse backgrounds into a polity capable of sustained collective action. Of course, racism and sexism remained pervasive on both institutional and grass roots levels, but the mass activity of the postwar era represented the stirrings of a class consciousness previously unknown in a proletariat deeply divided by ethnicity, race, and gender. By the 1950s, expanded consumer opportunities, suburbanization, and access to education offered positive inducements away from that class consciousness, while anti-Communism, purges, and restrictions on rank and file activism acted negatively to undercut trade unions as crucibles of class consciousness. Yet retentions of the incipient class formation of the 1940s percolated throughout the urban ethnic working-class situation comedies of the 1950s.

Jeannie Carson, the star of *Hey Jeannie,* began her career in show business by singing to Welsh miners as they came out of the pits. Appropriately enough, her U.S. television series adopted a working class locale—the home of Al Murray, a Brooklyn cab driver, and his sister Liz (*TV Guide* 1956:17). The setting imposed certain structural directions on the program's humor—directions that gave voice to sharp class resentments. One episode concerns Al Murray's efforts to hide his cab in a neighbor's garage so that he can take the day off from work to see his beloved Dodgers play baseball at Ebbets Field. Sensing Murray's dereliction of duty, the cab company president delivers a self-righteous harangue about the evils of such behavior to his secretary. Pontificating about the social responsibilities of a taxicab company, "a public utility," he asks his secretary if she knows what happens when one of his cabs is not operating. "No, what?" she inquires. "It cuts into my profits," he responds. (*Hey Jeannie:* "Jeannie The Cabdriver"). Humor based on such hypocrisy by employers has a long history in working-class culture, but it is rarely the subject of mass media comedy. As the episode continues, the boss' secretary (in an act of solidarity) calls Liz and Jeannie to warn them that the boss is out on the streets looking for Al's cab. Jeannie takes the taxi out of the garage to prevent Al's boss from finding it there, but accustomed to driving in her native Scotland, she drives on the left side of the street and gets stopped by a police officer. The policeman discovers that she is an immigrant and lets her off with a warning, remembering his own days as a newly arrived immigrant from Ireland. The resolution of the show finds Jeannie getting to the ballpark in time to get Al back to the cab where his boss finds him and apologizes for even suspecting his employee of misconduct. The episode vibrates with class consciousness, from the many acts of solidarity that get Al off the hook to the final victory over the boss—a victory gained by turning work time into play time, and getting away with it. That kind of collective activity in pursuit of common goals appears frequently in the urban ethnic working-class situation comedies of the 1950s, in incidents ranging from a rent strike by tenants in *The Goldbergs* to community protest against destruction of a favorite neighborhood tree in *Life with Luigi* (*The Goldbergs:* "The Rent Strike"; *Life with Luigi:* "The Power Line").

Even though the workplace rarely appears in television comedies about working-class life, when it does provide a focus for comic or dramatic tensions, it also seethes with class resentments. On one episode of *Mama,* Lars Hansen tells another worker that he prefers working for Mr. Jenkins to working for Mr. Kingsley because "Mr. Jenkins doesn't lose his temper so much." Mr. Kingsley also demands speed-ups from the men and tries to pressure Papa into making the other workers produce at a faster pace (*Mama:* "Mama and the Carpenter"). In this episode, the workplace appears as a place where workers with common interests experience fragmentation. Even after Jake Goldberg graduates from his job as a tailor to become owner of a small dressmaking firm, work prevents him from enjoying life. Business pressures take him away from his family and prevent him from developing recreational interests. When Molly's Uncle David starts playing pool, Jake confides that he never learned to play because "pool is a game that requires leisure." However, his business sense causes him to lean over the table, touch it, and murmur with admiration, "nice quality felt, though" (*The Goldbergs:* "Bad Companions"). Jake's work brings in a bigger financial reward than Al Murray's cab driving or Lars Hansen's carpentry, but it still compels him to trade the precious minutes and hours of his life for commodities that he hardly has time to enjoy. Work as a noble end in itself is almost entirely absent from these shows. No work ethic or pride in labor motivates these workers. In fact, Ed Norton's pride in his job as a sewer worker provides a recurrent comic premise in *The Honeymooners.* The object of work in these programs consists of material reward to enhance one's family status or to obtain some leisure time commodity.

Work not only appears infrequently in 1950s comedies about working-class life, but blue-collar labor often appears as a stigma—a condition that retards the acquisition of desired goods. But even demeaning portrayals of working-class people contain contradictions, allowing for negotiated or oppositional readings. Advertisers and network officials pointed to Chester A. Riley's "magnificent stupidity" as the key to the big ratings garnered by *The Life of Riley,* but that "stupidity" sometimes masked other qualities. At a fancy dinner where the Rileys are clearly out of place, they meet a blue blood named Cecil Spencer Kendrick III. "You mean there's two more of you inside?" Riley asks. The audience laughter at his gaffe comes in part from resentment against the antidemocratic pretensions of Kendrick and his associates (*Life of Riley:* R228). Similarly, when Riley's neighbor, Jim Gillis, tries to impress him with tales about the fancy food at an expensive restaurant, Riley gets Gillis to admit that crepes suzette are nothing more than "pancakes soaked in kerosene and then set on fire" (*Life of Riley:* R228). That sense of the unintentional insight also propels the malaprop-laden humor of Molly Goldberg. Who could dispute her self-sacrificing virtue when Molly vows to save money by getting old furniture: "I don't care how old, even antique furniture would be fine"? She complains that her cousin has been gone for two weeks and that she hasn't seen "hide nor seek of him," and she warns her uncle that she will give him only one word of advice, and that word is "be sure" (*The Goldbergs:* "Is There a Doctor in the House?"; *The Goldbergs:* "Boogie Comes Home"). When Molly says that "patience is a vulture," or that "it never rains until it pours," her misstatements carry wisdom (*The Goldbergs:* "Moving Day"; *The Goldbergs:* "Is There a Doctor in the House?").

Resentments about work, refusals to acknowledge the legitimacy of the upper classes, and creative word play abound in these programs, transmitting the texture of decades of working-class experience. Similarly, comedy about fraternal orders and ethnics lodges appear in television shows of the 1950s as a reflection of real historical experience. In history, fraternal orders and mutual aid societies comprised essential resources for working-class immigrants, often providing insurance, burial expenses, recreational facilities, and adult education at a time when the state accepted none of those responsibilities. In the urban ethnic working-class situation comedies of the early 1950s, the fraternal lodge appears as an archaic and anachronistic institution, a remnant of the past at odds with the needs of the family. Lars Hansen brings home officials of the Sons of Norway for dinner, thereby creating more work for Mama.[5] Chester A. Riley wastes his time and money on the Brooklyn Patriots of Los Angeles, an organization set up to revere the world he left behind when he moved his family west. The Mystic Knights of the Sea provide Kingfish with a theater of operations for bilking his "brothers" out of their money, and for indulging his inflated sense of self-importance. The Royal Order of Raccoons keep Ralph Kramden from spending time with Alice, and they divert his paycheck away from the family budget toward lodge dues. In one show Alice asks Ralph what benefit she derives from his lodge activities. He proudly informs her that his membership entitles both of them to free burial in the Raccoon National Cemetery in Bismark, North Dakota. With appropriate sarcasm, Alice replies that the prospect of burial in North Dakota makes her wonder why she should go on living (*The Honeymooners:* "The Loud Speaker").

In organic popular memory, lodges retained legitimacy as sources of mutuality and friendship. But in an age when suburban tract housing replaced the ethnic neighborhood, when the state took on welfare functions previously carried out by voluntary associations, and when the home sphere became increasingly isolated from the community around it, the lodge hall became a premise for comic ridicule. In television programs, the interests of the family took precedence over those of the fraternal lodge, and a binary opposition between the two seemed inevitable. Yet the very inclusion of lodges in these programs demonstrates the power of the past in the discourse of the present. Television programs validated the atomized nuclear family at the expense of the extended kinship and class relations manifested in the fraternal order. When successful, these shows undercut the ability of the past to provide legitimacy for contemporary social relations. When unsuccessful, these shows called attention to the possibility of other forms of community and culture than those that dominated the present.

Cultural specificity about working-class life provided credibility for early network television programs, but at the same time created problems for advertisers. Erik Barnouw points out that sponsors hardly relished the prospect of shows situated in lower-class environments—like the enormously successful teleplay, *Marty*—because "Sponsors were meanwhile trying to 'upgrade' the consumer and persuade him to 'move up to a Chrysler,' and 'live better electrically' in a suburban home, with help from 'a friend at Chase Manhattan.' The sponsors preferred beautiful people in mouth-watering decor to convey what it meant to climb the socioeconomic ladder. The commercials looked out of place in Bronx settings" (Barnouw 1979:106). When advertisers coasted on the borrowed legitimacy of working-class history to lend sincerity and authenticity to their appeals to buy coffee and soap, they also ran the risk of exposing contradictions between the past and present. Author Kathryn Forbes, who wrote the book on which *Mama* was based, complained that the television Hansen family had too much wealth to present accurately the circumstances she had written about. Forbes's book portrays the Hansen family with four children in a house shared with relatives and boarders; on television they have three children in a house to themselves. In the Forbes book, Mama represents a traditional mother raising independent daughters—using her traditional cooking skills to make social connections that allow Katrin to pursue an untraditional career as a writer. On television, tradition reigns as Mama instructs Katrin about cooking to help her land a husband, and Katrin becomes a secretary rather than a writer. Other shows made similar adaptations to the ideological norms of the 1950s. On radio and for most of their years on television, the Goldbergs lived in a multifamily Bronx dwelling where neighbors and relatives blended together to form an extended community. By the time the television show reached it last year of production in 1955–56, the Goldbergs moved to a suburban house in a Long Island subdivision where physical and emotional distances constituted the norm. The radio version of *Amos 'n Andy* began to neglect the solid family man and independent businessman Amos as early as the 1940s; but the television show which began in 1951 pushed Amos even farther into the background in order to zero in on the marital problems and home life of the shiftless and irresponsible Kingfish. In each of these shows, television versions tended to accentuate the dilemmas of atomized nuclear families and to downplay the dramas emanating from extended class and ethnic associations.

The working class depicted in urban ethnic working-class situation comedies of the 1950s bore only a superficial resemblance to the historical American working class. Stripped of essential elements of ethnic and class identity, interpreted through perspectives most relevant to a consumer middle class, and pictured in isolation from the social connections that gave purpose and meaning to working-class lives, the televised working-class family summoned up only the vaguest contours of its historical counterpart. Even in comparison to depictions of class in other forms of communication, like folklore, theater, music, literature, or radio, television presented a dessicated and eviscerated version of working-class life. Yet the legitimizing functions served by locating programs in working-class environments caused some attempts at authenticity that brought sedimented class tensions to the surface. While the producers of these television shows hardly intended to direct viewers' attentions toward real ethnic and class conflicts, the social location of the writers and actors most knowledgeable about working-class life served to make some of these programs focal points for social issues. When producers took on working-class settings as a form of local color, they burdened themselves with the contradictions of the communities that provided the color, as evidenced by public controversies over *The Goldbergs* and *Amos 'n Andy.*

Part of the convincing authenticity of *the Goldbergs* came from actors and writers who developed their skills within the Yiddish theater and the culture that supported it. An organic part of that culture included political activists, including Communists, socialists, and antifascists whose concerns found expression in a variety of community activities including theater. Philip Loeb, who played Jake Goldberg, became the center of controversy when an anti-Communist right-wing publication accused him of subversive connections arising from his appearance at antifascists rallies and his having signed a petition calling for the admission of Negroes into professional baseball. Nervous sponsors and advertising representatives, afraid of threatened boycotts by the anti-Communists, dropped their support of the show and demanded that its producer and star, Gertrude Berg, fire Loeb. At first she refused, pointing out that Loeb had never been a Communist, but ultimately Berg gave in to the pressure and fired her co-star in order to keep her show on the air. Sponsors resumed their support after Loeb left the program in 1952, and *The Goldbergs* ran for four more years. Loeb received a $45,000 settlement in exchange for dropping any legal actions against the show, but he never worked again as an actor because producers viewed him as "controversial." In 1956, Loeb committed suicide (Barnouw 1982: 126; Jezer 1982:193–194; Kanfer 1973:154; *New Republic* 1952A:8, 1952B:22). Similarly, Mady Christians played Mama in the Broadway play *I Remember Mama,* but could not play that role on television; anti-Communist pressure groups questioned her loyalty because she had worked on behalf of refugees from fascism in the 1930s and 1940s with individuals accused of subversion. Blacklisted from her profession, Christians sank into a severe depression that friends felt sapped her strength and made her unable to overcome health problems that led to her death in 1951. Loeb and Christians dismayed advertisers, not because of their political views, but because their presence provoked political controversy and interfered with the illusions created by their programs of a world without politics. Like the real Goldbergs and Hansens in American history, Philip Loeb and Mady Christians lived in a world where ethnicity connected them to complicated political issues. The controversy over their views and the public attention directed toward them threatened to unmask the world of *Mama* and *The Goldbergs* as a created artifact—depriving it of legitimating power.

Amos 'n Andy contained similar, but more culturally explosive, connections. Stereotyped and demeaning portrayals of black people have long constituted an obsessive theme in American theater, and for that matter, in American life. Historian Nathan Irvin Huggins points out that the minstrel show stereotypes enabled white society at the turn of the 20th century to attribute to black people the characteristics that it feared most in itself. At a time when industrialization demanded a revolutionary transformation in behavior that compelled Americans to accept Victorian standards about thrift, sobriety, abstinence, and restraint, the minstrel show emerged to present laziness, greed, gluttony, and licentiousness as traits singularly associated with black people. These images worked to legitimate the emerging Victorian code by associating opposition to the dominant ideology with the despised culture of Afro-Americans. The minstrel show "Negro" presented white society with a representation of the natural self at odds with the normative self of industrial culture. Uninhibited behavior could be savored by the ego during the minstrel performance, but overruled afterwards by the superego. The viewer could release tension by pointing to the minstrel show "darkie" and saying "It's him, not me." But the viewer came back, again and again. The desire to subjugate and degrade black people had political and economic imperatives of its own, but emotional and psychic reinforcement for that exploitation came from the ways in which racist stereotypes enabled whites to accept the suppression of their natural selves.

The centrality of racist images to white culture presented peculiar problems for Afro-Americans. Entry into white society meant entry into its values, and those values included hatred of blacks. In order to participate in the white world, blacks had to make concessions to white America's fantasy images. As Huggins notes, black people found it dangerous to step out of character, either on or off stage. The great black vaudeville entertainer Bert Williams demonstrated the absurd contradictions of this process; he donned blackface makeup to perform on stage—a black man imitating white men imitating black men. Williams's artistic genius and stubborn self-respect led him to inject subtle elements of social criticism into his act, but for most spectators, he merely reinforced their a priori conclusions about the stage Negro (Huggins 1978).

The black cast of *Amos 'n Andy* came out of the theatrical traditions that spawned Williams, and they perpetuated many of his contradictions. As a successful radio program, the all-black world of *Amos n' Andy* had been performed mostly by its white creators (Freeman Gosden and Charles Correll). With the move to television, Gosden and Correll hired an all-black cast, but they nonetheless faced protests from community groups. The National Association for the Advancement of Colored People and black actor James Edwards campaigned to have the program taken off the air because they felt that it made the only televised presentation of Afro-American life an insulting one. The NAACP complained in federal court that black citizens routinely suffered abuse from whites addressing them as "Amos" or "Andy," and that the program defamed black professionals by presenting them as liars and cheats. In response, black actors employed on the program and a few black intellectuals defended *Amos 'n Andy* as a harmless satire and an important vehicle for bringing much needed exposure to black actors (Cripps 1983; Macdonald 1983:27–28; *Newsweek* 1951:56).

Placed in historical context, *Amos 'n Andy* did for the values of the 1950s what the minstrel show accomplished for previous generations. Everything considered precious but contested in white society—like the family or the work ethic—became violated in the world of Kingfish. Ambition and upward mobility drew ridicule when pursued by blacks. In a society nurtured on Horatio Alger stories about rising from rags to riches, this lampooning of a black man's aspirations could function to release tensions about the fear of failure. It could redirect hostility away from the elite toward those on the bottom of society. When Kingfish pretends to be educated and uses grandiose language, the audience can howl derisively at his pretensions, but the same audience could glow with warm recognition when Mama Hansen uses her broken English to express her dreams for her son to grow up to be president. Ambition viewed as worthy and realistic for the Hansens becomes a symbol of weak character on the part of the Kingfish.

Consistent with the values of the 1950s as mediated through popular culture, family responsibilities—or neglect of them—define Kingfish even more than does his work. The glorification of motherhood pervading psychological and popular literature of the 1950s becomes comedy in *Amos 'n Andy*. Wives named for precious stones (Ruby and Sapphire) appear anything but precious, and "Mama" in this show appears as a nagging harpy screaming at the cowering— and emasculated—black man. Kingfish shares Ralph Kramden's dreams of overnight success, but his transgressions against bourgeois morality are more serious. Kingfish has no job, his late night revelries and lascivious grins hint at marital infidelity, and he resorts to criminal behavior to avoid what he calls "the horrors of employment."[6] He betrays his family and cheats his lodge brothers (and by implication the "brothers" of his race) with no remorse. But his most serious flaws stem from his neglect of the proper roles of husband and father. In one episode, Kingfish's late night excursions cause his wife, Sapphire, to leave home and live with her mother. Kingfish misses her and orders one of his lackeys to find out where she has gone. When the report comes back that Sapphire has been seen entering an obstetrician's office, Kingfish assumes that he is about to become a father. In reality, Sapphire has simply taken a job as the doctor's receptionist, but the misunderstanding leads Kingfish to tell Amos how much fun he plans to have as a father. When Amos warns him that fatherhood involves serious responsibilities, Kingfish replies, "What you mean serious? All you gotta do is keep 'em filled up wid milk an' pablum and keep chuckin' em under de chin" (*Amos 'n Andy:* "Kingfish Has a Baby"). Kingfish's ignorance plays out the worst fears of people in a society with a burgeoning obsession with family. By representing the possibility of incompetent parenting, Kingfish provides the audience with a sense of superiority, but one that can be maintained only by embracing parental responsibilities. Lest we miss the point of the show, when Kingfish and his friend Andy go to a clinic for prospective fathers, where they learn to bathe a baby by practicing with a doll, Kingfish lets his slip under the water and "drown" (*Amos 'n Andy:* "Kingfish Has a Baby").

Black protest made *Amos 'n Andy* a much debated phenomenon, unmasking the calculation that went into its creation. In the context of the 1950s, when migration to industrial cities created greater concentrations of black political and economic power, these protests could not be dismissed casually by advertisers or the networks. Blatz Beer decided to drop its sponsorship of *Amos 'n Andy* in 1954, knocking the show off prime time schedules and into syndication until 1966, when another wave of protests made it untenable even in reruns. As the program most thoroughly grounded in ideologically charged historical material, *Amos 'n Andy* lent itself most easily to critical historical interpretation and action, a capacity at odds with the interests of advertisers. But like shows rooted in white working-class histories, structural contradictions in black working-class life also held open the possibility for oppositional readings of the program's content. Black activist and author Julius Lester recalls his own formative experiences with *Amos 'n Andy* in his autobiography in a way that provides the quintessential act of reinterpreting hierarchically prepared and distributed mass culture. Ruminating on the seeming paradox of a home life that installed black pride into him but that also encouraged him to listen to the antics of the Kingfish, Lester recalls that

> In the character of Kingfish, the creators of Amos and Andy may have thought they were ridiculing blacks as lazy, shiftless, scheming and conniving, but to us Kingfish was a paradigm of virtue, an alternative to the work ethic. Kingfish lived: Amos made a living. It did not matter that my parents lived by and indoctrinated me with the Puritan work ethic, Kingfish had a *joie de vivre*

no white person could poison, and we knew that whites ridiculed us because they were incapable of such elan, I was proud to belong to the same race as Kingfish. [1976:14]

Whether through the careful decoding exemplified by Julius Lester, or through the politicization of *Amos 'n Andy* by mass protest, audience response to the program in some cases focused on the show's artifice and distortions of history. As was the case with *The Goldbergs,* the traditions needed to provide legitimacy for advertising messages surrounding *Amos 'n Andy* contained sedimented contestation that undermined their effectiveness, and instead provoked negotiated or oppositional readings. Dominant ideology triumphed on television in the 1950s, just as it did in political life, but historically grounded opposition remained possible and necessary for at least part of the audience.

The realism that made urban ethnic working-class situation comedies convincing conduits for consumer ideology also compelled them to present alienations and aspirations subversive to the legitimacy of consumer capitalism. As Antonio Gramsci insists, ideological hegemony stems from the ability of those in power to make their own interests appear to be synonymous with the interests of society at large. But appeals for legitimacy always take place within concrete historical circumstances, in contested societies with competing interests. In a consumer capitalist economy where unmet needs and individual isolation provide the impetus for commodity desires, legitimation is always incomplete. Even while establishing dominance, those in power must borrow from the ideas, actions, and experiences of the past, all of which contain a potential for informing a radical critique of the present.

DIALOGUE, NEGOTIATION, AND LEGITIMATION: METHOD AND THEORY

Recent scholarship in literary criticism, cultural studies, and sociology offers investigative methods and theoretical frameworks essential to understanding the historical dialogue about family, class, and ethnicity in early network television. The literary criticism of and "dialogic imagination" proposed by Mikhail Bahktin demonstrates how all texts inherit part of the historical consciousness of their authors and audiences (Newcomb 1984:37–41). Cultural studies theorist Stuart Hall notes that commercial mass media seek legitimacy with the audiences by effectively representing diverse aspects of social life, including memories of past experiences, current contradictions, and potential sources of division and opposition (Hall 1979). Sociologist Jürgen Habermas observes that contemporary capitalist culture destroys the very motivations that it needs to function effectively, such as the work ethic or the willingness to defer gratification. Consequently, capitalist societies draw upon the borrowed legitimacy of cultural values and beliefs from the past, like religion or the patriarchal family, in order to provide the appearance of moral grounding for contemporary forces inimical to the interests of tradition (Habermas 1975). Taken collectively, these approaches to culture provide a useful context for understanding the persistence of seemingly outdated and dysfunctional elements in early network television.

Bakhtin's analysis of text construction argues that communication does not begin in the present with a speaker or story; but rather that both speech and narrative come from a social matrix that is, at least in part, historical. Each speaker enters a dialogue already in progress; every work of art contains within it past, present, and future struggles over culture and power. Terms and forms of communication from the past not only make current discourse comprehensible and legitimate, but they also imbed within the present a collective historical experience rich with contradictions. The producers of early network television worked in a new medium, but they addressed an audience acclimated to specific forms of comedy and drama that reflected, however indirectly, the real texture of past struggles and present hopes.[7]

Structural unities underlie the seemingly divergent stories of different ethnic, working-class situation comedies. Viewers rarely saw Ralph Kramden's bus or Jake Goldberg's dressmaking shop, but the cameras introduced them to every detail of furnishing in the Kramden and Goldberg households. Difficulties encountered in the aircraft factory assembly line by Chester A. Riley or at the construction site by Lars Hansen paled in significance in contrast to the dilemmas of consumption faced in the Riley and Hansen families. The texture and tone of *Life with Luigi* and *Amos 'n Andy* came from the ethnic worlds they depicted, but the plots of those shows dealt with the aspirations of individuals as if ethnic rivalries and discrimination did not exist. Instead, ethnics attain a false unity through consumption of commodities: Jeannie MacClennan learns to "be an American" by dressing fashionably and wearing the right makeup; Luigi Basco hopes to prove himself a worthy candidate for citizenship by opening a checking account and purchasing an insurance policy; Molly Goldberg overcomes her fears of installment buying and vows to live above her means—which she describes as "the American way" (*Hey Jeannie:* "The Rock and Roll Kid"; *Life with Luigi:* "The Insurance Policy"; *The Goldbergs:* "The In-laws"). Comedies in this subgenre are clearly cases where, as Stuart Hall points out, the commercial mass media tend to direct popular consciousness toward consumption and away from production. They present social actions and experiences as atomized individual events in order to fragment groups into isolated consumers, and they resolve the tensions confronting their audiences by binding them together in false unities and collectivities defined for the convenience of capital accumulation (Hall 1979).

But Hall also shows that the imperial aspirations of the mass media, their imperative to attract as large an audience as possible, lead to a disclosure of contradictions that allows cultural consumers to fashion oppositional or negotiated readings of mass culture. In order to make their dramas compelling and their narrative resolutions dynamic, the media also reflect the plurality of consumer experiences. A system that seeks to enlist everyone in the role of consumer must appear to be addressing all possible circumstances: a system that proclaims consensus and unanimity must acknowledge and explain obvious differences within the polity, if for no other reason than to co-opt or trivialize potential opposition. Television and other forms of commercial electronic media so effectively recapitulate the ideology of the "historical bloc" in which they operate that they touch on all aspects of social life—even its antagonistic contradictions (Hall 1979). While the media serve to displace, fragment, and atomize real experiences, they also generate and circulate a critical dialogue as an unintended consequence of their efforts to expose the inventory of social practice.

Of course, mere disclosure of opposition does not guarantee emancipatory practice: ruling elites routinely call attention to "deviant" subcultures in order to draw a clear distinction between permitted and forbidden behavior. In urban ethnic working-class situation comedies in the 1950s, "deviant" traits—like Kingfish's aversion to work in *Amos 'n Andy* and Lars Hansen's lack of ambition in *Mama*—taught object lessons about the perils of unconventional behavior. Yet the operative premises and enduring tensions of each of these shows revolved around the "otherness" of the lead characters. The "old-world" attitudes of newly arrived immigrants in *Hey Jeannie* and *Life with Luigi* or the proletarian cultural innocence manifested in *The Life of Riley* or *The Honeymooners* led to comedic clashes that exposed the inadequacies and deficiencies of those on the margins of society. But at the same time, these clashes counterposed the conformity and materialism of the mainstream to the narratively privileged moral superiority of those with connections to the past. Traditional values and beliefs prevented protagonists in these shows from achieving success and happiness as defined by society, but those values and beliefs also facilitated a critical distance from the false premises of the present. As Gertrude Berg noted in explaining the popularity of her character Molly Goldberg, Molly "lived in the world of today but kept many of the values of yesterday" (Berg 1961:167).

The narrative sequence that framed every episode of *Mama* demonstrates the centrality of this dialogue between the past and present in early network television programs. As soon as Katrin Hansen introduced the show with the words "I remember Mama," a male narrator announced, "Yes, here's Mama, brought to you by Maxwell House Coffee." The camera then panned away from the photograph album to show Mama (played by Peggy Wood) making coffee for the Hansen family in their turn-of-the-century kitchen. The authority of the male narrator's voice established a connection between the continuity of family experience and the sponsor's product, between warm memories of the past and Mama in the kitchen making coffee. In this progression, the product becomes a member of the Hansen family, while tradition and emotional support become commodities to be secured through the purchase of Maxwell House coffee. The sponsor's introduction announced ownership of the television show, but it also laid claim to the moral authority and warmth generated by the concept of motherhood itself.[8]

Katrin Hansen's retrospective narrative and the pictures from the family album reassured viewers by depicting events that had already happened in the emotionally secure confines of the audience's collective childhood. This false authenticity encouraged viewers to think of the program as the kind of history that might be created in their own homes. A CBS press release during the program's first broadcast season proclaimed, "On 'Mama' we try to give the impression that nobody is acting," and went on to claim success for that effort, quoting an unnamed viewer's contention that the show depicted a real family because "nobody but members of a real family could talk like that" (Nelson 1949). Free from the real history of ethnic, class, and gender experience, the history presented on *Mama* located its action within the personal spheres of family and consumer choices. Within these areas, realism could be put to the service of commodity purchases, as when the narrator followed his opening introduction with a discourse about how Mama in her day "had none of the conveniences of today's modern products" like Minute Rice, Jello, or instant coffee (*Mama:* "T. R.'s New Home"). Thus the morally sanctioned traditions of hearth and home could be put to the service of products that revolutionized those very traditions—all in keeping with Ernest Dichter's advice to his fellow advertising executives: "Do not assert that the new product breaks with traditional values, but on the contrary, that is fulfills its traditional functions better than any of its predecessors" (Dichter 1960:209).

Every episode of *Mama* began and ended with Mama making coffee in the kitchen—but to very different effect. The opening sequence, with the announcer's statement about Maxwell House coffee, validates commodities; the ending sequence, however, validates both moralities and commodities. There Katrin, in the kitchen or as a voice-over, summarizes the meaning of that week's story for the audience by relating the lesson that she learned from it. Invariably these lessons belonged to the sphere of old-fashioned values, elevating human creations over commodities and privileging commitment to others over concern with self. In these lessons, the audience discovered that the toys Papa made with his hands meant more to the children than the fancy ones they saw in stores, or that loyalty to family and friends brought more rewards than upward mobility. These resolutions often directly contradicted the narratives that preceded them: after twenty-five minutes of struggle for happiness through commodity acquisition, the characters engaged in a one-minute homily about the superiority of moral goals over material ones. Then, with the high moral ground established, a voice-over by the announcer reminded viewers of the wonderful products that the sponsor of *Mama* had to offer.

The complicated dialogue in the opening and closing segments of *Mama* illumines the complex role played by historical referents in early network television. The past that brought credibility and reassurance to family dramas also contained the potential for undermining the commodified social relations of the present. The Hansen family interested advertisers because audiences identified their story as part of a precious collective memory resonating with the actual experiences and lessons of the past. The Hansens could not be credible representatives of that past if they appeared to live among the plethora of consumer goods that dominated the commercials, or if they appeared uncritical of the consumer world of the present that made such a sharp break with the values of the past. Yet the Hansen family had little value to advertisers unless their experiences sanctioned pursuit of commodities in the present. The creators of the program—like those engaged in production of the other urban ethnic working-class comedies on television—resolved this potential contradiction by putting the borrowed moral capital of the past at the service of the values of the present. They acknowledged the critique of materialism and upward mobility sedimented within the experiences of working-class families, but they demonstrated over and over again how wise choices enabled consumers to have both moral and material rewards. By positing the nuclear family as a transhistorical "natural" locus for the arbitration of consumer desires, television portrayed the value crises of the 1950s as eternal and recurrent. By collapsing the distinction between family as consumer unit and family as part of neighborhood, ethnic, and class networks, television programs in the early 1950s connected the most personal and intimate needs of individuals to commodity purchases. They implied that the past sanctioned rather than contradicted the ever-increasing orientation toward shopping as the cornerstone of social life, an orientation that characterized media discourse in the postwar era.

The reliance on the past to sanction controversial changes in present behavior forms the core of Jürgen Habermas's analysis of contemporary capitalism's "legitimation crisis." According to Habermas, the consumer consciousness required by modern capitalism revolves around "civil and familial-vocational privatism"—a syndrome that elevates private consumer decisions over social relations and public responsibility (Habermas 1975:71–75). Individuals see families as centers of consumption and leisure, while they regard employment as primarily a means of engaging in status competition. Instead of the rooted independence demanded by traditional family and community life, contemporary capitalist society encourages an atomized dependence on outside authorities—advertisers, self-help experts, and psychiatric, educational, and political authorities. Clearly useful for purposes of capital accumulation, this process undermines traditional motivations for work, patriotism, and personal relations, causing real crises in social relations. In addition, the infantile narcissism nurtured by this consumer consciousness encourages a search for validation from outside authorities—for communication which assures people that the impoverishment of work, family, and public life characteristic of late capitalism constitutes a legitimate and necessary part of progress toward a better life as defined by opportunities for more acquisition and more status.

For Habermas, the mass media play a crucial role in legitimation, but they do so imperfectly. The new forms of family and vocational consciousness cannot be justified on their own, but can be validated by invoking the moral authority of past forms of family and work identity. Thus the "work ethic" is summoned to justify a system based on commodified leisure, while mutual love and affection are called on to sanction families that exist primarily as consumer units. The social relations of the past are used to legitimate a system that in reality works to destroy the world that created those relations in the first place. Consequently, the invocation of the past in the service of the present is a precarious undertaking. Tradition used to legitimate untraditional behavior may instead call attention to the disparity between the past and the present; collective popular memory may see the manipulative use of tradition by advertisers as a conscious strategy, as an attempt to create artifacts that conflict with actual memory and experiences. As Habermas cautions, "traditions can retain legitimizing force only as long as they are not torn out of interpretive systems that guarantee continuity and identity" (Habermas 1975:71).

Habermas provides us with a framework capable of explaining both the presence of historical elements in early network television shows and their limitations. In conjunction with Bakhtin's emphasis on dialogue and Hall's delineation of negotiation, Habermas's analysis explains how portrayals of traditional, ethnic, working-class families might have been essential for legitimizing social forces that undermined the very values that made those families respected icons in popular consciousness. At the same time, Habermas directs our attention to the fundamental instability of this legitimation process, to the ways in which audiences might come to see manipulative uses of the past as prepared and created artifacts at war with the lessons of history as preserved in collective popular memory.

After 1958, network television eliminated urban ethnic working-class programs from the schedule. Marc Daniels, who directed *The Goldbergs,* recalls that a changing society less tied to class and ethnicity demanded different kinds of entertainment, and certainly the emergence of ethnically neutral, middle-class situation comedies between 1958 and 1970 lends credence to that view (Daniels 1984). The entry of major film studios into television production in the mid 1950s also had an impact, since the working-class shows tended to be produced by small companies like Hal Roach Studios. Major studio involvement in television production increased the proportion of action/adventure shows with production values ill-suited to the realism of urban ethnic working-class programs. In action and adventure shows, no embarassing retentions of class consciousness compromised the sponsors' messages, and no social associations with ethnic life brought up disturbing issues that made them susceptible to protests and boycotts.

One might conclude that television and American society had no need for urban ethnic working-class programs after 1958 because tensions between consumerist pressures and historical memories had been resolved. But the reappearance of race, class, and ethnicity in the situation comedies of the 1970s like *All in the Family, Chico and the Man,* and *Sanford and Son* testifies to the ongoing relevance of such tensions as existed in the 1950s to subsequent mass media dialogue. The programs of the 1970s reprised both aspects of the 1950s shows—legitimation through representation of the texture of working-class life, and commodification of all human relationships, especially within families. Like their predecessors, urban ethnic working-class shows of the 1970s mixed their commercial and consumerist messages with visions of connection to others that transcended the limits of civil and familial vocational privatism. They held open possibilities for transcending the parochialisms of traditional ethnicity and for challenging the patriarchal assumptions of both extended and nuclear families. The same communications apparatus that presented consumerism as the heir to the moral legacy of the working-class past also legitimized aspirations for happiness and community too grand to be satisfied by the lame realities of the commodity-centered world.[9]

In the early 1950s, an advertising instrument under the control of powerful monopolists established itself as the central discursive medium in American culture. With its penetration of the family and its incessant propaganda for commodity purchases, television helped erode the social base for challenges to authority manifest in the mass political activity among American workers in the

1940s. Yet television did not so much insure the supremacy of new values as it transformed the terms of social contestation. As mass culture gained in importance as an instrument of legitimation, oppositional messages filtered into even hierarchically controlled media constructions like network television programs. The internal contradictions of capitalism fueled this process by generating anxieties in need of legitimation, and by turning for legitimation to the very beliefs and practices most threatened by emerging social relations. Thus every victory for the ideology of civil and familial vocational privatism can also constitute a defeat. Every search for legitimacy can end in the dilution of legitimacy by unmasking media messages as prepared and fabricated ideological artifices. Even successful legitimation fails to a degree because the new social relations destroy their own source of legitimacy.

This is not to assume that the final outcome of television's ideological imperatives must be emancipatory. Inculcation of narcissistic desire coupled with destruction of traditional sources of moral restraint might well suit the needs of capital and produce a population eager for fascist authority. But structural conditions exist for an alternative future. As Joel Kovel argues, "The point is not that people desire the administrative mode, it is rather that administration protects them against the desires they can not stand, while it serves out, in the form of diluted rationalization, a hint of the desire and power lost to them" (Kovel 1978:19). The separation of individuals from political and community life, combined with the destruction of cultural traditions that previously gave direction and purpose to individuals, might make status competition and "possession" of a secure family role all that much more attractive. Certainly the neo-conservatism of the 1980s seems to hinge upon "protecting" the family from the increasing barbarism of society, and upon shifting the blame for the social disintegration caused by civil and familial vocational privatism onto the opposition movements formed to combat it.[10] But the sleight of hand inherent in the neo-conservative position allows for other possibilities. Reconnection to history and to motivational structures rooted within it is both desirable and possible. More than ever before, communication and criticism can help determine whether people accept the commodity-mediated desires that turn others into instruments and objects, or whether they build affirmative communities in dialogue with the needs and desires of others. By identifying the historical reality behind the construction of television texts in the early 1950s, we demystify their "organic" character and reveal their implications as created artifacts. We uncover sedimented critiques from the past and potential forms of opposition for the present.

The historical specificity of early network television programs led their creators into dangerous ideological terrain. By examining them as part of our own history, we learn about both the world we have lost and the one we have yet to gain. Fredric Jameson claims that "history is what hurts, what sets inexorable limits to individual as well as collective praxis" (Jameson 1981:102). But the unfinished dialogue of history can also be what helps, what takes us back into the past in order to break its hold on the present. By addressing the hurt, and finding out how it came to be, we begin to grasp ways of understanding the past, and ending the pain.

NOTES

Acknowledgments: I wish to thank Nick Browne, Gary Burns, Robert Deming, Tom Dumm, Michael Fischer, Jib Fowles, Mary Beth Haralovich, Susan Hartmann, Connie Labelle, Elizabeth Long, Barbara Tomlinson, and Brian Winston for their comments and criticisms on previous drafts of this article.

1. Stuart Ewen condemns these shows as hostile to immigrant life and imposing consumerism on it in his *Captains of Consciousness* (1976:208–210). Marty Jezer takes a more favorable view in *The Dark Ages* (1982:191–194).

2. Of course, class, ethnicity, and race remained important, but their relationship to individual identity changed radically at this time. The bureaucratization of trade unions and xenophobic anti-Communism also contributed to declines in ethnic and class consciousness.

3. See the discussion in this article of *Mama, The Goldbergs,* and *Amos 'n Andy.*

4. Neilsen ratings demonstrate television's view of the family as separate market segments to be addressed independently. For an analysis of the industry's view of children as a special market, see Patricia J. Bence (1985), "Analysis and History of Typology and Forms of Children's Network Programming from 1950 to 1980."

5. The *Mama* show relied on the Bay Ridge, Brooklyn chapter of the Sons of Norway for advice on authentic Norwegian folk customs and stories, according to Dick Van Patten and Ralph Nelson, in remarks made at the Museum of Broadcasting, New York City, on December 17, 1985.

6. The depiction of Kingfish's refusal to work had especially vicious connotations in an era where the crisis in black unemployment reached unprecedented depths.

7. For a discussion of the role of media borrowing from earlier forms see Daniel Czitrom (1983).

8. This is not to single out *Mama* as an especially commercial program. In fact, its advertisers allowed the show to run with no middle commercial, using only the opening and closing commercial sequences. Yet other shows incorporated commercial messages into dramatic program-like segments, especially *The Goldbergs* and *Life with Luigi.*

9. For an excellent discussion of 1970s television see the forthcoming book by Ella Taylor, *All in the Work-Family.*

10. Protection of the family represents an old social theme for conservatives and a traditional device for creating dramatic tension. But never before have they been as thoroughly unified as dramatic and political themes and never before have they dominated conservative thought as they have in the last decade.

WORKS CITED

Allen, Jeanne.

   1983. "The Social Matrix of Television: Invention in the United States." In *Regarding Television*. E. Ann Kaplan, ed. Pp. 109–119. Los Angeles: University Publications of America.

Allen, Robert

   1985. Speaking of Soap Operas. Chapel Hill: University of North Carolina Press.

Amos 'n Andy

   1951. Kingfish Has a Baby. Theater Art Library. University of California, Los Angeles.

   1953. Andy, The Godfather. Academy of Television Arts Collection. T 15645. University of California, Los Angeles.

Aronowitz, Stanley

1983. Working Class Hero. New York: Pilgrim.

Barnouw, Erik

1979. The Sponsor. New York: Oxford University Press.

1982. Tube of Plenty. New York: Oxford University Press.

Bence, Patricia J.

1985. Analysis and History of Typology and Forms of Children's Network Programming from 1950 to 1980. Paper presented at the Society for Cinema Studies Meetings. New York City. June 12.

Berg, Gertrude

1961. Molly and Me. New York: McGraw Hill.

Berger, Henry

1982. Social Protest in St. Louis. Paper presented at a Committee for the Humanities Forum. St. Louis, Missouri. March 12.

Boddy, William

1985. The Studios Move into Prime Time: Hollywood and the Television Industry in the 1950s. Cinema Journal 12(4):23–37.

Boorstin, Daniel

1973. The Americans: The Democratic Experience. New York: Vintage Press.

Chodorow, Nancy

1978. Reproduction of Mothering. Berkeley: University of California Press.

Cripps, Thomas

1983. The Amos 'n Andy Controversy. *In* American History and American Television. John O'Connor, ed. Pp. 33–54. New York: Ungar.

Czitrom, Daniel

1983. Media and the American Mind. Chapel Hill: University of North Carolina Press.

Daniels, Marc

1984. Presentation at the Director's Guild of America. July 11. Los Angeles, California.

de Cordova, Richard

1985. The Transition from Radio to Television. Unpublished paper presented at the Society for Cinema Studies Meetings. June 12. New York.

Dichter, Ernest

1960. The Strategy of Desire. Garden City: Doubleday.

Ewen, Stuart

1976. Captains of Consciousness: Advertising and the Social Roots of the Consumer Culture. New York: McGraw Hill Book Company.

Goldbergs, The

1949. The Rent Strike. Museum of Broadcasting. New York.

1955. Moving Day. Academy of Television Arts Collection. 35F341. University of California, Los Angeles.

1955. The In-Laws. Academy of Television Arts Collection. F3218. University of California, Los Angeles.

1955. Bad Companions. Academy of Television Arts Collection. F3219 University of California, Lost Angeles.

1955. Boogie Comes Home. Academy of Television Arts Collection. F3220. University of California, Los Angeles.

1955. Die Fledermaus. Academy of Television Arts Collection. F3222. University of California, Los Angeles.

1955. Is There a Doctor in the House? Academy of Television Arts Collection. F3225. University of California, Los Angeles.

Habermas, Jürgen

1975. Legitimation Crisis. Boston: Beacon Press.

Hall, Stuart

1979. Culture, The Media and the "Ideological Effect." *In* Mass Communication and Society. James Curran, Michael Gurevitch, and Janet Woollacott, eds. Beverly Hills: Sage Publications.

Hartmann, Susan

1982. The Home Front and Beyond. Boston: Twayne.

Hey Jeannie

1956. The Rock and Roll Kid. Academy of Television Arts Collection. University of California, Los Angeles.

1956. Jeannie the Cab Driver. Academy of Television Arts Collection. University of California, Los Angeles.

Honeymooners, The

1956. The Loud Speaker. Academy of Television Arts Collection. VT451. University of California, Los Angeles.

Huggins, Nathan

1978. Harlem Renaissance. New York: Oxford University Press.

Jameson, Frederic

1981. The Political Unconscious: Narrative as a Socially Symbolic Act. Ithaca: Cornell University Press.

Jezer, Marty

1982. The Dark Ages. Boston: South End.

Kanfer, Stefan

1973. A Journal of the Plague Years. New York: Atheneum Books.

Kovel, Joel

1978. Rationalization and the Family. Telos 37:5–21.

Ladies Home Journal

1956. September. Pp. 130–131.

Lester, Julius

1976. All is Well. New York: W. Morrow.

Life of Riley

1953. Academy of Television Arts Collection. R228. University of California, Los Angeles.

Life with Luigi

1952. The Insurance Policy. Script 2. Norman Tokar Papers. Special Collections Room. Doheny Library. University of Southern California, Los Angeles, California.

1952. The Power Line. Script 10. Norman Tokar Papers. Special Collections Room. Doheny Library. University of Southern California, Los Angeles, California.

Lipsitz, George

1981. Class and Culture in Cold War America: A Rainbow at Midnight. New York: Praeger.

Macdonald, J. Fred

1983. Blacks and White TV. Chicago: Nelson Hall.

Mama

1953. Mama and the Carpenter. Academy of Television Arts Collection. VT517. University of California, Los Angeles.

Meehan, Elizabeth and Bradford Ropes

1954. Mama's Birthday. Theater Arts Collection. University Research Library. University of California, Los Angeles.

Mitz, Rick

1983. The Great TV Sitcom Book. New York: Perigee.

Mollenkopf, John

1983. The Contested City. Princeton: Princeton University Press.

Moore, Geoffrey, and Phillip Klein

1967. The Quality of Consumer Installment Credit. Washington, D.C.: National Bureau of Economic Research.

Nelson, Ralph

1949. Press Release. Ralph Nelson Collection. Number 875. Box 44. Special Collections. University Research Library. University of California, Los Angeles.

New Republic

1952a. January 21. P. 8.

1952b. February 18, P. 22.

Newcomb, Horace

1978. TV: The Critical View. New York: Oxford University Press.

1984. On the Dialogic Aspects of Mass Communications. Critical Studies in Mass Communications 1:34–50.

Newsweek

1951. July 9. P. 56.

Romasco, Albert U.

1965. The Poverty of Abundance. New York: Oxford University Press.

Stone, Michael

1983. Housing the Economic Crisis. *In* America's Housing Crisis: What Is to Be Done? Chester Hartman, ed. Pp. 99–150. London and New York: Routledge and Kegan Paul.

Swanson, Charles E., and Robert L. Jones

1951. Television Ownership and Its Correlates. Journal of Applied Psychology 35:352–357.

Taylor, Ella

In Press All in the Work-Family. Berkeley: University of California Press.

TV Facts

1980. New York: Facts on File.

TV Guide

1953a. August 7. P. 7.

1953b. November 2. P. 17.

1954. May 7. P. 11.

1955. October 1. P. 14.

1956. December 29. P. 17.

Wolfenstein, Martha

1951. The Emergence of Fun Morality. Journal of Social Issues 7(4):15–25.

QUESTIONS FOR DISCUSSION

1. Lipsitz claims that representations of ethnic, working-class families were an important factor in legitimating the developing consumerist ideology of the post-war decades. Yet they also contained elements that critiqued the new suburban, consumerist lifestyle. How did the programs he discusses negotiate between these two positions? Why was it important that they do so?

2. Why did the working-class, ethnic comedies die out after 1958? What replaced them? Another genre very popular during the 1950s and 1960s was the Western. Can we account for its popularity along some of the same lines that Lipsitz uses?

 INFOTRAC COLLEGE EDITION

Search InfoTrac College Edition under "television and class" and "television and ethnicity" to explore this topic. Also look under "westerns." Search under the author's name for reviews of his other work.

7

Sitcoms and Suburbs
Positioning the 1950s Homemaker

MARY BETH HARALOVICH

Just as Lipsitz analyzed the sitcoms of the early 1950s along ethnic and class lines, Mary Beth Haralovich looks at the ways that gender representations lie at the heart of the domestic sitcoms of the late 1950s and 1960s. She argues that such programs combined with other ways of describing and positioning the middle-class homemaker—including housing development, the consumer products industry, and market research—to construct and "naturalize" a narrow definition of women as suburban, middle-class housewives—and little else.

Such shows as *Father Knows Best* and *Leave It to Beaver*, rather than reflecting and reinforcing surrounding social conditions—since many women worked outside the home during this period and many families differed substantially from the comfortable, "nonethnic," affluent suburban families on TV—emphasized instead the economic needs of American industry. They were helped in this task by the adoption of the realist *mise en scène* of classic film production, designed to hide television's former "live performance" aesthetic behind the "realism" of movie techniques. A new form of comedy emerged, substituting restrained, family-style narrative humor for the slapstick, gag-based comedy of earlier

From *Quarterly Review of Film and Video* 11(1989): 61–83. Reprinted by permission of Gordon and Breach Publishing.

television. At its center was the white, middle-class suburban homemaker, effectively repressing the nondomestic lives of the actual women who made the programs as well as the varied lives of those who watched them.

The suburban middle-class family sitcom of the 1950s and 1960s centered on the family ensemble and its home life: breadwinner father, homemaker mother, and growing children placed within the domestic space of the suburban home. Structured within definitions of gender and the value of home life for family cohesion, these sitcoms drew upon particular historical conditions for their realist representation of family relations and domestic space. In the 1950s, a historically specific social subjectivity of the middle-class homemaker was engaged by suburban housing, the consumer product industry, market research, and the lifestyle represented in popular "growing family" sitcoms such as *Father Knows Best* (1954–1963) and *Leave It to Beaver* (1957–1963). With the reluctant and forced exit of women from positions in skilled labor after World War II and during a period of rapid growth and concentration of business, the middle-class homemaker provided these institutions with a rationale for establishing the value of domestic architecture and consumer products for quality of life and the stability of the family.

The middle-class homemaker was an important basis of this social economy—so much so that it was necessary to define her in contradictions which held her in a limited social place. In her value to the economy, the homemaker was at once central and marginal.[1] She was marginal in that she was positioned within the home, constituting the value of her labor outside of the means of production. Yet she was also central to the economy in that her function as homemaker was the subject of consumer product design and marketing, the basis of an industry. She was promised psychic and social satisfaction for being contained within the private space of the home; and in exchange for being targeted, measured, and analyzed for the marketing and design of consumer products, she was promised leisure and freedom from housework.

These social and economic appeals to the American homemaker were addressed to the white middle class whom Stuart and Elizabeth Ewen have described as "landed consumers," for whom "suburban homes were standardized parodies of independence, of leisure, and most important of all, of the property that made the first two possible."[2] The working class is marginalized in and minorities are absent from these discourses and from the social economy of consumption. An ideal white and middle-class home life was a primary means of reconstituting and resocializing the American family after World War II. By defining access to property and home ownership within the values of the conventionalized suburban family, women and minorities were guaranteed economic and social inequality. Just as suburban housing provided gender-specific domestic space and restrictive neighborhoods, consumer product design and market research directly addressed the class and gender of the targeted family member, the homemaker.

The relationship of television programming to the social formation is crucial to an understanding of television as a social practice. Graham Murdock and Peter Golding argue that media reproduce social relations under capital through "this persistent imagery of consumerism conceal[ing] and compensat[ing] for the persistence of radical inequalities in the distribution of wealth, work conditions and life chances." Stuart Hall has argued that the ideological effects of media fragment classes into individuals, masking economic determinacy and replacing class and economic social relations with imaginary social relations.[3] The suburban family sitcom is dependent upon this displacement of economic determinations onto imaginary social relations that naturalize middle-class life.

Despite its adoption of historical conditions from the 1950s, the suburban family sitcom did not greatly proliferate until the late 1950s and early 1960s. While *Father Knows Best,* in 1954, marks the beginning of popular discussion of the realism of this program format, it was not until 1957 that *Leave It to Beaver* joined it on the schedule. In the late 1950s and early 1960s, the format multiplied, while the women's movement was seeking to release homemakers from this social and economic gender definition.[4] This "nostalgic" lag between the historical specificity of the social formation and the popularity of the suburban family sitcom on the prime-time schedule underscores its ability to mask social contradictions and to naturalize woman's place in the home.

The following is an analysis of a historical conjuncture in which institutions important to social and economic policies defined women as homemakers: suburban housing, the consumer product industry, and market research. *Father Knows Best* and *Leave It to Beaver* mediated this address to the homemaker through their representations of middle-class family life. They appropriated historically specific gender traits and a realist *mise en scène* of the home to create a comfortable, warm, and stable family environment. *Father Knows Best,* in fact, was applauded for realigning family gender roles, for making "polite, carefully middle-class, family-type entertainment, possibly the most noncontroversial show on the air waves."[5]

"LOOKING THROUGH A ROSE-TINTED PICTURE WINDOW INTO YOUR OWN LIVING ROOM"

After four years on radio, *Father Knows Best* began the first of its six seasons on network television in 1954. This program about the family life of Jim and Margaret Anderson and their children, Betty (age 15), Bud (age 13), and Kathy (age 8), won the 1954 Sylvania Award for outstanding family entertainment. After one season the program was dropped by its sponsor for low ratings in audience polls. But more than twenty thousand letters from viewers protesting the program's cancellation attracted a new sponsor (the Scott Paper Company), and *Father Knows Best* was promptly reinstated in the prime-time schedule. It remained popular even after first-run production ended in 1960 when its star, Robert Young, decided to move on to other roles. Reruns of *Father Knows Best* were on prime time for three more years.[6]

Contemporary writing on *Father Knows Best* cited as its appeal the way it rearranged the dynamics of family interaction in situation comedies. Instead of the slapstick and gag-oriented family sitcom with a "henpecked simpleton" as family patriarch (this presumably refers to programs such as *The Life of Riley*), *Father Knows Best* concentrated on drawing humor from parents raising children to adulthood in suburban America. This prompted the *Saturday Evening Post* to praise the Andersons for being "a family that has surprising similarities to real people":

> The parents . . . manage to ride through almost any family situation without violent injury to their dignity, and the three Anderson children are presented as decently behaved children who will probably turn into useful citizens.[7]

These "real people" are the white American suburban middle-class family, a social and economic arrangement valued as the cornerstone of the American social economy in the 1950s. The verisimilitude associated with *Father Knows Best* is derived not only from the traits and interactions of the middle-class family, but also from the placement of the family within the promises that suburban living and material goods held out for it. Even while the role of Jim Anderson was touted as probably "the first intelligent father permitted on radio or TV since they invented the thing,"[8] the role of Margaret Anderson in relation to the father and the family—as homemaker—was equally important to post-World War II attainment of quality family life, social stability, and economic growth.

Leave It to Beaver was not discussed as much or in the same terms as *Father Knows Best*. Its first run in prime-time television was from 1957 to 1963, overlapping the last years of *Father Knows Best*. Ward and June Cleaver raise two sons (Wally, 12; Theodore, the Beaver, 8) in a single-family suburban home which, in later seasons, adopted a nearly identical floor plan to that of the Andersons. Striving for verisimilitude, the stories were based on the "real life" experiences of the scriptwriters in raising their own children. "In recalling the mystifications that every adult experienced when he [sic] was a child, 'Leave It to Beaver' evokes a humorous and pleasurably nostalgic glow."[9]

Like *Father Knows Best*, *Leave It to Beaver* was constructed around an appeal to the entire family. The Andersons and the Cleavers are already assimilated into the comfortable environment and middle-class lifestyle that housing and consumer products sought to guarantee for certain American families. While the Andersons and the Cleavers are rarely (if ever) seen in the process of purchasing consumer products, family interactions are closely tied to the suburban home. The Andersons' Springfield and the Cleavers' Mayfield are ambiguous in their metropolitan identity as suburbs in that the presence of a major city nearby is unclear, yet the communities exhibit the characteristic homogeneity, domestic architecture, and separation of gender associated with suburban design.

Margaret Anderson and June Cleaver, in markedly different ways, are two representations of the contradictory definition of the homemaker in that they are simultaneously contained and liberated by domestic space. In their placement as homemakers, they represent the promises of the economic and social processes that established a limited social subjectivity for homemakers in the 1950s. Yet there are substantial differences in the character traits of the two women, and these revolve around the degree to which each woman is contained within the domestic space of the home. As we shall see, June is more suppressed in the role of homemaker than Margaret is, with the result that June remains largely peripheral to the decision-making activities of family life.

These middle-class homemakers lead a comfortable existence in comparison with television's working-class homemakers. In *Father Knows Best* and *Leave It to Beaver,* middle-class assimilation is displayed through deep-focus photography exhibiting tasteful furnishings, tidy rooms, appliances, and gender-specific functional spaces: dens and workrooms for men, the "family space" of the kitchen for women. Margaret Anderson and June Cleaver have a lifestyle and domestic environment radically different from that of their working-class sister, Alice Kramden, in *The Honeymooners.* The suburban home and accompanying consumer products have presumably liberated Margaret and June from the domestic drudgery that marks Alice's daily existence.

The middle-class suburban environment is comfortable, unlike the cramped and unpleasant space of the Kramdens' New York City apartment. A major portion of the comedy of *The Honeymooners'* (1955–1956) working-class urban family is derived from Ralph and Alice Kramden's continual struggle with outmoded appliances, their lower-class taste, and the economic blocks to achieving an easy assimilation into the middle class through home ownership and the acquisition of consumer goods. Ralph screams out of the apartment window to a neighbor to be quiet; the water pipe in the wall breaks, spraying plaster and water everywhere. The Kramden's refrigerator and stove predate the postwar era.

One reason for this comedy of *mise en scène* is that urban sitcoms such as *I Love Lucy* (1951–1957) and *The Honeymooners* tended to focus on physical comedy and gags generated by their central comic figures (Lucille Ball and Jackie Gleason) filmed or shot live on limited sets before studio audiences.[10] *Father Knows Best* and *Leave It to Beaver,* on the other hand, shifted the source of comedy to the ensemble of the nuclear family as it realigned the roles within the family. *Father Knows Best* was praised by the *Saturday Evening Post* for its "outright defiance" of "one of the more persistent clichés of television script-writing about the typical American family . . . the mother as the iron-fisted ruler of the nest, the father as a blustering chowderhead and the children as being one sassy crack removed from juvenile delinquency." Similarly, *Cosmopolitan* cited the program for overturning television programming's "message . . . that the American father is a weak-willed, predicament-inclined clown [who is] saved from his doltishness by a beautiful and intelligent wife and his beautiful and intelligent children."[11]

Instead of building family comedy around slapstick, gags and clowning, the Andersons are the modern and model American suburban family, one in which— judging from contemporary articles about *Father Knows Best*—viewers saw themselves. The *Saturday Evening Post* quoted letters from viewers who praised the program for being one the entire family could enjoy; they could "even learn something from it." In *Cosmopolitan,* Eugene Rodney, the producer of *Father Knows Best,* identified the program's audience as the middle-class and middle-income family. "It's people in that bracket who watch us. They don't have juvenile delinquent problems. They are interested in family relations, allowances, boy and girl problems."[12] In 1959 *Good Housekeeping* reported that a viewer had written to the program to thank *Father Knows Best* for solving a family problem:

> Last Monday my daughter and I had been squabbling all day. By evening we were both so mad that I went upstairs to our portable TV set, leaving her to watch alone in the living room. When you got through with us, we both felt like fools. We didn't even need to kiss and make up. You had done it for us. Thank you all very much.

Good Housekeeping commented fondly on the program's "lifelike mixture of humor, harassment, and sentiment that literally hits home with some 15 million mothers, fathers, sons, and daughters. Watching it is like looking through a rose-tinted picture window into your own living room." In this last season, *Father Knows Best* ranked as the sixth most popular show on television.[13]

The verisimilitude of *Father Knows Best* and *Leave It to Beaver* was substantially reinforced by being based at major movie studios (Columbia and Universal, respectively), with sets that were standing replications of suburban homes. The *Saturday Evening Post* described the living environment of *Father Knows Best*:

> The set for the Anderson home is a $40,000 combination of illusion and reality. Its two floors, patio, driveway and garage sprawl over Columbia Pictures Stage 10. One room with interchangeable, wallpapered walls, can be made to look like any of the four different bedrooms. The kitchen is real, however. . . . If the script calls for a meal or a snack, Rodney insists that actual food be used. . . . "Don't give me too much food," [Young said] "Jim leaves quickly in this scene and we can't have fathers dashing off without cleaning their plates."

The home is a space not for comedy riffs and physical gags but for family cohesion, a guarantee that children can be raised in the image of their parents. In *Redesigning the American Dream,* Dolores Hayden describes suburban housing

> as an architecture of gender, since houses provide settings for women and girls to be effective social status achievers, desirable sex objects, and skillful domestic servants, and for men and boys to be executive breadwinners, successful home handy men, and adept car mechanics.[14]

"THE HOME IS AN IMAGE . . . OF THE HOUSEHOLD AND OF THE HOUSEHOLD'S RELATION TO SOCIETY"

As social historians Gwendolyn Wright and Dolores Hayden have shown, housing development and design are fundamental cornerstones of social order. Hayden argues that "the house is an image . . . of the household, and of the household's relation to society."[15] The single-family detached suburban home was architecture for the family whose healthy life would be guaranteed by a non-urban environment, neighborhood stability, and separation of family functions by gender. The suburban middle-income family was the primary focus of this homogeneous social formation.

When President Harry Truman said at the 1948 White House Conference on Family Life that "children and dogs are as necessary to the welfare of this country as is Wall Street and the railroads," he spoke to the role of home ownership in transforming the postwar American economy. Government policies supported suburban development in a variety of ways. The 41,000 miles of limited-access highways authorized by the Federal Aid Highway Act of 1956 contributed to the development of gender-specific space for the suburban family: commuter husbands and homemaker mothers. Housing starts became, and still continue to be, an important indicator of the well-being of the nation's economy. And equity in homeownership is considered to be a significant guarantee of economic security in the later years of life.[16]

But while the Housing Act of 1949 stated as its goal "a decent home and a suitable living environment for every American family," the Federal Housing Administration (FHA) was empowered with defining "neighborhood character." Hayden argues that the two national priorities of the postwar period—removing women from the paid labor force and building more housing—were conflated and tied to

> an architecture of home and neighborhood that celebrates a mid-nineteenth century ideal of separate spheres for women and men . . . characterized by segregation by age, race, and class that could not be so easily advertised.[17]

In order to establish neighborhood stability, homogeneity, harmony, and attractiveness, the FHA adopted several strategies. Zoning practices prevented multi-family dwellings and commercial uses of property. The FHA also chose not to support housing for minorities by adopting a policy called "red-lining," in which red lines were drawn on maps to identify the boundaries of changing or mixed neighborhoods. Since the value of housing in these neighborhoods was designated as low, loans to build or buy houses were considered bad risks. In addition, the FHA published a technical bulletin titled "Planning Profitable Neighborhoods," which gave advice to developers on how to concentrate on homogeneous markets for housing. The effect was to "green-line" suburban areas, promoting them by endorsing loans and development at the cost of creating urban ghettos for minorities.[18]

Wright discusses how the FHA went so far as to enter into restrictive or protective covenants to prevent racial mixing and "declining property values." She quotes the 1947 manual:

> If a mixture of user groups is found to exist, it must be determined whether the mixture will render the neighborhood less desirable to present and prospective occupants. Protective covenants are essential to sound development of proposed residential areas, since they regulate the use of the land and provide a basis for the development of harmonious, attractive neighborhoods.

Despite the fact that the Supreme Court ruled in favor of the NAACP's case against restrictive covenants, the FHA accepted written and unwritten agreements in housing developments until 1968.[19]

The effect of these government policies was to create homogeneous and socially stable communities with racial, ethnic, and class barriers to entry. Wright describes "a definite sociological pattern to the household that moved out to the suburbs in the late 1940s and 1950s": the average age of adult suburbanites was 31 in 1950; there were few single, widowed, divorced, and elderly; there was a higher fertility rate than in the cities; and 9% of suburban women worked, as compared to 27% in the population as a whole. According to Hayden, five groups were excluded from single-family housing through the social policies of the late 1940s: single white women; the white elderly working and lower class; minority men of all classes; minority women of all classes; and minority elderly.[20]

The suburban dream house underscored this homogeneous definition of the suburban family. Domestic architecture was designed to display class attributes and reinforce gender-specific functions of domestic space. Hayden describes Robert Woods Kennedy, an influential housing designer of the period, arguing that the task of the housing architect was "to provide houses that helped his clients to indulge in status-conscious consumption . . . to display the housewife 'as a sexual being' . . . and to display the family's possessions 'as proper symbols of socio-economic class,' claiming that [this] form of expression [was] essential to modern family life." In addition to the value of the home for class and sexual identity, suburban housing was also therapeutic for the family. As Hayden observes, "whoever speaks of housing must also speak of home; the word means both the physical space and the nurturing that takes place there."[21]

A popular design for the first floor of the home was the "open floor plan," which provided a whole living environment for the entire family. With few walls separating living, dining, and kitchen areas, space was open for family togetherness. This "activity area" would also allow children to be within sight and hearing of the mother. Father could have his own space in a den or workroom and a detached garage for his car, while mother might be attracted to a modern model kitchen with separate laundry room. Bedrooms were located in the "quiet zone," perhaps on the second floor at the head of a stairway, away from the main activities of the household. While children might have the private space of individual bedrooms, parents shared the "master bedroom," which was larger and sometimes equipped with walk-in closets and dressing areas.[22]

This housing design, built on a part of an acre of private property with a yard for children, allowed the postwar middle-class family to give their children a lifestyle that was not so commonly available during the Depression and World War II. This domestic haven provided the setting for the socialization of girls into women and boys into men, and was paid for by the labor of the breadwinner father and maintained by the labor of the homemaker mother. The homemaker, placed in the home by suburban development and housing design, was promised release from household drudgery and an aesthetically pleasing interior environment as the basis of the consumer product industry economy.

"LEISURE *CAN* TRANSFORM HER LIFE
EVEN IF GOOD DESIGN CAN'T"

Like housing design and suburban development, the consumer product industry built its economy on defining the social class and self-identity of women as homemakers. But this industrial definition of the homemaker underwent significant changes during the 1950s as suburban housing proliferated to include the working class. Two significant shifts marked discussions among designers about the role of product design in social life. The first occurred in 1955, when, instead of focusing on practical problems, the Fifth Annual Design Conference at Aspen drew a record attendance to discuss theoretical and cultural aspects of design. Among the topics discussed were the role of design in making leisure enjoyable and the possibility that mass communications could permit consumer testing of products before the investment of major capital. Design was no longer simply a matter of aesthetically pleasing shapes, but "part and parcel of the intricate pattern of twentieth-century life." The second shift in discussion occurred in early 1958, when *Industrial Design* (a major trade journal in the field) published several lengthy articles on market research, which it called "a new discipline—sometimes helpful, sometimes threatening—that is slated to affect the entire design process."[23]

Prior to the prominence of market research in the United States, designers discussed the contribution of product design to an aesthetically pleasing lifestyle, to the quality of life, and to making daily life easier. The homemaker was central to the growth and organization of the consumer product industry, but the editors of *Industrial Design* introduced the journal's fourth annual design review (December 1957) with an article positioning the homemaker as a problematic recipient of the benefits of design. Entitled "Materialism, Leisure and Design," this essay is worth quoting at some length. It first summarized the contribution of design to the leisure obtained from consumer products:

> We care very much about this world of things, partly because we are design-conscious and partly because we are American: this country is probably unique in that a review of the year's products is actually a measure of the material improvement in the everyday life of most citizens. . . . We think there is a good side [to American materialism], and that it does show up here—in quality, in availability and in the implication of increased leisure. Traditionally American design aims unapologetically at making things easier for people, at freeing them.

The article went on to respond to cynics who questioned whether homemakers *should* be freed from housework. *Industrial Design* argued for the potentially beneficial emancipation of the homemaker gained by product design:

> Automatic ranges and one-step washer-dryers leave the housewife with a precious ingredient: time. This has come to be regarded as both her bonus and her right, but not everyone regards it with unqualified enthusiasm. Critics belonging to the woman's-place-is-in-the-sink school ask cynically what

she is free *for*. The bridge table? Afternoon TV? The lonely togetherness of telephone gossip? The analyst's couch? Maybe. But is this the designer's problem? Certainly it is absurd to suggest that he has a moral responsibility *not* to help create leisure time because if he does it is likely to be badly used. More choice in how she spends her time gives the emancipated woman an opportunity to face problems of a larger order than ever before, and this *can* transform her life, even if good design can't. In any case, the designer does have a responsibility to fill leisure hours, and *any* hours, with objects that are esthetically pleasing.[24]

These attempts to equate design aesthetics with leisure for the homemaker were occasionally challenged because they marginalized lifestyles other than the middle class. When Dr. Wilson G. Scanlon, a psychiatrist, addressed the 1957 meeting of the Southern New England Chapter of the Industrial Designers Institute, he argued that the act of "excessive purchasing of commodities [was] a form of irrational and immature behavior," that new purchases and increased leisure have not put anxieties to rest, and that "acceptance of some eccentricity rather than emphasis on class conformity should make for less insecurity [and for] a nation that is emotionally mature."[25]

Esther Foley, home services editor of MacFadden Publications, "shocked and intrigued" her audience at the "What Can the Consumer Tell Us?" panel at the 1955 conference of the American Society of Industrial Designers by discussing working-class homemakers. The flagship magazine of MacFadden Publications was *True Story*, with a circulation of two million nearly every year from 1926 through 1963. In addition to the confessional stories in the company's *True Romance, True Experience*, and other *True* titles, in the 1950s and 1960s some Mac-Fadden publications were "family behavior magazines," appealing to working-class homemakers who were "not reached by the middle-class service magazine such as *McCalls* and *Ladies Home Journal*."[26]

Foley introduce a "slice of life" into the theoretical discussions of design by showing color slides of the homes of her working-class readers. She showed

> their purchased symbols—the latest shiny "miracle" appliances in badly arranged kitchens, the inevitable chrome dinette set, the sentimental and unrelated living room furnishings tied together by expensive carpets and cheap cotton throw rugs.[27]

While Scanlon complained of the psychological damage to the nation from class conformity through consumerism (an issue the women's movement would soon raise), Foley illustrated the disparity between the working class and an aesthetics of product design articulated for the middle class. These criticisms recognized the social and economic contradictions in the growing consumer economy.

In the mid-1950s, *Industrial Design* began to publish lengthy analyses of product planning divisions in consumer product corporations. The journal argued that changes in industrial organization would be crucial to the practice of design. There were three important issues: 1) how large corporations could summon the resources necessary for analyzing consumer needs and habits in order to succeed in the increasingly competitive market for consumer products; 2) how product designers must become aware of the role of design in business organizations; and 3) how industrial survival in the area of consumer goods would increasingly depend on defining new consumer needs.[28]

The close relationship between research and design is illustrated by GE's 1952 "advance industrial design group" test of a wall-mounted refrigerator. The first stages of design testing measured the "maximum reach-in for average housewife's height." The article was illustrated with a picture of a woman standing with arm outstretched into a cardboard mockup of the refrigerator. While at first glance this is an amusing notion, the homogeneity of suburban development and housing design suggests that this physical identification of "the average housewife" is consistent with her placement within limited social definitions.[29]

This need for the consumer product industry to define the homemaker and, through her, its value to home life is well illustrated by a 1957 discussion among television set designers on whether to design television sets as furniture or as functional instruments like appliances. The designers talked about three aspects of this problem: 1) how to define the role and function of television in many aspects of daily life, not solely as part of living room viewing; 2) how to discover the needs of the consumer in television set design; and 3) the necessity of recognizing the role of television set design as part of an industry with a mass market. Whether modeled upon furniture or appliances, television set design should help the homemaker integrate the receiver into the aesthetics of interior decoration.[30]

The case for television as furniture was based on "better taste" on the part of consumers and the rapidly expanding furniture industry. Television set purchases exhibited a trend toward "good taste" and away from the "18th-century mahogany and borax-modern cabinets." In the previous year (1956), the furniture industry had had its best sales year in history. Given television's rapid installation rate in the 1950s (by 1960 it was in 87% of American households), designers agreed that people were spending more time at home and were more interested in the home's appearance. Designers needed to consider how the television set would play an important role in home redecoration and how they could assist homemakers in making aesthetic decision concerning, this new piece of furniture:

> There is not a homemaker who has not faced the problem of a proper room arrangement, lighting, color and decoration for television viewing—and even hi-fi listening. Yet let's be honest: the industry has not made an effort to solve this problem.[31]

The case for television as an instrument rested on its portability. Recent developments in the technology of television allowed for smaller, lighter sets that could be easily integrated into outdoor activities (on the deck behind the house) as well as into the kitchen decor (on the kitchen counter, color-coordinated with the appliances). For cues on how to proceed to fill this consumer need, television set designers suggested looking to the appliance industry, which had already proved effective in integrating products into complete and efficient packages for the kitchen.[32]

The consumer product design industry was aware of the significance of the homemaker in the economics of marketing and design. Before the introduction of systematic market research, her "needs" as a homemaker were partially determined by simply asking her what she wanted and then analyzing her responses. The 1957 Design Symposium at Silvermine invited five homemakers as conference participants, rather than merely as topics of discussion. The were not "typical housewives but five women with the ability to give serious thought and attention to shopping." These women helped the designers to analyze the way irons, washing machines, foreign cars, vacuum cleaners, and ranges functioned in their lives. But the feminine voice of the housewife was not the only voice heard at Silvermine. Four male "experts" discussed the need for consumers to communicate their "needs and wants" and described how the federal highway program, which fostered suburban expansion, would contribute to the development of a new mode of consumption: *the shopping center.* They also observed that deciding what product to buy produces tension that must be relived.[33]

Hayden points out that housework is status-producing labor for the family, but at the same time it lowers the status of the homemaker by separating her from public life. The "psychological conflict" engendered by "guarantee[ing] the family's social status at the expenses of her own . . . increases when women . . . come up against levels of consumption" that lie outside their potential for upward mobility.[34] Market research based its strength on turning these tension around, placing them in the service of the consumer economy.

"WOMEN RESPOND WITH FAVORABLE EMOTIONS TO THE FRESH, CREAMY SURFACE OF A NEWLY OPENED SHORTENING CAN"

By 1958, the "feminine voice" of the homemaker was even further enmeshed in expert opinion from the field of consumer science and psychology. With high competition in the consumer product industry, it was no longer adequate to determine the conscious needs of the homemaker through interviewing. Instead, market researchers sought to uncover the unconscious processes of consumption. *Industrial Design* described the market researcher as "a man with a slide rule in one hand and a copy of Sigmund Freud in the other," who quantified the unconscious motivations in purchasing.[35]

The class- and gender-related tensions inherent in consumer decisions could be identified through market research and alleviated through design. The status of the home and the identity of the homemaker, two important subjects of this research, were based on the development of suburban housing and the concomitant change in shopping patterns. With impersonal supermarkets replacing small retailers, market researchers argued that "sales talk had to be built into product and packaging."[36] Survey research, depth or motivational research, and experimental research sought to link design with class and gender characteristics, and ultimately to determine how product design could appeal to upward mobility and confirm the self-identity of homemakers. Survey research also helped to correlate the "social image" of products with their users in order to design products that would attract new groups as well as retain current buyers. The Index of Social Position, developed by August Hollingshead of Yale University, organized data on consumers into an estimation of their social status in the community. A multi-factor system rated residential position (neighborhood), power position (occupation), and taste level (education). The total score, he argued, would reveal a family's *actual* place in the community, replacing subjective judgments by interviewers.[37]

Other types of market research focused on the function of women as homemakers. Thus the economic responsibility for class status lay with the father while the mother was addressed through emotional connotations associated with homemaking. Depth research looked into the psychic motivations of consumers and revealed, for example, that "women reacted with favorable emotions to [the] fresh, creamy surface of a newly opened shortening can." Ernest Dichter redesigned the Snowdrift shortening label with this emotional response in mind. A swirl of shortening formed the letter *S* emerging from the can on a wooden spoon (to further associations with traditional cooking). The *s*-shape integrated the name of the product with the emotional appeal of the texture of the shortening. Proof of these researcher deductions and, presumably, the typicality of homemaker emotions was provided by IBM data-processing equipment, which could handle large samples and quantify the results.[38]

Experimental research included projective techniques that would elicit unconscious responses to market situations, on the theory that consumers would impute to others their own feelings and motivations. These techniques included word-association, cartoons in which word balloons were filled in, narrative projection in which a story was finished, role-playing, and group discussions. For example, women were shown the following two grocery lists and asked to describe the woman who used each list.

Shopping List 1	*Shopping List 2*
pound and a half of hamburger	pound and a half of hamburger
2 loaves of Wonder Bread	2 loaves of Wonder Bread
bunch of carrots	bunch of carrots
1 can Rumford's Baking Powder	1 can Rumford's Baking Powder
Nescafe instant coffee (drip)	1 lb. Maxwell House Coffee (ground)
2 cans Del Monte peaches	2 cans Del Monte peaches
5 lbs. potatoes	5 lbs. potatoes

Of the women polled, 48% described the first shopper as lazy, while only 4% attached that label to the second shopper. Women who considered using instant coffee a trait of the lazy housewife were less likely to buy it, "indicating that personality image was a motive in buying choice."[39]

In perception tests, machines measured the speed with which a package could be identified and how much of the design's "message" could be retained. Role-playing at shopping and group discussions at the Institute for Motivational Research's "Motivational Theater" were "akin to . . . 'psychodrama' " in that consumers would reveal product-, class-, and gender-related emotions that researchers would elicit and study. These techniques, it was noted in a contemporary article, "stimulate expression" by putting the subject "in another's position—or in one's own position under certain circumstances, like shopping or homemaking."[40]

Some designers complained that this application of science to design inhibited the creative process by substituting testable and quantifiable elements for aesthetics. In an address to the 1958 Aspen Conference, sociologist C. Wright Mills criticized designers for "bringing art, science and learning into a subordinate relation with the dominant institutions of the capitalist economy and the nationalist state." Mills's paper was considered to be "so pertinent to design problems today" that *Industrial Design* ran it in its entirety rather than publishing a synopsis of its major points, as it typically did with conference reports.[41]

Mills complained that design helped to blur the distinction between "human consciousness and material existence" by providing stereotypes of meaning. He argued that consumer products had become "the Fetish of human life" in the "virtual dominance of consumer culture." Mills attacked designers for promulgating "The Big Lie" of advertising and design, the notion that "we only give them what they want." He accused designers and advertisers of determining consumer wants and tastes, a procedure characteristic "of the current phase of capitalism in America . . . creat[ing] a panic for status, and hence a panic of self-evaluation, and . . . connect[ing] its relief with the consumption of specified commodities." While Mills did not specifically address the role of television, he did cite the importance of distribution in the post-war economy and "the need for the creation and maintenance of the national market and its monopolistic closure."[42]

TELEVISUAL LIFE IN SPRINGFIELD
AND MAYFIELD

One way that television distributed knowledge about a social economy that positioned women as homemakers was through the suburban family sitcom. These sitcoms promoted an image of the housewife and a mode of feminine subjectivity similar to those put forth by suburban development and the consumer product industry. In their representation of middle-class family life, series such as *Father Knows Best* and *Leave It to Beaver* mobilized the discourses of other social institutions. Realistic *mise en scène* and the character traits of family members naturalized middle-class home life, masking the social and economic barriers to entry into that privileged domain.

The heterogeneity of class and gender that market research analyzed is not manifested in either *Father Knows Best* or *Leave It to Beaver*. The Andersons and the Cleavers would probably rank quite well in the Index of Social Position.

Their neighborhoods have large and well-maintained homes; both families belong to country clubs. Jim Anderson is a well-respected insurance agent with his own agency (an occupation chosen because it would not tie him to an office). Ward Cleaver's work is ambiguous, but both men carry a briefcase and wear a suit and tie to work. They have the income that easily provides their families with roomy, comfortable, and pleasing surroundings and attractive clothing; their wives have no need to work outside the home. Both men are college-educated; the programs often discuss the children's future college education.

Father Knows Best and *Leave It to Beaver* rarely make direct reference to the social and economic means by which the families attained and maintain their middle-class status. Their difference from other classes is not a subject of these sitcoms. By effacing the separations of race, class, age, and gender that produced suburban neighborhoods, *Father Knows Best* and *Leave It to Beaver* naturalize the privilege of the middle class. Yet there is one episode of *Leave It to Beaver* from the early 1960s that lays bare its assumptions about what constitutes a good neighborhood. In doing so, the episode suggests how narrowly the heterogeneity of social life came to be defined.

Wally and Beaver visit Wally's smart-aleck friend, Eddie Haskell, who has moved out of his family's home into a rooming house in what Beaver describes as a "crummy neighborhood." Unlike the design of suburban developments, this neighborhood has older, rambling two-story (or more) houses set close together. The door to one house is left ajar, paper debris is blown about by the wind and left on yards and front porches. Two men are working on an obviously older model car in the street, hood and trunk open, tire resting against the car; two garbage cans are on the sidewalks; an older man in sweater and hat walks along carrying a bag of groceries. On a front lawn, a rake leans against a bushel basket with leaves piled up; a large canvas-covered lawn swing sits on a front lawn; one house has a sign in the yard: "For sale by owner—to be moved."

Wally and Beaver are uneasy in this neighborhood, one which is obviously in transition and in which work activities are available for public view. But everyone visible is white. This is a rare example of a suburban sitcom's demarcation of good and bad neighborhoods. What is more typical is the assumption that the homes of the Andersons and the Cleavers are representative of the middle class.

In different ways, the credit sequences that begin these programs suggest recurring aspects of suburban living. The opening of *Father Knows Best* begins with a long shot of the Anderson's two-story home, a fence separating the front lawn from the sidewalk, its landscape including trellises with vines and flowers. A cut to the interiors entryway shows the family gathering together. In earlier seasons, Jim, wearing a suit and with hat in hand, prepares to leave for work. He looks at his watch; the grandfather clock to the left of the door shows the time as nearly 8:30 A.M. Margaret, wearing a blouse, sweater, and skirt, brings Jim his briefcase and kisses him goodbye. The three Anderson children giggle all in a row on the stairway leading up to the second-floor bedrooms. In later seasons, after the long shot of the house, the Anderson family gathers in the entryway to greet Jim as he returns from work. Margaret, wearing a dress too fancy for housework, kisses him at the doorway as the children cluster about them, uniting the family in the home.

The opening credits of *Leave It to Beaver* gradually evolved from an emphasis on the younger child to his placement within the neighborhood and then the family. The earliest episodes open with childlike etchings drawn in a wet concrete sidewalk. Middle seasons feature Beaver walking home along a street with single-family homes set back behind manicured, unfenced lawns. In later seasons, the Cleaver family is shown leaving their two-story home for a picnic trip: Ward carries the thermal cooler, June (in a dress, even for a picnic) carries the basket, and Wally and Beaver climb into the Cleavers' late model car. While *Father Knows Best* coheres around the family ensemble, *Leave It to Beaver* decenters the family around the younger child, whose rearing provides problems that the older child has either already surmounted or has never had.

The narrative space of these programs is dominated by the domestic space of the home. *Father Knows Best* leaves the home environment much less often than does *Leave It to Beaver*, which often focuses on Beaver at school. This placing of the family within the home contributes in large measure to the ability of these programs to "seem real." During the first season of *Leave It to Beaver*, the Cleavers' home was an older design rather than a suburban dream house. The kitchen was large and homey, with glass and wood cabinets. The rooms were separated by walls and closed doors. By the 1960s, the Cleavers, like the Andersons, were living in the "open floor plan," a popular housing design of the 1950s. As you enter the home, to your far left is the den, the private space of the father. To the right of the den is the stairway leading to the "quiet zone" of the bedrooms. To your right is the living room, visible through a wide and open entryway the size of two doors. Another wide doorway integrates the living room with the formal dining room. A swinging door separates the dining room from the kitchen. The deep-focus photography typical of these sitcoms displays the expanse of living space in this "activity area."

While the Cleaver children share a bedroom, it is equipped with a private bathroom and a portable television set. Ward and June's bedroom is small, with twin beds. Since it is not a site of narrative activity, which typically takes place in the boys' room or on the main floor of the home, the parents' bedroom is rarely seen. These two small bedrooms belie the scale of the house when it is seen in long shot.

The Andersons' home makes more use of the potential of the bedrooms for narrative space. With four bedrooms, the Anderson home allows each of the children the luxury of his or her own room. Jim and Margaret's "master" bedroom, larger than those of their children, has twin beds separated by a nightstand and lamp, a walk-in closet, a dressing table, armchairs, and a small alcove. In this design, the "master" bedroom is conceived as a private space for parents, but the Anderson children have easy access to their parents' bedroom. The Andersons, however, have only one bathroom. Betty has commented that when she gets married she will have three bathrooms because "there won't always be two of us."

The Andersons and the Cleavers also share aspects of the decor of their homes, displaying possessions in a comfortably unostentatious way. Immediately to the left of the Andersons' front door is a large free-standing grandfather clock; to the right and directly across the room are built-in bookcases filled with hardcover books. In earlier seasons of *Leave It to Beaver,* the books (also hardbound) were on shelves in the living room. Later, these books were relocated to Ward's study, to line the many built-in bookshelves behind his desk.

The two families have similar tastes in wall decorations and furnishings. Among the landscapes in heavy wood frames on the Cleavers' walls are pictures of sailing vessels and reproductions of "great art," such as "Pinkie" by Sir Thomas Lawrence. While the Andersons do not completely share the Cleavers' penchant for candelabra on the walls and tables, their walls are tastefully decorated with smaller landscapes. Curiously, neither house engages in the prominent display of family photographs.

The large living room in each home has a fireplace. There is plenty of room to walk around the furniture, which is overstuffed and comfortable or of hardwood. The formal dining room in both homes includes a large wooden table and chairs that can seat six comfortably. It is here that the families have their evening meals. A sideboard or hutch displays dishes, soup tureens, and the like. The kitchen contains a smaller, more utilitarian set of table and chairs, where breakfast is eaten. Small appliances such as a toaster, mixer, and electric coffeepot sit out on counters. A wall-mounted roll of paper towels is close to the sink. The Andersons' outdoor patio has a built-in brick oven, singed from use.

While both homes establish gender-specific areas of women and men, *Father Knows Best* is less repressive in its association of this space with familial roles. Both Jim Anderson and Ward Cleaver have dens; Ward is often shown doing ambiguous paperwork in his, the rows of hardcover books behind his desk suggesting his association with knowledge and mental work. June's forays into Ward's space tend to be brief, usually in search of his advice on how to handle the boys. As Ward works on papers, June sits in a corner chair sewing a button on Beaver's shirt. Ward's den is often the site of father-to-son talks. Its doorway is wide and open, revealing the cabinet-model television that Beaver occasionally watches. While Jim also has a den, it is much less often the site of narrative action, and its door is usually closed.

Workrooms and garages are also arenas for male activity, providing storage space for paint or lawn care equipment or a place to work on the car. The suburban homemaker does not have an equivalent private space. Instead, the woman shares her kitchen with other family members, while the living and dining rooms are designated as family spheres. In typical episodes of *Leave It to Beaver,* June's encounters with family members generally take place in the kitchen, while Ward's tend to occur throughout the house. As her sons pass through her space, June is putting up paper towels, tossing a salad, unpacking groceries, or making meals. Margaret, having an older daughter, is often able to turn this family/female space over to her. She is also more often placed within other domestic locations: the patio, the attic, the living room.

Both Margaret and June exemplify Robert Woods Kennedy's theory that housing design should display the housewife as a sexual being, but this is accomplished not so much through their positioning within domestic space as through costume. June's ubiquitous pearls, stockings and heels, and cinch-waisted dresses area amusing in their distinct contradiction of the realities of housework. While

Margaret also wears dresses or skirts, she tends to be costumed more casually, and sometimes wears a smock when doing housework. Margaret is also occasionally seen in relatively sloppy clothes suitable for dirty work but marked as inappropriate to her status as a sexual being.

In one episode of *Father Knows Best,* Margaret is dressed in dungarees, sweatshirt, and loafers, her hair covered by a scarf as she scrubs paint from her youngest daughter, Kathy. When Betty sees her, she laughs, "If you aren't a glamorous picture!" As Jim arrives home early, Betty counsels Margaret, "You can't let Father see you like this!" Betty takes over scrubbing and dressing Kathy while Margaret hurries off to change before Jim sees her. But Margaret is caught, embarrassed at not being dressed as a suburban object of desire. Jim good-naturedly echoes Betty's comment: "If you aren't a glamorous picture!" He calms Margaret's minor distress at being seen by her husband in this departure from her usual toilette: "You know you always look great to me."

As this example shows, the agreement among Jim, Margaret, and Betty on the proper attire for the suburban homemaker indicates the success with which Betty has been socialized within the family. Yet even though both programs were created around "realistic" storylines of family life, the nurturing function of the home and the gender-specific roles of father and mother are handled very differently in *Father Knows Best* and *Leave It to Beaver.*

By 1960, Betty, whom Jim calls "Princess," had been counseled through adolescent dating and was shown to have "good sense" and maturity in her relations with boys. Well-groomed and well-dressed like her mother, Betty could easily substitute for Margaret in household tasks. In one episode, Jim and Margaret decide that their lives revolve too much around their children ("trapped," "like servants") and they try to spend a weekend away, leaving Betty in charge. While Betty handles the situation smoothly, Jim and Margaret are finally happier continuing their weekend at Cedar Lodge with all of the children along.

Bud, the son, participates in the excitement of discovery and self-definition outside of personal appearance. A normal boy in the process of becoming a man, he gets dirty at sports and tinkering with engines, replaces blown fuses, and cuts the grass. Unlike Betty, Bud has to be convinced that he can handle dating; Jim counsels him that this awkward stage is normal and one that Jim himself has gone through.

Kathy (whose pet name is "Kitten"), in contrast to her older sister, is a tomboy and is interested in sports. By 1959, *Good Housekeeping* purred that

> Kathy seems to have got the idea it might be more fun to appeal to a boy than to be one. At the rate she's going, it won't be long before [Jim and Margaret] are playing grandparents.[43]

Film and television writer Danny Peary was also pleased with Kathy's development, but for a very different reason: in the 1977 *Father Knows Best* "Reunion" show, Kathy was an unmarried gym teacher. Peary also felt that *Father Knows Best* was different from other suburban family sitcoms in its representation of women. "The three Anderson females . . . were intelligent, proud, and resourceful. Margaret was Jim's equal, loved and respected for her wisdom."[44] The traits that characterize Margaret in her equality are her patience, good humor, and easy confidence. Unlike Ward Cleaver, Jim is not immune to wifely banter.

In one episode, Jim overhears Betty and her friend Armand rehearsing a play, and assumes they are going to elope. Margaret has more faith in their daughter and good-naturedly tries to dissuade Jim from his anxiety: "Jim, when are you going to stop acting like a comic-strip father?" In the same episode, Jim and Margaret play Scrabble, an activity that the episode suggests they do together often. "Dad's getting beat at Scrabble again," observes Bud. Kathy notices, "He's stuck with the *Z* again." Margaret looks up Jim's *Z* word in the dictionary, doubting its existence. Margaret is able to continually best Jim at this word game and Jim is willing to play despite certain defeat.

In contrast to this easy-going family with character traits allowing for many types of familial interaction, *Leave It to Beaver* tells another story about gender relations in the home. June does not share Margaret's status in intelligence. In a discussion of their sons' academic performances, June remarks, "We can't all be *A* students; maybe the boys are like me." Ward responds, "No, they are *not* like you" and then catches himself. Nor does June share Margaret's witty and confident relationship with her husband. She typically defers to Ward's greater sense for raising their two sons. Wondering how to approach instances of boyish behavior, June positions herself firmly at a loss. She frequently asks, mystified, "Ward, did boys do this when you were their age?" Ward always reassures June that whatever their sons are doing (brothers fighting, for example) is a normal stage of development for boys, imparting to her his superior social and familial knowledge. Like her sons, June acknowledges the need for Ward's guidance. Unlike Margaret, June is structured on the periphery of the socialization of her children, in the passive space of the home.

Ward, often a misogynist, encourages the boys to adopt his own cynical attitude toward their mother and women in general. In an early episode, Ward is replacing the plug on the toaster. He explains to Beaver that "your mother" always pulls it out by the cord instead of properly grabbing it by the plug. Beaver is impressed by Ward's knowledge of " 'lectricity," to which Ward responds by positioning his knowledge as a condition of June's ineptness. "I know enough to stay about one jump ahead of your mother." Unlike *Father Knows Best, Leave It to Beaver* works to contain June's potential threat to patriarchal authority. When June asks why Beaver would appear to be unusually shy about meeting a girl, Ward wonders as well: "He doesn't know enough about life to be afraid of women."

In the episode in which Eddie Haskell moves out of the home, Ward sides with the Haskells by forbidding both his sons to visit Eddie's bachelor digs. As Ward telephones another father to ask him to do the same, June timidly asks (covering a bowl to be put in the refrigerator), "Ward, aren't you getting terribly involved?" Ward answers that if this were their son he would appreciate the support of other parents. June murmurs assent as Ward and June continue the process of defining June's function within the family in terms of passivity and deference.

While *Father Knows Best* and *Leave It to Beaver* position the homemaker in family life quite differently, both women effortlessly maintain the domestic space of the family environment. In their representation of women's work in the home, these programs show the great ease and lack of drudgery with which Margaret and June keep their homes tidy and spotlessly clean. In any episode, these homemakers can be engaged in their daily housework. June prepares meals, waters plants, and dusts on a Saturday morning. She brings in groceries, wipes around the kitchen sink, and asks Wally to help her put away the vacuum cleaner (which she has not been shown using). Margaret prepares meals, does dishes, irons, and also waters plants. While June is often stationary in the kitchen or sewing in the living room, Margaret is usually moving from one room to another, in the process of ongoing domestic activity.

While one could argue that this lack of acknowledgment of the labor of homemaking troubles the verisimilitude of these sitcoms, the realist *mise en scène* that includes consumer products suggests the means by which the comfortable environment of quality family life can be maintained. Margaret and June easily mediate the benefits promised by the consumer product industry. They are definitely not women of leisure, but they are women for whom housework is neither especially confining nor completely time-consuming.

The visible result of their partially visible labor is the constantly immaculate appearance of their homes and variously well-groomed family members. (The older children are more orderly because they are further along in the process of socialization than are the younger ones.) The "real time" to do piles of laundry or the daily preparation of balanced meals is a structured absence of the programs. The free time that appliances provide for Margaret and June is attested to by their continual good humor and the quality of their interactions with the family. Unrushed and unpressured, Margaret and June are not so free from housework that they become idle and self-indulgent. They are well-positioned within the constraints of domestic activity and the promises of the consumer product industry.

We have seen how the homemaker was positioned in the postwar consumer economy by institutions that were depended on defining her social subjectivity within the domestic sphere. In the interests of family stability, suburban development and domestic architecture were designed with a particular definition of family economy in mind: a working father who could, alone, provide for the social and economic security of his family; a homemaker wife and mother who maintains the family's environment; children who grow up in neighborhoods undisturbed by heterogeneity of class, race, ethnicity, and age.

The limited address to the homemaker by the consumer product industry and market research is easily understood when seen within this context of homogeneity in the social organization of the suburban family. Defined in terms of her homemaking function for the family and for the economy, her life could only be made easier by appliances. The display of her family's social status was ensured by experts who assuaged any uncertainties she may have had about interior decor by designing with these problems in mind. By linking her identity as a shopper and homemaker to class attributes, the base of the consumer economy was broadened, and her deepest emotions and insecurities were tapped and transferred to consumer product design.

The representation of suburban family life in *Father Knows Best* and *Leave It to Beaver* also circulated social knowledge that linked the class and gender identities of homemakers. Realist *mise en scène* drew upon housing architecture and consumer products in order to ground family narratives within the domestic space of the middle-class home. The contribution of the television homemaker to harmonious family life was underscored by the ease with which she negotiated her place in the domestic arena.

This brief social history has placed one television format—the suburban family sitcom—within the historical context from which it drew its conventions, its codes of realism, and its definitions of family life. Yet we must also ask about resistances to this social subjectivity by recognizing the heterogeneity of the social formation. For example, in the late 1950s and 1960s, when the suburban family sitcom proliferated on prime-time television, the women's movement was resisting these institutional imperatives, exposing the social and economic inequalities on which they were based.[45]

Oppositional positions point to the inability of institutions to conceal completely the social and economic determinations of subjectivity. But the durability of the suburban family sitcom indicates the degree of institutional as well as popular support for ideologies that naturalize class and gender identities. Continuing exploration of the relationship between the historical specificity of the social formation and the programming practices of television contributes to our understanding of the ways in which popular cultural forms participate in the discourses of social life and diverge from the patterns of everyday experience.

NOTES

I wish to thank Beverly O'Neil for suggesting and participating in the survey of design journals, and Robert Deming, Darryl Fox, and Lee Poague, who made helpful comments. An earlier version of this paper, entitled "Suburban Family sitcoms and Consumer Product Design: Addressing the Social Subjectivity of Homemakers in the 1950s," was presented to the 1986 International Television Studies Conference and appears in *Television and Its Audience: International Research Perspectives,* ed. Phillip Drummond and Richard Paterson (London: British Film Institute, 1988), pp. 38–60.

1. In *Women: The Longest Revolution* (London: Virago, 1984), p. 18, Juliet Mitchell argues that women are bound up in this contradiction: "[Women] are fundamental to the human condition, yet in their economic, social, and political roles, they are marginal. It is precisely this combination—fundamental and marginal at one and the same time—that has been fatal to them."

2. Stuart Ewen and Elizabeth Ewen, *Channels of Desire: Mass Images and the Shaping of American Consciousness* (New York: McGraw-Hill, 1982), p. 235.

3. Graham Murdock and Peter Golding, "Capitalism, Communication and Class Relations," and Stuart Hall, "Culture, Media and the 'Ideological Effect,'" in *Mass Communication and Society,* eds. James Curran, Michael Gurevitch, and Janet Woollacott (Beverly Hills: Sage, 1979), pp. 12, 36, 336–339.

4. I began this study by considering prime-time network sitcoms with runs of three seasons or more from 1948 through 1960. Fourteen of these thirty-five sitcoms were structured around middle-class families living in suburban single-family dwellings. Eight of these fourteen defined the family unit as a breadwinner father, a homemaker mother, and children growing into adults: *The Ruggles* (1949–1952), *The Aldrich Family* (1949–1953), *The Stu Erwin Show* (1950–1955), *The Adventures of Ozzie and Harriet* (1952–1966), *Father Knows Best* (1954–1963), *Leave It to Beaver* (1957–1963), *The Donna Reed Show* (1958–1966), and *Dennis the Menace* (1959–1963).

The other six suburban family sitcoms shared some of these traits, but centered their narratives on situations or characters other than the family ensemble: *Beulah* (1950–1953) focused on a black maid to an apparently broadly caricatured white middle-class family; *December Bride* (1954–1961) concerned an attractive, dating widow living with her daughter's family; *The Bob Cummings Show* (1955–1959) concentrated on the adventures of a playboy photographer living with his widowed sister and nephew in a suburban home; *I Married Joan* (1952–1955) focused on the zany adventures of the wife of a domestic court judge; *My Favorite Husband* (1953–1957) had a couple working for social status in the suburbs; and *Bachelor Father* (1957–1962) featured an attorney who cared for his young niece in Beverly Hills.

This information was derived from the following sources: Tim Brooks and Earle Marsh, *The Complete Directory of Prime Time Network Television Shows, 1946—Present* (New York: Ballantine Books, 1981); Les Brown, *The New York Times Encyclopedia of Television* (New York: Times Books, 1977); Henry Castleman and Walter J. Podrazik, *The TV Schedule Book* (New York: McGraw-Hill, 1984).

5. Kenneth Rhodes, "Father of *Two* Families," *Cosmopolitan* (April 1956), p. 125.

6. Rhodes, p. 125; Bob Eddy, "Private Life of a Perfect Papa," *Saturday Evening Post* (April 27, 1957), p. 29; Brooks and Marsh, pp. 245–246.

7. Rhodes, p. 125; Eddy, p. 29.

8. Newspaper critic John Crosby, quoted in Eddy, p. 29.

9. "TV's Eager Beaver," *Look* (May 27, 1958), p. 68.

10. Brooks and Marsh, pp. 340–341, 352–353.

11. Eddy, p. 29; Rhodes, p. 126.

12. Eddy, p. 29; Rhodes, p. 127.

13. "Jane Wyatt's Triple Threat," *Good Housekeeping* (October 1959), p. 48.

14. Eddy, p. 176; Dolores Hayden, *Redesigning the American Dream: The Future of Housing, Work and Family Life* (New York: Norton, 1984), p. 17.

15. Hayden, p. 40; see also Gwendolyn Wright, *Building the Dream: A Social History of Housing in America* (Cambridge: MIT Press, 1981).

16. Hayden, pp. 35, 38, 55; Wright, pp. 246, 248.

17. Hayden, pp. 41–42; Wright, p. 247.

18. Wright, pp. 247–248.

19. Wright, p. 248.

20. Hayden, pp. 55–56; Wright, p. 256.

21. Hayden, pp. 63, 109.

22. Hayden, pp. 17–18; Wright, pp. 254–255.

23. "The fifth international design conference at Aspen found 500 conferees at the crossroads, pondering the direction of the arts, and, every now and then, of the American consumer," *Industrial Design* 2:4 (August 1955), p. 42; Avrom Fleishman, "M/R, a Survey of Problems, Techniques, Schools of Thought in Market Research: Part 1 of a Series," *Industrial Design* 5:1 (January 1958), pp. 33–34.

24. "Materialism, Leisure and Design," *Industrial Design* 4:12 (December 1957), pp. 33–34.

25. Dr. Wilson G. Scanlon, "Industrial Design and Emotional Immaturity," *Industrial Design* 4:1 (January 1957), pp. 68–69.

26. "Eleventh Annual ASID Conference: Three Days of Concentrated Design Discussion in Washington, D.C.," *Industrial Design* 2:6 (December 1955), p. 128; Theodore Peterson, *Magazines in the Twentieth Century* (Urbana: University of Illinois Press, 1964), pp. 255, 298, 301–302.

27. "Eleventh Annual ASID Conference," p. 123.

28. Richard Tyler George, "The Process of Product Planning," *Industrial Design* 3:5 (October 1956), pp. 97–100. See also Deborah Allen, Avrom Fleishman, and Jane Fiske Mitarachi, "Report on Product Planning," *Industrial Design* 4:6 (June 1957), pp. 37–81; "Lawrence Wilson," *Industrial Design* 2:5 (October 1955), pp. 82–83; "Sundberg-Ferar," *Industrial Design* 2:5 (October 1955), pp. 86–87; "10 Work Elements of Product Planning," *Industrial Design* 4:6 (June 1957), p. 47.

29. Avrom Fleishman, "M/R: Part 2," *Industrial Design* 5:2 (February 1958), p. 42.

30. "IDI Discusses TV, Styling and Creativity," *Industrial Design* 4:5 (May 1957), pp. 67–68.

31. A. C. Nielsen Company, "The Nielsen Ratings in Perspective" (1980), p. 20; "IDI Discusses TV," pp. 67–68.

32. "IDI Discusses TV," pp. 67–68. On television technology and set design, see "Design Review," *Industrial Design* 6:9 (August 1959), p. 89; "TV Sets Get Smaller and Smaller," *Industrial Design* 4:1 (January 1957), pp. 39–43; "Redesign: Philco Crops the Neck of the Picturetube to Be First with Separate-Screen Television," *Industrial Design* 5:6 (June 1958), p. 52; "Design Review," *Industrial Design* 6:9 (August 1959), p. 88; Tenite advertisement, *Industrial Design* 6:7 (July 1959), p. 23; Tenite advertisement, *Industrial Design* 8:11 (November 1961), p. 25.

33. "The Consumer at IDI," *Industrial Design* 4:11 (November 1957), pp. 68–72.

34. Hayden, p. 50.

35. Fleishman, "M/R, a Survey of Problems," pp. 27, 29. While Fleishman recognized Paul Lazarsfeld's contribution to market research, this article did not mention Lazarsfeld's work in the television industry or his development of The Analyzer, an early instrument for audience measurement, for CBS. See Laurence Bergreen, *Look Now, Pay Later* (New York: New American Library, 1981), pp. 170–171.

36. Fleishman, "M/R, a Survey of Problems," p. 27.

37. Fleishman, "M/R, a Survey of Problems," p. 35.

38. Fleishman, "M/R, a Survey of Problems," p. 37.

39. Fleishman, "M/R, a Survey of Problems," p. 40.

40. Fleishman, "M/R, a Survey of Problems," pp. 41–42.

41. Fleishman, "M/R: Part 2," pp. 34–35; C. Wright Mills, "The Man in the Middle," *Industrial Design* 5:11 (November 1958), p. 70; Don Wallace, "Report from Aspen," *Industrial Design* 5:8 (August 1958), p. 85.

42. Mills, pp. 72–74.

43. "Jane Wyatt's Triple Threat," p. 48.

44. Danny Peary, "Remembering 'Father Knows Best,'" in *TV Book,* ed. Judy Fireman (New York: Workman, 1977), pp. 173–175.

45. Long-running suburban family sitcoms that ran on network prime time during the early years of the women's movement were *Father Knows Best* (1954–1963), *Leave It to Beaver* (1957–1963), *The Donna Reed Show* (1958–1966), *The Dick Van Dyke Show* (1961–1966), *Hazel* (1961–1966), *Dennis the Menace* (1959–1963), and *The Adventures of Ozzie and Harriet* (1952–1966). This information was obtained from Brooks and Marsh, pp. 15–16, 193, 199–200, 211, 245–246, 322, 423–424.

QUESTIONS FOR DISCUSSION

1. How did the centrality of women's representations in the domestic situation comedies of the late 1950s and early 1960s work both for and against women's power in the real world? Discuss the concept of "marginalized centrality."

2. Haralovich claims that the realistic *mise en scène* of these filmed sitcoms worked to naturalize middle-class home life. What did this naturalistic aesthetic conceal? Contrast this with Lipsitz's claims about the working class/ethnic comedies of the earlier period.

 INFOTRAC COLLEGE EDITION

Search InfoTrac College Edition for articles under "television and 1950s" and "television and gender."

❖

PART III

The Classic
Network System

8

From Domestic Space to Outer Space
The 1960s Fantastic Family Sitcom
LYNN SPIGEL

Sitcoms of the early to mid-1960s, now staples of nostalgic nighttime cable television programming, are often derided as prime examples of the "vast wasteland" that purportedly characterized television programming of that era, especially when juxtaposed to the high-minded social, technological, and cultural ideals of the Kennedy administration and its rhetorical "New Frontier." In this article, cultural historian Lynn Spigel situates the "fantastic family sitcoms" of the period, represented by programs such as *I Dream of Jeannie, My Favorite Martian,* and *Bewitched,* in the context of one of the Kennedy administration's key initiatives, the space program. Rather than dismissing these programs as escapist fantasy or worse, Spigel suggests that they were indicative of tensions and contradictions within American society and the domestic space of the American family. By incorporating aspects of the space-age future being enacted and promoted via the very active space program of the period, these situation comedies made the familiar strange and the strange familiar. In that way, they ameliorated anxieties over both the present and future states of American domesticity as well as the American nation.

From *Close Encounters: Film, Feminism, and Science Fiction,* ed. Constance Penley
(University of Minnesota Press, 1991) Reprinted by permission of the publisher.

t's a warm July night in 1969. and millions of Americans sit before their television sets, with a gleam of hope and a beer can in hand, awaiting the arrival of history. There, on the small screen of the living room console, a man steps out of his large white spaceship and onto a crater-covered surface. His limbs float in slow-motion gestures, his distant voice breaks through the static, and then, with a "giant leap for mankind," a small American flag anchors familiar meanings onto an alien landscape. This is Apollo 11, the mission to the moon, the realization of a decade-long American dream, the biggest crowd pleaser in television memory.

Like all technological triumphs, the moon landing was fully enmeshed in political, social, cultural, and economic struggles. What I find particularly interesting are the meanings space travel had for television itself—and for the burgeoning American culture based on watching TV. For above all, the public's knowledge of space was communicated through the procession of rocket take-offs and orbits broadcast during the 1960s. But more than just transmitting a privileged view of the universe, television offered the American public a particular mode of comprehension. It represented space, like everything else, as a place that the white middle-class family could claim as its own. Yet this epistemology of space was not merely an attempt to colonize the unknown with familiar values. In many ways the fascination with space served to defamiliarize the common myths of the "Golden Age" of the 1950s and the notions of domesticity that so pervaded television's "message" in that decade.

In the 1960s, television would construct for itself a new generic form founded on the merger between the troubled paradise of 1950s domesticity and the new-found ideals of the American future.[1] We might call this form the *fantastic family sitcom,* a hybrid genre that mixed the conventions of the suburban sitcom past with the space-age imagery of the New Frontier. Programs like *I Dream of Jeannie, My Favorite Martian, The Jetsons,* and *Lost In Space* were premised on an uncanny mixture of suburbia and space travel, while shows like *My Mother the Car, Mr. Ed, My Living Doll,* and *Bewitched* with a seemingly incongruous blend of suburban banality and science fiction fantasy.[2]

These programs have received little critical attention, most certainly because they seem to represent the "lower depths" of television's prime-time past. Typically in this vein, critics tend to view such shows within the logic of cultural hierarchies, seeing their value in negative terms—that is, as the opposite of high art. Rather than leading to knowledge, these programs are said to constitute an escape from reason. Consider David Marc's recent thesis that sees them as reflections of the turned-on, tuned-out ethos of 1960s drug culture and locates their popularity in "de-politicization through escapist fantasy."[3] Yet reading these sitcoms as transparent reflections of a desire to escape fails to explain their often satirical and critical aspects. These genre hybrids did not simply reflect a collective desire to flee from the present; rather, the collision of science fiction fantasy with domestic comedy resulted in programs that contested their own form and content. Fantastic sitcoms were a complex organization of contradictory ideas, values, and meanings concerning the organization of social space and everyday life in suburbia. To understand how they emerged, we should read them in relation to historical changes that created the conditions in which they could flourish. In the following pages, I discuss historical shifts that were crucial to the rise of the fantastic sitcom and then suggest ways to see these shows as popular texts that allowed for diverse, often critical, perspectives on the social world.

DYSTOPIAN VISIONS
AND A NEW SPACE-AGE FUTURE

The intricate bond between television and space-age imagery can be understood as a *response to a series of disillusionments* that began to be most deeply felt in the late 1950s. By the end of that decade, Americans were looking backward at the great white hopes that had somehow led them down a blind alley. The utopian dreams for technological supremacy, consumer prosperity, and domestic bliss were revealing their limits in ways that could no longer be brushed aside. With consumer debt mounting, the stock market felt its first major slide of the decade in 1957. In that same year, Americans witnessed the most stunning technological embarrassment of the times when the Soviet Union beat the United States into space with Sputnik. While these national failures signaled harder times, the promise of easy living and barbecues in every yard was turned into the substance of nightmarish visions as social critics wrote voluminously of the anomie and emptiness experienced in the mass-produced suburbs. And as the walls of Levittown came tumbling down, television, the central household fixture of suburban bliss, also joined the pantheon of fallen idols.

As James Baughman has argued, disappointment in American institutions and lifestyles was typical among liberals and intellectuals who felt disenfranchised in Eisenhower's America.[4] But importantly, I want to stress, such cultural anxieties were also voiced in popular venues. Magazines, newspapers, popular books, and films looked critically at the past and established a set of discursive conventions through which Americans might reflect on their experiences. These critical views anticipated a series of changes in the meanings and practices surrounding television in the next decade.

In this context, critiques of suburbia were especially bitter, particularly when we consider the hopes invested in this new "promised land" at the beginning of the decade. After World War II, suburban towns were a practical alternative to hardships in the city. A severe housing shortage in urban centers was soothed by Federal Housing Association (FHA) construction loans and low-interest mortgages provided through the GI Bill. These government-financed projects made it possible for builders like Levitt and Sons to offer mass-produced housing at extremely low prices, so low in fact that it cost less to buy a home than to rent an apartment in the city. The suburbs were essentially built for the white middle class, and FHA policies guaranteed the communities' racial make-up. Building loans were predicated on red-lining (or zoning) practices that effectively kept all "undesirables" out of the lily-white neighborhoods.

For the white middle class, the suburbs quickly became more than just a practical alternative to the urban housing crisis. They were glorified in popular culture as a new land of plenty—the answer to Depression and wartime shortages. Home magazines presented wondrous designs, spacious ranch houses with rolling green yards, shiny pink appliances, and happy white families at play inside. But practical realities of post-war life necessitated certain alterations of this middle-class ideal. Cramped quarters took the place of the magazines' spacious ranch homes, and rather than gazing out at rolling green yards, residents found themselves sandwiched between the identical houses of their next-door neighbors.

Early in the 1950s, a number of critics expressed doubts about the homogeneous living arrangements and conformist attitudes that characterized middle-class lifestyles, and by the end of the decade, the mass-produced suburbs had become the subject of widespread concern.[5] John Keats's *A Crack in the Picture Window* (1956) presented unflattering pictures of the new suburbanites, with characters like John and Mary Drone, whose lives were spent deciding how to buy washing machines and avoid their busy-body neighbors. William Whyte's *The Organization Man* (1956) was a damming critique of the new company boys, whose willingness to conform to job expectations was mirrored by the peer-pressure policies of their suburban lifestyles. And in *The City in History* (1961), Lewis Mumford criticized the new organization of social space and the homogeneous lifestyles it encouraged.

The *post-war cult of domesticity* was wearing especially thin for women, and their dissatisfaction began to gain ground in popular thought by the end of the decade. Despite the glorification of the housewife's role, women had joined the labor force at significant rates in the 1950s, and in particular, the number of married female workers rose substantially; by 1962 they accounted for about 60 percent of the female labor force.[6] Thus when Betty Friedan attacked domestic ideology and institutional sexism in the *Feminine Mystique* (1963), she received widespread support.

Popular entertainment forms also expressed dismay with middle-class lifestyles. Film melodramas like Douglas Sirk's *All That Heaven Allows* (1956) and *Imitation of Life* (1959) showed the rigid social codes of middle-class ideals and the devastating consequences that class, race, and gender expectations had for the public. Popular media aimed at youth especially questioned middle-class family values. Rock 'n' roll gave teenagers the chance to participate in a new youth culture, separate from their parents, while youth films like *Rebel Without a Cause* (1955) and *King Creole* (1958) made juvenile delinquents into popular heroes, thereby providing teenagers with role models that challenged the suburban family ideal.[7]

If the nation was keen on self-loathing by the end of the decade, one event would provide even more reason for angst. On October 4, 1957, Americans suffered a grave blow to their sense of national esteem when the Soviet Union beat the United States into space with Sputnik. Cold-war logic was predicated upon America's ability to prevail in all technological endeavors, especially those associated with national security. Thus the advent of a Russian rocket soaring into orbit sharply contrasted with previous conventions for representing American relations with the Soviets. Ironically, just three days after Sputnik's launch, *Life* presented the first of a multi-part issue entitled "Man's New World," which claimed that "the present lives and future fortunes of every American man, woman and child are directly and immediately affected by the gigantic technical strides of the past few years."[8]

As Walter McDougall has argued, Sputnik quickly became a major media crisis.[9] Critics expressed anxieties about the nation's technological agenda, claiming that American science had put its faith in consumer durables rather than concentrating on the truly important goals of national security. As Henry Luce of *Life* said, "For years no knowledgeable U.S. scientist has had any reason to doubt that his Russian opposite number is at least his equal. It has been doubted only by people—some of them in the Pentagon—who confuse scientific progress with freezer and lipstick output."[10] These criticisms grew out of and reinforced a more general dismay with consumer capitalism that was voiced over the course of the post-war years. Science fiction writers Cyril Kornbluth and Frederik Pohl told of a future dominated by advertisers in their popular book *The Space Merchants* (1953), while non-fiction books like Vance Packard's *The Hidden Persuaders* (1957) and John Kenneth Galbraith's bestseller *The Affluent Society* (1958) attacked various aspects of consumer culture. Such concerns were fueled by the recession of 1957–58, which created more general doubts about the consumer economy. Private debt increased from $73 billion to $196 billion during the 1950s, so when the Eisenhower administration suggested that the recession could be overcome by increased consumer purchases, not all Americans took solace in the buy now/ pay later recovery plan.[11] In this economic and discursive context, Sputnik seemed a particularly poignant symbol of America's misconceived goals.

Finally, the United States began a series of attempts to find its own path to glory. Two months after the launching of Sputnik I, on December 6, 1957, America made its first foray into space, with its own rocket, Vanguard I. Vanguard rose four feet off the launch pad and sank in front of swarms of newspaper reporters and television cameras. The popular press called Vanguard such derisive names as "Flopnik," "Kaputnik," and "Stayputnik."

Thus, by the end of the decade, anxieties about private and public goals were being voiced in both intellectual and popular culture. But, rather than simply signaling the end of a golden era, this historical conjuncture of disappointments provided the impetus for a new utopian future—one based on the rhetoric of Kennedy's New Frontier and fortified with the discourse of science and technology.

The ideology of the New Frontier promised Americans a way to join the march of history. This was accomplished, not through a radical revolution in contemporary lifestyles, but rather through a liberal blend of private ethics with national purpose. The New Frontier was in this sense a popular movement, one that forged an alliance between its own political agenda and the patterns, meanings, and values of the past. In fact, the degree to which the American people were actually fatigued with their existence is not at all certain. In 1960, a nationwide survey in *Look* suggested that "most Americans today are relaxed, unadventurous, comfortably satisfied with their way of life and blandly optimistic about the future." *Look* went on to explain that American plans for the future were "mainly concerned with home and family." As for the larger arena of national purpose and progress in space, *Look* summed up the attitude with the words of one Milwaukee woman who confided, "We are pretty far removed from outer space here on 71st Street." Indeed, as *Look* went on to describe, people were far more concerned with everyday realities. "The chief worry of a lumber dealer in South Dakota," *Look* reported, "was 'having only one channel to watch on TV.' " Importantly, however, the magazine packaged this national complacency within a new and more exciting image. *Look* called the issue "Soaring into the Sixties," and it displayed a rocket on the cover—one that, unlike the flopniks of the past, was clearly taking off.[12] Indeed, just as *Look*'s editors were able to turn a land of happy homebodies into a nation bound for glory, the construction of the New Frontier was largely accomplished through media discourses that envisioned new and potent ways to organize past experiences.

The Kennedy administration eagerly adapted its own political agenda to the new space-age metaphors—metaphors based on the tenets of progress, democracy, and national freedom. The forthright do-gooder citizen to whom Kennedy appealed was given the promise of a new beginning in abstract terms. Ideas like freedom need an image, and the ride into space proved to be the most vivid concretization of such abstractions, promising a newfound national allegiance through which we would not only diffuse the Soviet threat, but also shake ourselves out of the doldrums that 1950s life had come to symbolize.

As other historians have argued, the promise of reaching the moon by the end of the decade was a political coup for a president intent on garnering public support. After the embarrassments of the Bay of Pigs and the Soviet launching of Yuri Alekseyevich Gagarin into space, Kennedy was able to transform the scrutinizing gaze of defeat into a new look that reached upward to the heavens. Building on the firmly entrenched associations between space weaponry and national security (especially Congress's creation of the civilian-controlled National Aeronautics and Space Administration [NASA] in 1958), the Kennedy administration devised a solid technocratic plan through which to shift public consciousness away from our military expansionism overseas and onto the idea of space travel. In 1961, the President sent Congress a new budget that poured millions into NASA, and a new theatrics of space emerged with astronaut stars appearing on the covers of national magazines.

The goals of the Kennedy administration merged particularly well with those of the television industry, which at this time was facing a public image crisis of its own. By the latter half of the 1950s, the networks had become the target of attacks launched primarily by influential east-coast critics who began to mourn the passing of television's "Golden Age." As Baughman has argued, the critics, who were mostly liberals, saw television as an emblem of their disenfranchisement in Eisenhower's America.[13] Dismayed by programming trends that favored popular rather than elite (i.e., their) tastes, they were especially upset by the cancellation of "prestige" programs like anthology dramas and *See It Now* (whose ousting in 1958 sparked a particularly heated debate), and they protested the slew of sitcoms, westerns, and quiz shows that had taken the place of what they considered higher television art.

This situation was exacerbated in 1959 when Congress's investigation of the quiz-show scandals revealed that the sponsors had fed answers to contestants in the hope of heightening dramatic appeal. The critics seized the moment, blaming the breach of public trust on egg-head contestants like Professor Charles Van Doren, shady sponsors like Revlon, the money-grubbing networks, and the negligent regulators at the Federal Communications Commission (FCC). Having been one of the most popular program types, the quiz shows now were proof of the dangers of "low" television. As such, they enabled discourses on aesthetic and moral reform to emerge with a new purpose, creating a basis upon which critics, educators, the clergy and other cultural elites could ridicule popular tastes. After blaming the deceitful advertisers and negligent FCC, the *New Republic* concluded that

> a real investigation would center on a simple question: why is television so bad, so monotonous? The change over the past few years from Elvis Presley to Pat Boone is progress, from the obscene to the insipid. But is that the best TV can do? Must the majority of TV time be given to . . . the weary insouciance of the Bings and Frankies, the smiling but vacuous goings-on of Gale Storm, Donna Reed, Ernie Ford, Betty Hutton, June Allyson, Mickey Rooney, Ozzie and Harriet?[14]

In April of 1959, in the midst of these controversies, the FCC announced a new inquiry into network operations. Ultimately, however, rather than revamping the network system, the regulators adopted a reform strategy centered on program quality. In 1961, in his address to the National Association of Broadcasters, FCC Chair Newton Minow called television a "vast wasteland," attacking, in particular, popular entertainment formats. While he was critical about the networks' "concentration of power," his reform program did not attack the structure of commercial television; instead, it ridiculed its products. Popular formats like sitcoms, quiz shows, and westerns were "low TV," while his proposed educational and pay channels would ensure cultural uplift.[15] By focusing on issues of high and low TV, Minow placed himself squarely within the discourses of the culture-critics before him, and his position as FCC Chairman gave this kind of TV bashing an official stamp of approval.

In the wake of this public-image crisis, the networks found the look-ahead spirit of Kennedy's New Frontier to be a potent metaphor, one that might divert attention away from the scandals of the past and create a new utopian purpose for the medium. In their attempt to restore the cultural validity of television and to ward off the more practical threat of regulatory action, the networks cultivated information programming, lengthening their 15-minute news programs to half an hour in 1963 and showcasing hard-hitting documentaries.[16] Perhaps not surprisingly, at a time when the ontological status of the television image was thrown into question by the fraudulent histrionics of the quiz shows, the networks turned to reality-oriented formats with renewed vigor.

In this general programming context, the space race became a privileged-focus of attention. Documentary formats found space travel to be a particularly compelling subject of inquiry, and news teams eagerly covered rocket launchings throughout the decade.[17] Here, the political agenda of Kennedy's New Frontier and the networks' search for cultural validity merged harmoniously. Kennedy's promise to land on the moon before the end of the decade became television's promise as well. The space race gave television something to shoot for. It presented a whole new repertoire of images and created a whole new reason for looking at the living room console.

Information formats, in this and other ways, took up the challenge of national purpose and served, in large part, as an antidote to the attack on television's debased form. But the limits of public discourse foreclosed the possibility that entertainment television could be treated in the same vein. Indeed, as the critics (and Minow) had argued, sitcoms, quiz shows, westerns, and the like were resolutely low. While intended to infuse television with a set of "moral" guidelines, critical categories of high and low culture enabled the industry to divide its attention. With documentary and news formats to satisfy the reform demands of the wasteland critique, the industry continued to present its "low"—and markedly popular—money-making formats. Still, entertainment programming underwent its own peculiar transition. Although in distorted and circuitous ways, the progressive spirit of the New Frontier and its focus on space-age imagery serves as a launching pad for significant revisions in television's fictional forms.

TO THE MOON, ALICE!

In 1996, *Mad* magazine presented a cartoon saga of the perfect American television family, Oozie, Harried, Divot, and Rickety Nilson, who "lived completely and hermetically sealed off from reality." The story's opening panel showed Oozie comfortably reading his newspaper, which Harried had doctored-up in order to soothe the tensions of the day. Harried stands grinning in the foreground of the panel, where she tells her housewife friend, "I cut out all the articles that might disturb him"; as proof of her deed we see large cut-out areas under headlines that read "Vietnam," "Laos," and "race riots." Nevertheless, Oozie complains to Harried of his action-packed day. "First," he drones, "I pulled the wrong cord on the Venetian blind. . . . Then, Art Linkletter's House Party was preempted by a Space Shot. . . . It's been one thing after another."[18]

As *Mad* so humorously suggested, the middle-class suburban sitcom was vastly out of sync with the problems of the nation. Indeed, its codes of realism (the bumbling but lovable dads, the perfect loving wives, the mundane storylines) were, by this time, codes of satire and parody. If the suburban sitcoms had once explained the ideals and goals of the nation, they no longer seemed to matched the real world at all, as is vividly expressed by Oozie's choice of television programs. He prefers the family doldrums of Art Linkletter's *House Party* to the country's national goals in space.

Mad's TV spoof was part of a more general shift in popular representations of family life on television in the 1960s. Programs like *Bewitched, I Dream of Jeannie, Green Acres, The Beverly Hillbillies, The Jetsons, My Living Doll, The Addams Family,* and *The Munsters* poked fun at narrative conventions of the sitcom form and engaged viewers in a popular dialogue through which they might reconsider social ideals. In their own context, they took up the challenge of the New Frontier, but rather than providing a rational-scientific discourse on the public sphere (like that of the 1960s documentary), they presented a highly irrational, supernatural discourse on private life. In other words, they launched a critique of the American family in ways that were antithetical to the norms of television's "high" art forms.

These programs can be understood in the context of other media forms (magazines, rock 'n' roll, youth films, melodramas, and so on) that gave voice to critical perspectives on the social world. Borrowing from the discourses of previous texts and transmuting already established generic conventions, the fantastic sitcom provided a cultural space in which anxieties about everyday life could be addressed, albeit through a series of displacements and distortions. The sitcom format was an apt vehicle for this because it offered ready-made conflicts over gender roles, domesticity, and suburban lifestyles, while its laugh tracks, harmonious resolutions, and other structures of denial functioned as safety valves that diffused the "trouble" in the text. Moreover, its proclivity to deal with "contemporary" subject matter made the genre responsive to larger shifts in the social world.

In the most basic terms, changes in the family sitcom can be charted through a demographic analysis of family structure and living arrangements. In the early half of the 1950s, domestic comedies tended to present a varied demographic group that included families living in urban areas (such as *I Love Lucy, Make Room for Daddy,* and *My Little Margie,* suburban areas (such as *I Married Joan, Ozzie and Harriet,* and *My Favorite Husband*), and notably, ethnic and working-class types like Italian immigrants *(Life with Luigi),* Blacks *(Amos 'n' Andy, Beulah*) and working-class families *(The Honeymooners, The Life of Riley).* These programs appealed to television's early audience, which was located primarily in urban centers (especially the Northeast) and which could most strongly relate to these ethnic/urban types. As television became a national medium (by 1955 it was more evenly disseminated throughout the country), producers, networks, and advertisers tried to appeal to a more homogeneous, middle-class audience. In addition, as George Lipsitz has suggested, when the Hollywood majors rigorously entered into television production in the mid-1950s, these ethnic/working-class programs, which tended to be produced by small independents, began to wane.[19]

Concurrent with these shifts, the conventions for representing the family group changed over the course of the decade. Although these developments were somewhat uneven, significant trends can be tracked. Out of the seventeen different family sitcoms that aired on network prime time between 1957 and 1960, fourteen were set in the suburbs.[20] Meanwhile, the ethnic variations disappeared, so that by September 1960, they were all off the networks.[21] By the end of the decade, the middle-class suburban sitcom had become the primary form for representing family life. Programs like *Ozzie and Harriet, Leave It to Beaver, The Donna Reed Show, Father Knows Best,* and the more "moderne" *Dick Van Dyke Show* dramatized, with varying degrees of humor, the lives of nuclear families in suburban towns. The families included a modest number of children, a contented couple, and almost always lived near a group of friendly—if quirky—neighbors who were obviously of the same social class. Donna (Reed) Stone, for example, lived in the perfect suburban town of Hilldale with her physician-husband Alex Stone, her two children, and her next-door neighbor, Midge Kelsey (whose husband was also a doctor). Unlike such earlier zany sitcom characters as Lucy Ricardo *(I Love Lucy)* and Joan Stevens *(I Married Joan),* who tried desperately to break out of their domestic spaces, the women in these sitcoms were typically happy housewives who, despite the everyday strains of mothering, had put their faith in the suburban dream.

If these programs were out of sync with the widespread critique of suburbia at the end of the decade, they nevertheless remained on the networks through the early part of the 1960s, and until 1964, several ranked in the top twenty-five on the Nielsen charts. Most strikingly, however, by the fall 1966 season, all had been taken off the air.[22] This trend continued in the coming years; between 1966 and 1969 only three out of the thirty-two different domestic comedies aired on network prime time were suburban family sitcoms.[23] Taking their place were two new types that gained ground in the early to mid-1960s: the broken-family sitcom and the fantastic family sitcom.[24]

In the former, the middle-class family still constituted the focus of the show, but one parent was missing. This corresponded to the rising divorce rates of the 1960s, but in the fictional representation, the missing parent was never absent because of divorce (which was a network censorship taboo) but because he or she had died.[25] In this way, the broken-family sitcom signaled changes in family structure, but it also often smoothed over these social changes by including a character who functioned narratively as a surrogate parent. Thus, Uncle Charlie in *My Three Sons,* Aunt Bee in *The Andy Griffith Show,* and governess Katy Holstrum in *The Farmer's Daughter* were among a long list of stand-in parents.

In the fantastic sitcoms, families were also often formed in new ways. The genre was populated by unmarried couples such as Jeannie and Tony in *I Dream of Jeannie,* extended families such as *The Addams Family* (with Uncle Fester, Grandmama, and Cousin It), and childless couples such as Wilbur and Carol in *Mr. Ed.* But these sitcoms presented more than just demographic changes; they provided narrative situations and themes that suggested a clear departure from the conventions of the suburban family sitcoms that preceded them. These genre hybrids were parodic in nature because they retained the conventions of the previous form, but they made these conventions strange by mismatching form and content.

Bewitched, for example, employs the narrative conventions of the middle-class suburban sitcom. Its narrative structure revolves around the comedic complications and harmonious resolutions common to the sitcom genre as a whole. Typically, Darrin Stephens has an important advertising account at the office, but his domestic situation leads to complications. Often his mother-in-law Endora finds reason to spark a fight that creates havoc for the rest of the episode. This narrative complication is then neutralized by Samantha, who mediates the dispute, wins Darrin's ad account, and thus restores narrative harmony. The setting—an ideal two-story home located in a middle-class town—also borrows its conventions from the middle-class suburban sitcom. Similarly, the program retains clear gender divisions between public and private space, with Samantha taking the role of housewife and Darrin an executive in a high-rise office. Gladys and Abner Kravitz function as the neighbor characters of the earlier form. But in all of this, something is amiss. Samantha is a witch, and her supernatural powers recast the narrative situation so that the conventional becomes strange. Warlocks, witch doctors, and evil witches populate the traditionally decorated rooms of the Stephens's home, while powerful spells bring Ben Franklin, Mother Goose, and tooth fairies alive. In a similar way, programs like *Mr. Ed, My Mother the Car, I Dream of Jeannie, The Addams Family,* and *My Living Doll* retained the conventional forms of the suburban sitcom past but infused them with talking horses, conversing cars, genies, ghouls, and robots.

This peculiar mixture of domesticity and fantastic situations could be found outside the sitcom form in other popular venues. These series employed discursive strategies that were also used in representations of science and, in particular, space science. During the 1950s and 1960s, the American media communicated ideas about space through tropes of domesticity and family romance. National magazines mixed every-day situations with fantastic scenarios of space travel. In 1958, *Look* quoted lyrics from songs about space written by children of parents at the missile test program at Cape Canaveral. Another article showed how a vacationing family, dressed for summer fun, found Cocoa Beach a perfect place to watch for "imminent missile launchings" while "tak[ing] in the sun and the sights at the same time."[26]

The discursive conjuncture between domestic and outer space found its standard form in *Life*'s biographical essays, which presented technical information alongside multi-page spreads depicting family scenes and life histories of the astronauts. For example, in the May 18, 1962 issue, Scott Carpenter was pictured with his wife Rene on the cover, while the inside story showed family photos of Scott as a child with his grandfather, his pony, his friends, and finally his modern-day wife and children. The snapshots showed them as the ideal American family: playing at home, enjoying a family vacation, and finally in the last pages of the essay, saying their farewells just before the space flight.[27] In this way, the photographic narrative sequence suggested that Scott Carpenter's flight to the moon was one more in a series of "everyday" family activities. This became the conventional narration of *Life*'s astronaut profiles in the years to come.

In a practical sense, this essay format allowed the magazines to appeal to diverse audiences because it conveyed technical, scientific information in the popular format of family drama. Discussions of domesticity made space familiar, offering a down-to-earth context for the often-abstract reasoning behind space flights. When astronaut John Young went to space in 1965, this merger of science and domesticity was taken to its logical extreme. *Life* reported his flight by telling the story of his wife and children, who witnessed the event on television:

> The Youngs watch. In John Young's home outside Houston, the astronaut's family sits at the TV set as the seconds crawl toward launch time. Barbara Young fidgets, Sandy fiddles with a bit of string and Johnny, still getting over chicken pox, stares unsmiling at the screen. At lift off Mrs. Young hugs Sandy. "Fantastic," she crows . . . as ship soars skyward.

The accompanying photographs showed the Young family sitting before the television set, much like other Americans would have done that day.[28] Here as elsewhere, the "fantastic" is communicated through the domestic, and space technology is itself mediated through the more familial technology of television.

Even the space scientists seemed to recognize the popular appeal of domestic explanations for space travel. In 1958, Dr. Wernher von Braun told *Life* that "missile building is much like interior decorating. Once you decide to refurnish the living room you go shopping. But when you put it all together you may see in a flash it's a mistake—the draperies don't go with the slip covers. The same is true of missiles." And in 1969, NASA engineer John C. Houbolt told the same magazine that a "rendezvous around the moon was like being in a living room."[29]

The American public responded in kind, tying space-age imagery to their own domestic lives. In 1962, *Life* reported that parents across the country were naming their children in new ways. Lamar Orbit Hill, John Glenn Davis, John Glenn Donato, and John Glenn Apollo were among the list of space-age babies, and, as *Life* pointed out, the trend was so consuming that one couple "yielded to the headlines and named their new boy John Glenn—they'd been planning to call him Robert Kennedy."[30]

Big industry capitalized on and added to this space-age fever. In 1955, when going to the moon was more Technicolor fantasy than technocratic plan, Disneyland made space into family fun in its "Tomorrowland" section of the park. In the early 1960s, with the official space race now underway, the Seattle and New York World's Fairs opened their gates to families who wandered about futuristic pleasure gardens, peering at Ford's 100-passenger space ship and pondering the NASA exhibit. Meanwhile, women's home magazines included recipes for "blast-off" space cakes, promoted "space-age homes," and suggested building "space platforms" instead of porches.[31] Songwriters fashioned romantic tunes like "Space Ship for Two," "Earth Satellite," and "Sputnik Love."[32] Advertisers, eager to employ popular meanings, used space imagery to glorify family-oriented products. Ford, for example, showed a little boy dressed in a space suit, exploring his brand new Fairlane family sedan and telling consumers that "Ford interiors are . . . out of this world."[33]

This merger of science and domesticity thus became a conventional mode of thinking about the fantastic voyage into space, but as the above examples show, it also provided a new mode of expressing family relations. In the fantastic sitcom, science fiction fantasy invaded the discourses of the everyday, so that the norms of domesticity were made unfamiliar.

As Fredric Jameson has argued, science fiction tends less to imagine the future than to "defamiliarize and restructure our experience of our own *present*."[34] Although these sitcoms were not science fiction narratives per se, they engaged elements of science fiction fantasy for similar purposes. Rather than portraying the future, the fantastic sitcoms presented critical views of contemporary suburban life by using tropes of science fiction to make the familial strange.

Consider again the case of Samantha Stephens, who swore off her supernatural powers to marry a mere mortal. Episode after episode, we find the good witch in her Sears Roebuck outfits, masquerading as the perfect suburban housewife, happily scrambling eggs as Darrin deliberates over his next trite advertising slogan. Consider as well the beautiful Jeannie, who gleefully fulfills the wishes of her astronaut-master Tony as he desperately tries to hide her from his NASA bosses. And consider finally the exploits of the Jetsons, an average American cartoon family living in the twenty-first century, which turns out to be a space-odyssey version of Levittown. These sitcoms incorporated elements of science fiction to present a heightened and fantastic version of suburban life.

As Tzvetan Todorov has argued, the fantastic exists less as a genre than as a moment in a text, a moment characterized by hesitation.[35] The fantastic often occurs at the point at which the hero or heroine doubts the credibility of the situation (can this be happening, or am I dreaming this?). In the fantastic sitcom, the doubting Thomas character became a stock vehicle for this kind of hesitation. Gladys Kravitz, the busy-body neighbor in *Bewitched,* constantly doubted her own visions (or at least her husband Abner did). Similarly, Dr. Bellows, whose psychiatric discourse sought to explain all human aberrations, hesitated to believe the outlandish stories that Tony conjured up in his attempts to hide his genie from the boys at the space project. In addition to this hesitation within the mind of the character, the fantastic also makes the reader uncertain about the status of the text. The story calls its own conventions of representation into question and makes the reader wonder whether the narrative situation is possible at all. In the fantastic sitcom, the elements called into question are not the fantastic aspects per se (we are never made to question whether Jeannie is a genie, nor does the narrative ask if being a genie is possible in the first place). Rather, the moment of hesitation takes place in the realm of the natural. We are, in other words, made to question the "naturalness" of middle-class existence. We are asked to hesitate in our beliefs about the normative roles of gender, class, and race that so pervade the era's suburban lifestyles. In this sense, the fantastic unmasks the conventionality of the everyday.

These sitcoms expressed tensions about the classist, racist, and sexist premises of suburban life by revolving around fantastic situations that referred, in hyperbolic ways, to everyday practices of the middle class. In this sense, they can be seen as the 1960s answer to the ethnic, working-class family programs of the earlier decade. Although Italian immigrants, Jewish mothers, and working-class bus drivers might have disappeared from the screen, they returned in a new incarnation as genies, witches, and robots. In other words, fantastic hyperbolic representations of cultural difference took the place of the more "realistic" portrayals. At a time when the civil rights movement had gained ground, these programs dramatized the exclusionary practices of the middle-class suburbs, not in realistic ways, but through exaggerated, comedic representations.

In fact, fear of the "Other" became one of the central narrative motifs of the fantastic sitcom. In place of the idyllic neighbor characters of the suburban sitcom past, these genre hybrids presented unflattering images of the middle-class community. Instead of *Donna Reed's* best friend Midge or *Ozzie and Harriet's* affable Thorny, we had neighborhood snoops like *Bewitched's* Gladys Kravitz and *My Favorite Martian's* Detective Bill Brennan, characters who threatened to expose the alien's identity. In this regard the programs drew on earlier science fiction forms that dramatized the fear of aliens in our midst. Anthology shows like

Science Fiction Theater, The Twilight Zone, and *The Outer Limits* included episodes that revolved around aliens moving into suburban communities, while science fiction films like *War of the Worlds* and *Invasion of the Body Snatchers* based their plots on alien invasions.[36] The sitcoms incorporated this earlier strategy, but dramatized it in comedic terms.

These programs presented friendly, lovable aliens: good witches, flying nuns, glamorous genies, favorite Martians, humorous horses, motherly cars, and friendly ghosts were among the strange but kindly heroes and heroines. Rather than the aliens advancing a threat, it was the white middle-class suburbanites who revealed their darker sides. *The Addams Family* and *The Munsters* (which engaged the fantastic by turning to horror rather than science fiction) were particularly keen on this theme. These ghouls were friendly, kind, generous folks who welcomed strangers into their homes. But their difference from the white middle class made them unacceptable to suburbanites who feared deviations. Thus, after a glimpse at the cobwebbed decor, slimy pets, man-eating plants, and cream of toad soup, house guests typically fled from the haunted mansions in a panic.

Space aliens often presented similar commentary on the exclusionary tactics of white middle-class suburbanites. A 1967 episode of *The Beverly Hillbillies* is an emblematic example. This sitcom based its entire situation on the theme of cultural difference in a homogeneous, upper-class community. According to the story of the opening credit sequence, "poor mountaineer" Jed Clampet strikes oil in the Ozarks, after which he rounds up his "kinfolk" and takes them to the opulent California suburb. Their Southern hospitality provides a sharp contrast to their snobby banker neighbors, Mr. and Mrs. Drysdale, who socialize with the Clampets only in order to keep their oil money in the bank. In one particular episode, Mr. Drysdale hire a group of Italian-speaking midgets to pose as Martians in an advertising stunt for his bank. When the midgets, dressed in Martian suits, land their spacecraft in the Clampets' yard, the hillbilly family is at first alarmed. Granny, the most fearful of the bunch, calls the spacemen "little green varmints," but Jed's daughter, Ellie May, scolds her for this undue prejudice. "Well Granny," she says, "they can't help it if they's little and green," and taking this to heart Jed declares, "Ellie's right. We shouldn't let on that they's any different than us." After this bit of moralizing, their ideals of neighborliness and hospitality overcome their fears, and Granny invites the aliens in for "vittles." Thus, the kindly but naive hillbillies are more accepting of cultural differences than are their snobby Beverly Hills neighbors.

But this tolerance comes to a halt when cousin Jethro resparks the fear of strangers. Jethro, who constantly boasts of his sixth-grade education, is more schooled than the others. In the narrative logic, however, his education is his Achilles heel, for it makes him more vulnerable to the hollow ideals of middle-class life. In this episode, Jethro's schoolbook knowledge of Martians leads him to adopt the "get them before they get us" attitude that is reminiscent of middle-class rationales for social segregation. Having read that Martians can turn people into robots, he suggests a plan for extermination. Chilled by Jethro's warning, Granny reaches for her shotgun and shoots the alien spacecraft.

Often, the fantastic sitcoms represented aliens as being specifically female: Jeannies, witches, and sexy robots. These women had to be carefully guarded so as not to reveal their difference from the group outside. Snooping neighbors like Gladys Kravitz kept a constant vigil over the Stephens's home, hoping to catch the good witch in the act; Jeannie was hidden in her bottle, far away from next-door neighbor Roger (until the later episodes when he discovers her secret) and Dr. Bellows, who constantly pried into Tony's domestic life; the Flying Nun kept her aerodynamic secrets safely among the sisterhood at church; Dave Crabtree's mother clandestinely lived her second life in the form of a 1928 Porter automobile; and Dr. Robert McDonald kept the secret of his robot (played by the vampish Julie Newmar) hidden from his next-door neighbor, who had a powerful crush on the "living doll."

This woman-as-alien motif was indebted to earlier science fiction literature and films. In the 1950s, for example, stories that dealt with alien invasion often centered on relations of sexual difference. Science fiction thrillers like *War of the Worlds* (a librarian falls in love with a scientist who battles the space aliens), *Them!* (a woman scientist falls in love with the cop who kills the giant ants), and *Forbidden Planet* (an astronaut falls in love with the daughter of a psychotic scientist) presented tales that intertwined alien forces with gender dynamics. In such films, romance served to address the enigma in a way that scientific explanation could not. While the scientists try to understand the alien through the conventions of rational discourse, their success is always partial. They can destroy the alien, but the basis for explaining its origins and reproduction is never wholly scientific. Instead, the epistemological basis for diffusing the threat of difference is transposed onto romantic coupling. It is romantic love and marriage (the reproduction of the status quo and normal gender distinctions) that finally solve the crisis of the "Other." That is, sexual difference structures all other differences. The demise of the alien—whether it be Martian, giant ant, or psychotic parent—goes hand in hand with the bonding of hero and heroine and their acceptance of traditional marks of sexual identity. However, rather than serving a wholly conservative function, these films actually problematized the ideology of domesticity by making it strange.[37]

In fact, representations of the space race—whether offered in scientific or fantastic modes—often evoked this kind of defamiliarization. A perfect example is an episode from the syndicated series *Science Fiction Theater,* which was produced from 1955 to 1957 and funded in part by the Defense Department. The episode entitled "First Woman on the Moon" tells the story of Renza Hale and her astronaut-husband Joe who, upon the orders of his space department bosses, invites her to travel to the moon. Once Renza is on the moon, however, problems ensue. Renza is bored because the men will not let her leave the rocket, and her culinary talents go to waste since she cannot get the hang of anti-gravity cooking. One night, after her Yorkshire pudding is too tough, Renza breaks down. The next morning, she ventures out onto the lunar landscape without informing the crew. After a panicked search, Joe is furious and in a scolding tone tells his wife, "Your place is on earth at home where I know you're safe." In this episode, tropes of science fiction fantasy allow for an exposition of anxieties that women faced in more everyday circumstances. This program turns out to be a thinly veiled exploration of domesticity and the gendered division of spheres that so pervaded ideas about women's place in the 1950s.

If the space race provided a critique of gender in fictional forms, it also gave voice to feminist views in the culture at large. In 1960, *Look*'s cover story asked, "Should a Girl Be First in Space?" presenting the story of Betty Skelton, an American pilot who underwent a series of tests for space travel. But according to Betty, her fellow spacemen, who nicknamed her No. 7 ½, were not likely to take her along for the ride. As *Look* reported, "Some 2,000 American women, mostly teenagers, have volunteered for space flight," but, "what Miss Skelton and other possibly qualified women fear is not that they will be lofted out of the atmosphere, but that they won't." The article even went on to declare that "women have more brains and stamina per pound than men," and concluded as well that physical and psychological requirements for space travel "are so specialized that specific individual qualifications far outweigh any difference based on sex." In this case, the space race provided a photo-essay opportunity for deconstructing notions about biologically determined gender difference. However, this was recuperated within more conventional ideas about domesticity; later in the essay *Look* promised that the first woman in space would be "married," possibly even the "scientist-wife of a pilot engineer."[38]

In 1963, when the Soviet Union sent Valentina Tereshkova into space, *Life* ran an editorial that presented even more damning criticism of America's treatment of women. Written by Clare Boothe Luce (who was married to publisher Henry Luce), the article argued that

> Soviet Russia put a woman into space because Communism preaches and, since the Revolution of 1917, has tried to practice the inherent equality of men and women. The flight of Valentina Treshkova is, consequently, symbolic of the emancipation of the Communist woman. It symbolizes to Russian women that they actively share (not passively bask, like American women) in the glory of conquering space.

Boothe Luce went on to tell the story of the thirteen American women pilots who, while having proved their physical capacity for space flight in government tests, were barred from participating in the (aptly titled) manned space program.[39] The article (which most likely was published only because of Luce's family ties) pointedly attacked American sexism. The space race thus provided grounds upon which to question the gender-based decisions behind the New Frontier's march of progress.

Such blatant attacks on institutional sexism were atypical of mass media of the times, and 1960s television, which sought to appeal to broad-based audiences, was by no means a venue for this kind of dialogue. However, the domestic situation comedy was, by its very nature, predicated on the gender conflicts of the American family, and in the 1960s hybrid version, these conflicts were augmented by the fantastic scenarios of space-age situations. In a decade that began with Betty Friedan's criticisms of the mass media's "happy housewife heroine," these fantastic sitcoms offered exaggerated and humorous renditions of the June Cleaver syndrome. Thus, *Jeannie* and *Bewitched* revolved around super-powerful women who tried to efface their potential in return for the "rewards" of family life. Like Donna Reed, who sacrificed her nursing career for life with Dr. Alex Stone, these women traded their credentials for domestic bliss. But Samantha and Jeannie, unlike Donna, had more difficult transitions from career to housewife. Their supernatural powers called for exaggerated forms of self-imposed containment. Thus they became super-feminine. Jeannie referred to Tony as Master and scampered around the house in pink harem girl garb, while Samantha took the more conservative route of mini-skirts and aprons. In either case, they were perfect examples of Joan Rivière's seminal 1929 study "womanliness as a Masquerade," which showed how successful female professionals felt compelled to adopt a heightened veneer of femininity as a strategy for coping with their "transgression" of normative gender roles. By posing as super-feminine types, these women were able to minimize anxiety about the negative reactions they anticipated from male associates.[40] In the 1960s television version, powerful female characters were shown to threaten gender expectations of the patriarchal world; their masquerade as ideal housewives might well have alleviated audience tensions about the changing role of women at the time.

Although this basic situation was less than revolutionary, it did provide a premise for a more subversive kind of comedy that poked fun at social expectations about gender roles. The narratives continually showed how Samantha's and Jeannie's power could not be integrated into patriarchal norms, and they dramatized the impossibility of absolute containment. Notably in this regard, they provided an expressive outlet for women's "bottled-up" rebelliousness through a dopplegänger motif. Samantha's look-alike cousin and Jeannie's look-alike sister were wacky, wild, swinging singles who functioned as hyperbolic depictions of non-domestic roles for women. They had numerous lovers, visited maharajahs, and traveled the universe at their whim. Even if these characters were depicted as irresponsible party girls of the free-love decade, they often directly confronted their feminine counterparts, criticizing the boring lifestyles Samantha and Jeannie had chosen. Similarly, Samantha's bad witch mother, Endora (who was estranged from her warlock husband, Maurice), strongly opposed her daughter's marriage to "Durwood" and continually begged her to skip out to exotic locales like the French Riviera. Significantly here, these female doubles underscored the idea that the non-domestic woman was specifically of a jet-set class whose upper-crust lifestyles had little relationship to the everyday concerns of real working/independent women. Thus, while fantastic sitcoms allowed alternative female roles to be depicted, they bypassed the more threatening elements of women's economic and social power by confining that power to a small group of elites.

These programs also parodied middle-class men who strove to comply with bureaucratic dictates. Darrin Stephens, Tony Nelson, and Dr. Robert McDonald constantly tried to keep their strange and powerful secrets within the private sphere of their homes.[41] Like William Whyte's "organization man," these men had to hide any kind of social deviance behind a strict veneer of allegiance to the corporate ideal. In this way they very much adopted the structural position of the woman in the masquerade, only here the men hid their secret source of power by donning the exaggerated pose of the company boy. By dramatizing these scenarios, the fantastic sitcom often inverted the conventional power dynamics of masculinity and femininity, and in the process, they made viewers laugh at their own assumptions about gender.

In *Jeannie* this inversion of sexual identity was directly related to and reinforced by the program's burlesque of technological supremacy, specifically the space race. Not only did the sitcom poke fun at gender roles; it also mocked men's dominion over scientific progress. The program retains traditional divisions between public and private spheres. While the suburban home is the woman's place, NASA headquarters—and by extension space itself—is the male domain. However, Jeannie always manages to blur the gendered divisions of private and public spheres. She typically arrives incognito at NASA headquarters where she undermines its scientific breakthroughs with her greater powers. After all, she need only blink herself onto the moon.[42]

Take, for example, a 1968 episode in which Jeannie grants three wishes to Tony's astronaut pal Roger. Roger wishes to change places with Tony, who has been selected by NASA to travel to the moon. Upon his wish, Tony and Roger find themselves in each other's bodies, a situation resulting in confusion about male identity, a confusion that is typical of the series as a whole. In this case, as elsewhere, NASA psychiatrist Dr. Bellows tries to explain the rational causes behind this male identity crisis, but science fails to locate the "feminine" cause. Doctor Bellows, who assumes that Tony and Roger suffer from a deep personality disorder, becomes increasingly confused by the scenario. Finally, after Roger agrees to retract his wish, Jeannie restores the men to their proper bodies, and Tony takes off for the moon.

However, the final tag sequence defies this resolution, suggesting instead that Jeannie's female (supernatural) powers are more potent than those of the male scientists. Jeannie and Roger sit in the Nelson living room watching Tony on television as he travels to the moon. The camera lingers on a shot of the television set as documentary footage (apparently taken from an actual launching) displays a rocket take-off that is intercut with fictional shots of Tony in the spacecraft and Jeannie and Roger watching the broadcast. Dramatic music underscores the rocket footage, so that the viewer is led to marvel at the feats of contemporary space science. But this moment of revelry is interrupted when Roger reminds Jeannie that he is still entitled to another wish. After Jeannie's characteristic blink, the camera cuts back to the television set where Roger is pictured alongside Tony in the spacecraft. Thus the patriarchal splendors of the space project are ironically cast aside as a woman is able to accomplish the same task with mere wishful thinking.

In 1969, *Green Acres* presented a similar spoof of NASA's scientific domain when precocious child inventor, Dinky, sells a moon rock to Oliver Douglas's wife, Lisa. Douglas, who has left his New York law practice for the pastoral splendors of a Hooterville farm, is hopelessly caught in the scientific rationalism of his city-slicker past, and the moon rocks prove especially disturbing from this point of view. despite the claims of Lisa (who is always more in tune with Hooterville's anti-scientific, screwball logic), Oliver insists that Dinky's rocks aren't really from the moon. As in other episodes, Lisa adopts the attitude of her bizarre Hooterville neighbors, and through this she is better equipped to deal with the enigmatic laws of her universe. She is, in other words, placed on the side of the aliens, the television-watching pigs, inbred farm hands, and, in this case, whiz-kid inventors that comprise her community. Her husband, on the other hand, searches for "rational" solutions.

Finally, new "scientific proof" convinces Oliver that the rock is from the moon. The evidence is put forward by Mr. Kimball, the double-talking and clearly irrational agriculture scientist, who informs Oliver that several moon rocks were stolen from a traveling NASA exhibit. To Oliver, this seems a logical explanation. But when he calls NASA headquarters, the space officials assume he is just another crackpot and tell him to phone Alcoholics Anonymous. As is typical of the series, the episode reveals the limits of masculine rationalization. The final scene shows confused NASA officials listening to a closet full of beeping moon rocks, just as unable to explain the phenomenon as Lisa Douglas was. Gender dynamics are thus reworked, so that women's "alien" logic is just as rational as the conventions of scientific discourse in the male sphere.

In *Bewitched,* the woman's alien powers serve to invert the gender relations of suburban domesticity, and with this, the consumer lifestyles that characterize the suburbs are also parodied. Darrin's job as a junior executive in an advertising firm provides ample situations for a popular version of critical stances toward the consumption ethic to emerge. In a 1967 episode, for example, Darrin takes a cold tablet concocted by Samantha's witch doctor friend, Dr. Bombay. The magic pill instantly cures Darrin's cold, and upon seeing this, Darrin's greedy boss Larry decides to make a fortune overnight by packaging the miracle drug. But as Samantha and Darrin soon discover, there's an unfortunate side effect that leaves Darrin with a new, markedly feminine, high-pitched voice. As in *Jeannie,* magic works to transform Darrin's bodily functions, so that his sexual identity—and at times even his species classification—is thrown into question. Whether he's turned into a screeching soprano, a dog, a mule, or a little boy, Darrin has to be returned to his proper manly state before the episode can end.

So too, Samantha destabilizes the patriarchal structures of consumer capitalism. Since the 1920s advertisers have particularly targeted women, who they calculate are responsible for about 80 percent of the family's purchases. Women thus are institutionalized consumers, and advertisers are eager to promote specifically female uses for products. As Judith Williamson has argued, a central way in which advertisements promote product use is through the promise of magical transformation—cold pills instantly stop symptoms, Mr. Clean materializes in your kitchen, skin creams make wrinkles vanish, and dishwasher soap makes hands look younger.[43] *Bewitched* inverts this dynamic by giving a woman the power of transformation. In the above episode, not only Darrin but also Larry and a drug manufacturer have been afflicted by Dr. Bombay's magic pills, and thus all are at the mercy of Samantha's witchcraft. Being a good witch, she transforms them with an antidote, and their masculine voices are restored. This closure, however, is only temporary, because in the next episode Samantha will once again wreak havoc on the advertising executives.

More generally, these sitcoms poked fun at the consumer lifestyles of suburban culture, particularly new domestic technologies. Jeannie and Samantha, for example, did the housework the extra-easy way, by operating appliances with their magic touch. The Jetsons' push-button food dispensers, the Flintstones' prehistoric lawnmower, Mr. Ed's love affair with his television set, Gomez's proclivity for train wrecks, Grandpa Munster's mad scientist lab, and Jed Clampet's inability to distinguish a garbage disposal from a meat grinder are but a few in a long list of humorous parodies of the technological utopias Americans had hoped to find in their new suburban homes. Indeed, the consumer culture of the 1960s found a way to defamiliarize its own familiar logic.

CONCLUSION

In the 1960s, the rhetoric of the New Frontier set an agenda for international militarism and heavenly exploration by calling on the traditional moral fiber of the American family. By the same token, the outworn ideals of family life were reinvigorated with new goals of public life. The space race, in particular, provided a popular spectacle through which Americans could view the future in terms of the past and still feel as if they were going somewhere. No longer a nation of homebodies, we moved from domestic to outer space while still sitting in our easy chairs.

It was in this land of space-age familialism that the hybrid genre of the fantastic sitcom emerged. Blending science fiction fantasy with domestic situations, these programs foregrounded tensions about middle-class family lifestyles, tensions that were part of the culture at large. Their fantastic space-age imagery made the familial strange; it made people pause, if only to laugh, at what had once seemed natural and everyday. This unlikely collision of genres gave audiences the chance to reflect on their own expectations—not only about the sitcom's narrative conventions—but also about the social conventions by which they lived their lives. The extent to which viewers actually engaged in such thought is another question.[44] But when seen in this light, these programs clearly beg interpretations that go beyond the typical assumptions of their escapist, low-art nature.

Indeed, as I have tried to show, the fact that these programs have not been examined is itself a consequence of history. The "wasteland" critique applied to sitcoms in the 1960s makes it hard for us to break the patterns of the past. These programs were effectively the critics' proof of television's threat to "authentic" culture, and contemporary critics have inherited that binary logic. But television shows like *Bewitched* and *Jeannie* are, of course, part of history, and as such they can play a key role in our understanding of cultural transition. Despite the conventional wisdom of "high-brow" thinking, television's popular formats are not necessarily static; they are not doomed to an endless repetition of the same story. Perhaps their lack of reverence for the "classics" and the strictures of a pre-determined aesthetic canon gives them a certain flexibility that permits the development of recombinant genres and other unorthodox twists. Examining these programs in connection with other aspects of their cultural environment allows us to understand them in ways that go beyond the categories of high and low art. By reading these sitcoms alongside the more "culturally validated" texts of 1960s culture—especially here, popular scientific discourses on the space race—we can begin to see how the fantastic aims of space travel merged, in rather unexpected ways, with the everyday concerns of family life.

What is especially interesting in this regard is that by the end of the 1960s the "high" and mighty goals of going to space had themselves come under attack. Although the moon landing had attracted the most viewers in television history, the critics were restless once again. As an editorial in *Life* proclaimed, "The first requirement for a sensible post-Apollo 11 program is that President Nixon decline to sign the sort of blank check for an all-out manned Mars landing that vocal space agency partisans are urging on him." Critics particularly lamented the decidedly unpoetic sentiments that resulted from the exploration of the final frontier. *Saturday Review* complained about an "overly colloquial" reporter, who "when the lunar module successfully fired the engine that lifted it from the moon's surface, cried out 'Oh boy! Hot diggity dog! Yes sir!' " Even the astronauts had to admit their disappointment. Reflecting on their journeys in Apollo 8, astronauts Frank Borman, Jim Lovell, and Bill Anders clearly were at a loss for the kind of poetic language upon which high culture thrived. Borman admitted that while the moon was beautiful it was also "so desolate, so completely devoid of life. . . . Nothing but this great pockmarked lump of gray pumice." And while he hoped to find "secrets of creation," Lovell confided, "the moon was void." Anders apologized for making "a few poets angry" with his banal descriptions of the lunar landscape, but admitted nonetheless that "the long ride out to the moon was, frankly, a bit of a drag."[45]

If the space program was conceived by some as an empty venture, it nevertheless served a transformative function over the course of the decade. At least in television's fiction forms, discourses on space and tropes of the fantastic invaded the terrain of the everyday. Filling homes with domesticated witches, neighborly ghouls, and ravishing robots, these programs revolved around anxieties about middle-class social ideals. Even if the sitcom form defused these tensions with safe resolutions, the genre denied absolute closure, coming back each week to remind viewers that they too might be living in a suburban twilight zone.

I am grateful to Bill Forman for all his help with this essay, and I also wish to extend thanks to Mike Curtin, Henry Jenkins, Tom Streeter, and the *Camera Obscura* editors for their careful readings.

NOTES

1. Note that there were several sitcoms of the 1950s that included fantastic elements. *People's Choice,* which focused on the career and love life of a single man rather than a family situation, included the talking dog, Cleo. The hound was used as a special effect/sight gag rather than as an integral part of the story. Cleo talked in direct address to the audience, but could not be heard by the characters—a narrational device that functioned much like the self-reflexive direct address of *The Burns and Allen Show.* The latter also included a fantastic element in the later episodes, a magical television set through which George replayed portions of the program and commented on plot elements. Again, however, this was included as a running gag rather than as an integral part of the narrative situation. *Topper,* which revolved around ghosts who haunted a suburban home, was more skin to the 1960s version in its basic narrative premise, but it lasted for only two seasons. While one might see these programs as forerunners, it is in the 1960s that the hybrid genre cycle proliferates and formulates its particular narrative content and organization.

2. Although it did not use the sitcom form per se, *Lost in space* mixed family drama with elements of science fiction.

3. David Marc, *Comic Visions: Television Comedy and American Culture* (Boston: Unwin Hyman, 1989, pp. 121–156). Marc does suggest that some of these sitcoms reflected new cultural ideals, but he does not take this path of analysis into serious consideration.

4. James L. Baughman, "The National Purpose and the Newest Medium: Liberal Critics of Television, 1958–60," *Mid-America* 64 (April–July 1983), pp. 41–55. See also his *Television's Guardians: The FCC and the Politics of Programming, 1958–1967* (Knoxville: University of Tennessee Press, 1985). For more on dissident voices of the 1950s see Paul A. Carter, *Another Part of the Fifties* (New York: Columbia University Press, 1988) and Todd Gitlin, "Cornucopia and Its Discontents," in *The Sixties: Years of Hope, Days of Rage* (New York: Bantam, 1987), pp. 11–31.

5. Although not exclusively concerned with suburbia, books like David Reisman's *The Lonely Crowd* (1950) and C. Wright Mills's *White Collar* (1951) focused on middle-class consensus ideology.

6. For a discussion of this and other aspects of women's lives in post-war America, see Rochelle Gatlin, *American Women Since 1945* (Jackson and London: University of Mississippi Press, 1987).

7. The cycle of 1950s social problem films also highlighted domestic strife, often connecting it to a wider social unrest. See, for example, *Come Back Little Sheba* (1952), *The Country Girl* (1954), and *A Hatful of Rain* (1957). For more on these films see Jackie Byars, "Gender Representation in American Family Melodramas of the 1950s," Ph. D. diss., University of Texas-Austin, 1983. For discussions of popular culture and teenagers in the 1950s, see James Gilbert, *A Cycle of Outrage: America's Reaction to the Juvenile Delinquent in the 1950s* (New York: Oxford University Press, 1986) and Thomas Doherty, *Teenagers and Teenpics: The Juvenilization of American Movies in the 1950s* (Boston: Unwin Hyman, 1988).

8. "Man's New World: How He lives In It," *Life* (Oct. 7, 1957), p. 80.

9. Walter A. McDougall, . . . *the Heavens and the Earth: A Political History of the Space Age* (New York: Basic Books, 1985), pp. 141–156. See also Dale Carter, *The Final Frontier: The Rise and Fall of the American Rocket State* (London and New York: Verso, 1988), pp. 120–125.

10. Henry Luce, "Common Sense and Sputnik," *Life* (Oct. 21, 1957), p. 35. Soviets took the occasion to suggest this as well. For example, McDougall cites Leonid Sedov's condemnation of America's fixation on consumer durables: "It is very obvious that the average American cares only for his car, his home, and his refrigerator. He has no sense at all for his nation," p. 137.

11. Figures cited in Dewey W. Grantham, *Recent America: The United States Since 1945* (Arlington Heights, IL: Harlan Davidson, 1987), p. 143. For an interesting discussion of reactions to Eisenhower's economic recovery plan, see Carter (1988, pp. 35–40). Another recession occurred in 1960–61, but between 1962 and 1968 a long stretch of economic prosperity ensued.

12. William Atwood, "How America Feels as We Enter the Soaring Sixties." *Look* (Jan. 5, 1960), pp. 11–15. This survey was commissioned by the Gallup company and supplemented by *Look's* staff.

13. Baughman, "The National Purpose and the Newest Medium."

14. "Deception on TV," *New Republic* (Oct. 19, 1959), p. 4. For other examples on this, see Barbara Agee, "The Intruder in Our House." *American Mercury* (June 1959), pp. 129–130; Clare Booth Luce, "Without Portfolio: A Monthly Commentary: TV An American Scandal." *McCalls* (March 1960), pp. 18–19, 176, 178; "Where Are All the Sparkling Shows of Yesteryear?" *Newsweek* (July 3, 1961), pp. 70–71. For a discussion of related issues, see Baughman's *Television's Guardians*, pp.20–35, and "The National Purpose and the Newest Medium." Also note that while television critics became particularly dismayed about programming trends in the late 1950s, this attack on television developed out of on-going debates about television's aesthetic and cultural development. In the late 1940s and early 1950s influential east-coast television critics saw television as a medium that promised to channel the elite through the popular, and they formed aesthetic hierarchies based on this idea. In particular, anthology dramas, with their live origination and theatrical/literary base, as well as prestige programming like *Omnibus* and *See It Now,* were the darlings of the television critics, while filmed half-hour series were seen as the lowest form of television art. For more on this, see William Boddy, "From the 'Golden Age' to the 'Vast Wasteland': The Struggles Over Market Power and Dramatic Formats in 1950s Television," Ph. D. diss., New York University, 1984. For a discussion of the more general debates about television's impact on post-war culture and family life, see my "Installing The Television Set: The Social Construction of Television's Place in the American Home," Ph. D. diss., University of California-Los Angeles, 1988; and "Installing the Television Set: Popular Discourses on Television and Domestic Space," *Camera Obscura* 16 (March 1988), pp. 11–47.

15. Newton Minow, Address to the 39th Annual Convention of the National Association of Broadcasters, Washington DC, May 9, 1961. The address can in many ways be read as a reaction to the quiz-show scandals, and especially to the critics who attacked the FCC for their negligence in the matter. In a brief sentence, Minow deflected attention away from the scandals and onto the "more important" matters of reform: "I think it would be foolish and wasteful for us to continue any worn-out wrangle over the problems of payola, rigged quiz shows, and other mistakes of the past."

16. Documentary series included such titles as NBC's *White Papers,* ABC's *Close-up,* and *CBS Reports.* By suggesting that these programs were developed at a time when the status of the television image was thrown into question by the quiz shows, I am not trying to make a direct causal link between the scandals and the networks' turn to documentary. Rather, as James Baughman has shown in his work on *CBS Reports,* the turn to documentary has to be seen in the wider context of problems facing the networks in the late 1950s, and in the case of *CBS Reports,* especially the prospect of an FCC inquiry in 1959. See James L. Baughman, "The Strange Birth of CBS Reports Revisited," *Historical Journal of Film, Radio and Television* 2:1 (1982), pp. 27–38.

17. On the turn to objective science and the interest in the topic of the space race in the 1960s documentary, see Michael Curtin, "Defining the Free World: Prime-Time Television Documentary and the Politics of the Cold War, 1960–1964," Ph. D. diss., University of Wisconsin-Madison, 1990.

18. Mort Drucker and Stan Hart, "The Nilson Family." *Mad* (Jan. 1966), p. 13.

19. George Lipsitz, "The Meaning of Memory: Family, Class and Ethnicity in Early Network Television Programs," *Cultural Anthropology* 1:4 (Nov. 1986), pp. 381–382. Reprinted in *Camera Obscura* 16 (March 1988), pp. 79–117. Lipsitz argues that these programs used the memory of an ethnic/working-class past to legitimate the increasingly consumer society of the post-war era.

20. In this calculation I have included those sitcoms that revolved around domestic situations. Programs that included families, but focused on working life were not included, nor was the popular *The Many Loves of Doby Gillis,* which was mostly concerned with youth culture and student life. One program, *The Danny Thomas Show,* was set in an urban area, while two, *The Real McCoys* and *The Andy Griffith Show,* were set in rural areas.

21. Some of them did appear in re-runs. Note also that *The Danny Thomas Show,* which began under the title of *Make Room for Daddy* in 1953 and ended its original run in 1964, included an ethnic character. However, unlike the other ethnic comedies and dramas, this program did not usually focus on Danny Williams's Lebanese-ness as a major condition of the plot, but rather used it simply as a running gag.

22. By 1965, none of the classical family sitcoms ranked in the top twenty of the Nielsen charts. Only *The Dick Van Dyke Show,* which was a more updated version of the classical type, was still a Nielsen success. According to Tim Brooks and Earle Marsh, *The Dick Van Dyke Show* was canceled in the fall 1966 season due to creative decisions. See *The Complete Directory to Prime Time Network TV Shows, 1946–Present,* 3rd ed. (New York: Ballentine Books, 1985), p. 218. For more general rating information, see pp. 1030–1041.

23. These three were all substantially different from the classical suburban family sitcoms like *Donna Reed.* They include *Please Don't Eat the Daisies* (which was to some degree aberrant since the mother worked at home), *Blondie* (which also deviated from the norm since it was taken from the popular comic strip), and *The Debbie Reynolds Show* (which, like *I Love Lucy,* was based on a housewife who wanted to work; it was also extremely unpopular, lasting only one season).

24. I have not included certain rather idiosyncratic twists in the cycle in this calculation. These include sitcoms that depict childless couples (*He and She, Love on a Rooftop*) and one sit-com that depicted an extended family *(The Mothers In-Law).*

25. For divorce rates, see Gatlin, *American Women Since 1945,* p. 144; Winefred D. Wander-see, *On the Move: American Women in the 1970s* (Boston: Twayne, 1988), p. 131; Julie A. Matthaei, *An Economic History of Women in America: Women's Work, the Sexual Division of Labor, and the Development of Capitalism* (New York: Schocken, 1982), p. 311.

26. "A Child Writes a Space Song." *Look* (Dec. 23, 1958), p. 58; "The Strange Boom at Cocoa Beach." *Look* (June 24, 1958), p. 24.

27. Loudon Wainwright, "Comes a Quiet Man to Ride Aurora 7." *Life* (May 18, 1962), pp. 32–41.

28. Miguel Acoca, "He's On His Way. . . . and It Couldn't Be Prettier." *Life* (Apr. 2, 1965), pp. 36–37.

29. "The Seer of Space." *Life* (Nov. 18, 1957), pp. 134–135; "How An Idea No One Wanted Grew Up to Be the LEM." *Life* (March 14, 1969), p. 22.

30. "Meet Orbit Hill." *Life* (March 9, 1962), p. 2.

31. *American Home* (Sept. 1964), p. 54; *American Home* (Dec. 1962), p. 121; *House Beautiful* (June 1963), pp. 129–130.

32. By 1958, there were at least 300 such songs, and one music publisher even called his company "Planetary Music." See Gordon Cotler, "Songwriters Blast Off." *New York Times Magazine* (Feb. 16, 1958), pp. 19, 21.

33. *Life* (May 24, 1963), pp. 54–55.

34. Fredric Jameson, "Progress vs. Utopia: Or Can We Imagine The Future?" *Science Fiction Studies* 9:27 (1982), p. 151, emphasis his. Later in the article, Jameson more emphatically states that science fiction dramatizes "our incapacity to imagine the future" (153), and he goes on to discuss science fiction dystopias in this vein. My use of Jameson emphasizes his earlier point regarding the way science fiction provides opportunities imaginatively to restructure the present.

35. Tzvetan Todorov, *The Fantastic: A Structural Approach to a Literary Genre,* trans. Richard Howard (Ithaca, NY: Cornell University Press, 1970).

36. These programs often presented moralizing narratives that used the alien motif to drama-tize the exclusionary tactics of cold war America. See, for example, *Science Fiction Theater's* "The People at Pecos" and "Time Is Just Its Life," *The Twilight Zone's* "The Monsters Are Due on Maple Street," and *The Outer Limits'* "Galaxy Being."

37. In fact, many of these films specifically dramatized a threat to family formations. *Them!,* for example, introduces viewers to the giant ants by showing a stray little girl who has been traumatized by the creatures, Andre in *The Fly* destroys his happy home by turning himself into an alien being in a teleporting experiment, and relatives in *Invasion of the Body Snatchers* lose faith in the veracity of their family ties when the pod people replicate their kin.

38. "Should a Girl Be First In Space?" *Look* (Feb. 2, 1960), pp. 112–117.

39. Clare Boothe Luce, "But Some People Simply Never Get the Message." *Life* (June 28, 1963), pp. 31–33.

40. Joan Rivière, "Womanliness as a Masquerade." In *Formations of Fantasy,* edited by Victor Burgin et al. (London and New York: Methuen, 1986/1929), pp. 35–44.

41. As a variation on this plot, some male characters were forced to hide their secrets from both their private and their public worlds. Thus Wilbur hides Mr. Ed from his wife, his neighbor, and his clients; Dave Crabtree hides his mother the car from his wife, his neighbors, and his boss. In both these cases the male character reveals his secret to the viewer in a separate narrative space (a horse stable and a garage, respectively) that is somewhere in between the private and the public world.

42. A similar situation occurred in a 1967 episode of *Bewitched* when Samantha claims that she has beaten the astronauts to the moon through her magical powers of transportation.

43. Judith Williamson, *Decoding Advertisements: Ideology and Meaning in Advertising* (New York: Marion Boyars, 1979).

44. Along these lines, it is important to keep in mind that the genre attracted many child viewers who would have had a limited knowledge of the classic family sitcom as well as different social/historical backgrounds from adults in the audience.

45. "The New Priorities in Exploring Space." *Life* (Aug. 22, 1969), p. 30; Robert Lewis Shayon, "Cosmic Nielsens." *Saturday Review* (Aug. 9, 1969), p. 40; "Our Journey to the Moon." *Life* (Jan. 17, 1969), pp. 26–31.

QUESTIONS FOR DISCUSSION

1. Spigel links the "fantastic" sitcoms' critique of the "TV perfect family" of the early 1960s to the space race. What social phenomena might be inspiring the forms that recent "family critique" sitcoms take, such as *The Simpsons, Married . . . With Children,* or *Roseanne?*

2. Like Lipsitz, Spigel emphasizes that such comedies could be read two ways: as both a critique and a support of the conventions of the white middle-class nuclear television family. What happened to this balance between critique and support as the 1960s became the 1970s? What new comedic forms appeared, and what did they take as their central site of tension?

 INFOTRAC COLLEGE EDITION

Search InfoTrac College Edition under "television and science fiction" to follow up on this topic.

9

And That's the Way
It Was
The Vietnam War on the
Network Nightly News

CHESTER J. PACH, JR.

The conflict in Vietnam during the 1960s was the first televised war. As such, it raised issues about the presentation of images of and commentary about the war on television, including its impact on public opinion and its support or criticism of the U.S. government's policies and military strategy. Media historian Chester J. Pach, Jr., argues that television coverage of the Vietnam war portrayed it as the confused and questionable enterprise that it was. This representation of the war, he suggests, owed more to formal qualities and restrictions of television news programs than to explicit or implicit critiques of the government's Vietnam policy. For example, it was difficult to obtain combat film because of technological and logistical limitations, so network news teams often focused on human interest aspects of the war. The result was a smattering of combat footage intermingled with behind-the-lines stories presented in three-minute segments without critical analysis or commentary.

Pach observes that television news coverage of the war remained more or less the same even after the Tet Offensive of 1967, contradicting the widely held belief that television news coverage of the war after that series of battles helped

Reprinted from *The Sixties: From Memory to History*, ed. David R. Farber (University of North Carolina Press, 1994). Used by permission of the publisher.

to turn public opinion against U.S. involvement in Vietnam. Television, he suggests, affected public understanding of the war because by the late 1960s Americans got most of their news from television, and because televised images has such power to affect opinion, not because of an anti-Vietnam agenda among the news media.

"**A**s I sat in my office last evening, waiting to speak," Lyndon B. Johnson told the National Association of Broadcasters on 1 April 1968, the day after he announced he would not seek another term as president, "I thought of the many times each week when television brings the [Vietnam] war into the American home." What Americans saw each night in their living room, Johnson believed, was a distorted picture of the war, one dominated by "dramatic" events, such as the spectacular but temporary enemy successes during the recent Tet Offensive. Johnson conceded that it was impossible to determine exactly how "those vivid scenes" had shaped popular attitudes. He also acknowledged that "historians must only guess at the effect that television would have had . . . during the Korean war, . . . when our forces were pushed back there to Pusan" or during World War II when the Germans counterattacked at the Battle of the Bulge. Still, Johnson suggested that it was no accident that previous administrations had weathered these military reverses, but his had suffered a debilitating loss of popular support during the Tet Offensive. The reason for the "very deep and very emotional divisions" in public opinion was that Vietnam was America's first televised war.[1]

Johnson was one of many who have criticized, albeit for different reasons, TV coverage of the Vietnam War. Like Johnson, some observers have faulted television for oversimplifying the complexities of Vietnam or for emphasizing spectacular, but horrifying scenes of combat that shocked viewers into opposing the war.[2] In contrast, other commentators have denounced TV journalists for all too easily accepting official pronouncements of progress, at least until Tet, or for making the war's brutality seem so stylized, trivialized, or routine that the result was acceptance or ennui rather than revulsion.[3] Many scholars have argued that television news came of age during Vietnam, although one influential critic has insisted that fundamental weaknesses in American journalism produced a distorted assessment of the Tet Offensive as an American failure.[4] The most extreme critics blame television for reporting so ignorant, biased, or deceptive that it turned the victory American soldiers had won on the battlefields of Vietnam into defeat by producing irresistible political pressures for withdrawal.[5]

Television, however, did better at covering the war than many of these critics allow. To be sure, television's view of the war was limited, usually to what the camera could illustrate with vivid images. Too many film reports on the network newscasts dealt with American military operations, and too often they concentrated on immediate events—a firefight or an airstrike—with little, if any, analysis of how those incidents fit into larger patterns of the war. Yet television also showed the war as it was—a confused, fragmented, and questionable endeavor. Brief reports, usually no more than three minutes long, of isolated, disconnected military engagements, broadcast night after night, week after week, magnified the confusing features of a war that, at best, was hard to fathom—one usually without fronts, clearly identifiable enemies, reliable progress toward victory, or solid connections to American security. Because of the nature of the medium rather than any conscious effort, television nightly news exposed the irrationalities of a war that lacked coherent strategy or clear purpose.

When Johnson decided in 1965 to send American combat troops to Vietnam, TV journalists faced a unique challenge. Vietnam was television's first war. The three major networks rapidly enlarged their operations in Vietnam and by 1967 were each spending over $1 million annually on covering the war. The expansion of the nightly newscasts on CBS and NBC from fifteen to thirty minutes in September 1963—ABC did not follow suit until January 1967—provided more time for Vietnam news. The state of broadcast technology, however, made for substantial delays in airing stories from Vietnam. Not until February 1967 was it possible to relay film by satellite from Tokyo to New York, but then only at a cost of as much as $5,000 for a five-minute transmission. Thus all but the most urgent stories continued to be flown from Saigon to New York for broadcasting. Television viewers usually learned about the most recent developments in Vietnam from the anchor's summary of wire service copy. They commonly had to wait another two days to see film reports of those events.[6]

Unlike those who covered World War II or Korea, Vietnam correspondents did not have military censors review their reports, but they did face informal restrictions and pressures. Johnson was obsessed with the news—"television and radio were his constant companions," wrote one biographer—and he was determined to get reporters to promote his version of the national interest. "I'm the only president you've got, and . . . I need your help," he told members of the White House press corps. But if they did not cooperate, Johnson warned them, "I know how to play it both ways, too." Like Johnson, public information officers for the U.S. command in Vietnam tried to use informal pressures to shape reporting on Vietnam. They rejected censorship because they doubted its effectiveness and feared that it would anger correspondents. Instead, they outlined a series of guidelines that restricted identification of specific units or disclosure of the exact number of casualties in individual battles. They relied on daily news briefings, derisively known as the "Five O'Clock Follies," to influence the coverage of military operations. And they hoped that a vast array of incentives—transportation on military aircraft, interviews with commanders, lodging at bases—would secure or maintain a good working relationship with correspondents and thus favorable coverage of the war effort.[7]

The war that these reporters covered had a superficial, but ultimately specious logic. In South Vietnam, U.S. ground forces tried to win the war with a strategy of attrition. Their primary mission was to search out and destroy the main units of the Vietcong and the North Vietnamese army. The U.S. commander, General William C. Westmoreland, insisted that wearing down these conventional forces had to take precedence over rooting out guerrillas from populated areas. "It was, after all, the enemy's big units—not the guerrillas—that eventually did the South

Vietnamese in," he later explained. Although he would have preferred an invasion of North Vietnam—an option that Johnson refused to sanction—Westmoreland still believed that enormous advantages in mobility and firepower would enable American forces to win the big-unit war. Helicopters would allow American troops to bring the North Vietnamese or Vietcong to battle even in remote jungles or mountains, artillery and airpower would inflict enormous losses on enemy manpower and equipment, and seemingly inexhaustible stores of supplies would let American forces maintain the offensive. The combination of aggressive ground operations and the bombing of North Vietnam and the Ho Chi Minh Trail would push the enemy's main units beyond the crossover point, a level of casualties and equipment losses so great that they could not be replaced. This was war American-style—a high-tech, conventional way of fighting that accorded with U.S. army experience, training, and doctrine that the surest way to win was to pound the enemy into submission. Westmoreland's strategy of attrition, according to Earle Wheeler, the chairman of the Joint Chiefs of Staff, provided "the best assurance of military victory in South Vietnam."[8]

Despite Wheeler's assertion, the strategy of attrition utterly failed. The big battles that Westmoreland sought occurred only infrequently. Instead, by 1967 Vietnam had become a small-unit war in which 96 percent of the engagements involved an enemy force no larger than a company (150 soldiers). These battles usually took place only when the enemy chose to fight. By seizing the initiative, the North Vietnamese and the Vietcong were able to control their casualties and frustrate the strategy of attrition. Even though the body count always added up to an American victory, the more telling figures were in intelligence reports that showed that despite American bombing, Hanoi had increased the flow of reinforcements into South Vietnam and mobilized sufficient resources to carry on the war indefinitely.[9] Equally dismal were the results of the "other war," the effort to win the hearts and minds of the South Vietnamese. While American combat units engaged in search-and-destroy missions, the Vietcong stepped up guerrilla attacks on population centers. When U.S. forces mounted counterinsurgency operations, their heavy reliance on artillery, napalm, herbicides, and defoliants produced countless civilian casualties, hordes of refugees, environmental devastation, and untold resentment against the South Vietnamese government and its profligate patron.[10]

Attrition proved to be, at best, an incoherent strategy, at worst, no strategy at all. A study ordered by the army's chief of staff found that there was "no unified effective pattern" to U.S. military operations. Troops in the field reached the same conclusion through hard experience. The lack of front lines or territorial objectives made them frustrated and cynical. "Without a front, flanks, or rear, we fought a formless war against a formless enemy who evaporated like the morning jungle mists, only to materialize in some unexpected place," recalled Philip Caputo, a marine officer who saw action in 1965–66. "It was a haphazard, episodic sort of combat." Attrition produced a war of disconnected military operations, whose surest result was a relentless demand for more American soldiers and supplies. From 184,000 at the end of 1965, U.S. troop strength rose to 385,000 a year later and to 486,000 at the close of 1967. "Boiled down to its essence," as one official army historian has observed, "American 'strategy' was simply to put more U.S. troops into South Vietnam and see what happened."[11]

On television, the most important story about Vietnam was the fighting that involved U.S. forces. About half of the film reports on network newscasts concerned U.S. troops on foot or in helicopters searching out the enemy, exchanging fire with snipers, calling in air strikes on base camps and supply depots, or clearing guerrillas from hostile villages. This "bang, bang" coverage crowded out stories about pacification or the inefficiencies of the South Vietnamese government, reports that would have provided viewers a deeper understanding of the complexities of counter-insurgency warfare. Yet TV journalists thought that they were giving their audience the news it wanted. "There are approximately 500,000 American men there," one reporter explained. "When this is multiplied by parents, friends and other relatives, there is no doubt what is of most importance to Americans." TV journalists also believed that they were using their visual medium to best advantage. "The sensationalism in Vietnam is obviously in the combat," remarked one network reporter. "Editors want combat footage. They will give it good play." If forced to choose, declared ABC news executive Nick Archer, "a good fire fight is going to get on over a good pacification story." Indeed, the executive producer of the "CBS Evening News" considered "a really great piece of war film . . . irresistible."[12]

Such footage, however, was rare. Despite its potential to "describe in excruciating, harrowing detail what war is all about," the television camera only infrequently did so.[13] Obtaining combat film was difficult; the television crew had to get out to the field, be lucky enough to accompany a unit that made contact with the enemy, and make sure that its equipment worked properly. "Then, if the battle is fierce," noted NBC's John Paxton, "the cameraman does not get the film because he usually has his face in the dirt."[14]

If the camera operator did film the action, though, it might not be aired. In Saigon and Washington, military authorities cautioned television journalists that networks that showed objectionable scenes of American casualties might have their reporters barred from combat zones. Because of these warnings or their own scruples, editors hardly ever allowed ghastly pictures of the dead or dying into American homes during the dinner hour. Indeed, just 3 percent of news reports from Vietnam showed heavy fighting.[15] Those who remember graphic scenes of death and suffering simply recall a war that television did not show.

Instead, television provided only suggestive glimpses of the war. Typical was a report by Morley Safer on 17 November 1965 from the attack troop ship *Paul Revere,* which was carrying marines to beaches south of Danang to begin a search-and-destroy mission. Safer's film captured the anticipation of combat, but none of the fighting.[16] Network correspondents covered the Battle of the Ia Drang Valley, the first engagement between North Vietnamese regulars and U.S. soldiers in October–November 1965, mainly from rear areas. Viewers who watched ABC, for example, heard correspondent Ray Maloney describe the "very hard" fighting from the American base at Pleiku and listened to Lieutenant Colonel Hal Moore recount the action. But the only combat footage showed strikes against North Vietnamese positions by B-52s, which for the first time flew missions to support ground troops.[17] In a similar way, television provided only a flavor of other big American operations during 1966–67. During Operation Attleboro, a sweep through Tay Ninh province in November 1966 involving some 22,000 U.S. troops, ABC's Kenneth Gale and his crew filmed the defoliation of hedgerows with flamethrowers and the interrogation of a Vietcong prisoner. CBS reporter Ike Pappas opted for much lighter fare—the "seeming unreality" of performances by the First Infantry Division's band during pacification of a Vietcong village—while NBC's George Page took a familiar approach—an interview with General John Deane that summarized the accomplishments of the operation. When U.S. forces returned to the same area in February 1967 during Operation Junction City, some became the first Americans to make a combat jump in Vietnam, as Safer reported on the "CBS Evening News." His film showed the soldiers parachuting from the plane, but not their landing, which, as Safer mentioned, was "virtually unopposed." One of the great frustrations of Vietnam for Americans in the field was the elusiveness of the enemy. "Reporters," as Erik Barnouw has noted, "seldom saw 'the war' or 'the enemy.' "[18]

Often television focused not on battles but on the Americans who fought them. Human interest features reflected television's tendency to entertain as well as inform. A personalized story, TV journalists believed, appealed to their mass audience, perhaps because it often simplified—or avoided—complex or controversial issues.[19] A staple of network newscasts was the combat interview, either with a commander or a hero. NBC's George Page, for example, reported in May 1967 from the Mekong Delta, where he talked to soldiers in the Ninth Infantry Division whose bravery had saved the lives of their comrades. Several days later, the "CBS Evening News" carried an interview that correspondent Mike Wallace had conducted with Lieutenant Colonel Robert Schweitzer, who had been wounded eight times and decorated on eleven occasions.[20] Roger Staubach was no war hero, but he had been a college football star at Annapolis, and so his routine duties at a naval supply depot merited a film report by CBS's Ike Pappas in October 1966. Occasionally newsworthy were the lives of ordinary soldiers away from battle, as when Safer interviewed a group on rest and recreation traveling to Hong Kong to catch up, they said, on sleeping, letter writing, and drinking "good homogenized milk."[21] Stories about the air war frequently concentrated on the pilots rather than the bombing, since correspondents could not fly on the B-52 missions over North Vietnam. Typical was a report by CBS's Peter Kalischer in November 1965 from Andersen Air Base on Guam, which showed the preflight routines of the pilots and lauded each mission as a "minor masterpiece" of planning and execution. Television viewers, then, often saw the war from the perspective of the Americans in Vietnam who were experiencing it.[22]

Interpreting the war news was difficult, and television reporters often failed to provide analysis or commentary. The anchors of the nightly newscasts—Walter Cronkite on CBS, Chet Huntley and David Brinkley on NBC, and, successively, Peter Jennings, Bob Young, Frank Reynolds, and Howard K. Smith on ABC—offered no interpretation in more than half of the stories that they read. Their reticence was a result of their role in the program, which was to read short news items or introduce correspondents' reports. Less than one-fifth of their stories exceeded seventy-five words, which left little room for analytical comments. The canons of objective journalism—accuracy, balance, fairness, impartiality—

also encouraged anchors to limit interpretive remarks. So too did the importance of inspiring confidence and loyalty among viewers, who often chose which network newscast to watch on the basis of their reaction to the personal qualities of the anchor. Walter Cronkite did not earn his reputation as the most trusted man in America by making partisan, gratuitous, or controversial comments about the news, but by reporting it "the way it was."[23]

Network correspondents also did not supply much analysis in many of their stories about the war. Again, time limitations affected the content of their reports. With just twenty-two minutes each weekday night to present the news—commercials took up the rest of the half-hour program—television functioned as an electronic front page, covering little more than the day's most important occurrences, often in spare summaries. Correspondents' reports almost never ran more than three minutes and often considerably less. Television's preoccupation with the immediate—today's news—severely limited analytical reports intended to provide perspective. One of the infrequent attempts to do so, Morley Safer's wrap-up of the Battle of the Ia Drang Valley, failed to examine the effectiveness of search and destroy or the significance of new tactics of carrying troops to battle in helicopters. Instead, the only perspective came from the soldier in the field, as Safer interviewed members of a company of the Seventh Cavalry who had survived some of the deadliest combat with the North Vietnamese. Viewers of the nightly news, then, often got information about the Vietnam War without much analysis or interpretation.[24]

Yet television journalists did try to make sense of the war, frequently by comparing current military operations with previous ones. Measuring the size, scope, or cost of a military action was a convenient, albeit simplistic, way of assessing its importance. Network correspondents and anchors, for example, described the Battle of the Ia Drang Valley as the "biggest engagement yet," the "bloodiest, longest" battle since Korea, "classic infantry warfare," and "the biggest American victory yet in Vietnam."[25] Viewers learned that Operations Attleboro and Junction City were, successively, the largest of the war and that Operation Cedar Falls (January 1967) yielded the "biggest prize" so far, when U.S. troops captured the base camp of a Vietcong regiment.[26] Television journalists also imputed significance to military operations in Vietnam by comparing them with those in World War II. Reporting in November 1965 on marines preparing for an amphibious landing near Danang, Morley Safer thought that the scenes he witnessed resembled the Pacific war. CBS correspondent John Laurence suggested that the bloody, prolonged Battle of Hue in early 1968 looked like World War II action, a comparison endorsed by a marine battalion commander. On 4 July 1966 Dean Brelis closed his report from "the First Infantry Division, the Big Red 1 of North Africa, Omaha Beach, Normandy, Germany, and now the Cambodian border." Comparisons such as Brelis's, of course, associated intervention in Vietnam with a heroic and victorious tradition of American warfare.[27]

Television reporters also tried to understand current military events by speculating about their relationship with future developments in the war. Reasoning by extrapolation—projecting what happened today into next week or next month—was an easy, if risky, way of simplifying the complexities of Vietnam. Cronkite, for example, declared that the Battle of the Ia Drang Valley was a portent of "dramatic change" in the Vietnam War, while Dean Brelis considered it a harbinger of more big battles. Yet staggering losses encouraged the North Vietnamese to avoid major engagements after Ia Drang and utilize guerrilla tactics instead.[28] One year later, Cronkite predicted that a series of North Vietnamese and Vietcong military initiatives "could set the pattern of the war for months to come." But the anticipated major offensive did not occur. ABC's Bill Brannigan reported in February 1967 about the forced removal of villagers near Danang to a relocation center and speculated that such evacuations would become the preferred method of depriving the Vietcong of civilian support. Yet the American command began to modify its policy of mandatory relocation only two months later and abandoned it at the end of the year.[29] However logical or appealing to television journalists, extrapolation clearly was a dubious method of discerning the future in Vietnam.

Much of the information and many of the interpretive comments in television newscasts prior to the Tet Offensive suggested that the United States was winning the war. When TV journalists assessed the results of battles during 1965–67, they concluded that about two-thirds were American victories.[30] A key to this success, network correspondents frequently emphasized, was American firepower. In November 1965, for example, Ray Maloney informed viewers of the "ABC Evening News" that the Vietcong were defenseless against B-52 strikes and that airpower was "turning the tide in Vietnam." A year later, Bruce Morton covered the air attacks supporting Operation Attleboro and declared that firepower was a "principle" that had proved its worth. Reporting in January 1967 from the Iron Triangle northwest of Saigon during Operation Cedar Falls, NBC's George Page assured those who tuned into the "Huntley-Brinkley Report" that high-tech weaponry would destroy the region's elaborate tunnel system and so deprive the Vietcong of an important base area. The same night, CBS's John Hart explained how airstrikes with napalm had silenced Vietcong snipers that had pinned down American troops. Another major advantage, according to television reporters, was the high quality of American troops. During the Ia Drang fighting, for example, Brelis interviewed Lieutenant Colonel Hal Moore, who asserted that "we have the best soldiers that the world has ever seen." From time to time military officials appeared in news reports to assure the public that American troops were achieving their goals, as when General John Deane told Page in November 1966 that the war was going "very well."[31]

Television journalists also frequently reported that the air war was producing favorable results. Interviews with pilots always generated assurances that the bombing of North Vietnam was effective. That was what CBS's Bruce Morton heard, for example, when he talked to fliers in February 1967. Despite their objections to political restrictions on targets, the pilots were still making sure that the air campaign achieved its goals, Morton concluded, largely because of their professionalism in carrying out their missions. During the first year of the air war, television newscasts carried several stories that lauded the sophistication or superiority of American aircraft. Typical was Chet Huntley's narration in September 1965 of a Defense Department film of the A-4 Skyhawk, a fighter that eventually made more bombing raids in Vietnam than any other navy plane. The A-4 had produced "spectacular" results, Huntley exclaimed, and "should have even better shooting in the days ahead" because of improving weather.[32]

John Hart's report on the "CBS Evening News" in February 1967 on a lesser-known part of the air war, aerial defoliation and crop destruction, was so one-sidedly favorable that it bordered on propaganda. Hart asserted that the herbicides that the air force sprayed on jungles and forests were no stronger than dandelion killer and caused no damage to the soil. Air Force Major Charlie Hubbs added that Operation Ranch Hand, as the defoliation campaign was known, was not a form of chemical warfare, but a "humane" way of fighting. Although the toxic effects of Agent Orange, the principal herbicide, on the environment and humans were not yet fully known, many scientists had urged the Johnson administration to halt this form of warfare, something Hart did not mention. He simply noted that Ranch Hand pilots were "sensitive to criticism that came regularly from conservationists in the United States" but even more concerned about hostile fire from enemy guns. Yet the air force had not altered its Ranch Hand operations at all because of the objections of civilian scientists. Defoliation operations actually reached a peak in 1967.[33]

The favorable treatment of the war effort reflected television's acceptance of the cold war outlook that was responsible for U.S. intervention in Vietnam. TV journalists did not challenge President Johnson's conviction that the national interest required the containment of communism or the president's decision to commit U.S. combat troops to Vietnam. Those policies had such strong, mainstream support in 1965 that the network newscasts did not present them as matters of legitimate controversy. Instead, TV journalists responded to Johnson's decision to go to war in Vietnam less as objective journalists than as patriotic citizens. They reported the war effort in language that revealed a lack of detachment. Commonly in 1965–66, they referred to "our" troops, planes, and losses in Vietnam. The North Vietnamese or Vietcong were usually the "enemy," frequently the "Communists," and occasionally the "Reds." On one occasion Huntley mocked the term *National Liberation Front* as "Hanoi's name for its own forces." Editorial comments on television newscasts about the North Vietnamese or the Vietcong were overwhelmingly negative. Indeed, in one remarkable instance, the name of the Vietnamese revolutionaries became a synonym for deception and mendacity, when NBC correspondent Garrick Utley dismissed a National Liberation Front film as "unadulterated Vietcong."[34]

There were several reasons why the network newscasts seemed "to express a massive political consensus" at the beginning of the Vietnam War. Dependent on advertising revenues, subject to federal regulation, and vulnerable to pressure from affiliates, television networks were wary of controversial programming or discordant opinions. When J. William Fulbright (D-Ark.), the chair of the Senate Foreign Relations Committee, held hearings in February 1966 that disputed the Johnson Administration's Vietnam policies, CBS broke off its coverage in favor of reruns of "I Love Lucy," "The Real McCoys," and "The Andy Griffith Show." Network executives cited neither commercial nor ideological reasons for their decision, but—fantastically—the danger that extended telecasting of the hearings would "obfuscate" or "confuse" the issues about the war. Yet it is hard to believe that political considerations had no role in the network's action, since CBS president Frank Stanton considered a previous interview with Fulbright "a dirty trick . . . to play on the President of the United States."[35]

Such episodes have persuaded many observers that television in the mid-1960s was "the most timid" of the news media, the most willing to accept official statements at face value, the most reluctant to air dissenting opinions, the most likely to knuckle under to government pressure. Yet recent studies have cast doubt on the independence of newspaper reporting of the Vietnam War. One analysis of six newspapers of different sizes and political orientations revealed that reporters and editors relied heavily on government sources for information about military operations and tended not to doubt their credibility.[36] Another concluded that print journalists generally accepted "the assumptions and consensus of the foreign policy establishment" and hoped for the success of "foreign policies designed to meet the nation's problems," at least when those policies were first carried out.[37] Television newscasts may have expressed this consensual outlook in unique or distinctive ways—by focusing, for example, on "our boys" in Vietnam or stigmatizing the Vietcong as representatives of alien, evil ways. But the news media in general seems to have shared dominant core values that made it inclined in 1965–66 to support—or, at least, not to question—the fundamental reasons for American intervention in Vietnam.[38]

Television may have expressed those consensual values in unique or distinctive ways because network newscasts were not simply a source of information but also of entertainment. As media analyst Peter Braestrup has argued, the job of the network correspondent in Vietnam "was not to produce news in the sense of 'fact-finding' . . . , but to obtain and produce film vignettes" that were "presented as 'typical' or a 'microcosm' " of the entire war. The correspondents who submitted these film reports often had only the most rudimentary knowledge of Vietnamese politics and culture, since their overseas assignments usually lasted between six months and one year. Their expertise was not in Southeast Asian affairs or even in international relations, but in producing vivid, engaging, and dramatic stories. Even more than the correspondents, the editors and producers in New York who assembled the nightly newscasts were masters not of interpreting the news but of packaging it. Their concern was good television—reports from Vietnam that provided spectacular images that would attract large audiences and somehow encapsulate the entire war effort in one three-minute segment. This was neither adversarial nor even deeply analytical journalism. Instead, it was theatrical reporting, a reflection of the nature of the expertise of television journalists.[39]

Yet television journalists did question the implementation of American policy in Vietnam, and their stories occasionally caused controversy, as when CBS correspondent Morley Safer and his crew filmed a report in Cam Ne about a search-and-destroy operation. The mission was one of the first of its kind for U.S. marines, who had been previously concentrated on protecting air bases and other important military installations. On 3 August 1965 a marine company swept into Cam Ne, a village complex southeast of Danang that was supposed to be an enemy stronghold. "If there were Viet Cong in the hamlets," Safer asserted in his film report, "they were long gone" by the time the U.S. forces arrived.[40] The only certain Vietnamese casualties were a ten-year-old boy, who was killed, and four villagers, who were wounded, by the marine fire. The apparent lack of enemy resistance made all the more sensational the image of a marine using a cigarette lighter to set afire a thatched hut. The U.S. forces had orders to "level"

Cam Ne, Safer explained just before the camera showed another marine inciner-
ating a hut with a flamethrower. "There is little doubt that American fire power
can win a military victory here. But to a Vietnamese peasant whose home means
a lifetime of backbreaking labor, it will take more than presidential promises to
convince him that we are on his side."[41]

Enraged military authorities immediately accused Safer of inaccuracy and dis-
tortion. U.S. forces, they said, had faced not just the "burst of gunfire" that Safer
had reported, but snipers that had wounded four Americans and forced the
marines to withdraw under the cover of an artillery barrage. Cam Ne was no ordinary village, but an "extensively entrenched and fortified hamlet" with hundreds of booby traps and an elaborate network of tunnels. Although the marines
may have burned the huts of innocent civilians, they did so incidentally, according to the battalion commander, while trying "to neutralize bunkers, trenches,
and firing positions actually in use by the VC." The hut ignited by the cigarette
lighter appeared to be "a tactical installation rather than a peaceful dwelling," according to a military spokesperson in Saigon. The marines, another information
officer added, had not wantonly or callously used force but, like all American
troops in South Vietnam, followed Westmoreland's orders to exercise "the ut-
most discretion, judgment and restraint" in applying firepower.[42]

Safer stood by his story. In reply to the nervous inquiries of CBS news president Fred W. Friendly, he confirmed the accuracy of his film report before it aired
on 5 August. Despite the barrage of official criticism, he also maintained that
friendly fire, not Vietcong resistance, was responsible for the American casualties
at Cam Ne.[43] In a follow-up story several days later, Safer provided additional evidence that the marines entered Cam Ne determined to "teach [the villagers] a
lesson."[44] Was it necessary to burn "all the houses . . . to fulfill the mission?" he
asked a marine who had seen action at Cam Ne. It was, the marine replied, in
order "to show these people over a period of time that we're done playing with
them." Another marine declared. "You can't have a feeling of remorse for these
people. I mean, like I say, they are an enemy until proven innocent." A third dis-
closed that he entered villages such as Cam Ne, where marines had previously
faced hostile fire or suffered casualties, with a desire for revenge. Such statements
belied official assurances that U.S. policy was "to bend over backward" to avoid
harming civilians or their property, "even at possible cost of U.S. lives."[45]

Even more vehement than the official criticism of Safer's reporting was the
attack on his integrity. Leading the assault was Lyndon B. Johnson. "Are you trying to fuck me?" Johnson asked caustically in a telephone conversation with CBS
president Frank Stanton. "Your boys shat on the American flag." The president
was convinced that Safer was a communist, but an investigation proved only that
he was a Canadian. "Well, I knew he wasn't an American," Johnson sneered.
"Why do you have to use foreigners to cover that war?" inquired Bill Moyers, an
aide to Johnson, of another CBS correspondent. Canadian birth was reason
enough for Arthur Sylvester, the assistant secretary of defense for public affairs, to
demand Safer's relief. "I think that an American reporter," Sylvester wrote
Friendly, "would be more sensitive" to the need for "balance" in reporting U.S.
actions in Vietnam. Friendly dismissed Sylvester's letter as "character assassina-

tion," but Stanton repeatedly expressed doubts about Safer. A friend of Johnson, Stanton did not like having CBS accused of undercutting the president's war policies, especially since the source of trouble was a reporter who had been working for the network only a year and whose background he considered "sketchy." CBS news executives, however, kept Safer from learning about Stanton's reservations and Johnson's accusations while he remained in Vietnam.[46]

Nevertheless, Safer was terribly aware of the hostility he faced in Vietnam, and that pressure may have affected his reporting. Safer feared for his life and began carrying a gun after hearing a rumor that he might become the victim of "an accident" and after watching a drunk marine officer fire his pistol in front of the press center while yelling "Communist Broadcasting System."[47] Despite these threats, Safer insisted that he did not temper his reporting. Yet although he continued to cover the war's nasty side, he began describing it as part of the timeless brutality of warfare. Thus he explained the casualties that resulted from a mistaken U.S. bombing strike on the South Vietnamese village of Bong Son in October 1965 as an "inevitable" error. He also portrayed the Vietnamese hustlers and prostitutes who swarmed around the American installations at Danang as an "age-old misfortune of war." And in a report that must have pleased the American high command, he concluded that the South Vietnamese army regular, if led well, fought as effectively "as any other soldier."[48]

The upshot of Safer's Cam Ne story, then, was an intense debate, not over the effectiveness of search-and-destroy tactics but the legitimacy of critical television reporting of the war. Morley Safer raised all the right issues—the difficulty of identifying the enemy, the adverse effects of heavy firepower, and the problem of innocent victims of military action in populated areas. Yet an official expression of regret about civilian casualties and assurances of restraint in future missions effectively ended any discussion of whether operations such as Cam Ne could help win the war. Instead, government officials thought more about whether reports such as Safer's might help lose it. Pentagon officials began recording the network newscasts in order to monitor more effectively television's coverage of the war. Once more military authorities studied the feasibility of censoring war stories, but these reconsiderations only confirmed previous conclusions that such severe restriction of the news would be ineffective and counterproductive. Still, the inflamed reaction to Safer's story revealed the narrow limits of acceptable war reporting on television.[49]

Despite the furor over Cam Ne, television newscasts did occasionally examine problems with the war effort in 1965–66. Some of the most perceptive stories came from NBC correspondent Ron Nessen. After the first engagements in the Ia Drang Valley, Nessen was the only TV journalist who recognized that the North Vietnamese were dictating the terms of battle. Their attack had come as a surprise, he explained, and they had succeeded with the same tactics that had worked against the French. Even though they had retreated in the face of American and South Vietnamese reinforcements, the fighting "could break out again," Nessen correctly predicted, whenever the North Vietnamese wanted to resume it.[50] One year later, Nessen probed the difficulties of "the other war," when he reported from Voila, a village that had been "pacified" four times. The real problem at Voila was the ineffectiveness of South Vietnamese government efforts to win the loyalty of the villagers. For example, the revolutionary development cadre that was supposed to provide security, improve public services, and rally support for the government once had all but two of its fifty-nine members desert. Each night, Nessen declared, the Vietcong proved that government forces could not protect the village. Pacification would succeed, he concluded, only when Voila was secure.[51]

Another problem that attracted the attention of television journalists in 1965–66 was the sordid conditions of life in South Vietnam. On the "CBS Evening News" on 14 September 1965, Walter Cronkite introduced a film report about "one of the ugliest and saddest aspects of the Vietnam War." What followed was correspondent John Laurence narrating footage of South Vietnamese civilians who swarmed like "flies" and fought like "animals" in a U.S. marine garbage dump. Laurence explained that these "scavengers of war" risked crippling injury as well as infection, since the dump contained live ammunition. Seconds later, a grenade exploded, wounding a youth. The following month, Morley Safer described the degradation of the "once charming" city of Danang, the victim of con men and call girls who hustled for American dollars. A year later, he reported about an impending crackdown on the Saigon black market. Safer noted wryly, though, that business as usual would resume "next week at the latest."[52]

During 1967 network newscasts contained stronger and more frequent criticisms of American methods of warfare. New sources of information cast doubt on official evaluations of the war effort. At the end of 1966, Harrison Salisbury of the *New York Times* had become the first American correspondent to visit North Vietnam since the beginning of the air war. Salisbury said in interviews on the three networks in mid-January 1967 what he had written in articles for the *Times*—that the bombing had caused extensive civilian casualties but had not diminished the North's capacity to move war materiel to the South. By exposing the North Vietnamese to a common danger, Salisbury added, the bombing had actually raised civilian morale and united the country. One week later, Harry Ashmore, a Pulitzer Prize–winning former newspaper correspondent who had also traveled to Hanoi, endorsed Salisbury's conclusions in an interview with CBS's Charles Kuralt.[53]

Network correspondents made more interpretive comments in 1967 that cast doubt on the effectiveness of American military operations. Typical were David Burrington's stories in February about U.S. efforts to clear the Vietcong from their tunnel complexes. Experience showed, Burrington said, that the guerrillas would be back in a few days or weeks. During Operation Cedar Falls, NBC and ABC aired reports that pointed out the persistent problems in relocation camps and refugee resettlement programs. Adam Raphael informed CBS viewers in February about a failed search-and-destroy mission after which American troops took out their frustration on a suspected Vietcong prisoner. When the cameras were off, Raphael revealed, the suspect's treatment may not have been "exactly according to the Geneva Convention." Though common, such critical comments did not dominate the network newscasts in 1967. Indeed, favorable remarks about the American war effort were still far more numerous. But television journalists were more inclined to question American methods of warfare, perhaps because of their growing familiarity with the difficulties of achieving victory in Vietnam.[54]

There were far more profound doubts about American strategy in the White House and the Pentagon, and television newscasts revealed those reservations in sensational stories in May 1967. Several weeks earlier General Westmoreland had asked for an additional 200,000 troops, a request that added to the fears of Secretary of Defense Robert S. McNamara that the strategy of attrition would continue to produce a larger war, higher casualties, but no clear progress toward victory. "When we add divisions, can't the enemy add divisions? If so, where does it all end?" Johnson asked Westmoreland. With his own military advisers divided, Johnson denied Westmoreland the desired reinforcements. The administration's deliberations leaked out in a story on the "Huntley-Brinkley Report" on 8 May, and correspondent George Page concluded that Westmoreland's request showed that there was no limit to the number of troops that might be needed to protect South Vietnam. Two weeks later, ABC's Frank Reynolds reported on Johnson's Memorial Day proclamation, in which the president described the war as a "bloody impasse." This dramatic phrase, though, was misleading, since the president still clung to the hope that Westmoreland could make slow but steady progress toward victory without additional troops. Reynolds then added his own note of pessimism. The "isolated victories on the battlefield," he declared, "do not add up to any sort of overall victory against the North Vietnamese or Vietcong." Since enemy resolve had not lessened, the United States faced a "predicament from which there is no obvious escape."[55]

What kind of war, then, did a television viewer watch on the network nightly news during the American buildup in Vietnam from 1965 through 1967? He or she saw, as critic Michael Arlen has remarked, a "generally distanced overview of a disjointed conflict which was composed mainly of scenes of helicopters landing, tall grasses blowing in the helicopter wind, American soldiers fanning out across a hillside on foot, rifles at the ready, with now and then (on the soundtrack) a far-off ping or two, and now and then (as the visual grand finale) a column of dark, billowing smoke a half mile away, invariably described as a burning Vietcong ammo dump."[56] Night after night the American people peered at these scenes of battle from a war that had been domesticated by TV cameras. The war was always there on the screen, close enough to fascinate or repel but not so close as to spoil dinner. Most television battles ended in American victories, although increasingly they revealed problems that suggested that all might not be well. Rarely, though, could the viewer see beyond the battlefield. Television's war was a series of disconnected episodes of combat. Television reporters usually did not look for the connections, but when they did, they had trouble finding them. That was because the strategy of attrition had produced a war of isolated engagements. The fragmented war on television was precisely the war fought in Vietnam.

TV journalists reported the war this way not because of their perceptual acuity or analytical power, but because of the routines of their medium. Television consists of bits and pieces—segments, in the vocabulary of scholars who use semiotics to analyze communications. Each channel broadcasts a flow of programs, commercials, and announcements, and each program, in turn, consists of smaller segments. On a network newscast, those segments include reports, either by the anchor or correspondents, that together total only twenty-two minutes. Because of the shortness of time, these reports condense and simplify the news. And because of journalists' preoccupation with immediacy, the reports usually focus only on today's news, with little, if any, analysis of how recent events fit into larger patterns. Anchors may try to provide some context for the reports, but they usually must do so in a few sentences. Some studies have shown, however, that viewers often fail to make the intended connection between an anchor's introduction or conclusion and a correspondent's story. Brevity and segmentation thus made television likely to cover large events, such as the Vietnam War, through a series of largely self-contained reports. Television's fragmented reporting just happened to coincide with a disjointed war.[57]

Television suddenly had a different war to cover once the Tet Offensive began. On 30 January 1968 the North Vietnamese and Vietcong launched a coordinated series of attacks that seemed to turn almost all of South Vietnam into a battlefield. They struck with 100,000 troops in practically all major cities, most provincial and many district capitals, and quite a few hamlets—altogether more than 150 places. Vietcong sapper teams assaulted the most visible symbols of American and South Vietnamese authority—the embassy in Saigon and the presidential palace, respectively. At the last two locations, U.S. and South Vietnamese forces repelled the attacks within a few hours; almost everywhere else, they regained the advantage in a matter of days. Yet the breadth and fury of the Tet Offensive surprised American intelligence authorities and stunned public opinion. No one had imagined that the North Vietnamese and Vietcong were capable of such extraordinary action, especially since the Johnson administration had recently mounted a "progress campaign," a major public relations effort to show, as Westmoreland proclaimed, that the war had advanced into a new stage "when the end begins to come into view." Upon learning of the Tet attacks, Walter Cronkite expressed the bewilderment and betrayal felt by many Americans when he snapped, "What the hell is going on? I thought we were winning the war."[58]

Tet was high drama on television. No longer was the war in the background; instead, the fighting intruded into film reports in frightening and uncontrollable ways. Within a week, viewers saw two members of television crews suffer wounds while covering battle. During the fighting near the presidential palace, ABC's Piers Anderton and his camera operator recorded the anguish of an injured South Vietnamese soldier moaning in the street, while NBC's Douglas Kiker described the agony of Ban Me Thuot, as the film showed a city of rubble and refugees. "The nastiest kind of street fighting" occurred in Hue, CBS's Robert Schakne observed, and it exacted a heavy toll on U.S. marines, who had to clear out the enemy house by house, and on the city, which had ceased to function. From Danang, Saigon, Khe Sanh, and elsewhere correspondents reported that the fighting was hard and unpredictable. Not merely spectators at these engagements, yet not fully participants, they captured in words and images the surprise, horror, and confusion that engulfed South Vietnam during Tet.[59]

The most sensational story during Tet was the cold-blooded execution of a Vietcong officer in the streets of Saigon. The shooting followed a street battle between the Vietcong and South Vietnamese marines. An NBC crew recorded the fighting and the assassination in its entirety; an ABC camera operator stopped filming at the moment of death. Both reports aired on the nightly newscasts on

2 February; both contained commentary that was extraordinarily restrained. As the victim was led to his death, NBC's Howard Tuckner explained, "Government troops had captured the commander of the Viet Cong commando unit. He was roughed up badly but refused to talk. A South Vietnamese officer held the pistol taken from the enemy officer. The chief of South Vietnam's national police, Brigadier General Nguyen Ngoc Loan, was waiting for him." Neither Tuckner nor Roger Peterson, who narrated the ABC film, suggested that the shooting was an atrocity or a measure of the authoritarianism of the South Vietnamese regime. For Robert Northshield, the executive producer of the "Huntley-Brinkley Report," the film was newsworthy not because of its political implications but on account of its stunning images of death. Northshield, though, considered some of the scenes too "rough" for the television audience, and so he trimmed footage of blood spurting from the shattered skull of the victim. Perhaps as many as 20 million people watched the execution film on NBC; many more saw a photograph of the moment of death, published in almost every major newspaper.[60]

Although there is no way of knowing the impact on public opinion of this single story, the overall effect of the Tet Offensive in early 1968 was to deepen doubts about the war and destroy confidence in the Johnson administration's handling of it. Public support for the war did not suddenly vanish during Tet. Throughout 1967 more people had disliked Johnson's war policies than endorsed them, although the president won back some support during the "progress campaign" late in the year. The first public response to Tet was to rally behind the war effort, but that reaction lasted only briefly. By the time the enemy attacks had waned, 50 percent of the American people thought it had been a mistake to send troops to Vietnam, an increase of 5 percent over December 1967. Public support for the administration's management of the war plummeted from 39 percent in January 1968 to 26 percent by late March. Even more startling, those who thought that the United States was making progress in the war declined from half the population to less than one-third.[61]

The shift in attitudes toward the war, some observers maintain, occurred because the American people were misinformed about Tet. These critics blame the news media for reporting so sensational, inaccurate, or distorted that it prevented the public from realizing that the Tet Offensive was an American victory. The most influential of these critics is Peter Braestrup, a former war correspondent for the *New York Times* and *Washington Post,* who has argued that American journalists were so overwhelmed during Tet that they got the story wrong. "Essentially, the dominant themes of the words and film from Vietnam . . . added up to a portrait of defeat" for the United States and South Vietnam, Braestrup has written, when in fact Tet was "a severe military-political setback for Hanoi."[62]

Making sense of the welter of events during Tet was difficult, but television journalists were not overwhelmed. They dutifully reported official reactions in Washington and Saigon, which usually emphasized that enemy successes were transient and casualties enormous. Sometimes, though, they took issue with those interpretations, as when David Brinkley, in reaction to General Westmoreland's statement about heavy Vietcong losses, commented tersely, he "did not say it [the Tet Offensive] was not effective." Editorial comments, many of them openly skeptical of official pronouncements, were far more numerous in the nightly newscasts than before Tet. Often, journalists expressed the shock and disbelief so many people felt, as when ABC news analyst Joseph C. Harsch asserted that Tet was at odds with "what the government had led us to expect." CBS's Robert Schakne expressed the same idea more vividly when he exclaimed that Tet had turned the world upside down. Journalists occasionally tried to discern the long-term effects of Tet by projecting current developments into the future. Thus, Schakne declared that there could be another major offensive and warned that "our troubles in Vietnam may be just beginning." As the current wave of attacks waned, NBC's Douglas Kiker reported that U.S. intelligence authorities feared another Vietcong assault, this one even more effective. Yet these predictions were no more pessimistic than General Wheeler's private assessment of the situation for Johnson. "The enemy . . . has the will and capability to continue," Wheeler found after visiting in South Vietnam in late February. The Tet Offensive, the general concluded, was "a very near thing."[63]

Although pessimism was common, television journalists did not declare that Tet was a victory for the North Vietnamese and Vietcong. "First and simplest, the Vietcong suffered a military defeat," Walter Cronkite reported from Saigon on 14 February. Their suicidal attacks had produced staggering losses, and they had not succeeded in persuading large numbers of South Vietnamese to support their cause. Yet Cronkite also found that Tet had caused severe political problems by widening the Johnson administration's credibility gap and weakening the South Vietnamese government. "Pacification," he believed, "may have been set back by years, certainly months." Cronkite reiterated these conclusions two weeks later in a special evening program. "To say that we are closer to victory today is to believe, in the face of the evidence, the optimists who have been wrong in the past," he declared. "To suggest we are on the edge of defeat is to yield to unreasonable pessimism. To say that we are mired in stalemate seems the only realistic, yet unsatisfactory, conclusion." No other television journalist offered such a full evaluation of Tet. Yet the brief, fragmentary comments of other reporters and anchors did not fundamentally conflict with this assessment.[64]

The results of the Tet Offensive were by no means as clear as Braestrup has insisted. By the standards of conventional war—those that shaped the U.S. army's strategy of attrition—Tet was indeed a defeat for the North Vietnamese and the Vietcong. The attackers had absorbed huge losses and had failed to maintain control of the cities and towns they had seized. By the standards of revolutionary war, however, the North Vietnamese and Vietcong seem to have been victorious. The attack proved the vulnerability of practically every South Vietnamese city or hamlet. It set back pacification, and it dealt U.S. morale a withering blow. "At the time of the initial attacks, the reaction of our military leadership approached panic," reflected Clark Clifford, who took over as secretary of defense in March 1968. "There was, for a brief time, something approaching paralysis, and a sense of events spiraling out of the control of the nation's leaders." The Johnson administration was bitterly divided over how to react to the enemy initiative. Not until 31 March—two months after the Tet Offensive began—did Johnson make a major statement on Vietnam. Then he announced a partial bombing halt, a new peace initiative, and his own withdrawal from the presidential race. The administration sealed its own fate with misleading optimism, ineffective war making, and inaction. At the very least, then, Tet represented a major psychological triumph for the North Vietnamese and Vietcong.[65]

After Tet, TV reporting of the war in many ways followed earlier patterns. Most stories contained no editorial comments; again, television focused on Americans soldiers in the field. The portrayal of the war, though, was far less heroic than before. American troops began going home in 1969 under President Richard M. Nixon's strategy of Vietnamization. Really the mirror image of attrition, Vietnamization was no strategy at all; it consisted of pulling American troops out, hoping for peace, and seeing what happened. Those U.S. forces that remained frequently expressed their dissatisfaction with the war, and news stories reflected this disillusionment. CBS's Gary Shepard, for example, reported in October 1969 from Saigon about the use of marijuana in Vietnam, while on the same night NBC's Fred Briggs covered an antiwar protest in Fayetteville, North Carolina, by Vietnam veterans. Six months later, NBC's Kenley Jones did a story about soldiers in the Twenty-second Infantry who were "near revolt" over their orders to invade Cambodia. The troops complained that they did not understand what the United States was doing in Cambodia or, for that matter, Vietnam. "This is a different war," Jones concluded, and these soldiers wanted no part of it. Neither did a majority of the American people.[66]

Did it matter that the Vietnam War was covered on television? How did TV reporting affect public attitudes toward the war? These are important questions, but they cannot be answered as precisely as we might wish. Television did affect public understanding of the war, since by 1970 a majority of Americans got most of their news from television. Yet what they learned from nightly newscasts is by no means clear. Studies have revealed that most viewers have trouble remembering anything from news programs that they just finished watching. Perhaps that is because, as one scholar has observed, television "is designed to be watched intermittently, casually, and without full concentration. Only the commercials command and dazzle." Even if one does watch intently, the meaning one extracts from a news report is a product of individual values and attitudes. NBC's George Page recalled reporting on a battle in a way that he thought might create "a dovish attitude" among viewers. Then he got a letter from someone who had doubts about U.S. goals in Vietnam but who reacted to Page's story by saying, "Go, Marines. Go."[67]

Yet even if it cannot be precisely measured, television's influence during the Vietnam War was important. Images do have powerful effects, however much the reaction varies among individual viewers. It is no accident that Morley Safer's Cam Ne report created such a stir while similar stories in newspapers went almost unnoticed.[68] The reporting of the Tet Offensive on television undoubtedly shocked many people, especially after previous coverage of the war had been comparatively tame. Walter Cronkite's declaration that the war was a stalemate had a profound effect on at least one viewer, Lyndon Johnson, and, nearly a quarter century later, on George Bush. Certain that unrestricted reporting from Vietnam had undermined popular support of the war, Pentagon officials in the Bush administration restricted reporters' access to troops in the Persian Gulf and censored their reports.[69]

While the Bush administration vastly oversimplified the "lessons" of Vietnam, it does seem that nightly news coverage did contribute to popular dissatisfaction with the war. Television presented a war that was puzzling and incoherent—a series of disjointed military operations that were often individually successful but collectively disastrous. Night after night, television slowly exposed the illogic of attrition. If viewers grew weary or discontent or outraged, it was partly because television just happened to show them an important part of the Vietnam War "the way it was."

NOTES

1. *Public Papers of the Presidents of the United States: Lyndon B. Johnson, 1968–69,* 2 vols. (Washington, D.C.: GPO, 1970), 1:482–86.

2. William C. Westmoreland, *A Soldier Reports* (Garden City, N.Y.: Doubleday, 1976).

3. Michael Arlen, *Living-Room War* (New York: Penguin Books, 1982).

4. Peter Braestrup, *Big Story: How the American Press and Television Reported and Interpreted the Crisis of Tet 1968 in Vietnam and Washington,* 2 vols. (Boulder, Colo.: Westview Press, 1977).

5. Robert Elegant, "How to Lose a War," *Encounter* 57 (August 1981): 73–90.

6. Braestrup, *Big Story,* 1:36–40; Daniel C. Hallin, *The "Uncensored War": The Media and Vietnam* (New York: Oxford University Press, 1986), 105–6; Leonard Zeidenberg, "The 21-Inch View of Vietnam: Big Enough Picture?" *Television* 25 (January 1968): 28–32, 56–58; Edward Jay Epstein, *News from Nowhere: Television and the News* (New York: Random House, 1973), 33; George Bailey, "Television War: Trends in Network Coverage of Vietnam, 1965–1970," *Journal of Broadcasting* 20 (Spring 1976):150.

7. Doris Kearns, *Lyndon Johnson and the American Dream* (New York: Harper and Row, 1976), 7 (first quotation); Kathleen J. Turner, *Lyndon Johnson's Dual War: Vietnam and the Press* (Chicago: University of Chicago Press, 1985), 44–45 (second quotation); David Culbert, "Johnson and the Media," in *Exploring the Johnson Years,* edited by Robert A. Divine (Austin: University of Texas Press, 1981), 214–48; William M. Hammond, *Public Affairs: The Military and the Media, 1962–1968,* U.S. Army in Vietnam (Washington, D.C.: Center of Military History, 1988), 133–48, 233; Peter Braestrup, *Battle Lines: Report of the Twentieth-Century Fund Task Force on the Military and the Media* (New York: Priority Press Publications, 1985), 64–65.

8. Westmoreland, *A Soldier Reports,* 148; Andrew F. Krepinevich, Jr., *The Army and Vietnam* (Baltimore: Johns Hopkins University Press, 1986), 164–68 (quotation, p. 166); George C. Herring, *America's Longest War: The United States and Vietnam,* 1950–1975, 2d ed. (New York: Knopf, 1986), 145, 150.

9. When U.S. marines began Operation Harvest Moon in December 1965, south of Danang, they learned that one of the units they would be fighting was the First Vietcong Regiment. "Jesus Christ, that's the outfit we wiped out at Chu Lai," said one platoon leader, referring to a battle that had occurred four months earlier. "Guess you forgot to wipe out their recruiting department," cracked another marine. Philip Caputo, *A Rumor of War* (New York: Ballantine Books, 1977), 243–44.

10. Krepinevich, *The Army and Vietnam,* 177–214; Enthoven to McNamara, memorandum, 4 May 1967, in *The Pentagon Papers: The Defense Department History of United States Decision-making on Vietnam,* Senator Gravel Edition, 4 vols. (Boston: Beacon Press, n.d.), 4:461–63; Herring, *America's Longest War,* 150–56; Bruce Palmer, Jr., *The 25-Year War: America's Military Role in Vietnam* (New York: Simon and Schuster, 1984), 42–43; Mark Clodfelter, *The Limits of Air Power: The American Bombing of North Vietnam* (New York: Free Press, 1989), 134–46; Guenter Lewy, *America in Vietnam* (New York: Oxford University Press, 1978), 66.

11. *The Pentagon Papers,* 2:576–80; Caputo, *A Rumor of War,* 89; George Donelson Moss, *Vietnam: An American Ordeal* (Englewood Cliffs, N.J.: 1990), 377; Krepinevich, *The Army and Vietnam,* 165, 182–83; Harry G. Summers, Jr., *On Strategy: The Vietnam War in Context* (Carlisle Barracks, Pa.: U.S. Army War College, 1981), 56; Jeffrey J. Clarke, *Advice and Support: The Final Years, 1965–1973,* U.S. Army in Vietnam (Washington, D.C.: Center of Military History, 1988), 106.

12. Zeidenberg, "The 21-Inch View of Vietnam," 56 (quotations); Hallin, *The "Uncensored War,"* 111–12; Lawrence Lichty, "A Television War?," in *Vietnam Reconsidered: Lessons from a War,* edited by Harrison Salisbury (New York: Harper and Row, 1984), 86.

13. Morley Safer, quoted in Braestrup, *Battle Lines,* 67.

14. Arlen, *Living-Room War,* 97–98; Zeidenberg, "The 21-Inch View of Vietnam," 57.

15. Hammond, *Public Affairs,* 236–38; Braestrup, *Battle Lines,* 68–69.

16. Report by Safer, 17 November 1965, CBS, reel A15, Weekly News Summary, Assistant Secretary of Defense for Public Affairs, Record Group 330, National Archives, Washington, D.C. (hereafter cited as DOD Weekly News Summary).

17. Reports by Maloney, 17–19 November 1965, ABC, reels A15, A16, ibid.; George C. Herring, "The First Cavalry and the Ia Drang Valley, 18 October–24 November 1965," in *America's First Battles,* 1776–1965, edited by Charles E. Heller and William A. Stofft (Lawrence: University Press of Kansas, 1986), 300–326.

18. Reports by Pappas, 14 November 1966, CBS; Gale, 15 November 1966, ABC; Page, 16 November 1966, NBC, all on reel A68, DOD Weekly News Summary; report by Safer, 23 February 1967, CBS, reel A83, ibid.; Erik Barnouw, *Tube of Plenty: The Evolution of American Television,* 2d rev. ed. (New York: Oxford University Press, 1990), 378.

19. Daniel C. Hallin, "We Keep America on Top of the World," in *Watching Television,* edited by Todd Gitlin (New York: Pantheon Books, 1986), 11–15; Arlen, *Living-Room War,* 111–13.

20. Reports by Page, 5 May 1967, NBC, and Wallace, 8 May 1967, CBS, both on reel A94, DOD Weekly News Summary.

21. Reports by Pappas, 28 October 1966, CBS, reel A65, and Safer, 21 November 1966, CBS, reel A68, ibid. See also report by John Dancy, 21 November 1966, NBC, reel A68, ibid.

22. Report by Kalischer, 19 November 1965, CBS, reel A16, ibid.; Hallin, *The "Uncensored War,"* 124–25, 135–38; Hal Himmelstein, *Television Myth and the American Mind* (New York: Praeger, 1984), 197–206.

23. Bailey, "Television War," 147–58; Bailey, "Interpretive Reporting of the Vietnam War by Anchormen," *Journalism Quarterly* 53 (Summer 1976): 319–24; Daniel C. Hallin, "The American News Media: A Critical Theory Perspective," in *Critical Theory and Public Life,* edited by John Forester (Cambridge: MIT Press, 1985), 121–31; Hallin, *The "Uncensored War,"* 63–68.

24. Report by Safer, 22 November 1965, CBS, reel A16, DOD Weekly News Summary; Lawrence W. Lichty, "Video Versus Print," *Wilson Quarterly* 5 (Special Issue 1982): 52–53; Robert MacNeil, *The People Machine: The Influences of Television on American Politics* (New York: Harper and Row, 1968), 38–55.

25. Comments by anchors, 16 November 1965, NBC; 18 November 1965, CBS; report by Ray Maloney, 18 November 1965, ABC, all on reel A15, DOD Weekly News Summary; report by Dean Brelis, 22 November 1965, NBC, reel A16, ibid.

26. Comments by anchors, 11 November 1966, NBC, reel A68; 23 February 1967, NBC, reel A82; 12 January 1967, CBS, reel A77, all in ibid.

27. Reports by Safer, 17 November 1965, CBS, reel A15, and Laurence, 21 February 1968, CBS, reel A135, ibid.; Hallin, *The "Uncensored War,"* 142–43.

28. Comments by Cronkite, 16 November 1965, CBS, reel A15, and report by Brelis, 22 November 1965, NBC, reel A16, DOD Weekly News Summary; Herring, "The First Cavalry and the Ia Drang Valley," 322–23.

29. Report by Brannigan, 23 February 1967, ABC, reel A83, DOD Weekly News Summary; Krepinevich, *The Army and Vietnam,* 225–27; Hammond, *Public Affairs,* 304–5.

30. Based on his evaluation of a sample of network newscasts from August 1965 through January 1968, Daniel C. Hallin determined that when TV journalists assessed the outcome of battles, they found that 62 percent were American or South Vietnamese victories, 28 percent were losses, and 2 percent were inconclusive. There appears to be an error in Hallin's total of 92 percent, since he considered only those engagements that reporters or anchors assessed. Hallin, *The "Uncensored War,"* 146.

31. Reports by Maloney, 15 November 1965, ABC, reel A15; Morton, 21 November 1966, CBS, reel A68; Page, 17 January 1967, NBC, reel A78; Hart, 17 January 1967, CBS, reel A78; Brelis, 18 November 1965, NBC, reel A15; Page, 16 November 1966, NBC, reel A68, all in DOD Weekly News Summary.

32. Comments by Huntley, 10 September 1965, NBC, reel A6; report by Morton, 2 February 1967, CBS, reel A8o, both in ibid. See also report by Nessen on the F-5, 19 November 1965, NBC, reel A16, ibid.

33. Report by Hart, 20 February 1967, CBS, reel A83, ibid.; William A. Buckingham, Jr., *Operation Ranch Hand: The Air Force and Herbicides in Southeast Asia, 1961–1971* (Washington, D.C.: Office of Air Force History, 1982), 129, 138–40.

34. Comments by Huntley, 23 November 1965, NBC, reel A16, and Utley, n.d. (ca. 23 October 1965), NBC, reel A12, DOD Weekly News Summary; James Aronson, *The Press and the Cold War* (New York: Monthly Review Press, 1970), 218–30; Nicholas O. Berry, *Foreign Policy and the Pess: An Analysis of the New York Times' Coverage of U.S. Foreign Policy* (Westport, Conn.: Greenwood Press, 1990), 27–52, 139–50; Hallin, *The "Uncensored War,"* 114–26, 148; Bailey, "Interpretive Reporting of the Vietnam War," 322–23.

35. Barnouw, *Tube of Plenty,* 381–84 (quotations, pp. 381–82); Fred W. Friendly, *Due to Circumstances beyond Our Control . . .* (New York: Vintage Books, 1968), 212–40; Gary Paul Gates, *Air Time: The Inside Story of CBS News* (New York: Harper and Row, 1978), 123–24; Epstein, *News From Nowhere,* 44–59.

36. Clarence R. Wyatt, " 'At the Cannon's Mouth': The American Press and the Vietnam War," *Journalism History* 13 (Autumn–Winter 1986): 109–11.

37. Berry, *Foreign Policy and the Press,* xii–xiii.

38. Michael Mandelbaum, "Vietnam: The Television War," *Daedalus* 111 (Fall 1982): 160–61; Todd Gitlin, *The Whole World Is Watching: Mass Media in the Making & Unmaking of the New Left* (Berkeley: University of California Press, 1980), 252–82.

39. Braestrup, *Big Story,* 1:36–43; Hallin, "We Keep America on Top of the World," 9–15, 23–26.

40. Jack Shulimson and Charles M. Johnson, *U.S. Marines in Vietnam: The Landing and the Buildup, 1965* (Washington, D.C.: History and Museums Divisions, U.S. Marine Corps, 1978), 64.

41. Hammond, *Public Affairs,* 186–88.

42. Ibid.; Shulimson and Johnson, *U.S. Marines in Vietnam,* 63; *New York Times,* 6 August 1965.

43. Safer later claimed that the real reason for the operation in Cam Ne was that the province chief wanted the villagers punished for not paying their taxes. He said that he got this information months afterward from Richard Critchfield, a correspondent for the *Washington Star.* Critchfield, however, maintains that "Safer has his villages (or mine) confused. After the CBS telecast created such a stir, I went to Cam Ne and concluded that it had concealed a heavily fortified Viet Cong military post. . . . All I can say . . . is that Safer, in support of his own reporting of the burning of Cam Ne, somehow got it wrong." See Morley Safer, *Flashbacks: On Returning to Vietnam* (New York: Random House, 1990), 92; Richard Critchfield, *Villages* (Garden City, N.Y.: Anchor Press/Doubleday, 1981), 350; and David Halberstam, *The Powers That Be* (New York: Laural, 1979), 680.

44. Safer, *Flashbacks,* 89.

45. Hammond, *Public Affairs,* 188–90 (Safer/marine Q&A); Gates, *Air Time,* 160–62; *New York Times,* 4 August 1965.

46. Halberstam, *The Powers That Be,* 683–85; Gates, *Air Time,* 122–23, 161–62; Hammond, *Public Affairs,* 190–91; Safer, *Flashbacks,* 93–97.

47. Safer, *Flashbacks,* 88–93; Gates, *Air Time,* 162.

48. Reports by Safer, 23–24 October 1965, CBS, reel A12, and 30 October 1965, CBS, reel A13, DOD Weekly News Summary.

49. *New York Times,* 5 August 1965; Hammond, *Public Affairs,* 193–95.

50. Reports by Nessen, 28–29 October 1965, NBC, reels A12, A13, DOD Weekly News Summary.

51. Report by Nessen, 9 November 1966, NBC, reel A66, ibid.; Clarke, *Advice and Support,* 171–81.

52. Reports by Laurence, 14 September 1965, CBS, reel A6, and Safer, n.d. (ca. 23 October 1965 and 18 November 1966), CBS, reels A12, A68, DOD Weekly News Summary; Hammond, *Public Affairs,* 200–201.

53. Interviews with Salisbury, 11–12 January 1967, ABC; 12 January 1967, CBS; 12 January 1967, NBC, all on reel A77, DOD Weekly News Summary.

54. Reports by Page, 16 January 1967, NBC; Gale, 17 January 1967, ABC; Raphael, 16 February 1967, CBS; Burrington, 17, 20 February 1967, NBC, all on reels A78, A82–A83, ibid.; Hallin, *The "Uncensored War,"* 159–63.

55. Larry Berman, *Lyndon Johnson's War: The Road to Stalemate in Vietnam* (New York: Norton, 1989), 31–38 (LBJ quotation, p. 35); *Public Papers of the Presidents of the United States: Lyndon B. Johnson, 1967,* 2 vols. (Washington, D.C.: GPO, 1968), 1:554–55; Report by Page, 5 May 1967, NBC, reel A94, and comments by Reynolds, 22 May 1967, ABC, reel A98, DOD Weekly News Summary.

56. Michael J. Arlen, "The Air: The Falklands, Vietnam, and Our Collective Memory," *New Yorker,* 16 August 1982, 73.

57. Gitlin, *The Whole World Is Watching,* 265–66; John Fiske, *Television Culture* (London: Routledge, 1987), 99–105, and "Moments of Television: Neither the Text Nor the Audience," in *Remote Control: Television, Audiences, and Cultural Power,* edited by Ellen Seiter et al. (London: Routledge, 1989), 63–64; Robert C. Allen, *Channels of Discourse: Television and Contemporary Criticism* (Chapel Hill: University of North Carolina Press, 1987), esp. intro., chaps. 1–2; Jane Feuer, "The Concept of Live Television: Ontology as Ideology," in *Regarding Television: Critical Approaches—An Anthology,* edited by E. Ann Kaplan (Frederick, Md.: University Publications of America, 1983), 15.

58. Berman, *Lyndon Johnson's War,* 114–19 (Westmoreland quotation, p. 116); Don Oberdorfer, *Tet!* (New York: Da Capo, 1984), 21–33, 142, 158 (Cronkite quotation); Herring, *America's Longest War,* 189–80; Krepinevich, *The Army and Vietnam,* 239.

59. Reports by Ogonesof, 26 January 1968, CBS; Tuckner, 1 February 1968, NBC; Hall, 1 February 1968, NBC; Syvertsen, 1 February 1968, CBS; and Anderton, 1 February 1968, ABC, all on reel A132; report by Tuckner, 6 February 1968, reel A133; reports by Paul Cunningham, 14 February 1968, NBC; Fromson, 14 February 1968, CBS; and Schakne, 15 February 1968, CBS, all on reel A134; reports by Jaffe, 21 February 1968, ABC, and Laurence, 21 February 1968, CBS, reel A135, all in DOD Weekly New Summary; Braestrup, *Big Story,* 2:599–617.

60. Reports by Tuckner, NBC, and Peterson, ABC, 2 February 1968, reel A133, DOD Weekly News Summary; George A. Bailey, "Rough Justice on a Saigon Street: A Gatekeeper Study of NBC's Tet Execution Film," *Journalism Quarterly* 49 (Summer 1972): 221–29, 238; Braestrup, *Big Story,* 1:463–65.

61. Burns W. Roper, "What Public Opinion Polls Said," in Braestrup, *Big Story*, 1:674–704; John E. Mueller, *War, Presidents, and Public Opinion* (New York: Wiley, 1973), 54–58.

62. Braestrup, *Big Story*, 1:705.

63. Comments by Huntley, 31 January 1968, NBC, and Brinkley, 1 February 1968, NBC, and report by Harsch, 1 February 1968, ABC, reel A132; report by Schakne, 5 February 1968, CBS, and anchor comments, 6 February 1968, NBC, reel A133; report by Kiker, 21 February 1968, NBC, reel A135, all in DOD Weekly News Summary; *The Pentagon Papers*, 4:546–47.

64. Report by Cronkite, 14 February 1968, CBS, reel A134, DOD Weekly News Summary; Braestrup, *Big Story*, 2:180–89 (second quotation).

65. Krepinevich, *The Army and Vietnam*, 248–50; Clark Clifford with Richard Holbrooke, *Counsel to the President: A Memoir* (New York: Random House, 1991), 474–476.

66. Reports by Shepard, CBS, and Briggs, NBC, 13 October 1969, reel A221; reports by Shepard, CBS, and Jones, NBC, 6 May 1970, reel A250, all in DOD Weekly News Summary; Hallin, *The "Uncensored War,"* 174–80.

67. Lichty, "Video Versus Print," 53–54; Hallin, *The "Uncensored War,"* 107; Feuer, "The Concept of Live Television," 15; Zeidenberg, "The 21-Inch View of Vietnam," 32.

68. Hallin, *The "Uncensored War,"* 108, 123

69. John R, MacArthur, *Second Front: Censorship and Propaganda in the Gulf War* (New York: Hill and Wang, 1992), 112–45.

QUESTIONS FOR DISCUSSION

1. According to this author, what aspects of the Vietnam War did television coverage privilege? Is this still true of U.S. television war coverage?

2. How did the U.S. military try to shape and restrain coverage? How have those methods changed compared, for instance, to the Gulf War?

3. How did the Tet Offensive change coverage of the war? Why? Does this undercut the author's argument that TV's "disjointed, fragmentary" nature accurately reflected a disjointed, directionless war?

 INFOTRAC COLLEGE EDITION

Search InfoTrac College Edition for more articles on "media and war" and "media and Vietnam."

10

High Concept, Small Screen
Reperceiving the Industrial and Stylistic Origins of the American Made-for-TV Movie

GARY EDGERTON

Made-for-TV movies are often castigated by film scholars as being on the same level as B films, those low-budget and exploitative features made by Hollywood to turn a quick profit. They are therefore judged according to cinematic ideals and aesthetics. Television scholar Gary Edgerton refutes that analysis, locating made-for-TV movies squarely within the contexts and traditions of television programming. Edgerton argues that made-for-TV movies, which first appeared in the mid-1960s, were envisioned, designed, and budgeted as and for television.

By the mid-1960s, there was a shortage of appropriate theatrical releases for exhibition on television. In addition, Hollywood films were evolving beyond television's norms for the depiction of sex and violence. Television networks already had the production personnel and talent in place for the creation of made-for-TV movies, as well as appropriate generic and formal conventions. Made-for-TV movies did not function as a "farm system" for the movie industry but as a genre specific to the needs and constraints of television. As such, the genre was able to evolve by taking advantage of the nature of television

From the *Journal of Popular Film and Television* 19 (Fall 1991): 114–27. Reprinted by permission of HELDREF Publications.

production. For example, because television programs take less time to produce than theatrical releases, made-for-TV movies were able to reflect current issues and events, leading to the creation of the docudrama.

MIXING APPLES AND ORANGES

TV films . . . are increasingly cinema films in all but name;
they rely upon cinematic techniques, and they invite their audiences
to try to view them with the attitudes and intensity of concentration
that is more characteristic of cinema. For broadcast TV, the culturally
respectable is increasingly equated with the cinematic.

—JOHN ELLIS, 1982[1]

The made-for-TV movie is consistently the most misunderstood and maligned genre on television. No doubt a worse fate was accorded the once-lowly soap opera more than a decade ago before a move in the related fields of television and cinema studies began resurrecting this form from critical oblivion.[2] The number of publications on the television movie remains relatively small, however, especially when considering the major impact this genre has had on the economics, topicality, and production values of primetime programming in America over the last three decades.

Indeed, the few sources that do exist on television movies are typically polarized in nature, ranging from outright repugnance to a few instances of lavish praise.[3] The term itself, "TV movie," is often used pejoratively by movie critics to describe what bad theatrical pictures tend to resemble; even a recent reassessment in *American Film* entitled "TV Movies—Better Than the Real Thing (Are You Kidding?)," which heralds a "Golden Age [for] today's TV movies and miniseries," tends to exhibit the kind of ambivalence that is characteristic about this subject from most film quarters.[4] The made-for-TV movie is invariably judged against some higher "cinematic" and "culturally respectable" ideal, while, ironically, preferences in TV movie style, technique, propriety, preferred themes, budgets, shooting schedules, talent, target audiences, and administrative supervision have all along been more a reflection of the customs and priorities of television than the separate market and industrial sphere of the theatrical movie business.

It is crucial at the outset, therefore, to reconsider the tendency of most film scholars to frame the made-for-TV movie within an agenda set by the movie business: the television movie is thus conceived of as a byproduct of the motion picture industry, rather than as a fundamental programming staple of network TV. Another case in point is Douglas Gomery's skillful examination of *Brian's Song,* which, nevertheless, situates the television movie firmly within the traditions of the classical Hollywood style:

The made-for-TV movie in the early 1970s had become what the B film was to Hollywood in earlier eras. Contending with restrictions in budgets, language and sex, rating-minded networks, and a format demanding an opening "teaser" and six climactic "act curtains" before commercial breaks, creators had to work quickly and efficiently.[5]

The positioning of the telefeature within the context of the film industry almost always leads to the conclusion that the TV movie is today's "B" picture, an inferior feature film form modeled on the Hollywood paradigm. From this perspective, television movies are viewed as having comparatively meager budgets (generally five times smaller than theatrical films), paltry shooting schedules (four times smaller), and tame and antiseptic presentations. This supposition, however, misrepresents the industrial origins and stylistic conventions that are most common of movies made exclusively for television.

The made-for-TV movie needs, first and foremost, to be reperceived as a product of network TV. When Hollywood's movie companies expanded their services and identities during the 1950s to become primetime program suppliers, these studios created new telefilm divisions that operated firmly under the purview of ABC, CBS, and NBC; likewise, NBC was the commissioning force that sponsored Universal TV when it produced the first telefeature in 1964. Asserting this distinction is more than splitting hairs; it also place television movies squarely within the context and traditions of network programming, where this genre has extended the acceptable boundaries of dramatic length, thematic concern, and production value for primetime. From this adjusted vantage point, the TV movie was never a "B" product; in contrast, it was always envisioned, designed, and budgeted as a prestige vehicle for television. It is also more accurate to liken inferior telefeatures to overblown TV series episodes than to the "formula quickies" that were churned out decades ago by the old Hollywood studio system.

The subindustry that manufactures the made-for-TV movie is solidly beholden to the presidents of primetime programming at ABC, CBS, and NBC because television has always served this sector as its primary distribution venue. Programming executives at the networks, including the respective vice presidents for telefeature and mini-series production, acquire contractual rights to approve scripts, budgets, above-the-line personnel, shooting schedules, and promotional strategies. Even at the inception of this TV genre in the mid-1960s, a newer group of small-screen moguls, who had been enculturated within the milieu and dictates of primetime television, dominated the creation and development of made-for-TV movies, although Hollywood and network radio drama were certainly secondary influences with respect to story ideas and production techniques.

By 1991, the total number of television movies made in America has now reached 2,500, including such innovations in product variations from the 1970s as the docudrama and the miniseries.[6] More than 15 telefeature and mini-series episodes, in fact, have attracted audiences of more than 100 million, placing them among the most watched television programs ever.[7] TV movies have also been regularly honored with Emmy and Peabody awards since the early 1970s, while the Museum of Modern Art in New York formally recognized the maturation of this television genre with a symposium in 1979, just 15 short years after the broadcast of the first telefeature.[8] These indicators of widespread popularity and institutional recognition were doubtlessly inconceivable 27 years ago when NBC in 1964, and later ABC in 1969, first began responding in earnest to the growing cost and impending shortage of appropriate theatrical films for primetime scheduling by nurturing the brainchild of an executive at Universal TV, Jennings Lang.

THE GREENING OF THE MADE-FOR-TV
MOVIE, 1964–1969

> For network-movie watchers, in the beginning there were movies.
> Then came the nonmovies. And now it's minimovies. For the audience,
> it's a puzzlement and a frustration. For the networks, it's big business.
> And where it's all leading no one will guess.
>
> —JUDITH CRIST, 1969[9]

The precise birthdate of the American made-for-TV movie is arguable, although only a handful of pretenders exists before the 1964–1965 television season. Claims range from Ron Amateau's B-Western, *The Bushwackers,* which first appeared for public consumption on CBS in 1951; to Disney's *Davy Crockett, King of the Wild Frontier,* which was initially broadcast as three separate segments during the 1954–1955 debut season of *The Wonderful World of Disney;* to the theatrical offering, *The Scarface Mob* (1962), which was shown on television in 1959 a the two-part pilot for the ABC series, *The Untouchables.*[10] By the late 1950s, several of television's dramatic anthologies, for instance *Bob Hope Presents, the Chrysler Theatre,* and *Alfred Hitchcock Presents,* were frequently producing their teleplays on film, and it was not uncommon for a number of these presentations to be expanded into a second hour for airing the following week as a finale of a two-part drama.[11] These sporadic and haphazard examples, however, predate the systematic and conscious development of feature-length motion pictures exclusively for the small screen.

Propitious conditions for the birth of the made-for-TV movie began to take shape in the mid-1950s and became imminent during the early 1960s. When Hollywood's major studios entered the fray of series television production between 1955 and 1958, all of the smaller telefilm companies were either hurt by the added competition, driven from the business, or absorbed by larger firms. These independents, most notably MCA's Revue, Columbia's Screen Gems, United Artists' Ziv-TV, Hal Roach Productions, and Desilu, had composed a modest, though burgeoning production sector in Hollywood that successfully provided the television industry with episodic TV on film since 1948. Jennings Lang began promoting longer and more novel programming formats in the final years of the 1950s as his way of counteracting Warner Brothers, Paramount,

Twentieth Century-Fox, and MGM's influential move into TV production; his motivation was a desire to create an advantage for Revue in the face of this newly emerging challenge from the major movie studios.

Lang was ideally positioned between two merging traditions when he started to innovate on two TV programming concepts: the "special-event" and the "long-form" (which refers to television programming that extends past a 60-minute time slot). He had already established himself as one of the leading talent agents in the film industry when he joined the Music Corporation of America (MCA) agency in 1950. The next year, MCA created Revue, and Lang was placed in charge of TV program development. Toward the end of the decade, his dual experiences in both the motion picture and television industries led him to consider feature-length storytelling at a time when growing competition between NBC and CBS first motivated NBC to start funding program proposals for film that extended the usual conventions of primetime scheduling.[12]

Lang "began his [two-parter] experiments with anthology shows like 'The Alfred Hitchcock Hour' and 'The Chrysler Theater,' in the one-hour format, and he had a big hand in the first 90-minute regularly scheduled series, 'The Virginian,' " which premiered on NBC in September 1962.[13] This was also the year that MCA, the most powerful talent agency in Hollywood at this juncture, purchased Universal Pictures. As a result, Revue was consolidated as Universal TV in this corporate takeover, and Jennings Lang was selected to direct what immediately became a more expanded and influential operation.

Now coming from Universal TV, NBC programmers were simply more receptive to Lang's proposals for repackaging the anthology format as a series of "TV epic[s] (or special events), when an entire evening [would] be given over to a single spectacular, made for the occasion."[14] Lang and Universal TV convinced NBC to invest in what were originally called "mini-movies" in 1963. Although Jennings Lang is the man most responsible for championing the telefeature as a viable programming form for television, the made-for-TV movie was really an idea whose time had come. It is clear in retrospect that once television production moved to the West Coast for good during the mid-1950s, it was simply a matter of years before one of the new television executives who also had contacts and experience with the motion picture industry, such as Lang, would induce some company to produce features on film for TV.

For its part, NBC initially considered Lang's overtures for "mini-movies" because theatrical films were performing well in primetime beginning in 1961. NBC finally decided to invest in telefeature production two years later because of both an impending shortage of theatrical motion pictures for nighttime scheduling and the rapidly escalating price of leasing these movies from the studios. Appendix 1 suggests the increasing cost effectiveness of TV movies: Bidding competition between ABC, CBS, and NBC had actually caused the cost of leasing a theatrical feature film for television to increase twice as fast as the average telefeature budget between 1965 to 1971. TV movies were not only an economical alternative, they also held three other key incentives for the networks by 1970: movies made for TV were virtual ratings equals to theatricals on TV from their inception; their style and content were better shaped to the priorities of television, especially when considering the growing sexual and violent explicit-ness that was evident in theatrical films during the late 1960s and early 1970s; and their production supported in-house staffs within the television industry.

Some personnel crossover did, in fact, exist between made-for-TV movies and films produced for theaters, although most above- and below-the-line em-ployees in both telefeatures and later mini-series stayed within this unique genre or worked in series TV for most of their careers. Despite glamorous examples, such as Steven Spielberg, the television movie has not so much served as a kind of "farm system" for the theatrical feature, which is implied by the B movie label, as it has developed its own cadre of more than 2,000 actors, actresses, producers, directors, and screenwriters, most of them borrowed from primetime series pro-duction or originally supplanted from the "live" dramatic anthologies of TV's so-called Golden Age during the 1950s.[15]

The success of *The Virginian* during the 1962–1963 season, telecast on NBC between 7:30 and 9:00 P.M. on Wednesdays, was the final impetus that motivated this network to contract with Lang and Universal to produce self-contained, feature-length films that would fit into a two-hour time slot to be tentatively scheduled during the 1963–1964 television year under the title *Project 120,* a never fully actualized weekly series whose very name echoed the "live" dramatic anthologies of the previous decade. NBC allotted $250,000 in 1963 for its first planned telefeature (which was the same average amount of money budgeted that season for two 1-hour primetime episodes), as Universal TV hired Holly-wood journeyman Don Siegel to direct " 'Johnny North,' an adaptation of Ernest Hemingway's short story, 'The Killers,' starring John Cassavetes, Lee Marvin, Angie Dickinson, and Ronald Reagan" in his last role.[16] The movie that resulted eventually cost more than $900,000, and was deemed by the network "too spicy, expensive, and violent for TV screens."[17]

In early 1964, *Johnny North* was retitled *The Killers* (like its 1946 Hollywood predecessor), and this motion picture was subsequently released that spring to movie theaters nationwide by Universal Pictures. Mort Werner, NBC-TV vice president in charge of programming at the time, reflected in May 1964 on this whole experience: "We've learned to control the budget. Two new 'movies' will get started soon, and the series (*Project 120*) probably will show up on televi-sion in 1965."[18]

The first made-for-TV movie, *See How They Run,* premiered on 17 Octo-ber 1964, a few months earlier than Werner suggested in his public pronounce-ment. This telefeature appeared under the aegis of MCA-Universal and NBC's *Project 120. See How They Run* follows the murder of a father by an interna-tional crime syndicate and the subsequent pursuit of his three teenaged daugh-ters who unwittingly stumble upon some damaging evidence. This routine crime melo-drama was quickly followed six weeks later by the NBC broadcast of Don Siegel's next excursion into the made-for-TV genre, *The Hanged Man.* Like *The Killers* before it, Siegel's second assignment for *Project 120* is another remake of a classic *film noir, Ride the Pink Horse* (1947). Although television movies were now a reality, there would be a two-year hiatus before NBC and MCA-Universal presented another telefeature to the American viewing public.

ABC began its sponsorhip of the made-for-TV movie during the 1965–1966 season with the March 10th telecast of *Scalplock*. This Western, starring Dale Robertson and produced by Columbia's Screen Gems, deals with a gambler who wins a railroad in a poker game and then assumes control over his new enterprise. *Scalplock* is actually characteristic of many subsequent telefeatures in that it is a pilot as well as a TV movie, meaning that this telefilm also served as the first episode of a prospective primtime series (in this case, *The Iron Horse,* 1966–1968) by introducing an original storyline and a new set of characters. This strategy of creating telefeatures as pilots provided primetime suppliers, such as Screen Gems, with a way of recouping more of their initial investment by encouraging greater network participation in financing a property with more than one scheduling purpose; the TV production company would then seek additional distribution opportunities through the overseas television and theatrical markets.

Programming executives at the major networks were alerted to the ratings potential of the made-for-television movie as early as the 1966–1967 season. On Saturday evening during the 1966 Thanksgiving weekend, NBC hyped its two-hour pilot, *Fame Is the Name of the Game,* as a "World Premiere" on *NBC Saturday Night at the Movies* rather than as part of *Project 120*. Corporate wisdom had now decided that it was better not to remind target audiences that stars and story types would not recur on a regular basis, even though a semi-frequent series of telefeatures was an obvious reprise of the anthology format. Extensive pretesting had instead convinced NBC to emphasize that these telefeatures were being presented to the public for the very first time. No one at the network would later argue with what turned out to be windfall results.

Fame Is the Name of the Game, a series pilot (*The Name of the Game,* 1968–1971), starring Tony Franciosa, Jill St. John, and Susan Saint James, which involves an enterprising reporter investigating the murder of a prostitute, surprised everyone at NBC by attracting nearly 35 million viewers. A staggering figure about the nine "World Premieres" that NBC broadcast during the 1966–1967 season is that each and every one had a Nielsen rating over 20 (which at the time meant approximately 25 million viewers); and "they [also] had, on the average, an audience of 20 percent more people than the average of all other movies (142 theatricals and two telefeatures) shown on the networks."[19] "The 1967–68 season" would be an even greater source of optimism as " 'World Premiere' movies attracted 42.2 percent of the audience, while the theatrical films claimed 38 percent" in comparison.[20]

The success of NBC's "World Premieres" merely serves to counterpose a continuing problem: Hollywood's leasing price to ABC, CBS, and NBC for its "blockbuster" pictures increased 250 percent between 1965 and 1970; at the same time, network demand for theatrical movies kept well ahead of the available supply through 1968.[21] In response, CBS and ABC felt compelled to take a different kind of initiative than the partnership entered into between NBC and Universal TV. In the summer of 1967, CBS and ABC created subsidiaries, CBS Cinema Center and ABC Pictures, for the express purpose of producing features for theaters that would eventually be made obtainable for broadcast use at a more reasonable rate. This foray into the motion picture business, which lasted until 1972, was an unmitigated disaster for both networks, costing each tens of millions of dollars in losses. The move did prove to be one crucial part of the corrective for the feature shortage on primetime, however, glutting the market with product and thus stabilizing lease prices as network inventories remained overstocked with theatricals through 1972.

The other component that filled the need for more movies on TV was, of course, the rise of the telefeature. Neither CBS Cinema Center nor ABC Pictures was ever an important player in television movie production, accounting for only 4 percent and less than 1 percent, respectively, of the 228 made-for-TV [movies] that were telecast from 1964 through the 1971–1972 season.[22] Following NBC's lead, ABC and CBS decided against using ABC Pictures and CBS Cinema Center for further telefeature production after January 1972; they learned from experience that sponsorship of the major TV movie suppliers afforded them greater control and fewer legal problems in the long run.[23]

During the first decade (1964–1973) of the made-for-TV movie, in fact, six firms generated more than 70 percent of the genre's output. Ranked according to productivity, these companies were Universal TV, Aaron spelling Productions or Danny Thomas/Aaron Spelling Productions, Paramount TV, 20th Century-Fox TV, Columbia's Screen Gems, and Metromedia.[24] Together, the networks and these major TV movie suppliers rapidly propelled the made-for-TV movie beyond its humble beginnings during the early 1970s. Many of the better producers, writers, actors, and directors in the television industry experimented with the telefeature in this period as their way of progressing past the relentless work regimen of series TV. As a result, the made-for-TV movie started evincing what would become its primary aesthetic strategy: Continuing efforts at producing NBC's "World Premiere" movies, ABC's *Movie of the Week* (1969–1975), and later *The New CBS Friday Night Movie* (1971–1975) forged the identity of the tele-feature into a feature-length, small screen form that personally dramatizes high-profile concepts and topical themes.

THE REALIZATION OF THE MADE-FOR-TV MOVIE, 1970–1977

For every social and moral problem there is an equal and apposite TV movie.

—DANIEL MENAKER, 1980.[25]

The American made-for-television movie came of age in the 1970s. This maturation process proceeded rapidly on several fronts, as the TV movie genre was decisively fulfilled as both a viable industrial product and a distinctly televisual form by the end of the decade. Theatricals remained the film of choice on primetime until 1972–1973 when the seasonal output of made-for-TV movies began to inch past its predecessor for three critical reasons: the number of available theatrical films from the major movie studios plummeted from an average of 180 during the late 1960s to around 120 by the mid-1970s[26]; second, theatrical films were both more dated and less appropriate for primetime audiences than TV movies (between 1970s and 1975, the average age of a theatrical film was more than four years old before its first exposure on the networks, and 35 percent to 40 percent of MPAA-rated films during this same period were awarded either an R or X rating[27]); and, lastly, the overall quality of made-for-TV movies continued to improve throughout the 1970s.

CBS joined NBC and ABC by starting to seriously invest in telefeature production during the 1971–1972 season. All three networks had now institutionalized positions for a vice president of television movies within the hierarchy of their entertainment divisions, signaling the newly arrived importance of this genre in planning their primetime schedules. In retrospect, NBC and ABC were also the proven leaders in creating innovations in the TV movie form during the decade (i.e., the docudrama and the mini-series), although all of network TV was quick to copy each new programming breakthrough within a season or two of its first appearance.

In like manner, made-for-television movies have never varied much in design, practice, or ideology from network to network. The inclination of ABC, CBS, and NBC to follow similar lines of program development is a long established pattern that results from the high degree of insularity and interdependence within their oligopoly. The networks pioneered the TV movie genre with an identical group of suppliers; and they virtually geared their primetime features toward the same general target audience (i.e., women from 18 of 49 with slight demographic variations depending on which evening the made-for-television movies were being scheduled[28]). The overall growth of the TV movie genre is, therefore, best understood as a shared experience—allowing for brief break-out periods for experimentations in topical subject matter, the docudrama, and the mini-series—shaped in large part by the common traditions and mutual priorities of all three networks.

The differences between theatrical and television movies were readily apparent from the outset of the genre. Made-for-TV movies were always more suggestive of the scale and techniques of series TV and the "live" anthology dramas from the 1950s and early 1960s that the larger-than-life narratives and protagonists that are typically associated with the classical Hollywood style. Even those early television movies that most reminded film critics of the Hollywood B movie, such as the aforementioned Western *Scalplock,* had televised antecedents that were well established, numerous, and tailored to primetime long before the broadcast of the first telefeature. The tendency in *Scalplock,* for example, toward a more sociable cowboy hero, plenty of conversation, and intimate camerawork rather than epic sweep and physical action is expressly derivative of the literally dozens of "live" Western teleplays (e.g., Rod Serling's "A Town Has Turned to Dust" for *Play-house 90*) and the more than 50 Western series (e.g., *Gunsmoke,* 1955–1975) that abounded on primetime during the 1950s.

The proponents of the new television movie were evidently working within a different set of strictures from what had ever been standardized in the motion picture industry. The constraints of creating drama for a 25-inch screen had always inspired producers to stress performance over plot; now the telefeature discovered its own unique voice within the contours of this long-standing tradition. The individualized and informal depiction of everyday characters in an assortment of medium shots and close-ups quickly became the forte of the TV movie, more so than in any other feature film form. Plot structure and setting were accordingly scaled back as a means of better shaping these conventions to the shorter length and commercial segmentation of primetime and the lower definition and smaller ratio of the TV screen. As writer-producer Rod Serling recalled in 1969, "the key to television is intimacy. The facial study on a small screen carries with it a meaning and power far beyond its usage in motion pictures."[29] A case in point is the first major critical success of the genre—Universal TV and NBC's *My Sweet Charlie,* which premiered 20 January 1970.

My Sweet Charlie is characteristic of the TV movie form in many important ways. This telefilm is a small, social melodrama that concentrates its primary focus on a limited number of characters; in this specific instance, two principals dominate the entire program. The story is "soft" by motion picture standards, meaning there is no graphic sex, very little violence, and a minimum of action clichés that demand elaborate special effects. The premise, based on a successful novel and Broadway play of the same name, is also decidedly topical for the time this telefeature was made, addressing race relations, runaways, and unwed motherhood.

My Sweet Charlie concerns a young white woman, Marlene Chambers (Patty Duke), who is forced by circumstances to share an abandoned summer house in a rural town on the Texas coast for several days with a black lawyer from New York, Charles Roberts (Al Freeman, Jr.), who has just killed a white man in self-defense at a nearby civil rights demonstration. Marlene has been cast-off by her father because she is pregnant and unwed. Both characters are, therefore, hiding out, forced into being outsiders for different reasons.

One of the most interesting aspects of this TV movie is that the usual stereotypes of the period are reversed as Marlene is presented as a poor and ignorant member of the Southern underclass, whereas Charlie is an accomplished, sophisticated, and intelligent professional. Marlene is also a scared and angry bigot, hurling the epithet "nigger" at Charlie whenever she is cornered; the hostility in her characterization was a television breakthrough, especially considering the climate of primetime prior to *All in the Family* (which was first telecast 12 January 1971). Charlie is similarly more than just a noble black prototype; he is racist in his own right, as the two individuals learn to recognize their prejudices and identify somewhat with their respective fates on the periphery of society. Both Duke's and Freeman's performances are resilient even today, underplaying sentiment and creating two desperate characters with honesty and compassion.

The key to understanding the fundamental nature of any TV movie, such as *My Sweet Charlie,* is to assess its position as a creation of the television industry, not as a motion picture byproduct. Bob Banner, an independent television producer, actually attempted to first package *My Sweet Charlie* as a theatrical film property with Sidney Poitier and Mia Farrow in the lead roles. No movie studio was interested, though, because *My Sweet Charlie* is essentially a two-character sketch, however well drawn, with very little happening. This apparent large-screen liability was, in fact, the central reason why the story appeared attractive to two screenwriter-producers, Richard Levinson and William Link. Their conventional wisdom dictated that "television can usually deal with an intimate personal story better than a large-scale event."[30]

Levinson and Link were eight-year veterans of TV (writing for such series as *Alfred Hitchcock Presents, Burke's Law,* and *The Fugitive*) when they were hired by Jennings Lang and placed under contract at Universal TV in 1967. After creating the successful program *Mannix,* Levinson and Link were rewarded by Universal TV with an opportunity to "liberate [themselves] from the constraints of series television" by producing their first made-for-TV movie.[31] Attracted by the story elements and relevancy of *My Sweet Charlie,* they secured its rights for Universal TV from Bob Banner, who remained on the project as the executive producer. Levinson and Link then wrote the script themselves.

The rest of the cast and crew selection, budgeting, and shooting schedule are all examples of extending the usual conventions of primetime TV. For instance, Levinson and Link procured their above-the-line talent from within the ranks of the television sector and were provided with in-house, below-the-line workers from Universal TV. They first hired an experienced television director, Lamont Johnson (who had directed for several anthologies, *Peter Gunn, Have Gun—Will Travel, The Twilight Zone,* and *The Defenders,* among others), because they admired his understated and intimate style, his feeling for character, and his liberal sensibility.

Levinson and Link next selected Patty Duke to star in *My Sweet Charlie* because she was an accomplished and bankable TV performer with credits earned on "live" anthology dramas, commercials, and *The Patty Duke Show* (1963–1966). Her casting is especially indicative of a new cadre of home-grown TV movie stars (e.g., Jane Alexander, Ed Asner, Richard Chamberlain, Hal Holbrook, Elizabeth Montgomery, Stephanie Powers, Dennis Weaver, etc.), who consistently eclipsed comparable theatrical stars in television movie ratings even in the early 1970s. (For example, ABC was the first network to learn that motion picture stardom did not necessarily translate into success in TV movies when Elizabeth Taylor and Richard Burton "bombed out in 'Divorce His/Divorce Hers' " in 1973.[32])

Comparative figures in Appendix 1, moreover, indicate that *My Sweet Charlie*'s $450,000 budget was approximately four times less than the average cost of a theatrical feature in 1970. The rationale for NBC and Universal TV's investment must, nevertheless, be evaluated within the context of primetime dramatic programming to be understood clearly. *My Sweet Charlie* was always considered a prestige project in television terms and its budget was actually calculated "high" for April 1969.[33] The allocation of $450,000 for a projected 90-minute TV movie easily exceeded the cost-per-minute ratio for two episodes of the most expensive one-hour series on television at the time, including *The Wonderful World of Disney* ($450,000), *Gunsmoke* ($430,000), and *Mission: Impossible* ($420,000).[34] Likewise, the shooting schedule (5 May to 27 May 1969) was 50 percent longer than what was typically allotted for the production of 120 minutes of primetime drama. As is customary with most made-for-television movies, *My Sweet Charlie* was always envisioned and designed as a first-class, quality production, surpassing in resources any other kind of project being developed by the networks.

The production values of most TV movies are correspondingly closer to series television than to the technical finesse and state-of-the-art sophistication of a major theatrical film. The lighting quality in *My Sweet Charlie,* for instance, is often slightly underexposed, while its soundtrack is similarly problematic, employing very little sound sweetening and almost no incidental music. Still, TV movie producers are never expected by primetime audiences to approach the quality and style of a major motion picture. As Pauline Kael so perceptively stated in 1971, "We almost never think of calling a television show 'beautiful,' or even complaining about the absence of beauty, because we take it for granted that television operates without beauty."[35]

On 7 June 1970, *My Sweet Charlie* became the first made-for-TV movie to be recognized by the Television Academy of Arts and Sciences by winning three Emmys for Best Actress in a Single Performance (Patty Duke), Best Dramatic Screenplay (Richard Levinson and William Link), and Best Editing (Ed Abroms). These awards affirmed the acceptance and position of the TV movie genre within the television industry. *My Sweet Charlie's* congruent popularity (41 million viewers) with the American viewing public also encouraged the proliferation of scores of other telefeatures whose main purpose was to dramatize social issues. NBC and Universal TV had taken the first step in establishing an indigenous voice for the TV movie; now ABC in tandem with the major TV movie suppliers would offer a different innovation of its own.

ABC's Tuesday *Movie of the Week,* the most popular movie series in television history, premiered on 23 September 1969. Barry Diller, a former advertising agency executive and newly appointed head of primetime programming at ABC, is the man responsible for devising the "TV movie of the week" concept at his network. Diller and his boss, Leonard Goldberg, the vice president in charge of programming, negotiated a deal with Universal TV that in effect doubled the combined output of telefeatures on commercial television in just one year. "It was an innovative twenty-six week series of original, ninety-minute 'world premiere' movies specially produced (at an average cost of $375,000 per movie) for television, and it became a roaring success."[36] In 1970–1971, ABC's *Movie of the Week* was TV's sixth most-watched program; the next season this series climbed to number 5. In 1980, Barry Diller remembered

> In the early period, we did a lot of junk movies, but we also proved that you could do movies every week. And some of what we did was truly landmark for television—the first thing on television about homosexuality [*That Certain Summer* (1972)], about the Vietnam War [*The Ballad of Andy Crocker* (1969)], about drugs [*Go Ask Alice* (1973)]. It gave people in television a way to grow.[37]

The ABC *Movie of the Week's* most significant contribution to the TV movie genre was converting the topicality of the new telefeature into the fact-based formula of the docudrama between 1971 and 1973. The growth of the topical telefeature had indeed changed the entertainment landscape of the made-for-television movie forever. Older narrative types (e.g., Westerns, crime melodramas, etc.) were quickly abandoned in favor of an abundance of present-day stories inspired by social controversies, cultural trends, or whatever was on the public agenda. Appendix 2 suggests the totality of this transformation in its listing of the most popular telefeatures in television history.

Programmatic planning by TV movie executives at the networks now affirmed the conventional wisdom that higher concept subject matter was required because "there is no word of mouth" for a TV movie. It has "only one shot at an audience."[38] In turn, ABC, CBS, and NBC remained on the lookout during the rest of the 1970s for "a strong story premise and a promotable hook—something that [could] be summed up in one line in TV Guide."[39] The contemporaneousness of the docudrama lent itself perfectly to this new demand: ABC introduced this innovation in 1971–1972 by extending the strategies of the topical telefeature to include the recreation of "real" events, people, and places.

ABC's reasons for sponsoring the first docudramas were threefold. First, this network was directing its appeal toward the same young adult and urban demographics that all three networks were concerned with cultivating after 1971. ABC began addressing the tastes of this target audience by probing America's headlines and popular culture for TV movie topics that were both relevant and attention-grabbing. Second, the telefeature form was ideally geared to the currency of most docudramatic ideas by having a gestation period of only six months to a year; in this way, a television movie could be created and telecast while the newsworthiness of the subject was still fresh in the public's consciousness. And most important, made-for-television movie production skyrocketed in the 1970s, leaving all three networks desperate for 30 to 50 workable TV movie ideas a season. (The yearly output of television movies soared from approximately 50 in 1970 to 120 by 1975 to around 150 by 1980.) The ABC *Movie of the Week,* in particular, labored under the rigorous imperative of producing a movie a week for 39 weeks over six straight seasons. The docudrama, therefore, resulted in large part from this relentless demand for more producible and easily accessible TV movie concepts.

ABC's origination of the telefeature-as-docudrama cannot be considered a radical departure, in retrospect, because the history of the docudrama is long and varied and includes examples from literature, theater, film, radio, and even a few "live" anthology dramas from the 1950s and early 1960s for such series as *Hallmark Hall of Fame, Armstrong Circle Theater,* and *Profiles in Courage.* ABC first started its experiments in feature-length reality programming with Columbia's Screen Gems when they premiered *Brian's Song* on 30 November 1971. This "real-life" melodrama, an adaptation of *I Am Third* by Gayle Sayers with Al Silverman, is an excellent example of how the made-for-television docudrama blends aspects of the documentary and narrative modes with the demands of fiction usually dominant on primetime.

Brian's Song chronicles the interracial friendship between two professional football players, Brian Piccolo (James Caan) and Gale Sayers (Billy Dee Williams), and the slow cancerous deterioration and death of Piccolo. In a broad sense, this scenario is a fact-inspired drama, meaning that it promises to be an accurate retelling of a historical, socially significant, or controversial story. *Brian's Song* neutralizes the latter criterion, however, by characterizing the racial interaction between Sayers and Piccolo as much more comforting than discordant (e.g., in one scene Sayers even good naturedly laughs at being called a "nigger" by Piccolo, who is trying to motivate him to work harder). Piccolo's illness is, moreover, presented in typical "disease-of-the-week" manner, complete with bedside goodbyes and an excess of tears and sentiment.

Brian's Song was, nevertheless, the popular (44 million viewers) and critical success of the 1971–1972 television season, capturing the 1972 Best Dramatic Program Emmy as well as being the first TV movie to ever receive a George Foster Peabody Award for Outstanding Achievement in Entertainment, the most prestigious nonindustry acknowledgment that is available for a broadcast program. These accolades and the overwhelming viewer numbers for *Brian's Song* were important catalysts in convincing ABC to permanently pursue its new departure in TV movie form with more fact-based subjects in 1972–1973 and thereafter. NBC and CBS soon followed suit by commissioning docudramas of their own during 1973–1974.

The docudrama actually flourished so rapidly that it comprised one-third of the total output for all TV movies by 1975–1976. That season was the verifiable turning point on which the notion of fact-inspired recreations was broadened to include famous events and figures from history. ABC again led the way with *Eleanor and Franklin,* which aired on 11 and 12 January 1976 and dramatized the early formative years and beginning political career of FDR (Edward Herrmann) and Eleanor Roosevelt (Jane Alexander), winning nine Emmys in the process. The historical approach raised both the profile of the docudrama as well as the number of complaints from journalists and historians over distortions in dialogue and fabrications in plot structure. The major controversy over the docudrama has always been and still remains the inveterate tension between fact and fiction that is embodied in its very name.

The mid-1970s were years of impending flux for both the supply side of the television movie subindustry as well as the three networks. Five out of the top-six telefeature producers from 1964 to 1973 continued their major status for the remainder of the decade. Universal TV, Aaron Spelling Productions or Spelling/Goldberg Productions, Paramount TV, Columbia TV, and 20th Century-Fox TV were now joined by a bevy of new program providers, most notably ABC Circle Films, David L. Wolper Productions, Lorimar Productions, Quinn Martin Productions, Charles Fries Productions, and Filmways.[40] This group of 11 suppliers usually furnished from half (1973–1976) to one-third (1977–1980) of all TV movies annually (as opposed to 70 percent for the top-six firms between 1964 and 1973).[41] This drop in market share is directly attributable to the rapid rise in the number of independent producers that entered the television movie marketplace beginning in 1973.

The TV movie production sector experienced a 12-year transformation between 1973 and 1984 in which the major suppliers virtually relinquished their dominance to literally dozens of independent companies.[42] The reason for this slow abdication was simply due to the limited profitability of TV movie product in syndication (which is where suppliers recoup their production deficits and generate most of their profits). The ratings responses to most television movies in rerun were consistently poor. Between 1975 and 1980, in fact, only 43 percent of all primetime TV movies were ever repeated by the networks; comparatively,

91 percent of theatricals had encore showings and performed respectably.[43] As a result, the first generation of major made-for-television movie suppliers grew increasingly disenchanted with TV movie production and shifted more of their attention toward the windfall syndication potential of sitcoms and one-hour series. "The independents," in turn, became "specialists in TV movies" by the early 1980s "because they often [didn't] have any other business."[44]

ABC, CBS, and NBC's interest in made-for-television movies remained strong and abiding by contrast. TV movies continued to meet the long-form programming demands of the networks by continuously outpointing theatricals during their first-runs in primetime. CBS first inaugurated *The New CBS Friday Night Movie* in 1971–1972 and instantly matched the TV movie output of ABC and NBC. Appendix 1 also indicates how production costs continued to rise because of the increased efforts of concept testing, developing, and promoting variations in TV movie product, especially the docudrama and, beginning in earnest in 1976, the mini-series.[45]

The structural and stylistic roots of the mini-series are directly traceable to programming innovations explored a decade earlier by the British Broadcasting Corporation (BBC) in both its originally scripted productions and its novels-to-television. American audiences had their initial taste of this longer format when National Education Television (NET) programmed the 26-part, BBC-produced *Forsyte Saga* on a weekly basis beginning in October 1969. On 5 October 1970, the newly formed Public Broadcasting System (PBS) next brought the mini-series to stay on domestic television when it began telecasting the perennially popular *Masterpiece Theatre,* hosted by Alistair Cooke.

The first American production to approach the scope and style of the British mini-series was ABC and Universal TV's 12-hour *Rich Man, Poor Man,* which was scheduled in six 2-hour segments over seven weeks between February and March of 1976. *Rich Man, Poor Man* captured and translated the British strategy of creating a primetime soap opera with socio-historical resonances: the story follows two brothers, Rudy (Peter Strauss) and Tom Jordache (Nick Nolte), and their dual pursuit of professional success and the same woman (Susan Blakely) from World War II through the late 1960s. The immense popularity of *Rich Man, Poor Man* (41 million viewers) encouraged ABC to proceed with the even more ambitious plan of contracting with David L. Wolper Productions for $6 million to produce a 12-hour version of Alex Haley's *Roots.*[46]

Roots ran on eight consecutive evenings from Sunday, 23 January, through Sunday, 30 January 1977. In reporting this media and cultural phenomenon, *Broadcasting* proclaimed "television may never be the same again."[47] *Roots* so completely captured the imagination of middle-America that seven of the eight segments placed in the top-ten list of most-watched television programs of all time, while the other remaining episode ranked 13th. Overall, "the A. C. Nielsen Co. recorded an average 66 share of the audience—130 million people—more than had watched anything, anytime, anywhere."[48] A case can be made that *Roots* was the programming peak of the network era. ABC, CBS, and NBC were at their apex as the nations' purveyors of family-oriented, mass entertainment in the mid-1970s. *Roots* provided the network system with its greatest success in its most prestigious genre. The made-for-TV movie was indisputably realized with this mini-series, fulfilling with a vengeance its earliest promise of becoming a television "special event" in "longform."

ABC, NBC, and, to a lesser degree, CBS combined to sponsor 68 first-run mini-series over the next decade in their haste to reconstruct the success of *Roots*.[49] Appendix 3 suggests the analogous levels of popularity for nearly 20 percent of these efforts, although *Roots* still remains the highest rated mini-series in the history of American television. The mini-series stretched the limits of the TV movie genre, staking out a midpoint between the longform and the television series. This program innovation also became the primary scheduling strategy that the three major networks employed in counteracting the incessant erosion of their share of the primetime audience (from 90 percent in 1975 to 61 percent in 1991) by the ever-growing number of cable networks after 1975.

Outside media forces assure the continued longevity of the television movie genre. The pay-TV portion of the cable industry grew astronomically in the decade following 1977, soon replacing the three major networks as the second window of distribution for Hollywood's theatrical features. ABC, CBS, and NBC responded by increasing their already strong reliance on television movies, since their comparative interest in expensive, cable-saturated theatricals waned steadily. HBO also premiered the first made-for-pay TV movie, *The Terry Fox Story,* in May 1983. This story of a young Canadian athlete (Eric Fryer) who completes a cross-country marathon after losing a leg to cancer is obviously derivative of many network counterparts. Showtime, the Disney Channel, the USA Network, the Family Channel, and Turner Network Television (TNT) soon joined HBO in producing approximately 30 television films annually with budgets averaging 50 percent higher than network movies, but these cable-features have contributed little to the form in terms of stylistic and topical inventiveness.

The TV movie genre actually entered a mature phase after 1977. Appendix 1 illustrates how budgets have more than tripled since the mid-1970s; product variation and innovation has virtually ceased; and the cable industry now is a secondary developer of television product. ABC, CBS and NBC still combine to produce around 150 TV movies annually, as this genre has comprised approximately 15 percent of primetime programming since the 1977–1978 season. In the most recent attempt to establish a viable and competitive fourth network, in fact, Fox Broadcasting now presents a two-hour Monday night block devoted to original television movies and mini-series produced by Fox TV. For the foreseeable future, at least, the principal economic and creative habitat for the American made-for-TV movie continues to be primetime network television.

CONCLUSIONS

America is the impression I get from looking in the television set.
—ALLEN GINSBERG FROM HIS POEM "AMERICA"[50]

From humble beginnings in 1964, the TV movie quickly flourished through cycles that spotlighted a "disease-of-the-week," then, an "issue-of-the-week," and has since proved to be among the most resilient and popular primetime staples, along with sitcoms and crime shows. Born of propitious mingling between NBC, ABC, CBS, and several of Hollywood's more ambitious telefilm companies, the made-for-TV movie soon developed two distinct structural subsets—the telefeature and the mini-series. Television films fast became identifiable with a small-screen, televisual style and a high-concept approach to subject matter. Newsworthy events, national issues and controversies, and bits of historical lore and legend promptly became this genre's stock-in-trade. Headline hunting even spawned the docudrama, a logical extension of the high-concept formula, whose accessible style adapted equally well to the telefeature and the mini-series.

Contrary to popular opinion, television movies have never functioned as byproducts of the motion picture industry, even though many examples from this genre were once produced by several of the more established and prominent corporate names in Hollywood, including Universal TV, Columbia's Screen Gems, Paramount TV, and 20 Century-Fox TV. Likewise, TV films were never designed as "B" products by the executives and above-the-line talent from the television industry who worked within this genre; nor were telefeatures and mini-series ever presumed to be second-rate forms by the tens of millions of American television watchers who have regularly tuned into these feature-length TV programs over the past 27 years. ABC, CBS, and NBC presently attract an average of more than 30 million viewers for a typical primetime made-for-TV film, whereas only 20 million people attend all the movies in all the theaters nationwide each week. Like the television medium itself, the popularity of television movies in sheer numbers is truly revolutionary.

The core audience for movies made-for-TV (generally women between the ages of 18 and 49) also varies widely from the distinctly younger grouping (67 percent are 12 to 29, with the most targeted segment being teenaged males between 17 and 19) that most frequently attends theatrical motion pictures in the United States. Besides nudity, profanity, and graphic violence, matures themes and message pictures are actually more common on the small screen today, reflecting the more seasoned perspective of TV's older and broader audience. As early as 1969, the television movie has served as a pioneer into bolder and untapped subject areas on primetime. The broadcast standards departments at the three networks traditionally allowed this genre more freedom in its handling of controversial topics because of its noncontinuous format and because of the TV movie's special quality and higher status within the sphere of nighttime programming.

Not all television films have challenged the strictest parameters of primetime, of course, as many have fallen victim to the ratings imperative and rendered the controversial sentimental, triviazed the poignant, and turned scores of high concepts into clichés. To renew our understanding of TV movies, however, it is fundamental to remember the economic and industrial conditions in which television films are made (just as it is critical for future research to begin analyzing the core viewers who most attend to this genre). The best made-for-TV movies of any year, such as *Playing for Time* (1980), *Something About Amelia* (1984), or *Lonesome Dove* (1989), are as meaningful to their viewers within the dictates of television as any theatrical motion picture is to its audience within the separate context of cinema.

Appendix 1 Estimated Cost per Episode of First-Run Primetime Fare (in Hundred of Dollars)

Season	Thirty-minute sitcom	One-hour drama	Two-hour made-for-TV movie	Theatrical movies	
				Production cost for major movie studios	Lease price to networks
1955–1956	30.0	67.5	—	1,100.0	100.0
1960–1961	49.5	105.5	—	1,300.0	180.0
1965–1966	72.5	155.0	300.0	1,500.0	290.0
1970–1971	98.5	205.0	400.0	1,750.0	725.0
1975–1976	115.0	255.0	775.0	4,000.0	1,100.0
1980–1981	265.0	525.0	1,475.0	8,500.0	Not available
1985–1986	365.0	765.0	2,275.0	12,000.0	2,300.0
1989–1990	455.0	925.0	2,475.0	18,500.0	Not available

SOURCES: Compiled from data found in Charles S. Aaronson, ed., *1965 International Motion Picture Almanac,* 37th ed. (New York: Quigley, 1965), p. 64A; "Curtain Falling on Theatrical Films on TV," *Broadcasting,* 3 September 1984, pp. 42, 44; John Dempsey, "Majors Pass or Vidpix, Minis," *Daily Variety,* 17 October 1984, pp. 1, 11; Richard Gertner, ed., *1987 International Motion Picture Almanac,* 58th ed. (New York: Quigley, 1987), p. 32A; Lawrence W. Lichty and Malachi C. Topping, eds., *A Source Book on the History of Radio and Television* (New York: Hastings, 1975), p. 440; "Prime-Time Program Costs: A Three Decade Analysis," *Media Matters: The Newsletter for the Media and Advertising Industries,* August 1986, pp. 8–9; "The Returning Shows," *Channels,* September 1986, pp. 58–59; and "Can the Major Networks Curb Primetime Program Costs Over "Long Haul?" *Media Matters: The Newsletter for the Media and Advertising Industries,* November 1989, pp. 8–9.

Appendix 2 The Most Popular Telefeatures, 7 October 1964 through 10 June 1990

Rank	Show name	Date	Network	Rating	Share
1	*The Day After*	11/20/83	ABC	46.0	62
2	*Helter Skelter* (Part 2)	4/2/76	CBS	37.5	60
3	*Little Ladies of the Night*	1/16/77	ABC	36.9	53
4	*The Burning Bed*	10/8/84	NBC	36.2	52
5	*Helter Skelter* (Part 1)	4/1/76	CBS	35.2	57
6	*The Waltons' Thanksgiving Story*	11/15/73	CBS	33.5	51
7	*Night Stalker*	1/11/72	ABC	33.2	48
8	*A Case of Rape*	2/20/74	NBC	33.1	49
9 (tie)	*Return to Mayberry*	4/13/86	NBC	33.0	49
	Dallas Cowboys Cheerleaders	1/14/79	ABC	33.0	48
11	*Brian's Song*	11/30/71	ABC	32.9	48
12	*Fatal Vision* (Part 2)	11/19/84	NBC	32.7	49
13 (tie)	*Women in Chains*	1/24/72	ABC	32.3	48
	Jesus of Nazareth (Part 1)	4/3/77	NBC	32.3	50
15	*Something About Amelia*	1/9/84	ABC	31.9	46
16	*Heidi*	11/17/68	NBC	31.8	47
17 (tie)	*Guyana Tragedy: The Story of Jim Jones* (Part 2)	4/16/80	CBS	31.7	50
	My Sweet Charlie	1/20/70	NBC	31.7	48
19	*Feminist and the Fuzz*	1/26/71	ABC	31.6	46
20 (tie)	*Something for Joey*	4/6/77	CBS	31.5	51
	Dawn: Portrait of a Teenage Runaway	9/27/76	NBC	31.5	46

SOURCES: Compiled from data found in "Hit Movies on U.S. TV Since '61," *Variety,* 24 January 1990, pp. 160, 162; and "The Best and Worst by the Numbers," *TV Guide,* 7 July 1990, p. 13.

Appendix 3 The Most Popular Mini-Series, 13 November 1973 Through 10 June 1990

Rank	Show name	Date	Network	Rating	Share
1	*Roots*	1/77	ABC	45.0	66
2	*The Thorn Birds*	3/83	ABC	41.9	59
3	*The Winds of War*	2/83	ABC	38.6	53
4	*Shogun*	9/80	NBC	32.6	51
5	*How the West Was Won*	2/77	ABC	32.5	50
6	*Holocaust*	4/78	NBC	31.1	49
7	*Roots: The Next Generation*	2/79	ABC	30.2	45
8	*Pearl*	11/78	ABC	28.6	45
9	*Rich Man, Poor Man*	4/76	ABC	27.0	43
10 (tie)	*79 Park Avenue*	10/77	NBC	26.7	40
	Master of the Game	2/84	CBS	26.7	39
12	*Masada*	4/81	ABC	26.5	41
13	*Scruples*	2/80	CBS	26.3	40
14	*Lonesome Dove*	2/89	CBS	26.1	39
15	*North and South*	11/85	ABC	26.0	38
16	*The blue and the Gray*	11/82	CBS	25.9	39
17	*East of Eden*	2/81	ABC	25.7	37

SOURCES: Compiled from data found in Alvin H. Marill, ed., *Movies Made for Television: the Telefeature and the Mini-Series, 1964–1986* (New York: Zoetrope, 1987); David L. Wolper, "Yes, *A.D.* and *Space* Died—but don't Bury the Miniseries Form Yet," *TV Guide*, 5 October 1985, pp. 6–11; "The Best and Worst by the Numbers," *TV Guide*, 27 June 1987, p. 13; " 'Dove' Pulls CBS Up the Ladder," *Broadcasting*, 20 February 1989, p. 39; and "The Best and Worst by the Numbers," *TV Guide*, 7 July 1990, p. 13.

NOTES

1. John Ellis, *Visible Fictions: Cinema, Television, Video* (London: Routledge & Kegan Paul, 1982), p. 116.

2. For two of the better examples, see Christine Geraghty, *Women and Soap Operas* (Cambridge: Polity Press, 1991); and Robert Allen, *Speaking of Soap Operas* (Chapel Hill: Univ. of North Carolina Press, 1985).

3. For a review of the literature on the made-for-television movie, see Gary Edgerton, "The American Made-for-TV Movie," In *TV Genres: A Handbook and Reference Guide,* ed. Brian G. Rose (Westport, CT: Greenwood, 1985), pp. 173–175; and the works cited in Gregory Waller, "Re-placing *The Day After,*" *Cinema Journal* 26 (Spring 1987), pp. 3–20. Also see Laurie Schulze, "Getting Physical: Text/Context/Reading and the Made-for-Television Movie," *Cinema Journal* 25 (Winter 1986), pp. 35–60; and Elayne Rapping, "Made for TV Movies: The Domestication of Social Issue," *Cineaste* 14, No. 2 (1985), pp. 30–33.

4. Laurence Jarvik and Nancy Strickland, "TV Movies—Better Than the Real Thing (Are You Kidding?)," *American Film,* December 1988, pp. 40–43, 56.

5. Douglas Gomery, "*Brian's Song:* Television, Hollywood, and the Evolution of the Movie Made for Television," in *American History/American Television: Interpreting the Video Past,* ed. John E. O'Connor, with a foreword by Erik Barnouw (New York: Ungar, 1983), pp. 215–216.

6. A *telefeature* is a self-contained filmed or videotaped narrative for television of four hours or fewer that is scheduled over no more than two primetime evenings. The *mini-series* further extends the sweep of the made-for-television movie into at least "three broadcast parts,"

according to the National Academy of Television Arts and Sciences, and typically presents a historical saga or a literary epic in more than four hours.

7. "All-Time Top 75 Programs," *Variety,* 17–23 May 1989, p. 66.

8. Judith Crist, "The 10-Best TV-Movies of 1979," *TV Guide,* 29 December 1979, p. 2.

9. Judith Crist, "Tailored for Television," *TV Guide,* 30 August 1969, p. 6.

10. Darrell Y. Hamamoto, "Interview with Television Producer Rod Amateau of *Dukes of Hazzard,*" *Journal of Popular Film and Television* 9 (Winter 1982), p. 166; and Alvin H. Marill, ed., *Movies Made for Television* (New York: De Capo, 1980), p. 10.

11. Douglas Brode, "The Made-for-TV Movie: Emergence of an Art Form," *Television Quarterly* 156 (Fall 1981), p. 55.

12. "Specials, Specials," *The Hollywood Reporter: Television's Fall Issue,* September 1978, pp. 29–30. Longform spectaculars were developed at NBC but soon became popular with all three networks. These specials routinely exhibited the ability to attract viewers from the opposition, allowing NBC, for example, to "stunt" or promote itself and its upcoming programming to a newer and wider audience.

13. Bill Davidson, "Every Night at the Movies," *Saturday Evening Post,* 7 October 1967, p. 32.

14. Henry Ehrlich, "Every Night at the Movies," *Look,* 7 September 1971, p. 62.

15. Alvin H. Marill, ed., *Movies Made for Television: The Telefeature and the Mini-Series, 1964–1986* (New York: Zoetrope, 1987), pp. 459–566.

16. "Johnny North," *TV Guide,* 2 May 1964, p. 8.

17. Henry Harding, "First Attempts at Making Movies for TV," *TV Guide,* 4 July 1964, p. 14.

18. "Johnny North," p. 9.

19. Davidson, p. 32.

20. Crist, "Tailored for Television," p. 7.

21. John Izod, *Hollywood and the Box Office, 1895–1986* (New York: Columbia Univ. Press, 1988), pp. 173–174.

22. These percentages are compiled from data found in Alvin H. Marill, ed., *Movies Made for Television,* pp. 11–99.

23. For background information on the legal problems experienced by the networks as a result of their production activities, see Michael Conant, "The Paramount Decrees Reconsidered," in *The American Film Industry,* rev. ed., ed. Tino Balio (Madison: Univ. of Wisconsin Press, 1985), pp. 537–573; and Gary Edgerton and Cathy Pratt, "The Influence of the Paramount Decision on Network Television in America," *Quarterly Review of Film Studies* 8 (Summer 1983), pp. 9–23.

24. Marill, *Movies Made for Television,* pp. 11–99.

25. Daniel Menaker, "Television: Apposite Reactions," *Film Comment,* July–August 1980, p. 76.

26. Thomas Guback, "Theatrical Film," in *Anatomy of the Communications Industry: Who Owns the Media?* ed. Benjamin M. Compaine (White Plains, NY: Knowledge Industry, 1982), p. 247.

27. Christopher H. Sterling and Timothy R. Haight, eds., *The Mass Media: Aspen Institute Guide to Communication Industry Trends* (New York: Praeger, 1978), pp. 297–298.

28. Women are highlighted because research data support the contention that they make most of the buying decisions in American households, except for a few product such as cars, life insurance, and beer. In addition, counterprogramming strategies determine the demographic variation; for example, *NBC Monday Night at the Movies* has long emphasized family dramas and strong women characters to compete against the traditionally male-oriented, action entertainment of *ABC Monday Night Football.*

29. William I. Kaufman, ed., *Great Television Plays,* with an introduction by Ned E. Hoopes (New York: Dell, 1969), p. 10.

30. Richard Levinson and William Link, *Stay Tuned* (New York: Ace, 1981), p. 28.

31. Levinson and Link, p. 4.

32. Dwight Whitney, "The Boom in Made-for-TV Movies: Cinema's Stepchild Grows Up," *TV Guide,* 20 July 1974, p. 26.

33. Levinson and Link, p. 41.

34. Cobbett Steinberg, *TV Facts,* rev. and updated (New York: Facts on File, 1985), pp. 79–81.

35. Pauline Kael, *Kiss Kiss Bang Bang* (New York: Bantam, 1971), p. 277.

36. Patrick Milligan, "Movies Are Better Than Ever—On Television," *American Film,* March 1980, p. 52.

37. Milligan, p. 52.

38. Benjamin Stein, "Words That Sell in TV-Movie Titles," *TV Guide,* 25 July 1981, p. 34.

39. "Movies on the Tube," *Newsweek,* 10 April 1972, p. 87.

40. ABC Circle Films is ABC's telefilm subsidiary and was wholly separate from ABC Pictures, the theatrical film entity. Similarly, CBS Cinema Center was part of the film industry, whereas CBS Entertainment and NBC Production are part of the television industry.

41. These estimates are compiled from data found in Marill, *Movies Made for Television,* pp. 147–315.

42. John Dempsey, "Majors Pass on Vidpix, Minis," *Daily Variety,* 17 October 1984, pp. 1, 11.

43. Joseph D. Zaleski, "Successful Syndication of Completed Motion Pictures to Television," in *The Selling of Motion Pictures in the '80s: New Producer/Distributor/Exhibitor Relationships,* eds., Peter J. Dekom, Michael I. Adler, David Ginsburg, and Michael H. Lauer (Los Angeles: The Regents of the University of California, 1980), p. 292.

44. Dempsey, p. 11.

45. The first move toward extending the telefeature beyond two nights was NBC and Lorimar's *The Blue Knight,* which telecasted from 13 November through 16 November 1973. This drama was not longer than the four-hour requirement for a mini-series, though, nor did NBC follow it up until 30 September, 7, 14, 28 October, 4, 11 November 1976 with the nine-hour *Captains and Kings.*

46. Stephen Zito, "Out of Africa," *American Film,* October 1976, pp. 8–17.

47. "The Effects of 'Roots' Will Be with TV for a Long Time," *Broadcasting,* 7 February 1977, p. 52.

48. Dwight Whitney, "When Miniseries Become Megaflops," *TV Guide,* 19 July 1980, p. 3.

49. "Running the Numbers: Megadrop in Miniseries," *Channels,* March 1989, p. 72.

50. Allen Ginsberg, *Howl and Other Poems* (San Francisco: City Lights Books, 1956), p. 34.

QUESTIONS FOR DISCUSSION

1. Why are made-for-TV movies more closely associated with exploring social issues than are series TV shows? Does this still hold true?

2. What is a "docudrama" and how does it differ from both documentary and drama? Why did the 1970s see a rise in this form?

3. This author does not specifically mention the strong emphasis on female characters and issues of particular concern to women in the made-for-TV movies, but it
can be seen in his list of the most highly rated. Race, too, is frequently a narrative
element. How do these emphases mesh with the industrial framework discussed?

4. How did the passage of the financial interest and syndication (fin/syn) rules affect
made-for-TV movie production? What about the introduction of PBS?

INFOTRAC COLLEGE EDITION

Look under "miniseries" and "docudrama" on InfoTrac College Edition to follow
up on this topic. Also see titles of specific made-for-TV movies and series.

11

Feeding Off the Past
The Evolution of the
Television Rerun

PHIL WILLIAMS

Reruns are a ubiquitous, economically crucial, and underanalyzed aspect of U.S.
television. In this article, media historian Phil Williams brings the history and
significance of the television rerun out of the shadows. Williams places its roots in
the nascent television syndication industry of the 1950s. During that period,
syndicators provided movie packages and later independently produced television
series to local affiliate stations to fill time between network feeds, and to
independent stations to fill their schedules. With the switch to filmed
programming in the late 1950s and the discovery that viewers would watch
programs more than once, the rerun emerged, first as a way to save network
money during the summer by obviating the need for summer replacement series.
Williams documents the economic importance of the rerun to the television
industry, especially in the development of the off-network strip. By the early
1960s, networks began to package their canceled programs for sale to
independent and affiliate stations. The sale of off-network programs by networks
supported the system of deficit financing, in which the profit made from
syndication offset the loss incurred in production. The mandatory introduction
of UHF channels on all television sets provided even more opportunities for the

From the *Journal of Popular Film and Television* 21 (Winter 1994): 162–75. Reprinted by
permission of HELDREF Publications.

syndication of off-network programming. The Financial Interest and Syndication Rules of the 1970s (limiting the number of programs a network could own and barring networks from controlling syndication rights) pushed networks out of the syndication market while paradoxically increasing the importance of reruns to television programming and economics. The expansion of cable television in the 1980s and 1990s, as well as the creation of three new television networks, were all fueled, in large part, by the availability of off-network reruns.

U p and down the dial, day and night, the television rerun glows as a rarely appreciated byproduct of mass culture. Within the television industry, however, the rerun is a product in and of itself. For more than four decades, the marketing and programming practices surrounding the rerun have evolved, first cautiously, then by aggressive leaps and bounds. The stories of the rerun's evolution form particularly revealing, and mostly unnoticed, chapters in the history of American television.

"NO SOUND REASON":
CONCEPT AND PRACTICE

As the new medium of television stood at the edge of exponential growth at mid-century, valuable precedents for repetition were provided by the film and radio industries. Hollywood, since Edison's day, had battled for profits along aggressive distribution and exhibition lines. This competition, waged among a handful of industry giants, was conducted on a weekly basis. Repeat audience attendance was desirable, but maintaining a constant flow of individual patrons week after week remained a greater priority.

Until World War II, reissues were infrequent. As the supply from the studios ebbed during the war years, however, a small syndication industry appeared on Hollywood's perimeter. These companies met the demand of theaters searching to round out double features and Southern movie-houses where twin bills had never flourished to the extent that they had elsewhere. Consequently, these films could be promoted as first-run products (Pryor B3; "Film Classics" 15). After the war, anti-trust decrees pushed the uncertain majors increasingly toward reissues as a means to supplement the continued decline in first-run product. In 1947, the entire industry released 53 reissues, 105 in 1948, and 136 in 1949 ("Box Score" 6; "Reissues Ease" 7).

Wartime exigencies also unleashed the possibility of sustained broadcast repetition in the radio industry. Programmers had 16-inch disk recordings at their disposal since the dawn of the industry in the 1920s. Yet these program recordings were expensive, frequently marred by cracks and scratches, and—due to FCC requirements that such shows be identified as a transcription—thought to be anathema to audiences. The effective development and application of tape in Armed Forces Radio broadcasts promised to solve these difficulties and, indeed, the networks turned to magnetic tape recorders after the war.

Still, the transition was not immediate. ABC and Mutual began recording their broadcasts in 1946. CBS and NBC, fearing dead air mishaps, waited until 1948. ABC and NBC, also in 1948, were the first networks to opt for the new taping systems. These delays were partially attributable to the cost of taping machinery, which, unlike the actual tapes, remained formidable. More important, audience acquiescence toward taped programming remained in doubt. Not until 1950 was the public's acceptance of the technology conventional wisdom within the industry. By that time, the ascendancy of television had thrown the established radio industry into disarray. The veterans of radio programming who flocked to the new medium brought a developed appreciation of taped broadcasts. Whether the broadcasts could be re-aired remained in doubt (Baughman, *The Republic* 67; "Disks Catch On" 68–69; "Transcription Boom" 58–59; "Tape" 52).

The issue, in fact, had been addressed a decade earlier before conflict relegated the nascent television industry to a dormant state. These observers adopted the existing logic of Hollywood: Television would be dependent upon filmed programming—and such programming could not be rerun. In a 1939 *Public Opinion Quarterly* piece, Jack Western argued, "Rarely does a moviegoer see a film more than once. There is no reason to believe that the looker will consent to see a telecine transmission more frequently. Afterwards, the film must be relegated to the vaults." A year later, NBC President Lenox R. Lohr echoed these concerns: "It appears to be inadvisable to broadcast most programs more than once. On the second broadcast, the audience is likely to become hypercritical and to lose interest" (qtd. in Boddy 67).

Despite earlier predictions, the industry, led by the networks, did not adopt filmed programming during its first explosive years. This was both a measure of preference—film was viewed as having greater production costs—and necessity— the networks were not yet willing to strike deals with Hollywood. The result was the live programming, with each show airing 52 weeks of the year, that defined the medium's mischievous Golden Age.

It was also during this brief era that local stations enjoyed their most autonomous moments. The networks' daily schedules were limited, coaxial cables remained on the drawing board, and local advertisers proved eager sponsors of the new medium. One result of this relative freedom was the hours of cooking shows, talent showcases, and interview programs that were produced.

Another result—given the costs associated with the production of live programming—was a scramble by the stations for additional material. This product, the first influx of filmed programming into the medium, was supplied by the young television syndication industry. The role of Hollywood in the development of this industry—production units and aged stars flocking toward the networks as the film industry staved off Supreme Court rulings and witch hunts—has been well documented (Baughman, *The Republic* 77–90; Boddy 132–54). For the rerun's purpose, however, the resulting product and its applications deserve examination.

First, syndicators offered movie packages. Stations, as an analyst indicated in 1950, were particularly eager for Hollywood features: "The surest bet in television programming is sponsorship of Hollywood movies and westerns. No other category has consistently come up with such high ratings at such low cost" (Kugel 15). Until the mid-1950s, when lasting unions between the networks and Hollywood were struck, the flow of features consisted of badly dated efforts from lesser studios.

Battling to meet the expectations of hundreds of thousands of new TV sets, the quality of these films became something of a moot concern. Moreover, the supply was limited and, in bidding scrambles, a considerable strain was placed on even the healthiest station's budget. Almost immediately, local stations re-aired these features, pausing afterwards to provide justification. "Let's concede that television is in the fortunate position of finding itself the recipient of the products of an established medium and being able to adapt these for its own needs," stated Carol Levine, film supervisor of New York's powerful independent station WPIX in 1953. Levine's adaptive strategy was the station's *First Show,* an attractive movie aired Monday to Friday in the 7:30 to 9 P.M. time slot, with a fresh feature introduced each Wednesday. Ratings, she noted, had "shown a tendency not to suffer appreciably on re-runs, and . . . the individual cost of each showing is considerably lower" (89).

In addition, syndicators marketed independently produced filmed series—the "westerns" that spellbound the 1950 insider—to the local stations. At this stage of the industry the syndication companies faced competition from the networks. As early as 1950, CBS had migrated "upstream" to produce series such as *Strange Adventure* and *The Gene Autry Show* for distribution (Kugel 16).

But the bulk of syndicated programs came from independent companies. Of these, Ziv Television Programs was the most successful. Ziv's success suggests that the burgeoning television syndication industry was as indebted to radio as it was to the film colony. Formed in 1937, Frederick W. Ziv Inc. boasted 24 programs on 850 radio stations, generating a gross of $10 million (a dollar amount questioned by competitors) when its founder decided to strike at television a decade later. Throughout the 1950s, Ziv rolled out one stock action half-hour program after another—*The Cisco Kid, Boston Blackie, Highway Patrol, Mr. District Attorney,* and *I Led Three Lives.* As an independent syndication company, Ziv needed a substantial capital outlay to begin operation, faced increasing production costs, and had to be aware of competition in pricing its products. As a result, the revenue generated by repeated showings quickly became necessary to earn a profit ("Transcription Boom" 58; "Millions" 44, 48–49; Moore).

Stations discovered—as they had with movies—that re-airing syndicated series did not necessarily equate lost viewers and advertisers. *Television Magazine* answered its February 1954 article "Are Re-Runs a Good Buy?":

> There's no valid argument against the re-run concept, *if the show is good and used properly.* The record shows that it is possible for a return engagement program of almost any type to reach a sizable audience, comparable to that of high-rated network programming. (24)

The "record" received further support from the A. C. Nielsen Company. Surveying 254 repeat broadcasts from the 1953–1954 season, Nielsen concluded that the audience share dropped only 9 percent from the original broadcasts while the average minutes of viewing time fell 6 percent ("Nielsen" 30).

In assessing rating successes, industry insiders saw reruns as proof of the public's love affair with television. At times, especially from syndicators, the vision was an upbeat, if faintly sadistic one. Saul J. Turell, president of Sterling Television, stated in 1952, "We feel people not only can take an indefinite amount of film, but never tire of the same film, if it's good. One of ours, *Sandy,* has been shown in N.Y. alone 37 times, and the stations obviously are happy with it" ("Syndicated Film" 63). Others drew attention to the explosive demand for the medium. As early as 1950, distributor Robert D. Wolfe noted, "Running a film a year after its first run, the sponsor can reach millions who missed the first showing, or have bought their sets since then" ("Trend" 12). WPIX's Levine drew a comparison to a suddenly endangered Hollywood: "Reissues are money in the bank for movie production companies. There is no sound reason why the same principle cannot be applied to television" (93).

NETWORK SUMMER: "SOME PEOPLE JUST HAVE TO WATCH TELEVISION"

As regional programmers and their syndicated partners backed into programming repetition, the networks gravitated toward the economics of the summer rerun. Production costs, especially for the favored live productions, became increasingly difficult to bear over a 52-week run. Quickly, 39 weeks of original programming became the norm, and the summer lull was mostly populated with less costly variety shows.

In a spirited defense of local programming, WSB-TV assailed this phenomenon in an advertisement in the 25 June 1951 issue of *Broadcasting.* Under the heading "No Summer Doldrums in Atlanta," the station reminded the potential advertiser: "The primary interest of WSB-TV is still audience . . . and lots of it. Despite the normal difficulties of summer programming (hiatuses, replacements, and replacements for replacements), WSB-TV has resisted the take-it-easy convenience of network scheduling." WSB's clients, instead of substandard network fare, were treated to locally produced programming (*Broadcasting* 67).

The networks countered such budding heresy. CBS and NBC launched "Operation Summer" in 1951 to retain sponsors. Rates were cut and NBC provided a brochure reporting that, for sponsors who stayed with the network through the 1950 summer, "an idle summer became a summer idyll" as "virtually all piled up more TV homes during the summer months than they had during the April, May and June just preceding" (" 'Operation Summer' " 62).

"Operation Summer," however, proved an ineffective campaign. *Broadcasting* reported in its 13 August 1951 issue that "June marked the first sign of a summer decline in TV network billings comparable to the traditional summer slump of radio broadcasting" as the combined gross sales for the four networks fell from the May total of $10,011,144 to $8,996,940 ("June" 72).

Such numbers, and the growing suspicion that alliances with independent production facilities—if not the major studios—would prove more cost effective than the growing inflexibilities and expenses associated with live programming, provided the impetus to finally accept filmed programs. The direction was sensed by one analyst in the 10 September 1951 issue of *Broadcasting:* "While the networks continue to talk up live TV shows, the fact remains that they are in the foreground of film production, either present or future" (Glickman 94). Led by such sitcoms as *I Love Lucy* and *The Adventures of Ozzie and Harriet,* the movement toward film steadily progressed. By the 1956–1957 season, 44 percent of all network primetime programming was on film ("Now—More" 54). Four years later, the total stood at 83 percent (MacDonald 118).

Filmed programs were adaptable for virtually any programming needs. And, by the time *TV Guide* editorialized on the subject in September 1956, filmed reruns had replaced live replacement shows: "Not too many years ago the networks were using the summer months as a try-out time for different kinds of programs. Now they save their 'different' shows for their regular winter season." However, repeats or not, viewers remained glued to the set: "Some people just have to watch television and if only reruns are on, they watch reruns" ("As We See It" 2).

Film was still a rather rare commodity in the first years of the summer repetition. Many reruns were remnants from previous seasons. Highlighting the resurrection of ABC's failed 1959 sitcom *Hey, Jeanie,* CBS's 1959 summer flop *Peck's Bad Girl,* and the drab 1957 NBC play *Wedding Present* for the 1960 summer, *Newsweek* struck an already familiar chord: " 'April is the cruelest month,' wrote T. S. Eliot, but obviously he never reckoned with television in June, July, and August. This TV summer is shaping up as a wasteland of stupefying familiarity . . . [and] . . . neither quality nor popularity necessarily has anything to do with the choice of revivals" ("Thirsty" 92).

Lacking competition and facing increasing production costs—the $50,000 cost of the average half-hour and the $100,000 cost for the average hour in 1960 doubled by 1973—deeper cuts occurred in original programming (Davidson 8). In 1960, the networks began to offer only 26 weeks of original programming. When, a dozen years later, this number fell to 22 or 24 weeks, the summer rerun inched into March.

Only the emergence of competition from cable and the Fox network forced the established networks to consider fewer reruns.[1] John Severino, ABC president, told *Broadcasting* in 1983, "We can't kid ourselves. We can't think we can go into summer reruns and still retain the audience" ("New Network" 35). Seven years later, Warren Littlefield, an executive vice president at NBC Entertainment, confessed to an industry gathering, "We've put crap on the air in the summer. That's got to change" ("Networks Promise" 52).

The networks were true to their promises. During the 1991–1992 season, reruns accounted for 17 percent of NBC's programming, 16 percent of ABC's, and 9 percent of CBS's (significantly, the young Fox network had the highest total at

26 percent). Specials had chipped away at the rerun base. CBS's share of such programming had risen to 31 percent (a figure inflated by the 1992 Winter Olympics and a seven-game World Series and one that helped the network win the season's rating sweepstakes) while specials accounted for 11 percent of NBC's slate, 10 percent of ABC's, and 8 percent of Fox's. Furthermore, the networks increasingly aired reruns in non-sweep periods outside the summer. In December 1991, for example, reruns accounted for 27 percent of the total programming for the four networks. In December 1982, this figure stood at only 4 percent. The number of original program episodes had rarely increased but, relegated to non-sweep periods and often preempted by specials, reruns began to disappear from the warmer months (especially in the sweep periods of May and July). The summer rerun had, slowly but steadily, become an endangered species ("Study Blames" 36; Mandese 54).[2]

THE IMPACT OF THE OFF-NETWORK STRIP

The American television viewer also became familiar with another brand of rerun in the mid-1950s: off-network strips, the showing of a previously broadcast network program five times a week in a particular time slot. It appears that the first strip was *Amos 'n' Andy,* available to local stations in the fall of 1953 after concluding a two-year run on CBS (Ely 239–42; "Hot Market" 27). Another early off-network product was NBC's *My Little Margie.* After a three-year network run, Official Films began to market *Margie's* 126 episodes in the fall of 1955. WPTZ, a Philadelphia independent looking to compete against CBS's strong daytime lineup, was one such buyer. The contract was for two-and-a-half years, allowing for five showings of each episode. Reporting on WPTZ's use of *Margie, Television Magazine* noted a "most satisfactory" initial return on the sponsors' investment and concluded, "The key to the economics of this daytime strip, as it is to the financing of all syndicated films, is the rerun. And as long as the rerun is delivering satisfactorily, the advertiser is getting a good buy" (" 'Nighttime' " 77–78).

Strips took off. *Broadcasting,* surveying 60 markets, concluded that combined network and independent strips rose from 440.5 hours per week in 1956 to 800.5 hours per week in 1957 and to 1,070.5 hours per week in 1958 ("Syndicators Off" 162). Still, the real growth had not occurred. After only seven network programs totaling 423 half-hours were released for syndication in 1960, "the flood of 1961" brought 23 programs totaling 1,528 half-hours and 146 hours into the marketplace by July of that year ("Hot Market" 27). Before the pace finally slowed in 1964, 100 network programs hit the market in a five-year period ("Off-Network Scarcity" 52).

The impact was tremendous. The networks grabbed many of the most valuable commodities for their daytime programming, beginning a trend that introduced many of the best loved reruns. The most famous, *I Love Lucy,* first appeared in CBS's daytime schedule on 5 January 1957, where it ran for almost eight years before it was cast toward the open market (Simon 51).

For individual stations, especially the independents, the off-network strip was an even greater blessing. A network product, usually deemed a superior product, could grab a better time period, was more attractive as a proven product, and was more durable in reruns than a syndicated offering. More important, perhaps, the product existed. Unless a package contained approximately 100 half-hour episodes, the minimal optimal six-month run was impossible. Shorter, more frequent cycles, the stations had discovered, would usually exhaust both audience and advertiser ("Timebuying" 17).

For the syndicator of non-network programming, this was a considerable hurdle to pass. If fortunate enough to possess an adequate cache of episodes, the syndicator faced the equally difficult task of selling an increasingly unattractive product to a substantial number of markets to fully recoup production costs. Locked into this cycle, independent syndicators usually responded by cutting costs, falling further and further behind.

Therefore, as a 1961 *Broadcasting* survey indicated, a "virtual breakdown in new production for syndication" resulted ("Program Sources" 20). From a 1956 high of 29, the number of first-run series offered by independent syndicators plunged to six five years later with little indication that the trend would be halted ("Hot Market" 27). On the other hand, network programming, now mostly produced by powerful Hollywood studios, survived by largely defining the industry's economies of scale. This network/studio alliance, and the reruns that it left in its wake, virtually destroyed the independent syndicator.

In addition to the syndicated product, the well of theatrical films, even as the vaults spilled open, was also running dry. In August 1956, *Broadcasting* estimated that half of the 12,000 to 14,000 old features had been released. Because television's appetite for these films was still increasing, it was noted that the source might be exhausted by 1962 ("Films for Fall" 40).

The journal was only slightly more optimistic five years later, predicting that the backlog would be "substantially" exhausted by the end of 1964 and completely exhausted by 1967 ("Will First-Run Films" 27). The networks, by that time, began to produce their own "TV movies." For individual stations, however, it was, as Albert Kroeger observed in the April 1964 *Television Magazine,* "a seller's market and distributors tell balky station buyers, 'Haven't you heard? There aren't any more movies behind this batch.' And they're right" (96).

As the supply of non-network syndicated programs and the first-run movie backlog evaporated, it was becoming increasingly difficult for individual stations to produce their own programming. Again, the industry's economies of scale were the deciding factor. Bernard Smith perceptively argued in a 1962 *Harper's* piece that:

> It is a fallacy to think of TV as chiefly a medium for "local" talent and interests. . . . Good TV programming is just too expensive for the resources of a single station, and it is getting costlier all the time. Nor will the local advertiser foot the bill. A local Chicago program, for instance, can reach less than 5 percent of TV homes in America. For it an advertiser will not pay more than 5 percent of what he would pay for a national network show. (29)

Although never abundant, quality local programming became the exception to the rule.

In the decade following the debut of *My Little Margie* on WPTZ, therefore, a hierarchical programming structure took firm root. At the peak was network programming—increasingly filmed and limited to half-hour sitcoms and hour-long westerns or adventure series. The networks netted the best of this material after its original run for their own use during the daytime and, after these shows lost their luster, they were released to individual stations where they were aired yet again. But most off-network shows went straight to the WPTZs of the dial where the rerun was no longer the hesitant, almost humble, force of the early 1950s. On the local level, the abundance and popularity of strips were quickly driving, either by direct competition or indirect opportunities, other forms of programming—syndicated non-network shows, movies, and local productions—from the playing field.

"FREEZING THE WASTELAND"

Few moments capture the essence of the New Frontier more convincingly than FCC Chairman Newton Minow flaunting the sins of television's "vast waste-land" at the podium of the 39th Annual Convention of the National Association of Broadcasters on 2 March 1961. For several years, a flow of indictments from disgruntled postwar liberals, an increasingly disenchanted viewing public, and those displaced by the industry's film wave had been targeted at the medium.[3] Minow's rallying call to arms led aspirations for a richer and more informative medium into uncharted areas of federal regulation. As the FCC moved forward on two fronts to improve first-run programming, the promises inherent in greater competition quickly cemented the hierarchical programming structure and the reruns that largely defined it for the next two decades.

A day before his speech to the NAB, Minow spoke to John Bartlow Martin of the *Saturday Evening Post:*

> We're only using twelve channels, Two through Thirteen. We could use thirty more, the ones in the ultrahigh frequency band. It's the only way to increase competition in television. If we used the ultrahigh frequencies, you might have ten or twelve stations in Chicago instead of four. (Martin 64)

The history of UHF television had taken a decisive turn when, during the closing months of World War II, the FCC froze the development of UHF channels until 1953. When the freeze was lifted, only a third of all televisions produced in the United States could receive UHF signals. Consequently, many of the stations that set up shop past channel 13 after the freeze hoping to lure audiences away from the network affiliates and established independents of the VHF spectrum faced an uphill battle for survival. Within two years 123 of these stations folded and the number of televisions that could tune in UHF fell to 15 percent ("Hopes Fade" 27). By the time the 1962 All-Channel Act requiring all domestic televisions to have UHF capabilities was passed, there were 85 UHF stations in operation and five million of the 55 million sets in the U.S. could receive such signals ("TV Trade" 40).

Two years after the "wasteland" speech, Minow, claiming that "the time has come for more than speeches," again addressed the NAB convention. While a UHF dial, under the terms of the All-Channel Act, would not be mandatory on sets produced in the United States until 30 April 1964, Minow saw a number of roles it could play. These included an educational network, a system of pay TV, and a base for a fourth network. He also envisioned a relationship between "first-run" VHF network affiliates and "second-run" affiliates on the UHF dial. The first-run stations would air original network programming; the UHF second-run stations would allow the public "a [second] chance to see the best the networks have to offer" and a scattering of foreign programming. Moreover, in such a system, advertisers unable to afford network fees could find a new source, program costs could be more effectively amortized, and producers could receive additional rerun fees ("Minow Proposes" 60).

Minow's salesmanship was effective. *Broadcasting* reported that the growth of UHF stations had been "the single brightest development in the syndication industry" in 1966, as their total sales had quadrupled since 1965 and grown to 10 percent of the total domestic syndicated market ("U's Newest" 31). There were 265 UHF stations by the end of the decade and 60 percent of all sets could tune them in ("UHF Band" 61). A number of these stations provided bilingual, public affairs, and quality foreign programming. Also, the UHF dial served as a friendly habitat for struggling educational channels. The majority of these new stations, however, veered toward the second-run path, using off-network reruns and syndicated film packages to fill most of their programming day. The base of the hierarchical programming structure had been widened considerably, creating more demand for the off-network product.

The discrepancy between Minow's original vision of UHF and the vaster wasteland that it largely led to illustrates the ineffectiveness of the FCC as a means to an end of better television in the early 1960s. One obstacle was the holdover commissioners from the Eisenhower years who represented a daunting majority. This bloc, Minow quickly discovered, would support rulings that forwarded increased competition as a solution to the industry's programming shortcomings but balked at any direct interventions by the federal government. Also, haunted by the agency's fumbling of the UHF question in the early 1950s, the entire commission was tentative and inconsistent in its efforts a decade later (Baughman, *Television's Guardians* 153–59).

But, in fact, Minow's FCC was largely unconcerned with reruns and, insofar as they prospered in the wake of the agency's actions, their growing role in American television. Nowhere in the "wasteland" address did the chairman allude to reruns. Rather, in an era of quiz show scandals, hordes of derivative westerns, and fewer and fewer "quality" efforts such as *See It Now* and *Omnibus,* Minow had captured the essence of existing criticism in damning the networks. Building tangible regulatory legislation from this base was not only unpalatable to the entrenched Eisenhower appointees but a policy of initiating showdowns with corporate America was unlikely to gain approval in Camelot. Consequently, Minow's vision of increased competition was one of promise: Prisoners to an unimaginative programming hierarchy in the short run, it was possible that, in the long run, the young UHF stations could gain firm financial footing and pose an alternative from below.

The FCC also began to struggle with the question of how much involvement the networks should have "downstream" in the syndication market. As early as 1957, the agency issued studies concerning the vertical reach of ABC, CBS, and NBC. When concrete proposals came in 1965, the networks promptly joined forces to counter the threat. First, they claimed that their share of the syndicated market amounted to only 12 percent of the total, down from 25 percent in 1958 ("In Defense" 33). Second, they launched a prolonged legal campaign to protect what *Broadcasting* called "an estimated $30 million-a-year bonanza" ("$30-Million Plum" 26). The networks staved off the threat until 1 June 1973. By then CBS, considerably more involved in the syndicated market than ABC or NBC, had created a corporate spin-off, Viacom, to handle the network's syndication and fledgling cable efforts.[4] In 1971, its first year, Viacom pulled in almost $21 million in revenue from these two sources, a figure that increased eightfold by 1980 ("Viacom" 32).

With the onset of the Reagan deregulatory revolution, the FCC, under the captaincy of Mark Fowler, moved to strike the syndication rulings from the books. Again, legal action and lobbying ground legislation to a halt. A break came in 1991 when a U.S. Court of Appeals ruled that the law was unconstitutional and, after yet several more delays, the networks were allowed, on 1 April 1993, to reenter the syndication market (Jessell 7, 10).

Convoluted even by FCC standards, the push to remove the networks from the syndication market had a great impact on the development of the rerun. Although they could, and did, pressure producers to grant them distribution rights, the networks' first priorities were ratings and advertising revenues.[5] Whether a program remained on the air long enough to prove attractive as a product for off-network stripping was, at best, a secondary concern.[6] In fact, a quickening of cancellations in the late 1970s and early 1980s in the face of completion from other programming sources contributed to a crucial drought in the off-network market.

For the producers who capitalized on the FCC's rulings against the networks, the length of a program's run on the networks was the greatest of concerns. The production of network programming was, and remains, a deficit-financed operation. Broadcast fees from the networks covered only part of production costs. Reruns brought a break-even point or, if the program enjoyed a lengthy network run, profits as stations would eagerly bid for a popular series with enough episodes to ensure successful stripping.[7] Large producers, such as Universal and Paramount, or independent syndication companies, if the producer lacked the resources to follow operations downstream, were left to scavenge fiercely as the networks weathered and then fell to the FCC's fire.

The insights of those who occupied the industry's trenches reveal what was at stake as the FCC began to fumble with the UHF and syndication dilemmas. Several months after Minow's indictment of the networks, *Broadcasting* surveyed industry leaders for their opinions of the crossroads where American television had arrived:

> "If we have a wasteland in television programming now," said one station executive, "then what we're doing is freezing the wasteland for a long time to come." Another put the same thought in this way: "What we're doing is perpetuating the 'sameness' in television programming and stretching it out over a longer period of time. If a western is taken off the network and put into syndication and then is replaced on the network by a new western, what you have is summer reruns 40 times over." ("Program Sources" 20)

As the off-network programming chokehold continued, such prognoses became more pessimistic. In the aforementioned 1964 Kroeger piece, Jay Faragan, program director and film buyer for WFLA Tampa, reckoned that, of the rerun cycle, "The audience will get used to it and we'll get by with it—for a while, but without a doubt we're going to have to come up with something new." Samuel S. Carey, holding the same positions at WRVA Richmond, warned, "The end of the road is coming on rerunning reruns . . . shows like *My Little Margie,* run in local time for years, are wearing out. Once they could maintain most of the audience, but no more" (Kroeger 102–4).

"I'D SELL MY SOUL FOR A HALF-HOUR"

Audiences and stations were, however, increasingly locked into a rerun cycle as FCC actions led to the crystallization of the hierarchial programming structure. Network programming had not been improved and the syndication industry broke from the gate at a breakneck pace that has not diminished to this day. It is this competitive force that has defined the rerun's role in television over the last three decades.

Immediately after the flood of off-network programs glutted the market in the early 1960s, the flow slowed to a trickle. After 30 shows hit the market in 1963, only 19 became available in 1964 and 12 in 1965 ("Syndicators Confident" 68; "Off-Network Bonanza" 25). Although the number rose again in 1966—with 22 shows offered—variances of supply in this era were exacerbated by other factors ("Syndicators Have" 100). Residual payments increased as the Screen Actors Guild contracted concessions from the Association of Motion Picture and Television Producers during union/industry showdowns and as actors, writers, and directors with the greatest leverage independently struck even more costly payment schedules ("Those TV Reruns" 62; "Color Tones Up" 69). Also, starting in 1966, syndicators began to scramble for color off-network programs as the American viewer began to demand the fruits of this long-awaited breakthrough ("Color Tones Up" 69).

With quality color products a scarcity, contingency selling became the norm. Richard Wollen, vice president of programming of Metromedia Television, introduced this strategy in 1967. Seeking to purchase topnotch off-network products for the stations under the Metromedia umbrella, he grabbed *The Man from U.N.C.L.E.* and *Mission Impossible* while the shows were in the midst of their network run. The latter was an especially risky move because the show had only been on the air for 10 weeks. As Wollen told *Television Magazine* a year later: "If *Mission* had run only one season I would have had my neck out. . . . But my instincts told me it was too good to run only one season. I just figured this thing has got to be a barn burner and it's going to run at least two years and maybe four" ("What Stations Want" 63). Six years later, Wollen's gamble bore fruit and Metromedia's stations, rather than their competitors, possessed the program for stripping.

Contingency selling, however, threatened to dampen the appetite of stations. In waiting for a program to conclude a lengthy network run before picking up rerun rights, datedness might offset the show's popularity with viewers. An ingenious solution was not long in appearing. In 1973, Louis Friedland, chairman of MCA's syndication efforts, as *Forbes* told the story five years later,

> had a bright idea. Why not, he reasoned, take a series while it was going strong on the network and sell its reruns for a definite delivery date in the future? "Before, stations didn't get a shot at a show until it had been publicly executed," says Friedland. "They were prepared to pay much more for something that might still be punching it out when they got it." (Jaffee 98)

Thus, *Happy Days, M*A*S*H, All in the Family,* and *Laverne & Shirley* led the way in what *Forbes* concluded had become "a true futures market in this most volatile of entertainment commodities" (Jaffee 98).

For individual stations, the risks, now dictated by the possibility of an early cancellation, increased accordingly. Production companies, seeking to offer a safer product and combat a new off-network drought in the early 1980s, responded in a twofold manner. First, in 1983, the production runs of two cancelled network shows with only 63 episodes apiece, *Fame* and *Too Close for Comfort,* were continued. Revenues were quickly garnished from both selling the first-run property and by marketing a larger, and thus more attractive, package for stripping ("How Independents" 62). Second, larger companies, as Paramount did with *Family Ties* and *Cheers,* began to guarantee—for which they extracted a surcharge from stations—a certain number of episodes. If the networks cancelled such programs, they would follow *Fame* and *Too Close for Comfort* into nonnetwork production runs ("The World of TV" 55). Yet, no less than they had been in the early 1950s with an independent product, local stations were as resourceful as their syndicator partners in molding the off-network strip as a programming tool. On the networks, such programs had been primetime entities molded by the nobility of American mass culture—network executives and Hollywood producers—with the aggressive intent to grab the attention of advertisers by capturing the loyalties of the public. On their off-network run, the appeal of these programs to advertisers was far more powerful than the cartoons and unsophisticated syndicated programs they replaced ("Off-Network Bonanza" 26).

Therefore, in an ironic turn consistent with Minow's aspirations for the UHF dial, increased dependence on the off-network rerun provided an opening for independent stations to make a bid for the entire adult market. After solidifying the hierarchial programming structure, the rerun emerged as a threat to its health. Specifically, this threat was counterprogramming: the running of attractive off-network strips by independents in the early fringe period (5 to 7:30 P.M., 5 to 8 after 1971 when the FCC forced the networks to give the 7:30 to 8 slot back to their affiliates) to compete with the network news and other non-primetime programming of the affiliates.

An NBC study of the early 1980s traced the damage that counterprogramming inflicted upon its affiliates. From a 7.4 share in 1971, the average UHF independent's early fringe ratings rose to a 13.5 share in 1982 ("Independent TV" 26).[8] In 1981, Bud Hirsch, a vice president in NBC's sales division, told *New York* that, in the nation's largest market, "The independents, predominantly WNEW and WPIX, keep growing every season, and I'm worried. . . . They are mainly successful now in the 6-to-8 P.M. slot, when they can program reruns of *M★A★S★H* or *Laverne & Shirley* against local and network news. We just can't compete with independents in that period" (Nobile 26).

Advertising revenues followed the ratings. In 1972, for the first time, the average UHF channel turned a profit ("UHF" 35). All independents earned a combined $7 million in profits in 1973; by 1977 the amount leapt to $131 million (Jaffee 98). In 1984 there were 193 independents, twice the number of 1979 ("Happy Days" 74).

In this wildly competitive environment the price of the off-network product rocketed. When *I Love Lucy* first became available to local stations in 1967, WNEW paid just over $4,300 per episode (Jaffee 98).[9] WPIX, in 1976, paid $35,000 for each episode of *Happy Days* (Mariani 27). Two years later, 33-year-old Randy Reiss, a vice president for domestic syndication at Paramount, launched the *Laverne & Shirley* campaign. Labeled "one of those upwardly mobile types whose nervous stomach could no longer accommodate 16-ounce steaks at expensive Manhattan restaurants" by *TV Guide,* Reiss knew that the show would be especially desirable to stations seeking to take on competitors who had snatched up *Happy Days* (Mariani 27). The show was also powerful enough to become a station's "hooker spot," forcing advertisers to buy packages that included time for less-attractive spots in addition to the precious *Laverne & Shirley* presence. Reiss set the minimum bid at $50,000 for New York stations; other markets, as is the case with syndication sales, would bid after this benchmark had been set. WPIX outbid its New York rivals, purchasing the show for $54,000 per episode, while KTLA earned Los Angeles rights for $61,000 per half-hour (Mariani 30).

The ideal counterprogramming product is maneuverable and capable of appealing to a wide demographic viewer base. Sitcoms, at half the length of the hour-long drama and more easily digested by young adults, had long since been established as the staple of the syndication market by the time Reiss leapt to proto-Yuppie fame. Yet, led by the success of *Dallas* and *Hill Street Blues* and the demise of mainstay half-hour comedies, the networks swung toward hour-long dramas while producers and critics pronounced the sitcom to be dead as a network entity.

The effect on the off-network market was not difficult to gauge: Syndicators and local stations knew that only a single network sitcom would be available in both 1985 *(Gimme a Break)* and 1986 *(Facts of Life)*. Putting cancelled programs such as *Too Close for Comfort* and *It's a Living* on non-network syndication runs was, at best, a minimal response to the drought. The development of first-run syndicated material as an alternative to the entrenched rerun was an obvious solution, but the products that rolled off the assembly line were painfully weak. Of *Small Wonder,* a landmark pilot produced in 1984 by a consortium of five of the industry's largest station groups, one wag noted: "All those brains and they come up with a show about an 8-year-old girl who's a robot?" (Rosenthal 44). Thoroughly mediocre, by both aesthetic and ratings yardsticks, the scarce off-network sitcoms went for top dollar (*Gimme a Break* fetched a top price of $77,000). The mood of the industry was captured by a chief programmer from a major station group: "I'd sell my soul for a half-hour" ("Off Network Sitcoms" 34).

Then what *TV Guide* called the "most shamelessly arrogant exercise in hard-ball salesmanship the television industry had ever seen" was launched to sell *The Cosby Show* (Hill, "The *Cosby* Push" 3). The show was marketed as having a "halo" effect: so popular that programs in surrounding time periods would gain and retain *Cosby* viewers. It was also sold as having a "halo" effect: bids set so high that stations could only hope to offset the costs with heightened advertiser interest in the surrounding programs. A Machiavellian marketing campaign stressed that, whatever the costs, non-*Cosby* stations would be at the mercy of competitors who possessed the program. Furthermore, Viacom demanded a minute of the six-and-half minutes of advertising (during its network run, the program had four-and-half minutes of advertising space—editing more ad space into a rerun was an established practice) for its own use. Barter deals had been commonly struck for first-run independent programming; *Cosby,* however, represented the first application of this practice for an off-network product. When the feeding frenzy of bidding passed, barter time generated approximately $100 million of the $600 to $650 million of revenue from the *Cosby* sale (" 'Cosby' " 76). New York's superstation WOR-TV submitted the top bid, $350,000 an episode ("The 'Cosby' Numbers" 58).

DENOUEMENT AND REBIRTH

Cosby's ratings in syndication did not, in the eyes of industry analysts, justify its price. Nor did it have a significant "halo" effect ("Mixed Results" 38; Hill, "*Cosby* Reruns" 32). The boom market in independent stations, fueled by FCC rulings allowing more stations to be owned by individual companies and easier sales of stations within the industry, went belly up in 1987 as several dozen went into Chapter 11 or were incorporated into the Home Shopping Network (Grillo 64; Cray 44). If there was any room for hope for the independents in the post-*Cosby* era, it was, as Jean Bergantinni Grillo scolded in a January 1988 *Channels* piece, that they "have studied the primer on how *not* to run a station that they helped write during their wild expansion and painful contraction over the past few years" (Grillo 64).

One of the chief lessons was to avoid deadly bidding wars for off-network programs. "*Cosby* told us how to say 'no.' " observed Rick Lowe, general manager of KOKI, Fox's Tulsa outpost (Heuton 37). Such discipline, and the fruits of the resurrected sitcom, drove prices down for syndicated material. For example, whereas *Cosby* went for $100,000 an episode in the Detroit market, *Perfect Strangers* was bought for less than $20,000 and *ALF* for less than $30,000 ("Sitcoms" 36).

Also, Lowe and other station managers could shed their independent status and align themselves with the Fox network. Although Fox shows eventually flowed down the programming hierarchy—witness *Married . . . With Children*—the network offered a source of first-run material that had proved so illusive during the previous three decades. First-run material also began to blossom in the form of dramas such as *Baywatch* and a new wave of talk shows. Furthermore, there was the appeal of products produced by individual stations. Greg Nathanson, general manager of KTLA, told *Broadcasting* in 1993: "I think our whole future is in local programming . . . when we run a movie or an off-network sitcom, even though we run a lot and we're very successful with it, every cable system, every USA Network or Nickelodeon can bring you rerun programming." ("To Live and Program" 74).

Nathanson's cable examples are especially relevant to the present and future state of the rerun. USA led the way in pulling recent off-network strips away from individual stations, adding *Riptide* to its schedule in 1986, *Miami Vice* in 1987, and—in the first case of a cable network acquiring a network program ranked in the top 10—*Murder, She Wrote* in 1988 (Brown 26; "USA Network" 45; " 'Murder, She Wrote' " 102). For syndicators this trend helped to salvage some of the costs associated with the largely unwanted off-network hour-long drama in an era of sitcom demand. But not always enough to put a show in the black. *Miami Vice,* for example, cost MCA Inc. a reported $1.3 million per episode to produce, of which $850,000 was covered by the license fee paid by NBC. The USA deal did not cover the $450,000 deficit. This, in turn, led MCA and other companies away from the production of hour-long dramas, especially those that were particularly topical and expensive ("USA Network" 46).

In 1985, Nickelodeon judged its evening slate of children's programming expendable, opted for a slate of network relics, and launched its *Nick at Nite* programming (Schneider B22). The decision coincided with the appearance of "evergreen" divisions within several nervous syndication companies scavenging for products in the midst of the drought of recent off-network strips. Individual stations and superstations have continued to snap up dated shows—often, given the cost of the most attractive strips and the need to flesh out a programming schedule, out of necessity ("New Life" 54–59). Nonetheless, *Nick at Nite* has arguably cornered the market of vintage reruns.

A long-standing relationship with the nostalgic consciousness of the American viewing public has carved a broad swath through the rerun's history. The recycling of movies in the 1950s—in particular B Westerns and the Little Rascals and Three Stooges series—attracted both younger audiences and the adults who had flocked to the theaters in the days before television.[10] In the mid-1970s, a wave of programs from the 1950s such as *The Mickey Mouse Club* and *You Bet Your Life* grabbed both ratings and the attention of the media (Doan 10; "Second Childhood" 48). *Leave It to Beaver* and *The Brady Bunch,* although perennial rerun success stories, enjoyed renaissances of sorts in, respectively, the early 1980s and early 1990s (Friedman 18–21; Stengal 76; Briller 13–20).

It is difficult to imagine, however, a friendlier habitat for the rerun than *Nick at Nite.* Through its clean-cut promotional jingles the rerun itself is exalted and the viewer's memories of dusty UHF dens and a family's summertime bewilderment with *TV Guide* listings are affectionately coddled. For example, before being dethroned by Dick Van Dyke, Dr. Will Miller served as *Nick at Nite's* chairman, providing soothing psychological insights into the viewer's relationship with programs being viewed for the umpteenth time. Gilligan's failed efforts to leave his island are attributable to his reluctance to leave the stranded community, no more than the viewer can abandon yet another escapade of coconuts and gorillas. Meanwhile, in-house giggles follow the bottom line: reruns helped to boost Nickelodeon's advertising revenues to $78.5 million in 1991, an increase of 34 percent from the previous year (Winski S-2).

But the secret of *Nick at Nite's* success would seem to lie more in the atomization of American television in the age of cable than in the average viewer's sophisticated appreciation of postmodern camp. Traditionally, whimsical midlife crises equated only partial rerun success. Unless younger viewers were also attracted, a rerun would wither on the dial. DLT Entertainment's recent marketing campaign for the "new" *Three's Company* illustrates this objective in no uncertain terms:

> So why do we call it new? Because every season *THREE'S COMPANY's* audience completely re-generates itself! *THREE'S COMPANY* and *MASH* are the only two sitcoms to stay on the top 10 syndication sitcom list for 29 consecutive sweeps!
>
> That's why. . . . For 20 million teenagers, *THREE'S COMPANY* is this season's *newest* hit!
>
> For 68 million young adults, it's still their all time favorite program!
>
> For 36 million kids, every episode is first run!
>
> *That's* why we call it new! (*Channels* 67)

For Nickelodeon this concern is largely a secondary one. Aiming for a specific niche—movies, music videos, news, sporting events and summaries, cartoons and comedians, infomercials and shopping market-places—few cable channels bother to submit a full week's, or a full day's, worth of original programming. Instead, they seek a minimal hold on a targeted audience to attract enough local and national advertisers to off-set this selected and cost-effective programming. Thus the feasibility of *Nick at Nite.*

And thus, the art form saluted by Nickelodeon is wildly embraced by its cable brethren. Constant, albeit increasingly specialized, repetition flows from the modern American TV set. Conspiring is the viewer, armed with remote control and a VCR, an independent programmer free to finicky repeat at will. Tom Shales, in labeling the 1980s "The Re Decade," provided a definitive encapsulation of a future that has come to pass:

> With so many more channels out there, we are more than ever before feeding off the work of the past. We are even more parasitical of the past, and the past is more easily accessed than ever. We're accessin' it like crazy, all the time; you can get a fix of yesterday at almost any hour of the day and night, whereas it's not quite so easy to get a fix on, or a fix of, Right Now, This Minute. (72)

In this expanding environment, delineations on the rerun continuum fade. Summer reruns dissipate across the calendar. Off-network strips seep from traditional UHF havens into one cable outpost after another. A fresh wave of repetition foams about these products of postwar mass culture as they gradually melt into the concept that they began to define some 40 years ago. The reverence shown to the rerun by Dr. Miller and his cohorts is wholly fitting. After an elusive trek through our television heritage, the rerun basks in its blinding, omnipresent triumph.

ACKNOWLEDGMENT

The author is indebted to Professor Randy Roberts of the Department of History at Purdue University for his assistance and encouragement with this study.

NOTES

1. An ineffective flurry of presidential interest in summer reruns, however, emanated from the 1972 Nixon re-election campaign in its efforts to court Hollywood unions dissatisfied with residual payments for rebroadcasts. See "Don't Play It Again," *Newsweek* 25 Sept. 1972: 105; "The Rerun Syndrome," *Time* 2 Oct. 1972: 63; Peter Funt, "Are Viewers Getting the Old Rerun-Around?" *TV Guide* 1 Feb. 1975: 2–5.

2. In 1972, *Broadcasting* estimated that 44.8 percent of CBS's schedule consisted of reruns, 42.2 percent of NBC's, and 36 percent of ABC's ("The Realities of Reruns in Network TV," *Broadcasting* 2 Oct. 1972: 15). Although this study included reruns of theatrical films and the study two decades later ignored such repeats choosing instead to include them in the "specials" category, the rerun share had clearly diminished.

3. For detailed analysis of this criticism, see Baughman's "The National Purpose and the Newest Medium: Liberal Critics of Television, 1958–60," *Mid-America* 64 (1982): 41–55.

4. ABC's spinoff, Worldvision, was in place by 1972, as was NBC's NTA.

5. For a discussion of the tactics and results of such network intrusions see A. Frank Reel, *The Networks: How They Stole the Show* (New York: Charles Scribner's Sons, 1979): 125–27.

For a rare insight into the hegemonic reach of the networks from an industry insider during the initial FCC/network clashes, see independent producer Don McGuire's "Another View on 50–50 Rule," *Broadcasting* 7 Mar. 1966: 34+.

6. A noted example: Todd Gitlin's description of *Lou Grant*'s demise in *Inside Prime Time* (New York: Pantheon, 1985): 3–11.

7. Producers also depend upon foreign sales. This was especially true before the massive rise of off-network products and the increased production capabilities and programming protectionism of other nations in the late 1960s and early 1970s. See "World Laps Up U.S. TV Fare," *Business Week* 23 Apr. 1960: 129–131; Ross Drake, "From *Daniel Boone* to *Mod Squad*," *TV Guide* 29 Apr. 1972: 33–36.

8. The study also concluded that the late fringe strategy of placing local newscasts versus the final primetime hour also led to substantial ratings gains.

9. Until the 1980s, the terms of a rerun purchase allowed each episode to be aired six times within a given time period.

10. An interesting analysis of the beginnings of the Stooges' revival may be found in "Out of Vault, Into Limelight," *Broadcasting* 16 Feb. 1959: 62.

WORKS CITED

"A $30-Million Plum to Be Picked?" *Broadcasting* 3 May 1965: 26–28.

"Are Re-Runs a Good Buy?" *Television Magazine* Feb. 1954: 24–25.

"As We See It." *TV Guide,* 8 Sept. 1956: Inside front cover.

Baughman, James. "The National Purpose and the Newest Medium: Liberal Critics of Television, 1958–60." *Mid-America* 64 (1982): 41–55.

———. *The Republic of Mass Culture: Journalism, Filmmaking, and Broadcasting in America Since 1941.* Baltimore: Johns Hopkins UP, 1992.

———. *Television's Guardians: The FCC and the Politics of Programming, 1958–1967.* Knoxville: U of Tennessee P, 1985.

Boddy, William. *Fifties Television: The Industry and Its Critics.* Urbana: U of Illinois P, 1990.

"Box Score of 1947 Releases." *Variety* 31 Dec. 1947: 6.

Briller, Bert. "Will the Real Live Brady Bunch Stand Up?" *Television Quarterly* 26 (1992): 13–20.

Broadcasting 25 June 1951: 67.

Brown, Rich. "Off-Net Hours Find Good Home on Cable." *Broadcasting* 29 June 1992.

Channels Feb. 1990: 67.

"Color Tones Up Syndication Sales Picture." *Broadcasting* 21 Mar. 1966: 69–76.

"The 'Cosby' Numbers in Syndication." *Broadcasting* 27 Apr. 1987: 58–64.

" 'Cosby': Off-Network's Biggest Deal Ever." *Broadcasting* 12 Sept. 1988: 76–8.

Cray, Ed. "The Toughest Year." *Channels* Feb. 1988: 44–46.

Davidson, Bill. "The Facts Behind Those Network Reruns." *TV Guide* 8 June 1973: 6–13.

"Disks Catch On." *Business Week* 21 June 1947: 68–9.

Doan, Richard K. "All Together, Now—M-I-C-K-E-Y. . . ." *TV Guide* 21 June 1975: 9–11.

"Don't Play It Again." *Newsweek* 25 Sept. 1972: 105.

Drake, Ross. "From *Daniel Boone* to *Mod Squad*." *TV Guide* 29 Apr. 1972: 33–6.

Ely, Melvin Patrick. *The Adventures of Amos 'n' Andy.* New York: Free Press, 1991.

"Film Classics Sticks with Reissues." *Variety* 16 Mar. 1946: 15.

"Films for Fall." *Broadcasting* 13 Aug. 1956: 37–48+.

Friedman, Elise. "Never Say 'Bye.' " *TV Guide* 18 June 1983: 18–21.

Funt, Peter. "Are Viewers Getting the Old Rerun-Around?" *TV Guide* 1 Feb. 1975: 2–5.

Gitlin, Todd. *Inside Prime Time.* New York: Pantheon, 1985.

Glickman, Dave. "Film in the Future." *Broadcasting* 10 Sept. 1951: 79+.

Grillo, Jean Bergantini. "The Cautious Survivors." *Channels* Jan. 1988: 64–5.

"Happy Days for the 'Indies.' " *Newsweek* 5 Mar. 1984: 74.

Heuton, Cheryl. "An Enviable Situation." *Channels* 17 Dec. 1990: 36–8.

Hill, Doug. "The Cosby Push Wasn't Going for Laughs: 'We Gotta Confuse 'Em and Scare 'Em.' " *TV Guide* 7 May 1988: 3–10

———. "Cosby Reruns: Was the Big Bill Worth It?" *TV Guide* 29 July 1989: 32.

"Hopes Fade for UHF Television." *Business Week* 19 Nov. 1955: 27.

"The Hot Market in Used Shows." *Broadcasting* 17 July 1961: 27–9.

"How Independents See Their Fates." *Broadcasting* 20 Feb. 1984: 62.

"In Defense of Network Programs." *Broadcasting* 7 Mar. 1965: 31–3.

"Independent TV: It's Come a Long Way." *Broadcasting* 27 June 1983: 49–54.

Jaffee, Thomas. "The Great TV Hold-up." *Forbes* 18 Sept. 1978: 98–100.

Jessell, Harry A. "Networks Victorious in Fin-Syn Fight." *Broadcasting* 5 Apr. 1993: 7+.

"June Gross Lags." *Broadcasting* 13 Aug. 1951: 72.

Kroeger, Albert R. "Programming: Short Supply, Big Demand." *Television Magazine* Apr. 1964: 72+.

Kugel, Fred. "The State of Film." *Television Magazine* Aug. 1950: 15+.

Levine, Carol. "Film Re-Runs Can Pay Off." *Broadcasting* 10 Aug. 1953: 89+.

MacDonald, J. Fred. *One Nation Under Television: The Rise and Decline of Network TV.* New York: Pantheon Books, 1990.

Mandese, Joe. "More Reruns Creeping Into Regular Season." *Advertising Age* 4 May 1992: 54

Mariani, John. "Waiting For the Ring—and the 'Sale of the Century.' " *TV Guide* 12 May 1979: 26–30.

Martin, John Bartlow. "The Big Squeeze." *Saturday Evening Post* 11 Nov. 1961: 62–72.

McGuire, Don. Another View on 50–50 Rule." *Broadcasting* 7 Mar. 1966: 34+.

"Millions in TV Film." *Broadcasting* 4 June 1956: 44–52.

"Minow Proposes Second Run UHF Network." *Broadcasting* 8 Apr. 1963: 60.

"Mixed Results for Off-Network 'Cosby,' " *Broadcasting* 10 Oct. 1988: 38–9.

Moore, Barbara. "The Cisco Kid and Friends: The Syndication of Television Series from 1948 to 1952." *Journal of Popular Film and Television* 8 (1980): 26–34.

" 'Murder, She Wrote' to Appear on Cable." *Broadcasting* 8 Feb. 1988: 102.

"Networks Promise Summer Punch." *Broadcasting* 19 Feb. 1990 52–6.

"New Life in Old TV Shows." *Broadcasting* 18 Mar. 1985: 54–9.

"A New Network Summer Song." *Broadcasting* 7 Feb. 1983: 35–6.

"Nielsen: Film Re-Runs Hold Audience." *Broadcasting* 24 Jan. 1955: 30.

" 'Nighttime in the Daytime' with Film." *Television Magazine* Dec. 1955: 49+.

Nobile, Philip. "The Greening of Channels 5, 9, 11." *New York* 26 Oct. 1981: 26+.

"Now—More Innovations, More Film Than Ever." *Television Magazine* July 1956: 54–6.

"Off-Network Bonanza for Buyers." *Broadcasting* 2 May 1966: 25–7.

"Off-Network Program Scarcity Ahead?" *Broadcasting* 30 Sept. 1963: 52–5.

"Off Network Sitcoms Set for Syndication." *Broadcasting* 29 July 1985: 34–7.

" 'Operation Summer.' " *Broadcasting* 9 Apr. 1951: 15+.

"Out of Vault, Into Limelight." *Broadcasting* 16 Feb. 1959: 62.

"Program Sources Drying Up?" *Broadcasting* 18 Sept. 1961: 19–21.

Pryor, Thomas M. "Boom Market for Yesteryear's Movies." *New York Times* 30 Jan. 1944: B3.

"The Realities of Reruns in Network TV." *Broadcasting* 2 Oct. 1972: 15–16.

Reel, A. Frank. *The Networks: How They Stole the Show.* New York: Charles Scribner's Sons, 1979.

"Reissues Ease Off as Quality Lags, Though Top Pix Continue Strong." *Variety* 16 Nov. 1949: 7+.

"The Rerun Syndrome." *Time* 2 Oct. 1972: 63.

Rosenthal, Sharon. "$77,000 for 30 Minutes? *Gimme a Break!" TV Guide* 8 Dec. 1984: 43–5.

Schneider, Steve. "Nickelodeon Branches Out." *New York Times* 30 June 1985: B22.

"Second Childhood." *Newsweek* 3 Mar. 1975: 48.

Shales, Tom. "The Re Decade." *Esquire* Mar. 1985: 67–72.

Simon, Ronald. "The Eternal Rerun: Oldies but Goodies." *Television Quarterly* 22 (1986): 51–8.

"Sitcoms: The (Lower?) Price of Success." *Broadcasting* 7 May 1990: 36–7.

Smith, Bernard B. "A New Weapon to Get Better TV." *Harper's* July 1962: 27–34.

Stengal, Richard. "When Eden Was in Suburbia." *Time* 9 Aug. 1982: 76.

"Study Blames Network Viewer Drop on Repeats." *Broadcasting* 4 Nov. 1991: 36.

"Syndicated Film." *Television Magazine* July 1952: 27+.

"Syndicators Confident of Future." *Broadcasting* 25 Jan. 1965: 68–71.

"Syndicators Have Pitches Ready." *Broadcasting* 27 Mar. 1967: 99–102.

"Syndicators Off and Running Toward New Highs." *Broadcasting* 24 Feb. 1958: 162.

"Tape for the Networks." *Time* 3 May 1948: 52.

"Thirsty TV Summer." *Newsweek* 13 June 1960: 92+

"Those TV Reruns to Cost More." *Broadcasting* 13 July 1964: 62.

"Timebuying Key to Re-Runs." *Television Magazine* Feb. 1953: 17.

"To Live and Program in L.A." *Broadcasting* 18 Jan. 1993: 42+.

"Transcription Boom." *Newsweek* 19 Jan. 1948: 58–9.

"The Trend Toward Films." *Television Magazine* Dec. 1950: 11+.

"TV Trade Bends on UHF." *Business Week* 17 Feb. 1962: 40.

"The UHF Band Strikes Up." *Newsweek* 3 Mar. 1969: 60–1.

"UHF: Out of the Traffic and Heading for the Open Road." *Broadcasting* 10 June 1974: 35–45.

"U's Newest Syndicator Prospect." *Broadcasting* 14 Nov. 1966: 31–34.

"USA Network Buys 'Miami Vice.' " *Broadcasting* 16 Nov. 1987: 45–6.

"Viacom: In Position to Go With the Flow of Telecommunications Future." *Broadcasting* 10 Aug. 1981: 32–4.

"What Stations Want." *Television Magazine* Apr. 1968: 49+.

"Will First-Run Films Be Extinct?" *Broadcasting* 27 Nov. 1961: 27–9.

Winski, Joseph M. " 'Addicted' to Research, Agency Exec Says Net Hits the Hot Button." *Advertising Age* 10 Feb. 1992: 52+.

"World Laps Up U.S. TV Fare." *Business Week* 23 Apr. 1960: 129–31.

"The World of TV Programming: Syndication." *Broadcasting* 22 Oct. 1984: 54+.

QUESTIONS FOR DISCUSSION

1. What impact did the UHF boom have on syndication? What about the advent of cable?

2. It seems that syndicated programs and locally produced programs are viewed as competing and mutually exclusive. How might this conflict be reduced? (Hint: look at PBS).

 INFOTRAC COLLEGE EDITION

Search InfoTrac College Edition under "television and syndication" for more articles on this subject.

PART IV

The Multichannel Universe

12

Cable Television and the Public Interest

PATRICIA AUFDERHEIDE

Cable television now delivers programming to the majority of American homes with television. Despite its distribution of hundreds of channels, it does not deliver the diversity of programming choices that its numbers seem to suggest. As a result, the utopian hopes that cable television would facilitate a vibrant public sphere and public activity in electronic spaces are unfulfilled. Media concentration of the cable industry by a handful of multiple systems operators (MSOs), combined with increased competition for scarce advertising dollars, results in fewer rather than more possibilities for public, as opposed to consumer, participation in an electronic public sphere.

In this article, Patricia Aufderheide discusses possibilities for using cable television in the public interest, building on resources that already exist: public, educational, and governmental (PEG) access channels. Aufderheide argues for a subsidized public access system that does not have to conform to the familiar production values and genres of commercial television, but is used and appreciated for its facilitation of civic, noncommercial communication. Potential sources of funding include a national video production fund, financing projects

From *Journal of Communication* 42 (Winter 1992): 52–65. Reprinted by permission of Oxford University Press.

in the public interest across the range of programming distribution vehicles, or the extension or enhanced used of cable franchise fees. What is most necessary, Aufderheide suggests, is telecommunications policy that speaks to the First Amendment rights of citizens as well as media producers.

Since passage of the Cable Communications Policy Act of 1984, the cable industry has thoroughly demonstrated its failure to serve the public interest, as measured minimally in diversity of sources. Regulating cable's monopolistic tendencies could improve rates and service, and increase the range of sources within the constraints of the commercial marketplace. However, to fulfill the promise of the First Amendment, subsidized noncommercial public spaces also need to be universal on cable services, as sites not merely of individual expression but for the practice of civic life.

Cable television is an appropriate site to raise questions of the public interest in telecommunications, because it is such a pervasive medium, because its recent record so boldly demonstrates rapid concentration of control over information, and because policy discussions about the industry are under way. In this article I propose that the public interest can be served, not only by regulatory mechanisms that check market power and enhance diversity in the commercial marketplace, but also by mechanisms that guarantee and protect electronic spaces—channels, centers, and services—exclusively for public activity. This is because the public interest is broader than that of consumers, or even protection of the individual speaker; the public has its own interests, separate from those of government or business.

Cable is now the primary delivery medium for television in a majority of American homes. Currently more than 90% of the American homes with television can receive cable, and more than 60% do receive it. The cable industry, aiming to deflect regulation, argues that cable is not nearly as important as it appears, because consumers have alternatives (newspaper, videocassettes, broadcast, and theaters) to the various elements of its communications package. But this ignores questions of accessibility, comparative cost, and consumer habits. Neither does the promise of new transmission technologies on the horizon (Pepper, 1988) change the need to deal with social and economic realities of the present.

Historically, cable policy has been hammered out among a handful of special interests, all of whom have invoked the public interest. The Cable Communications Policy Act of 1984 was passed with a minimum of public participation. This law, a hasty resolution to a three-year argument between the largest cable operators and the municipalities that control franchises, created a national cable policy for the first time. The law attempted to encourage the growth of cable, partly "to assure that cable communications provide, and are encouraged to provide, the widest possible diversity of information sources and services to the public" (Cable Communications Policy Act, 1984). It also attempted to balance the cables' desire for minimal regulation and the cities' desire for accountability (Meyerson, 1985).

The cable industry grew dramatically once the law went into effect. However, even the law's modest public interest provisions—for example, leased access and public access—offered poor enforcement, and sometimes were worse than the status quo ante. Furthermore, partly because of a deregulatory Federal Communication Commission's (FCC) interpretation of Congress' mandates, partly because of sloppy language, and partly because of confusion over First Amendment rights— all of which were conditioned by the growing clout of the cable industry—the act gave even greater leeway to cable than it had originally seemed. Consumers' resulting outrage over prices and services, and municipalities' indignation over violated contracts, triggered current policy discussions in which, once again, the public interest was universally invoked but rarely represented.

THE PUBLIC SPHERE

The public and its interest is not the same thing as consumers and their interest, nor is it the sum total of individual opinions on the events of the day. The public is that realm of society that shares in common the consequences of private and state action, and that acts effectively in its own defense (Dewey, 1983 [1927]). For example, when citizens of a locality suffer the effects of industrial pollution and find ways to redress the problem—perhaps through a labor-parents-environmental coalition that challenges a complacent city council with alternative development proposals—they act as the public. We are all, in some aspects of our lives, members of the public. But when we cannot find each other and act on our common problems, we are members of a dangerously weak public.

The public sphere, a social realm distinct both from representative government and from economic interest (Habermas, 1989 [1962]), daily becomes a living reality in "free spaces" (Boyte & Evans, 1986), in which people both discuss and act on their conclusions. In town meetings, community groups, and non-local communities such as national environmental organizations working in the public interest, citizens carve out public spaces with ingenuity, against the odds, and are rarely noticed in national media.

The public sphere in American society is nearly inchoate at a rhetorical level. But when members of the public have resources to raise issues of public concern, debate them among themselves and develop ways to act on them, telecommunications becomes a tool in the public's organizing of itself. Otherwise, the public's interest in television easily becomes reduced to ex-FCC commissioner Mark Fowler's view of the public interest as what the "public" (i.e., consumers) is interested in watching.

First Amendment as a Tool

The First Amendment provides an important tool for defense of the public sphere, for protecting the right of the citizenry to "understand the issues which bear upon our common life" (Meiklejohn, 1948, p 89). Ruling in the context of broadcasting, the Supreme Court has said that the ultimate objective of the First

Amendment is to create a well-informed electorate, and that the public's rights are paramount over all (*Red Lion Broadcasting Co. v. FCC,* 1969; reinforced in *Metro Broadcasting, Inc. v. FCC,* 1990).

Concern for the quality of public life has marked other judicial decisions, such as the Supreme Court's ruling supporting free and open airing of contemporary issues so that "government may be responsive to the will of the people and that changes may be obtained by lawful means" (*Stromberg v. California,* 1931). It is the basis for Judge Learned Hand's celebrated statement that:

> [The First Amendment] presupposes that right conclusions are more likely to be gathered out of a multitude of tongues, than through any kind of authoritative selection. To many this is, and always will be, folly; but we have staked upon it our all. (*U.S. v. Associated Press,* 1943, p. 372).

"A multitude of tongues" has social utility; it is not a good in itself. What is involved is not mere data delivery, but a process in which many are involved as producers and presenters as well as receivers.

This concept has been given a shorthand definition as diversity of sources, a longstanding measure of the First Amendment in communications policy (Melody, 1990a, 1990b). Diversity's primary value is to offer ranges of viewpoints and sources on problems affecting the public sphere. In recent years, the notion that the marketplace of ideas is well-served in the commercial marketplace without regulatory protection for such diversity has become popular. However, a public without a thriving marketplace of ideas may not be educated to demand it either (Entman & Wildman, 1990).

CABLE, DIVERSITY, AND THE PUBLIC INTEREST

Cable today is hardly a thriving marketplace of ideas. There are harsh limitations on the current cable industry's ability to provide diversity of sources and viewpoints on issues of public concern, much less to be a service that fortifies civic activism. Those limitations lie in the conditions of commercial television programming, whatever the delivery vehicle, as well as the current structure of the cable industry.

Cable was once trumpeted as the "technology of abundance," a medium so expansive that no social engineering would be needed for a multitude of tongues to flourish. But this turned out to be another instance in a longstanding tradition of blind optimism in technologies to bring about social change (Streeter, 1987; Winston, 1986; Le Duc, 1987; Sinel et al., 1990). Although cable has ushered in new formats, from CNN to Nickelodeon to Court TV, the unforgiving logic of commercial production has shaped them all, and ownership has increasingly centralized in a few hands. C-SPAN I and II function as a kind of insurance policy with legislators, and thus say nothing about the capacity of the television marketplace to function in the public interest.

Most television programming, including cable programming, is supported by advertising. Programming is designed to attract the audience for the advertising; the public interest may lie in the opposite direction, and the public as a concept is virtually erased in favor of the consumer—who is often referred to as "the public" nonetheless. The most vulnerable members of the public—the young—have been long slighted. Even with the stimulus of legislation mandating children's programming, educational programming for children is still mostly dependent on the slim resources of public television. An issue of great public importance that commercial television never frankly addresses is its own social effect. Bill Moyers' *The Public Mind,* which did address this issue, was on public television, and was not even carried by all public stations.

Cable's increased channel capacity does not miraculously create new opportunities for public participation in this technology, nor even for greater diversity of sources (Le Duc, 1987; Winston, 1990). Television viewing overall has increased by only minutes a day since the wide distribution of cable, and this fact affects the available universe of advertising (Garnham, 1990, p. 158). As networks brainstorm cost-cutting measures—including "reality" programming—to lower the high costs of production, the total amount of production dollars is being spread ever more thinly. Compression technologies, multiplying the possible channels, threaten to spread the viewers out even further, to programmers' dismay ("Filling the upcoming channel cornucopia," 1991).

Producers know that new technologies do not bring new creative options, new voices, or new viewpoints. One study surveying 150 television producers on the options for creativity in the "new television marketplace" found several biases pushing programming away from creativity, including bottom line strategies and horizontal and vertical integration (Blumler & Spicer, 1990).

Cable's current industry structure also powerfully discourages diversity of sources and perspectives, and leaves virtually no opening for use of the system as a public space. A few multiple-system operators (MSOs) control the marketplace today. Currently four companies control, at a conservative estimate, 47% of all cable subscribers—a national figure that grossly underestimates often-total regional control (FCC, 1990a, Appendix G, p. 1; FCC, 1990b, Association of Independent Television Stations Comments, April 6, pp. 15–16).

With their market power, cable MSOs have militated against programming diversity, even within the limits of what advertisers want and what viewers find entertaining. Cable companies favor programs they own. They discourage new, competing programming, and cable operators also often refuse to carry all the local broadcast channels. Since viewers must disconnect cable to pick up those broadcast signals, this effectively sends smaller stations' signals to Siberia.

Cable's approach to leased access likewise manifests a choice for control over diversity (Lampert, Cate, & Lloyd, 1991; U.S. Senate, 1990b). In theory, cable companies with more than 36 channels have to keep between 10% and 15% of their space open for any purchaser, according to section 612(b) of the 1984 act. But leased access is a virtual dead letter (Meyerson, 1990, pp. 252–254), because the cable companies also get to set the price and terms of carriage and do not have to handle billing.

The large MSOs have also clipped the wings of distribution competitors, such as direct broadcast satellite and wireless cable. Competing services find that programmers, many partly owned by MSOs, refuse to sell to them (FCC, 1990a, Wireless Cable Association Comments, May 23, Alan Pearce and Stuart M. Whitaker, "Video Programming Availability and Consumer Choice," pp. 7–14). MSOs have also purchased equity in potential competitors, thus placing them in a position to preempt competition.

Checking Cable's Power

Policy reform checking the cable industry's power could lay the groundwork for other uses of the service as a public space. It could increase individual access to the service at reasonable rates, and could increase the potential for a variety of sources on the service. One recent policy change—the FCC's stiffening of its "effective competition" rule (FCC, 1991)—may affect some consumer rates. Other reforms—some of them incorporated into congressional bills S. 12 and H.R. 1303—would face stiff challenges from a strong cable lobby and a White House opposed to sterner regulation.

Universal service issues could be addressed largely in the franchise process and by the creation of a "basic basic" tier, offered at the cost of installation and maintenance. This would include all local broadcast services (should a cabler accept any) and public services. Carrying all, if any, local broadcast stations is one well argued solution to broadcast carriage (FCC, 1990a, Action for Children's Television Comments, March 1). A weaker version of this basic basic service was proposed in earlier legislation, and cable companies themselves have also established an even weaker basic basic service on many systems, apparently in an attempt to create a "throwaway" service for regulators (Burgi, 1990). Rates for commercial services beyond that tier can be addressed by establishing a rigorous, effective competition standard on the order of the recommendations of the Consumer Federation of America (FCC, 1990b, CFA Comments, February 14) and, as the FCC itself suggests, leaving enforcement and terms to the franchiser.

Cable's current tight control over information could be addressed in a variety of ways. One long-touted option, common carrier status—a frequent recommendation until the late 1970s (Parsons, 1987, pp. 131–134; Kalba et al., 1977)—seems "about as likely to get a second hearing as the Articles of Confederation" (Brenner, 1988, p. 329), given the current shape and clout of the industry. The 1984 act explicitly prohibits regulation of cable as a common carrier or public utility. But common carrier status continues to make as much sense as it did when it was recommended by policy analysts and scholars alike, and would dramatically simplify regulation. It would be particularly appropriate should telephone companies enter the field (Winer, 1990), and would dramatically restructure regulatory options.

A modified, limited form of common carrier access—already legally ratified—is viable leased access. To trust to compression technologies to make the problem of commercial access go away is to repeat the technology-of-abundance fallacy. Viable leased access would provide an incentive to program producers in the commercial marketplace; a combination of tariff-setting and arbitration to resolve disputes would improve enforcement (Lampert et al., 1991, pp. 20–21).

Restrictions on horizontal integration and, with greater difficulty, cross-ownership might also be a salutary return to regulatory techniques that check concentration of control over information. They would most likely have to be undertaken as part of an industry-wide policy reform.

These measures would create some common channels for public access to information, such as the full range of commercial broadcast and particularly public television. They could check the cost spiral that disenfranchises sectors of the population. They could spur programming entrepreneurs and create an entry point, in leased access, for programmers out of favor with the cable company.

ELECTRONIC PUBLIC SPACES

The commercial programming marketplace on cable is still hostage to the economic realities of programming and advertising, however. If electronic media policy is to fortify the public sphere, members of the public must be able to use this resource as a public space and in support of other public spaces. The success of this use of the medium would not be measured by commercial criteria but by its ability to promote relationships within its communities of reference, on issues of public concern. Ratings numbers should be less important than contributing to the never-ending process of constructing the public sphere.

One of many potential resources already exists: public, educational, and governmental (PEG) access channels. They exist thanks largely to grassroots activism resulting in local regulation, and a since revoked 1972 FCC rule requiring access channels (Engelman, 1990). Such channels—especially public access—have long been portrayed as electronic soapboxes, where the goal is simple provision of a space in which to speak. The 1984 act continued this tradition, describing public access as:

> the video equivalent of the speaker's soap box or the electronic parallel to the printed leaflet. They provide groups and individuals who generally have not had access to the electronic media with the opportunity to become sources of information in the marketplace of ideas. (House report, cited in Meyerson, 1985, p. 569)

But what if everybody can speak but nobody cares? The real value of such services has been and must be in helping to build social relationships within which such speech would be meaningful—constructing that "marketplace of ideas." Such a service needs to be seen and used not as a pathetic, homemade version of entertainment, but as an arm of community self-structuring.

Public Access as a Public Space

Access programs often have been, in the words of one tired access director, "programmed to fail." This is less remarkable than the fact that they exist at all. Only canny, ceaseless, locality-by-locality citizen activism wrested access centers and channels in the franchise process in the first place (Engelman, 1990), and all such victories are temporary. The 1984 act sabotaged some of those victories. It had capped localities' franchise fees and required them to be unrestricted. It did not require access channels. Points of confusion in the law—particularly the definition of "service"—as well as restrictions on renewal procedures, among others, made it easy for cable operators to pay more attention to their bottom line and for franchisers to pay more attention to road paving than to cable access (Meyerson, 1990; U.S. Senate, 1990a, pp. 453–490; Ingraham, 1990; Brenner, Price, & Meyerson, 1990, sec. 6.04[3][c], 6.04[4]).

Even under starvation conditions, access has carved out a significant role in the minority of communities where it exists. Currently only 16.5% of systems have public access; 12.9% have educational access, and 10.7% have governmental access (*Television and Cable Factbook,* 1990, p. C-384). An abundance of local programming is produced in some 2,000 centers—about 10,000 hours a week (Ingraham, 1990), far outstripping commercial production. The Hometown USA Video Festival, showcasing local origination and PEG channel production annually, in 1990 attracted 2,100 entries from 360 cities in 41 states.

These channels are often perceived to be valued community resources, using traditional measures. One multisite study shows that 47% of viewers watch community channels, a quarter of them at least three times in two weeks; 46% say it was "somewhat" to "very" important in deciding to subscribe to or remain with cable (Jamison, 1990). Another study, commissioned by Access Sacramento, showed that two-thirds of cable subscribers who knew about the channel watched it (Access Sacramento, 1991). Access centers provide resources and services typically valued at many times what they cost. Access Sacramento, for instance, estimates a community value of its equipment, training, and consultation at $4.5 million, ten times its budget (Access Sacramento, 1990), an estimate corroborated by the experience of access cable in Nashville and Tucson.

But the most useful measure is not, and should not be, numbers of viewers or positive poll results, but the ability of access to make a difference in community life. Access cable should not function like American public television does. Public television offers a more substantial, thoughtful, challenging, or uplifting individual viewing experience than a commercial channel. Access needs to be a site for communication among and between members of the public as the public, about issues of public importance.

Beyond a basic technical level of quality, the entertainment value of such programming comes far secondary to its value as a piece of a larger civic project, whether it is citizen input into actions the local city council is making, or discussions of school reform, or a labor union's donation of services to low-income residents, or the viewpoints of physically challenged people on issues affecting them. This is because viewers are not watching it as individual consumers, but as citizens who are responding to a controversy. In each case, the program—unlike a commercial broadcast or cable service—is not the end point, but only a means toward the continuing process of building community ties.

In small and incremental ways, the access cable channel acts as a public space, strengthening the public sphere. In Tampa, Florida, for instance, public access cable provided the primary informational vehicle for citizens concerned about a county tax that was inadequately justified. Major local media, whose directors shared the interest of politicians, had failed to raise accountability issues. The tax was defeated in a record voter turnout. Also in Tampa, the educational cable access system's airing of school board meetings has resulted in vastly increased public contact with school board members and a children's summer reading program in which libraries', schools', and the access center's work together has resulted in the committee members, officers of 13 different institutions, finding other common interests.[1]

Access does not need to win popularity contests to play a useful role in the community. It is not surprising if people do not watch most of the time. (Indeed, given the treatment access gets by cable operators, it is a kind of miracle that viewers find the channel at all.) It is indicative of its peculiar function that people find the channel of unique value when they do use it. Different kinds of access are used for very different purposes. Government and educational channels may feature such programming as the city council meeting, the school board meeting, the local high school's basketball game, religious programming or rummage-sale announcements on a community billboard. Some colleges have sponsored oral history sessions that illuminate immigrant history (Agosta, Rogoff, & Norman, 1990; Nicholson, 1990).

Public access channels, run on a "first-come, first-served" basis, are responsible for much of access cable's negative image, and some of its most improbable successes. There is often a strong element of the personalist and quixotic in the programming. Public access channels are sometimes a source of scandal and legal controversy, as for instance when the Ku Klux Klan started circulating national programs for local viewing (Shapiro, 1990, pp. 409f; Brenner et al., 1990, sec. 604[7]). Less reported is that often the Klan programs spurred civil liberties and ethnic minorities organizations to use the access service for their own local needs, and these groups have continued to do so. Voluntary associations—for instance, the Humane Society's adopt-a-pet program in Fayetteville, Arkansas—and a musical education series sponsored by the Los Angeles Jazz Society (Nicholson, 1990), also use public access. In a some places—for instance, New York City, where Paper Tiger television regularly produces sharply critical programs on the media; or Austin, Texas, home of one of access cable's oldest talk shows—public access has become an established alternative voice in public affairs. Public access is host to viewpoints as diverse as those of leftist critics of the Gulf War (in Deep Dish TV's national series) and those of conservative Rep. Newt Gingrich (R–GA), who hosts half-hour shows produced by the Washington, DC-based American Citizens' Television (ACTV).

Thus access has a history of fulfilling a role of community service and has been recognized in law as performing a useful First Amendment function. Access cable could, in every locality, provide an unduplicated, local public forum for public issues.

Public Access under Assault

Since the 1984 act, however, access cable has been under relentless assault, both by cable companies and by cities under financial pressure to use nontargeted franchise fees (Ingraham, 1990). In municipalities such as Pittsburgh, Pennsylvania; Milwaukee, Wisconsin; and Portland, Oregon, cable companies immediately rescinded or renegotiated franchise terms regarding cable access, once the act went into effect.

Even when access was established or reestablished, the cost was significant. For instance, in Austin, Texas, the Time-owned company announced that it could not afford to meet its franchise obligations—especially its $400,000-a-year funds for access television and the provision of eight channels—only two weeks after deregulation went into effect. It took 11 months of civic organizing and city council pressure, and some $800,000, to restore the provisions.

In localities beset with fiscal crisis—a widespread problem, since in the 1980s many costs of government were shifted downward—revenues once designated to access have gone into general revenues. For instance, when Nashville found itself in a budget crisis in 1988, a program by a gay and lesbian alliance on public access triggered a city council debate. The cable company, a Viacom operator, supported city council members trying to rechannel access funds into general operating funds. The upshot was near-total defunding of the access center. In Eugene, Oregon, and Wyoming, Michigan, among others, municipalities have drastically cut or eliminated access budgets in favor of other city projects.

Cable policy in the public interest might well improve the dismal legal situation for access, as well as define clearly its role as a site where the public sphere can be strengthened. Policy could go further still, creating new mechanisms for use of the medium as an electronic public space. So far, legislative reform proposals have been virtually silent on access, much less on any as yet untested mechanisms to create new public spaces.

A percentage of channel capacity—in a fixed, low range of numbers—could be reserved for public use on all cable systems. Such reservation would guarantee universal, local, and multiple access channels, and as well provide for nontraditional services as technology evolves. Access centers would also need to be funded adequately—for facilities, professional production assistance, local public production funds, and promotion—through the franchise and through annual franchise fees.[2]

Centers should universally have funding for professional staff, which would not mitigate access's value as a public space. There is no need to fetishize the amateur and the homemade; professional craftsmanship can improve the functioning of a public forum and enliven the public sphere as much as it can the realm of commerce. Professionals' tasks, however, would be as facilitators of communication rather than promoters of expression for its own sake.

National public cable channel capacity, with protected funds to avoid both censorhip and the distortions of corporate underwriting, could further broaden the public forum. C-SPAN's admirable record, and that of a foundation-funded regional public affairs channel focusing on the state legislature, CAL-SPAN: The California Channel (Western & Givens, 1989) might serve as prototypes for such an effort. The service would not, however, have to be limited to legislative or judicial issues. Nor would it be beholden to the whims of the cable industry, as C-SPAN is. This service would differ from public television—another valuable service—not only in its subject matter but in its primary mandate to respond to the moment, a flexibility public television does not exercise except in extremity.

Such national channel capacity would boldly raise the perennial problem of who should broker information and how, a problem that in itself could become another opportunity for civic organizing and creative rethinking of how television is and can be used. It too would, without doubt, require professional staff, with rules and structures guiding their work. For instance, users might have to meet a minimum standard of organization; public interests least likely to be served in the commercial marketplace might be prioritized. Arenas of concern such as educational and health policy, multicultural questions, environmental and workplace issues, and the arenas of public discourse themselves (e.g., events of public interest groups) could be the basis for ongoing electronic workshops.

Another resource for such a reinvigorated public interest could be a national video production fund, with its products available for distribution through all televisual vehicles, including cable, broadcast television, and videocassette. Such a fund could be paid for in a variety of ways, such as spectrum fees; revenues from profits from sales of broadcast stations and cable systems; and charges on videocassettes, VCRs, and satellite dishes. Its goal too, would be to promote citizen organizing. Some of the early projects of Britain's Channel 4, particularly in workshops and special programming sections, could provide useful models.

PUBLIC ACCESS, POLICY, AND PRACTICALITY

But would protection for access channels and other public spaces even survive the cable companies' claim to First Amendment priority? It is true that in the 1980s, many, but not all, courts have supported operators' First Amendment rights over cable access (Shapiro, 1990). And commercial media laid a legitimate claim to First Amendment rights, one recognized extensively in law since the mid-1970s (Robinowitz, 1990, p 313, fn. 29). However, First Amendment rights are not absolute, nor the special preserve of economic as opposed to public interests; and there is powerful precedent for the democratic state structurally promoting the public's right to speak (Holmes, 1990, p. 55). In many of their aspects, cable operators are not speakers or even editors (Brenner, 1988, p. 329f). Policy mandating access centers certainly would not abridge "expression that the First Amendment was meant to protect" (*First National Bank of Boston v. Bellotti,* 1978); it would foster the opposite, and furthermore withstand constitutional scrutiny (Meyerson, 1981, pp. 33–59). Congress has also found that leased and PEG access regulation meet First Amendment and constitutional standards (U.S. Senate 1990b, p. 46; U.S. House of Representatives, 1990, p. 35).

Is it reasonable to assume that people want to "make their own media," when the record shows so decisively that people prefer to pay someone to make it for them? No, and that argument is not made here. For entertainment, most people do and will choose high-quality products paid for mostly by their purchase of advertisers' products. Indeed, that is why it is important not to abandon that arena to the iron grip of a few MSOs. But people using cable as a public space are using it to communicate with others about particular issues and projects of public interest. Whatever the level of their involvement, they perceive it and use it—as producers, viewers, or organizers of viewers—not as a consumer experience but as a participatory step in a relationship that is not, typically, either electronic or commercial.

Why should we assume a demand for something that's been around so long to so little effect? This question builds on the negative image of access cable, which like all stereotypes has an origin in some kind of truth. A variety of answers, substantiated above, address different facets of that negative image. One is that some programming, primarily in public access, has indeed been trivial, self-indulgent, and derivative, and that those uses often reflect an interpretation of access that sees the First Amendment as an end rather than a means to democratic vitality. More important is access's gross underfunding, its abandonment by legislators and regulators, and the unrelenting attacks by cablers and cities on centers. In that light, it is much more shocking that access centers survive anywhere. It is particularly impressive that access channels have been able to do as much as they have with so little professional staff. Finally, access—lacking a national substructure as public television did until 1967—is still in its pre-history.

But can we afford to have such ambitious programs? One answer is to ask if we can afford not to. Less rhetorically, this is a question that needs as yet ungathered data. Cable and other mass media interests would probably make substantial contribution to the costs. Operators have powerful arguments against any of these proposals, and they all hinge on inability to afford them—an argument unprovable without accounting evidence. So telecommunications media, especially cable MSOs and broadcast stations, should open their books for the public record.

Finally, are access and other mechanisms to promote the use of the medium as a public space cost effective? This is a wildly speculative area of economics, because it deals with externalities such as the health of a democratic polity. In the absence of social cost-benefit studies—an area begging for more economic research—one can make some basic points. The technological level of equipment and expertise needed to do so is comparatively low; the price of even a lavish subsidy cannot compare to even a small road-paving job; and the benefits are widespread and incremental. Television, and increasingly cable television, has a central role in American consumer habits, and has unique capacities to transmit complex, multisensory messages. Why should that capacity be used exclusively to sell things and not for civic projects?

The performance of cable television since 1984 thus exposes larger issues in public interest telecommunications policy. One of the goals of such policy should be creating vehicles for activity within the public sphere, where citizens can be more than consumers of media.

NOTES

1. Interviews with the following people between September 1990 and August 1991 informed the analysis of access cable: Andrew Blau, then communications policy analyst, United Church of Christ Office of Communication, New York; Alan Bushong, executive director, Capital Community TV, Salem, OR; Gerry Field, executive director, Somerville Community Access Television, Somerville, MA; Ann Flynn, Tampa Educational Cable Consortium: Nicholas Miller, lawyer, Miller and Holbrooke, Washington, DC; Elliott Mitchell, ex-executive director, Nashville Community Access TV, TN; Randy Van Dalsen, Access Sacramento, CA.

2. Corrective proposals to the 1984 act's haziness, lacunae, and crippling clauses on access, such as those proposed by Meyerson (1990), the NFLCP (Ingraham, 1990). The United Church of Christ Office of Communication (FCC 1990a, UCCOC et al. Reply Comments, p. 7) and Miller (1988) bear consideration to clear the legislative underbrush.

REFERENCES

Access Sacramento. (1990). *Access Sacramento annual report: 1990, the year in review.* Sacramento: Coloma Community Center.

Access Sacramento. (1991). *1991 Audience survey findings report.* Sacramento: Coloma Community Center.

Agosta, D., Rogoff, C., & Norman, A. (1990). *The PARTICIPATE study: A case study of public access cable television in New York state.* New York: Alternative Media Information Center.

Blumler, J. G., & Spicer, C. (1990). Prospects for creativity in the new television marketplace: Evidence from program-makers. *Journal of Communication, 40,* 78–101.

Boyte, H. C., & Evans, S. M. (1986). *Free spaces: The sources of democratic change in America.* New York: Harper and Row.

Brenner, D. (1988). Cable television and the freedom of expression. *Duke Law Journal, 1988,* 329–388.

———, Price, M., & Meyerson, M. (1986). *Cable television and other nonbroadcast video: Law and policy.* New York: Clark Boardman.

Burgi, M. (1990, October 8). No piece of cake: Explaining tiering to cable subscribers isn't so easy. *Channels,* pp. 21–22.

Cable Communications Policy Act of 1984, Sec. 601[4], U.S.C. Sec. 532[4].

Dewey, J. (1983). *The public and its problems.* Athens, OH: Swallow Press. (Originally published 1927).

Engelman, R. (1990). The origins of public access cable television. *Journalism Monographs,* No. 123.

Entman, R. M., & Wildman, S. (1990). *Toward a new analytical framework for media policy: Reconciling economic and non-economic perspectives on the marketplace for ideas.* Paper presented at the annual Telecommunications Policy Research Conference, Airlie, VA, October 1–2.

Federal Communications Commission. (1990a, July 31). In the matter of competition, rate deregulation, and the Commission's policies relating to the provision of cable television service, MM Docket No. 89-600, FCC 90-276.

Federal Communications Commission. (1990b, December 31). Reexamination of the effective competition standard for the regulation of cable television basic service rates, MM Docket No. 90-4, FCC 90-412, Further Notice of Proposed Rule Making.

Federal Communications Commission. (1991, June 13). Reexamination of the effective competition standard for the regulation of cable television basic service rates, MM Docket No. 90-4, FCC 90-412, Report and Order and Second Further Notice of Proposed Rule Making.

Filling the upcoming channel cornucopia. (1991, May 27). *Broadcasting.* 44–47.

First National Bank of Boston v. Bellotti, 435 U.S. 765 (1978).

Garnham, N. (1990). *Capitalism and communication.* London: Sage.

Habermas, J. (1989). *The structural transformation of the public sphere: An inquiry into a category of bourgeois society.* (T. Burger, with the assistance of F. Lawrence, Trans.). Cambridge: MIT Press. (Originally *Strukturwandel der Offentlicheit,* 1962).

Holmes, S. (1990). Liberalism and free speech. In J. Lichtenberg (Ed.). *Democracy and the mass media* (pp. 66–101). New York: Cambridge University Press.

Ingraham, S. B. (1990, May 16). Testimony before the U.S. House of Representatives Subcommittee on Telecommunications and Finance of the Committee on Energy and Commerce, on behalf of the National Federal of Local Cable Programmers.

Jamison, F. R. (1990). Community programming viewership study composite profile. Kalamazoo, MI: Western Michigan University Media Services Department.

Kalba, K. (1977). *Separating content from conduit? Market realities and policy options in non-broadcast cable communications.* Cambridge, MA: Kalba Bowen Associates.

Lampert, D., Cate, F. H., & Lloyd, F. W. (1991). *Cable television leased access.* Washington, DC: Annenberg Washington Program.

Le Duc, D. (1987). *Beyond broadcasting: Patterns in policy and law.* New York: Longman.

Meiklejohn, A. (1948). *Free speech and its relation to self-government.* New York: Harper.

Melody, W. H. (1990a). The information in I.T.: Where lies the public interest? *Intermedia, 18,* 10–18.

———. (1990b). Communication policy in the global information economy: Whither the public interest? In M. Ferguson (Ed.), *Public communication: The new imperatives* (pp. 16–39). London: Sage.

Metro Broadcasting, Inc. v. FCC, 110 S. Ct. 2997 (1990).

Mayerson, M. I. (1981). The First Amendment and the cable operator: An unprotective shield against public access requirements. *Comm/Ent, 4,* 1–66.

———. (1985). The Cable Communications Policy Act of 1984: A balancing act on the coaxial wires. *Georgia Law Review, 19,* 543–622.

————. (1990). Amending the oversight: Legislative drafting and the Cable Act. *Cardozo Arts and Entertainment Law Journal, 8,* 233–255.

Miller, N. P. (1988). The Cable Act revisited: The public interest vs. the cable monopoly— A white paper. In F. Lloyd (Ed.), *Cable television 1988: Three years after the Cable Act* (pp. 41–54). Washington, DC: Practicing Law Institute.

Nicholson, M. (1990). Cable access: A community communications resource for nonprofits [Monograph]. *Benton Foundation Bulletin, 3.* Washington, DC: Benton Foundation.

Parsons, P. (1987). *Cable television and the First Amendment.* Lexington, MA: Lexington Books.

Pepper, R. M. (1988). Through the looking glass: Integrated broadband networks, regulatory policy and institutional change. OPP Working Paper 24. Washington, DC: Federal Communications Commission.

Red Lion Broadcasting Co. v. FCC, 395 U.S. 367 (1969).

Robinowitz, S. (1990). Cable television: Proposals for reregulation and the First Amendment. *Cardozo Arts and Entertainment Law Journal, 8,* 309–335.

Shapiro, G. H. (1990). Litigation concerning challenges to the franchise process, programming and access channel requirements, and franchise fees. In F. Lloyd (Ed.), *Cable television law 1990: Revisiting the Cable Act, Vol. 1.* Washington, DC. Practicing Law Institute.

Sinel, N. M., et al. (1990). Current issues in cable television: A re-balancing to protect the consumer. *Cardozo Arts & Entertainment Law Journal, 8,* 387–432.

Streeter, T. (1987). The cable fable revisited: Discourse, policy and the making of cable television. *Critical Studies in Mass Communication, 4,* 174–200.

Stromberg v. California, 283 U.S. 359, 369 (1931).

Television and cable factbook. (1990). Washington, DC: Warren.

U.S. House of Representatives. (1990). Cable Television Consumer Protection and Competition Act of 1990. House Report, H.R. 5267. Report 101-682, 101st Congress, 2d Session.

U.S. Senate. (1990a). Cable TV Consumer Protection Act of 1989: Hearings before the Subcommittee on Communications of the Committee on Commerce, Science, and Transportation, U.S. Senate. 101st Congress, 2nd session, on S. 1880, March 29 and April 4. Washington: GPO.

U.S. Senate. (1990b). Cable Television Consumer Protection Act of 1990: Report on S. 1880. Report 101-381, 101st Congress, 2d Session.

U.S. v. Associated Press, 52 F. supp 362, 372 (S.D.N.Y. 1943).

Westen, T., & Givens, B. (1989). *A new public affairs television network for the state: The California Channel.* Los Angeles: Center for Responsive Government.

Winer, L. H. (1990). Telephone companies have First Amendment rights too: The constitutional case for entry into cable. *Cardozo-Arts and Entertainment Law Journal, 8,* 257–307.

Winston, B. (1986). *Misunderstanding media.* Cambridge, MA: Harvard University Press.

————. (1990). Rejecting the Jehovah's Witness gambit. *Intermedia, 18,* 21–25.

QUESTIONS FOR DISCUSSION

1. Can "consumers" and the "public" never be the same? What is the key distinction? Can we think about readers of newspapers or magazines in the same way? What is the difference in the public service capacities or obligations of cable versus print media?

2. Aufderheide claims that cable's multiplicity of channels has done nothing to encourage "diversity of sources or perspectives." Do you agree? What aspects of cable programming confirm, or contradict, this statement?

3. How might public access and other access channels strengthen the existence of local, regional, and national public spheres? What steps, according to Aufderheide, should be taken to ensure their continuing viability?

 INFOTRAC COLLEGE EDITION

See other articles by Patricia Aufderheide on InfoTrac College Edition. Also, search under "cable television and public interest" and "public access cable."

13

Recodings
Possibilities and Limitations in Commercial Television Representations of African American Culture

HERMAN GRAY

Since its inception, American television has economically targeted and represented the white middle-class viewer. Representations of other ethnicities and races have served to naturalize white middle-class experience as the American social norm. In particular, African American culture has been misrepresented. On television, African Americans are represented as either thoroughly assimilated into the conventions and mores of the white middle-class or mired in lower-class poverty, with little exploration of the broader scope of African American culture and lived experience.

Every so often, a prime-time program attempts to break this representational mold. In this article, media historian Herman Gray examines one of those programs, *Frank's Place,* which aired on CBS during the fall 1987 television season. *Frank's Place* is notable because of its attempt to recode television's representations of African American culture by innovating within the prime-time situation comedy format. The program is notable in that its producers created a "structure of feeling" that used formal aspects of television production, such as the setting, script, camera placing, and editing, to situate the viewer in a

From *Quarterly Review of Film and Video* (1/3 1991): 117–30. Reprinted by permission of Gordon & Breach.

position of African American subjectivity. Central to the show's representational strategy was the attention paid to its geographical location, New Orleans, long a center of African American culture, and the concerns and characteristics of its African American working class. The program's narrative content therefore expressed a range of themes not usually seen on situation comedies designed for the white middle class.

Nevertheless, according to Gray, the progressive aspects of the program were contained by the conventions of prime-time television as well as the race relations in American society. Although critics praised the program, it was a ratings failure and was subsequently canceled by CBS. Gray determines that the program's narrative and aesthetic innovations forced the typical white middle-class television viewer to "work too hard," leading to rejection of the show. The commercial failure of *Frank's Place,* Gray concludes, ultimately reveals the limitations of the American television audience as well as the limitations of commercial television within the United States.

> There is great drama in our lives, in our past, in our culture and in our Africanisms. I'd like to see more of that portrayed.
>
> ROSALIND CASH (ACTRESS WHO APPEARED ON *FRANK'S PLACE*)

Actress Rosalind Cash has identified one of the persistent and dominant assumptions in commercial television's representation of African American culture.[1] American commercial television programs about blacks position viewers to experience African American culture from the vantage point of the white middle class experience, which is assimilationist (Gans 1979) or pluralist—blacks simply function, in outlook, character, and setting as copies of whites (Gray 1990). In a society such as the United States which remains characterized by social inequality and racism, such representations of black life and culture function, ideologically, to sharpen the "normativeness" of the white middle class experience.

Frank's Place, a novel but short lived commercial television treatment of black life in America, breaks significantly with this pattern. *Frank's Place* achieves this departure precisely because African American culture and black American subjectivity are central to the series' content, aesthetic organization, setting, narrative, characters, and assumptions (Childs 1984).

In *Frank's Place* we see an attempt to rewrite and reposition African American culture and black subjectivities. By rewriting and repositioning I refer to the strategy of appropriating (or re-appropriating) existing formal, organizational, and aesthetic elements in the commercial culture in general and television in particular and refashioning them into different representations. These different representations often serve as alternatives to (and occasionally critique) the dominant forms of existing culture (Foster 1985, Williams 1977).

Television representations of blacks in *Frank's Place* activated African American sensibilities that were historically experienced on television, through absence, silence, and invisibility. Since the televisual reality is dominated by "normative" representations of white middle class subjectivities and sensibilities, blacks and other communities of color have had to create and fill in the televisual spaces where African American representations might otherwise fit. For various sectors of the black American community *Frank's Place* worked through affirmation rather than silence. And it is not just the fact that the show featured blacks at the level of character and setting. The show achieved this affirmative stance through its complex treatments of social class, gender, region, and theme—all of which were rooted in an African American point of view.

In commercial television culture where assumptions and representations of African Americans continue to operate largely within the limits of assimilation and pluralism (Gray 1990), I regard *Frank's Place* as a moment of displacement, an attempt to push the limits of existing television discourses about blacks. The representations on *Frank's Place* are expressions of the most recent struggles over the representations of race in general and African American culture in particular. (These struggles are expressed in other arenas of contemporary television, most notably cable—where music television, Black Entertainment Network, and sports continue to be the areas that are the most open and available for the expression and articulation of a Black American cultural sensibility.)

THE SOCIAL PRODUCTION
OF *FRANK'S PLACE*

Frank's Place aired on CBS during the fall 1987 television season with a 14.9 rating and a 25 share. The series was produced by co-executive producers Hugh Wilson and Tim Reid for Viacom Studios.[2] Reid and Wilson developed a friendship and working relationship on *WKRP Cincinnati,* which Wilson produced and in which Reid starred. The results of that collaboration and friendship led to the development of *Frank's Place.*

The concept for the show was developed by Wilson, Reid, and by former CBS Television Head of Entertainment Kim LeMasters. Because of its drop in the ratings the previous season CBS needed a show for its new season. The network was therefore willing to take a chance with an innovative show such as *Frank's Place.* Moreover, network executives were familiar with Wilson's record as a producer/writer/director and with Reid's work in the successful series *WKRP Cincinnati,* and *Simon and Simon.* Indeed, Reid and Wilson were able to extract a hands off deal in most areas in the development and production of the series. This unusual control over the show afforded Wilson and Reid the opportunity to develop the show with minimal interference from network executives. It was an important element in the innovative (and risky) character of the show. One other manifestation of this kind of control was that both Wilson and Reid were committed to (and hired) a multiracial crew.

The central premise of the show was this: Frank Parrish, a Professor of Renaissance History from Boston, inherited his father's restaurant (The Chez Louisianne) in New Orleans. Parrish knows little about New Orleans and even less about managing a restaurant. Over the course of the series we, along with Parrish, learn the nuances of managing a restaurant and about aspects of a local black community in New Orleans. The primary characters in the show included the staff at the restaurant—Miss Marie, an elderly black woman; Big Arthur, the chef and his white assistant, Shorty; Anna, a middle aged black waitress; Tiger, the elderly black bartender and his assistant, Cool; the regular cast also included members of the local community—a local entrepreneur (a black female funeral home director and her daughter Hannah—played by Daphne Maxwell Reid); The Reverend Deal, a colorful local minister; and Bubba, a white lawyer.

Once the concept for the show was set Wilson and Reid took several trips to New Orleans to get a feel for the ambience and the texture of life in that city. On these trips both Reid and Wilson visited with members of the local black community. They were especially interested in getting an interior sense of New Orleans from members of the black business community. Wilson likened their activities on these trips to the field work of oral historians.

After setting the story concept, Wilson established a certain look for the show which he then let dictate the writing, editing, and dramatic approach. As producer/writer/director Wilson wanted to get as much of New Orleans on the television screen as he possibly could. This required that Wilson, a former film director, get away from the existing conventions of television direction, camera work, and lighting (Barker 1985).[3] As a result Wilson developed a more self consciously cinematic look for the show, shooting with film instead of video tape, treating the main camera ('B') as the major narrative voice rather than using three cameras to achieve this as is usually done in filming for television, using a faster and crisper editing technique, eschewing the use of sweeteners and a laugh track, and using original music on the show (Barker 1985). (To achieve the look that they wanted Wilson was especially meticulous about lighting the show. He hired an award winning film cinematographer—William A. Fraker—to shoot the pilot, and then had the lighting for the subsequent episodes approximate the look of the pilot. This look provided one of the consistent and defining qualities for the series.)

The production schedule was even dictated by the look and feel that Wilson and Reid were trying to achieve. Thus, as Wilson described it

> We had to start shooting at seven o'clock in the morning. By then the lights were on. We just shot it film style. We'd rehearse it, shoot it and shoot it out of order so they (the network) couldn't send anybody over. There was no run through to see and so consequently we were left totally free.[4]

This strategy, in addition to creating the look of the show, was also a way of maintaining control over production of the project.

To achieve the look and feel of the show that Wilson wanted was an expensive proposition (by television standards for half hour situation comedies). *Frank's Place* cost $650,000 an episode to produce.[5] According to Wilson, they began the series at a deficit since CBS paid Viacom $425,000 to produce the show. In retrospect Wilson believes that part of the commercial failure of the show, at least in terms of network support and their unwillingness to ride out the early storm of low ratings, was due to the cost involved in producing the show. At some point in the season, CBS decided that the costs and the risks of the show were too high and they decided "to cut their losses."[6]

Wilson's and his production team's commitment to creating a different kind of show was evident not just in the aesthetic look and texture of the show's content, but also in the social relations of its production. The crew was multiracial and composed of men and women. More importantly, the entire production team served as an important barometer for monitoring the pulse of the show. The most immediate place (and impact) for the collaborative style that defined the show (especially with respect to the representations of black cultural sensibilities), occurred among the writers, the crew, and the actors. (On this point Tim Reid's relationship with Wilson, the crew, and the actors was crucial). Wilson assembled a team of four writers, two of whom he had previously worked with on other projects and two of whom he had not. For a short period there was one female on the team (she did not work out), and a black writer who wrote regularly for the show.

Wilson described the writing for the show as truly collaborative, save the fact that as the chief writer he exercised final authority to shape a story:

> We would discuss these stories in a group. And we would talk and talk. And sometimes we would talk about a story for days and then decide to abandon it. But then if we had something we liked whoever the writer was who had that assignment would then write an outline and we would all read the outline. And then talk that to death. Then the writer would write a draft and sometimes a second draft. Then he would give it to me and I would write the third draft. That's why the shows sort of have a singularity of viewpoint. Because they all, with the exception of one show, would come through my final filter.[7]

They did occasionally take scripts from outside the writing staff, but even these had to go through this process of refinement and collaboration by Wilson and his team.[8] With respect to the representations of African American culture, I believe that this collaborative process (at all stages of production) is an important way to insure a variety of viewpoints, sensibilities, and visions.

Finally, two important personal and biographical points about Wilson's and Reid's roles ought to be emphasized as they specifically concern cultural sensibilities that appeared on *Frank's Place*. Wilson is a Southerner who identifies himself primarily as a writer. Since Wilson grew up, was educated, and worked in the South (where he also participated in the Civil Rights Movement), he remained sensitive to Southern race relations as well as the sensibilities that defined African American culture there. Secondly, working with Tim Reid and other black members of the crew, Wilson not only trusted their inputs and their sensibilities (seeking them out), but he seems to have been able to effectively use his own position as a Southern white male to monitor the show's representations of black Southern life and culture. This willingness to collaborate on these matters is important, especially in the production and presentations of black life in commercial television.

Critically, *Frank's Place* received rave reviews. It was hailed by television critics and various segments of the public as innovative and refreshing television. Because of the absence of a laugh track, the absence of traditional resolutions at the end of each episode, and its blending of comedy and drama the show was referred to by many critics and industry observers as a dramedy.[9] Unfortunately, the show failed to receive sufficient ratings throughout its run and was eventually canceled by CBS.[10] The final episode aired October 1, 1988 with a 5.6 rating and a 10 share. In January 1990, The Black Entertainment Network (BET) began broadcasting all twenty-two existing episodes of *Frank's Place*.

THE LOCATION OF *FRANK'S PLACE* IN TELEVISION DISCOURSES ABOUT RACE

> I think blacks are looked upon in this country in a very peculiar way. . . . I don't think we are taken seriously as a group that has something to say in film or theater. . . . I think musically we're more apt to be accepted, musically and in comedy.
>
> ROSALIND CASH

Socially and aesthetically the distinctive character of *Frank's Place* derives from a variety of historical, generic, and aesthetic elements: situation comedy, the workplace family, American racial memory, shows about region and location, and the tradition of black situation comedy. To understand the lineage of black representations that made a series like *Frank's Place* possible (and with which it remained in dialogue), I want to situate the show in relationship to series that preceded it as well as to other contemporary black oriented series.[11]

Frank's Place and the aesthetic and cultural representations which it expressed were possible because *The Cosby Show* effectively cleared the contemporary commercial and aesthetic television landscape (Downing 1988, Gray 1990). Also included in the lineage of shows about blacks that eventually helped make *Frank's Place* possible are programs from the late seventies and early eighties including *The Jeffersons, Benson, Webster,* and *Different Strokes.* In these shows upward social mobility and middle class affluence replaced urban poverty as both setting and theme (Gray 1989, 1986).

Television programs about black life such as *Good Times, Florence, Baby I'm Back, That's My Mama,* and *Sanford and Son,* which were set in lower class poverty and which appeared in the nineteen seventies, were themselves a response to the social protest and petitions by blacks against American society in general and the media in particular for the absence of black images in the media (MacDonald 1983, Winston 1982). Black programs in the nineteen seventies were a response to network attempts to soften (i.e., whiten) black stars like Bill Cosby *(I Spy),* Diahann Carroll *(Julia),* Nat King *(The Nat King Cole Show),* and Greg Morris *(Mission Impossible)* who appeared on television in the fifties and sixties (MacDonald 1983). These programs and the representations of blacks that they presented anticipated a set of discourses that I have elsewhere called assimilationist (Gray 1990). In contrast to pluralist and recoded discourses, assimilationist discourses present blacks as invisible and for all practical purposes just like whites.[12] Finally these more acceptable representations developed in response to stereotypes of blacks which appeared in the earliest days of television in shows such as *Amos and Andy* and *Beulah* (MacDonald 1983, Montgomery 1989, Winston 1982).

Reading the *Bill Cosby Show* (and subsequently *Frank's Place*), against these early programs and the discourses in which they were embedded helps account for its middle class focus and more importantly for its consistent reappropriation of the stable black middle class family.[13] That the *Cosby* show features a black family is, ideologically at least, significant evidence of American racial equality and pluralism. African American culture, whether expressed as language, music, or style of life, provides props along the narrative path of social mobility—small nonthreatening indicators of difference that confirm the possibility of a benign pluralism (or postmodernism) rooted in the ideology of middle class equality (Miller 1988). In cultural and social terms the show is just black enough not to offend and middle class enough to comfort.

Many of the qualities of *The Cosby Show* are also found on other contemporary black oriented programs such as *227, Family Matters,* and *AMEN,* which offer comfortable nonthreatening renderings of black life. These shows seldom explore the centrality of African American culture as guides for action or clues for what happens to people of African American descent in modern American society.

By contrast, in *Frank's Place,* African American culture is central to the lives of the characters and the structure of the show. As I show in the next section, it is the cultural and historical ground from which the show operated. In this respect the show was different from the others that form part of its lineage, including *The Cosby Show.* At the same time, *Frank's Place* can only be read against these shows, their familiarity, advances, and silences (Gates 1989).

In addition to the history of black television shows, *Frank's Place* also drew on and remained in dialogue with the lineage of shows about place.[14] The culture and location of New Orleans was central to the show's identity. In *Frank's Place,* food, language, setting, dress, and music are collectively used to establish the centrality of black New Orleans to the theme and feel of the show.

Frank's Place also owed much of its formal character to a previous generation of television programs about the workplace and to those that used comedy and drama innovatively in the half-hour format (Taylor 1989). Norman Lear's *Soap* and *Mary Hartman, Mary Hartman* are often cited as the forerunners in the innovative use of comedy and drama in the comedic format as well as in the use of endings that lack resolution (Barker 1985, Feuer 1986, Newcomb and Alley 1983). The workplace family on *Frank's Place* was also very similar to those found on *Mary Tyler Moore*, *M*A*S*H*, *Barney Miller,* and *Cheers* (Feur 1987, Taylor 1989).

Frank's Place, then, forms part of a continuing strategy of adjustment, displacement, and reappropriation of television representations of black life. It momentarily transformed and occasionally challenged rather than reproduced the conventional representations of black Americans in commercial network television.

RECODING AFRICAN AMERICAN CULTURE
IN *FRANK'S PLACE*

> In my neighborhood I saw people who I respected: the shopkeeper,
> the butcher, the cobbler . . . the man who used to come through
> and sharpen knives. . . . I never saw that on the screen.
>
> ROSALIND CASH

Before examining the central role of African American culture in *Frank's Place,* I want to clarify my view of culture and its specific application to the African American experience. What I intend is some specification of the way that mass mediated commercial culture in general and television in particular expresses the impulses, tones, and consciousness of contemporary black lives in American society (i.e., those qualities described by Rosalind Cash in the epigraph which begins this section)—especially as these as are lived and practiced in everyday life.

I am interested in the way that the practices and sensibilities of people in marginalized and subordinated positions vis-à-vis the dominant culture are expressed, especially in the realm of mass mediated popular culture. The aim is to identify the specific ways that these sensibilities get articulated, mediated, and appropriated in contemporary mass produced and distributed popular culture.

What are the elements of African American cultural sensibilities present in *Frank's Place?* First, compared to existing television programs about blacks, the series was distinguished by its explicit recognition and presentation of the habits, practices, manners, nuances, and outlooks of black Americans located in New Orleans. In subtle matters of language, dress, sense of place, the relationship to time, pace, body movements (especially nonverbal expressions), the show expressed a distinct sensibility or "structure of feeling" (Williams 1977).

Consider one episode's rendering of the following scene:

A group of white male New York corporate executives enter The Chez for a late night dinner meeting. They are dressed in business suits that signal their social class and professional status. They present themselves in the formal manner and demeanor of urban businessmen—formal, reserved, controlled. In a relaxed but deliberate manner a young black waiter slowly approaches the table. In the process of taking their order, he strikes up a conversation. "Yall from New York City?" he asks. "Yes," one of them replies. The waiter continues, "Thought so. My brother lives up there but he don't like it much." "How come?" asks one of the businessmen. "Because some dude knocked out his eye, that's how come," answers the waiter before continuing to disclose more details of the incident, its location, and so on to his surprised patrons.

This exchange is significant because it points up the contrast in language, pace, detail, and relationship to public talk between these white Northern businessmen and this Southern black man. Reading this scene from a white middle class view one might regard the waiter's behavior as slovenly, even rude. As a black American born and raised in the South, I see his behavior in contrast to the public formality and reserve of the white professional businessmen as black and Southern. The young man does not think about his warrant to offer or solicit private information from these complete strangers. Rather, as public talk it is an assumed part of the folkways of the community where he lives. The businessmen are in The Chez and in New Orleans which is the young black man's turf. It is they, not him, who are made uncomfortable by the exchange.

As I've noted, in the content and structure of the program, setting, approach to production, organization of the cast, themes addressed (voodoo, jazz, basketball recruitment, homelessness) lie the elements and expressions of a distinctive African American orientation. Formally, viewers are positioned through the setting, the script, camera placement, editing, and coding to understand the show from the point of view of black New Orleans' residents. We *must* negotiate the world of *Frank's Place* through the experiences of black subjects. In this sense the show is not simply didactic nor does it merely offer a voyeuristic tour of black experiences which disempowers or exoticizes black subjects.

Since the program explicitly operated from an African American subject position, the multiracial cast (and viewing audience), remains grounded in assumptions that structure an African American reality. To make sense of and appreciate the show, viewers (especially whites and others outside of this specific cultural milieu), cannot simply operate outside of the "structure of feeling" that defined the show. The white members of the cast, Shorty (the cook) and Bubba (the lawyer), participate as full members of this community. In language, habits, and assumptions, they actively participate in the cultural definitions and sensibilities that ordered the world of *Frank's Place*.[15]

The show's setting also expressed elements of an African American sensibility. The historical and social significance of New Orleans in the American past (slavery and the origins of black American music), was represented and repeatedly reinforced through the musical and visual montage that opened the show. This montage works almost viscerally to establish New Orleans as a concrete place of cultural location in America and African Americans as a significant cultural community.[16] The tightly edited sepia-tone stills of New Orleans' life include scenes of Mississippi Riverboats, the Mississippi River, Louis Armstrong, The Preservation Jazz Orchestra, The French Quarter, and Congo Square. These scenes move rapidly across the screen to strains of Louis Armstrong's classic recording "Do You Know What It Means to Miss New Orleans." The combined effect is to aurally and visually place the viewer into the experience of black New Orleans. In constructing this representation, the producers foreground African American New Orleans, thereby situating its location and identity within an African American sensibility. This is not just anywhere USA populated by anonymous folk, but black New Orleans with its own particular history and story.

Food was also central to the program's identity. The cuisine featured was Creole (rather than the French Canadian derived cajun which enjoyed a period of trendy culinary popularity in the mid-1980s). The centrality of food to the show and its location within African American culture is revealed in a telling scene from an episode (described below) on African musicians and jazz. Upon their arrival at The Chez, a group of touring African musicians are treated to dinner. After dinner the troupe is given a tour of the kitchen and introduced to the staff. Immediate rapport and cultural commonality is established between the musicians and the staff of The Chez through their discussion (and lessons) about foods, especially those which they have in common. In the dialogue between the two groups the symbolic connections (and distinctions) between Africans and African Americans is established.

Also central to explicitly establishing the show's preferred cultural point of view were nuances about the people and socio-economic characteristics of the community. Indeed, I think it is significant that the restaurant is a small black business located in a black working class community (rather than the French Quarter), frequented mainly by blacks. The complex class character of the program was explored in an early episode when Frank asked Tiger (the bartender) about the absence of local restaurant patrons during the middle of the week. In response to Frank's inquiry Tiger notes, "These are all working people in our neighborhood; they don't go out to dinner on week nights. White folks are afraid to come down here after dark." A simple and clear observation rendered from the viewpoint of a working member of a community who knows his customers and his neighbors.

By highlighting aspects of working class life in New Orleans, the show moved a considerable distance from other programs that remain contained by "normative" middle class cultural sensibilities. With its serious, ironic, and humorous exploration of issues such as drugs, sports, voodoo, middle class status, and homelessness, the show tilted toward a more noble and serious representation of black working class experience. The aspirations, pressures, joys, and troubles of waiters, cooks, and regular folk were represented with integrity in this show rather than the derision, exaggeration, and marginalization that is too often the case in other television representations of blacks and working class people. Finally, while set in a working class context, the show moved between various class positions and experiences even as it addressed tensions between these different classes.[17]

What distinguished the use of cuisine, language, and music in *Frank's Place* from other programs with similar themes was the use of these elements as expressions of an African American "structure of feeling." These elements were the subjects of various episodes and more significantly they consistently provided the context and setting for action. In at least one episode each, both food and music were dominant themes. Formally music was used, as it has been conventionally in television, to begin and end each episode as well as to suggest emotion, cue action, and segue from scene to scene. The show's particular use of black popular musical forms such as blues, jazz, and rhythm and blues reproduced the central relationship between the role of music and African American culture. Music was a constant in the show—it was always there, whether formally as a background device, on the jukebox as entertainment in the club, or as the subject of an episode.

What is more, *Frank's Place* (with the exception of *The Bill Cosby Show*) was one of the few places on commercial network television which actively used blues and jazz performed by original artists in settings like those found in black communities. Reid's and Wilson's commitment to present the original music by Louis Armstrong, Lightnin Hopkins, Jimmy Reed, Slim Gallard, Slam Stewart, B. B. King, Muddy Waters, and Dizzy Gillespie represents a rare moment of commercial network television's treatment of African American music as a cultural resource and the African American musician as a cultural hero.

Aside from these formal uses, black music was also the major motif of at least one episode. Written by novelist and screen writer Samm-Art Williams, this episode brought members of an African music and dance troupe to The Chez Restaurant. During their New Orleans visit, one of the troupe's members (Adele), a master African musician and devout jazz lover, discovers that Dizzy Gillespie is scheduled to perform in town. As the narrative develops it is revealed that Adele is so enamored of jazz that he plans to defect to the United Stated in order to play professionally.

Viewed against marginalization and trivialization of things African by the dominant commercial media, this was an unusual moment in American commercial network television's representations of blacks. As a black American, I find this representation especially significant because the narrative adopted a "pan African" recognition of music, culture, food, and customs.[18] (The representation of Adele's desire to play American jazz with Dizzy Gillespie is also significant from the viewpoint of African American cultural history, since Gillespie was the first American jazz musician to incorporate African and Afro-Caribbean influences into his music (Gillespie 1979).[19]

At the level of narrative content *Frank's Place* explored an extraordinary range of themes—homelessness, greed and exploitation, basketball recruitment, voodoo, music, and personal relationships. The program's critical appeal and aesthetic innovation owed much to this rich thematic range. Aside from the explicit representations of African American culture, the jazz episode stands out for its attempt at cross cultural understanding and the location of living African American cultural practices (food, music, dance) at the center of the narrative.

An episode about the recruitment of a black high school All American basketball player (Calvin) addressed issues—sports, education, male culture— "relevant" to significant segments within black communities. The show examined the aspirations and complicated connections between Calvin and a white middle aged recruiter named Chick. The episode explored the stakes, excesses, confusion, exploitation, and competition involved in recruiting black high school athletes. By using humor and irony to focus on the exploitation and absurdity in the athletic recruitment game, the episode called attention to the need for community resources to help Calvin (and countless others like him) through this process—the politics of recruiting, the balance between academics and public relations, excessive hype and reliable information, and the destinies of young black athletes.

The narrative, organized as a montage, followed Calvin's initial recruitment through the announcement of his selection of a college. The visual montage (risky for the genre of situation comedy) was presented from the vantage points of the various people (and interests) involved in the recruitment process—the athlete (Calvin), the adviser (Frank), the coach, the recruiter (Chick), and the mother. By moving from one perspective to another, we learn the motives of the various people involved. From the angle of these different interests we come to appreciate the enormous pressures, frustrations, and risks of exploitation that young black athletes like Calvin face.[20]

This episode was unusually explicit about the racial exploitation and arrogance which accompanies the circus atmosphere of college athletic recruitment. In this exchange between two elderly black women, Calvin's mother and Miss Marie (one of the major characters in the show), notice the sense of personal and cultural violation these women feel at the hands of insensitive white male recruiters.

> **Calvin's mother:** "Some (recruiters) just write, but others, they call my house all hours of the day and night. They drive by my house."
>
> **Miss Marie:** "And they even come by the church."
>
> **Calvin's mother:** "Yea! All these white men dropping money in the collection plate so I can see."

This exchange reveals the clash of culture and the different assumptions that order each world. Viewers are forced to choose sides, and those who identify and sympathize with these women quickly become suspicious of the recruiters and impatient with the process. Emotionally the suspicion, impatience, and identification with the plight of these elderly women is an articulation of the episode's critique of the recruitment process, especially the precarious terms on which the decisions about the futures of black youngsters rest.

A number of other qualities from this episode suggest its operation and location within a black American cultural sensibility. As Calvin's adviser, Frank, the middle class university professor, represents many of the concerns of a black parent about sending a young adult to college—ratio of students to faculty, ration of blacks to whites, school population, the background of the students, the graduation rates for black athletes. Significantly, Frank also mentioned "the small all black college" as an option for Calvin. Although much of this seems lost on Calvin, it was not lost on black viewers especially those for whom historically black colleges remain a major route for the eduction of young blacks.[21]

When taken together these explicit articulations of concerns relevant to black Americans reveal elements of African American experiences which are usually silent and absent in American commercial network television. It is not enough that such concerns are explicitly mentioned however; it is in the specific selection, organization, and use of these elements that their legitimacy and resonance operate.

FRANK'S PLACE AND THE LIMITS OF TELEVISION REPRESENTATION OF AFRICAN AMERICAN CULTURE

While *Frank's Place*'s rewriting of African American representations in commercial network television offer alternatives to dominant representations, there are even limits to this most hopeful set of representations. After all, the series operated within the slippery and contested terrain of commercial television. Therefore even this welcome corrective does not constitute a complete break (Foster 1985, Taylor 1988). As *Frank's Place* pressed the limits of dramatic and comedic television representations of black Americans, it illustrates the hegemonic strategies of containment operating in the commercial television system. Thus while it challenged conventional aesthetic and generic boundaries and offered new ways to represent aspects of black life in America, *Frank's Place* failed to find resonance in the high stakes world of commercial popularity.

In addition to its muted commercial appeal, the show's critical insights were often contained and limited. For example, in its incisive critique of high school basketball recruitment, it is not clear where the critique was directed—the college recruitment system, urban public school education which produces students like Calvin, parents, individual recruiters, individual coaches, or students. (In an episode on homelessness, a sympathetic and insightful portrait of a homeless person is drawn, but the question of homelessness as a complex social problem remains essentially Frank's moral problem.)

Within this structure of containment the character of Frank is important. It was usually Frank who expressed critical insight and moral outrage. He expressed these responses in a variety of ways: by looking away in disgust at the offending character's (Reverend Deal's) indiscretions; by sanctioning Cool for his errant drug dealings; by judging Bubba's need to mislead his family (about his and Frank's homosexual relationship) to get out of a difficult situation. Frank, the sophisticated but naive college professor, represents the critique and strategies for change. (Consistent with the conventions of character development in commercial television, Frank was not infallible; he too suffered loss, disappointment, and bad judgment (Fiske 1987.)

Significantly the show was also contained by the social and cultural limitations of an American social order where racism, social inequality, and deep suspicions of cultural differences remain. *Frank's Place* required its audience to engage directly the issue of cultural difference. The show also demanded the necessary competence, patience, and engagement to produce pleasure and maintain interests. The narrative structure, thematic approach, and cinematic look of the show disturbed the normal television experience. In a sense the show required too much work; it asked too much of an audience for whom African American culture remained a fuzzy and distant experience. Its potential audience simply had to work too hard to make sense of the African American life and culture represented in the show (and never mind that they also had to work to find the show in the network's programming schedule.)

The show's commercial failure resecured the center of the genre of situation comedy, rather than inviting explorations of the margins. It reinforced the limited terms within which the general American television audience can explore the interiors of black social and cultural life. *Frank's Place*'s daring but short life is perhaps the exception that proves the rule in commercial television as it concerns blacks: representations of African Americans will remain an active part of American commercial television offerings to the extent that we remain contained, nonthreatening, and familiar.

NOTES

1. Thanks to the following colleagues and friends for critical readings, discussions, and support in the preparation of this paper: Clyde Taylor, Tommy Lott, George Lipsitz, Rosa Linda Fregoso, Teshome Gabriel, Hamid Naficy, Valerie Smith, Jimmie Reeves, Richard Campbell, Horace Newcomb, and The Center for African American Studies at UCLA.

2. Most of the information in this section was taken from a day long seminar and discussion with *Frank's Place* co-executive producer Hugh Wilson. The seminar was held in New Orleans, Louisiana, in November 1988. Many of the details of the production of the show are more fully reported and developed in Richard Campbell's and Jimmie L. Reeves's "Television Authors: The Case of Hugh Wilson" (unpublished paper 1989).

3. Wilson's most well known and commercially successful film was *Police Academy I.*

4. Seminar discussion with Wilson, November 1988.

5. Even this figure seems modest compared to the reported $1 million dollars per episode cost of *The Cosby Show.* See Lippman 1990.

6. In the course of its twelve month run CBS moved the show to six different time slots and four different nights.

7. Seminar discussion with Wilson, November 1988.

8. It is not surprising that Wilson used this approach since he honed his writing and directing skills at MTM studios, where this approach was widely used.

9. Some observers in the television industry attribute the show's commercial failure to its blurring of these genres and its failure to develop a clear identity.

10. The cancellation of *Frank's Place* prompted widespread protests and letter writing campaigns from organizations such as the National Urban League and the NAACP.

11. Discussions with Tommy Lott and Clyde Taylor helped shape many of the ideas in this section.

12. See Gray, "Watching Television, Reading Race" (unpublished manuscript 1989).

13. The recently acclaimed *Arsenio Hall Show* is similar in this respect. The chatty and occasionally gossipy format is really about the class and mobility aspirations of a new generation of young blacks and whites.

14. Other notable programs about place include *Dallas* (Texas), *The Bob Newhart Show* (Vermont), *The Andy Griffin Show* (North Carolina), *Designing Women* (Atlanta), *Spencer For Hire* and *St. Elsewhere* (Boston).

15. This universe of African American cultural sensibilities is rare in commercial television; one other site where such representation occurs is music television, namely music video.

16. My observations on this point are indebted to Rosalinda Fregoso who offers a similar analysis about the use of music to establish cultural location and significance in Chicano film. For her analysis of the role of music in Chicano film see: Rosalinda Fregoso (1990) "Hybridity in Chicano Cinema" paper presented at the International Association for the Study of Popular Music. New Orleans (May).

17. One episode explored color caste and class conflicts within the Southern black experience. In this particular episode, Frank was faced with the difficult choice of choosing between two black male fraternal organizations which were distinguished, in this case, by class background and skin color. A similar theme was, of course, at the center of Spike Lee's *School Daze.*

18. The presentation of music was also significant because of the space in the program given both to traditional African music and dance and to American jazz. Musicians and dancers performed in traditional African costumes. A further affirmation of the close relationship between Africans and African Americans was expressed by Hannah's mother, who during the performance by the African troupe, explained to Tiger (and the audience) the origins of various costumes and the symbolism of the instruments.

19. In the nineteen fifties Gillespie hired the Cuban drummer Chano Pozo to play in his band.

20. For example, as a family acquaintance and adviser, Frank is interested in securing the best academic environment for Calvin; Calvin's mother, who is both proud and tired, wants Calvin to make the right decision and for the circus act to end; Calvin's high school coach wants a university coaching position; Chick, the university recruiter wants a successful

basketball program and to compete in the final four NCAA basketball tournament; Calvin wants "to wear #17, to play on national television, to start [his] freshman year, and a twelve million dollar NBA contract." In contrast to these collective pressures and interests, Calvin's aspirations seem simple albeit poorly prioritized. Against the background of his eighth grade reading ability and weak high school preparation his goals seem out of reach.

21. *The Bill Cosby Show* must also be credited with introducing references to historically black colleges into the plots and narrative of situation comedy. For a while Denise attended Hillman, a fictitious black college. Filmaker Spike Lee's influence on this issue should not be lost since his successful musical *School Daze* was also set in a Southern Black college.

REFERENCES CITED

Barker, David. 1985. "Television Production Techniques as Communication." In *Critical Studies in Mass Communication*. 2:234–246.

Childs, John Brown. 1984. "Afro-American Intellectuals and the People's Culture." *Theory and Society*. 13

Downing, John H. 1988. "The Cosby Show' and American Racial Discourse." In Geneva Smitherman-Donaldson and Teun A. Van Dijk. 46–74. *Discourse and Discrimination*. Detroit: Wayne State University Press.

Feur, Jane. 1987. "The MTM Style." In Horace Newcomb, ed. 52–84. *Television: The Critical View*. 4th ed., New York: Oxford University Press.

———. 1986. "Narrative Form in American Network Television." In Colin MacCabe, Ed. *High Theory/Low Culture: Analyzing Popular Television and Film*. New York: St. Martin's.

Fiske, John. 1987. *Television Culture*. London: Methuen.

Foster, Hal. 1985. *Recodings: Art, Spectacle, and Cultural Politics*. Port Townsend, Washington: Bay Press.

Gans, Herbert. 1979. *Deciding What's News: A Study of the CBS Evening News, NBC Nightly News, Newsweek and Time*. New York: Pantheon.

Garfinkel, Perry. 1988. "*Frank's Place:* The Restaurant as Life Stage." *New York Times* (February 17):C1.

Gates, Henry Louis. 1989. "TV's Black World Turns—But Stays Unreal." *New York Times* (November 12): Arts and Leisure Section, 1.

Gillespie, Dizzy. 1979. *To Be or Not to Bop*. New York: Doubleday.

Gitlin, Todd. 1986. *Watching Television*. New York: Pantheon.

Gray, Herman. 1990. "Watching TV: Reading Race." Presented at the Annual Convention of the American Sociological Association. Washington, D.C. (August).

———. 1989. "Television, Black Americans and the American Dream." *Critical Studies in Mass Communication*. 6, 4: 376–387.

———. 1986. "Television and the New Black Man: Black Male Images in Prime-time Situation Comedy." *Media Culture and Society*. 8: 223–242.

Hall, Stuart. 1981. "Notes on Deconstructing the Popular." Pp. 227–240 in Raphael Samuel, ed. *People's History and Socialist Theory*. London: Routledge and Kegan Paul.

Lippman, John. 1990. "Cosby Makers Ask NBC for a $1 Million Bonus." *Los Angeles Times*. (March 22): A1.

MacDonald, J. Fred. 1983. *Blacks and White TV.* Chicago: Nelson-Hall.

McClaurin-Allen, Irma. 1987. "Working: the Black Actress in the Twentieth Century: Interview with Rosalind Cash." *Contributions in Black Studies: A Journal of African and Afro-American Studies.* 8:67–77.

Miller, Mark Crispin. 1988. "Cosby Knows Best." In his *Boxed In: The Culture of TV.* Evanston, IL: Northwestern University Press.

Montgomery, Katheryn. 1989. *Target Prime Time.* London: Oxford.

Newcomb, Horace. 1984. "On the Dialogic Aspects of Mass Communication." *Critical Studies in Mass Communication.* 1: 34–50.

Newcomb, Horace, and Robert S. Alley. 1983. *The Producer's Medium.* New York: Oxford.

Taylor, Clyde. 1988. "We Don't Need Another Hero: Anti-thesis on Aesthetics." Pp. 80–85 in Mbye B. Cham and Claire Andrade-Watkins, eds. *Critical Perspectives on Independent Black Cinema.* Cambridge, Massachusetts: MIT University Press.

Taylor, Ella. 1989. *Prime Time Television Families.* Berkeley: University of California Press.

Reeves, Jimmie L. 1988. "Rewriting Newhart: A Dialogic Analysis." *Wide Angle.* 10, 1: 76–91.

Williams, Raymond. 1977. *Marxism and Literature.* New York: Oxford University Press.

Wilson Hugh. 1988. "Observations on Making of *Frank's Place.*" Seminar on *Frank's Place.* Speech Communications Association. New Orleans (November).

Winston, Michael. 1982. "Racial Consciousness and the Evolution of Mass Communication in the United States." *Daedalus.* 111:171–182.

QUESTIONS FOR DISCUSSION

1. Gray argues that *Frank's Place*'s credibility and depth in representing the African American experience comes from the free creative hand given to a production company with a considerable number of African American writers, producers, and other creative personnel. Contrast this to other shows involving minority groups, such as Margaret Cho's *All American Girl* or the Wayans brothers' *In Living Color.*

2. According to Gray, certain of the show's elements contributed to the show's primarily African American "structure of feeling." What are these elements, and why are they repressed in the majority of network programming?

3. Has cable television opened up the opportunities for representations of African American culture? How have these changed the "normativity" of the white middle class experience? How might they have reinforced it?

4. Not only was *Frank's Place* innovative in its representations of race, class, gender, and place, it also employed an innovative narrative form, the "dramedy," or intertwining of comedy and drama in a half-hour format. How did this narrative structure add to the depth and complexity of the show? How might it have both furthered and weakened the program's messages?

5. Often, an innovative program experiences "scheduling problems"—the network cannot seem to find a "good" time slot in which to air it. Why might this be? What other problems are concealed behind a "scheduling" dilemma?

INFOTRAC COLLEGE EDITION

Search InfoTrac College Edition under "African Americans and television" for more articles on this subject. Also combine the terms "Asian American," "Hispanic" and "Latino," or names of other groups, with "television" for more on television and ethnicity.

14

U.S. Broadcasting
and the Public Interest
in the Multichannel Era
The Policy Heritage
and Its Implications

WILLARD D. ROWLAND, JR.

Almost from its inception, broadcasting in the United States has been owned and controlled by private enterprises in the public interest. Such corporate stewardship of an ostensibly public resource was, until very recently, unique to the United States. Willard Rowland, Jr., places the philosophical origins of U.S. broadcasting policy not at its inception in the early twentieth century but well before that, in the libertarian ideals that were codified in the U.S. Constitution and the Bill of Rights. These ideals led to the institutionalization of the belief that the nascent American press of the early nineteenth century would better serve the public interest if held in private, not governmental hands.

In this article, Rowland traces the incorporation of these ideals and their implications for and institutionalization in regulatory policy, from the invention of the telegraph through radio, television, and to the contemporary multichannel, Internet era. At all stages, he argues, the private and commercial orientation of American communications technologies has remained virtually unquestioned, while the already small role of public broadcasting is increasingly eroded. The current multichannel era, Rowland suggests, is no exception, as an

First published in *Studies of Broadcasting* 33, (February 1997): 89–130. Reprinted by permission of NHK Broadcasting Culture Research Institute.

increased governmental focus on industry deregulation, allegedly in the service of technological innovation, leads to a hypercommercialized and concentrated media environment with little room for alternatives, or for the delivery of services to a diverse population in their, rather than corporate, interest.

> The American system takes an extreme, indeed, distorted Millian view of the central dilemmas of broacasting; it takes the purest and most abstract conceptions of freedom of expression and places them inside a high-pressured commercial tyranny.
>
> ANTHONY SMITH (1973)

INTRODUCTION

The history of U.S. broadcasting is a story of the attempt to balance public and private interests in a context of capitalistic, "free" enterprise economics, First Amendment legal theory, individualistic and utilitarian social philosophy, and countervailing positive and negative concerns about the cultural implications of electronic media technology. U.S. broadcasting has been owned primarily in the private sector and supported as a commercial enterprise, much in the model of most other American media institutions (newspapers, publishing, film). Yet it has also been regulated by the federal government through a public trusteeship (fiduciary) licensing process premised on the assumption of spectrum scarcity and on social anxiety about the putative power of radio and television. The regulatory mechanism for U.S. broadcasting has been closely associated with that for telecommunications (telegraph, telephone) and public utilities (power, water), though not to the extent of outright public ownership, as in the PTTs of other countries, nor even to the rates and services prescriptions or any of the local and state government authority typical for other such industries and services in the U.S.

Meanwhile, there has never been provision for a strong, centrally placed noncommercial, public broadcasting enterprise in the U.S. This situation derives from the deep social and legal tradition favoring private enterprise in communication, and the closely related, powerful American belief system in the public service potential of such forms of ownership and control, especially under the fiduciary regulation system. Noncommercial public service broadcasting exists in the U.S., but with nowhere near the same degree of widespread social and policy support as in most other industrialized democratic societies.

Shaped by all these conditions and beliefs, broadcasting and most of the electronic media in the U.S. have historically been perceived primarily as instruments of commerce rather than as institutions of culture. As reflected in the traditional American appeal to the "marketplace of ideas," the dominant metaphor has been economic, to understand people more as consumers than as citizens. Social concerns have not been absent in the debates about communication, but unlike the situation in most other economically advanced nations, the presumption about the commercial role of broadcasting and telecommunications has been so dominant as to relegate the social and cultural to secondary consideration in applied U.S. policy.

The balance of this paper traces the history of those policy trends and how they define the contemporary condition and behavior of U.S. broadcasting and the integrated forms of electronic communication.

THE LEGACY OF U.S. MEDIA AND POLICY HISTORY

The Libertarian Heritage

The prospects for U.S. broadcasting were established early in the history of the republic, a full century or more before radio and television were technologically possible and well before they were beginning to be imagined in the late-nineteenth century. The principal factor was an overarching, classically liberal, Lockean-Smithian social and political economic ideology, with its emphases on reason, natural order, individual rights of expression and private property ownership, parliamentary and representative forms of democratic governance, religious freedom and the due process of law (Jensen, 1957; Rivers, et al., 1971). Most of those tenets were widely debated and institutionalized through such events as the Constitutional Convention and the publication of and debates around the *Federalist* papers in 1787–88 (Lodge, 1888); some were enshrined in the U.S. Constitution (1789), others in its first ten amendments, the Bill of Rights (1791).

By the early nineteenth century and the initial phases of the industrial revolution, the libertarian ideals had framed certain enduring conditions for the ownership, control and purpose of communications media in the country. During the colonial period the printing press had come to be understood primarily as an enterprise of private commerce. There was a strong belief that as institutionalized in journalistic and manuscript publication forms the press would far better serve the broad public interest were it to be held largely in private hands and to operate in a commercial marketplace as with most other enterprises.[1] In late-eighteenth century America, government was understood to be the principal barrier to free expression and to the full realization of the prospects for enlightenment of the citizenry and an effective democratic process. Hence the explicit articulation of freedoms of speech and press in the First Amendment to the Constitution.[2]

Yet, despite the power of that world view, the separation of the private and public was never as thorough as this sketch suggests. To begin with, there always had been other forms of ownership and purpose in printing. Churches, political groups and even colonial and eventually state and federal governments all owned presses and were involved in various forms of publication.

At the same time, most democratic governments retained the state's historical responsibility for the postal service. Much of the rationale for public ownership of such a key means of communication was to insure affordable, universal public access to news and information. But another important consequence of public ownership of the postal system was to provide public subsidy of all the private business carried out through the exchange of mailed correspondence, including that of the press (Kielbowicz, 1989, p. 182). The fiscal health of the press thus has always depended to a great extent on the mailing rate discounts provided by the government through the postal service.[3]

Democratic government was deeply involved in the interests of the private press in other ways. Politicians might complain about the specifics of press behavior, but in a broad institutional sense they were deeply dependent on a commercially successful journalistic enterprise. The most elemental processes of democracy, in the forms of electoral politics and the actions of governments, required coverage by the press. Incumbents and challengers alike found it generally more advantageous than not to have a commercially supported journalistic enterprise, their critiques of accuracy and bias notwithstanding. Additionally, governments came to find it necessary to purchase space in the press to publish notices thought to be essential public information. Government was thereby materially supporting the private press in several ways.[4]

Commercial Telecommunications and Popular Media

It was in this environment that the first electronic media emerged in mid-nineteenth century America. As a result, the control pattern in the U.S. was much different than in other industrializing democracies where first the electric telegraph and then the telephone were quickly and universally identified as extensions of the posts. The U.S. Post Office was never given the authority, or resources, to develop the comprehensive range of services more typical of the European PTTs (Smythe, 1957, p. 16).

Instead, the U.S. telegraph and telephone industries were almost immediately privatized and given over to commercial ownership (Thompson, 1947, pp. 20–24), much in the model of such other major industries as the railroads, shipping, banks, insurance and petroleum. The concentrated powers of such enterprises engendered forms of antitrust legislation and regulation that were likewise applied to the telecommunications industries (Schwartz, 1973, Vol. I, pp. 3–13). In a new pattern of oversight, drawn from the states, the federal government attempted to establish a fiduciary licensing and regulatory system, granting telecommunications franchises to private parties on the grounds of their promised stewardship as public trustees providing service in "the public interest." The fiduciary system permitted private ownership of telegraph and telephone services in return for such regulatory requirements that they provide universal access and that they be subject to certain controls on rates and services.

There were moments when telecommunications was thought of as possibly being a proper sphere for public ownership. One was at the very outset, when

Congress sponsored construction of the first public, experimental Morse telegraph line, between Baltimore and Washington, D.C. in the early 1840s. But that arrangement was principally one of testing and facilitation; it lasted only a few months, ending with the federal government declining to purchase the Morse patent rights, deferring further telegraph development to the private sector and permitting a series of consolidations that led to the creation of the Western Union monopoly in 1866.

During the decades after the Civil War, in the wake of the growing linkages between the telegraph and wire service monopolies, there were dozens of legislative initiatives to create a government telegraph service (Czitrom, 1982, pp. 24–29; Harlow, 1936, pp. 333–334, 338). But Western Union, in close association with the Associated Press, brought considerable pressure to bear on publishers and editors, effectively stymieing any open debate about the merits of public ownership.

As the industrial revolution continued its geometric expansion during the post-bellum period, the U.S. government began to address communications policy more explicitly. Beginning with legislation in 1866 (U. S. Congress, 1866) that policy established a middle ground between public ownership and totally unrestricted private monopoly ownership in the form of a rudimentary "common carrier" status for the telegraph industry. The common carrier arrangement constituted a trade-off between government grants of monopoly use of the public rights-of-way and publicly sanctioned rate and service regulations. By the 1890s that accommodation for the telegraph and telephone industries would be joined to the "public interest" principle emerging as the central antitrust federal policy doctrine for a number of other large, national-scale industries.

The federal government briefly became re-involved in telecommunications administration, as part of the industrial planning and oversight associated with the entry of the U.S. into World War I. During 1918–19 the Postal Department was given authority over the telegraph and telephone systems, and the Navy over the wireless telegraphy and telephony services of the day. But even then it was clear that the government never intended the post office or the military to serve in anything more than supervisory roles. The assets of the wired and wireless telecommunications enterprises remained in private, corporate hands, and their managements remained those of the owning companies, principally AT&T and Western Union (Danielian, 1939, pp. 243–270).

During the late Progressive period there was some policy debate suggesting the possibility of public ownership of telecommunications (U.S. Post Office Department, 1914). But the dominant policy expectation always was that U.S. telecommunications would remain in private hands and be supported commercially. In fact, the brief wartime interlude of federal supervision of the telephone company turned out to be highly advantageous to it, guaranteeing AT&T certain rate and service concessions it had long sought and been denied through the prewar regulatory process of the Interstate Commerce Commission (Danielian, 1939, p. 243).

Faced with the opportunity to reassess the situation after the Armistice, the federal government demurred from pursuing any means of public ownership of the electronic media. To the contrary it had already shown its strong willingness to establish conditions whereby the private manufactures and telecommunications service providers could pool their patents to facilitate production of U.S. radio equipment for the war effort and not be beholden to the patent and manufacturing leads held by competitors chartered in foreign countries (Barnouw, 1966, pp. 47–61; Czitrom, 1982, pp. 69–70). That policy carried over into the immediate postwar period and led the federal government to help establish the first major wireless telecommunications trust, the Radio Corporation of America.[5]

Meanwhile the industrialization of communications in the late-nineteenth century had led to the formation of largely private, commercial forms of popular theater (vaudeville and burlesque), music (performance and recordings) and film, and to an increasingly commodified popular culture (Gilbert, 1940; Green and Laurie, 1951; Jowett, 1976). Combined with the already overwhelmingly private, commercial system of the press and publication in general (newspapers, magazines, books), the popular mass audience media at the turn of the century were thoroughly defined in light of commercial interests.

This approach was firmly ingrained in telecommunications during the first two decades of the twentieth century. Some federal regulation was introduced during those years, along the line of antitrust, transportation, utility and other forms of economic legislation adopted between 1887 and 1916. Such "trust-busting" and the related new federal administrative agencies (e.g., the Interstate Commerce Commission, the Federal Reserve System, and the Federal Trade Commission) were products of the Progressive political themes of the day and were seen as ways of protecting individual consumers and citizens against the predatory policies of large, concentrated national capital as in the railroad, banking and petroleum industries. But while such regulation may have curbed the worst abuses of monopoly capitalism, it had little capacity for restraining oligopoly. Indeed, it may have actually enhanced such arrangements through its inherent protectionism (Schwartz, 1973, Vol. I, pp. 10–11). Whatever the actual contribution of early federal regulation in that regard, it did have the additional effect of muting calls for public ownership of telecommunications.

The experience of World War I also contributed to that dampening. Much of the popular mythology about the Great War was that it was a product of the corruption of the European states and that it had been resolved by the far more vigorous and, as was widely presumed, more virtuous American socio-economic order. The early and mid-1920s were marked by an unprecedented economic prosperity. Yet at the same time there were great fears in the U.S. about the putative power and influence of domestic socialism and international communism (Allen, 1931, pp. 18–20, 45–75). The contradictions of industrial capitalism in the U.S. remained unresolved and those conditions in association with heavy waves of rural-to-urban migration and foreign immigration during the preceding generation had fostered considerable labor and social unrest. Much of the Progressive reform agenda had gone unfilled, and in spite of the apparent global success of the U.S. as an emerging economic and cultural power, there were serious domestic doubts and anxieties. The Bolshevik revolution in Russia and the apparent threat of an increasingly strong global socialist movement only exacerbated those fears and encouraged the search for a new order in the U.S. (Wiebe, 1967, pp. 275–276).

The result was an attempt to overwhelm the doubts and contradictions by resort to a highly positive celebratory form of self-congratulation. The dominant U.S. beliefs about democracy and industry in the postwar period came to be a combination of traditional libertarian though and pragmatism, now redefined by Herbert Hoover as "progressive individualism" (Schlesinger, 1957, pp. 77–89). Theories of freedom of individuals, speech and enterprise were thoroughly intertwined with one another; the practical, positive capacities of American technology, science and management seemed to be self-evident and uncritically promoted, and there was an emerging faith that well-educated, professionalized business and political leaders would be able to join together to insure socially responsible industrial behavior and public welfare.

In that light there was considerable confidence in the practical and moral superiority of "the American way," fostering an attitude toward things foreign as antiquated, inefficient and inferior. Such "nativism" was not new in American experience, but perhaps because of the continuing postwar contradictions and lingering social doubts, the self-assurance it expressed tended to be overstated, and in this latest incarnation it militated strongly against notions of public ownership or ever more vigorous public regulation in any sector of the economy. Such concepts were seen as hopelessly out of date, and as they bore on communications and telecommunications, with their free expression associations, they were unthinkable.

Altogether, then, the popular media and telecommunications in the early twentieth century existed in a pattern of ownership and purpose that was thoroughly private and commercial. There were provisions for government, public interest regulation of the "natural monopoly," utility-like portions of the emerging communications complex. But fiduciary regulation proved to be relatively light touch and protectionist, as much supportive as restrictive of the industries, and it came nowhere near the extent of public ownership and noncommercial purpose associated with telecommunications in other democracies. Such were the policy conditions, an emerging pattern of technocratic libertarianism, that had set the stage for any new for of communication, such as radio broadcasting.

U.S. BROADCASTING
AS COMMERCIAL ENTERPRISE

Radio as Mass Audience Business

When radio began to emerge in the early twentieth century it was widely imagined to be a form of radio telegraphy and telephony; not a mass audience medium of journalism and entertainment.[6] Accordingly, the initial policy approaches to it in the U.S. and internationally were those for the telecommunications industries; radio was treated as a private enterprise, not as a publicly owned medium. In keeping with its utility image radio remained subject to certain public interest regulations deriving from the federal transportation and commerce legislation of the 1892–1912 period, but those were limited restrictions, largely oriented around technical, safety and economic issues (Rowland, 1989). They reflected no threat to the fundamental commitment to private, commercial ownership of radio.

It was not until after World War I, in the early 1920s, that the uses of radio began to demonstrate large audience, broadcast characteristics (Barnouw, 1966, pp. 64–74, 79–114). But in either respect, whether as a medium of telecommunications or broadcasting, the pattern for radio ownership and regulation had already largely been set. As popular, mass audience, radio broadcasting emerged in the mid-1920s, there was overwhelming official policy faith in the public interest adequacy of private, commercial forms of control and use. The ideology of a progressive, socially responsible private-enterprise economy had been so successfully resuscitated during the antitrust reform era of the preceding generation (1890–1920), and it became so closely associated with equally optimistic expectations about the positive values of commercial forms of modern, popular communication, that throughout the decade before the Great Depression there was little support for fashioning radio under any other template. The assumption remained that there was such considerable identity between private and public interests in broadcasting that, as in the simple models of eighteenth-century libertarianism, the best public services would emerge in a largely unfettered private enterprise.

Occasionally doubts were expressed about such prospects, and there were even explicit attempts to develop alternative, noncommercial radio services, typically under the auspices of educational, religious, labor, or municipal government institutions. But those concerns and institutional alternatives were at such odds with the predominant world view, and they had such little official government support (Barnouw, 1966, pp. 172–176), that they remained relatively weak and ineffectual during the crucial period of the mid-1920s when the basic structure of American broadcasting was being erected. As a result, the Radio Act of 1927 (U.S. Congress, 1927) made no provision for supporting or developing noncommercial broadcasting, and much of the work of the new Federal Radio Commission (FRC) also militated against the few existing public service efforts (Barnouw, 1966, pp. 259–263); Blakely, 1979, pp. 54–55).

The formal, core policy document defining U.S. broadcasting policy continues to be the Communications Act of 1934 (U.S. Congress, 1934), as amended. But insofar as radio and television are concerned the key legislation was the Radio Act of 1927. Its provision for broadcasting were reincorporated almost verbatim in the new statute. The policy for broadcasting of the mid-1930s and beyond was therefore one, not of the Depression and the New Deal, but of the free-wheeling, "ballyhoo," mid-1920s. The U.S. approach to broadcasting was shaped in a highly entrepreneurial, speculative climate of "Coolidge prosperity" boosterism and increasingly commercialized, popular entertainment, not by strong public regulation or directed social purpose.

It is in this light that one understands the failure of the proponents of a more noncommercial, public service approach to broadcasting in the U.S. By the mid-1930s, the noncommercial interests had been reduced to a loose amalgam of stations licensed to schools, colleges and universities. They had no broad-ranging national service authority and they were not chartered by the federal government in the pattern common for national public broadcasting services emerging in other industrialized democracies. Nor did they benefit from any sort of national funding, as in the license fee mechanism that was widely introduced elsewhere during the 1920s and 1930s. Also, because the public interest was thought to inhere naturally in the regulated commercial broadcasting system, the noncommercial stations had none of the broad-ranging popular program service authority invested in most national broadcasters abroad.

Elsewhere public broadcasting was being built on the expansive doctrine of universal service, quality, choice, balance, education and entertainment espoused most forcefully in Britain (Reith, 1924; Briggs, 1965, pp. 20–48, 75–121). In the U.S. the mandate was to be only "noncommercial and educational," a definition that was narrower, dryer and more forbiddingly pedagogical than the mandate for other national public service broadcasters. Finally, because they were not seen as a central, indispensable element of U.S. radio, a heavily disproportionate share of the noncommercial broadcasters were forced off the air during the FRC's major restructuring of the licensee assignments in the late-1920s and early 1930s. The educational stations did eventually receive the benefit of reserved space on the spectrum allocations for television, but those were only in the then unused FM band.[7]

These developments explain why the noncommercial stations had little presence in U.S. radio during its heyday (1927–1955), particularly in large population centers. There was no public funding that approached anything like the resources typical abroad, which meant that there were no national, interconnected public radio networks, no major sources of large volumes of high quality programming, nor any attempt to reach large audiences. With this poor heritage the noncommercial radio service was so narrowly defined, locally based, and technologically limited that well into the 1970s it was barely audible in U.S. media culture.

By contrast with other countries U.S. broadcasting was dominated by commercial networks and a form of mass entertainment programming inherited more from vaudeville, musical entertainment, film and popular literature. Radio comedy, variety programs, soap operas, action-adventure dramas, and westerns were forms of popular culture that had been well rehearsed in the preceding generation of commercial mass media. Advertising-based radio developed elements of education, high culture music and drama in its first decade or two, but such forms were never dominant, and as the commercial potential of radio continued to reveal itself through the 1940s they atrophied and were marginalized.

Commercial radio also was slow to develop serious forms of journalism. Part of the reason was the deliberate resistance of the newspaper industry, which saw broadcasting as a direct threat to itself and which initially went to great lengths to deny radio stations and networks the wire service resources and public identity as a legitimate journalistic medium that were more typical of the national public radio services abroad. In time that situation changed, and with the outbreak of World War II commercial radio found itself becoming more thoroughly a medium of news, public affairs and political information. The press itself also finally came to invest in broadcasting, to the extent that "by 1940 newspapers owned or controlled one-third of all radio stations" (Griffith, 1989, p. 6). But the overwhelming orientation of U.S. radio remained light, popular and commercial. While its journalistic efforts were an increasingly important feature of the medium, its presence in education and public service information was less central.

The public policy environment at mid-century helped insure the maintenance of that heavily commercialized characteristic of U.S. broadcasting. Throughout the 1930s and 1940s the compromises in the fiduciary regulatory system had continued to manifest themselves. Despite criticism of commercial radio performance the FCC had declined to exert much pressure on the networks or other holders of station licenses, and it did not get much encouragement from either Congress or the White House to do otherwise.

In light of some criticism of broadcasting the Commission did undertake a major investigation of the power of the networks in the 1938–1943 period (National Broadcasting, 1943), and in 1945–46 it conducted a close examination of the programming performance of several radio stations (Federal Communications Commission, 1946). But, although the network investigation led to the breakup of the NBC network duopoly in 1943, there were virtually no significant program service changes as a result. The programming of the new ABC radio network that emerged from the sale of the NBC "Blue" network did not differ all that much from the pattern already established by CBS and the remaining NBC network.[8] Likewise and even more tellingly, although the FCC's station programming study, the so-called "Blue Book," constituted a strong indictment of the commercial industry's failure to live up to the promises in its station license applications, the Commission never adopted the report as official policy and it renewed the licenses of all of the stations reviewed in the study without requiring any changes in their programming (Kahn, 1984, p. 149).

Communications policy debate was dominated at mid-century by a loose ethic known as "social responsibility theory" (Commission on Freedom of the Press, 1947; Peterson, 1956). This doctrine was drawn from the post-progressive efforts in business and the professions to reconcile private and public interest by emphasizing the obligations of industrial leaders to consider the social good while yet competing in the commercial marketplace. In social responsibility theory the traditional libertarian insistence on near-absolute freedom for the communicator was tempered by consideration of the needs of the audience in a complex modern world and the obligation of publishers, filmmakers and broadcasters to return to society some special consideration as compensation for the constitutional privileges they possessed. This theory seemed particularly relevant to broadcasting because of spectrum scarcity and its implication that not all who so wished might be able to use the medium. It also implicitly contained a new emphasis on communications technology as an increasingly central, liberating phenomenon of the modern era.

However, as a neo-libertarian doctrine the social responsibility theory was never able to transcend the implications of its classically liberal roots (Nerone, 1995, pp. 82, 99–100). It remained committed to private ownership and predominantly commercial purposes in the media. While it might flirt with elements of public regulation as in broadcasting and telecommunications, it could not articulate a complete rationale for strong, authoritative oversight of the media, nor for alternative systems of ownership and financial support. It could render critiques of the effects of commercialization and marketplace imperatives in the media, but it could not quite bring itself to insist on major noncommercial, public service structures at the heart of U.S. communications. Public service doctrines were more sustainable in other democratic societies where the imagination of the hard ideological division between the private and the public was not as firm as in the U.S. In this context the federal regulatory mechanism through the FCC could never be particularly demanding of its broadcast licensees, and it would therefore tend to defer to the industry's definitions of everything from technological standards to appropriate forms of fiscal support and programming services.[9]

Broadcast Television and the Policy
of Commercial Entertainment

The light touch regulatory policy carried over into the era of broadcast television, the period from roughly the late-1940s to the late-1970s, before the ascendancy of cable television, satellites and interactive telecommunications. Television excited deeper concerns about its social impact than had radio, and those sentiments led to a long pattern of congressional and academic investigation and debate about its content, particularly in relationship to violence, obscenity, service to children, and diversity of access (Skornia, 1965; Cowan, 1978; Rowland, 1983). Despite those concerns the pattern for television's regulation remained largely the same as it had been in radio. From the first comprehensive spectrum allocation plan, the *Sixth Report and Order* (Federal Communications Commission, 1952), through the second network investigation (U.S. House, 1958) and the first programming policy statement about television (Federal Communications Commission, 1960), to the various children's service policies of the 1970s–90s, the FCC tended not to exert much more than rhetorical pressure on the networks or station licensees. As a result their popular entertainment, commercial orientation was at least as strong, if not more so, as in the radio period.

The prospects for public service television were only slightly better than those for public radio. The noncommercial interests did receive about eleven percent of the initial spectrum allocations, but again those assignments were less desirable, as in this instance they were much more heavily in the little used UHF band than was the case for commercial television.[10] Also, as before, the public service efforts were dominated by a relatively narrow educational approach ("ETV") without benefit of any federal funding or major national networking and program production capacity.

News and public affairs did come to play an important role in commercial television. U.S. television inherited the radio news experience, as with other programming genres, and that legacy lent to the new medium an earlier, stronger journalistic flavor than had been the formative case for radio. By the end of television's first decade in the late 1950s large network news operations defined much of the U.S. television culture, and over time local news became a staple, and even eventually profitable element, of television station programming. But throughout the broadcast era the total amount of television news programming remained a small proportion of the overall schedule, and serious in-depth public affairs coverage constantly struggled for sufficient and desirable airtime. The overwhelming orientation of U.S. broadcast television was to light entertainment, taking on most of the popular programming forms and themes from commercial radio that had in turn been adapted from mass audience film, vaudeville and popular literature (Sterling and Kittross, 1990, pp. 278–287, 341–348).

Meanwhile a growing social and political ferment began to focus questions about television in the society. During the decade defined roughly by the mid-1960s to mid-1970s the U.S., as much of the rest of the globe, was deeply engaged in a series of serious social debates. That turmoil involved widespread discord about such matters as the Vietnam War, domestic civil rights, consumerism and the environment. The media were never far from the heart of these debates, and in each official national commission or academic report about those matters there were indictments of television, and frequently recommendations about how its performance might be improved (U.S. Kerner Commission, 1968; Surgeon General's, 1972).

Whether or not television was a seriously causal element in the social unrest of the period continues to be debated. More important for our purposes here is the observation that whatever the reality of television's responsibility, the widespread impression of culpability never actually led to a thoroughgoing review of the fundamental terms under which television was to operate in U.S. society.

For a brief period it did appear that there might be significant change in the approach to television. There were two primary indications of such a possible shift. One was a series of challenges to the licenses of commercial television stations and the reorientation of the FCC toward support of citizens' or public interest group action in such challenges, and the other was an effort to build a more major U.S. public broadcasting enterprise.

The license challenges came in the late 1960s with three cases in which the government appeared to be exerting more pressure on the television industry (Federal Communications Commission, 1969; Office of Communication, 1966; Red Lion, 1969). Collectively these cases dealt with Fairness Doctrine concerns, minority ownership and program service problems, and press cross-ownership issues. One of their major implications seemed to be that the federal courts would sustain the challenges of public interest groups and force the FCC to give them official standing, thereby ending its traditional approach of making it difficult for any but financially interested broadcasting parties to be heard in regulatory proceedings. Further, it appeared that the FCC was actually beginning to deny license renewals on the basis of poor and unfair programming practices and media concentration.

At about the same time the first Carnegie Commission on public television issued its report (1967), and later that year Congress passed, and President Johnson signed, a major piece of legislation setting the stage for direct federal support for U.S. public broadcasting (U.S. Congress, 1967). The new legislation created the Corporation for Public Broadcasting (CPB), it authorized federal funding for public broadcast programming, and it provided for the establishment of systems of network interconnection for public television and radio, a provision that would lead shortly to the creation of the Public Broadcasting Service (PBS) and National Public Radio (NPR).

These measures emerged at the height of the Great Society legislation of the 1960s, and for many observers and participants at the time they seemed to signal the ascension of many of those aspects of the social responsibility theory that had never been fully implemented in broadcasting policy at mid-century. Here, finally, seemed to be a collection of public policy steps that would, on the one hand, hold commercial television more accountable for the quality of its service and, on the other, support a noncommercial enterprise that would help broaden television's contribution to society.

COMMUNICATIONS POLICY IN THE ERA OF NEW TECHNOLOGIES AND THE MARKETPLACE RESURGENT

In the end, however, there were other forces at work in the U.S. communications policy environment that would lead in other directions. One of these was technological; the other ideological.

Changing Technologies

Throughout the late-1960s and early 1970s U.S. communications policy reoriented itself around an increasing interest in the emerging new electronic technologies. Much of that interest was spurred by the prospects for cable television and the emerging understanding that the original, typically six-to-twelve channel, community antenna television systems (CATV) might soon give way to a much larger, multichannel broadband cable universe (Sloan Commission, 1971; Smith, 1972; Cabinet Committee, 1974). Up until the late-1960s CATV had been mostly a means for extending existing broadcast television signals where they were difficult to receive, as for instance in central cities where large buildings interfered with transmissions or in nearby rural regions where the signals did not reach.

For many the newer broadband prospects heralded a revolutionary communications environment for all television users, "the wired nation," and for some it suggested a radical reordering of society, nationally and beyond, "the global village" (McLuhan and Fiore, 1968). At the very least, broadband cable was touted as the medium that would overcome the narrow commercialism of broadcasting and break its monopoly on television services. It was thought that many of the more diverse services and "social goods" of communication that were being lamented as absent in traditional broadcast television now would be readily available. That thinking became all the more prevalent by the mid-1970s with the arrival of the geostationary satellite and its harnessing to the delivery of both broadcast and cable television across the nation.

Meanwhile a similar pattern of change was beginning to be felt in the broader realm of telecommunications, principally in the telephone and computer industries. Fundamental changes in electronic technology such as miniaturization and higher frequency transmission capacities were leading to new opportunities for faster, cheaper systems of information processing of all kinds, not just conventional broadcast television. So, for instance, many large, private users of telecommunications services, such as the financial, oil and transportation industries, had begun to develop their own data networks and to seek new forms of equipment and transmission to connect to or bypass the existing telephone system (Schiller, 1982). Together, these challenges to the conventional technological infrastructures of broadcast television and basic telephone service began to raise interest in the possibility for a whole new order of multiple industry competition, lower cost and diverse services in all aspects of electronic communication.

Marketplace Ideology Reprised

Those prospects for technology coincided with a widespread ideological shift, principally in the form of a reassessment of federal economic and social regulatory policy. For all the seeming power and authority of the New Deal and Great Society programs, there had remained in much of U.S. politics a substantial resistance to what was perceived from some quarters as undesirable increases in the size and role of government. By the late-1960s much of the political agenda was beginning to be redefined in line with neo-conservative, marketplace orientations and in association with well-funded, business oriented academic journals and institutes.[11]

While much of the initial business community opposition to regulation turned on social issues, throughout the 1970s deregulation tended to occur mostly in the economic sector in such rate-regulated industries as transportation and finance (Horwitz, 1989, pp. 212–213). There was a similar pattern in the communications industries. Although there were underlying broadcast and cable industry concerns about such content and socially oriented regulations as those having to do with the Fairness Doctrine, community ascertainment, public access, and affirmative action, the broadcasters and established telephone companies, principally AT&T, were interested in maintaining their protections under traditional FCC policies. Yet it was in the realm of industrial restructuring and changed rate and service regulations that deregulation was first most firmly felt in communications.

As with the other business sectors, the initial deregulation thrust in communications centered on proposals for increasing industrial competition through wider, readier applications of new technologies in what was hoped would be a more open, vigorous marketplace of communications hardware and services. The federal communication regulatory and legislative initiatives emerging during the 1970s were based on attacks on traditional statutory and regulatory assumptions about spectrum scarcity and other information technology realties. Those propositions were developed and made ever more central to the policy debate through a vast amount of private, official, and academic literature (see, for instance, Sloan Commission, 1971; Cabinet Committee, 1974; and U.S. House, 1977). They included internal efforts at the FCC first to "re-regulate" then deregulate, they involved Justice Department investigations of the AT&T telephone monopoly, and they led to several years of effort to revise the basic communications legislation (Rowland, 1982).

The late-1970s legislative "rewrite" effort failed in the sense that Congress did not immediately adopt the wholesale statutory changes proposed in the draft bills at the time. Yet much of the legislative agenda found its way into public policy during the following decade and a half. Telephone deregulation was implemented in the early 1980s, principally through the court-supervised settlement of a divestiture suit between the U.S. Department of Justice and AT&T (Horwitz, 1989, pp. 237–243). Already moving toward deregulation in the Ford and Carter administrations, the FCC stepped up its efforts in the Reagan years, with a leadership that was avowedly committed to marketplace ideology and increased opportunities for private commercial uses of the spectrum and all aspects of broadcasting and telecommunications (Fowler and Brenner, 1982; Horwitz, 1989, pp. 260—263). Throughout the 1970s the FCC had continued to loosen the restrictions on cable television, softening its historical position of protecting the broadcasting industry. By 1984 Congress passed and President Reagan signed a major piece of cable legislation (U.S. Congress, 1984) profoundly restricting the power of local franchise authorities in rates and services regulation (the historic cornerstone of U.S. utility regulation) and fostering a period of franchise trafficking and ownership consolidation that continued at least into the late-1990s. In broadcasting the FCC had eliminated all but the most minimal technical regulation of radio by 1983, it steadily loosened its station ownership rules, it permitted more entry by direct satellite television delivery systems, it eliminated the Fairness Doctrine in 1987 and it adopted more permissive commercial "underwriting" (sponsorship) rules for public broadcasting.

Meanwhile the underlying softness of federal policy support for public broadcasting was revealed in the large cuts in federal funding for the public service enterprise in the early 1980s and the initial success of the Reagan administration (Rowland, 1993, p. 177). It took much of the next decade for those reductions to be reinstated, but by the mid-1990s, under the Clinton administration, the pattern of reduced federal support, not unlike the early Reagan years, had reemerged. Much of that attack could be attributed to the overall budget reduction fever that dominated Congress in the wake of the Republican capture of both houses in the 1994 elections. But in its first two years, 1992–94, the Clinton administration had already shown little interest in building public broadcasting beyond the modest funding recovery that had been achieved during the Bush administration, 1988—92. Its unwillingness to confront the needs of public broadcasting during its second two years, 1994—96, reflected both the age-old difficulty in the U.S. of advancing the notion of public broadcasting as a necessarily large, well supported core of broadcasting culture and the particular political calculus of a Democratic administration fearful of its chances for a second term.

BROADCAST POLICY AND STRUCTURE
AT CENTURY'S END

By the mid-1990s the triumph of technocratic ideology seemed to be nearly complete in the U.S. Faith in the liberating power of the marketplace and newer technologies had reached its highest point in the history of American communications and industrial policy. Well rehearsed during the preceding two decades, the positive rhetoric extolling unregulated commercial competition had come to dominate the discourse about communications. That view had strengthened by tapping deeply into the libertarian heritage and by fostering an ever larger, interrelated complex of interested industrial parties for whom the emerging terms of "deregulation" and interlocking capital power were not only thoroughly acceptable, but also essential.

Broadcasting during the 1980s had been marked by increasingly concentrated cross-media ownership, further institutionalization of its large, corporate character, and continued abandonment of social and cultural expectations for it. By the early 1990s those patterns had been joined by the emergence of the Internet and further attempts by the federal government to promote economic and social progress through the integration and reconfiguration of the communications industries. Building on the trends of the preceding two decades the approach of the Clinton/Gore administration was to fold broadcasting into the broader policy for telecommunications with its increasing emphasis on the putative revolution expected from continuing construction of the "information superhighway." By the late 1990s the issue had become not so much whether further concentration in broadcasting would occur, but how thoroughly integrated the various communications industries would become. In close interaction with the dominant policy themes, the traditional broadcasting companies were becoming absorbed in a large complex of telecommunications, cable, and computer giants which themselves also were increasingly involved in a wide array of publishing, film, music and other industrial interests, in the U.S. and globally.

Concentration and Multimedia Cross Ownership:
The Re-Cartelization of U.S. Telecommunications
and Broadcasting

U.S. broadcasting had always had elements of cross-ownership and industrial integration. Its ties to the telecommunications and other communications industries were intimate from the outset. The history of NBC is illustrative. From the outset in 1926 NBC had been a child of RCA which in turn had been originally (1920–21) a government sanctioned patent pool cartel of General Electric, Westinghouse, AT&T, American Marconi and United Fruit (Barnouw, 1966, pp. 57–61, 72–73; Smythe, 1957, pp. 49–51). RCA began as the pool manager and radio equipment sales arm for its electrical industry owners and, in keeping with its government sponsorship and the growing economic and political significance of telecommunications, it was deeply implicated in national industrial and defense policy. By the mid-1920s, as public and commercial pressure mounted for new legislation to accommodate the rapidly developing commercial radio broadcasting business, some in Congress did raise concerns about the antitrust implications of the pooling arrangement, leading to a Federal Trade Commission investigation. A quid pro quo for the new law appears to have been the severing of AT&T's ownership (though not pool) interests. Subsequently, in the depths of the Depression and under further antitrust review by the Justice Department and a 1932 consent decree, RCA was separated from the remaining pool members. By then, however, RCA had itself already become vertically integrated as an equipment manufacturer, musical recording producer and distributor, radio program producer, and owner of two national broadcast networks and ten radio stations. It also had become a major defense contractor, and through its co-formation of RKO in 1928 it had likewise become integrated into the film industry. Little noticed in the disputes about RCA and the patent pool is that the formal antitrust action by the government was necessitated in large part by the monopoly practices that the government itself had fostered.

The RKO/RCA episode reveals a typical set of political economic and cultural linkages (see Gilbert, 1940, p. 394; and Green and Laurie, 1951, pp. 92, 247, 271–272). RKO had its origins in what was first the Keith-Albee-Murdock, then Keith-Albee-Orpheum (KAO) vaudeville and musical theater chain that in the 1880s and 1890s had forged many elements of the national industrial character of modern popular culture (production formulas, exclusive bookings, the star system and national syndicates or networks) and which in the early twentieth century was one of the country's most powerful cultural production and exhibition combines. By the 1920s the KAO interests were becoming increasingly part of the motion picture business (purchasing Pathé and F.B.O. Pictures in 1927 and developing film sound recording and playback equipment), which itself was building on many of the industrial practices vaudeville had helped shape.[12] RCA's manufacturing interests and its linkages to Hollywood, the visual entertainment industries, publishing and the popular arts generally were developed even further with its role in television in the 1940s and 1950s.

Over and above the issue of interlinked ownership, the structure and profitability of the U.S. radio and television networks have always depended deeply on the technological capacities and rates and services of the telephone industry. A major provision of the dissolution of the original RCA ownership group was an agreement that AT&T would be the supplier of network lines to the NBC duopoly. For the next half-century AT&T would have that exclusive role for all the broadcast networks.

Meanwhile substantial ties between the telecommunications and film industries had been well established as early as the late 1920s. Even as it was withdrawing from formal ownership interests in RCA and NBC, AT&T was extending its influence in the motion picture business through its Electrical Research Products, Inc. subsidiary. ERPI managed the telephone company's patent interests (developed by another AT&T subsidiary, Western Electric) as the film industry moved into sound, leading to a series of direct and indirect financial controls of such companies as Fox, Loews, MGM, Paramount and United Artists, particularly during the Depression (Danielian, 1939, pp. 138–165).

The newspaper industry was initially ambivalent about the incursion of broadcasting into advertising and journalism, yet by the late 1920s publishers were becoming a significant component among owners of broadcasting stations.[13] That relationship continued to expand to the extent of raising some political concern and pressure on the FCC during the late 1930s to conduct an investigation of press ownership of radio stations. That study took place in the early 1940s, but it led to no new rules (Sterling and Kittross, 1990, pp. 105, 237–238). In that respect the press cross-ownership issue was handled by the FCC and the general policy establishment in much the same way as they were dealing with the near simultaneous Blue Book. The weak results of both studies reflected the similarly limited-impact significance of the Network Study. Altogether these inquiries constituted a clear indication of the overall limitations of the public interest and social responsibility doctrines in applied practice.

Broadcasting became increasingly involved in the film industry with the arrival of television. It did so through explicit cross-ownership, as in the merger of ABC and United Paramount Theaters in 1953. But another more defining form was the increasing interdependence between the networks and the Hollywood film production studios, as reflected in the programming contract between ABC and Disney in 1954.

Even without such forms of institutional intertwining, the commercial entertainment expectations and mass audience entertainment role of U.S. broadcasting were deeply shaped by the forms of popular publishing, theater, recorded music and film that had emerged before radio and that then in some cases had co-evolved with it.

Each of the major broadcasting networks demonstrated aspects of such vertical and horizontal integration over the decades. The radio and television industries were always part of a larger complex of communications equipment manufacturing, multimedia commercial entertainment production and distribution and related aspects of national and global industrial and defense policy. In that respect the fact that in the mid-1980s the three major networks were purchased by large commercial interests is not surprising.

For its part RCA came full circle when in 1986 it was repurchased by General Electric for $6.3 billion. That step brought RCA, and its NBC news operations, even more fully into a broad, global corporate enterprise worth tens of billions of dollars of sales and direct or indirect ownership interests in manufacturing and services that include electronics, electrical equipment and generation, nuclear power, automotive, railroad, aircraft and spacecraft supplies and components, department stores, wood products, textiles, insurance, and banking, (Bagdikian, 1992, pp. 11, 24, 208). In 1987 GE-RCA spun off its radio network, but shortly thereafter it began to enter directly and heavily into domestic cable television by purchasing the Financial News Network and re-establishing it as the CNBC channel; by forming a number of national and regional sports channels, including Prime Sports; and in league with other media interests by investing in a series of other cable program channels such as Bravo, the Independent Film Channel and American Movie Classics, all with Rainbow/Cablevision; Arts and Entertainment with Disney and Hearst; and the History channel with ABC and Hearst. In 1996 it established a link with the computer and interactive information industries by creating a partnership with Microsoft, the world's largest computer software manufacturer, to launch MSNBC, a multichannel cable and Internet news service to compete directly with CNN. By the mid-1990s NBC had also begun to expand abroad with satellite and cable television ventures in Europe and Asia.

Meanwhile, after fighting off acquisition bids from Ted Turner, Senator Jesse Helms and others, CBS was taken over initially in 1985–86 by Laurence Tisch and the Loews hotel, theater and financial corporation (Auletta, 1991, pp. 136–185). It was then put through a process of restructuring and dismemberment that among other things seriously undermined its strong network news division and what remained of the proud Murrow tradition of broadcast journalism (Katz, 1995).

Then in 1995–96 CBS was sold again, this time to Westinghouse. The new arrangement combined Westinghouse's large array of electrical manufacturing, nuclear power, satellite, telecommunications and defense industry interests with a broadcast complex of fourteen television and thirty-nine radio stations. Westinghouse had had a formative role in shaping U.S. broadcasting through its original partnership in the 1920s RCA combine and in its experimentations with advertising and popular programming on its own stations. It had remained in broadcasting over the decades after the RCA divestiture, through its continued ownership of its station group. Now, in the merger with CBS, it had returned to the national network and major market station ownership business. The size and range of its politically sensitive non-broadcast holdings, in conjunction with the prior reduction in the CBS news operations raised questions about the prospects for reinvigorating journalism in the new corporation.

A parallel takeover pattern was reflected in the fortunes of ABC. It was sold to Capital Cities in 1986 for $3.5 billion, a merger that combined the ABC network and ABC-owned radio and television stations with another group of radio and television stations, and a series of other media interests including partial or complete ownership of chains of U.S. newspapers, national trade publications, local cable television franchises, national cable program services and film companies (Bagdikian, 1992, p. 242; Maney, 1995a, p. 159). Then a decade later, in 1995, the new Capital Cities/ABC, still working out the implications of its merger, was purchased by the Disney Corporation for $19 billion. The new organization would combine ABC's television "network, ten television stations, twenty-one radio stations, six radio networks, ESPN and a variety of other [cable] assets [including Arts & Entertainment and Lifetime]" with Disney's "film, television, and animation studios and the Disney cable channel, theme parks, publishing enterprises, and retail stores" to create "the world's largest media company—one with a market value of fifty billion dollars" (Auletta, 1996c, p. 27). The deal would also enhance ABC's prior efforts to develop interactive programming, multimedia software and other products linked with the computer and Internet industries (Maney, 1995a, pp. 159–162).[14]

With the spread of more independent broadcasting television stations and their wider availability on cable television, new interests began to develop fourth, fifth and sixth broadcast television networks in the U.S. and to integrate them into larger media complexes. Perhaps the most significant of those was Rupert Murdoch's purchase in 1984–85 of 20th Century-Fox (film) and Metromedia (broadcasting) to create the Fox network (Blumler and Nossiter, 1991, p. 58). Fox thereby became the U.S. broadcasting component of Murdoch's global media empire, News Corporation, which by the mid-1990s had come to include major newspapers, film studios and distribution services, broadcast radio and television stations and networks, and satellite television services throughout Australia, North America, Great Britain, Europe, Latin America, India and considerable portions of Asia, including China (Maney, 1995a, pp. 173–179; Auletta, 1996a, pp. 31–32). The reach and power of these media assets permitted Murdoch a series of special legal and regulatory concessions throughout the world, including the U.S. (Bagdikian, 1992, p. 245).

The Fox network was built on the multichannel assumption that in an age of cable and improved broadcast reception the distinctions between VHF and UHF transmission were no longer so important. That situation was recognized by other interests, particularly in Hollywood, leading to creation of additional networks such as WB and UPN in 1995, each of which represented a marriage among some combination of major film, broadcast, cable and publishing interests, e.g., Time Warner and Paramount respectively. These networks were constituted of collections of affiliate broadcast stations, but it is clear that as with Fox their success would depend as much on their availability on cable as on the strengths of their programming niches and their associations with much larger media combines.

Meanwhile the cable television industry had grown from a modest disconnected series of small "mom and pop" CATV companies on the margins of the U.S. broadcast industry in the 1950s and 1960s, to a vast core enterprise in U.S. telecommunications. During that period cable had become highly regulated, largely as a matter of protection for the broadcast television industry. As interest grew in the prospects for a broader range of program services and as federal regulation in general became increasingly suspect, the situation for cable began to change. The FCC began to deregulate cable in the mid-1970s. That trend and the 1984 legislation provided by Congress and the Reagan administration (U.S. Congress, 1984) created for cable a special status that gave it unprecedented freedom in U.S. electronic communications. On the one hand it was relieved of most restrictions faced by broadcasters (limits on numbers of local franchises, Fairness Doctrine and political broadcasting rules), while on the other it was not to be considered a common carrier in the conventional telephone model. The latter provision meant that the industry was free to integrate vertically, i.e., to own its own program production sources, and not be required to be an open platform for other content providers. Meanwhile, as the federal government was deregulating cable, it also began to restrict the cable oversight and regulation rights of local and state governments. As a result, cable had a great deal of freedom to grow and develop, with only minimal public service requirements, as in the provision of a few public, education and government (PEG) access channels and modest franchise fees to support them. By the late 1980s cable was available in over fifty percent of U.S. households, its many different owners were consolidating into a relatively few large multiple system owning corporations (MSOs), four of whom controlled service to over twenty-five percent of cable households, and all the large MSOs in turn were beginning to expand vertically, particularly into content production.

Examples of their growth were reflected in the two largest MSOs, Telecommunications, Inc. (TCI) and Time Warner. The two represented quite different examples of the way cable television emerged in the U.S. TCI was self-grown; it had begun as a small group of isolated rural systems in Texas and the Mountain West, and through an aggressive process of re-investment it steadily leveraged itself into the country's largest MSO, with 16 percent of the subscribers by 1993. By the early 1990s TCI also had expanded into dozens of co-ventures, all oriented around the cable industry. It had reorganized itself into four divisions, separately handling its domestic, international, programming and technology activities. Through its Liberty Media division and the parent company TCI had become a significant partner in many cable program services, such as Cable News Network, TBS, Encore, The Discovery Channel, The Learning Channel, Home Shopping Network, QVC, Prime Network (sports), Black Entertainment Television, American Movie Classics, The Cartoon Network, Your Choice TV, The Family Channel and Court TV.

With most of these investments in place TCI was prepared to take a much bigger step on the national stage. In 1993 TCI entered into a merger agreement with Bell Atlantic, one of the post-AT&T divestiture regional Bell operating companies. That plan drew considerable press and congressional attention (U.S. Senate, 1993), as it seemed to represent the epitome of the mega-merger tendency in the communications industries of the late 1980s and early 1990s. The deal fell through over differences in the final asset valuations, but whether successful or not it was a harbinger of the increasingly large mergers that were occurring in communications as deregulation proceeded, raising concerns about the sheer capital size of all future such combines and the power they would exert in the telecommunications and media industries, as well as the political process. Indeed shortly thereafter an undaunted TCI entered into another joint venture, this time with Cox Communication, Comcast and Sprint to develop integrated, interactive telephone, cable and wireless technology.

Time Warner became a major player in cable by another route (Clurman, 1992). Time-Life had been one of the world's largest publishing enterprises, a central fixture in American journalism and politics. It had been uncomfortable in the broadcast television business, but by the early 1970s it was beginning to invest in cable (in what was to become its American Television Corporation division). Warner Communications was the heir of the Kinney services corporation and Warner Brother-Seven Arts film company. By the mid-1970s it had become a large, wide ranging media and entertainment company that also was developing cable (Warner-Amex). In addition to movies, records, popular publications, professional sports, cosmetics, video games (Atari) and its growing number of cable franchises, Warner was developing various program enterprises such as Home Box Office, MTV, Nickelodeon, and Qube. Between the mid-1970s and mid-1980s the two corporations had become directly competitive in cable franchising throughout the country.[15] In 1989–90 in spite of quite different histories and cultures the two merged, blending their heritages of traditional publishing, Hollywood entertainment and cable in what at the time was the largest media conglomerate in the world (Clurman, 1992, pp. 338–339).

Thereafter Time Warner was prepared to expand more widely in telecommunications and general media, particularly through its ventures in telephony and its efforts to acquire a major cable news service. The telephone excursion began when US West acquired a 25.5 percent interest in Time Warner ($2.4 billion), in a pattern parallel to that sought by TCI with Bell Atlantic. The news approach would be made by attempting to purchase the Turner Broadcasting System, a key property of which is CNN. But it also was recognition of Turner's expansion in other areas, such as professional sports and film studios (e.g., Castle Rock and New Line). Because TCI already owned 25 percent of the Turner properties, this offer revealed much about the increasingly interlocked, backdoor character of the major communications interests in the U.S.

By 1996 TCI and Time Warner together controlled about 34 percent of all cable subscribers in the U.S. and a vast array of television program ventures. Apart from the various backdoor partnerships in which they might be mutually involved, they were both engaged throughout the mid-1990s in a series of cable franchise trades, with one another and with many other major MSOs, in an effort to concentrate their respective regions of cable dominance in various major urban centers across the U.S.

With the breakup of AT&T, the local Bell telephone companies had been re-aggregated in the mid-1980s into a collection of seven regional operating companies (RBOCs). Those firms had as their primary business the maintenance of local telephone services, but they did not long remain static purveyors only of those. For the most part the post-divestiture policy environment continued to support an emerging model of multiple competitors in telecommunications. Throughout the 1980s the telephone companies re-oriented themselves in that light and as they did so they also began to work with the FCC and Congress to effect further regulatory changes that would permit them increasing freedoms not only in traditional telephony, but also in a wider range of data, information and entertainment services.

A major policy question was whether multiple, competing services implied multiple delivery systems into households and business. The telephone companies began to rebuild their core backbones and trunks with ISDN and fiber optics. Their last step "drops," however, remained low capacity, "twisted pair" copper wire, which without digital transmission severely restricted the range and speed of what actually could be delivered to customers. Meanwhile the cable companies had built their systems largely around networks of microwave transmission, satellite distribution and coaxial cable, providing them with a broadband delivery capacity into homes, but which in their infrastructures did not have the same degree of high speed, large volume and switching capacity as the telephone systems.

Much of the policy debate turned around the extent to which the telephone and cable industries would be permitted entry into one another's businesses. During the 1980s they remained restricted from one another in the U.S., but in anticipation of the electronic media continuing to open, the RBOCs and other telephone interests (primarily the major competing long distance carriers such as AT&T, MCI and Sprint) established experimental partnerships abroad with U.S. cable companies. So, for example, by the mid-1980s the Thatcher government in Britain had permitted the boroughs of London to be divided among a series of U.S. partnerships, in each case pairing one telephone company with one major cable firm, to provide cable television. That is, while they were otherwise struggling with one another domestically on Capitol Hill and in the courts, the telephone and cable companies were working together abroad in a series of new venture colonizations, testing their different technological and management cultures, all in preparation for the day when they would be working at home in a more thoroughly deregulated and concentrated multimedia environment.

By the early 1990s, and in anticipation of further statutory changes, all of the RBOCs had become multimedia corporations. Having already acquired a major interest in Time Warner in 1993, US West went another major step farther in 1996 by purchasing all of Continental Cablevision, at the time the nation's third largest cable company, for $5.3 billion, plus assumption of $5.6 billion in debt. The merger with Continental and the prior ties with Time Warner (the second largest MSO) immediately provided US West with the largest subscriber reach in the country and the possibility of providing "combined television and local telephone service in 66 of the top 100 cable markets" (Landler, 1996). The matter of Time Warner's proposed purchase of Turner broadcasting and CNN, and a suit over it by US West (Fabrikant, 1996), complicated the arrangement, but whatever the ultimate resolution of that dispute the tendency among the major cable and telecommunications interests to conflate their multimedia and journalistic enterprises was clear.

The computer industries had likewise become major players in the telecommunications industry complex that was increasingly enveloping U.S. broadcasting. The chief example was Microsoft which had become the dominant program software force in the personal computer business during the 1980s. By the mid-1990s Microsoft had begun to integrate vertically, engaging in various telecommunications, media and journalistic enterprises. In 1996 alone, it invested $500 million in the MSNBC cable television and on-line news service partnership with GE/RCA; it launched an on-line, Internet, public affairs "magazine," *Slate* (Auletta, 1996b); and it entered the Internet browser market to compete directly with Netscape and other services that had been providing consumer access to the World Wide Web. There were traditional concerns that Microsoft's sheer size would threaten the competitive prospects of other browser providers (*New York Times,* 1996), but in light of its increasing integration into news and media content production, the public interest questions about Microsoft appeared to be much greater than antitrust issues.

All these trends in the industries were reflections of how federal policy for communications had become dominated by a resurgent combination of new technology fever and marketplace ideology. As in previous phases of U.S. public policymaking for broadcasting, the need for a stronger public service effort was discounted in the face of the continuing, underlying and resurgent techno-libertarian expectations.

The history, terms, and ultimate contradictions of these policy premises had begun to come under closer critical review in the late-1980s and early 1990s (e.g., Bagdikian, 1983–92; Bogart, 1995; Gitlin, 1996; Horwitz, 1989; McChesney, 1994; Miller and Biden, 1996; Rowland, 1996). The more critical communication literature began to raise questions about the universal adequacy of marketplace models in communication, the truly revolutionary potential for new technology, the actual applied meanings of diversity and service in the deregulated environment, and the nature of the primary interests being served by the new orthodoxy.

But such perspectives were widely ignored in the applied policy process. The old contradictions of neo-libertarianism were resolved not by a direct confrontation with the weakened state of the social and cultural definition of communications, but by an embrace of more traditional, libertarianism with its reinforcement both of the material, commercial, business aspects of the media and telecommunications and of the social benefits expected of a more abundant technological capacity.

As a result the policy climate for broadcasting and telecommunications throughout the 1990s continued to be dominated by marketplace approaches and deregulatory initiatives with an ever further deepening of their commercial aspects, a growing concentration of ownership among broadcasting, cable, telephone, film and computer industries, and a further weakening of the already marginal noncommercial, public service structure.

The New Legislation

All these developments were reflected in the Telecommunications Act of 1996 (U.S. Congress, 1996), a massive piece of legislation that had strong bipartisan support and that was readily endorsed by the Clinton administration. The bipartisan policy approach had two thrust for broadcasting. One was to continue to encompass broadcasting in the overarching domain of telecommunications policy and its heavy emphasis on building the so-called "National Information Infrastructure" (NII). The other was to press the rhetorical crituque of televisions's violence and low moral standards.

To many the 1996 law was the appropriate, natural outcome of the deregulation trends of the preceding twenty years. Its proponents argued that it would break down the barriers to competition among communications industry sectors and encourage faster development of the NII. It would, for instance, permit telephone carriers to compete more with one another (locally, nationally, and internationally; wire and wireless), and it would allow cable, satellite broadcasting, telephone and other interests to compete more directly in each other's markets, in theory encouraging more competition and lower prices throughout electronic communications.

The law also was seen as a major victory for those concerned with violence, pornography and children's programming. Apart from providing for easier competition and inter-penetration among the telecommunications industries, the act variously encouraged or required development of digital advanced television (ATV), adoption of V-chip technology in future television set manufacturing, implementation of a program rating system for violence and sexual content in television programming, and a ban on "indecency" on the Internet. The law also encouraged the FCC to develop a regulatory requirement for children's programming in broadcasting, a provision that led to the adoption of an agreement between the Commission and the industry that broadcasters would guarantee up to three hours of children's programming a week (Mifflin, 1996).

The dual approach had been championed for the Clinton administration by Vice President Al Gore. During the 1980s then Senator Gore (D-Tenn.) had been associated with strong rhetorical critiques of popular culture and the quality of children's television. An "Atari Democrat" and "futurist" from the freshman congressional classes of the mid-1970s, the Senator also had become a strong proponent of the "information superhighway," of promoting the development of the new communications technologies as the way to increased economic and social progress.[16] In his respect his views were similar to those of another mid-1970s Tofflerite, Representative Newt Gingrich (R-Georgia), who after the Republican capture of Congress in 1994 was to become the Speaker of the House (Heilemann, 1995). They appeared to differ on the paths to be taken to the new world of competitive, open access cyberspace, with Gore remaining more cautious about the relative size and power of the competitors and the speed with which government deregulation could occur. Yet in the end the futures they envisioned seemed to be identical—a competitive, private enterprise marketplace of communications that, in the libertarian model of old, would somehow yield a true diversity of access and content that in turn would improve the public discourse and commonweal.

Critics of the legislation were less sanguine about its progressive social implications. Aspects of the critique drew from a literature that has patiently noted the longstanding tendency in U.S. discourse to over-state the revolutionary sociopolitical consequences of changes in communications technology (see Carey, 1989; Dery, 1996; Marvin, 1988). Development of ATV, for instance, had no inherent implications for improved content and social service. Permitting further expansion of both vertical and horizontal integration among multi-billion dollar communications combines might hasten the "500-channel" universe, but it begged the question of who would have access to those channels and what diversity of interest, voice and view they would accomodate (Gitlin, 1996, pp. 2, 6). There was concern that the bureaucracy of concentration would inhibit novelty, creativity, and quality of ideas (Bogart, 1995, p. 46).

From these perspectives the primary effect of the law was to permit Congress and the administration to appear to be democratizing the media while they were in fact helping the larger, pre-existing telecommunications interests rationalize among themselves the deployment of the profits from the ever expanding communications markets. This concern concluded that the law actually would continue to encourage precisely the sort of corporate integration and national-scale conglomeration that had historically been responsible for discouraging competition in telecommunications and broadcasting and undermining their prospects for quality of content.

Related criticism also pointed to the continuing primary association of U.S. communications with technocratic and economic issues, as opposed to matters social and cultural. In that light the information superhighway image is contradictory. While to many it bespeaks a great engine of economic activity, as the federal highway program surely has been, to others the highway system has stood for considerable urban destruction, visual blight, increased auto pollution, the degradation of public transportation and social dislocation. The superhighway image also firmly links information technologies to the transportation and industrial models of communication, weakening its association with notions of social and cultural process.

Other approaches suggested that the programming provisions in the law were largely symbolic, without much capacity for challenging the fundamental structure and character of U.S. broadcasting. The V-chip technology was not actually available at the time of the law, and it appeared to be several years away from integration into set manufacture (Maney, 1995b). The program ratings system would do little more than offer a guide to content; in an environment of otherwise near total deregulation in broadcasting it could not provide much incentive for change in program behavior. Enthusiasm for the children's content provisions was likewise tempered by recollections of the previous history of children's program regulation, wherein broadcasters had been regularly threatened, yet invariably forgiven and routinely re-licensed despite questionable performance in serving children (Kunkel and Watkins, 1987; Kunkel, 1988).[17] And, finally, the "indecency" ban in the portion of the law known as the Communications Decency Act was widely viewed as unconstitutional, a judgment quickly reinforced by the Pennsylvania federal district court in the law's initial court test (American Civil Liberties Union, et al., 1996).

Additional criticism suggested that the law was missing a major element, in that it contained no provisions relative to public service communications. This perspective noted that in freeing most of telecommunications and broadcasting from all but the most minimal of requirements, the law failed to provide for any structural alternatives to the purely commercial exploitation of the new media. The act provided for no public dividend for use by public service institutions such as might be derived from the proceeds of the ATV reassignment program or spectrum auctions, or from taxes on commercial license sales and the increased profits of the telecommunications industries.

This line of critique also noted that while the 1996 act was being passed, Congress and the administration were simultaneously reducing federal funding for public broadcasting and driving it even further into commercialization. Spectrum auctions were occurring in the mid-1990s, but the proceeds were going solely into deficit reduction; they were not being used to offset the deficiencies of the communications marketplace. During 1995–96 Congress did consider creating a public broadcasting trust fund (Behrens, 1996). But that proposal was a weak measure. Its proposed endowment of only $1.0 billion would yield even lower amounts of federal support for public broadcasting than had been the case in the Bush years. The proposal was unclear about the source of that endowment, and it dealt too narrowly with the question of multiple station communities.

What is most telling about the 1996 proposal for public broadcasting legislation is that it was not considered as part of the Telecommunications Act. In no other major nation is it conceivable that such a sweeping piece of national policy would have been debated, let alone passed, without serious attention to the situation of public broadcasting. To have ignored public broadcasting in the principal media law of the era and then to have tried to deal with it only as an afterthought was to reiterate the old pattern of a continuingly small, under-funded vision for public service communications in the U.S.

Altogether, then, the new law may be most significant for the way it reflected the deeper historical tendencies in U.S. communications policy. Whether oriented more toward the neo-libertarian, fiduciary licensing, social responsibility philosophy of broadcasting's first half century, or toward the more explicitly classically liberal approach that linked the subsequent quarter-century of deregulated new technologies with an older, pre-industrial eighteenth century marketplace model of communications, the core faith was always that a commercially driven, private enterprise media system would provide all the range of choice, quality and public service necessary in the electronic media, particularly in an era of technological abundance.

The 1996 act did reflect two needs of the then troubled Clinton administration. One was to associate itself with the powerful rhetoric of industrial communications technocracy—"the bridge to the twenty-first century." The other was to be able early in an election year to demonstrate the administration's ability to accomplish some legislation. Prior failure in health care reform and other areas required an image of success in other sectors. It appeared that the public interest, including freedom of speech, could be compromised in communication policy making in order to create an image of legislative capacity. The administration's support of the act also suggested the political power of the status quo in U.S. media and telecommunications. No U.S. president has evern been elected on a campaign platform arguing for a major realignment of underlying federal communications policy.

In keeping with the previous two decades of technocratic libertarianism the 1996 act was marked by a thorough unwillingness to confront the continuing public interest and journalistic contradictions for U.S. broadcasting posed by its increasing integration into a steadily growing, concentrated, global, commercial telecommunications cartel. As had long been the case in the U.S. there was little capacity to see the need for affirmative structural measures that would provide institutional alternatives to the historic failures of reliance on either a system of light touch, fiduciary licensing or the marketplace. Broadcasting would continue to exist, but regardless of the pace of its absorption into a digital and even cyberspace nexus, the prospects for its multichannel capacity would continue to be constrained by its exclusively commercial purpose. Whether oriented toward mass or niche audiences, whether supported by advertising or subscription, the fundamental purposes would remain to increase revenues, enhance asset values and treat people primarily as consumers. Those conditions would continue to vex the likelihood of broadcasting's ability to deliver truly diverse services dedicated to a broadly defined public interest in which the values of citizenship and social growth would be central ethics.

NOTES

1. There appears never to have been much explicit debate about the relative merits of private vs. public ownership of the press during the colonial and early republican periods. The context of an emerging private enterprise economy and liberal democracy seems to have settled the question implicitly. The occasional struggles over censorship focused attention on the rights of individual writers and editors as private citizens, and the First Amendment clearly assumed conditions of predominantly private ownership for the press. From within this legal and economic milieu it seems to have been nearly impossible to have posed questions about contradictions and unmet public interest needs in the private marketplace of communication.

2. Much of the broadcasting literature traces the origins of the technology and industry, and some of its relates those issues to the emerging cultural imagination and social concerns about mass communication. So, for instance, it is common to find broadcasting portrayed as the fulfillment of one of the early misunderstandings by Alexander Graham Bell himself and many of his journalist celebrators about how the telephone would work as a mass medium (Barnouw, 1966; Czitrom, 1982). Likewise much of the policy literature (including this paper) traces the relationship between broadcasting law and the legal and regulatory nexus established around telecommunications, utility and antitrust developments by the turn of century. But for a clear understanding of the U.S. policy environment it is important to look behind the technology to rediscover the power of libertarian ideology and its contradictions as they had already begun to work themselves out in the press and in public beliefs about what was steadily becoming an industrialized communications system.

3. The special rate policy for newspapers was formally established by the Post Office Act of 1792 (John, 1995, pp. 30–42; Kielbowicz, 1989, pp. 31–36), and by the mid-nineteenth century it began to be extended to magazines and books. While occasionally debated since, the policy was not significantly challenged until Congress, the Postal Rate Commission, and the Postal Service became engaged in a series of debates about postal competitiveness, privati-

zation and deregulation in the mid-1990s. Among the concerns about the various legislative and rate "reforms" were their threats to the public service character of the postal system and the role therein of special rates for journalistic publications (Hernandez, 1996).

4. The intertwining of the private and public in U.S. communications was perhaps most tellingly symbolized in the frequent co-location of the village printing press and post office. It was not uncommon in the colonial and early republican periods to find the private printer/publisher/editor also holding the community's postal franchise (Kielbowicz, 1989, pp. 13–19, 40–41). Moreover, the public post office/private printing establishment frequently also served as a trading post, village store and coffee house. Altogether such establishments were major public gathering places wherein the interests of private individuals, commerce, politics, and government were all served and intimately implicated in one another.

5. The U.S. Navy was the primary federal sponsor of the RCA plan. A chief proponent of the arrangement was the then Assistant and Acting Secretary of the Navy, Franklin Delano Roosevelt (Barnouw, 1966, pp. 47–48, 57–58). His approval of government sanctioned patent pooling among major U.S. telecommunications interests provides telling insight into how the private-public ownership issue for broadcasting would be addressed in the New Deal after he became President fourteen years later.

6. Images of service to large simultaneous audiences were not entirely foreign in radio. There had been proposals for and experiments with radio *broadcasting* prior to the 1920s, but they had been isolated and unorganized, without adequate financial backing (Barnouw, 1966, pp. 33–38, 78–79). The predominant image of radio was as wireless, point-to-point signaling between two individuals or transmission stations, not as a mass medium. Note the irony of how this misperception is the reverse of that for the telephone at its outset; see fn. 2.

7. To this day there are no reservations for public radio in the AM "standard" band frequencies.

8. There is a view that in forcing NBC to give up one of its networks, the government might actually have eliminated more programming diversity than it fostered. This argument contends that, because RCA owned both and did not need them to compete with one another, it was content to permit the two NBC networks to develop different, complementary strains of programming, thereby serving a broader range of tastes and interests. With the profits of one network cross-subsidizing the costs of the other it may have been possible for the latter to be more of a high culture, educative service in the mold of the national public service broadcasters abroad, than direct commercial competition among separate companies normally permits.

9. The image of federal regulation portrayed by the broadcast industry, and uncritically accepted by much of the literature, suggests a more meddlesome FCC pushing the bounds of its constitutional authority. However, any careful comparison with the nature of broadcast regulation in virtually all other democracies would suggest that government "interference" in the U.S. has been far less onerous and, indeed, far more protectionist than is commonly understood.

10. This takes the 1952 ruling as the initial allocation. In fact, allocations began as early as 1939 when television service was first authorized, continuing after World War II on twelve VHF channels between 1945 and 1948. All during that period and then through the entire "freeze" of 1948–1952, when the commercial television system was largely established, there were no noncommercial reservations.

11. As, for instance, with the founding of the journal, *The Public Interest* in 1965; see also Horwitz, pp. 206–207 and fns. 25–28 on the role of the Olin Foundation, the Rand Corporation, the American Enterprise Institute, the Hoover Institution and other corporately sponsored think tanks.

12. RCA's agent in the KAO purchase and transformation was industrialist, financier, Boston political figure, and FBO executive Joseph P. Kennedy, who also was the father of a future U.S. president (John F. Kennedy), a major contributor to the campaigns of Franklin D. Roosevelt, a putative presidential candidate himself and eventually ambassador to Great Britain. The senior Kennedy's role signaled the growing ties among Hollywood, Wall Street, broadcasting, telecommunications and national politics.

13. A characteristic example came in 1924 with the acquisition of a radio station by the McCormick family, owners of *The Chicago Tribune*. The station was to become one of the few, and therefore highly valuable, 50,000 watt licenses which at night had large regional and frequently almost national propaganda coverage. The McCormick/Tribune station was granted the call letters WGN, standing for "World's Greatest Newspaper." In the mid-1990s the Tribune stations remain a major division of a large media corporation consisting of four other radio stations, eight television stations, five newspapers, a regional news cable channel and the Tribune Entertainment Company.

14. It also formalized and brought to much larger fruition the ABC-Disney-Hollywood associations that had begun in the mid-1950s.

15. While it was growing as a major cable MSO and program developer in the mid-to-late 1970s, Time-Life had become among the first U.S. television interests to use the satellite for national program delivery, initially to develop HBO as a national movie channel. The others first exploring the satellite possibilities were public television (PBS) and Turner broadcasting in its initial "superchannel" (WTBS) effort. The traditional commercial broadcasting networks were much slower to adopt satellite delivery technology, only disengaging from their old AT&T terrestrial system in the 1980s.

16. The Vice President is often credited with coining the "information superhighway" term. In fact, the concept has an earlier history (e.g., Smith, 1972). Regardless of the term's origins, Mr. Gore intended its adoption to link the information technology developments to the image of the national interstate highway system championed by his father, Senator Albert Gore, Sr., in the 1950s (Heilemann, 1995).

17. Among the most egregious examples were the way in which in spite of a formal piece of legislation (U.S. Congress, 1990), the FCC had permitted the industry such wide latitude in the definition of children's programming as to lead to the counting of adult entertainment programming and program-length commercials as part of its children's service.

REFERENCES

Allen, Frederick L. (1931). *Only Yesterday: An Informal History of the Nineteen Twenties,* New York: Harper.

American Civil Liberties Union vs. Janet Reno, Attorney General of the United States, (1996). 929 F. Supp. 824 (E.D. Pa. 1996), June 11, 1996.

Auletta, Ken (1991). *Three Blind Mice: How the TV Networks Lost Their Way,* New York: Random House.

———. (1996a). "Fourteen Truisms for the Communications Revolution," *Media Studies Journal,* 10:2–3, Spring/Summer, pp. 29–38.

———. (1996b). "The Reëducation of Michael Kinsley," *New Yorker,* May 13, 1996, pp. 58–73.

———. (1996c). "Marriage, No Honeymoon," *New Yorker,* July 19, 1996, pp. 26–31.

Bagdikian, Ben H. (1992). *The Media Monopoly,* 4th Ed., Boston: Beacon [earlier editions in 1983, 1987, and 1990].

Barnouw, Erik (1966). *A History of Broadcasting in the United States, Vol. 1, A Tower in Babel,* New York: Oxford University Press.

Behrens, Steve (1996). "Trust Fund Bill Motionless in Last Rush of Congress," *Current,* 15:16, September 2, pp. 1, 11.

Blakely, Robert J. (1979). *To Serve the Public Interest: Educational Broadcasting in the United States,* Syracuse, NY: Syracuse University Press.

Blumler, Jay G. and T. J. Nossiter, eds. (1991). *Broadcasting Finance in Transition: A Comparative Handbook,* New York: Oxford University Press.

Bogart, Leo (1995). *Commercial Culture: The Media System and the Public Interest,* New York: Oxford University Press.

Briggs, Asa (1965). *The History of Broadcasting in the United Kingdom, Vol. II: The Golden Age of Wireless,* London: Oxford University Press.

Cabinet Committee on Cable Communications (1974). *Cable: Report to the President,* Washington, D.C.: U.S. Government Printing Office.

Carey, James W. (1989). *Communication as Culture: Essays on Media and Society,* Boston: Unwin Hyman.

Carnegie Commission on Educational Television (1967). *Public Television: A Program for Action,* New York: Bantam Books.

Clurman, Richard M. (1992). *To the End of Time: The Seduction and Conquest of a Media Empire,* New York: Simon & Schuster.

Commission on Freedom of the Press (1947). *A Free and Responsible Press,* Chicago: University of Chicago Press.

Cowan, Geoffrey (1978). *See No Evil: The Backstage Battle over Sex and Violence on Television,* New York: Simon & Schuster.

Czitrom, Daniel J. (1982). *Media and the American Mind: From Morse to McLuhan,* Chapel Hill: U. North Carolina Press.

Danielian, N. R. (1939). *A. T. & T.: The Story of Industrial Conquest,* New York: Vanguard Press.

Dery, Mark (1996). *Escape Velocity: Cyberculture at the End of the Century,* New York: Grove Press.

Fabrikant, Geraldine (1996). "A Bold Gamble or Tit-for-Tat?," *New York Times,* February 28, pp. C1, C4.

Federal Communications Commission (1946). "Public Service Responsibility of Broadcast Licensees," March 7, 1946 [Kahn, pp. 148–163].

——— (1952). "Sixth Report and Order," 17 Reg. 3905, 3908 (41 FCC 148, 158), April 14, [Kahn, pp. 182–190].

——— (1960). "Report and Statement of Policy re: Commission en banc Programming Inquiry," 25 Fed. Reg. 7291 (44 FCC 2303), July 29, 1960 [Kahn, pp. 191–203].

——— (1969). "WHDH, Inc.," 16 FCC 2d l.

Fowler, Mark S. and Daniel L. Brenner (1982). "A Marketplace Approach to Broadcast Regulation," *Texas Law Review,* 60:2, pp. 207–257.

Gilbert, Douglas (1940). *American Vaudeville: Its Life and Times,* New York: Whittlesey House (McGraw-Hill).

Gitlin, Todd (1996). "Not So Fast," *Media Studies Journal,* 10:2–3, Spring/Summer, pp. 1–6.

Green, Abel and Joe Laurie (1951). *Show Biz: From Vaude to Video,* New York: Henry Holt and Company.

Griffith, Thomas (1989). "Press Lords and Media Barons," *Gannett Center Journal,* 3:1, pp. 1–10.

Harlow, Alvin F. (1936). *Old Wires and New Waves: The History of the Telegraph, Telephone, and Wireless,* New York: D. Appleton-Century Co.

Heilemann, John (1995). "The Making of the President 2000," *Wired,* December, pp. 152–155, 218–230.

Hernandez, Debra Gersh (1996). "Proposed Postal Rates Save, Skewer Newspapers;" "Postal Rate Debate Continues;" "Postal Reform Process Begins;" *Editor and Publisher,* February 3, 1996, pp. 17, 31; April 20, 1996, pp. 14–15; July 27, 1996, pp. 17, 36.

Horwitz, Robert Britt (1989). *The Irony of Regulatory Reform: The Deregulation of American Telecommunication,* New York: Oxford University Press.

Jensen, Jay W. (1957). "Liberalism, Democracy and the Mass Media," unpublished doctoral dissertation, Department of Journalism, College of Communications, University of Illinois at Urbana-Champaign.

John, Richard R. (1995). *Spreading the News: The American Postal System from Franklin to Morse,* Cambridge, MA: Harvard University Press.

Jowett, Garth (1976). *Film: The Democratic Art,* Boston: Little, Brown.

Kahn, frank J., ed. (1984). *Documents of American Broadcasting,* 4th ed., Englewood Cliffs, NJ: Prentice-Hall.

Katz, Jon (1995). "CBS Mourning News," *Gentleman's Quarterly,* December, pp. 112–115+.

Kielbowicz, Richard B. (1989). *News in the Mail: The Press, Post Office and Public Information, 1700–1860s,* Westport, CT: Greenwood Press.

Kunkel, Dale and Bruce Watkins (1987). "Evolution of Children's Television Regulatory Policy," *Journal of Broadcasting and Electronic Media,* 31:4, Fall, pp. 367–389.

——— (1988). "From a Raised Eyebrow to a Turned Back: The FCC and Children's Product-Related Programming," *Journal of Communication,* 38:4, Autumn, pp. 90–108.

Landler, Mark (1996). "US West's Continental Ambitions," *New York Times,* February 28, pp. C1, C4.

Lodge, Henry Cabot, ed. (1888). *The Federalist: a commentary on the Constitution of the United States, reprinted from the original text of Alexander Hamilton, John Jay and James Madison,* New York & London: G. P. Putnam's Sons.

Maney, Kevin (1995a). *Megamedia Shakeout: The Inside Story of the Leaders and the Losers in the Exploding Communications Industry,* NY: J. Wiley.

——— (1995b). "One Teensy Little Problem with This New V-chip," *USA TODAY,* August 9, 1995, B, 1:2.

Marvin, Carolyn (1988). *When Old Technologies Were New: Thinking About Electric Communication in the Late Nineteenth Century,* New York: Oxford University Press.

McChesney, Robert W. (1994). *Telecommunications, Mass Media & Democracy: The Battle for the Control of U.S. Broadcasting, 1928–1935,* New York: Oxford University Press.

McLuhan, Marshall and Quentin Fiore (1968). *War and Peace in the Global Village,* New York: McGraw-Hill.

Mifflin, Lawrie (1996). "U.S. Mandates Educational TV for Children," *New York Times,* August 9, 1996, A, 16:4; "TV Broadcasters Agree to Three Hours of Children's Educational Programs a Week," *New York Times,* July 30, 1996, A, 8:1.

Miller, Mark C. and Janine Biden (1996). "The National Entertainment State," *The Nation* 262:22, June 3, 1996.

National Broadcasting Co., Inc., et al. v. United States et al. (1943). 319 U.S. 190, May 10, 1943 [Kahn, pp. 124–147].

Nerone, John C., ed. (1995). *Last Rights: Revisiting Four Theories of the Press,* Urbana: University of Illinois Press.

New York Times (1996). "The Browser Duel," September 16, 1996, A-14.

Office of Communication of the United Church of Christ v. Federal Communications Commission (1966). 359 F. 2d 994 (D.C. Cir.) March 25, 1966 [Kahn, pp. 233–249].

Peterson, Theodore (1956). "The Social Responsibility Theory of the Press" in Fred S. Siebert, et al., *Four Theories of the Press,* Urbana: University of Illinois Press.

Red Lion Broadcasting Co., Inc., et al. v. Federal Communications Commission (1969). 395 U.S. 367, June 9, 1969 [Kahn, pp. 274–293].

Reith, J. C. W. (1924). *Broadcast over Britain,* London: Hodder & Stoughton.

Rivers, William L., Theodore Peterson and Jay W. Jensen (1971). *The Mass Media and Modern Society, 2d ed.,* San Francisco: Rinehart Press.

Rowland, Willard D., Jr. (1982). "The Process of Reification: Recent Trends in Communications Legislation and Policy-Making," *Journal of Communication,* 32:4, Autumn pp. 114–136.

——— (1983). *The Politics of TV Violence: Policy Uses of Communication Research,* Beverly Hills: Sage.

——— (1989). "The Meaning of 'The Public Interest' in Communications Policy—Part I: Its Origins in State and Federal Regulation," Presentation to the International Communications Association, Annual Conference, San Francisco, CA.

——— (1993). "Public-Service Broadcasting in the United States: Its Mandate, Institutions and Conflicts," in Robert K. Avery, ed., *Public-Service Broadcasting in a Multichannel Environment,* New York: Longman/Annenberg Program in Communication Policy.

——— (1996). "Television Violence Redux: The Continuing Mythology of Effects," Chapter 7 in Martin Barker and Julian Petley, eds., *Challenging the 'Effects' Tradition,* London: Routledge, in press.

Schiller, Dan (1982). *Telematics and Government,* Norwood, NJ: Ablex.

Schlesinger, Arthur M., Jr. (1957). *The Age of Roosevelt: The Crisis of the Old Order,* 1919–1933, Boston: Houghton Mifflin.

Schwartz, Bernard (1973). *Economic Regulation of Business and Industry,* Vol. I. New York: Chelsea House.

Skornia, Harry Jay (1965). *Television and Society: An Inquest and Agenda for Improvement,* New York: McGraw-Hill.

Sloan Commission on Cable Communications (1971). *On the Cable: The Television of Abundance,* New York: McGraw-Hill.

Smith, Anthony (1973). *The Shadow in the Cave; A Study of the Relationship between the Broadcaster, his Audience and the State.* London: Allen & Unwin.

Smith, Ralph Lee (1972). *The Wired Nation—Cable TV: The Electronic Communication Highway,* New York: Harper & Row.

Smythe, Dallas (1957). *The Structure and Policy of Electronic Communication,* Urbana: University of Illinois Press.

Sterling, Christopher H. and John M. Kittross (1990). *Stay Tuned: A Concise History of American Broadcasting,* 2d ed., Belmont, CA: Wadsworth.

Surgeon General's Scientific Advisory Committee on Television and Social Behavior (1972). *Television and Growing Up: The Impact of Televised Violence,* Washington, DC: Government Printing Office.

Thompson, Robert L. (1947). *Writing a Continent: The History of the Telegraph Industry in the United States, 1832–1866,* Princeton: Princeton University Press.

U.S. Congress (1866). "An Act to aid in the construction of telegraph lines, and to secure to the Government the use of the same for postal, military and other purposes," 14 Stat. 221, 39th Congress, Session 1, Chapter 230, July 24, 1866.

——— (1927). "Radio Act of 1927," P.L. 69-632, Feb. 23, 1927 [Kahn, pp. 40–56].

———— (1934). "Communications Act of 1934," P.L. 73-416, June 19, 1934 [Kahn, pp. 417–485].

———— (1967). "Public Broadcasting Act of 1967," P.L. 90-129, 102 Stat. 3207, November 7, 1967.

———— (1984). "Cable Communications Policy Act of 1984," P.L. 98-549, 98 Stat. 2779, (47 U.S.C. §601), October 30, 1984.

———— (1990). "Children's Television Act of 1990," P.L. 101-437, H.R. 1677, October 18, 1990.

———— (1992). "Cable Television Consumer Protection and Competition Act of 1992," P.L. 102-385, October 5, 1992.

———— (1996). "Telecommunications Act of 1996," P.L. 104-104, S. 652, February 8, 1996.

U.S. House (1958). *Network Broadcasting,* Report of the Committee on Interstate and Foreign Commerce, Report No. 1297, 85th Congress, 2d Session, January 27, 1958, U.S.G.P.O.

U.S. House, Subcommittee on Communications (1977). *Options Papers* (Staff Report), 95th Congress, 2d Sess. U.S.G.P.O.

U.S. Kerner Commission (1968). "Report of the National Advisory Commission on Civil Disorders," U.S.G.P.O.

U.S. Post Office Department (1914). "Government ownership of electrical means of communication," Letter from the postmaster general, in response to a Senate resolution of January 12, 1914, 63d Congress, 2d Sess., Senate, Doc. 399, U.S.G.P.O.

U.S. Senate (1993). *Examining the Effect of Megamergers in the Telecommunications Industry,* Hearings, Subcommittee on Antitrust, Monopolies, and Business Rights, Committee on the Judiciary, 103rd Congress, 1st Session, October 27, November 16, and December 17, 1993, U.S.G.P.O.

Wiebe, Robert (1967). *The Search for Order, 1877–1920,* New York: Hill & Wang.

QUESTIONS FOR DISCUSSION

1. Contrast the Libertarian heritage discussed by Rowland with the Progressive heritage analyzed by Goodman and Gring. Are there contradictions in these accounts? Where and how do the two perspectives come together? Relate both to "social responsibility theory."

2. What, according to Rowland, are the main factors behind the United States' failure to set up a significant public broadcasting service? What changed to allow the creation of PBS in the late 1960s? What happened to undercut these efforts?

3. How well do Rowland's conclusions about the nature and probable effects of the Telecommunications Act of 1996 hold up in the light of recent events? How does his conclusion relate to either the Libertarian or Progressive heritage discussed above?

INFOTRAC COLLEGE EDITION

Look in InfoTrac College Edition under "television and regulation" for more information on this topic. Also try "deregulation and television."

15

Prime-Time Television
in the Gay '90s
Network Television, Quality
Audiences, and Gay Politics[1]

RON BECKER

The mid to late 1990s were dubbed "the Gay '90s" by a popular entertainment magazine, in part because of the increased presence of gay and lesbian characters on television. In this article, Ron Becker examines why, after little presence on television prior to the 1990s, gay and lesbian characters and issues are now a regular part of prime-time television. Becker argues that this phenomenon is due less to liberal cultural and political impulses of network executives than to their desire to retain a quality audience in the increasingly competitive era of cable television and narrowcasting.

According to Becker, the quality audience sought by network programmers consists of the elusive 18- to 49-year-old consumer, gay or straight, with liberal attitudes and disposable income. Becker dubs this audience "socially liberal, urban-minded professionals," or "slumpies." In order to appeal to this imagined audience, network television constructs representations of gays and lesbians as upscale, white, and witty urbanites, thus creating new and potentially damaging stereotypes. These stereotypes, Becker argues, are

From *Velvet Light Trap* 42 (Fall 1998): 36–47. © 1998 by the University of Texas Press. All rights reserved.

detrimental to gay politics and progressive social movements in that they erase the real lived experience of gays and lesbians who do not conform to television's images of them, especially people of color and of lower socio-economic status.

———————

In 1994, *Entertainment Weekly* dubbed the decade "the Gay '90s."[2] A look at the period's prime-time network-television programming seems to prove the announcement prophetic. Throughout its first four decades, television virtually denied the existence of homosexuality. The families, workplaces, and communities of most network programming were exclusively heterosexual. As recently as the early '90s, in fact, even the most astute television viewers could likely spot only a handful of openly gay, lesbian, and bisexual characters in an entire year of network television. After only a few television seasons, however, gay-themed episodes and references to homosexuality were everywhere. By the 1995–96 season, for example, even the relatively casual viewer might have spotted several openly gay characters in just one night. At least two dozen openly gay, lesbian, and bisexual recurring characters were featured on almost 20 shows, including *Roseanne, In the Pursuit of Happiness, Mad About You, Spin City, Chicago Hope, Melrose Place, N.Y.P.D. Blue, My So-Called Life, Fired Up, The Crew, Style & Substance,* and *High Society.* Hit shows such as *Wings, Veronica's Closet, Suddenly Susan, Grace Under Fire, Dr. Quinn—Medicine Woman, Beverly Hills 90210, Coach, Cosby, Homicide: Life on the Street, Murphy Brown, E.R., The Nanny,* and *Law & Order,* as well as short-lived programs like *Hudson Street* and *The Faculty,* all had specific episodes focused on gay topics and many others were riddled with gay references and jokes. In addition to the dramatic increase of openly and lesbian characters, a good number of avowedly straight characters were mistaken (or not) as being gay or lesbian, including just about every male cast member on *Friends, The Single Guy, Frasier,* and *Seinfeld.* The expansion of gay and lesbian issues on prime-time television reached a new level with the April, 1997, coming-out episode of *Ellen.* Gay-themed television, it seems, was the programming trend of the '90s.

In this essay I explore a major force behind this recent trend—namely network desire to target a quality audience in the increasingly competitive era of '90s narrowcasting. The recent representations of gays and lesbians certainly existed within wider social contexts. The gays-in-the-military debate, the Clinton presidency, anti-gay legislation battles, lesbian chic, and openly gay and lesbian celebrities were only a few of the multiple and interwoven factors at play behind television's fascination with homosexuality. Yet such cultural and political impulses interacted with the structures, constraints, and imperatives of network television. Here, I focus specifically on industry conceptions of its quality audience and argue that network executives incorporated gay and lesbian material into their prime-time line ups in order to attract an audience of "sophisticated," upscale, college-educated and liberally-minded adults.[3] For the networks, this programming strategy also had the advantage of targeting a distinct segment of

→ narrowcasting

that demographic group—namely middle and upper-class gays and lesbians. While examining the relationship between the industry's conception of its audiences and the recent deluge of prime-time homosexuality helps explain some of the forces at play behind one of the decade's dominant programming trends, it also leads to a consideration of the serious consequences at stake for gay politics.[4]

The audience is crucial to the business of television. As the commodity sold by networks to advertisers, it constitutes the economic raison d'être of the industry. Yet, as many critics point out, the television audience doesn't simply exist out there for network executives to find; it isn't, as Ien Ang asserts "an ontological given."[5] Instead, networks use tools such as ratings and marketing research to produce a specific understanding of its audience. Although influenced by the social conditions in which real viewers live, industry conceptions of the television audience are also shaped by the economic imperatives of an advertiser-based medium. Consequently, for the American television industry, at least, the audience is a collection of consumers, known by their demographic profiles—consumers which it tries to attract through specific programming.

While the industry sees the television audience as a commodity to be drawn in, packaged and sold, critics have encouraged us to see television audiences from alternative perspectives. Feminist media scholars have looked at the lived social experiences of female viewers and at how watching television contributes to the construction of women's gendered identities. Similarly, many involved in the gay and lesbian civil rights struggle have seen the television audience as a collection of political constituents that can be mobilized not to buy consumer products but rather to participate in supporting gay rights—a perspective that is especially important as gay and lesbian characters and gay-themed material become increasingly prevalent on network television. Work on television audiences, however, must also analyze how industry conceptions of its audience help influence the ways socially-situated viewers engage with television. Integrated approaches to media studies, most notably Julie D' Acci's examination of *Cagney & Lacey* and the struggles among producers, networks executives, writers, and viewers to define notions of feminity through the program, have begun to explore these relationships, yet more work needs to be done.[6] Consequently, this paper focuses on the economic imperatives behind television's use of gay material and begins to examine the subsequent tensions that develop between industry notions of consumers and a gay civil rights notion of politicized citizens.

TARGETING A QUALITY AUDIENCE
IN THE '90s

As an industry, network television has always been driven by selling viewers to sponsors, and although anxious to claim possession of the mass audience, especially in prime time, the networks have, at least since the 70s, consistently been interested in the appeal of their programs to certain demographic groups. The so-called "quality audience," broadly comprised of upscale adults, 18 to 49—those assumed to be the most active consumers with the most disposable income—has been the underlying target demographic of all three networks for several decades.[7] Research, however, has shown that highly-educated and upscale viewers tend to watch less television than their lower-income counterparts and that those who do watch are increasingly switching to cable channels.[8] Consequently, networks have been forced to work particularly hard in order to attract these hard-to-reach viewers. Although the industry maintains an idea of a broad audience of upscale adults, in practice, the networks have had to work from a narrow and fluid conception of the quality audience. Reacting to changes in social and cultural contexts, the networks have continually updated their notion of this most prized audience segment and have repeatedly developed new programming strategies to target those specific viewers. In the early 70s, CBS, concerned with the revenue of its urban-centered owned-and-operated stations, used *All in the Family* and *Mary Tyler Moore* to attract a distinctly urban demographic. In the 1980s, as cable television and changes in women's employment patterns forced them to reassess their audiences and programming strategies, the networks used shows like *Cagney & Lacey, Kate and Allie,* and *Designing Women* to target a quality audience of upscale working women.

In the 1990s, the networks, adapting to both industrial and social changes, once again updated both their profile of the quality audience and their programming strategies. The increasing pressure from intense competition forced the networks to target even narrower audience segments and to court them more aggressively with programming geared to their specific interests. Between 1984 and 1996, the big three networks' audience share dropped from 73.9% to 50.5%.[9] At the same time, Generation X-ers—with tastes and attitudes shaped by record levels of college enrollment, the AIDS epidemic, Reaganomics, and childhoods saturated with cable television and marked by high divorce rates—came of age. Believed to be critical individualists and cynical libertarians with seen-it-all attitudes, these latest members of the 18-to-34 demographic forced many companies to rethink their conception of the adult market. Consequently, in the mid-90s, the quality demographic that became the most widely sought after wasn't simply upscale adults, 18 to 49, but more specifically "hip," "sophisticated," urban-minded, white, college-educated, upscale 18-to-49 year olds with liberal attitudes, disposable income, and a distinctively edgy and ironic sensibility—a group basically comprised of segments of the aging yet still socially progressive and upwardly mobile baby boomers and the youthful twenty and thirty-somethings that followed in their wake.[10] While the industry never found a name for the members of this new psychographic market, I will dub them slumpies: socially-liberal, urban-minded, professionals. As networks worked to cultivate the slumpy audience, prime-time schedules saw a slew of programs featuring what network executives believed the world of this audience looked like—a world that, in many cases, included gays and lesbians.

NBC was the network that has targeted this specific quality audience most forcefully. In the early '90s, NBC was a weak third in the ratings. ABC, on the other hand, was the top-rated network in prime time—its success partially built on strong family sitcoms like *Full House, Grace Under Fire, Home Improvement,* and *Family Matters.* Working within the broadcasting industry's twenty-year-old de facto Family Hour policy, ABC scheduled shows with kid appeal during the early evening hours. Scheduling executives hoped to attract children who, in turn, would bring the parents—the network's real target audience—as the family watched TV together. While shows with strong kid appeal helped ABC capture first place in 1994, NBC gained enormous ground by abandoning the family-hour strategy and blatantly going after 18-to-49-year-olds—especially the young, hip, urban, professional segment.[11] Shows like *Friends, Seinfeld, Frasier,* and *Mad About You* successfully appealed to the new quality audience.

NBC's new strategy was encouraged by a perceived change in viewing practices among the industry's audience. Ted Harbert, president of ABC Entertainment, explains, "Seventy percent of households now have more than one TV set. . . . You now have parents putting their kids in one room to watch their show and they can go in the other room and watch a more adult show designed for them."[12] Unconcerned with kid appeal, NBC was able to target its key adult demographic more efficiently by placing sitcoms filled with so-called adult situations and themes throughout its entire prime-time line up—not just after 9 P.M. Advertisers, glad to reach these highly prized consumers, rushed to spend their dollars at the rejuvenated NBC.

By the 1995–96 season, the other networks eagerly followed NBC's lead, resulting in a noticeable trend in programming. More shows targeted to the perceived interests of a hip, cosmopolitan, professional, adult audience appeared throughout prime-time. ABC dropped family sitcoms like *Full House,* moved shows considered to have more adult appeal such as *Roseanne* and *Ellen* to earlier time slots, and added *The Naked Truth* and *Murder One.* CBS, which had long targeted a slightly older and perhaps more rural and conservative audience of 25-to-54 year olds with *Murder She Wrote, In the Heat of the Night,* and *Evening Shade,* joined the trend with *Central Park West, Almost Perfect,* and *Can't Hurry Love*—shows clearly targeted at a younger, more urban-minded demographic. Similarly, Fox picked up shows like *The Crew, Partners,* and *Ned and Stacey.* Meanwhile, NBC placed *Caroline in the City, The Single Guy,* and *In the Pursuit of Happiness* on a schedule already heavy with similar programs.

As new shows flooded the fall schedule, prime time was filled with programs about the lives of childless, often single, almost exclusively urban, white, upscale twenty and thirty-year-olds. Characters usually lived in big city apartments and work as often directionless yet still well-off professionals whose lives revolved around the trials of urban living, dating, and sex. Frequently displaced, of course, were the standard family sitcom preoccupations with suburban living, child rearing, and marriage. This preoccupation with the slumpy audience ignored the interests of viewers both younger and older than the target market; rural, conservative, and working class adults; and many minority audiences. Conversely, such programming likely appealed to a segment of the lucrative upscale 18-to-49 market once unserved by the family-hour strategy—specifically, adults without children.

Many of these programs were also populated with significant numbers of openly gay and lesbian characters and filled with numerous gay references. With children, as well as older and more conservative viewers increasingly out of the loop, writers, producers and networks were able to take greater risk with what was previously risqué material. In 1990, for example, a great deal of controversy surrounded an episode of ABC's *thirtysomething* in which two gay characters appeared in bed together. Even after ABC forced producers to edit out a same-sex kiss, numerous advertisers pulled their sponsorship. The network lost $1.5 million in revenue and refused to air the episode in summer reruns. Four years later, a similar controversy started to brew around a proposed lesbian kiss on *Roseanne*. The kiss remained, however, and the program was a ratings smash for ABC. Seemingly a quick learner, NBC consciously used gay and lesbian material as part of its strategy to rise from its third-place ratings slump and attract its quality audience. In a 1994 episode of *Frasier*, Frasier Crane, in a classic sitcom series of misunderstandings, ends up on a date with his new gay boss. The show was such a big hit that NBC reran the episode in the November sweeps period accompanied by a large promotional campaign.[13] A year later, during the November, 1995, sweeps, NBC promoted its Thursday night sitcom line up with a gimmick called "Star-Crossed Thursday" in which characters from each program made guest appearances on one of the other shows. The evening line up was also linked by the repeated appearance of gay material. *Caroline in the City*'s Lea Thompson assumed *Friends*' Joey and Chandler were a gay couple. On *The Single Guy,* Jonathan stayed with his gay neighbors and went on a date with *Friends*' Ross, while on *Seinfeld,* Elaine's armoire was stolen by two apparently gay thugs.[14] Both NBC's characters and its audience were caught up in a world in which gays and lesbians clearly belonged.

As all four networks worked to reach the same target audience, incorporating gay and lesbian characters and plot lines was a shrewd business decision. When the key demographic was one that prided itself on being politically progressive, in general, or gay friendly, in particular, including a gay neighbor, a lesbian sister, or some queer plot twist was not only possible but also lucrative for those networks and producers anxious to differentiate their product in a saturated market of *Friends* and *Seinfeld* imitators. Network executives appeared convinced that this new quality audience of white, urban sophisticates was not only comfortable with, but was even drawn to, programming featuring gay material. With such a perspective, bringing controversial issues from current headlines could give a show the politically-correct and in-the-know quality helpful in attracting a hard-to-reach audience uninspired by warm-hearted family sitcoms and other standard network fare. Thus, while Roseanne went to a gay bar to show how "cool" she really is on an episode of the ABC sitcom, network executives hoped that viewers from its target audience would tune in to prove how "hip" they were.

The desire to reach the quality audience was most certainly a factor in Disney/ABC's decision to allow Degeneres and her writers to out Ellen Morgan in an April, 1997, episode that, at the time, marked the climax for gay and lesbian characters on prime time. When it first appeared as *These Friends of Mine* in 1994, the program was clearly seen as ABC's attempt to compete with NBC for the slumpy quality audience. As one critic pointed out, "It was *Seinfeld* with women."[15] Observers, however, argued that the program never gained an identity of its own; it was always "following trends but never setting them (first it was a female *Seinfeld*, then a *Friends* clone)."[16] Throughout its short history, producers dramatically retooled the show in an attempt to attract the socially-liberal, urban-minded, white, adult audience. In the 1995–96 season, for example, producers decided to highlight the program's Los Angeles setting to exploit further the possibilities of its big-city surroundings.[17] That same season saw the increased importance of two gay characters, Peter and Barrett, whose send up of traditional gay stereotypes tested the audience's hipness and progressive politics.

Opening the closet door for the lead character was a logical step in revamping the program. As the immense media attention and high ratings recently generated by the coming-out story illustrates, a gay Ellen Morgan certainly distinguished the show not only from family sitcoms like *Step by Step* and *Home Improvement* but also from clones like *Caroline in the City* or *Suddenly Susan*. Many observers argued the move gave the show the much-needed "identity" required to attract the target demographics. Paraphrasing a high-ranking studio executive, one media observer claimed that "Commercially, making Ellen Morgan a lesbian would give *Ellen* an edginess that might bring back its sophisticated *Seinfeld*-type viewers."[18] Even the immense backlash by Christian conservatives—a reaction that would most definitely have scared any network away from a coming out story just a few years ago—may actually have worked in *Ellen* and ABC's favor; watching a new "controversial" Ellen and, thus thwarting the extreme conservative agenda of a Pat Robertson or Donald Wildmon, may offer liberally-minded, "sophisticated" viewers that "edginess" in which they seem to find so much pleasure.

TARGETING THE GAY AND LESBIAN
AUDIENCE IN THE '90s

While networks and producers used gay and lesbian material to attract an audience of urbane and upscale adults, the recent programming trend could also be particularly effective at appealing to a highly lucrative segment of that quality audience—specifically upscale gay and lesbian viewers.[19] As network audience shares decreased and the imperatives of narrowcasting intensified in the '90s, it would have been poor business for the networks not to at least consider gay and lesbian viewers as a profitable market. Narrowcasting often encourages a network to discover markets currently being underserved by other outlets. In this case, television programming's ubiquitous heterosexuality had turned away many in the gay and lesbian community. At the same time, the dissolution of television's so-called mass audience and the segmentation of viewership had reduced the risk networks face by airing gay material. While still somewhat fearful of controversy, the networks were under less pressure to please all viewers. Consequently, if Christian conservatives, demographically more rural and Southern, weren't part of a network's target audience, including gay and lesbian material became less hazardous. While many sponsors appeared more cautious than the networks, the dynamics of niche marketing worked in similar ways for them. Thus, the danger of offending certain viewers/consumers by sponsoring a controversial program featuring gay material could be outweighed by the benefits of reaching a prime target market.

Ultimately, however, both networks and sponsors only targeted gays and lesbians if they thought doing so would be worth their while. In the early '90s, economic and social changes, self-serving promotion on the part of a new gay press and marketing firms, and coverage in the business press worked together to focus more and more of the business world's attention on what gay men and lesbians did with their money. In the process, they constructed the gay community as not only a viable but also an important market in the highly competitive business world of the 1990s. In April, 1994, for example, over 150 consumer products companies paid up to $1,500 each to put up booths at the Meadowlands Convention Center in Secaucus, New Jersey, in what was billed as the First National Gay and Lesbian Business Expo. The event, according to *New York Times* advertising columnist, Stuart Elliott, was yet one more "indication of one of the least expected business trends of the 1990's: the growing efforts by many mainstream marketers to reach consumers who are homosexuals."[20]

Similar economic changes that led network television to alter its programming policies led businesses in general to change how they sold their products to consumers. Ray Mulryan, a partner in the Mulryan/Nash advertising agency explained that in the 1990s, "the mass market just doesn't exist. . . . If you want to reach America, you've got to identify them by group—and then you have to talk to them."[21] Faced with greater competition, then, more companies had to specialize their sales pitches to appeal to ever narrower groups. Stuart Elliott asserts such economic incentives led mainstream companies to look to new markets previously ignored: "The need to attract dollars from consumers have become so overwhelming that they're willing to target messages to consumers that they might not have been willing to talk to in previous years."[22] As the 1994 expo illustrates, one such segment was the gay and lesbian community.

Although economic incentives led many companies to turn to niche markets, other forces were at play to convince them that the gay and lesbian community was a commercially viable niche. A political and social shift that took place in the 1990s concerning the position of gays and lesbians opened the door for advertisers to openly target gay dollars. In the late 70s and early 80s numerous companies had begun pitching campaigns to the gay market. With the emergence of AIDS in the mid-80s and the social stigma generated around the gay community, however, advertisers retreated.[23] By 1990, companies like Johnnie Walker and K Mart gradually made guarded overtures to gay consumers with ambiguous ads.[24] Nevertheless, in 1990, one media analyst was still warning retailers to "be careful with niche segmentation, so you don't offend some old customers who . . . might think, 'That's where the gays shop.' "[25] Yet as one observer pointed out four years later, such caution "was pre-Clinton, -gays-in-the-military, -Colorado-legislation headlines."[26] By the 1992 election, presidential candidate Clinton actually hired an advertising and PR firm specializing in reaching the gay and lesbian community to help him get the gay vote. As news coverage after the election has reframed gay men and women, moving them closer to the mainstream, more and more advertisers decided to follow Clinton's example and turned to the gay market.

If a new social context made the gay market viable, the emergence of new gay magazines, advertising agencies, and research firms made it attractive. Traditionally comprised of local magazines produced on newsprint, focused on covering politics, and supported by locally gay-owned business and explicit sex ads, the gay and lesbian press saw a dramatic change in 1992. National magazines like *Out, Genre, Deneuve,* and *10 Percent* debuted on glossy paper and were filled with trendy layouts, full-color photos, and articles from nationally recognized writers. Faced with the new competition, the nation's oldest national magazine, *The Advocate,* followed suit, getting rid of its sexually explicit personals section and moving to glossy print. All these magazines needed to attract mainstream, national advertisers willing to pay the writers, designers, printing fees, and circulation overhead of a nation-wide periodical.[27] Consequently, these magazines rapidly began touting the attractive demographics of its readership, trying to convince Madison Avenue and its clients that buying space in their magazine was a smart investment.

The magazines quickly turned to research firms like Overlooked Opinions and advertising agencies like Mulryan/Nash and aka Communications—all of which specialized in promoting the gay and lesbian community—to provide the sterling demographics needed to woo national companies. A widely reported study by Overlooked Opinions claimed that American's estimated 18 million gay and lesbians were spending over $500 billion dollars annually.[28] Profiles of gay and lesbian consumers were almost always compared to data for average Americans. Data compiled by aka Communications from research by Simmons Market Research, the U.S. Census Bureau and Overlooked Opinions, claimed that 40 percent of lesbians and 47 percent of gay men hold managerial jobs compared with 15 percent and 31 percent nationwide. Twenty percent of gay people are frequent fliers compared to a national average of 2 percent, while 66 percent are overseas travelers compared to 14 percent nationwide.[29] According to a report by Mulryan/Nash, "61 percent of gay people have a four-year college degree, as opposed to 18 percent of average Americans. . . . forty-three percent of gay people work out in a gym as opposed to 8 percent of average Americans. . . . sixty-four percent of gay people drink sparkling water as opposed to 17 percent of [average] Americans."[30] Other surveys claimed that a typical gay male couple earns $51,600 a year, while the average straight couple earned only $37,900. The average lesbian couple reportedly earned $42,800.[31] According to aka Communications, 18 percent of gay households had incomes over $100,000.[32] Not only did gay men and lesbians have all this income, these reports suggested, they also tended not to have children. Without the worries of braces, college tuition, and medical bills, gay men and women's disposable income was even greater.

As if such stellar statistics weren't enough to convince blue-chip firms, many reports claimed that gays and lesbians were amazingly loyal to businesses that openly court their patronage. According to a poll of its readers, *The Blade,* a Washington DC gay weekly, found that 80 percent of its readers claimed to be loyal to *Blade* advertisers and that 70 percent said they would change their shopping habits if a retailer advertised in the paper.[33] According to *American Demographics,* "gay men and lesbians show their gratitude to marketers who have the courage to serve them. In return for what they see as acceptance and respect, gay consumers will go out of their way to patronize these companies. Furthermore, they will actively spread the word through an amazingly efficient network that circulates not only through word of mouth, but through 200 electronic bulletin boards."[34] Finally, other reported but less tangible qualities of the gay community made it a particularly important demographic segment. According to the report by Mulryan/Nash, because of their prominent position in the fields of fashion, design, media, and the arts, gay men and lesbians "occupy a special sphere of influence and shape national consumer tastes. Gay men have been credited with popularizing blow-dryers, painter's pants, the gentrification of urban neighborhoods, disco music, Absolut Vodka, Levi's 501 jeans, Doc Martin boots, and Santa Fe home-style furnishings."[35] What better target market could a profit hungry company have wanted?

Madison Avenue and its clients seem to have been convinced. When Hirman Walker & Sons were marketing their Tuaca liqueur, according to Laurie Acosta, group product manager, they wanted to reach young, hip consumers, "and by definition, that includes the gay and lesbian market."[36] BMG Records and RCA Victor began selling gay-targeted classical compilations like "Out Music" and "Out Classics," and Atlantic Records established a department dedicated to marketing music to gay audiences. Articles informed banks, booksellers, radio stations, travel agents, and retail stores of the importance of tapping into the gay and lesbian demographic. In addition to the traditional ads from entertainment, clothing and liquor companies, gay magazines were being filled with full page ads selling everything from Apple computers, Naya spring water, and Xerox copiers, to Continental Airlines, Swatch watches, and MCI-long distance. The gay press had even been able to tap into the lucrative automotive market; Saab and Subaru both placed print ads in gay periodicals. A number of data lists of people assumed to be gay or lesbian—lists compiled from magazine subscriptions, gay credit card holders, single-ticket buyers for plays like *Jeffrey,* and even lists of AIDS organization donors—were sold to companies interested in direct mailing.[37] IKEA, a Sweden-based furniture company, produced a now-famous television ad featuring a gay male couple shopping for a dining table. The 30-second spot aired in a number of big city markets.

When asked why their companies were targeting gays and lesbians, the responses of company spokespeople dramatically illustrate how widely-accepted and influential the demographic picture of the gay market had become. According to a marketing vice-president, CJ Wray believed "it's a market that has money." Virgin Atlantic Airlines' ad executive asserted that "They're an audience that we believe will give us a great return on our advertising investment." Benetton's director of communication claimed that "Anyone who would pass over this market without giving it thorough analytical treatment is remiss and probably guilty of knee-jerk discrimination. . . . Ultimately it comes down to not mind-ing the shop." Linda Sawyer, executive v.p. for a New York ad agency, best summed up the attitude of many companies in the mid-90s: "Now including gays seems safe—and smart."[38]

While widely circulating discourses about the affluence of the gay market encouraged many companies to target gay and lesbian consumers, their influence on television advertising and network television executives was more complicated. While once presenting a rather unified front against any overt images of homosexuality on the programs they sponsor, some sponsors were increasingly willing to break rank. While a home goods company like Procter & Gamble may have been very hesitant to risk offending Christian conservatives by linking themselves too close to gay issues, high-tech computer firms like Apple and IBM—whose target audiences were very different—could take more risks. Although some companies pulled out of the coming-out episode of *Ellen,* for example, many more were glad to take their place and to pay premium prices to do so. Of Volkswagen of America, Inc.'s decision to buy time on the episode Tony Foulad-pour, company spokesperson, explained "It's about advertising our products to a target audience of drivers, which matches the viewers of *Ellen* and which would include many different life styles."[39] Rebecca Patto, senior v.p. at E-Trade Group, an on-line brokerage firm who aired spots during the show in New York and San Francisco, felt the program would reach its desired audience: "We really appeal to people who think for themselves."[40] Such comments are certainly far less overt in acknowledging a desire to target the gay market, and few if any advertisers sponsored gay-inclusive TV in order to specifically target gay and lesbian viewers. The economics of network broadcasting just didn't support such a marketing strategy. The high cost of a 30-second prime-time network ad spot determined its use. In order to get one's money's worth, marketers couldn't feasibly use prime-time network television to narrowly target a niche audience as small as gays and lesbians, even if they were disproportionately highly active and affluent consumers. Gay publications, direct marketing, and special event advertising were far more cost effective vehicles for reaching them than an episode of *Seinfeld* or *Ellen.* Even with a gay-themed commercial like the 1994 IKEA spot, the target audience was not merely gay men. According to IKEA's advertising executive Linda Sawyer, the gay-inclusive ad was meant to appeal to a group of consumers the agency dubbed "wanna-bes": basically upwardly mobile consumers highly concerned about establishing a sense of style.[41] Surely, IKEA felt that gay men were part of that market, but more importantly IKEA and its ad agency felt that a gay couple would be an effective tool to speak to the broader market.

Discourses of the gay market also influenced network television executives similarly. With the extensive attention paid to the statistical profiles of gays and lesbians, it is hard to believe that the demographic-obsessed marketing, advertising and programming executives at work behind the networks remained unaware of and unaffected by the numbers.[42] In 1993, just as the trend of gay programming began, *Mediaweek,* a major trade journal, cited the same demographic figures, quoted the same gay-owned advertising firms, and included the same targeting-the-gay-market-is-smart-business advice circulating in other business magazines.[43] Reportedly loyal, highly-educated, and affluent with disposable incomes greater than the national average, gay men and women represented the perfect market for networks eager to deliver a quality audience to advertisers. In many ways, the reported demographics of gays and lesbians were strikingly similar to those of the upscale, "hip," urban, white, college-educated, liberal audience networks and advertisers were so anxious to reach; in fact, they seem even better. Nevertheless, network executives have never admitted to targeting gay and lesbian viewers, and considering the economics of network television, their silence most likely isn't entirely disingenuous.[44] Despite the dramatic erosion of network audience shares in the early '90s, gays and lesbians, at least in the minds of network executives, remained too small a market segment to target too narrowly. Even in the age of narrowcasting, network broadcasting functioned on a different scale than more niche-oriented media like magazines, direct marketing, or cable; network television's niche audiences remain significantly larger than those targeted by other media.[45] Moreover, A. C. Nielsen's television ratings reports didn't breakdown audiences by sexual orientation, so no data were available about the viewing behavior of gays and lesbians, making it difficult, if not impossible, to sell and buy gay TV viewers in the network TV ad market. Granted some producers consciously created programming to appeal to a gay and lesbian audience. However, such efforts were driven by a desire to serve rather than target gay viewers and don't really account for the overall increase of gay-inclusive programming. More often than not, gay material was used to target a significantly larger audience of socially liberal, urban-minded professionals. The fact that it could also be particularly effective at appealing to a highly lucrative gay segment of that quality audience was a collateral if ultimately unmeasurable benefit.[46] Affluent gay viewers, I'd argue, entered the equation, but most likely only in an auxiliary function.[47] The highly attractive demographic profile of the gay and lesbian market, then, enabled networks to push television's conventions and use gay material in order to aggressively target its broader quality audience—an audience that apparently finds a gay twist with their television appealing. When such a strategy had the advantage of appealing to an audience that was as lucrative as gays and lesbians appear to be, it was much easier to risk offending more conservative viewers whose demographics weren't as attractive and who weren't part of the target audience.

CONCLUSIONS

In the 1990s, gay men and women had an increasingly visible role in the world of prime-time television. But just how were gay characters and issues presented? Used as textual selling points, gay and lesbian characters and their lives often mirrored both the demographic profile of the urban, upscale, white and adult quality audience networks sought and the demographic profiles of the gay community created in the marketing press. Frasier's gay boss, for example, was an upwardly mobile radio station manager who moved to Seattle from London after a messy breakup that included a dispute over opera recordings. Paul's sister on *Mad About You* and her obstetrician partner were upscale professional Manhattan-ites who became romantically involved while on a ski weekend. *Spin City* was somewhat unusual in that it offered one of the few African-American gay characters on prime time; yet Carter's race seemed less important to his characterization than his sexual identity, and his background as a political activist was repeatedly downplayed in story lines that focued on the lives of young professionals working in the New York mayor's office. And, although *Ellen*'s Peter and Barrett weren't decidedly professional, they lived and worked in the decidedly urban world of Los Angles and trendy Hollywood.[48]

Many observers, including some from the gay and lesbian community, wholeheartedly praised the programming trend. Loren Jarvier, a spokesperson for GLAAD asserted, "It's great because television is finally saying, 'We're not a sideshow. We're just like you. We're your friends and your family. We go to school with you.'"[49] Paul Witt, co-creator of *Soap* and WB Television's *Muscle* agreed, "You're beginning to see openly gay characters portrayed just like everyone else, who don't embody stereotypes."[50] The problem, of course, as with nearly all television representation, is that they did embody stereotypes. Instead of images of nelly queens or motorcycle dykes, we were presented with images of white, affluent, trend-setting, Perrier-drinking, frequent-flier using, Ph.D.-holding consumer citizens with more income to spend than they knew what to do with. For many, such a stereotype is equally frightening.

The gay characters featured on shows like *Friends, Ellen,* and *NYPD Blue* and the highly touted statistical profiles featured in *Fortune, Mediaweek,* and *The New York Times* worked together to construct a specific view of the gay and lesbian community. Television's representations are imbricated within the economic imperatives of major production companies and networks anxious to attract a quality audience to sell to advertisers. Driven by similar economic forces, national gay and lesbian magazines and ad firms devoted to marketing to the gay community—institutions for which profit, not gay liberation, is the bottom line—generated and promoted much of the market research. Consequently, the results of reader surveys done by the gay press were often conflated with profiles for the entire community, and the gay men and lesbians who couldn't afford to buy the magazines or didn't identify with the images of gay life presented in them were increasingly excluded from the mainstream's understanding of what it meant to be gay or lesbian in the '90s—an understanding reinforced by television's recent prime-time representations. The results of broader surveys based on random samples were similarly skewed. Because of homophobia, gay men and women, particularly gay teens, older gay men and women, and those in less urban areas and with less financial security, were far less likely to identify themselves as gay or lesbian and were consequently ignored. Finally, both television representations and market researchers excluded the significant numbers of bisexual men and women.[51] While helping to construct an industry knowledge of gays and lesbians as a consumer audience, such sampling biases also resulted in a demographic picture that badly misrepresented the gay community.

The exclusion of a range of gay and bisexual men and women from both prime-time television and statistical profiles has serious consequences for gay politics and underscores the conflict between industrial conceptions that commodify individuals as an audience of consumers and politicized notions that try to mobilize people into a social movement. While appearing to have economic clout can translate into real political progress, it is not the same as actually having real economic power.[52] In fact, misleading data touting the size of the gay pocketbook has worked against gay civil rights struggles in states like Oregon and Colorado where anti-gay advocates used the statistics to discredit the assertion that gays and lesbians were socially oppressed. Effaced from market reports and most television programs, of course, are the real lived experiences of thousands of gay and bisexual people who do face economic discrimination every day. The economic oppression faced by lesbians and gay people of color is even more egregiously erased. The conflation of the gay, lesbian, and bisexual community with a specific quality audience of gays and lesbians moves the entire debate to the realm of consumption, disregards all notions of wider social oppression, and threatens to fracture the gay community along axes of class, gender, race, and sexual identity even more than it currently is.[53] Such problems are exacerbated when such incomplete images of gay and lesbian experience are targeted at a quality audience of liberal television viewers, both straight and gay, who may feel that by watching "sophisticated" programs with gay and lesbian characters or gay-themed programs, they are somehow supporting the struggle for gay rights.[54] But when that world is nearly always devoid of serious discrimination and hate crimes, as is true of most television programming, little change and thus little effort on the part of viewers is called for.[55]

Thus, while marking a significant change in the representation of gays and lesbians on television, the deluge of gay material in prime time calls as much for caution as for celebration. Situated within the specific industrial forces driving television, images of gays and lesbians have consistently been constructed with a highly straight, white, affluent audience in mind. We must also be wary of constructing a progress narrative for gay and lesbian visibility on television. Just because there are more images doesn't mean they are inherently better, and even the few advances made can quickly be lost. As industrial situations and network motivation change, programming trends come and go. As with all programming, shows using "edgy" gay material to attract a quality audience are situated within an innovation-imitation-saturation cycle that drives prime-time television.[56] The same imperative to reach a new audience in new ways that helped propel gay material onto dozens of shows could also lead to its demise.[57]

While economic forces clearly were and continue to be at work behind the spate of gay content on prime time, this examination has been only the first step in understanding the reasons behind and impact of this programming trend. Television is not only a profit-generating industry. It is also a site of cultural negotiation, and as the struggle for gay and lesbian rights has heated up, television has become one important front along which that battle has been played out. For both the gay and lesbian community and those studying television, it is important to understand the complex interaction among industrial forces, social movements, cultural conflict, and political aims.

NOTES

1. I would like to thank Elana Levine and an anonymous reader for their insightful comments during the writing process.

2. *Entertainment Weekly* 8 September 1995: cover.

3. I don't want to suggest that the recent outbreak of gay and lesbian material is limited to network prime-time programming. HBO's *The Larry Sanders Show,* MTV's *The Real World,* NBC's *Saturday Night Live,* ABC's *All My Children,* The Discovery Channel's *Interior Motives,* and the syndicated hit *Xena,* for example, all reflect the growing importance of gay material across the television landscape. However, I have chosen to focus on network prime-time television because these hours still represent the peak viewing period where most advertising revenue is at stake.

4. Throughout the paper, I will use the term gay and lesbian to refer to the characters and issues represented on television and to the community/market described by a variety of magazines and marketing firms. The selection of such terms is not meant to deny the presence of bisexual men and women in the gay community and political movement, but to best reflect the images and discourses constructed in these texts. The consequences such images and discourses hold for the community they describe/construct are explored below.

5. Ien Ang, *Desperately Seeking the Audience* (London: Routledge, 1991), 3. Also see Thomas Streeter and Wendy Wahl, "Audience Theory and Feminism: Property, Gender, and the Television Audience," *Camera Obscura* / 33–34 May–September–January 1994–95: 243–246.

6. Julie D'Acci, *Defining Women: Television and the Case of Cagney & Lacey* (Chapel Hill: University of North Carolina Press, 1994).

7. For work on quality audiences see Julie D' Acci; Eileen R. Meehan, "Why We Don't Count: The Commodity Audience," in Patricia Mellencamp, ed., *Logics of Television: Essays in Cultural Criticism* (Bloomington: Indiana University Press, 1990), 117–137; Jackie Byars and Eileen R. Meehan, "Once in a Lifetime: Constructing 'The Working Woman' through Cable Narrowcasting," *Camera Obscura* / 33–34 May–September–January 1994–95: 13–41; Pamela Wilson, "Upscale Feminist Angst: Molly Dodd, the Lifetime Cable Network and Gender Marketing," *Camera Obscura* / 33–34 May–September–January 1994–95: 103–130; Jane Feuer, Paul Kerr, and Tise Vahimagi, eds., *MTM: Quality Television* (London: British Film Institute, 1984); Todd Gitlin, *Inside Prime Time* (New York: Pantheon, 1983): 203–220.

8. Xiaoming Hoa, "Television Viewing among American Adults in the 1990s," *Journal of Broadcasting and Electronic Media* Summer (1994): 353–360; Byars and Meehan, 21–22.

9. Keith Marder "Cable television gaining fat on big 3 networks," *State Journal Register* 10 October 1996: 25.

10. The adjective "hip" is certainly far from precise. Nevertheless, I use it here because marketers, network executives and media observers employ it so frequently. They find it useful, I feel, because, in the '90s, it serves as a safe way to refer to a somewhat socially-liberal audience with a cynical, urban-minded sensibility. The term "rural" seems to function in similar ways to refer to an audience of conservative and even Christian viewers.

11. Rick DuBrow, "Television; Networking, '90s Style," *Los Angeles Times* 9 April 1995: Calendar 6.

12. Ibid.

13. Rex Poindexter, "Laughing Matters," *The Advocate* 13 December 1994: 56–58.

14. Not only does the evening line up reflect a consistent interest in presenting gay material, the ability of each character to seamlessly move from the diagetic world of his/her hip, Manhattan neighborhood to that of the next show indicates the interchangeable qualities that have resulted from a unified goal of attracting the quality audience. Further, NBC's use of gay material to promote its shows is more recently evident in its fall 1997 promo for the premier of *Working.* The oft-run commercial featured a joke in which Fred Savage's new boss offers an attractive male secretary as a perk for a new job.

15. Graham Jefferson, "Ellen Happy with Women at Helm/Finding Fun with Female Point of View," *USA Weekend* 19 December 1995: D3.

16. Bruce Fretts, "This Week," *Entertainment Weekly* 25 October 1996: 102.

17. Promotional material from ABC illustrates this shift and indicates the show's relationship to *Friends*. Describing Ellen Morgan, for example, they say she is a "thirty-something urbanite . . . striving to find her niche in L.A." John Carmody, "The TV Column," *The Washington Post* 16 September 1996: D6.

18. Gail Shister, "Gay Producers, Actors Urge *Ellen* to Come Out," *Wisconsin State Journal* 18 September 1996: 7D.

19. In the early 70s urban-centered programming like *All in the Family* and *The Jeffersons* attracted not only the white urban audience CBS so badly wanted but also the increasingly prosperous black middle class. Further, for work examining issues surrounding targeting gays and lesbians in other industries see Danae Clark, "Commodity Lesbianism," in Henry Abelove, Michele Asina Bardale, and David M. Halperin, eds., *The Lesbian and Gay Studies Reader* (New York: Routledge, 1993), 186–201; and Gregory Woods, "We're Here, We're Queer and We're Not Going Catalogue Shopping," in Paul Burston and Colin Richardson, eds., *A Queer Romance: Lesbians, gay men and popular culture* (London: Routledge, 1995), 147–163; Eve M. Kahn, "The Glass Closet," *Print* (v.48 n.5) September–October 1994: 21–32.

20. Stuart Elliott, "This weekend a business expo will show the breadth of interest in gay consumer," *New York Times* 14 April 1994: D-18.

21. Jeffrey Scott, "Media Talk; Formerly standoffish advertisers openly courting gay consumers," *Atlanta Journal and Constitution* 5 April 1994: B-3.

22. Charles Feldman, "Advertising Aimed at Gay Community Surges," CNN 7 October 1992: Transcript #200-1.

23. Ibid.

24. See Paul Colford, "The Scotch Ad That's Got 'Em Buzzing," *Newsday* February 1989: II-2; and Bernice Kanner, "Normally Gay," *New York* 4 April 1994: 24.

25. Kara Swisher, "Gay Spending Power Draws More Attention," *Washington Post* 18 June 1990: F1.

26. Kanner 24.

27. See Rodger Streitmatter, *Unspeakable; The Rise of the Gay and Lesbian Press in America* (Boston: Faber and Faber, 1995), 308–337; Daniel Harris, *The Rise and Fall of Gay Culture* (New York: Hyperion, 1997), 64–85.

28. See Diane Cyr, "The emerging gay market," *Catalogue Age* November 1993: 112.

29. Kathy Kalafut, "Alternative Demos; Profile on Aka Communications Inc," *Mediaweek* 14 September 1992: 32.

30. Sarah Schulman, "Gay Marketeers," *The Progressive* July 1995: 28.

31. Rodger Streitmatter, 314.

32. Teresa Carson, "Agencies Push Gay Market Ads to Banks," *The American Banker* 21 May 1992: 6.

33. Swisher F1.

34. Hazel Kahan and David Mulryan, "Out of the Closet," *American Demographics* May 1995: 46–47. In this lengthy article, the writers declare the "gay and lesbian market [to be] an untapped goldmine" and basically provide a guidebook for marketers who want to get started examining the gay community.

35. Schulman 28.

36. Cyndee Miller, " 'The Ultimate Taboo,' Slowly But Surely, Companies Overcome Reluctance to Target the Lesbian Market," *Marketing News TM* 14 August 1995: 1. Miller uses the term "hip, young consumer" to introduce the quote from Laurie Acosta.

37. Gary Levin, "List-generating hot—to direct mail's delight," *Advertising Age* 30 May 1994: S-1+.

38. Gary Levin, "Mainstream's domino effect: Liquor, fragrance, clothing advertisers ease into gay magazines," *Advertising Age* 18 January 1993: 30; Martha Moore, "Courting the gay market—Advertisers: It's business, not politics," *USA Today* 23 April 1993: B1; Susan Reda, "Marketing to Gays & Lesbians: The Last Taboo," *Stores* September 1994: 19; Kanner 24.

39. Dana Canedy, "As the main character in *Ellen* comes out, some companies see an opportunity; others steer clear," *New York Times* 30 April 1997: D8.

40. Ibid. The E-Trade Group may also be motivated to sponsor a lesbian Ellen Morgan by demographic statistics which claim disproportionately high on-line computer use in the gay community. forty-eight percent of *Out* magazine readers, for example, subscribe to an on-line computer service compared to a national average of 11%. See Michael Wilke, "Wired Lesbian/Gays Lure Marketers," *Advertising Age* 11 December 1995: 33.

41. John Gallagher, "Ikea's Gay Gamble," *The Advocate,* 3 May 1994: 24–26.

42. One brief article in *Advertising Age* illustrates the kind of information executives must be aware of. The factoid gives the top ten rated shows in $60,000-plus households. *Roseanne,* which had recently included two openly gay/lesbian recurring characters was, despite its decidedly blue-collar tenor, the number one rated show in that lucrative demographic, gaining 13% over the previous season. Reading this kind of industry information may be leading executives to put two and $60,000 together. "Hey, big spender," *Advertising Age* 15 March 1993: 29.

43. Mark Hudis, "Gays Back in Prime Time," *Mediaweek* 13 December 1993: 14. Also see David W. Dunlap, "Gay Images, Once Kept Out Are Out Big Time," *New York Times* 21 January 1996: I-29.

44. Of course targeting a gay audience would have been politically difficult for the Big 3 network still framed by their long history as the nation's mass medium—the medium supposedly designed for everyone. While it never had been that, aggressively targeting a political minority like gays and lesbians was in many ways inconceivable at the time. The networks, in fact, weren't willing to admit that gay material was linked to competitive economics at all. Most network explanations for the spate of gay and lesbian characters claimed that the trend was simply mirroring social reality. Marc Cherry, executive producer of *The Crew,* for example, asserts, "Gay people are now more than ever becoming a part of American life. . . . You can't deny the existence of gay people throughout the country. They should be represented." John Carman, "Gay characters get a life on TV," *San Francisco Chronicle* 17 August 1995: E1. Such comments efface the hard-nosed economics behind television programming and reflect the power of a long-lasting discursive construction of television as a medium meant to serve the public interest.

45. Cable most certainly has considered gay viewers as a target market. For one, there has been repeated effort to create a cable channel targeted explicitly at the gay market in the style of BET. At the same time, other cable networks, most notably E! and Showtime seem to have developed programming geared to the perceived interests of the gay market.

46. In the early 70s urban-centered programming like *All in the Family* and *The Jeffersons* attracted not only the white urban audience CBS so badly wanted but also the increasingly prosperous black middle class. Further, for work examining issues surrounding targeting gays and lesbians in other industries see Danae Clark, "Commodity Lesbianism," in Henry Abelove, Michele Asina Bardale, and David M. Halperin, eds., *The Lesbian and Gay Studies Reader*

(New York: Routledge, 1993), 186–201; and Gregory Woods, "We're Here, We're Queer and We're Not Going Catalogue Shopping," in Paul Burston and Colin Richardson, eds., *A Queer Romance: Lesbians, gay men and popular culture* (London: Routledge, 1995), 147–163; Eve M. Kahn, "The Glass Closet," *Print* (v.48 n.5) September–October 1994: 21–32.

47. Granted, that fact may have started to change with the continuing erosion of audience shares in the late '90s. When a show like *Will & Grace,* for example, was a hit and drew top advertiser dollars with only 16 million viewers, the interests of a gay audience, especially when it was considered to be disproportionately affluent, may have become a more primary consideration.

48. The representation of gay and lesbian characters on prime time is certainly not entirely homogenous. *Cosby* included an episode with elderly gay men that were African-American and Asian-American. *My So-Called Life* featured a Hispanic gay teen. And both *Roseanne* and *Grace Under Fire* have featured a variety of gay, lesbian, and bisexual characters who live and work in mid-sized Midwestern towns. Nevertheless, these examples mark the exception to the rule. In most shows, gay material is part of a world defined by the white, urbane, upscale people populating it.

49. Tom Hopkins, "Gays on TV, " *Dayton Daily News* 20 August 1995: IC.

50. Susan Karlin, "TV Discovers Gay Characters," *Electronic Media* 13 February 1995: 6.

51. Lee Badgett from the University of Maryland, for example, has done research that indicates gay men make less, nearly one third less, than their straight male counterparts. See M. V. Lee Badgett, "Beyond Biased Samples: Challenging the Myths on the Economic Status of Lesbians and Gay Men," in Amy Gluckman and Betsy Reed, eds., *Homo Economics: Capitalism, Community, and Lesbian and Gay Life* (New York: Routledge, 1997), 73–86. Also see Urvashi Vaid, *Virtual Equality: The Mainstreaming of Gay and Lesbian Liberation* (New York: Anchor, 1995), 249–259.

52. While many companies have been anxious to take advantage of gay economic power and actively court it, others have faced the consequences of offending the gay community. In 1990, Woodies, a local retail chain in Washington, DC, was the target of a gay boycott when it refused to give the partner of a gay employee the same family discount as straight employees. As the gay community quickly organized its clout, Woodies examined the situation and decided to concede. Besides granting the discount, they also agreed to include nondiscrimination based on sexual orientation in its employment policy, add sensitivity training on homophobia for all employees and managers, and promised to engage in public advocacy for legislation that would extend spousal benefits to gay partners. Joseph Culver, v.p. for personnel at Woodies' parent company states, "We found there was an articulate and financially important gay and lesbian community in Washington." Illustrating what impact such economic muscle flexing can have, Culver claims, "the incident gave us all an awareness in the organization that some of our thinking was archaic and needed to change." Woodies' decision influenced the nine-store Garfinkel's chain to follow suit. George Kelly, president and chairman, states, "We looked at what went on with Woodies and thought it was the right thing to do, considering the realities of today. We did it for business reasons too, since I have seen surveys that show that the gay community is one that shops and spends money way beyond the necessities." Swisher F1.

53. For further discussion see Amy Gluckman and Betsy Reed, "The Gay Marketing Moment," in Amy Gluckman and Betsy Reed, eds., *Homo Economics: Capitalism, Community, and Gay and Lesbian Life* (New York: Routledge, 1997), 3–10. While the vast majority of prime-time programs contribute to the problem, *Roseanne* has done more than any show to actually overcome such fractures. Besides including gay men and lesbians within a decidedly blue-collar context, they also work to construct alliances between gays, lesbians, African-Americans, and working-class whites. More work needs to be done analyzing the different ways gays and lesbians are presented on specific programs and in different genres.

54. Network television's use of gay characters as a tool to attract a quality audience of straight consumers in the '90s bears resemblance to the strategy of some assimilationist gay politics which tries to win social and political acceptance by marginalizing the more unconventional elements of the gay community in an attempt to appeal to straight Americans. More work needs to be done to explore the relationship between the industrial forces at play behind mass media images of gay life and the political and social forces behind certain political aims. Particularly salient, it seems, is the relationship between identity politics and consumer marketing. Since both marketers and some political activists are concerned with constructing definitions of the gay community and what it means to be gay or lesbian, the two endeavors can easily become intertwined. As Gregory Woods points out, "Considering that one of capitalism's principal means of inveigling individuals into the cycle of production and consumption is the commercialisation of identity, one has to recognise that there is a seamless logic to the process by which, within a capitalist economy, identity politics likewise become commercialised and commodified." Gregory Woods, 160.

55. A relatively common story line in the '90s involves a show's central characters discovering an acquaintance is gay or lesbian. While certain characters have some problems dealing with it, the show's most sympathetic character quickly take the stance that (to paraphrase Jerry Seinfeld and Gorge Costanza) "There's not anything wrong with it." In fact, a character's problem with someone else's sexuality is often set up as the problem. By the end of the show, the specter of homophobia is usually stamped out; at least the audience is told to believe that the gay character is okay. *Suddenly Susan, Grace Under Fire, Coach, Hudson Street, Dr. Quinn—Medicine Woman, Mad About You, Wings, Cosby, Murphy Brown,* and *Beverly Hills 90210* all have had such episodes. Further, in a number of other shows, a character's homosexuality is virtually a non-issue within the program's diagetic world—i.e., *Seinfeld, Chicago Hope, Fired Up, Suddenly Susan, Relatively, Style & Substance.*

56. In his analysis of television documentary in the 1960s, Michael Curtin offers and extended discussion of that genre's saturation cycle. See Michael Curtin, *Redeeming the Wasteland* (New Brunswick: Rutgers UP, 1995).

57. After a disastrous 1995–96 season in which it wholeheartedly copied NBC and ABC, CBS, for example, returned to targeting a decidedly older, less urban and more conservative audience with its "Welcome Home" campaign and a line up of shows like *Touched by an Angel, Walker, Texas Ranger, Promised land,* and *Cosby.* Nevertheless, gay-themed television seemed to sustain its viability in the 1997–1998 season. NBC's *Veronica's Closet* and *Homocide: Life on the Streets,* for example, have included gay material as significant plot elements. Even CBS's *Cosby* had an episode in which the title character played baseball with an over-50 gay men's group, attended a gay line-dancing party, and was assumed to be gay by almost everyone including his wife.

QUESTIONS FOR DISCUSSION

1. Think about Becker's claims in terms of Eileen Meehan's article. What are the implications if television's only effort to represent "difference" from the white, middle-class norm comes attached to the construction of audiences as affluent and upscale?

2. Becker's analysis of the "discourse of gay marketing" illustrates how the various media work together to create trends that affect programs, advertising, and publication in a variety of genres. How does this relate to synergies in the media industry of the 1990s?

3. This article clearly resonates with those of Lipsitz, Haralovich, and Spigel in drawing connections between larger social contexts, utopian or dystopian views of the past (or future), and programs that result. Contrast and compare their various claims. What is the difference between Lipsitz's claims about the working of nostalgia and Becker's argument about the use of "socially liberal" values?

 INFOTRAC COLLEGE EDITION

Look in InfoTrac College Edition under "gays and television" and also "television and homosexuality" for more articles on this subject. Also try the names of individual television programs discussed.

16

U.S. Television Abroad
Market Power and
National Introspection

WILLIAM BODDY

Throughout the "network era" of American television, roughly 1960 to 1990, the United States dominated the creation and international distribution of television programming. By the late 1980s, the United States contributed 5 percent of the global television audience, but the U.S. television industry was by far the major supplier of programming worldwide. Since the early 1990s, rapid technological, economic, and structural change has resulted in a shift in relations between U.S. media industries and the rest of the world.

In this article, media historian William Boddy discusses the impact of the changing global context on industrial constructions and perceptions of the American nation and its audiences. He observes, for example, that the purchase of major American media software producers (e.g., film studios, television production companies, music labels) by Japanese multinational corporations in the early 1990s resulted in Hollywood's definition of an American "self" against cultural and racial "others." At the same time, global audiences for U.S. media products are increasingly important economically, and new technologies

From *Quarterly Review of Film and Video* 49, no. 2 (Spring 1999): 55–70. Reprinted by permission of Gordon and Breach.

facilitate the construction of global, rather than local or national, markets. He cites the example of the new transnational youth market as a product of the new global media culture. Nevertheless, he argues that issues of national identities and audiences will become even more important as transnational media companies transcend the physical borders of countries.

Contemporary film and television historians often address those historical moments marked by the dissemination of new media technologies within particular national and industrial contexts, such as the development of the early film industry, radio broadcasting in the 1920s, the transition to sound in the Hollywood film industry, and the beginnings of commercial television. Such conjunctures offer privileged case studies of technological innovation, financial and market restructuring, and challenges to traditional representational practices. The late 1980s and early 1990s represent—in both the U.S. and Europe, in both public service and commercial television systems—a similar moment of crisis in political and economic legitimation for broadcast institutions and a reconfiguration of the previously stable institutional representations of nation and audience. Parallel to the crisis in the three-network TV oligopoly in the U.S., a distinct era of public service broadcasting came to a close in many Western European nations by the end of the 1980s.[1] The recent upheaval on both sides of the Atlantic can perhaps most acutely be read as a crisis in the manner in which the respective television institutions have constructed what John Hartley has called the twin "imaginary communities" of nation and audience.[2]

The U.S. role in the unsettled arena of international television at the start of the 1990s suggests an intriguing parallel to the position of the American TV industry during the boom years of early global TV programming trade in the early 1960s, an era which defined U.S. network hegemony in both international and domestic markets. The two historical moments which bracket the "network era" of U.S. television can be unpacked via the shifting public and trade discourses addressing television, especially in the way in which such discourses have proposed new definitions of the nation and the television audience. In each case, a period of sustained growth in U.S. market power in the international media market, combined with the crisis in a consensus vision of the U.S. government's global political and military roles, created unusual occasions of national introspection as media-industry and political leaders redefined the stakes and position of U.S. media around the globe.

It is ironic, though not entirely unexpected, that the precise attributes and operations of the "network era" of American television have been more fully explicated only recently, at the same time that the networks' tight-fisted grip on their American domestic audience slips. Likewise, the contrasting moments of U.S. self-consciousness as an actor on the international media stage during the periods of crisis in market power and public relations of the early 1960s on the one hand and the late 1980s and early 1990s on the other may suggest wider issues concerning the economic and ideological constructions of the nation in contemporary film and television studies. There is an urgent need for contemporary media historians to address the U.S. film and television industries as part of a global market and system, sensitive not only to transnational economic forces but also to the nature of representations of the national audience produced by television and film institutions around the world.

Television culture has long inhabited a curious contradictory context, where the national boundary-indifferent paths of broadcast signals have, since the beginnings of radio broadcasting, triggered utopian visions of international understanding, even a withering away of the nation-state in a kind of one-world oral and image community, while at the same time the legal, economic, and discursive constructions of broadcast institutions and audiences have been resolutely national in design. It is the playing out of these discursive tensions under the shifting economic, political, and technological conditions of contemporary media that I would like to address.

The U.S. media's role in the 1991 U.S.-Iraq War crystallized some of these recent tensions of nation and audience. Joshua Muravchik, a resident scholar at the right wing American Enterprise Institute, wrote euphorically in the *New York Times* in January 1991 about what he saw as the fallout of the military success of Operation Desert Storm on chastised Democrats at home, on Arab malcontents who "believed that . . . the humiliations of colonialism and underdevelopment could be redeemed," and on those around the globe who would doubt America's new willingness to use force in a post-Vietnam syndrome era. Most optimistically, however, Muravchik saw in the ashes of the lopsided Gulf War the long-sought fulfillment of the post-WWII U.S. dream of a Pax Americana, now sovereign in a new unipolar world. He proclaimed:

> This Pax Americana will rest not on domination but on persuasion and example as well as power. It will consist not of empire but of having won over a large and growing part of the world not only to the joys of jeans and rock and Big Macs but also to our concept of how nations ought to be governed and to behave.[3]

But just as the U.S. military's carefully-managed image repertory of smart-bomb nosecone footage and uniformed talking heads could not entirely erase the presence of the war's actual victims, the technological muscle-flexing of CNN's new global reach during the Gulf War showcasing the carrots and sticks of a new Pax Americana failed to assuage recent U.S. anxieties about its role in the new global media system. The Gulf War, along with recent economic changes in the international landscape of television, what *Fortune* magazine at the end of 1990 called "a one-world pop-tech civilization," have brought anxious new institutional configurations of the nation and the TV audience, at a time when television serves a predominant role as both a product and producer of the nation around the world.[4]

By the second half of the 1980s, the implications of the long-heralded "technological revolution" in the electronic media were made manifest in distinct ways in the United States and Western Europe, and an examination of the trade and public discourses which anticipated and accompanied the technological and market changes in TV broadcasting can illuminate larger cultural processes involved in constructing national identities on both sides of the Atlantic. The new TV delivery systems represented by cable and direct broadcast satellites, the ongoing consolidation of the telecommunications and computer industries, the shifting political and regulatory policies regarding broadcasting, and the growth of significant new transnational entrepreneurs in the new media environment all point to the mid- and late-1980s as the period of greatest change in broadcasting since the widespread international adoption of television in the 1950s.

The study of international television today presents challenges not only of responding to a rapidly changing economic environment but also to major shifts within the premises and methods of critical media research, a clash of generations, disciplines, ideologies, and national contexts. There have been twenty years of sustained critical scrutiny of the massive export of U.S. television programming, long enough for some of the fundamental assumptions about the implications of international program flows to be challenged during a time when European nations have undergone a decade of significant changes in their own institutions of national broadcasting. Recent international debates in television studies may in turn inform U.S. critics increasingly sensitive to the domestic implications of the altered international TV landscape.[5]

One striking contrast between the discussions of television policy in the U.S. and Western Europe is the degree to which such debates abroad, in contrast to the general insularity in the U.S., have spilled into the popular press and into wider debates over national identity and public policy. The early 1980s, for example, saw across Europe a general panic at the prospect of what one British TV critic called *TV Today and Tomorrow: Wall to Wall Dallas,* invoking the American prime-time serial that French Cultural Minister Jack Lang called "the symbol of American cultural imperialism."[6] The ensuing debates among European media scholars usefully questioned received definitions of public service broadcasting, the national, the politics of popular pleasure and the functions of television melodrama.[7] In the U.S., by contrast, an entire earlier generation of TV critics and intellectuals saw their polemical investment in television's "golden age" of live drama dashed at the end of the 1950s in the traumas of the quiz show scandals and a rising tide of filmed action adventure shows. Until recently, the post-1960s interventions of American intellectuals into popular discourses on television have too often been limited to drop-dead broadsides, rudimentary content analysis, and the perennial hot button topics of TV sex and violence, journalistic objectivity, and the propriety of the TV docudrama.

However, at the same time that the New York-based TV critics were lamenting the death of live drama at the hands of filmed action adventure shows and frequently abandoning altogether what they viewed as a disloyal and corrupted medium, the American television industry was exploiting the booming world market for the same easily-exported filmed series. In 1961 for the first time there were more TV sets in use outside the U.S. than inside the country, and the three American networks eagerly looked abroad for new program markets, foreign partnerships and direct investments. ABC, for example, used a newly-created international division to acquire a majority interest in a private TV network in Central America and minority interests in Australian and Latin American stations.[8] But the most significant international sector for the U.S. television industry quickly became the export of television programming; by 1970 the three networks had become the world's largest TV program traders. The head of ABC told *The Saturday Evening Post* in 1961:

> Television has a great future. ABC is out in front on the international front. We have acquired a minority interest in twenty-two stations abroad. *The Untouchables, 77 Sunset Strip, Maverick* are the most popular programs in Australia. In Bangkok they watch *Wyatt Earp.* Half the people in the world are illiterate. Television can penetrate that barrier. . . . Television is a worldwide medium. You have to think globally. If you own a show, you own it worldwide.[9]

By 1963 CBS's film sales division had become the world's largest exporter of TV programming and for the first time that year its foreign sales exceeded domestic syndication revenues.[10] CBS's experience with the Japanese market is illustrative. The network began supplying news film to Japan in 1955; between 1955 and 1961 CBS sold over 2700 different programs in Japan, and by 1961 50 percent of network prime time programming in Japan (then the world's second largest TV market after the U.S.) was supplied by American firms, a "direct result," CBS Chairman Frank Stanton noted at the time, "of the removal of restrictions on how much programming the Japanese networks could accept, and how much they were permitted to pay for it." In 1964 CBS set up CBS Japan, Inc. to distribute TV programming; in 1967 CBS Records entered a 50/50 joint venture with Sony Corporation to manufacture and market records in Japan and elsewhere.[11]

Meanwhile the global penetration of U.S. programming in the early 1960s brought a new anxiety and self-consciousness about the image of America abroad, the fear, as CBS Chairman Frank Stanton told a Japanese-American group in 1963 (speaking in place of an ailing Edward R. Murrow), "that what entertains us at home may embarrass us abroad."[12] As film critic J. Hoberman recently argued, "a dozen years after the end of World War II, the United States was suffering from a new sort of malady, namely an 'image problem,' " as works such as the 1959 best-seller *The Ugly American* adopted the domestic introspection of 1950s popular fiction and nonfiction and "took this self-doubt global." *The Ugly American,* according to Hoberman, struck a responsive chord in the U.S. public and was used by Democrats to construct a New Frontier foreign policy, perhaps the high point of the original postwar Pax Americana.[13]

The high-profile Washington hearings in 1961 and 1962 into sex and violence in prime time TV programming led by Senator Thomas Dodd exposed widespread anxieties about the detrimental effects of such programming on the U.S. image abroad. Clara Logan, president of the National Association for Better Radio and Television, told the Subcommittee: "Worst of all, the Communists the world over use gangsterism in American telefilms for their own political ends, propagandizing that this TV gangsterism and violence really is America." Witnesses before Dodd's committee repeatedly, expressed concern about the harmful effects of American television programming on what they viewed as more impressionable foreign audiences.[14]

A 1961 *Broadcasting* magazine article entitled "TV, Movies Cast as Villains of Delinquency," reflected the dual nascent moral panics about impressionable television audiences at home and abroad. The magazine reported that one Congressman inserted critic John Crosby's charge that "we teach juvenile delinquency on television" into the *Congressional Record*. The article also noted, in the coincidental confirmation hearings for Edward R. Murrow as U.S. Information Agency director, another elected official's worries about the harmful effects of American television program exports on the U.S. image abroad. Could Murrow "persuade" leaders of the industry to stop exporting them, the Senator asked; Murrow said he would try.[15] In a potent symbol of the new political sensitivity about American TV exports and the industry-government alliances typical of the New Frontier, President John F. Kennedy had, in 1961, first offered the directorship of the United States Information Agency (USIA) to CBS's Frank Stanton and only to Edward R. Murrow when Stanton declined. Murrow promptly attempted to prevent the BBC from airing his own *CBS Reports: Harvest of Shame* and later removed the unflattering documentary from all USIA programs abroad.[16]

Nevertheless, what is striking in these expressions of official anxiety as the U.S. moved to predominance in world image markets in the early 1960s is the general confidence in the structural role of the U.S. as program exporter, with the occasional misgivings reflecting either narrow partisan disputes or the muted ambivalence of a delicate imperialist sensibility. Historian Herbert Schiller has identified the early 1960s as the high point of the confident cold war consensus of government officials, media industry leaders and academic researchers about the role of U.S. media exports in what one communication scholar at the time called "the persuasive transmission of enlightenment . . . [as] . . . the modern paradigm of international communication."[17]

The early 1960s also witnessed the emphatic institutional construction of the domestic U.S. television audience along the lines of what John Hartley has termed a paedocratic regime (with the audience imagined as having childlike qualities and needs), constructed simultaneously from the good-parent, bad-parent discourses of CBS head James Aubrey's widely-reported program directive of "broads, bosoms and fun" on the one hand and the paternalistic inquisitions into TV and juvenile delinquency by ex-seminarian, ex-Nuremberg prosecutor and ex-FBI agent Senator Thomas Dodd on the other.[18] Both Hartley and Ien Ang have noted the colonialist and orientalist quality of the institutional discourse of the American TV industry concerning knowledge about and address to its audience, a discourse which created an objectified, dominated and often childlike "other" as audience. This regime of knowledge, functional to the network industry's need for profit maximization and self-preservation, characterized an ascendant U.S. television industry supremely confident of its domestic and international hegemony.[19]

The American television industry grew, prospered and remained structurally unaltered through the 1960s and most of the 1970s. At the same time, the unequal growth rates of the domestic and foreign program markets widened in the 1970s and 1980s; between 1970 and 1988, the number of TV households worldwide grew from 80 million to 500 million. Nevertheless, in the late 1980s the U.S. remained the predominant supplier in the international programming market; with less than 5 percent of the global TV audience, the U.S. television industry represented one third of the world's total TV program expenditures in 1989. The extended period of profits and stability of the network television industry from the late 1950s through the 1970s, along with the continued marginalization of public television and the virtual absence of foreign programming on American commercial TV, made domestic evidence of U.S. television's reciprocal links to the rest of the TV world extremely tenuous. Large U.S. audiences cozily divided among three network firms, a high proportion of U.S. gross national product spent on advertising (2.4 percent in 1986, the highest in the world), nearly double-digit annual growth rates in advertising expenditures (from $5 billion to $100 billion between 1948 and 1988, with nearly a quarter of the spending going to television), and the one-way nature of the U.S. trade in TV programs (the U.S. imported about 2 percent of its programming in 1983) all contributed to an international profile for the U.S. television industry which recalls the boastful sign along the rusting New Jersey industrial corridor of an earlier era: "Trenton Makes, The World Takes."[20]

However, despite the continued dominance of U.S. firms in world image markets, as the 1990s began there was a noticeable shift in the popular and industry view of the relation of U.S. television to the rest of the world. The early roots of this anxiety can be sensed in CBS Chairman Frank Stanton's 1963 speech to the United States-Japan Conference on Cultural and Educational Interchange when he noted prophetically:

> It is true, and I would be the first to concede the point, that for the moment at least the exchange is lopsided: we export far more than we import. But I also believe that Japanese television film product will increasingly find its way into the world market. . . . Recall, if you will, that only a little over a decade ago world manufacturers of optical and electronic components and devices never dreamed what Japanese inventiveness and industry would mean to them competitively in an astoundingly short time. . . . Habits, no matter how deeply entrenched, have a way of changing.[21]

In the early 1990s context of sustained economic recession and growing anxiety about the nation's ability to thrive in changing global markets, U.S. media-industry and government leaders reconfigured the domestic stakes of the new international media landscape. These trade and public policy discourses recast the

U.S. media industry in industrial-policy terms as the rare success story of American ingenuity and market appeal, but one increasingly threatened by international software piracy on the one hand and by a Japanese financial takeover of U.S. media firms on the other.[22] In 1990 U.S. trade surpluses from media exports were outpaced only by the aerospace sector in an otherwise bleak balance of trade picture; when combined with the export of the high-profile mass consumer goods of Joshua Muravchik's new Pax Americana (Ninja Turtles, Coke, Big Macs and Levis) whose demand is driven by American media exports, the combined pop culture sector represents the largest single contributor to U.S. exports.[23]

The contemporary construction of the U.S. media industry along industrial-policy terms, often combined with more or less explicit nationalist appeals, has brought a new reciprocal consciousness of America's place in the international media market among leaders of the U.S. film and television industries. The infamous "leaked" 1991 memorandum from Disney head Jeffrey Katzenberg noted lyrically:

> In a way, there is something quite noble in what we do. Our potential impact can not be minimized and should never be trivialized. At the same time that America has lost its dominance of the world's economy, it has become a pre-eminent force in the world's culture. And this is largely because of what we do. People around the world may no longer drive in American cars, build with American steel, or listen to American radios. But they do go see American films. They share our hopes and dreams and values when they experience the joy of a *Pretty Woman,* the enchantment of a *Little Mermaid* or the inspiration of a *Dead Poet's Society.*[24]

A fearful and defensive tone in contemporary conceptions of the U.S. media industry was rarely far from the surface of such brave statements of national pride. Recent purchases by foreign-based multinationals of major U.S. media software producers (four of the eight major motion picture studies are owned by firms based outside the U.S., as are four of the five global record labels), culminating in Sony's purchase of Columbia Pictures and CBS Records and Matsushita's $7 billion buyout of MCA, the largest acquisition ever of a U.S. company by a Japanese firm, have provoked new discursive configurations of "nation" and "other" within the U.S. media industry.[25] Economist George Gilder worried in 1990 that "as the 1980s roared and tumbled to a close, sirens wailed and moods darkened in Japanese-America relations. . . . For the first time since World War II, the underpinnings of friendship and prosperity between the U.S. and Asia appeared to be in serious jeopardy. . . . A consensus emerged that the U.S. was a graying and gullible nation, slipping into churlish senility, and that Japan was a mercantilist shyster, seizing power by unfair trade."[26]

Most U.S. media industry observers view the recent acquisitions as driven by the desire of Japanese media–hardware manufacturers to exploit horizontal integration via control or ownership of complementary software firms in the form of movie studios, record labels, and TV production companies. Michael Schulhof, president of Sony USA, citing the lessons of the VCR and the audio CD, told

Fortune: "Unless you have software to support your hardware, you can't have a successful industry." But the move by Japanese firms into software production provoked a new self-consciousness in Hollywood of American cultural identity as defined against a cultural and racial other. The CEO of Coca-Cola, which sold Columbia Pictures to Sony for $3.4 million told the magazine: "Hollywood, unlike Detroit, has found a product that the Japanese can't improve upon."[27] But Disney's Katzenberg warned in his 1991 memo that Sony and Matsushita were getting into a business "out of their cultural context" in acquiring Hollywood studios, explaining:

> Filmmaking in its essence is about the conveyance of emotion. Not coincidentally, filmakers by their nature are an emotional group—from the actors on the screen to the dealmakers behind the scenes. It is said to be a crazy business and most of its practitioners admittedly are, by normal standards, a bit eccentric.
>
> The Japanese, on the other hand, culturally err on the side of withholding emotion. In saying this, I am not simply offering an American perspective. The Japanese are the first to tell you this about themselves.[28]

Such racialist suggestions of national character aside, the economic and institutional boundaries between the U.S. motion-picture and television industries, eroded by converging financial ownership structures and textual practices, have become increasingly tenuous in the new international media landscape. Despite the financial success of "character-driven" sleeper hits in 1990, for example, the U.S. domestic theatrical box office continues to represent a diminishing share of total studio revenues. A decade before Katzenberg's memo, *Variety* pointed out, the U.S. domestic box office represented 80 percent of a film's total revenues; now it represents only about 30 percent. Notwithstanding disingenuous proclamations by studio heads of the new centrality of character and story, studio management remains focused on what are seen as the star-, action-, and special effects-driven demands of home video and the foreign box office; as one studio executive told *Variety:* "It's almost like theatrical distribution is your loss leader."[29]

Some of the implications of such shifts in the figuration of "nation" and "other" in the contemporary U.S. media industry are worth suggesting. As David Morley and Kevin Robins argue, the new media technologies are deeply transgressive of traditional discursive boundaries of the nation and the audience, disaggregating "fixed national audiences and communities and creating new ones across national boundaries."[30] In *Fortune*'s "one-world pop-tech civilization," media firms have constructed a new global media culture as transnational youth market. Bill Roedy, the CEO of MTV Europe, which captured 20 million viewers in its first three years with the support of major advertisers such as Coke, Levi's, Nike, and the Hollywood studios, explained: "An 18-year old in Denmark has more in common with an 18-year old in France than either has with elders in their own country." Roedy continued: "The programming has been so regulated over here, we're like an oasis in the desert. And our idea is so simple: English language music programming works regardless of the culture or the language. It's an international art form."[31] Similarly, Coca Cola CEO Roberto Goizueta explained his company's international marketing strategy:

> Our message has been consistent since 1923, and it's been a very emotional one: family, friends, good times. What they're buying is the good things in life. Americans may say, well, that's the American way, but it's not really. There's a thirst out there everywhere to have a good time. It's *everybody's* way.[32]

The recent growth of the international TV program market, besides creating new opportunities for U.S.-based (if no longer U.S.-owned) program producers, has also had significant implications for European broadcasters and audiences. The 1980s and early 1990s brought not only new financial and competitive pressures on European public service broadcasters, but also a new crisis of political legitimacy for established broadcast institutions. As Ien Ang has argued, European public service broadcasting's traditional forms of institutional knowledge about television audiences, based on the philosophical certainties of paternalism and an imputed public sphere, have been gradually replaced by the bureaucratic self-validating values of professionalism and balance and, as a result, public service broadcasters have increasingly relied upon the market-oriented empiricist constructions of the TV audience common to commercial broadcasting. In the face of newly contested audience representations for European public service broadcasters, the political challenge for defenders of public service broadcasting remains, as Nicholas Garnham wrote in 1983, that of addressing

> a crisis in imagination—an inability to conceive of an alternative to broadcasting controlled by profit-seeking private capital other than as centralised, bureaucratic, inefficient, arrogantly insensitive to the people's needs, politically subservient to the holders of state power . . .[33]

At the same time, the U.S. television industry in the 1980s began a wrenching, discursive reconstruction of its audience accompanied by industry hostility to what it viewed as the new fickle and irresponsible multichannel viewer.[34] As several contemporary media critics have noted, the commodification of commercial television's audience brought with it the structural imperative for continuous audience surveillance and quantification. Far from the more perfected panopticon ideal of audience surveillance and control represented by ever-improved technologies of spectator visibility, however, the continuous methodological refinements of the reigning empirically-constructed commercial TV audience have instead only pointed out the hopelessly vague and slippery nature of actual audiencehood. While contemporary commentators such as John Fiske, Ian Connell, and Lydia Curti have opted, with varying degrees of explicitness and commitment, to endorse commercial television as promising fuller satisfaction of popular pleasures than public service broadcasting, Ien Ang sees a wider complicity between the two systems in their institutional constructions of the TV audience.[35] From the ruins of the increasingly non-functional traditional institutional constructions of the audience in both U.S. and European television, Ang calls for communication scholars to construct non-totalizing ethnographic accounts of audiencehood from what she terms "the side of the audience."[36]

Despite the increasingly globally-integrated marketing campaigns of the multi-national consumer goods industry and the transnational medial networks they support, issues of the nation are unlikely to lose relevance in the continuing debates over television policy around the globe. As David Morley and Kevin Robins point out, notions of national identity—themselves constructed in part by specific cultural technologies—are always ideologically defined against other: the U.S. and Japan, Europe and the U.S.[37] Despite the current obsession in U.S. policy and financial circles for an over-hyped domestic "information superhighway" (promising interactive access to American homes by the newly-integrated sectors of telecommunications, cable and Hollywood studios), issues of national identity are unlikely to be displaced for long. As multinational media firms reach audiences in an ever more intimate and global fashion, the issues of nation and audience seem instead likely to grow more pressing, even in nations like the United States, where questions of cultural technologies and national identity have long seemed so nearly isomorphic as to be axiomatic. The secure bravado of an earlier, and extinct, U.S. industrial era reflected in "Trenton Makes, The World Takes," which served so long as the implicit paradigm for the U.S. communication industry in relation to its domestic and international audiences, is likely to enter increasing crisis in the future, notwithstanding rosy visions by some of a resuscitated consumerist Pax Americana in a putative one-world pop-tech civilization.

NOTES

1. For material on the contemporary crisis in European public service broadcasting, see Dennis McQuail, "Western Europe: 'Mixed Model' Under Threat?," in John Downing, Ali Mohammadi, and Annabelle Sreberny-Mohammadi, eds., *Questioning the Media: A Critical Introduction* (Newbury Park: Sage, 1990), pp. 125–38; Willard D. Rowland and Michael Tracey, "Worldwide Challenges to Public Service Broadcasting," *Journal of Communication* 40:2 (Spring 1990); 8–27; Steven S. Wildman and Stephen E. Siwek, "The Privatization of European Television: Effects of International Markets for Programs," *Columbia Journal of World Business* (Fall 1987), pp. 71–76; Ien Ang, *Desperately Seeking the Audience* (London: Routledge, 1991), pp. 99–152; Edward Buscombe, "Coca-cola Satellites? Hollywood and the Deregulation of European Television," in Tino Balio, ed., *Hollywood in the Age of Television* (Cambridge MA: Unwin and Hyman, 1990), pp. 393–415; Jay Blumer and T. J. Nossiter, eds., *Broadcasting Finance in Transition: A Comparative Handbook* (New York: Oxford University Press, 1991); Kenneth Dyson and Peter Humphreys, eds., *The Political Economy of Communications: International and European Dimensions* (London: Routledge, 1990); Kenneth Dyson, Peter Humphreys, Ralph Negrine and Jean-Paul Simon, eds., *Broadcasting and New Media Policies in Western Europe* (London: Routledge, 1988); Preben Sepstrup, *Transnationalization of Television in Western Europe* (London: John Libbey, 1990); R. Negrin and S. Papathanassopoulos, *The Internationalization of Television* (London: Pinter Publishers, 1990).

2. John Hartley, *Tele-ology: Studies in Television* (London: Routledge, 1992), pp. 101–18; see also Benedict Anderson, *Imaginary Communities: Reflections on the Origins and Spread of Nationalism* 2nd edition (London: Verso, 1991).

3. Joshua Muravchik, "At Last, Pax Americana," *New York Times,* January 24, 1991, p. A23.

4. John Huey, "America's Hottest Export: Pop Culture," *Fortune,* December 31, 1990, p. 50; for a discussion of the media's role in the Gulf War, see Kevin Robins and Les Levidow, "The Eye of the Storm," *Screen* 32:3(Autumn 1991): 324–28.

5. On the changing international scholarship as represented by papers from the International Television Studies Conferences organized by the British Film Institute, see Philip Drummond and Richard Paterson, eds., *Television in Transition* (London: BFI, 1986); Drummond and Paterson, eds., *Television and Its Audience: International Research Perspectives* (London: BFI, 1988); Drummond, Paterson and Janet Willis, eds., *National Identity and Europe: The Television Revolution* (London: BFI, 1993).

6. Chris Dunkley, *TV Today and Tomorrow: Wall to Wall Dallas* (London: Penguin, 1985); Land is quoted in Ien Ang, *Watching "Dallas": Soap Opera and the Melodramatic Imagination* (New York: Methuen, 1985), p. 2.

7. See, for example, David Morley, "Changing Paradigms in Audience Studies," in Ellen Seiter, Hans Borchers, Gabriele Kreutzner and Eva-Maria Warth, eds., *Remote Control: Television, Audiences and Cultural Power* (London: Routledge, Chapman and Hall, 1989), pp. 16–43; Nicholas Garnham, "Public Service Versus the Market," *Screen* 23:2 (July/August 1983): 6–27; Ian Connell, "Commercial Broadcasting and the British Left," *Screen* 24:6 (November/December 1983): 70–80; Ian Connell and Lydia Curti, "Popular Broadcasting in Italy and Britain: Some Issues and Problems," in *Television in Transition*, pp. 87–111; Richard Collins, "Wall to Wall Dallas? The US-UK Trade in Television," in Cynthia Schneider and Brian Wallis, eds., *Global Television* (Cambridge: MIT Press, 1988), pp. 79–94; Richard Collins, *Culture, Communication and National Identity: The Case of Canadian Television* (Toronto: University of Toronto Press, 1990); John Tomlinson, *Cultural Imperialism* (Baltimore: Johns Hopkins, 1991); John Caughie, "Playing at Being American: Games and Tactics," in Patricia Mellencamp, ed., *Logics of Television: Essays in Cultural Criticism* (Bloomington: Indiana University Press, 1990), pp. 44–58.

8. "Income and Earnings Reach Record High," *Broadcasting*, April 4, 1960, pp. 76–77.

9. John Bartlow Martin, "Television USA": Part 1: "Wasteland or Wonderland?," *The Saturday Evening Post,* October 21, 1961, p. 24.

10. Columbia Broadcasting System, *Annual Report* for year ending December 28, 1963 (New York: Columbia Broadcasting System, 1964), pp. 4, 19; for contemporary accounts of American telefilm exports, see "World Laps Up U.S. TV Fare," *Business Week,* April 23, 1960, p. 129; "TV Abroad Thrives on U.S. Ways," *Business Week,* September 3, 1960, pp. 105–07; Robert Lewis Shayon, "Breakthrough in International TV," *Saturday Review of Literature,* January 14, 1961, p. 35.

11. Frank Stanton, Keynote Address, Second United States-Japan Conference on Cultural and Educational Interchange, Washington, D.C., October 16, 1963, p. 2. Collection of the CBS Reference Library. Columbia Broadcasting System, *Annual Report* for year ending January 2, 1965 (New York: Columbia Broadcasting System, 1965), p. 4; Columbia Broadcasting System, *Annual Report* for year ending December 30, 1967 (New York: Columbia Broadcasting System, 1968), p. 3. The percentage of U.S.-produced programming on Japanese television fell significantly after the early 1960s for a variety of reasons.

12. F. Stanton, Keynote Address, p. 3.

13. J. Hoberman, "Believe it or Not: J. Hoberman on *The Ugly American*" *Artform,* April 1991, pp. 27–28.

14. U.S. Congress, Senate, Committee on the Judiciary, Subcommittee to Investigate Juvenile Delinquency, *Hearings Part 10 Effects on Young People of Violence and Crime Portrayed on Television* 87th Cong; June–July 1961; January, May 1962, pp. 1678–81, 1883; see also Val Adams, "Stanton Defends TV Sent Overseas," *New York Times,* May 4, 1962, p. 67.

15. "TV, Movies Cast as Villains of Delinquency," *Broadcasting,* March 20, 1961, p. 76.

16. James L. Baughman, *Television's Guardians: The FCC and the Politics of Programming 1958–1967* (Knoxville: University of Tennessee Press, 1985), p. 56.

17. Daniel Lerner quoted in Herbert Schiller, *Culture, Inc.* (New York: Oxford University Press, 1989), p. 139.

18. *Tele-ology,* p. 108; for a discussion of Aubrey's alleged dictum, see "Networks Offer Definitions of Sex," *New York Times,* May 12, 1962, p. 51; Aubrey told Dodd's subcommittee: "I do not believe I have ever used the term 'broads, bosoms, and fun' in connection with a CBS television network program. But I believe it is quite easy for people who work in this particular business to interpret a request for attractive girls, wholesome, attractive girls, rather than neurotic, unhappy, unattractive women as 'broads,' and also, because you want them attractive, I believe you use the word 'bosoms.' " *Hearings,* pp. 2481–82.

19. *Tele-ology,* p. 105; *Desperately Seeking the Audience,* pp. 22–23.

20. The data in this paragraph are found in Peter Dunnett, *The World Television Industry* (London: Routledge, 1990), pp. 1, 4, 6, 25, 41.

21. Stanton, Keynote Address, pp. 4, 5–6.

22. See "America's Hottest Export," pp. 51, 58; also see David Morley and Kevin Robins, "Techno-Orientalism: Foreigners, Phobias and Futures," in *New Formations* 16 (Spring 1992): 136–56.

23. *Ibid.,* p. 50.

24. "The Teachings of Chairman Jeff," *Variety,* January 21, 1991, p. 5.

25. "America's Hottest Export," p. 51.

26. George Gilder, *Life After Television: The Coming Transformation of Media and American Life* (Knoxville: Whittle, 1990).

27. "America's Hottest Export," p. 51.

28. "The Teachings of Chairman Jeff," p. 5.

29. *Ibid.*

30. David Morley and Kevin Robins, "Spaces of Identity," *Screen* 30:4 (1989): pp. 11–12.

31. "America's Hottest Export," p. 52.

32. *Ibid.,* p. 58 (emphasis added).

33. "Public Service Versus the Market," p. 21.

34. For a discussion of the new viewing practices, see Carrie Heeter and Bradley S. Greenberg, *Cableviewing* (Norwood, NJ: Ablex, 1988).

35. John Fiske, "Popular Television and Commercial Culture: Beyond Political Economy," in *Television Studies,* pp. 34–35; "Commercial Broadcasting and the British Left"; "Popular Broadcasting in Italy and Britain."

36. *Desperately Seeking the Audience,* pp. 164–70.

37. "Spaces of Identity," p. 10.

QUESTIONS FOR DISCUSSION

1. How have changes in technology and in national broadcasting systems since the early 1990s changed this one-sided dynamic that Boddy describes?

2. How "American" are U.S. media forms: film, TV shows, music? If the global audience is central to economic success, can U.S. media products afford to be too specifically "American?"

3. Why does the United States import so little TV from other countries? What might change this?

INFOTRAC COLLEGE EDITION

To search for more information on this subject on InfoTrac College Edition try combining the term "global" with other terms like "media," "television," and "Hollywood." Also search under "globalization and television." Also try under names of countries combined with "television". "France and television," "Japan and television," and so on.

17

Feminine Desire
in the Age
of Satellite Television

MICHAEL CURTIN

The increased conglomeration of media industries in the 1990s and 2000s leads many media and social critics to decry the subsequent homogenization of public media cultures. According to these critiques, profit-driven international media giants rob media images and texts of their cultural specificity in order to ensure their popularity with the largest possible audience. In this article, Michael Curtin argues that such thinking, based on assumptions about the media industries formed during the high network era of the 1960s to 1980s, is out of date and inadequate for the analysis of the media landscape of the new century.

Curtin instead argues that the current neo-network era is characterized by the seemingly paradoxical corporate strategies of both the globalization and fragmentation of media texts and audiences. He suggests that neo-network era culture industries are far from being "well-oiled machines" that operate according to a coherent and mature logic, and are therefore capable of creating and circulating content that is sometimes subversive. To support his argument, Curtin examines two case studies of how corporate strategies in the neo-network era have facilitated, perhaps unwittingly, the circulation of transgressive

From *Journal of Communication* 49, no. 2 (Spring 1999): 55–70. Reprinted by permission of Oxford University Press.

images of feminine desire in two very different cultural sites. Curtin is careful not to celebrate the neo-network era as a triumph of popular and local cultures over corporate control but suggests that the current period provides opportunities, perhaps but not necessarily fleeting, in which women and other subordinate groups may imagine and enact different and more advantageous social roles and desires.

Television texts around the world increasingly feature female characters who resist or reformulate conventional gender roles. This trend seems to defy expectations that the concentration of media ownership leads to a conservative, homogeneous flow of popular imagery. Such an apparent contradiction can be explained by close analysis of the strategies, operations, and discourse of culture industries in the neo-network era of satellite and cable media. This era is paradoxically characterized by corporate conglomeration and by strategies of flexibility and decentralization. Consequently, media firms actually benefit from the transnational circulation of multiple and alternative representations of feminine desire. Although this does not necessarily democratize media, in most societies its significantly expands the rage of feminine imagery available in popular culture.

The original version of *Macarena,* the transnational popular music hit, was released in April 1993 by a couple of flamenco singers, Antonio Romero and Rafael Ruiz, who perform under the name Los del Rio. They have worked together for over 30 years, churning out more than 300 songs during their career. Because flamenco is a rather localized genre, they are by no means major pop icons. Indeed, legend has it that the origins of *Macarena* were rather modest. The song was written one night by Romero after he and his partner had performed with a flamenco dancer named Diana Patricia Cubillan, a good friend of theirs, at a Caracas hotel in 1992.

The song is a tribute to Cubillan and briefly became a modest hit in Spain during the summer of 1993. This original version was especially popular with older listeners, who tend to appreciate the traditional music of Andalusia, but it failed to capture the attention of younger mainstream audiences. Nevertheless, several remixes of *Macarena* were commissioned by the Zafiro label based on the song's limited success, and it slowly began to migrate to dance clubs throughout Europe and Latin America. In 1994, Zafiro was bought by Bertelsmann, the German media conglomerate that also owns BMG and RCA records. A young BMG executive in Paris reportedly took notice of the song's popularity on the European disco scene and decided to escalate the international marketing of *Macarena* by ordering the production of a music video and by commissioning a dance instructor to choreograph a set of moves that could easily be learned by viewers of all ages.

In an explicit attempt to crack the U.S. market, BMG then hired a Miami hip-hop group, the Bayside Boys, to do an English-language remix of the song, hoping to attract a crossover audience. *Macarena* hit number one on the U.S. music charts in the summer of 1996 and was played in heavy rotation on radio and music television for the next few months. Some claim it surpassed the Beatles's song *Yesterday* as the most frequently played single in U.S. radio history. It also generated perhaps the biggest dance craze since John Travolta's disco film, *Stayin' Alive*. Ultimately, *Macarena* enjoyed extensive transnational circulation, traveling to the top of the world where it was featured in the nightclubs of Lhasa and Tibet, and in the schoolyards in Australia, where children methodically practiced and performed the dance steps in synchrony (DuLac & Smith, 1996; Hinckley, 1996; Lannert, 1995; Llewellyn, 1996; Navarro, 1995; Smith, 1996).

The global success of *Macarena* owes much to the video and to the Bayside Boys's remix, featuring a techno beat with a heavy bass line and synthesizer accompaniment, which moves the song close to the *MTV* mainstream. Although the remix was obviously targeted at the music television market, the beat was intentionally made slower than the average techno hit to make it danceable for a broad audience. The lyrics were also retooled to blend the original Spanish text with a new set of English-language lyrics that bring the song closer to a Madonna-esque version of femininity. According to the remixed version, Macarena likes to shop and she likes to chase boys, regardless of what her absent lover, Vitorino, might think. Indeed, Macarena seems to exercise power both in her relationship with Vitorino and in her relationships with young men whom she invites to dance. "Move with me, chant with me," she sings in English, "and if you're good, I'll take you home with me." To this, Ruiz and Romero respond, "Dale a tu cuerpo alegria Macarena" (give your body pleasure, Macarena).

This mixture of fantasy, desire, and feminine power is, of course, open to other interpretations. The video is liberally sprinkled with what male executives in the entertainment industry often refer to as "eye candy," in this case, a dance troupe of suggestively dressed young women from a range of racial and ethnic backgrounds, wearing trendy street fashions that appropriate design elements from a range of ethnic apparel. Looking somewhat like a Benetton ad, the video is both a United Nations of hip hop and a masculine fantasy of scantily clad young women gyrating around two middle-aged White men (Romero and Ruiz) in three-piece suits who applaud the lascivious sensibilities of their female collaborators.

Macarena seemingly has a little something for everyone and represents a very calculated effort to move a product through the elaborate circuits of global popular culture. In the parlance of the industry, *Macarena* was "leveraged every which way imaginable" to wring out every ounce of profitability by thoroughly exploiting it throughout the value chain of the Zafiro-Ariola-BMG-RCA-Bertelsmann music empire.

This example raises several significant issues for media critics. First, *Macarena* unambiguously directs our attention to media representations of feminine desire. Throughout this century, as capitalist economies around the world have entered a consumerist phase, marketing strategies increasingly focus their attention on women as the key arbiters of family purchasing decisions. What is more, as disposable income rises among the general population, hygiene and beauty products industries become especially conscious of the role that feminine desire plays in promoting their products. Consequently, radio, television, and print media are important sites where codings of woman as homemaker and romantic partner have been produced, circulated, and conventionalized. As many scholars have demonstrated, however, alternative and even subversive images of women's desires have become more widespread recently, with the literature on Madonna generating perhaps the greatest amount of attention (Bradby, 1992; Brown & Campbell, 1986; Curry, 1990; Fiske, 1992; Kaplan, 1987; Leung, 1997; Lewis, 1990; Miller, 1991; Schwichtenberg, 1992; Watts, 1996; Wilson & Markle, 1992; Young, 1991).

Why and how have these transgressive images of feminine desire emerged? Certainly one can tie them to feminist struggles since the early 1970s to challenge dominant assumptions about women's roles in society. But how and why do images of feminine power and desire become marketable products in the increasingly globalized culture industries? In this essay I show how the changing discourse and structure of the culture industries accommodate, nurture, and even benefit from the circulation of transgressive images of feminine desire.

Second, *Macarena* is an important departure point for analysis, because it seems to represent much of what is feared about global media conglomerates. It serves as an example of a song that expresses local cultural tastes and values, but which takes on another life as it is repackaged and endlessly exploited in a seemingly cynical and calculated fashion. Rather than celebrating or promoting a distinctive genre of music, the Bertelsmann media conglomerate apparently dipped into its semiotic toolbox to refashion the product for mass, transnational consumption. The implication is that all culture is headed the way of *Macarena,* that there is little room for authentic difference or alternative cultural forms of expression. The homogenizing power of media conglomerates seems insurmountable, as they tighten the bolts on a well-oiled system of production, circulation, and exchange.

Curiously, we find this characterization of transnational media in the work of postmodern and postcolonial scholars such as Fredric Jameson (1991), Masao Miyoshi (1996), Arif Dirlik (1996), and Edward Said (1994), as well as in the scholarly writings of political economists such as Herbert Schiller (1992), Nicholas Garnham (1990), and Ben Bagdikian (1992). All these critics focus their attention on a supposed correlation between the emergence of huge media conglomerates and what they take to be a homogenization of public culture. In their eyes, ownership is the crucial concern. The actual operation of media industries is treated as epiphenomenal. Ownership is equated with control, and control is maintained by forging ever larger markets for particular cultural forms through a process of homogenization.

In this essay I first argue that these assumptions about the homogenizing power of huge media conglomerates are based on residual concepts from the classical or high network era of television. Such an approach fosters a misrecognition of the actual forces at work in the contemporary culture industries and obscures the ways in which popular culture serves as a site for reimagining social relations during periods of cultural and political changes. A better way to understand the actual operations of media conglomerates is to delineate the corporate logic of what I refer to as the neo-network era, which most prominently features decentralizing strategies via multiple circuits of production, distribution, and consumption. The emerging principles of this new era also help to explain contradictory tendencies toward conglomeration and specialization, toward globalization and fragmentation.

In the second part of this essay I examine a cult television hit, *Absolutely Fabulous,* which provides an example of an unruly text that never would have been produced or distributed during the high network era but has proven extremely lucrative during the neo-network era. This example not only suggests a new textual and corporate logic to television programming practices, it reveals the relative immaturity and incoherence of corporate responses to the new media environment.

In the final section I explore the political implications of the neo-network era on the Indian subcontinent, where huge media conglomerates are wrestling with local music, television, and film producers for the attention of hundreds of millions of viewers. If *Macarena* shows us a very calculated effort to leverage profitably a local cultural form into a transnational phenomenon, then Alisha Chinai's gender-bending pop music shows the reverse: the opportunity for local producers to appropriate elements of cosmopolitan media in ways that produce distinctive and alternative forms of cultural expression in national and local contexts.

THE NEO-NETWORK ERA

In many ways television, more than any other popular form of communication, seems to embody the defining features of a mass medium. During its first 3 decades in the United States, for example, television stood at the intersection of entertainment and information, of imagination and consumption, and of private leisure and public life. Huge mass audiences engaged it on a daily, simultaneous basis, making it arguably the most central institution in U.S. history.[1] Even though the audience has been splintering for close to 20 years, the heyday of network television continues to shape much of our thinking about the culture industries. The "classical" or "high network" era of television emerged during the early 1950s and lasted roughly until the early 1980s, when cable satellite television began to siphon off significant portions of the audience. During this time, television seemed to represent both everything that was good and bad about a mass medium. It was widely available, relatively inexpensive, and offered a showcase for some of the best talent in the history of modern entertainment. It also "brought us together" for some of the most densely textured moments of political and cultural exchange.

Nevertheless, it is difficult for those who have lived through these moments not to see the television industry as controlled by a small coterie of White males who have the ability to shape popular consciousness in profound ways. Our imagination of how the industry operates is still influenced by the imposing shadows cast by the likes of Sarnoff, Paley, and Goldenson. Yet, despite the supposed power of these media moguls, the high network era also seemed to be governed by the inexorable logic of a mass medium, premised upon an inter-locking system of mass production, mass marketing, mass consumption, and na-tional regulation (Curtin, 1996). The "shared sense of experience" that television seemed to provide during the high network era was less a matter of consensus than it was a manifestation of a particular set of capitalist relations of production and exchange. Such relations have been described by scholars under the rubric of Fordism.

This era was also dominated by the belief that huge, integrated enterprises could serve the needs of vast national and international markets. Even though television audiences of this period were fragmented along many axes, network executives aspired to represent their audiences as a unified entity in ratings, mar-keting reports, and promotions. Moreover, they characterized their overaching mission as integrative (i.e., pulling people together, uniting various regions, forg-ing ever larger markets). Of course, niche markets existed then as now, but they were not celebrated in trade discourse among the major corporate players who controlled the medium.

The operative principles of the high network era still exercise a powerful hold on our imaginations. As we have witnessed the merging of gigantic media firms into huge conglomerates over the past decade, many scholarly and popular critics seem to have assumed that this concentration of ownership means greater control at the top of the corporate pyramid and an increasing homogenization of cultural products. They revert to past stereotypes of media moguldom to convey a sense of the organizing intentions behind firms like News Corporation, Disney, and Viacom. Each conglomerate is represented as an institutional extension of the personality of its chief corporate officer (e.g., Rupert Mudoch, Michael Eisner, Sumner Redstone).

As conglomeration has intensified over the past couple decades, the power of these moguls has supposedly assumed transnational proportions, reaching into virtually every culture and society. Critics like Bagdikian (1989) have suggested that what we are witnessing is the continuation of a trend toward concentration that began earlier in this century. Whereas media moguls once controlled popu-lar culture and public opinion on a national scale, they now control it on a global scale. This presumption is also widely featured in popular narratives, like the most recent James Bond film, *Tomorrow Never Dies.*

Despite frightening apparitions of gigantic media octopuses, Fordist princi-ples seem to be undergoing a period of significant transformation. Changes in national and global economies over the past 2 decades have fragmented the mar-ketplace and pressured the culture industries to reorganize and restrategize. As opposed to the relative stability of huge, nationally based media corporations during much of this century, the current period of transition is paradoxically characterized by both transnationalization and fragmentation. New technologies, deregulation, and relentless competition have undermined national frameworks and are reconfiguring the cultural landscape.

Although mass markets continue to attract corporate attention, industry dis-course about the mass audience no longer refers to one simultaneous experience so much as a shared, asynchronous cultural milieu. In part, this is because the culture industries exercise less control over the daily scheduling of popular entertainment. Audiences time-shift and channel surf, or they pursue a myriad of other entertainment options. Consequently, trends and ideas now achieve prominence in often circuitous and unanticipated ways.

Media executives therefore strive for broad exposure of their products through multiple circuits of information and expression. They also seek less to homogenize popular culture than to organize and exploit diverse forms of creativity toward profitable ends. Besides their heavily promoted mass products, media corporations cultivate a broad range of products intended for more specific audiences. Flexible corporate frameworks connect mass market operations with more localized initiatives.

Therefore, two strategies are now at work in the culture industries. One focuses on mass cultural forms aimed at broad national or global markets that demand low involvement and are relatively apolitical (e.g., Hollywood films or broadcast television). Media operations that deal in this arena are cautious about the prospect of intense audience responses either for or against the product they are marketing. By comparison, those products targeted at niche audiences actively pursue intensity. They seek out audiences that are more likely to be highly invested in a particular form of cultural expression. These firms do not aim to change niche groups. They aim instead to situate their products within them. Among industry executives, these are referred to as products with "edge." They received little attention 30 years ago, but product today development meetings are peppered with references to attitude and edge, that is, references to products that sharply define the boundaries of their intended audience.

We are therefore witnessing the organization of huge media conglomerates around the so-called synergies that exploit these two movements. This is what I refer to as the neo-network era, an era characterized by the multiple and asynchronous distribution of cultural forms. It is an era that operates according to neo-Fordist principles, what Harvey (1989) referred to as a flexible regime of accumulation. Rather than a network structure anchored by highly centralized systems of national finance, production, and regulation, the neo-network era features elaborate circuits of cultural production, distribution, and reception.

This transformation is not a radical break with the past. Rather, it is a transitional phase in which Fordist and neo-Fordist principles exist side-by-side. Blockbuster films that appeal to a transnational audience are still the desideratum of major Hollywood studios, but the same conglomerate that may own a studio may also own a cable service, a specialty music label, and a collection of magazines that target very specific market niches.[2] "As you get narrower in interest," one media executive observed, "you tend to have more intensity of interest [and] the person is more likely to pay the extra money" (quoted in Ohman, Averill, Curtin, Shumway, & Traube, 1996, p. 137).[3] The key to success is no longer the ownership and control of a centralized and highly integrated media empire, but the management of a conglomerate structured around a variety of firms with different audiences and different objectives. According to media executives, these firms are simply following a marketing strategy that is strictly capitalistic and generally disinterested in content issues.

Ideally, this neo-network strategy will present opportunities whereby a micromarket phenomenon crosses over into a mainstream phenomenon, making it potentially exploitable through a greater number of circuits within the media conglomerate. Some rap artists' careers obviously followed this trajectory. This may be best represented by the success of a performer like Will Smith, who has scored hits in both Hollywood film and broadcast television. The converse is also true, however. A product that was originally a mass phenomenon can be spun out through myriad niche venues, which has been Viacom's strategy behind *Star Trek,* one of its profitable brands.[4] In an interview while he was in charge of the Turner Entertainment Group, Scott Sassa elaborated on this approach and pointed out that his job was to exploit the profitability of copyrighted material throughout the so-called value chain of the conglomerate. Sassa said that, "Every copyright that starts out anywhere in the system gets leveraged every which way imaginable" (quoted in Kline, 1995, p. 112). The key to profitability in the neo-network era is still distribution, but the distribution system is more diverse and decentered. It also remains highly volatile, given the unpredictable nature of popular responses to new cultural forms.

AN ERA OF INDETERMINACY

These corporate strategies help to explain the seemingly contradictory impulses toward globalization and fragmentation. They suggest how a niche product like *Macarena* might be leveraged into a mass global phenomenon. However, they also show how a television program like *Absolutely Fabulous* might never become a mass phenomenon, but could nevertheless prove enormously profitable if it were cleverly managed within the multiple and asynchronous circuits of global distribution. Another reason to turn our attention to *Absolutely Fabulous* is that this example reminds us that the seemingly tidy logic of the neo-netowork era, so elegantly laid out by executives like Sassa, is still at a very formative stage. We need to recognize that gaps, contradictions, and inconsistencies are much more characteristic of this era than what might be suggested by more common representations of highly integrated media juggernauts run by powerful moguls like Rupert Murdoch.

Interestingly, this era of indeterminacy also engenders unexpected opportunities to explore, criticize, and undermine dominant representations of feminine desire. It is therefore instructive to examine carefully the production, circulation, and textual logic of television programs like *Absolutely Fabulous.* The series features the omniholic Patsy Stone and Edina Monsoon—two aging flower children cum fashion divas with enormous appetites—who are bent on consuming every trendy drug, garment, and comestible on which they can lay their hands. This campy, ironic, and some argue queer take on contemporary consumer society had a bit too much edge for broadcast television executives when it was first pitched to them, but, then, that was exactly the point.

Absolutely Fabulous was designed from the outset to represent feminine desire as so voracious and uncontrollable that it was unlike most anything that has ever graced the airwaves of popular television. Conventional television texts, like the *Macarena* music video, will usually contain feminine desire or transform it into a mirror image of masculine fantasies, a tendency that has prevailed from the very earliest years of the medium (Doty, 1990; Mellencamp, 1991; Ritrosky-Winslow, 1998; Rowe, 1995; Spigel, 1992). *Absolutely Fabulous* not only resisted these conventions, it directly assaulted them, savaging the tidy little bows and wrappers of mass television on its way to ripping open a Pandora's box of kinky feminine desire.

Edina and Patsy, the lead characters, represent the exact opposite of everything the domestic comedy has ever imagined for adult women. They are neither nurturing nor self-sacrificing. Rather than mediating conflicts among the characters, they incite sensational confrontations. Edina is not a good mother to her daughter Saffy. Instead, she is manipulative, self-indulgent, and appallingly neglectful. Instead of guiding her adolescent daughter along the path to adulthood, Edina is racing backwards in a frantic attempt to recover her own youth. Her vodka-swilling best friend, Patsy, chain-smokes her way through the series with only occasional interruptions to pursue cynically her seemingly insatiable sexual desires. These are not nice people, and their physical appearance is not conventionally pretty.

Indeed, the series was developed from the outset as a hyperparodic niche product that would invite intense reactions from viewers. Only with the greatest reluctance did the BBC produce the series for a limited run of 18 episodes. ABC was so skittish about a U.S. prime-time adaptation of *Absolutely Fabulous* that the network declined to pick it up, despite considerable pressure from ABC's then comedy superstar, Roseanne, a strong supporter of the series (Bellafante, 1995; Jacobs & Nashawaty, 1996).

Absolutely Fabulous clearly is not a mass product. Unlike *Macarena,* in which feminine desire is represented through fairly conventional images of a "liberated" woman whose licentious behavior also appeals to masculine fantasies of the naughty temptress, *Absolutely Fabulous* makes few concessions aimed at broadening its appeal. In addition to the intriguingly repulsive gender, generational, and family dynamics, the dialogue is laden with in-jokes about everything from high fashion to tabloid celebrity gossip to New Age health practices. It seems to beg viewers, who are not on the inside, to stay away. Of course, this strategy makes the programs even more attractive to those who appreciate the jokes. However, these very qualities limit the ways that media executives might market the series. Attempts to reconstitute it as a mass product for U.S. network television failed, and one could imagine that such a program would never have been considered, much less broadcast, 30 years ago at the height of the classical network era.

Absolutely Fabulous proved to be a cult favorite that BBC's niche marketing operation successfully hawked in more than 20 countries around the globe, including sales to Norway's NRK network, Northwest Airlines' in-flight entertainment, and TM3 (a women's cable channel in Germany). Videotape episodes of the show were among the top three sellers at Virgin Megastores in 1995, and they made the *Billboard* sales charts for more than 40 weeks. At the Comedy Central cable network in the U.S., a joint venture of Time-Warner and Viacom, *Absolutely Fabulous* was far and away the ratings leader during its three-season run (BBC Programme Purchases, 1996; Berger, 1995; King, 1996).

The series seems to demonstrate a cultural shift in representations of feminine desire facilitated by a transformation in the strategies and operations of the culture industries. Yet, before we begin to write paeans to the corporate geniuses of the neo-network era who exploited this trend, a couple of observations highlight the messiness of this current moment of transformation in the culture industries. First, although *Absolutely Fabulous* was marketed successfully by the sales division of the BBC, the series almost failed to make it into production because of reservations expressed by male network executives who found it difficult to reconcile the program's imagery with their own notions of femininity and with industry conventions for representing feminine desire. They worried the program had too much edge for a prime-time audience. The series ultimately was approved only because it was coded as an "alternative" offering on the noncommercial, highly regulated airwaves of Great Britain (Bellafante, 1995). Thus, the series was not initially conceived and developed with a commercial, neo-network strategy in mind.

The marketing phase was not a clearly organized campaign either. In the United States, Comedy Central almost passed on the series because executives at the newly established cable network imagined their target demographic as a niche audience of young men. They believed that women simply would not find the series among the clutter of cable offerings, and that their target audience of young male viewers would fail to appreciate the humor. Although the latter proved true, female viewers flocked to the series in droves, a response that ran contrary to the market research done in preparation for launching the new network. The ensuing success of *Absolutely Fabulous* was such a boon to the fortunes of Comedy Central that the cable network went through a period of significant readjustment after Jennifer Saunders, the series' creator and lead actress, retired from the series. During the early years of Comedy Central, *Absolutely Fabulous* was without a doubt the network's breakthrough success. Yet executives failed to recognize the potential value of the show when it was first offered to them (Bellafante, 1995; Berger, 1995).

Consequently, one must be careful not to characterize the neo-network culture industries as well-oiled corporate machines operating according to a coherent, mature logic. The popularity of specific products is still notoriously unpredictable, and the content is often unruly and even subversive. Likewise, one would be foolish to imagine this era as the most advanced stage of the co-optative or incorporative powers of the culture industries. The landscape has changed, but popular culture remains an active site of social and political contest. In fact, the media industries may be more open to alternative forms of cultural expression today, simply because executives are not certain from where the next hit will come

(Curtin, in press). Unlike the high network era in which executives exercised some control over product popularity because of their monopoly control of limited distribution channels, this new era is characterized by a cluttered marketplace of niche offerings and the constant fragmentation of audiences. By jettisoning a narrowly defined approach to political economy that primarily focuses on ownership issues, a more specific analysis of the operations and strategies of neo-network media firms reveals the existence of opportunities that are not readily apparent.

One could argue, however, that the social significance of programs like *Absolutely Fabulous* is relatively modest. Even if it does in fact undermine prevailing representations of gender relations, it nevertheless appeals primarily to middle-class women in advanced industrial and postindustrial societies. On a global scale, these are television's most privileged viewers. One might wonder if the logic of the neo-network era is likewise affecting popular images of feminine desire in other parts of the world.

SUBCONTINENTAL IMPLICATIONS

In April 1995, Alisha China's music video *Made in India* rocketed to the top of the national charts soon after it premiered across the subcontinent on the Hong Kong-based STAR TV satellite network. Credited with sparking the current Indo-Pop craze, this video foregrounded a young Indian woman's desires in ways that are both global and local and both subversive and traditional. The success of the video and the rapidly growing popularity of satellite television has been discussed more thoroughly in other research (Kumar & Curtin, 1997). In this section I briefly sketch our critique of the video and connect it with the foregoing analysis of the neo-network era.

Since the beginning of the decade, Indian television has changed from a government media monopoly to a rapidly expanding selection of satellite services that now draws large audiences in major cities and most large towns across the country. In 1991, satellite or cable services were available to 330,000 Indian homes. According to recent estimates, the number has grown to 15 million, with an average of 5 viewers to each household (Duncan, 1995; Popham, 1997). Satellite systems in Bombay, for example, feature more than 36 channels and similar services are available in most cities and large towns, even some rural areas. With an estimated 40 million television households nationwide, the market is considered large enough to invite fierce competition between regional, national, and transnational program providers. This means that Indian television has changed from an educational, public service medium to a panoply of services that includes the same range of program genres available in most industrialized societies.

According to Emma Duncan (1995), South Asia editor of the *Economist,* the rise of satellite television "gets the blame (or the credit)" for all the changes taking place in India over the past few years, especially changes in gender relations. Many young women are now wearing "western, not Indian, clothes" and "some advanced cosmopolitan couples" are now living together before they are married because "it's easier to explain it to a mother who has seen *The Bold and The Beautiful*" on satellite TV (Duncan, 1995, p. 3). According to Dhillon (1996),

> No one has remained unaffected by the transformation brought about by satellite TV. . . . For the first time, viewers [are seeing] the kind of scenes that westerners consider tame—kissing, love-making, nudity, homosexuality—but that are shocking in India. Consider that this is a nation where celluloid kisses were banned until three years ago, where most women feel uncomfortable in sleeveless tops and few know the Hindi word for sex. (p. A7)

Without a doubt, the growth of satellite television has played a role in the naked display of bodies and commodities in India. Yet, to describe these changes solely as a response to satellite television would be a gross simplification. For several decades, well before the advent of satellite television, Indian cinema—primarily based in Bombay and, therefore, commonly referred to as Bollywood—provided desiring audiences many avenues of exposure, in all senses of the term. Indian cinema was, and continues to remain, the most popular mass medium. It has always thrived on fantastic displays of luxury, wealth, and consumption, as well as the blatant exploitation of women as titillating objects of sexual desire. The predominant Bollywood genre is the film musical in which romantic complications are ultimately resolved in a series of lavish song and dance numbers.

By comparison, Indian pop music, especially a single album like *Made in India,* is a very recent phenomenon, emerging only in the last few years. Despite the rapid rise of this new genre, what some refer to as Indo-Pop, the music industry continues to be dominated by the sale of songs from film musicals, accounting for about 70% of all sales, compared to Indo-Pop's much more modest share of 7%. Nevertheless Indo-Pop is the fastest growing part of the market, jumping 25% to 30% annually (Dua & Bhat, 1997). BMG-Crescendo, one of the largest firms in the Indian music business, estimates that Indian pop music should push past a 20% share of the $572 million music market by the year 2000 (Fernandes, 1996).

The rapid growth of this new musical genre can be tied directly to the rise of satellite television services, like MTV and STAR. In 1991, when Hong Kong-based STAR TV started its pan-Asian broadcasts, it tapped the resources of MTV with its familiar line-up of Beavis and Butthead, Nirvana, Madonna, and other Generation-X icons. Three years later, when MTV and STAR TV announced their parting of the ways, STAR TV decided to launch its own music service called Channel V. Initially, Channel V seemed content playing an MTV clone. However, it soon became clear that the STAR-based service was charting a new course as part of an effort to distinguish itself from its competition. Claire Marshall, Channel V manager in Hong Kong, contended,

MTV's philosophy is international programming. It has a very Westernized . . . very American image. They pick up Western youth trends and establish those as the norm in their programming. But a lot of what they produce has no relation to the Asian context. It is a copycat culture for Asian youth. So we had to go Asian; we had to localize. (quoted in Bavadam, 1995, p. 69)

Consequently, Channel V saw its mandate as creating a local channel with an international flavor, a clear contrast to MTV's approach of being an international channel with a local flavor. In its efforts to localize, Channel V established production facilities in Delhi and Bombay. It also appropriated MTV's verité camera work, cacophonous editing style, provocative animation, and Top 40 song rotation, which Channel V then infused with iconographic elements of the Bollywood musical and the self-deprecating humor and slapstick comedy that are hallmarks of Indian cinema. Channel V thus promoted the rise of a new hybrid satellite channel, casually mixing elements from East and West. Channel V then pushed the market even further by nurturing its own pop music stars outside the circuits of the Bollywood film musical. Alisha Chinai's *Made in India,* the first big hit of the Indo-Pop genre, sold 2 million albums, plus an estimated 6 million pirated copies. The phenomenal success of Alisha's album was primarily ascribed to the popularity of the Channel V-produced video ("Channel V," 1997; Fernandes, 1996; "Synergy," 1997).

The video begins in ornate palatial surroundings similar to those commonly found in Bollywood films. Princess Alisha is watching an elaborate performance by dancers and musicians at the royal court, yet she seems distracted and indifferent. Ultimately, she breaks into song, lamenting a boredom that springs from the fact that, despite her travels around the world, the princess has yet to find one true love. In desperation, she summons a sorcerer, whose fervent incantations over a boiling cauldron conjure up steamy apparitions of the handsome young man of Alisha's dreams. A montage of shots that most prominently feature erotic poses of his naked torso startle and titillate the desirous princess, who orders her minions to bring her the man at once. Her wish is fulfilled when a wooden shipping crate—prominently emblazoned *Made in India*—is portered to Alisha's lair containing the cargo of her desire. Out of the crate springs the muscular, forthright man of her dreams, naked to waist, who literally sweeps Alisha off her feet. At this moment of closure, she playfully turns to the camera and offers a knowing smile to the audience as the image cuts to a closing shot of the final page of a storybook that reads, "and the handsome prince carried the princess away and they lived happily ever after. The End."

At this point of narrative closure, the video seems a rather conventional text by the standards of Bollywood musical. Yet, *Made in India* inverts dominant representations of desire in rather profound ways. Traditionally, in Bollywood musicals, dream sequences are used to foreground transgressive masculine desire featuring spectacular displays of the female body. A powerful masculine gaze encourages the viewer to accept a hierarchy of gender relations that indulges male fantasies while effectively silencing feminine desire. *Made in India* inverts these conventions by transforming the male body into the sight of spectacle, so as to fix the attention of the viewer on questions of feminine desire: What does an Indian woman want, need, and deserve?

These are not inconsequential issues in a society where most women exercise few choices about labor and family relations. In such a context, the very act of fantasizing about feminine desire has such subversive implications that the narrative must recuperate this moment of textual transgression by literally sweeping the protagonist off her feet and restoring some semblance of masculine dominance to this counterhegemonic fantasy. Yet, even this moment of recuperation is undermined when Alisha, swaddled in the arms of her prince, playfully acknowledges the camera as if to say it is she who ultimately controls the trajectory of the narrative.

In short, the subversive possibilities of this text and their implications for women across India are in large part a product of the intersecting forces at work in Asian television. As such, the new worldliness of Indian media imagery that has been sparked by the invasion of transnational media firms need not be reductively interpreted as homogenizing nor as constraining popular modes of expression. Indeed, the transformation of India's media economy created the very opportunities from which Indo-Pop emerged and thereby created a context in which young women might fantasize about their futures outside the patriarchal representational norms of traditional religion, Bollywood film, and government television.

CONCLUSION

This analysis does not attempt to project a particular politics onto alternative images of feminine desire. Rather my aim is to understand the growing circulation of such images and the political potential that they may present. If our attention remains primarily fixed on the global march of gigantic media conglomerates like News Corporation—the parent company of STAR TV—then we will fail to recognize the potential spaces in which alternative gender politics might be constructed. If one wants to comprehend the dynamic interactions between global and local forces, and if one wants to locate the fleeting but significant cultural spaces in which women might imagine a more liberated future, then one would do well to explore the specific operations of neo-network media industries and the textual possibilities they present.

The growing prominence of huge media conglomerates does not automatically herald the homogenization of culture, the death of free expression, or the end of public life. Ownership does not necessarily equal control. As suggested earlier, cultural conditions are always shifting and uncertain. Even though media conglomerates have fashioned their strategies to accommodate these uncertainties, the second section of this essay reminds us that these strategies are in many ways immature and incoherent if not inadequate. The final part of this paper suggests how one local artist has embraced the opportunities of this era to fashion a sly challenge to the masculine conventions of Indian popular culture.

At the same time, we should take care to recognize this moment of opportunity for what it is: fleeting, contingent, and indeterminate. History reminds us that the public sphere, which has received such conspicuous attention in recent scholarly discussions, was not an intentional outcome of the transition to capitalism, and it did not become a stable feature that would endure for centuries. Instead, it was an opening that was exploited by an emergent class at a specific historical moment (Habermas, 1962/1989).

Likewise, the current reorganization of the culture industries provides fluid and ephemeral spaces in which to imagine new gender roles, political affinities, and sexual orientations. An understanding of the neo-network era asks us to rethink our assumptions about the homogenizing power of global media conglomerates, pressing us instead to explore this terrain as a site of contest, and a productive space within civil society. Such an approach neither denies corporate power nor uncritically celebrates popular culture. Instead it suggests how scholarly criticism might help us identify locations in which to construct alternative images of feminine desire.

REFERENCES CITED

BBC programme purchases. 1996, (March 11). *Information Access Company Newsletter.*

Bagdikian, B. 1989, (June 12). Lords of the global village. *Nation,* 805–820.

———. 1992. *The media monopoly.* Boston: Beacon Press.

Batelle, J. 1995, (April). Viacom doesn't suck. *Wired,* 110–115.

Bavadam, I. 1995, (January 1). V for variety. *Sunday* (India), 68–71.

Bellafante, G. 1995, (June 12). Carousing women. *Time,* 79.

Berger. W. 1995, (July 23). At Comedy Central, a serious revolution. *New York Times,* 29.

Box office. 1997, (October 27). *Variety,* 16.

Bradby, B. 1992. Like a virgin-mother?: Materialism in the songs of Madonna. *Cultural Studies,* 6(1), 73–96.

Brown, J. D., & Campbell, K. 1986. Same beat but a different drummer: Race and gender in music videos. *Journal of Communication, 36*(1), 94–106.

Channel V listens to a new song. 1997, (January). *Cable and Satellite Asia,* 18.

Curry, R. 1990. Madonna from Marilyn to Marlene—pastiche and/or parody? *Journal of Film and Video, 42*(2), 15–30.

Curtin, M. 1996. On edge: Culture industries in the neo-network era. In R. Ohmann, G. Averill, M. Curtin, D. Shumway, & E. Traube (eds.), *Making and selling culture* (181–202). Hanover, NH: Wesleyan University Press.

———. (in press). Gatekeepers of the neo-network era. In M. Suman (ed.), *Advocacy groups and prime-time television.* Westport, CT: Praeger.

Dhillon, A. 1996, (January 28). Sexual revolution shakes India to its traditional foundations. *Ottawa Citizen,* A7.

Dirlik, A. 1996. The global in the local. In R. Wilson & W. Dissanayake (eds.), *Global/local: Cultural production and the transnational imaginary* (21–45). Durham, NC: Duke University Press.

Doty, A. 1990. The cabinet of Lucy Ricardo: Lucille Ball's star image. *Cinema Journal, 29*(4), 3–22.

Dua, A., and V. Bhat. 1997, (January 1). Developing an eye for music. *Business Standard,* 8.

DuLac, J. F., and A. D. Smith. 1996, (August 24). Heeey Macarena! *Rocky Mountain News,* D7.

Duncan, E. 1995, (January 21). Hello, world. *Economist,* 3.

Fernandes, N. 1996, (June 14). Indo-pop: New east-west music rocks urban India. *Associated Press.*

Fiske, J. 1992. British cultural studies and television. In R. C. Allen (Ed.), *Channels of discourse, reassembled: Television and contemporary criticism* (284–326). Chapel Hill: University of North Carolina Press.

Garnham, N. 1990. *Capitalism and communication: Global culture and the economics of information.* Newbury Park, CA: Sage.

Habermas, J. 1989. *The structural transformation of the public sphere* (T. Burger, Trans.). Cambridge, MA: MIT Press. (Original work published 1962)

Harvey, D. 1989. *The condition of postmodernity: An enquiry into the origins of cultural change.* Cambridge, MA: Basil Blackwell.

Hinckley, D. 1996, (August 15). Out of the blue, a dance craze. *Daily News,* 108.

Jacobs, A. J., and C. Nashawaty. 1996, (February 2). Where are they now? *Entertainment Weekly,* 6.

Jameson, F. 1991. *Postmodernism, or, the cultural logic of late capitalism.* Durham, NC: Duke University Press.

Kaplan, E. A. 1987. *Rocking around the clock: Music television, postmodernism and consumer culture.* London: Methuen.

King, S. 1996, (February 11). Private lives: Home entertainment. *Los Angeles Times,* 67.

Klady, L. 1997, (October 27). Sony sent soaring by "summer," *Variety,* 16.

Kline, D. 1995, (March). Savvy Sassa. *Wired,* 110–113.

Kumar, S., and M. Curtin. 1997, (May). *Miss world(ly): Desiring discourse "made in India."* Paper presented at Console-ing Passions: Television, Video, Feminism Conference, Montreal.

Lannert, J. 1995, (July 29). Tale of "Macarena" and her sisters. *Billboard,* 30, 33.

Leung, L. 1997. The making of matriarchy: A comparison of Madonna and Margaret Thatcher. *Journal of Gender Studies, 6*(1), 33–42.

Lewis, L. (ed.). 1990. *Gender politics and MTV: Voicing the difference.* Philadelphia: Temple University Press.

Llewellyn, H. 1996, (July 27). BMG's "Macarena" fever spreads around the world. *Billboard,* 7, 102.

Mellencamp, P. 1991. Situation comedy, feminism and Freud: Discourses of Gracie and Lucy. In J. Butler (ed.), *Star texts: Image and performance in film and television* (80–95). Detroit, MI: Wayne State University Press.

Miller, J. 1991. Madonna. *Ploughshares, 17*(4), 221–231.

Miyoshi, M. 1996. Borderless world? From colonialism to transnationalism and the decline of the nation-state. In R. Wilson & W. Dissanayake (eds.), *Global/local: Cultural production and the transnational imaginary* (78–106). Durham, NC: Duke University Press.

Navarro, M. 1995, (December 27). Macarena madness now has the floor. *New York Times,* A10.

Ohmann, R., G. Averill, M. Curtin, D. Shumway, and E. Traube (eds.). 1996. *Making and selling culture.* Hanover, NH: Wesleyan University Press.

Popham, P. 1997, (September 1). Murdoch stumbles in the passage to India. *Independent,* 6.

Ritrosky-Winslow, M. 1998. *"Polished like a gem": Loretta Young's marketing strategy.* Unpublished doctoral dissertation, Indiana University, Bloomington.

Rowe, K. 1995. *The unruly woman: Gender and the genres of laughter.* Austin: University of Texas Press.

Said, E. W. 1994. *Culture and imperialism.* New York: Knopf.

Sandler, A. 1996, (February 26). MCA finishes interscope odyssey. *Variety,* 62.

Schiller, H. I. 1992. *Mass communication and American empire* (2nd ed.). Boulder, CO: Westview Press.

Schwichtenberg, C. (ed.). 1992. *The Madonna connection: Representational politics, subcultural identities, and cultural theory.* Boulder, CO: Westview Press.

Smith, A. D. 1996, (August 26). Virgin saint of cool entices the world on to dance floor. *Observer,* 17.

Spigel, L. 1992. *Make room for TV: Television and the family ideal in postwar America.* Chicago: University of Chicago Press.

Synergy of sight and sound. 1997, (March 1). *Hindu,* 39.

Thigpen, D. E. 1997, (November 10). A sound rebound. *Time,* B2.

Watts, M. 1996. Electrifying fragments: Madonna and postmodern performance. *New Theatre Quarterly, 12*(46), 99–107.

Wilson, J. L., and G. E. Markle. 1992. Justify my ideology: Madonna and traditional values. *Popular Music and Society, 16*(2), 75–84.

Young, S. E. 1991. Like a critique: A postmodern essay on Madonna's postmodern video *Like a prayer. Popular Music and Society, 15*(1), 59–68.

NOTES

1. By comparison, the film studios dealt only with entertainment. Although widely popular, films were not enjoyed as a simultaneous mass experience. Radio in many ways anticipated the television era by generating huge national audiences, yet most stations remained independent and programming was primarily in the hands of sponsors and ad agencies, not the networks. Neither the newspaper nor music industries have been as centralized as television, and their audiences have been subdivided by geography or taste. As for the general circulation magazine, it has been national in scope, but its audience skewed more toward the educated and affluent.

2. For example, Interscope, an "independent" music company formerly owned by Time-Warner, became very controversial because one of its niche labels. Death Row Records, prominently featured "gangster rap" artists like Snoop Doggy Dog and the late Tupac Shakur. After intense public pressure, Time-Warner put Interscope up for sale. This quickly attracted the attention of Sony and MCA/Universal, with the later taking control after a high-stakes bidding war. Rather than actually going independent, Interscope is now racking up record-breaking sales in new niche markets that include punk-ska and Gospel music (Sandler, 1996; Thigpen, 1997).

3. Quoted in interview with Mark Edmiston (Ohmann et al., 1996).

4. Smith starred in the NBC prime-time series, *Fresh Prince of Bel Air,* and the Sony Pictures blockbuster, *Men in Black,* which earned over $500 million in global box office revenues

4 months after its premier, making it the 10th highest grossing film in Hollywood history ("Box Office," 1997; Klady, 1997). The aim behind new corporate strategies is for a star like Smith to score his various successes under a single corporate umbrella. Regarding Viacom's strategy for the exploitation of product brands like *Star Trek,* see Batelle, 1995.

QUESTIONS FOR DISCUSSION

1. Curtin claims that the "neo-network" era is marked by increasing trends towards both concentration and fragmentation. What is the evidence of this dual movement?

2. Why might it be that women, as a group both locally and globally, are the ones to benefit most greatly from the "neo-network" industrial/representational system? Are there limits to this benefit?

3. Are there certain existing tendencies that could tip the current global media situation back in a direction of concentration and centralized control? What forces work against this?

 INFOTRAC COLLEGE EDITION

Search InfoTrac College Edition under "satellite television," "Start TV," and "MTV Asia" for articles that relate to this subject. Also look under "media concentration."

Index of Authors
and Readings